HTML5 and CSS3

ALL-IN-ONE

FOR

DUMMIES®

A Wiley Brand

3rd Edition

by Andy Harris

FOR

DUMMIES®

A Wiley Brand

HTML5 and CSS3 All-in-One For Dummies® 3rd Edition

Published by:
John Wiley & Sons, Inc.,
111 River Street,
Hoboken, NJ 07030-5774,
www.wiley.com

Contents at a Glance

Table of Contents

Introduction

I love the Internet, and if you picked up this book, you probably do, too. The Internet is dynamic, chaotic, exciting, interesting, and useful, all at the same time. The web is pretty fun from a user's point of view, but that's only part of the story. Perhaps the best part of the Internet is how participatory it is. You can build your own content — free! It's really amazing. There's never been a form of communication like this before. Anyone with access to a minimal PC and a little bit of knowledge can create his or her own homestead in one of the most exciting platforms in the history of communication.

The real question is how to get there. A lot of web development books are really about how to use some sort of software you have to buy. That's okay, but it isn't necessary. Many software packages have evolved that purport to make web development easier — and some work pretty well — but regardless what software package you use, there's still a need to know what's really going on under the surface. That's where this book comes in.

About This Book

You'll find out exactly how the web works in this book. You'll figure out how to use various tools, but, more importantly, you'll create your piece of the web. You'll discover:

- **How web pages are created:** You'll figure out the basic structure of web pages. You'll understand the structure well because you build pages yourself. No mysteries here.

- **How to separate content and style:** You'll understand the foundation of modern thinking about the Internet — that style should be separate from content.

- **How to use web standards:** The web is pretty messy, but, finally, some standards have arisen from the confusion. You'll discover how these standards work and how you can use them.

- **How to create great-looking web pages:** Of course, you want a terrific-looking website. With this book, you'll find out how to use layout, style, color, and images.

- **How to build modern layouts:** Many web pages feature columns, menus, and other fancy features. You'll figure out how to build all these things.

- **How to add interactivity:** Adding forms to your pages, validating form data, and creating animations are all possible with the JavaScript language.

✔ **How to write programs on the server:** Today's web is powered by programs on web servers. You'll discover the powerful PHP language and figure out how to use it to create powerful and effective sites.

✔ **How to harness the power of data:** Every web developer eventually needs to interact with data. You'll read about how to create databases that work. You'll also discover how to connect databases to your web pages and how to create effective and useful interfaces.

✔ **How AJAX is changing everything:** The hottest web technology on the horizon is AJAX (Asynchronous JavaScript and XML). You'll figure out how to harness this way of working and use it to create even more powerful and interesting applications.

Foolish Assumptions

I don't have any foolish assumptions: I'm not assuming anything in this book. If you've never built a web page before, you're in the right hands. You don't need any experience, and you don't have to know anything about HTML, programming, or databases. I discuss everything you need.

If you're reasonably comfortable with a computer (you can navigate the web and use a word processor), you have all the skills you need.

If you've been around web development for a while, you'll still find this book handy.

If you've used HTML but not HTML5, see how things have changed and discover the powerful combination of HTML5 and CSS3.

You'll see how new HTML and CSS features can literally make your web pages sing and dance, with support for advanced tools like audio and video embedding, animation, and much more.

If you're already comfortable with HTML and CSS, you're ready to add JavaScript functionality for form validation and animation. If you've never used a programming language before, JavaScript is a really great place to start.

If you're starting to get serious about web development, you've probably already realized that you'll need to work with a server at some point. PHP is a really powerful, free, and easy language that's extremely prominent on the web landscape. You'll use this to have programs send e-mails, store and load information from files, and work with databases.

If you're messing with commercial development, you'll definitely need to know more about databases. I get e-mails every week from companies looking for people who can create a solid relational database and connect it to a website with PHP.

If you're curious about AJAX, you can read about what it is, how it works, and how to use it to add functionality to your site. You'll also read about a very powerful and easy AJAX library that can add tremendous functionality to your bag of tricks.

I wrote this book as the reference I wish I had. If you have only one web development book on your shelf, this should be the one. Wherever you are in your web development journey, you can find something interesting and new in this book.

Use Any Computer

One of the great things about web development is how accessible it can be. You don't need a high-end machine to build websites. Whatever you're using now will probably do fine. I tested most of the examples in this book with Windows 7, Ubuntu Linux, and a Macbook pro. I've tested on computers ranging from cutting-edge platforms to mobile devices to a $35 Raspberry Pi. Most of the software I use in the book is available free for all major platforms. Similar alternatives for all platforms are available in the few cases when this isn't true.

Don't Buy Any Software

Everything you need for web development is on the companion website. I've used only open-source software for this book. Following are the highlights:

- ✔ **Komodo Edit:** Komodo Edit is my current favorite editor. It's a solid free text editor well suited to the many text-editing tasks you'll run across in your programming travels. It also works exactly the same on every platform, so it doesn't really matter what computer or operating system you're running.

- ✔ **XAMPP:** When you're ready to move to the server, XAMPP is a complete server package that's easy to install and incredibly powerful. This includes the incredible Apache web server, the PHP programming language, the MySQL database manager, and tons of useful utilities.

- ✔ **Useful tools:** Every time I use a tool (such as a data mapper, a diagram tool, or an image editor) in this book, I make it available on the companion website.

There's no need to buy any expensive web development tools. Everything you need is here and no harder than the more expensive web editors.

How This Book Is Organized

Web development is about solving a series of connected but different problems. This book is organized into eight minibooks based on specific technologies. You can read them in any order you wish, but you'll find that the later books tend to rely on topics described in the earlier books. (For example, JavaScript doesn't make much sense without HTML because JavaScript is usually embedded in a web page written with HTML.) The following describes these eight minibooks:

✔ **Book I: Creating the HTML Foundation** — Web development incorporates a lot of languages and technologies, but HTML is the foundation. Here I show you *HTML5,* the latest incarnation of HTML, and describe how it's used to form the basic skeleton of your pages.

✔ **Book II: Styling with CSS** — In the old days, HTML had a few tags to spruce up your pages, but they weren't nearly powerful enough. Today, developers use Cascading Style Sheets (CSS) to add color and formatting to your pages as well as zing and pizazz. (I'm pretty sure those are formal computer programming words.)

✔ **Book III: Building Layouts with CSS** — Discover the best ways to set up layouts with floating elements, fixed positioning, and absolute positioning. Figure out how to build various multicolumn page layouts and how to create dynamic buttons and menus.

✔ **Book IV: Client-Side Programming with JavaScript** — Figure out essential programming skills with the easy and powerful JavaScript language — even if you've never programmed before. Manipulate data in web forms and use powerful regular expression technology to validate form entries. Also discover how to create animations with JavaScript with the powerful new <canvas> element.

✔ **Book V: Server-Side Programming with PHP** — Move your code to the server and take advantage of this powerful language. Figure out how to respond to web requests; work with conditions, functions, objects, and text files; and connect to databases.

✔ **Book VI: Managing Data with MySQL** — Most serious Web projects are eventually about data. Figure out how databases are created, how to set up a secure data server, the basics of data normalization, and how to create a reliable and trustworthy data back end for your site.

✔ **Book VII: Integrating the Client and Server with AJAX** — Look forward to the technology that has the web abuzz. AJAX isn't really a language but rather a new way of thinking about web development. Get the skinny on what's going on here, build an AJAX connection or two by hand, and read about some really cool libraries for adding advanced features and functionality to your pages.

✔ **Book VIII: Moving from Pages to Sites** — This minibook ties together many of the threads throughout the rest of the book. Discover how to create your own complete web server solution or pick a web host. Walk through the process of designing a complex multipage web site. Discover how to use content management systems to simplify complex websites and, finally, to build your own content management system with skills taught throughout the book.

New for the Third Edition

This is actually the third edition of this book. (The previous editions were called *HTML, XHTML, and CSS All in One For Dummies.*) I have made a few changes to keep up with advances in technology:

- **Focus on HTML5:** The first edition of the book used HTML4, the second edition used XHTML, and this edition uses HTML5. I'm very excited about HTML5 because it's easier to use than either of the older versions, and quite a bit more powerful.

- **Integration with CSS3:** CSS3 is the latest incarnation of CSS, and it has some wonderful new features too, including the ability to use custom fonts, animation, and new layout mechanisms.

- **Improved PHP coverage:** PHP has had some major updates reflected in this book. I have modified all form input to use the safer `filter_input` mechanism, and all database connectivity now uses the PDO library.

- **Enhanced jQuery coverage:** jQuery has become even more important as a utility library than it was before. The coverage updates some of the nice new features of this library.

- **A new mobile chapter:** Mobile web development is increasingly important. I provide a new chapter with tips on making your pages mobile-friendly, including use of the jQuery mobile library and building responsive designs that automatically adjust based on screen size.

- **Support for the WebsiteBaker CMS:** I use this CMS quite a bit in my web business, and I find it especially easy to modify. I changed Book VIII, Chapter 3 to explain how to use and modify this excellent CMS.

- **Various tweaks and improvements:** No book is perfect (though I really try). There were a few passages in the previous edition that readers found difficult. I tried hard to clean up each of these areas. Many thanks to those who provided feedback!

Icons Used in This Book

This is a *For Dummies* book, so you have to expect some snazzy icons, right? I don't disappoint. Here's what you'll see:

This is where I pass along any small insights I may have gleaned in my travels.

I can't really help being geeky once in a while. Every so often, I want to explain something a little deeper. Read this to impress people at your next computer science cocktail party or skip it if you really don't need the details.

A lot of details are here. I point out something important that's easy to forget with this icon.

Watch out! Anything I mark with this icon is a place where things have blown up for me or my students. I point out any potential problems with this icon.

Beyond the Book

You can find additional features of this book online. Visit the web to find these extras:

- **Companion website:** www.aharrisbooks.net/haio

  This is my primary site for this book. Every single example in the book is up and running on this site so you can see it in action. When necessary, I've also included source code so you can see the source code of anything you can't look at with the ordinary View Source command. I've also posted a link to every piece of software that I mention in the book. If you find any example is not working on your site, please come to my site. If there was a problem with an example in the book, I'll update the site right away, so check my site to compare your code to mine. I also have links to my other books, a forum where you can ask questions, and a form for emailing me any specific questions you might have.

- **Cheat Sheet:** Go to www.dummies.com/cheatsheet/html5css3aio to find this book's Cheat Sheet. Here, you can find primers on selected HTML syntax, CSS attributes, JavaScript syntax, and MySQL commands.

- **Dummies.com online articles:** Go to www.dummies.com/extras/ html5css3aio to find the Extras for this book. Here you can find articles on topics such as using HTML entities, resetting and extending CSS, JavaScript libraries, using templates with PHP, SQLite and alternative data strategies, fun with jQuery plug-ins, and what's next for the web.

- **Updates:** *For Dummies* technology books sometimes have updates. To check for updates to this book, go to www.dummies.com/extras/ html5css3aio.

Where to Go from Here

Well, that's really up to you. I sincerely believe you can use this book to turn into a top-notch web developer. That's my goal for you.

Although this is a massive book, there's still more to figure out. If you have questions or just want to chat, feel free to e-mail me at andy@ aharrisbooks.net. You can also visit my website at www.aharrisbooks. net/ for code examples, updates, and other good stuff.

I try hard to answer all reader e-mails, but sometimes I get behind. Please be patient with me, and I'll do my best to help.

I can't wait to hear from you and see the incredible websites you develop. Have a great time, discover a lot, and stay in touch!

Part I
Creating the HTML Foundation

getting started
with
HTML5 and
CSS3

Contents at a Glance

Chapter 1: Sound HTML Foundations

In This Chapter

✔ **Creating a basic web page**

✔ **Understanding the most critical HTML tags**

✔ **Setting up your system to work with HTML**

✔ **Viewing your pages**

This chapter is your introduction to building web pages. Before this slim chapter is finished, you'll have your first page up and running. It's a humble beginning, but the basic web technology you learn here is the foundation of everything happening on the web today.

In this minibook, you discover the modern form of web design using HTML5. Your web pages will be designed from the ground up, which makes them easy to modify and customize. Although you figure out more advanced techniques throughout this book, you'll take the humble pages you discover in this chapter and make them do all kinds of exciting things.

Creating a Basic Page

Here's the great news: The most important web technology you need is also the easiest. You don't need any expensive or complicated software, and you don't need a powerful computer. You probably have everything you need to get started already.

No more talking! Fire up a computer and build a web page!

1. **Open a text editor.**

   You can use any text editor you want, as long as it lets you save files as plain text. If you're using Windows, Notepad is fine for now. If you're using Mac, you'll really need to download a text editor. I like Komodo Edit (www.activestate.com/komodo-edit) or TextWrangler (www.barebones.com/products/textwrangler/). It's possible to make TextEdit work correctly, but it's probably easier to just download something made for the job. I explain text editors more completely in Chapter 3 of this mini-book.

Don't use a word processor like Microsoft Word or Mac TextEdit. These are powerful tools, but they don't save things in the right format. The way these tools do things like centering text and changing fonts won't work on the web. I promise that you'll figure out how to do all that stuff soon, but a word processing program won't do it correctly. Even the Save as HTML feature doesn't work right. You really need a very simple text editor, and that's it. In Chapter 3 of this minibook, I show you a few more editors that make your life easier. You should not use Word or TextEdit.

2. Type the following code.

Really. Type it in your text editor so you get some experience writing the actual code. I explain very soon what all this means, but type it now to get a feel for it:

```
<!DOCTYPE HTML>
<html lang="en-US">
<head>
<meta charset="UTF-8">
<!-- myFirst.html -->

<title>My very first web page!</title>
</head>

<body>

<h1>This is my first web page!</h1>

<p>
This is the first web page I've ever made,
and I'm extremely proud of it.
It is so cool!
</p>

</body>
</html>
```

3. Save the file as `myFirst.html`.

It's important that your filename has no spaces and ends with the `.html` extension. Spaces cause problems on the Internet (which is, of course, where all good pages go to live), and the `.html` extension is how most computers know that this file is an HTML file (which is another name for a web page). It doesn't matter where you save the file, as long as you can find it in the next step.

4. Open your web browser.

The *web browser* is the program used to look at pages. After you post your page on a web server somewhere, your Great Aunt Gertrude can use her web browser to view your page. You also need one (a browser, not a Great Aunt Gertrude) to test your page. For now, use whatever browser you ordinarily use. Most Windows users already have Internet Explorer installed. If you're a Mac user, you probably have Safari. Linux folks generally have Chrome or Firefox. Any of these are fine. In Chapter 3 of this minibook, I explain why you probably need more than one browser and how to configure them for maximum usefulness.

5. **Load your page into the browser.**

   You can do this a number of ways. You can use the browser's File menu to open a local file, or you can simply drag the file from your Desktop (or wherever) to the open browser window.

6. **Bask in your newfound genius.**

   Your simple text file is transformed! If all went well, it looks like Figure 1-1.

Understanding the HTML in the Basic Page

The page you created in the previous section uses an extremely simple notation — HTML (HyperText Markup Language), which has been around since the beginning of the web. HTML is a terrific technology for several reasons:

✦ **It uses plain text.** Most document systems (like word processors) use special *binary encoding schemes* that incorporate formatting directly into the computer's internal language, which locks a document into a particular computer or software. That is, a document stored in Word format can't be read without a program that understands Word formatting. HTML gets past this problem by storing everything in plain text.

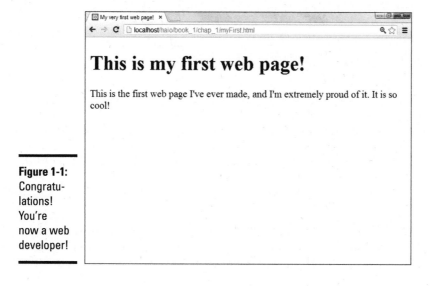

Figure 1-1:
Congratu-
lations!
You're
now a web
developer!

✦ **It works on all computers.** The main point of HTML is to have a universal format. Any computer should be able to read and write it. The plain-text formatting aids in this.

✦ **It describes what documents *mean*.** HTML isn't really designed to indicate how a page or its elements look. HTML is about describing the meaning of various elements (more on that very soon). This has some distinct advantages when you figure out how to use HTML properly.

✦ **It *doesn't* describe how documents *look*.** This one seems strange. Of course, when you look at Figure 1-1, you can see that the appearance of the text on the web page has changed from the way the text looked in your text editor. Formatting a document in HTML does cause the document's appearance to change. That's not the point of HTML, though. You discover in Book II and Book III how to use another powerful technology — *CSS* — to change the appearance of a page after you define its meaning. This separation of meaning from layout is one of the best features of HTML.

✦ **It's easy to write.** Sure, HTML gets a little more complicated than this first example, but you can easily figure out how to write HTML without any specialized editors. You only have to know a handful of elements, and they're pretty straightforward.

✦ **It's free.** HTML doesn't cost anything to use, primarily because it isn't owned by anyone. No corporation has control of it (although a couple have tried), and nobody has a patent on it. The fact that this technology is freely available to anyone is a huge advantage.

Meeting Your New Friends, the Tags

The key to writing HTML code is the special text inside angle braces (< >). These special elements are *tags*. They aren't meant to be displayed on the web page, but offer instructions to the web browser about the meaning of the text. The tags are meant to be embedded into each other to indicate the organization of the page. This basic page introduces you to all the major tags you'll encounter. (There are more, but they can wait for a chapter or two.) Each tag has a beginning and an end tag. The end tag is just like the beginning tag, except the end tag has a slash (/):

✦ `<!DOCTYPE HTML>`: This special tag is used to inform the browser that the document type is HTML. This is how the browser knows you'll be writing an HTML5 document. You will sometimes see other values for the doctype, but HTML5 is the way to go these days.

✦ `<html lang = "en"></html>`: The `<html>` tag is the foundation of the entire web page. The tag begins the page. Likewise, `</html>` ends the page. For example, the page begins with `<html>` and ends with `</html>`. The `<html></html>` combination indicates that everything in the page is defined as HTML code. In HTML5, you're expected to tell the browser which language the page will be written in. Because I write in English, I'm specifying with the code "en."

TIP

Some books teach you to write your HTML tags in uppercase letters. This was once a standard, but it is no longer recommended.

✦ `<head></head>`: These tags define a special part of the web page called the *head* (or sometimes *header*). This part of the web page reminds me of the engine compartment of a car. This is where you put some great stuff later, but it's not where the main document lives. For now, the only thing you'll put in the header is the document's title. Later, you'll add styling information and programming code to make your pages sing and dance.

✦ `<meta charset="UTF-8">`: The meta tag is used to provide a little more information to the browser. This command gives a little more information to the browser, telling it which character set to use. English normally uses a character set called (for obscure reasons) UTF-8. You don't need to worry much about this, but every HTML5 page written in English uses this code.

✦ `<!--/-->`: This tag indicates a *comment,* which is ignored by the browser. However, a comment is used to describe what's going on in a particular part of the code.

✦ `<title></title>`: This tag is used to determine the page's title. The title usually contains ordinary text. Whatever you define as the title will appear in some special ways. Many browsers put the title text in the browser's title bar. Search engines often use the title to describe the page.

Throughout this book, I use the filename of the HTML code as the title. That way, you can match any figure or code listing to the corresponding file on the web site that accompanies this book. Typically, you'll use something more descriptive, but this is a useful technique for a book like this.

WARNING!

It's not quite accurate to say that the title text always shows up in the title bar because a web page is designed to work on lots of different browsers. Sure, the title does show up on most major browsers that way, but what about cellphones and tablets? HTML never legislates what will happen; it only suggests. This may be hard to get used to, but it's a reality. You trade absolute control for widespread capability, which is a good deal.

✦ `<body></body>`: The page's main content is contained within these tags. Most of the HTML code and the stuff the user sees are in the body area. If the header area is the engine compartment, the body is where the passengers go.

✦ `<h1></h1>`: H1 stands for *heading level one.* Any text contained within this markup is treated as a prominent headline. By default, most browsers add special formatting to anything defined as H1, but there's no guarantee. An H1 heading doesn't really specify any particular font or formatting, just the *meaning* of the text as a level one heading. When you find out how to use CSS in Book II, you'll discover that you can make your headline look however you want. In this first minibook, keep all the default layouts for now and make sure you understand that HTML is about semantic meaning, not about layout or design. There are other levels of headings, of course, through <h6> where <h2> indicates a heading slightly less important than <h1>, <h3> is less important than <h2>, and so on.

Beginners are sometimes tempted to make their first headline an <h1> tag and then use an <h2> for the second headline and an <h3> for the third. That's not how it works. Web pages, like newspapers and books, use different headlines to point out the relative importance of various elements on the page, often varying the point size of the text. You can read more about that in Book II.

✦ **<p></p>:** In HTML, p stands for the paragraph tag. In your web pages, you should enclose each standard paragraph in a <p></p> pair. You might notice that HTML doesn't preserve the carriage returns or white space in your HTML document. That is, if you press Enter in your code to move text to a new line, that new line isn't necessarily preserved in the final web page.

The <p></p> structure is one easy way to manage spacing before and after each paragraph in your document.

Some older books recommend using <p> without a </p> to add space to your documents, similar to pressing the Enter key. This way of thinking could cause you problems later because it doesn't accurately reflect the way web browsers work. Don't think of <p> as the carriage return. Instead, think of <p> and </p> as defining a paragraph. The paragraph model is more powerful because soon enough, you'll figure out how to take any properly defined paragraph and give it yellow letters on a green background with daisies (or whatever else you want). If things are marked properly, they'll be much easier to manipulate later.

A few notes about the basic page

Be proud of this first page. It may be simple, but it's the foundation of greater things to come. Before moving on, take a moment to ponder some important HTML principles shown in this humble page you've created:

✔ **All tags are lowercase.** Although HTML does allow uppercase tags, modern developers have agreed on lowercase tags in most cases. (<!DOCTYPE> is one notable exception to this rule.)

✔ **Tag pairs are containers, with a beginning and an end.** Tags contain other tags or text.

✔ **Some elements can be repeated.** There's only one <html>, <title>, and <body> tag per page, but a lot of other elements (<h1> and <p>) can be repeated as many times as you like.

✔ **Carriage returns are ignored.** In the Notepad document, there are a number of carriage returns. The formatting of the original document has no effect on the HTML output. The markup tags indicate how the output looks.

Setting Up Your System

You don't need much to make web pages. Your plain text editor and a web browser are about all you need. Still, some things can make your life easier as a web developer.

Displaying file extensions

The method discussed in this section is mainly for Windows users, but it's a big one. Windows uses the *extension* (the part of the filename after the period) to determine what type of file you're dealing with. This is very important in web development. The files you create are simple text files, but if you store them with the ordinary `.txt` extension, your browser can't read them properly. What's worse, the default Windows setting hides these extensions from you, so you have only the icons to tell you what type of file you're dealing with, which causes all kinds of problems. I recommend you have Windows explicitly describe your file extensions. Here's how to set that up in Windows 7:

1. **Click the Start button.**

   This opens the standard Start menu.

2. **Open the Control Panel.**

   The Control Panel application allows you to modify many parts of your operating system.

3. **Find Appearance and Personalization.**

   This section allows you to modify the visual look and feel of your operating system.

4. **Choose Folder Options.**

   This dialog box lets you modify the way folders look throughout the visual interface.

5. **Find Advanced Settings.**

   Click the View tab and then look under Advanced Settings.

6. **Display file extensions.**

   By default, the Hide Extensions for Known File Types check box is selected. Deselect this check box to display file extensions.

The process for displaying file types is similar in Windows 8:

1. **Go to Windows Explorer.**

   Use the Windows Explorer tile to view Windows Explorer — the standard file manager for Windows.

2. **Click the View tab.**

   This tab allows you to modify how directories look.

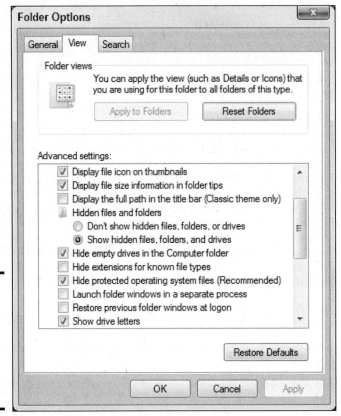

Figure 1-2:
Don't
hide file
extensions
(deselect
that Hide
Extensions
check box).

3. **De-select filename extensions.**

   If this button is checked, file extensions are shown (which is what you want.) (See Figure 1-2.) Note this is the opposite of Windows 7's behavior.

Although my demonstration uses Windows 7 and 8, the technique is similar in older versions of Windows. Just do a quick search for "displaying file extensions."

Setting up your software

You'll write a lot of web pages, so it makes sense to set up your system to make that process as easy as possible. I talk a lot more about some software you should use in Chapter 3 of this minibook, but for now, here are a couple of easy suggestions:

✦ **Put a Notepad icon on your Desktop.** You'll edit a lot of text files, so it's helpful to have an icon for Notepad (or whatever other text editor you use) available directly on the Desktop. That way, you can quickly edit any web page by dragging it to the Desktop. When you use more sophisticated editors than Notepad, you'll want links to them, too.

✦ **Get another web browser.** You may just *love* your web browser, and that's fine, but you can't assume that everybody likes the same browser you do. You need to know how other browsers interpret your code. Chrome is an incredibly powerful browser, and it's completely free, as well has having a lot of great programmer's features. If you don't already, I suggest having links to at least two browsers directly on your Desktop.

Understanding the magic

Most of the problems people have with the web are from misunderstandings about how this medium really works. Most people are comfortable with word processors, and we know how to make a document look how we want. Modern applications use WYSIWYG technology, promising that *what you see is what you get.* That's a reasonable promise when it comes to print documents, but it doesn't work that way on the web.

How a web page looks depends on a lot of things that you don't control. The user may read your pages on a smaller or larger screen than you. She may use a different operating system than you. She may have a slower connection or may turn off the graphics for speed. She may be blind and use screen-reader technology to navigate web pages. She may be reading your page on a tablet, smart phone, or even an older (not so smart) cellphone. You can't make a document that looks the same in all these situations.

A good compromise is to make a document that clearly indicates how the information fits together and makes suggestions about the visual design. The user and her browser can determine how much of those suggestions to use.

You get some control of the visual design but never complete control, which is okay because you're trading total control for accessibility. People with devices you've never heard of can visit your page.

Practice a few times until you can easily build a page without looking anything up. Soon enough, you're ready for the next step — building pages like the pros.

Chapter 2: It's All About Validation

In This Chapter

✔ **Introducing the concept of valid pages**

✔ **Using a doctype**

✔ **Setting the character set**

✔ **Meeting the W3C validator**

✔ **Fixing things when they go wrong**

✔ **Using HTML Tidy to clean your pages**

*W*eb development is undergoing a revolution. As the web matures and becomes a greater part of everyday life, it's important to ensure that web pages perform properly — thus, a call for web developers to follow voluntary standards of web development.

Somebody Stop the HTML Madness!

In the bad old days, the web was an informal affair. People wrote HTML pages any way they wanted. Although this was easy, it led to a lot of problems:

✦ **Browser manufacturers added features that didn't work on all browsers.** People wanted prettier web pages with colors, fonts, and doodads, but there wasn't a standard way to do these things. Every browser had a different set of tags that supported enhanced features. As a developer, you had no real idea if your web page would work on all the browsers out there. If you wanted to use some neat feature, you had to ensure your users had the right browser.

✦ **The distinction between meaning and layout was blurred.** People expected to have some kind of design control of their web pages, so all kinds of new tags popped up that blurred the distinction between describing and decorating a page.

✦ **Table-based layout was used as a hack.** HTML didn't have a good way to handle layout, so clever web developers started using tables as a layout mechanism. This worked, after a fashion, but it wasn't easy or elegant.

✦ **People started using tools to write pages.** Web development soon became so cumbersome that people began to believe that they couldn't do HTML by hand anymore and that some kind of editor was necessary to handle all that complexity for them. Although these editing programs introduced new features that made things easier upfront, these tools also made code almost impossible to change without the original editor. Web developers began thinking they couldn't design web pages without a tool from a major corporation.

✦ **The nature of the web was changing.** At the same time, these factors were making ordinary web development more challenging. Innovators were recognizing that the web wasn't really about documents but was about applications that could dynamically create documents. Many of the most interesting web pages you visit aren't web pages at all, but programs that produce web pages dynamically every time you visit. This innovation meant that developers had to make web pages readable by programs, as well as humans.

✦ **XHTML tried to fix things.** The standards body of the web (there really is such a thing) is called the World Wide Web Consortium (W3C), and it tried to resolve things with a new standard called XHTML. This was a form of HTML that also followed the much stricter rules of XML. If everyone simply agreed to follow the XHTML standard, much of the ugliness would go away.

✦ **XHTML didn't work either.** Although XHTML was a great idea, it turned out to be complicated. Parts of it were difficult to write by hand, and very few developers followed the standards completely. Even the browser manufacturers didn't agree exactly on how to read and display XHTML. It doesn't matter how good an idea is if nobody follows it.

In short, the world of HTML was a real mess.

XHTML had some great ideas

In 2000, the World Wide Web Consortium (usually abbreviated as W3C) got together and proposed some fixes for HTML. The basic plan was to create a new form of HTML that complied with a stricter form of markup, or *eXtensible Markup Language (XML)*. The details are long and boring, but essentially, they came up with some agreements about how web pages are standardized. Here are some of those standards:

✦ **All tags have endings.** Every tag comes with a beginning and an end tag. (Well, a few exceptions come with their own ending built in. I'll explain when you encounter the first such tag in Chapter 6 of this minibook.) This was a new development because end tags were considered optional in old-school HTML, and many tags didn't even have end tags.

✦ **Tags can't be overlapped.** In HTML, sometimes people had the tendency to be sloppy and overlap tags, like this: `<a><b>my stuff</a></b>`. That's not allowed in XHTML, which is a good thing because it confuses the browser. If a tag is opened inside some container tag, the tag must be closed before that container is closed.

✦ **Everything's lowercase.** Some people wrote HTML in uppercase, some in lowercase, and some just did what they felt like. It was inconsistent and made it harder to write browsers that could read all the variations.

✦ **Attributes must be in quotes.** If you've already done some HTML, you know that quotes used to be optional — not anymore. (Turn to Chapter 3 for more about attributes.)

✦ **Layout must be separate from markup.** Old-school HTML had a bunch of tags (like `<font>` and `<center>`) that were more about format-ting than markup. These were useful, but they didn't go far enough. XHTML (at least the strict version) eliminates all these tags. Don't worry, though; CSS gives you all the features of these tags and a lot more.

This sounds like strict librarian rules, but really they aren't restricting at all. Most of the good HTML coders were already following these guidelines or something similar.

Even though you're moving past XHTML into HTML5, these aspects of XHTML remain, and they are guidelines all good HTML5 developers still use.

HTML5 actually allows a looser interpretation of the rules than XHTML strict did, but throughout this book I write HTML5 code in a way that also passes most of the XHTML strict tests. This practice ensures nice clean code with no surprises.

You validate me

In old-style HTML, you never really knew how your pages would look on various browsers. In fact, you never really knew if your page was even writ-ten properly. Some mistakes would look fine on one browser but cause another browser to blow up.

The idea of *validation* is to take away some of the uncertainty of HTML. It's like a spell checker for your code. My regular spell checker makes me feel a little stupid sometimes because I make mistakes. I like it, though, because I'm the only one who sees the errors. I can fix the spelling errors before I pass the document on to you, so I look smart. (Well, maybe.)

It'd be cool if you could have a special kind of checker that does the same things for your web pages. Instead of checking your spelling, it'd test your page for errors and let you know if you made any mistakes. It'd be even cooler if you could have some sort of certification that your page follows a standard of excellence.

That's how page validation works. You can designate that your page will follow a particular standard and use a software tool to ensure that your page meets that standard's specifications. The software tool is a *validator*. I show you two different validators in the upcoming "Validating Your Page" section.

The browsers also promise to follow a particular standard. If your page validates to a given standard, any browser that validates to that same standard can reproduce your document correctly, which is a big deal.

The most important validator is the W3C validator at `http://validator.w3.org`, as shown in Figure 2-1.

A validator is actually the front end of a piece of software that checks pages for validity. It looks at your web page's doctype and sees whether the page conforms to the rules of that doctype. If not, it tells you what might have gone wrong.

You can submit code to a validator in three ways:

✦ **Validate by URI.** This option is used when a page is hosted on a web server. Files stored on local computers can't be checked with this technique. Book VIII describes all you need to know about working with web servers, including how to create your own and move your files to it. (A *URI*, or uniform resource identifier, is a more formal term for a web address, which is more frequently seen as URL.)

✦ **Validate by file upload.** This technique works fine with files you haven't posted to a web server. It works great for pages you write on your computer but that you haven't made visible to the world. This is the most common type of validation for beginners.

✦ **Validate by direct input.** The validator page has a text box you can simply paste your code into. It works, but I usually prefer to use the other methods because they're easier.

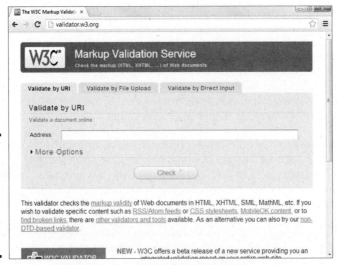

Figure 2-1:
The W3C validator page isn't exciting, but it sure is useful.

Validation might sound like a big hassle, but it's really a wonderful tool because sloppy HTML code can cause lots of problems. Worse, you might think everything's okay until somebody else looks at your page, and suddenly, the page doesn't display correctly.

 As of this writing, the W3C validator can read and test HTML5 code, but the HTML5 validation is still considered experimental. Until HTML5 becomes a bit more mainstream, your HTML5 pages may get a warning about the experimental nature of HTML5. You can safely ignore this warning.

Validating Your Page

To explain all this, I created a web page the way Aesop might have done in ancient Greece. Okay, maybe Aesop didn't write his famous fables as web pages, but if he had, they might have looked like the following code listing:

```html
<!DOCTYPE HTML>
<html lang="en-US">
<head>
    <meta charset="UTF-8">

<!-- oxWheels1.html -->

<!-- note this page has deliberate errors! Please see the text
     and oxWheelsCorrect.html for a corrected version.
-->

</head>
<body>
<title>The Oxen and the Wheels</title>
<h1>The Oxen and the Wheels
<h2></h1>From Aesop's Fables</h2>

<p>
    A pair of Oxen were drawing a heavily loaded wagon along a
    miry country road. They had to use all their strength to pull
    the wagon, but they did not complain.
<p>

<p>
    The Wheels of the wagon were of a different sort. Though the
    task they had to do was very light compared with that of the
    Oxen, they creaked and groaned at every turn. The poor Oxen,
    pulling with all their might to draw the wagon through the
    deep mud, had their ears filled with the loud complaining of
    the Wheels. And this, you may well know, made their work so
    much the harder to endure.
</p>

<p>
    "Silence!" the Oxen cried at last, out of patience. "What have
    you Wheels to complain about so loudly? We are drawing all the
    weight, not you, and we are keeping still about it besides."
</p>

<h2>
They complain most who suffer least.
```

```
</h2>

</body>
</html>
```

The code looks okay, but actually has a number of problems. Aesop may have been a great storyteller, but from this example, it appears he was a sloppy coder. The mistakes can be hard to see, but trust me, they're there. The question is, how do you find the problems before your users do?

You might think that the problems would be evident if you viewed the page in a web browser. The various web browsers seem to handle the page decently, even if they don't display it in an identical way. Figure 2-2 shows oxWheels1.html in a browser.

Chrome appears to handle the page pretty well, but `From Aesop's Fables` is supposed to be a headline level two, or *H2,* and it appears as plain text. Other than that, there's very little indication that something is wrong.

If it looks fine, who cares if it's exactly right? You might wonder why we care if there are mistakes in the underlying code, as long as everything works okay. After all, who's going to look at the code if the page displays properly?

The problem is, you don't know if it'll display properly, and mistakes in your code will eventually come back to haunt you. If possible, you want to know immediately what parts of your code are problematic so you can fix them and not worry.

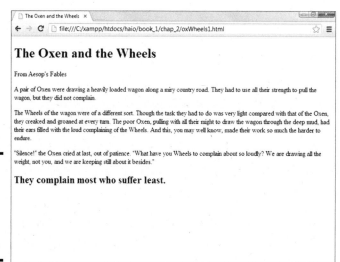

Figure 2-2:
The page looks okay, but the headings are strange.

Aesop visits W3C

To find out what's going on with this page, pay a visit to the W3C validator at `http://validator.w3.org`. Figure 2-3 shows me visiting this site and uploading a copy of oxWheels1.html to it.

Hold your breath and click the Check button. You might be surprised at the results shown in Figure 2-4.

The validator is a picky beast, and it doesn't seem to like this page at all. The validator does return some useful information and gives enough hints that you can decode things soon enough.

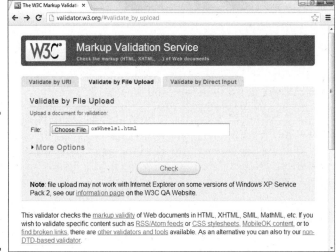

Figure 2-3:
I'm checking the oxWheels page to look for any problems.

Figure 2-4:
Five errors? That can't be right!

Examining the overview

Before you look at the specific complaints, take a quick look at the web page the validator sends you. The web page is chock-full of handy information. The top of the page tells you a lot of useful things:

✦ **Result:** This is really the important thing. You'll know the number of errors remaining by looking at this line. Don't panic, though. The errors in the document are probably fewer than the number you see here.

✦ **File:** The name of the file you're working on.

✦ **Encoding:** The text encoding you've set. If you didn't explicitly set text encoding, you may see a warning here.

✦ **Doctype:** This is the doctype extracted from your document. It indicates the rules that the validator is using to check your page. This should usually say HTML5.

✦ **The dreaded red banner:** Experienced web developers don't even have to read the results page to know if there is a problem. If everything goes well, there's a green congratulatory banner. If there are problems, the banner is red. It doesn't look good, Aesop.

Don't panic because you have errors. The mistakes often overlap, so one problem in your code often causes more than one error to pop up. Most of the time, you have far fewer errors than the page says, and a lot of the errors are repeated, so after you find the error once, you'll know how to fix it throughout the page.

Validating the page

The validator doesn't always tell you everything you need to know, but it does give you some pretty good clues. Page validation is tedious but not as difficult as it might seem at first. Here are some strategies for working through page validation:

✦ **Focus only on the first error.** Sure, 100 errors might be on the page, but solve them one at a time. The only error that matters is the first one on the list. Don't worry at all about other errors until you've solved the first one.

✦ **Note where the first error is.** The most helpful information you get is the line and column information about where the validator recognized the error. This isn't always where the error is, but it does give you some clues.

✦ **Look at the error message.** It's usually good for a laugh. The error messages are sometimes helpful and sometimes downright mysterious.

✦ **Look at the verbose text.** Unlike most programming error messages, the W3C validator tries to explain what went wrong in something like English. It still doesn't always make sense, but sometimes the text gives you a hint.

✦ **Scan the next couple of errors.** Sometimes, one mistake shows up as more than one error. Look over the next couple of errors, as well, to see if they provide any more insight; sometimes, they do.

✦ **Try a change and revalidate.** If you've got an idea, test it out (but only solve one problem at a time.) Check the page again after you save it. If the first error is now at a later line number than the previous one, you've succeeded.

✦ **Don't worry if the number of errors goes up.** The number of perceived errors will sometimes go up rather than down after you successfully fix a problem. This is okay. Sometimes, fixing one error uncovers errors that were previously hidden. More often, fixing one error clears up many more. Just concentrate on clearing errors from the beginning to the end of the document.

✦ **Lather, rinse, and repeat.** Look at the new top error and get it straightened out. Keep going until you get the coveted Green Banner of Validation. (If I ever write an HTML adventure game, the Green Banner of Validation will be one of the most powerful talismans.)

Examining the first error

Look again at the results for the oxWheels1.html page. The first error message looks like Figure 2-5.

Figure 2-5: Well, that clears everything up.

Figure 2-5 shows the first two error messages. The first complains that the head is missing a title. The second error message is whining about the title being in the body. The relevant code is repeated here:

```
<!DOCTYPE HTML>
<html lang="en-US">
```

```
<head>
    <meta charset="UTF-8">

<!-- oxWheels1.html -->

<!-- note this page has deliberate errors! Please see the text
    and oxWheelsCorrect.html for a corrected version.
-->

</head>
<body>
<title>The Oxen and the Wheels</title>
```

Look carefully at the `head` and `title` tag pairs and review the notes in the error messages, and you'll probably see the problem. The `<title>` element is supposed to be in the heading, but I accidentally put it in the body! (Okay, it wasn't accidental; I made this mistake deliberately here to show you what happens. However, I have made this mistake for real in the past.)

Fixing the title

If the `title` tag is the problem, a quick change in the HTML should fix it. oxWheels2.html shows another form of the page with my proposed fix:

```
<head>
<meta http-equiv="Content-Type" content="text/html; charset=iso-8859-1" />

<!-- oxWheels2.html -->

<!-- Moved the title tag inside the header -->
<title>The Oxen and the Wheels</title>

</head>
<body>
```

Note: I'm only showing the parts of the page that I changed. The entire page is available on this book's website. See this book's Introduction for more on the website.

The fix for this problem is pretty easy:

1. **Move the title inside the head.** I think the problem here is having the `<title>` element inside the body, rather than in the head where it belongs. If I move the title to the body, the error should be eliminated.

2. **Change the comments to reflect the page's status.** It's important that the comments reflect what changes I make.

3. **Save the changes.** Normally, you simply make a change to the same document, but I've elected to change the filename so you can see an archive of my changes as the page improves. This can actually be a good idea because you then have a complete history of your document's changes, and you can always revert to an older version if you accidentally make something worse.

4. **Note the current first error position.** Before you submit the modified page to the validator, make a mental note of the position of the current first error. Right now, the validator's first complaint is on line 12, column 7. I want the first mistake to be somewhere later in the document.

5. **Revalidate by running the validator again on the modified page.**

6. **Review the results and do a happy dance.** It's likely you still have errors, but that's not a failure! Figure 2-6 shows the result of my revalidation. The new first error is on line 17, and it appears to be very different from the last error. I solved it!

Solving the next error

One down, but more to go. The next error (refer to Figure 2-6) looks strange, but it makes sense when you look over the code.

This type of error is very common. What it usually means is you forgot to close something or you put something in the wrong place. The error message indicates a problem in line 17. The next error is line 17, too. See if you can find the problem here in the relevant code:

```
<body>
<h1>The Oxen and the Wheels
<h2></h1>From Aesop's Fables</h2>
```

After you know where to look, the problem becomes a bit easier to spot. I got sloppy and started the `<h2>` tag before I finished the `<h1>`. In many cases, one tag can be completely embedded inside another, but you can't have tag definitions overlap as I've done here. The `<h1>` has to close before I can start the `<h2>` tag.

Figure 2-6:
Heading cannot be a child of another heading. Huh?

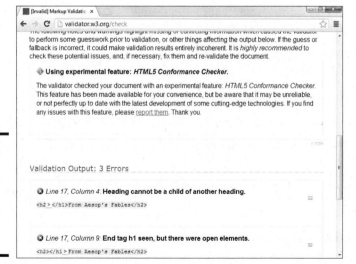

This explains why browsers might be confused about how to display the headings. It isn't clear whether this code should be displayed in H1 or H2 format, or perhaps with no special formatting at all. It's much better to know the problem and fix it than to remain ignorant until something goes wrong.

The third version — oxWheels3.html — fixes this part of the program:

```
<!-- oxWheels3.html -->
<!-- sort out the h1 and h2 tags at the top -->
<title>The Oxen and the Wheels</title>
</head>
<body>
<h1>The Oxen and the Wheels</h1>
<h2>From Aesop's Fables</h2>
```

The validator has fixed a number of errors, but there's one really sneaky problem still in the page. See if you can find it, and then read ahead.

Using Tidy to repair pages

The W3C validator isn't the only game in town. Another great resource — HTML Tidy — can be used to fix your pages. You can download Tidy or just use the online version at `http://infohound.net/tidy`. Figure 2-7 illustrates the online version.

Is validation really that big a deal?

I can hear the angry e-mails coming in. "Andy, I've been writing web pages since 1998, and I never used a validator." Okay, it's true. A lot of people, even some professional web developers, work without validating their code. Some of my older web pages don't validate at all. (You can run the W3C validator on any page you want, not just one you wrote. This can be a source of great joy if you like feeling superior to sloppy coders.) When I became more proficient and more prolific in my web development, I found that those little errors often caused a whole lot of grief down the road. I really believe you should validate every single page you write. Get into the habit now, and it'll pay huge dividends. When you're figuring out this stuff for the first time, do it right.

If you already know some HTML, you're gonna hate the validator for a while because it rejects coding habits that you might think are perfectly fine. Unlearning a habit is a lot harder than learning a new practice, so I feel your pain. It's still worth it.

After you discipline yourself to validate your pages, you'll find you've picked up good habits, and validation becomes a lot less painful. Experienced programmers actually like the validation process because it becomes much easier and prevents problems that could cause lots of grief later. You may even want to re-validate a page you've been using for a while. Sometimes a content update can cause mistakes.

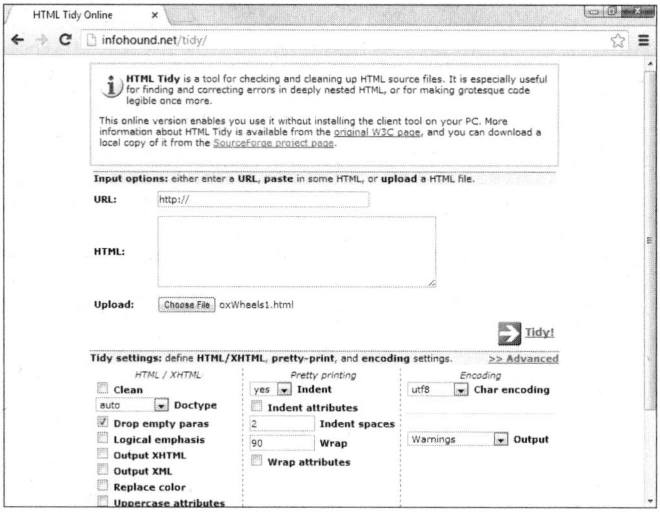

Figure 2-7:
HTML
Tidy is an
alternative
to the W3C
validator.

Unlike W3C's validator, Tidy actually attempts to fix your page. Figure 2-8 displays how Tidy suggests the oxWheels1.html page be fixed.

Tidy examines the page for a number of common errors and does its best to fix the errors. However, the result is not quite perfect:

✦ **It outputs XHTML by default.** XHTML is fine, but because we're doing HTML here, deselect the Output XHTML box. The only checkbox you need selected is Drop Empty Paras.

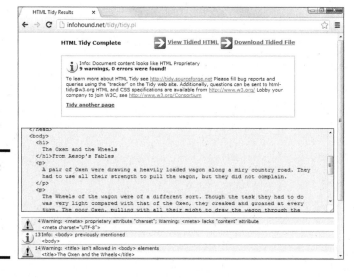

Figure 2-8:
Tidy fixes
the page,
but the fix
is a little
awkward.

✦ **Tidy got confused by the headings.** Tidy correctly fixed the level one heading, but it had trouble with the level two heading. It removed all the tags, so it's valid, but the text intended to be a level two heading is just sort of hanging there.

✦ **Sometimes, the indentation is off.** I set Tidy to indent every element, so it is easy to see how tag pairs are matched up. If I don't set up the indentation explicitly, I find Tidy code very difficult to read.

✦ **The changes aren't permanent.** Anything Tidy does is just a suggestion. If you want to keep the changes, you need to save the results in your editor. Click the Download Tidied File button to do this easily.

I sometimes use Tidy when I'm stumped because I find the error messages are easier to understand than the W3C validator. However, I never trust it completely. Until it's updated to truly understand HTML5, it sometimes deletes perfectly valid HTML5 tags. There's really no substitute for good old detective skills and the official W3C validator.

Did you figure out that last error? I tried to close a paragraph with <p> rather than </p>. That sort of thing freaks out an XHTML validator, but HTML takes it in stride, so you might not even know there is a problem. Tidy does notice the problem and repairs it. Remember this when you're working with a complex page and something doesn't seem right. It's possible there's a mistake you can't even see, and it's messing you up. In that case, consider using a validator and Tidy to figure out what's going wrong and fix it.

Chapter 3: Choosing Your Tools

*W*eb development is a big job. You don't go to a construction site without a belt full of tools (and a cool hat), and the same thing is true with web development (except you don't normally need a hard hat for web development). An entire industry has evolved trying to sell tools that help make web development easier. The funny thing is that the tools you need might not be the ones that people are trying to sell you. Some of the very best web development tools are free, and some of the most expensive tools aren't that helpful.

This chapter tells you what you need and how to set up your workshop with great programs that simplify web development.

What's Wrong with the Big Boys: Expression Web and Adobe Dreamweaver

Many web development books are really books about how to use a particular type of software. Microsoft's Expression Web and Adobe Dreamweaver are the two primary applications in this category. These tools are powerful and offer some *seemingly* great features:

✦ **WYSIWYG editing:** *What you see is what you get* is an idea borrowed from word processors. You can create a web page much like a word-processing document and use menus as well as tools to handle all the formatting. The theory is that you don't have to know any icky codes.

✦ **Templates:** You can create a template that stays the same and build several pages from that template. If you need to change the template, everything else changes automatically.

✦ **Site management:** The interaction between the various pages on your site can be maintained automatically.

These sound like pretty good features, and they are. The tools (and the newer replacements, like Microsoft's Expression suite) are very powerful and can be an important part of your web development toolkit. However, the same powerful programs introduce problems, such as the following:

✦ **Code maintenance:** The commercial editors that concentrate on visual design tend to create pretty unmanageable code. If you find there's something you need to change by hand, it's pretty hard to fix the code.

✦ **Vendor lock-in:** These tools are written by corporations that want you to buy other tools from them. If you're using Dreamweaver, you'll find it easy to integrate with other Adobe applications (like ColdFusion), but it's not as simple to connect to non-Adobe technology. Likewise, Microsoft's offerings are designed to work best with other Microsoft technologies.

✦ **Cost:** The cost of these software packages keeps going up. Although there are free versions of Microsoft's web development tools, the commercial versions are very expensive. Likewise, Dreamweaver weighs in at $400. Both companies encourage you to buy the software as part of a package, which can easily cost more than hundreds more.

✦ **Complexity:** They're complicated. You can take a full class or buy a huge book on how to use only one of these technologies. If it's that hard to figure out, is it really saving you any effort?

✦ **Code:** You still need to understand it. No matter how great your platform is, at some point, you have to dig into your code. After you plunk down all that money and spend all that time figuring out an application, you still have to understand how the underlying code works because things still go wrong. For example, if your page fails to work with Safari, you'll have to find out why and fix the problem yourself.

✦ **Spotty standards compliance:** The tools are getting better here, but if you want your pages to comply with the latest standards, you have to edit them heavily after the tool is finished.

✦ **Display variations:** WYSIWYG is a lie. This is really the big problem. WYSIWYG works for word processors because it's possible to make the screen look like the printed page. After a page is printed, it stays the same. You don't know what a web page will look like because that depends on the browser. What if the user loads your page on a cellphone or handheld device? The editors tend to perpetuate the myth that you can treat a web page like a printed document when, in truth, it's a very different kind of beast.

✦ **Incompatibility with other tools:** Web development is now moving toward content management systems (CMS) — programs that create websites dynamically. Generally, CMS systems provide the same ease-of-use as a visual editor but with other benefits. However, transitioning code created in a commercial editor to a CMS is very difficult. I describe CMS systems in detail in Book VIII.

How About Online Site Builders?

A lot of modern websites are built with a content management system (CMS). Content management systems are software programs that allow you to build and modify a page right in your web browser. Some CMS systems are free, and some cost money to use. I go over how to install and modify a CMS (and even build your own) in Book VIII. A CMS system can be nice because it allows you to build a website visually without any special tools or knowledge.

The CMS approach is a very good solution, but I still recommend you discover how to build things by hand. Ultimately even a CMS uses HTML and CSS, and you'll need these skills to make your site look and perform well even if you have help.

Alternative Web Development Tools

For web development, all you really need is a text editor and a web browser. You probably already have a basic set of tools on your computer. If you read Chapters 1 and 2 of this minibook, you've already written a couple of web pages. However, the very basic tools that come with every computer might not be enough for serious work. Web development requires a specialized kind of text editor, and a number of tools have evolved that make the job easier.

I've found uses for four types of programs in web development:

✦ **Enhanced text editors:** These tools are text editors, but they're souped-up with all kinds of fancy features, like syntax checkers, code-coloring tools, macro tools, and multiple document interfaces.

✦ **Browsers and plug-ins:** Some browsers are better than others for development. You'll also need a full suite of browsers to ensure your code works in all of them. Some browsers can be extended with plug-ins for advanced performance.

✦ **Programming technologies:** This book covers all pertinent info about incorporating other technologies, like Apache, PHP, and MySQL. I show you how to install everything you need for these technologies in Book VIII, Chapter 1. You don't need to worry about these things yet, but you should develop habits that are compatible with these enhanced technologies from the beginning.

✦ **Multimedia tools:** It's very common for a web page to feature various types of images, as well as other multimedia like custom fonts, sound effects, and video. You'll need some tools to manage these resources.

Picking a Text Editor

As a programmer, you come to see your text editor as a faithful companion. You spend a lot of time with this tool, so use one that works with you.

A text editor should save plain text without any formatting at all. You don't want anything that saves colors, font choices, or other text formatting because these things don't automatically translate to HTML.

Fortunately, you have several choices, as the following sections reveal.

Tools to avoid unless you have nothing else

A text editor may be a simple program, but that doesn't mean they're all the same. Some programs have a history of causing problems for beginners (and experienced developers, too). There's usually no need to use some of these weaker choices.

Microsoft Word

Just don't use it for web development. Word is a word processor. Even though, theoretically, it can create web pages, the HTML code it writes is absolutely horrific. As an example, I created a blank document, wrote "Hello World" in it, changed the font, and saved it as HTML. The resulting page was non-compliant code, was not quite HTML or XHTML, and was 114 lines long. Word is getting better, but it's just not a good web development tool. In fact, don't use any word processor. They're just not designed for this kind of work.

Windows Notepad

Notepad is everywhere, and it's free. That's the good news. However, Notepad doesn't have a lot of the features you might need, such as line numbers, multiple documents, or macros. Use it if you're on an unfamiliar machine, but try something else if you can. Many people begin with Notepad, but it won't be long until you outgrow its limitations.

Mac TextEdit

Mac has a simple text editor built in — TextEdit — that's similar to Notepad, but closer to a word processor than a programmer's text editor. TextEdit saves files in a number of formats. If you want to use it to write web pages, you must save your files in plain-text format, and you must not use any of TextEdit's formatting features. It's probably best not to use TextEdit unless you really have to.

Suggested programmer's editors

If Notepad, Word, and TextEdit aren't the best choices, what are some better options?

Good question. Because a text editor is such an important tool, it might depend a bit on your preferences, so I'll highlight a few of my favorites. Note that every editor I mention here is entirely free, so don't go paying for something until you've tried some of these first.

A noteworthy editor: Notepad++

A number of developers have come up with good text editors. Some of the best are free, such as Notepad++ by Don Ho. Notepad++ is designed for text editing, especially in programming languages. Figure 3-1 shows Notepad++ with an HTML file loaded.

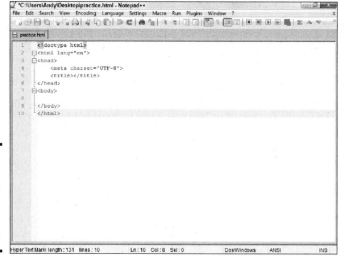

Figure 3-1:
Notepad++
has many of
the features
you need in
a text editor.

Notepad++ has a lot of interesting features. Here are a few highlights:

✦ **Syntax highlighting:** Notepad++ can recognize key HTML terms and put different types of terms in different colors. For example, all HTML tags are rendered blue, and text is black, making it easy to tell if you've made certain kinds of mistakes, such as forgetting to end a tag. Note that the colors aren't saved in the document. The coloring features are there to help you understand the code.

✦ **Multiple files:** You'll often want to edit more than one document at a time. You can have several different documents in memory at the same time.

✦ **Multi-language support:** Currently, your pages consist of nothing but HTML. Soon enough, you'll use some other languages, like SQL, CSS, and PHP. Notepad++ is smart enough to recognize these languages, too.

✦ **Macros:** Whenever you find yourself doing something over and over, consider writing a keyboard macro. Notepad++ has a terrific macro feature. Macros are easy to record and play back a series of keystrokes, which can save you a lot of work.

✦ **Page preview:** When you write a page, test it. Notepad++ has short-cut keys built in to let you quickly view your page in Internet Explorer (Ctrl+Alt+Shift+I) and Firefox (Ctrl+Alt+Shift+X).

✦ **TextFX:** The open-source design of Notepad++ makes it easy to add features. The TextFX extension (built into Notepad++) allows you to do all sorts of interesting things. One especially handy set of tools runs HTML Tidy on your page and fixes any problems.

Sadly, Notepad++ is a Windows-only editor. If you're using Mac or Linux, you need to find something else. The closest alternative in the Mac and Linux world is gedit.

gedit

One simple but effective editor available free for all major operating systems is gedit. It is the default editor for many versions of Linux, but you can download it for Mac and Windows from `http://projects.gnome.org/gedit/`.

It has all the standard features including syntax highlighting (which colors different parts of code in different colors to help with debugging), line numbers, and a tag list, which is a special menu which allows you to pick common HTML tags from a list if you forget some syntax. (You may need to play with the plugins from the edit-preferences menu to activate all these features.)

Sadly, gedit does not have a macro editor. This may not be a deal-breaker for you, but often I find a macro tool to be extremely useful, and I'm happiest when my editor has this feature. (If you're especially geeky, it does expose the entire Python language and allow you to modify anything with this language, but that's a topic for another day.) If you need a very nice general-purpose editor, consider gedit. It does much of what you might want without getting terribly complicated.

Figure 3-2 shows gedit in action.

Figure 3-2: gedit is a very nice but simple tool.

The old standards: VI and Emacs

No discussion of text editors is complete without a mention of the venerable UNIX editors that were the core of the early Internet experience. Most of the pioneering work on the web was done in the UNIX and Linux operating systems, and these environments had two extremely popular text-editor families.

Both might seem obscure and difficult to modern sensibilities, but they still have passionate adherents, even in the Windows community. (Besides, Linux is more popular than ever!)

VI and VIM

VI stands for VIsual Editor. That name seems strange now because most developers can't imagine an editor that's *not* visual. Back in the day, it was a very big deal that VI could use the entire screen for editing text. Before that time, line-oriented editors were the main way to edit text files. Trust me, you have it good now. Figure 3-3 shows a modern variant of VI (called GVIM) in action.

Figure 3-3:
VI isn't pretty, but after you know it, it's very powerful.

VI is a *modal* editor, which means that the same key sometimes has more than one job, depending on the editor's current mode. For example, the I key is used to indicate where you want to insert text. The D key is used to delete text, and so on. Of course, when you're inserting text, the keys have their normal meanings. This multimode behavior is baffling to modern users, but it can be amazingly efficient after you get used to it. Skilled VI users swear by it and often use nothing else.

VI is a little too obscure for some users, so a number of variants are floating around, such as VIM, or VI Improved. (Yeah, it should be VII but maybe they were afraid people would call it the Roman numeral seven.) VIM is a little friendlier than VI, and GVIM is friendlier yet. It tells you which mode it's in and includes such modern features as mouse support, menus, and icons. Even with these features, VIM is not intuitive for most people.

Versions of VI are available for nearly any operating system being used. If you already know VI, you might enjoy using it for web page development because it has all the features you might need. If you don't already know VI, it's probably more efficient for you to start with a more standard text editor, such as Notepad++.

Emacs

The other popular editor from the UNIX world is Emacs. Like VI, you probably don't need this tool if you never use Linux or UNIX. Also like VI, if you know it already, you probably don't need anything else. Emacs has been a programmer's editor for a very long time (it has been in continuous development since 1976) and has nearly every feature you can think of.

Emacs also has a lot of features you haven't thought of, including a built-in text adventure game and even a psychotherapist simulator. I really couldn't make this stuff up if I tried.

Emacs has very powerful customization and macro features and allows you to view and edit more than one file at a time. Emacs also has the ability to view and manipulate the local file system, manage remote files, access the local operating system (OS) shell, and even browse the web or check e-mail without leaving the program. If you're willing to invest in a program that takes some effort to understand, you'll have an incredibly powerful tool in your kit. Versions of Emacs are available for most major operating systems. Emacs is one of the first programs I install on any new computer because it's so powerful. A version of Emacs is shown in Figure 3-4.

An enhanced version — XEmacs — (shown in the figure) uses standard menus and icons like modern programs, so it's reasonably easy to get started with.

Figure 3-4: Emacs is powerful but somewhat eccentric.

WARNING!

Emacs has an astonishing number of options and a nonstandard interface, so it can be challenging for beginners. However, those who have made the investment (like me) swear by it.

My personal choice: Komodo Edit

Personally I really like Komodo Edit (www.activestate.com/komodo-edit). This editor is extremely powerful, but is not quite as intimidating as some of the older tools. It has a modern streamlined interface, but more power than you might realize at first. Komodo Edit is actually the open-source cousin to a commercial Integrated Development Environment (IDE) called Komodo IDE. Komodo IDE costs hundreds of dollars, but Komodo Edit has almost as many features, and is entirely free. Figure 3-5 illustrates Komodo Edit.

Komodo Edit has a number of really intriguing features that make it stand out in my mind:

✦ **All the standard features:** Komodo Edit has all the features I've mentioned as necessary for a programmer's editor, including syntax highlighting, line numbers, and saving in plain text format.

✦ **Code completion:** A number of higher-end programmer's editors have this feature, but it's not as common in text editors. Here's how it works: When you set up a page as HTML5 (by choosing from the menu on the bottom right), Komodo "watches" as you type and provides hints. So, if you begin typing <h, Komodo pops up a little dialog box showing all the tags that begin with h. If you pick <html> and then move to the next line and type an angle bracket (<) character, you'll get a pop-up menu with <head> and <body> listed because these are the two tags valid in this context. Komodo is pretty smart about knowing what tags you can use when. This can be a helpful feature when you're starting out.

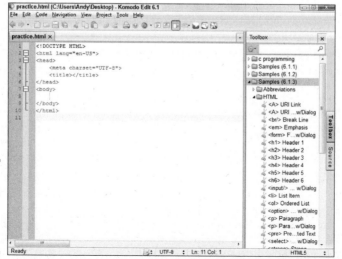

Figure 3-5:
Komodo Edit
is a really
powerful
editor.

✦ **Multiple file support:** Your first few web pages will be single documents, but most websites incorporate many pages. Komodo allows you to have several pages at once and to compare any two pages at the same time.

✦ **Page Preview:** Just use `ctrl-K-V` to preview the current web page in a second tab. This is a quick way to see how your page is going.

✦ **Multiple language support:** This book (and web development in general) requires a whole bunch of different languages. Komodo Edit is just as good at the languages you'll be using as it is with HTML. Komodo has native support for HTML, CSS, JavaScript, PHP, MySQL and many more. (In fact, I also use it for working in other languages like Python, C++, and Java, so you might end up using it beyond even web development.)

✦ **Multi-platform:** It might not be a big deal to you right now, but Komodo works the same on all major operating systems – Windows, Mac, and Linux. This really matters in web development because you will encounter new operating systems in your web travels. I use all three major OS types and use Komodo on all of them.

✦ **Remote file support:** Eventually, you'll be posting your sites on a remote web server. (See Book VIII for details on how to set up a server.) Komodo makes it easy to edit a web page even when it's not on your own machine!

✦ **Page templates:** If you don't remember exactly how to start a page, you can choose New ➪ File from Template from the File menu to start a file with some starter code in it. Note that the HTML5 code provided with Komodo does not include everything the validator wants, but you can add the features you want and save it as your own template (File ➪ Save As ➪ Template).

✦ **Code sample library:** Komodo comes with a complete code sample library. To see it, pick View ➪ Tabs and Sidebars➪Toolbox. The toolbox appears and contains a number of interesting tools. Choose `samples-HTML` from the tree structure and you'll see several useful HTML snippets. You can double-click on any of these to add a code snippet directly to your page. This can be helpful when you don't remember exactly how to type something.

✦ **Powerful macro system:** As you spend more time with your editor, you'll probably want to add some custom features. The Macro and command feature is especially powerful. This system allows you to record a series of keystrokes and play them back. This is handy when you find yourself doing something repetitive (for example, if you have a list of filenames and you want to turn them into links). I love a good macro system. If you create a particularly good macro, you can save it for later reuse and even attach a keystroke to it so it becomes a permanent part of your Komodo system.

✦ **Tools and commands:** Explore the Tools panel to see some very useful tools that are installed by default. These tools are often used to send commands to the underlying operating system. You can use the tool system to view the contents of a particular directory, preview the current document in a specific browser, or pretty much anything you can do from the command line.

Super-charging Komodo with Emmet

As you begin coding, the basic features of Komodo Edit are more than enough for your needs. However, you'll soon become more adept at coding, you may want some tools to improve your efficiency. My favorite add-on for Komodo is a tool called Emmet (formerly known as Zen Coding). It's a neat tool for writing HTML and CSS super-quickly.

Essentially, this tool allows you to enter a code snippet and Emmet expands it to complete code. For example, take a look at the following code:

```
html:5>h1{my page}+ul>li*5>{item $}
```

With Emmet installed, you can simply invoke Emmet's `expand abbreviation` command, and the following HTML snippet is created:

```
<!doctype html>
<html lang="en">
<head>
    <meta charset="UTF-8">
    <title>Document</title>
</head>
<body>
```

```
<h1>my page</h1>
<ul>
    <li>item 1</li>
    <li>item 2</li>
    <li>item 3</li>
    <li>item 4</li>
    <li>item 5</li>
</ul>
</body>
</html>
```

Of course, you might not understand the Emmet code or the HTML it generates yet, so don't worry about installing Emmet until you're a little more fluent with HTML and CSS. However, when you're ready, you'll find that Emmet is one of the most powerful tools in your library. You can install Emmet (and many other interesting add-ons) by searching for it in the Tools ⇨ Add-ons menu.

I actually use Emmet more often than the code snippets built into Komodo because I find it faster and more flexible. With this tool and a little practice, I can build a web page far more quickly and accurately in a text editor than I ever would with a graphical tool like Dreamweaver.

✦ **Extensions and add-ons:** Komodo uses the same general architecture as the Firefox web browser. The developers of Komodo made it very easy to extend, so there are hundreds of really great add-ons you can install quite easily. After you have a feel for the stock version of Komodo, you may want to investigate some add-ons to make it even better. See the nearby sidebar "Super-charging Komodo with Emmet" to find out about my favorite add-on.

Other text editors

Many other text editors are used in web development. The most important thing is to find one that matches the way you work. If you don't like any of the editors I've suggested so far, here are a few more you might want to try:

✦ **SynEdit:** Much like Notepad++ and very popular with web developers

✦ **Scintilla:** Primarily a programming editor, but has nice support for HTML coding

✦ **jEdit:** A popular text editor written in Java with nice features, but some developers consider it slower than the other choices

The bottom line on editors

There is a dizzying array of editors for you to choose from. Which is the best for you is something of a personal decision. As your coding style develops, you'll know more about which is the best editor for you. If you're not sure, I recommend starting with gedit (if you want simple and fast) or Komodo Edit (if you're ready for a bit more power). Then as you spend more time with an editor, try some of the others out to see what best fits your needs.

Finding a Good Web Developer's Browser

Web pages are meant to display in a browser; so, of course, you need browsers for testing. Not all browsers are the same, though, so you need more than one. There are a number of important browsers in use right now, and you need to understand how they are related because they are how the user will see your work.

A little ancient history

You've probably already noticed that browsers are inconsistent in the way they display and handle web pages. It's useful to understand how we got into this mess.

Mosaic/Netscape: The killer application

In the beginning, browsers were written by small teams. The most important early browser was Mosaic, written by a team based at the National Center for Supercomputing Applications (NCSA) in Champaign–Urbana, Illinois.

Several members of that NCSA team decided to create a completely commercial web browser. Netscape was born and it quickly became the most prominent and important browser, with 97 percent market share at the peak of its popularity.

Microsoft enters (and wins) the battle

Microsoft came onto the scene with Internet Explorer (IE). A bitter fight (sometimes called the First Browser Wars) ensued between Microsoft and Netscape. Each browser added new features regularly. Eventually, entire sets of tags evolved, so a web page written for IE would not always work in Netscape and vice versa. Developers had three bad choices: pick only one browser to support, write two versions of the page, or stick with the more limited set of features common to both browsers.

Netscape 6.0 was a technical disappointment, and Microsoft capitalized, earning a nearly complete lock on the browser market. Microsoft's version of standards became the *only* standards because there was virtually no competition. After Microsoft won the fight, there was a period of stability but very little innovation.

Firefox shakes up the world

A new browser rose from the ashes of Netscape (in fact, its original name was Firebird, after the mythical birds that rise from their own ashes). The name was later changed to Firefox, and it breathed new life into the web. Firefox has several new features that are very appealing to web developers:

✦ **Solid compliance to standards:** Firefox followed the W3C standards almost perfectly.

✦ **Tabbed browsing:** One browser window can have several panels, each with its own page.

✦ **Easy customization:** Firefox developers encouraged people to add improvements and extensions to Firefox. This led to hundreds of interesting add-ons.

✦ **Improved security:** By this time, a number of security loopholes in IE were publicized. Although Firefox has many of the same problems, it has a much better reputation for openness and quick solutions.

WebKit messes things up again

The next shakeup happened with a rendering engine called *WebKit*. This tool is the underlying engine shared by Apple's Safari and Google's Chrome browser. These browsers changed things again by being even more aggressive about standards-compliance and by emphasizing the programming capabilities built into a browser. Chrome and Safari are each extensions of the same essential technology. It gets messier. Recently Google announced that they are developing a new rendering engine called 'blink' based on WebKit. It's still not clear what this will mean, but for the time being, WebKit is a solid place to start.

HTML5 ushers in the second browser war

It is now becoming clear that the web is far more than a document mechanism. It is really becoming more like an operating system in its own right, and increasingly the web is about applications more than documents. HTML5 is at the center of this innovation, and today there are again many browser choices. It's a better situation, as developers are insisting on compliance with HTML5 standards, and any browser that follows these standards will be acceptable. The real question today isn't which browser the user prefers, but does the user have a browser that's reasonably complaint with today's standards?

Overview of the prominent browsers

The browser is the primary tool of the web. All your users view your page with one browser or another, so you need to know a little about each of them.

Microsoft Internet Explorer 10

Microsoft Internet Explorer (IE) remains a dominant player on the Internet. Explorer is still extremely prevalent because it comes installed with Microsoft Windows. Of course, it also works exclusively with Microsoft Windows. Mac and Linux aren't supported (users don't seem too upset about it, though).

Version 10 of IE finally has respectable (if not complete support) for the major parts of the HTML5 standard. If you write pages according to the version of HTML5 described in this book (using a reasonably universal subset of the HTML5 standard), you can expect your page to work well in IE10. Most features will also work in IE9, but not all.

Older versions of Internet Explorer

The earlier versions of IE are still extremely important because so many computers out there don't have 10 installed yet. Version 6 was the dominant player in the Internet for some time, and it refuses to die. However, it will not play well with modern standards, so it's considered obsolete by most developers. (There are some software packages built on the proprietary features of IE6, so it refuses to die away completely, but there is no need for consumers to use this version.)

Mozilla Firefox

Firefox is a major improvement on IE from a programmer's point of view, for the following reasons:

✦ **Better code view:** If you view the HTML code of a page, you see the code in a special window. The code has syntax coloring, which makes it easy to read. Some versions of IE display code in Notepad, which is confusing because you think you can edit the code, but you're simply editing a copy.

✦ **Better error-handling:** You'll make mistakes. Generally, Firefox does a better job of pointing out errors than IE, especially when you begin using JavaScript and other advanced technologies.

✦ **Great extensions:** Firefox has some wonderful extensions that make web development a lot easier. These extensions allow you to modify your code on the fly, automatically validate your code, and explore the structure of your page dynamically.

✦ **Multi-platform support:** IE works only on the Windows operating system, so it isn't available to Mac or Linux users. Even if you're a Windows-only developer, your users may use something else, so you need to know how the other browsers see things.

WebKit/Safari

The default browser for Mac and the iPhone/iPad Operating System (iOS) is called Safari. It's a very powerful browser built on the WebKit rendering engine. Safari was designed with standards-compliance and speed in mind, and it shows. Your Mac and iOS users will almost certainly be using Safari, so you should know something about it. Fortunately, Chrome uses WebKit (or a variant) as well, so if things look good on Chrome, you're likely to be fine with your Apple users.

Google Chrome

Google sees the future of computing in browser-based applications using AJAX technologies. (AJAX is described in Book VII.) The Chrome browser is extremely fast, especially in the JavaScript technology that serves as the foundation to this strategy. Chrome complies quite well with common standards. In addition, Chrome has a number of developer toolkits that makes it the hands-down favorite browser for many web developers (including me). Many of the features of the developer tools make sense only when you have a bit more experience, but here are the highlights:

✦ **Real-time page editing:** You can go to any web page, right click 'inspect this element' and modify the text of that element in real time. You can then see what the element looks like with new content. You can select a part of the page to see which page corresponds to the code, and you can select the code and see which part of the page that code represents. Figure 3-6 illustrates this feature in action.

Figure 3-6: The ability to inspect an element is a powerful feature of Chrome.

✦ **Page Outline:** A well-designed web page is created in outline form, with various elements nested inside each other. The elements view allows you to see the web page in this format, with the ability to collapse and expand elements to see your page's structure clearly.

✦ **Realtime CSS Edit:** As you discover how to apply CSS styles in Books II and III, you'll want to be able to see how various CSS rules change your page. In the Inspect Element view, you can highlight a part of your page and change the CSS while seeing how the change affects your page in real time.

✦ **Network Tab:** This feature allows you to examine how long each piece of your page takes to load. It can be helpful for troubleshooting a slow-loading page.

✦ **Sources View:** This allows you to see the complete code of your page. It's especially useful when you get to JavaScript programming (in Book IV) because it includes a powerful debugging suite.

✦ **Console:** The console view is a little command-line tool integrated directly into your browser. This can be very helpful because it often shows errors that are otherwise hidden from view. The console is most useful when using JavaScript, so it is described in more detail in Book IV.

Other notable browsers

Firefox and IE are the big players in the browser world, but they certainly aren't the only browsers you will encounter.

Opera

The Opera web browser, one of the earliest standards-compliant browsers, is a technically solid browser that has never been widely used. If you design your pages with strict compliance in mind, users with Opera have no problems accessing them. Opera has very good HTML5 compliance. Many gaming consoles and mobile devices have browsers based on Opera, so it's worth looking into.

WebKit/Safari

Apple includes a web browser in all recent versions of Mac OS. The current incarnation — Safari — is an excellent standards-compliant browser. Safari was originally designed only for the Mac, but a Windows version is also available. The WebKit framework, the foundation for Safari, is used in a number of other online applications, mainly on the Mac. A modified version of Safari is the foundation of the browsers on the iPhone and iPad.

Text-only browsers

Some browsers that don't display any graphics at all (such as Lynx) are intended for the old command-line interfaces. This may seem completely irrelevant today, but these browsers are incredibly fast because they don't display graphics. Auditory browsers read the contents of web pages. They were originally intended for people with visual disabilities, but people without any disabilities often use them as well. Fire Vox is a variant of Firefox that reads web pages aloud.

Worrying about text-only readers may seem unnecessary because people with visual disabilities are a relatively small part of the population, and you may not think they're part of your target audience. You probably should think about these users anyway because it isn't difficult to help them (and if you're developing for certain organizations, support for folks with disabilities is required). There's another reason, too. The search engines (Google is the main game in town) read your page just like a text-only browser. Therefore, if an element is invisible to a text-based browser, it won't appear on the search engine.

The bottom line in browsers

Really, you need to have access to a couple browsers, but you can't possibly have them all. I tend to do my initial development testing with Chrome. I look over my page in IE version 10 and I try to keep an older computer around with IE7 or 8 just to see what will happen.

I also check the built-in browser on an Android phone and iOS tablet to see how the pages look there. Generally, if you follow the subset of HTML5 outlined in this book, you can be satisfied that it works on most browsers. However, there's still no guarantee. If you follow the standards, your page displays on any browser, but you might not get the exact layout you expect.

Chapter 4: Managing Information with Lists and Tables

In This Chapter

✔ **Understanding basic lists**

✔ **Creating unordered, ordered, and nested lists**

✔ **Building definition lists**

✔ **Building basic tables**

✔ **Using rowspan and colspan attributes**

*Y*ou'll often need to present large amounts of organized information, and HTML has some wonderful tools to manage this task. HTML has three kinds of lists and a powerful table structure for organizing the content of your page. Figure out how these tools work, and you can manage complex information with ease.

Making a List and Checking It Twice

HTML supports three types of lists. *Unordered* lists generally contain bullet points. They're used when the order of elements in the list isn't important. *Ordered* lists usually have some kind of numeric counter preceding each list item. *Definition* lists contain terms and their definitions.

Creating an unordered list

All the list types in HTML are closely related. The simplest and most common kind of list is an unordered list.

Looking at an unordered list

Look at the simple page shown in Figure 4-1. In addition to a couple of headers, it has a list of information.

This list of browsers has some interesting visual characteristics:

✦ **The items are indented.** There's some extra space between the left margin and the beginning of each list item.

✦ **The list elements have bullets.** That little dot in front of each item is a *bullet*. Bullets are commonly used in unordered lists like this one.

Figure 4-1:
An
unordered
list of web
browsers.

✦ **Each item begins a new line.** When a list item is displayed, it's shown
  on a new line.

These characteristics help you see that you have a list, but they're just
default behaviors. Defining something as a list doesn't force it to look a particular way; the defaults just help you see that these items are indeed part of
a list.

Remember the core idea of HTML here. You aren't really describing how
things *look*, but what they *mean*. You can change the appearance later when
you figure out CSS, so don't get too tied up in the particular appearance of
things. For now, just recognize that HTML can build lists, and make sure you
know how to use the various types.

Building an unordered list

Lists are made with two kinds of tags. One tag surrounds the entire list and
indicates the general type of list. This first example demonstrates an unordered list, which is surrounded by the `<ul></ul>` pair.

Note: Indenting all the code inside the `<ul>` set is common. The unordered
list can go in the main body.

Inside the `<ul></ul>` set is a number of list items. Each element of the list
is stored between a `<li>` (list item) and a `</li>` tag. Normally, each
`<li></li>` pair goes on its own line of the source code, although you can
make a list item as long as you want.

Look to Book II, Chapter 4 for information on how to change the bullet to all
kinds of other images, including circles, squares, and even custom images.

The code for the unordered list is pretty straightforward:

```html
<!doctype html>
<html lang="en">
<head>
    <meta charset="UTF-8">
<title>basicUL.html</title>
</head>
<body>
    <h1>Basic Lists</h1>
    <h2>Common Web Browsers</h2>
    <ul>
      <li>Firefox</li>
      <li>Chrome</li>
      <li>Internet Explorer</li>
      <li>Opera</li>
      <li>Safari</li>
    </ul>
</body>
</html>
```

Creating ordered lists

Ordered lists are almost exactly like unordered lists. Ordered lists tradition-ally have numbers rather than bullets (although you can change this through CSS if you want; see Book II, Chapter 4).

Viewing an ordered list

Figure 4-2 demonstrates a page with a basic ordered list — basicOL.html.

Figure 4-2 shows a list where the items are numbered. When your data is a list of steps or information with some type of numerical values, an ordered list is a good choice.

Figure 4-2:
A simple ordered list.

Building the ordered list

The code for basicOL.html is remarkably similar to the previous unordered list:

```
<!doctype html>
<html lang="en">
<head>
    <meta charset="UTF-8">
    <title>basicOL.html</title>
</head>
<body>
    <h1>Basic Ordered List</h1>
    <h2>Top ten dog names in the USA</h2>
    <ol>
      <li>Max</li>
      <li>Jake</li>
      <li>Buddy</li>
      <li>Maggie</li>
      <li>Bear</li>
      <li>Molly</li>
      <li>Bailey</li>
      <li>Shadow</li>
      <li>Sam</li>
      <li>Lady</li>
    </ol>

    <p>
      data from http://www.bowwow.com.au
    </p>
</body>
</html>
```

The only change is the list tag itself. Rather than the `<ul>` tag, the ordered list uses the `<ol>` indicator. The list items are the same `<li></li>` pairs used in the unordered list.

You don't indicate the item number anywhere; it generates automatically based on the position of each item within the list. Therefore, you can change the order of the items, and the numbers are still correct.

This is where it's great that HTML is about meaning, not layout. If you specified the actual numbers, it'd be a mess to move things around. All that really matters is that the element is inside an ordered list.

Making nested lists

Sometimes, you'll want to create outlines or other kinds of complex data in your pages. You can easily nest lists inside each other, if you want. Figure 4-3 shows a more complex list describing popular cat names in the U.S. and Australia.

Figure 4-3 uses a combination of lists to do its work. This figure contains a list of two countries: the U.S. and Australia. Each country has an H3 heading and another (ordered) list inside it. You can nest various elements inside a list, but you have to do it carefully if you want the page to validate.

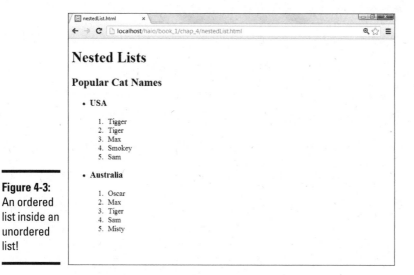

Figure 4-3:
An ordered
list inside an
unordered
list!

In this example, there's an unordered list with only two elements. Each of these elements contains an <h3> heading and an ordered list. The page handles all this data in a relatively clean way and validates correctly.

Examining the nested list example

The entire code for nestedList.html is reproduced here:

```
<!doctype html>
<html lang="en">
<head>
    <meta charset="UTF-8">
    <title>nestedList.html</title>
</head>
<body>
    <h1>Nested Lists</h1>

    <h2>Popular Cat Names</h2>
    <ul>
      <li>
        <h3>USA</h3>
        <ol>
          <li>Tigger</li>
          <li>Tiger</li>
          <li>Max</li>
          <li>Smokey</li>
          <li>Sam</li>
        </ol>
      </li>

      <li>
        <h3>Australia</h3>
        <ol>
          <li>Oscar</li>
          <li>Max</li>
          <li>Tiger</li>
```

```
        <li>Sam</li>
        <li>Misty</li>
      </ol>
    </li>
  </ul>
</body>
</html>
```

Here are a few things you might notice in this code listing:

✦ There's a large `<ul>` set surrounding the entire main list.

✦ The main list has only two list items.

✦ Each of these items represents a country.

✦ Each country has an `<h3>` element, describing the country name inside the `<li>`.

✦ Each country also has an `<ol>` set with a list of names.

✦ The indentation really helps you see how things are connected.

Indenting your code

You might have noticed that I indent all the HTML code in this book. The browsers ignore all indentation, but it's still an important coding habit.

There are many opinions about how code should be formatted, but the standard format I use in this book will serve you well until you develop your own style.

Generally, I use the following rules to indent HTML code:

✦ **Indent each nested element.** Because the `<head>` tag is inside the `<html>` element, I indent to indicate this. Likewise, the `<li>` elements are always indented inside `<ul>` or `<ol>` pairs.

✦ **Line up your elements.** If an element takes up more than one line, line up the ending tag with the beginning tag. This way, you know what ends what.

✦ **Use spaces, not tabs.** The tab character often causes problems in source code. Different editors format tabs differently, and a mixture of tabs and spaces can make your carefully formatted page look awful when you view it in another editor.

Most editors have the ability to interpret the tab key as spaces. It's a great idea to find this feature on your editor and turn it on, so any time you hit the tab key, it's interpreted as spaces. In Komodo Edit, you do this in Edit ➪ Preferences ➪ Editor ➪ Indentation.

✦ **Use two spaces.** Most coders use two or four spaces per indentation level. HTML elements can be nested pretty deeply. Going seven or eight layers deep is common. If you use tabs or too many spaces, you'll have so much white space that you can't see the code.

✦ **End at the left margin.** If you finish the page and you're not back at the left margin, you've forgotten to end something. Proper indentation makes seeing your page organization easy. Each element should line up with its closing tag.

Building a nested list

When you look over the code for the nested list, it can look intimidating, but it isn't really that hard. The secret is to build the list *outside in:*

1. **Create the outer list first.** Build the primary list (whether it's ordered or unordered). In my example, I began with just the unordered list with the two countries in it.

2. **Add list items to the outer list.** If you want text or headlines in the larger list (as I did), you can put them here. If you're putting nothing but a list inside your primary list, you may want to put some placeholder `<li>` tags in there just so you can be sure everything's working.

3. **Validate before adding the next list level.** Nested lists can confuse the validator (and you). Validate your code with the outer list to make sure there are no problems before you add inner lists.

4. **Add the first inner list.** After you know the basic structure is okay, add the first interior list. For my example, this was the ordered list of cat names in the U.S.

5. **Repeat until finished.** Keep adding lists until your page looks right.

6. **Validate frequently.** It's much better to validate as you go than to wait until everything's finished. Catch your mistakes early so you don't replicate them.

Building the definition list

One more type of list — the definition list — is very useful, even if it's used infrequently. The definition list was originally designed to format dictionary-style definitions, but it's really useful any time you have name and value pairs. Figure 4-4 shows a sample definition list in action.

Definition lists don't use bullets or numbers. Instead, they have two elements. *Definition terms* are usually words or short phrases. In Figure *4-4*, the browser names are defined as definition terms. *Definition descriptions* are the extended text blocks that contain the actual definition.

The standard layout of definition lists indents each definition description. Of course, you can change the layout to what you want after you understand the CSS in Books II and III.

You can use definition lists any time you want a list marked by key terms, rather than bullets or numbers. The definition list can also be useful in other situations, such as forms, figures with captions, and so on.

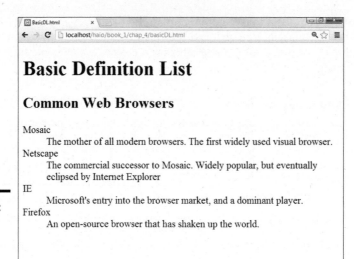

Figure 4-4:
A basic
definition
list.

Here's the code for basicDL.html:

```
<!DOCTYPE HTML>
<html lang="en-US">
  <head>
    <meta charset="UTF-8">
    <title>BasicDL.html</title>
  </head>
  <body>
    <h1>Basic Definition List</h1>
    <h2>Common Web Browsers</h2>
    <dl>
      <dt>Mosaic</dt>
      <dd>
        The mother of all modern browsers. The first widely used
        visual browser.
      </dd>

      <dt>Netscape</dt>
      <dd>
        The commercial successor to Mosaic. Widely popular, but
        eventually eclipsed by Internet Explorer
      </dd>

      <dt>IE</dt>
      <dd>
        Microsoft's entry into the browser market, and a dominant
        player.
      </dd>

      <dt>Firefox</dt>
      <dd>
        An open-source browser that has shaken up the world.
      </dd>
    </dl>
  </body>
</html>
```

As you can see, the definition list uses three tag pairs:

✦ `<dl></dl>` defines the entire list.

✦ `<dt></dt>` defines each definition term.

✦ `<dd></dd>` defines the definition data.

Definition lists aren't used often, but they can be extremely useful. Any time you have a list that will be a combination of terms and values, a definition list is a good choice.

Building Tables

Sometimes, you'll encounter data that fits best in a tabular format. HTML supports several table tags for this kind of work. Figure 4-5 illustrates a very basic table.

Sometimes, the best way to show data in a meaningful way is to organize it in a table. HTML defines a table with the (cleverly named) `<table>` tag. The table contains a number of table rows (defined with the `<tr>` tag). Each table row can consist of a number of table data (`<td>`) or table header (`<th>`) tags.

Compare the output in Figure 4-5 with the code for basicTable.html that creates it:

```
<!doctype html>
<html lang="en">
```

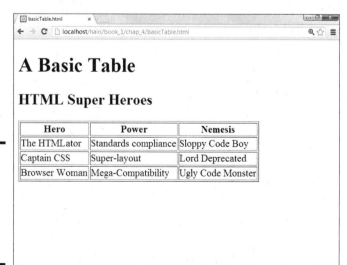

Figure 4-5:
Tables are useful for certain kinds of data representation.

```
<head>
    <meta charset="UTF-8">
    <title>basicTable.html</title>
</head>
<body>
    <h1>A Basic Table</h1>
    <h2>HTML Super Heroes</h2>
     <table border = "1">
      <tr>
        <th>Hero</th>
        <th>Power</th>
        <th>Nemesis</th>
        </tr>

      <tr>
        <td>The HTMLator</td>
        <td>Standards compliance</td>
        <td>Sloppy Code Boy</td>
      </tr>

      <tr>
        <td>Captain CSS</td>
        <td>Super-layout</td>
        <td>Lord Deprecated</td>
      </tr>

      <tr>
        <td>Browser Woman</td>
        <td>Mega-Compatibility</td>
        <td>Ugly Code Monster</td>
      </tr>

    </table>
</body>
</html>
```

Defining the table

The HTML table is defined with the `<table></table>` pair. It makes a lot of
sense to indent and space your code carefully so you can see the structure
of the table in the code. Just by glancing at the code, you can guess that the
table consists of three rows and each row consists of three elements.

In a word processor, you typically create a blank table by defining the
number of rows and columns, and then fill it in. In HTML, you define the table
row by row, and the elements in each row determine the number of columns.
It's up to you to make sure each row has the same number of elements.

By default (in most browsers, anyway), tables don't show their borders. If
you want to see basic table borders, you can turn on the table's `border`
attribute. (An *attribute* is a special modifier you can attach to some tags.)

```
<table border = "1">
```

This tag creates a table and specifies that it will have a border of size `1`. If
you leave out the `border = "1"` business, some browsers display a border

Building Tables **61**

Book I
Chapter 4

Managing
Information with
Lists and Tables

and some don't. You can set the border value to 0 or to a larger number. The larger number makes a bigger border, as shown in Figure 4-6.

Although this method of making table borders is perfectly fine, I show a much more flexible and powerful technique in Book II, Chapter 4.

Setting a table border is a good idea because you can't count on browsers to have the same default. Additionally, the border value is always in quotes. When you read about CSS in Book II (are you getting tired of hearing that yet?), you discover how to add more complex and interesting borders than this simple attribute allows.

Adding your first row

After you define a table, you need to add some rows. Each row is indicated by a `<tr></tr>` pair.

Inside the `<tr></tr>` set, you need some table data. The first row often consists of *table headers*. These special cells are formatted differently to indicate that they're labels, rather than data.

Table headers have some default formatting to help you remember they're headers, but you can change the way they look. You can change the table header's appearance in all kinds of great ways in Books II and III. Define the table header so when you discover formatting and decide to make all your table headers chartreuse, you'll know where in the HTML code all the table headers are.

Indent your headers inside the `<tr>` set. If your table contains three columns, your first row might begin like this:

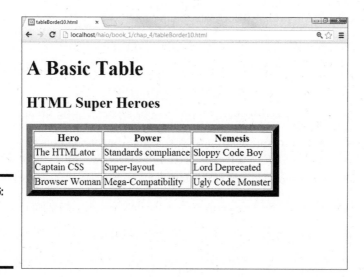

Figure 4-6:
I set the border attribute to 10.

```
<tr>
  <th></th>
  <th></th>
  <th></th>
</tr>
```

Place the text you want shown in the table headers between the `<th>` and `</th>` elements. The contents appear in the order they're defined.

 Headings don't have to be on the top row. If you want headings on the left, just put a `<th></th>` pair as the first element of each row. You can have headings at both the top and the left, if you want. In fact, you can have headings anywhere, but it usually makes sense to put headings only at the top or left.

Making your data rows

The next step is to create another row. The data rows are just like the heading row, except they use `<td></td>` pairs, rather than `<th></th>` pairs, to contain the data elements. Typically, a three-column table has blank rows that look like this:

```
<tr>
  <td></td>
  <td></td>
  <td></td>
</tr>
```

Place the data elements inside the `<td></td>` segments and you're ready to go.

Building tables in the text editor

Some people think that tables are a good reason to use WYSIWYG (what you see is what you get) editors because they think it's hard to create tables in text mode. You have to plan a little, but it's really quite quick and easy to build an HTML table without graphical tools if you follow this plan:

1. **Plan ahead.** Know how many rows and columns will be in the table. Sketching it on paper first might be helpful. Changing the number of rows later is easy, but changing the number of columns can be a real pain after some of the code has been written.

2. **Create the headings.** If you're going to start with a standard headings-on-top table, begin by creating the heading row. Save, check, and validate. You don't want mistakes to multiply when you add more complexity. This heading row tells how many columns you'll need.

3. **Build a sample empty row.** Make a sample row with the correct number of td elements with one `<td></td>` pair per line. Build one td set and use copy and paste to copy this data cell as many times as you need. Make sure the number of `<td>` pairs equals the number of `<th>` sets in the heading row.

Building Tables **63**

Book I
Chapter 4

Managing
Information with
Lists and Tables

4. **Copy and paste the empty row to make as many rows as you need.**

5. **Save, view, and validate.** Be sure everything looks right and validates properly before you put a lot of effort into adding data.

6. **Populate the table with the data you need.** Go row by row, adding the data between the `<td></td>` pairs.

7. **Test and validate again to make sure you didn't accidentally break something.**

Spanning rows and columns

Sometimes, you need a little more flexibility in your table design. Figure 4-7 shows a page from an evil overlord's daily planner.

Being an evil overlord is clearly a complex business. From a code standpoint, the items that take up more than one cell are the most interesting. Designing traps takes two mornings, and improving the hideout takes three. All Friday afternoon and evening are spent on world domination. Take a look at the code, and you'll see how it works:

```
<!doctype html>
<html lang="en">
<head>
    <meta charset="UTF-8">
    <title>tableSpan.html</title>
</head>
<body>
    <h1>Using colspan and rowspan</h1>
    <table border = "1">
      <caption><p>My Schedule</p></caption>
       <tr>
        <th></th>
        <th>Monday</th>
        <th>Tuesday</th>
        <th>Wednesday</th>
        <th>Thursday</th>
        <th>Friday</th>
      </tr>

      <tr>
        <th>Breakfast</th>
        <td>In lair</td>
        <td>with cronies</td>
        <td>In lair</td>
        <td>in lair</td>
        <td>in lair</td>
      </tr>

      <tr>
        <th>Morning</th>
        <td colspan = "2">Design traps</td>
        <td colspan = "3">Improve Hideout</td>
      </tr>

      <tr>
        <th>Afternoon</th>
        <td>train minions</td>
```

```
            <td>train minions</td>
            <td>train minions</td>
            <td>train minions</td>
            <td rowspan = "2">world domination</td>
        </tr>

        <tr>
            <th>Evening</th>
            <td>manaical laughter</td>
            <td>manaical laughter</td>
            <td>manaical laughter</td>
            <td>manaical laughter</td>
        </tr>

    </table>
</body>
</html>
```

The secret to making cells larger than the default is two special attributes: rowspan and colspan.

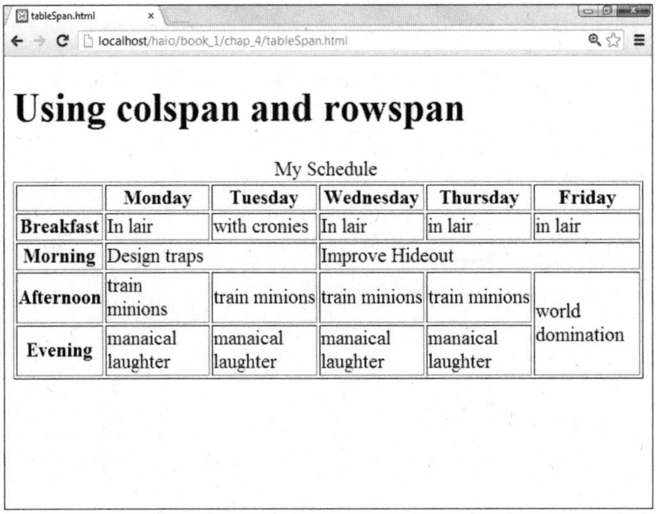

Figure 4-7: Some of these activities take up more than one cell.

Spanning multiple columns

The morning activities tend to happen over several days. Designing traps will take both Monday and Tuesday morning, and improving the hideout will occupy the remaining three mornings. Take another look at the Morning row; here's how this is done:

```
<tr>
    <th>Morning</th>
    <td colspan = "2">Design traps</td>
    <td colspan = "3">Improve Hideout</td>
</tr>
```

The Design Traps cell spans over two normal columns. The `colspan` attribute tells how many columns this cell will take. The Improve Hideout cell has a `colspan` of 3.

The Morning row still takes up six columns. The `<th>` is one column wide, like normal, but the Design Traps cell spans two columns and the Improve Hideout cell takes three, which totals six columns wide. If you increase the width of a cell, you need to eliminate some other cells in the row to compensate.

Spanning multiple rows

A related property — `rowspan` — allows a cell to take up more than one row of a table. Look back at the Friday column in Figure 4-7, and you'll see the World Domination cell takes up two time slots. (If world domination was easy, everybody would do it.) Here's the relevant code:

```
<tr>
  <th>Afternoon</th>
  <td>train minions</td>
  <td>train minions</td>
  <td>train minions</td>
  <td>train minions</td>
  <td rowspan = "2">world domination</td>
</tr>

<tr>
  <th>Evening</th>
  <td>maniacal laughter</td>
  <td>maniacal laughter</td>
  <td>maniacal laughter</td>
  <td>maniacal laughter</td>
</tr>
```

The Evening row has only five entries because the World Domination cell extends into the space that would normally be occupied by a `<td>` pair.

If you want to use `rowspan` and `colspan`, don't just hammer away at the page in your editor. Sketch out what you want to accomplish first. I'm pretty good at this stuff, and I still needed a sketch before I was able to create the tableSpan.html code.

Avoiding the table-based layout trap

Tables are pretty great. They're a terrific way to present certain kinds of data. When you add the `colspan` and `rowspan` concepts, you can use tables to create some pretty interesting layouts. In fact, because old-school HTML didn't really have any sort of layout technology, a lot of developers came up with some pretty amazing layouts based on tables. You still see a lot of web pages today designed with tables as the primary layout mechanism.

Using tables for layout causes some problems though, such as

✦ **Tables aren't meant for layout.** Tables are designed for data presentation, not layout. To make tables work for layout, you have to do a lot of sneaky hacks, such as tables nested inside other tables or invisible images for spacing.

✦ **The code becomes complicated fast.** Tables involve a lot of HTML markup. If the code involves tables nested inside each other, it's very difficult to remember which `<td>` element is related to which row of which table. Table-based layouts are very difficult to modify by hand.

✦ **Formatting is done cell by cell.** A web page could be composed of hundreds of table cells. Making a change in the font or color often involves making changes in hundreds of cells throughout the page. This makes your page less flexible and harder to update.

✦ **Presentation is tied tightly to data.** A table-based layout tightly intertwines the data and its presentation. This runs counter to a primary goal of web design — separation of data from its presentation.

✦ **Table-based layouts are hard to change.** After you create a layout based on tables, it's very difficult to make modifications because all the table cells have a potential effect on other cells.

✦ **Table-based layouts cause problems for screen-readers.** People with visual disabilities use special software to read web pages. These screen-readers are well adapted to read tables as they were intended (to manage tabular data), but the screen-readers have no way of knowing when the table is being used as a layout technique rather than a data presentation tool. This makes table-based layouts less compliant to accessibility standards.

✦ **Table-based layouts do not adapt well.** Modern users expect to run pages on cell phones and tablets as well as desktop machines. Table-based designs do not easily scale to these smaller form-factors.

Resist the temptation to use tables for layout. Use tables to do what they're designed for: data presentation. Book III is entirely about how to use CSS to generate any kind of visual layout you might want. The CSS-based approaches are easier, more dependable, and much more flexible.

Chapter 5: Making Connections with Links

In This Chapter

✔ **Understanding hyperlinks**

✔ **Building the anchor tag**

✔ **Recognizing absolute and relative links**

✔ **Building internal links**

✔ **Creating lists of links**

*T*he basic concept of the hyperlink is common today, but it was a major breakthrough back in the day. The idea is still pretty phenomenal, if you think about it: When you click a certain piece of text (or a designated image, for that matter), your browser is instantly transported somewhere else. The new destination might be on the same computer as the initial page, or it could be literally anywhere in the world.

Any page is theoretically a threshold to any other page, and all information has the ability to be linked. This is still a profound idea. In this chapter, you discover how to add links to your pages.

Making Your Text Hyper

The hyperlink is truly a wonderful thing. Believe it or not, there was a time when you had to manually type in the address of the web page you wanted to go to. Not so anymore. Figure 5-1 illustrates a page that describes some of my favorite websites.

In Figure 5-1, the underlined words are hyperlinks. Clicking a hyperlink takes you to the indicated website. Although this is undoubtedly familiar to you as a web user, a few details are necessary to make this mechanism work:

✦ **Something must be linkable.** Some text or other element must provide a trigger for the linking behavior.

✦ **Things that are links should look like links.** This is actually easy to do when you write plain HTML because all links have a standard (if ugly) appearance. Links are usually underlined blue text. When you can create color schemes, you may no longer want links to look like the default appearance, but they should still be recognizable as links.

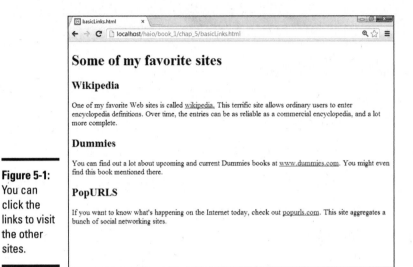

Some of my favorite sites

Wikipedia

One of my favorite Web sites is called wikipedia. This terrific site allows ordinary users to enter encyclopedia definitions. Over time, the entries can be as reliable as a commercial encyclopedia, and a lot more complete.

Dummies

You can find out a lot about upcoming and current Dummies books at www.dummies.com. You might even find this book mentioned there.

PopURLS

If you want to know what's happening on the Internet today, check out popurls.com. This site aggregates a bunch of social networking sites.

Figure 5-1:
You can
click the
links to visit
the other
sites.

+ **The browser needs to know where to go.** When the user clicks the link, the browser is sent to some address somewhere on the Internet. Sometimes that address is visible on the page, but it doesn't need to be.

+ **It should be possible to integrate links into text.** In this example, each link is part of a sentence. It should be possible to make some things act like links without necessarily standing on their own (like heading tags do).

+ **The link's appearance sometimes changes.** Links sometimes begin as blue underlined text, but after a link has been visited, the link is shown in purple, instead. After you know CSS, you can change this behavior.

Of course, if your web page mentions some other website, you should provide a link to that other website.

Introducing the anchor tag

The key to hypertext is an oddly named tag called the *anchor* tag. This tag is encased in an `<a></a>` set of tags and contains all the information needed to manage links between pages.

The code for the `basicLinks.html` page is shown here:

```
<!DOCTYPE html>
<html lang = "en-US">
  <head>
    <meta charset = "UTF-8">
    <title>basicLinks.html</title>
```

```
</head>

<body>
  <h1>Some of my favorite sites</h1>
    <h2>Wikipedia</h2>
    <p>
      One of my favorite websites is called
      <a href = "http://www.wikipedia.org">wikipedia.</a>
      This terrific site allows ordinary users to enter
      encyclopedia definitions. Over time, the entries
      can be as reliable as a commercial encyclopedia,
      and a lot more complete.
    </p>

    <h2>Dummies</h2>
    <p>
      You can find out a lot about upcoming and current
      Dummies books at <a href = "http://www.dummies.com">
      www.dummies.com</a>. You might even find this
      book mentioned there.
    </p>

    <h2>PopURLS</h2>
    <p>
      If you want
      to know what's happening on the Internet today,
      check out <a href = "http://popurls.com">
      popurls.com</a>. This site aggregates a bunch of
      social networking sites.
    </p>
  </body>
</html>
```

As you can see, the anchor tag is embedded into paragraphs. The text generally flows around an anchor, and you can see the anchor code is embedded inside the paragraphs.

Comparing block-level and inline elements

All the tags described so far in this book have been *block-level* tags. Block-level tags typically begin and end with carriage returns. For example, three `<h1>` tags occupy three lines. Each `<p></p>` set has implied space above and below it. Most HTML tags are block-level.

Some tags are meant to be embedded inside block-level tags and don't interrupt the flow of the text. The anchor tag is one such tag. Anchors never stand on their own in the HTML body. This type of tag is an *inline* tag. They're meant to be embedded inside block-level tags, such as list items, paragraphs, and headings.

Analyzing an anchor

The first link shows all the main parts of an anchor in a pretty straightforward way:

```
<a href = "http://www.wikipedia.org">wikipedia.</a>
```

✦ **The anchor tag itself:** The anchor tag is simply the `<a></a>` pair. You don't type the entire word *anchor,* just the *a.*

✦ **The hypertext reference (`href`) attribute:** Almost all anchors contain this attribute. It's very rare to write `<a` without `href`. The `href` attribute indicates a web address will follow.

✦ **A web address in quotes:** The address that the browser will follow is encased in quotes. See the next section in this chapter for more information on web addresses. In this example, `http://www.wikipedia.org` is the address.

✦ **The text that appears as a link:** The user will typically expect to click specially formatted text. Any text that appears between the `<a href>` part and the `</a>` part is visible on the page and formatted as a link. In this example, the word *wikipedia* is the linked text.

✦ **The `</a>` marker:** This marker indicates that the text link is finished.

Introducing URLs

The special link addresses are a very important part of the web. You probably already type web addresses into the address bar of your browser (`http://www.google.com`), but you may not be completely aware of how they work. Web addresses are technically URLs (Uniform Resource Locators), and they have a very specific format.

Sometimes, you'll see the term *URI* (Uniform Resource Identifier) instead of URL. URI is technically a more correct name for web addresses, but the term URL has caught on. The two terms are close enough to be interchangeable.

A URL usually contains the following parts:

✦ **Protocol:** A web *protocol* is a standardized agreement on how communication occurs. The web primarily uses HTTP (hypertext transfer protocol), but occasionally, you encounter others. Most addresses begin with `http://` because this is the standard on the web. Protocols usually end with a colon and two slashes (`://`).

✦ **Host name:** It's traditional to name your primary web server www. There's no requirement for this, but it's common enough that users expect to type **www** right after the `http://` stuff. Regardless, the text right after `http://` (and up to the first period) is the name of the actual computer you're linking to.

✦ **Domain name:** The last two or three characters indicate a particular type of web server. These letters can indicate useful information about the type of organization that houses the page. Three-letter domains usually indicate the type of organization, and two-letter domains indicate a country. Sometimes, you'll even see a combination of the two.

✦ **Subdomain:** Everything between the host name (usually www) and the domain name (often .com) is the subdomain. This is used so that large organizations can have multiple servers on the same domain. For example, my department web page is http://www.cs.iupui.edu. www is the name of the primary server, and this is the computer science department at IUPUI (Indiana University–Purdue University Indianapolis), which is an educational organization.

✦ **Page name:** Sometimes, an address specifies a particular document on the web. This page name follows the address and usually ends with .html. Sometimes, the page name includes subdirectories and username information, as well. For example, my web development course is in the N241 directory of my (aharris) space at IUPUI, so the page's full address is http://www.cs.iupui.edu/~aharris/n241/index.html.

✦ **Username:** Some web servers are set up with multiple users. Sometimes, an address will indicate a specific user's account with a tilde (~) character. My address has ~aharris in it to indicate the page is found in my (aharris) account on the machine.

The page name is sometimes optional. Many servers have a special name set up as the default page, which appears if no other name is specified. This name is usually index.html but sometimes home.htm. On my server, index.html is the default name, so I usually just point to www.cs.iupui.edu/~aharris/n241, and the index page appears.

Domain	Explanation
.org	Non-profit institution
.com	Commercial enterprise
.edu	Educational institution
.gov	Governing body
.ca	Canada
.uk	United Kingdom
.tv	Tuvali

Making Lists of Links

Many web pages turn out to be lists of links. Because lists and links go so well together, it's good to look at an example. Figure 5-2 illustrates a list of links to books written by a certain (cough) devilishly handsome author.

This example has no new code to figure out, but the page shows some interesting components:

✦ **The list:** An ordinary unordered list.

✦ **Links:** Each list item contains a link. The link has a reference (which you can't see immediately) and linkable text (which is marked like an ordinary link).

✦ **Descriptive text:** After each link is some ordinary text that describes the link. Writing some text to accompany the actual link is very common.

Figure 5-2:
Putting links
in a list is
common.

This code shows the way the page is organized:

```
<!DOCTYPE html>
<html lang = "en-US">

  <head>
    <meta charset = "UTF-8">
    <title>listLinks.html</title>
  </head>

  <body>
    <h1>Some nice programming books</h1>
    <ul>
      <li><a href = "http://www.aharrisbooks.net/haio">
          HTML / CSS / JavaScript ALL in One for Dummies</a>
          A complete resource to web development</li>
      <li><a href = "http://www.aharrisbooks.net/jad">
          JavaScript / AJAX for Dummies</a>
          Using JavaScript, AJAX, and jQuery</li>
      <li><a href="http://www.aharrisbooks.net/pythonGame">
          Game Programming - the L Line</a>
          Game development in Python</li>
      <li><a href="http://www.aharrisbooks.net/h5g">
          HTML5 Game Development for Dummies</a>
          Building web and mobile games in HTML5</li>
    </ul>
  </body>
</html>
```

The indentation is interesting here. Each list item contains an anchor and some descriptive text. To keep the code organized, web developers tend to place the anchor inside the list item. The address sometimes goes on a new line if it's long, with the anchor text on a new line and the description on succeeding lines. I normally put the `<li>` tag at the end of the last line, so the beginning `<li>` tags look like the bullets of an unordered list. This makes it easier to find your place when editing a list later.

Working with Absolute and Relative References

There's more than one kind of address. So far, you've seen only absolute references, used for links to outside pages. Another kind of reference — a relative reference — links multiple pages inside your own website.

Understanding absolute references

The type of link used in basicLinks.html is an *absolute reference*. Absolute references always begin with the protocol name (usually `http://`). An absolute reference is the complete address to a web page, just as you'd use in the browser's address bar. Absolute references are used to refer to a site somewhere else on the Internet. Even if your website moves (say, from your desktop machine to a web server somewhere on the Internet), all the absolute references will work fine because they don't rely on the current page's position for any information.

Introducing relative references

Relative references are used when your website includes more than one page. You might choose to have several pages and a link mechanism for moving among them. Figure 5-3 shows a page with several links on it.

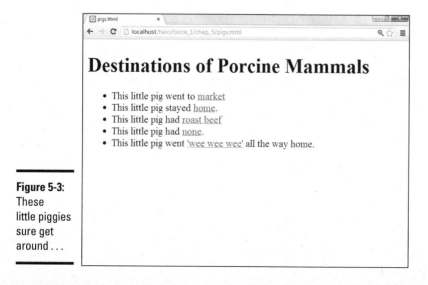

Figure 5-3:
These little piggies sure get around . . .

The page isn't so interesting on its own, but it isn't meant to stand alone. When you click one of the links, you go to a brand-new page. Figure 5-4 shows what happens when you click the market link.

The market page is pretty simple, but it also contains a link back to the initial page. Most websites aren't single pages at all, but an interconnected web of pages. The relative reference is very useful when you have a set of pages with interlacing links.

The code for pigs.html shows how relative references work:

```
<!DOCTYPE html>
<html lang = "en-US">

  <head>
    <meta charset = "UTF-8">
    <title>pigs.html</title>
  </head>

  <body>
    <h1>Destinations of Porcine Mammals</h1>
    <ul>
      <li>This little pig went to
          <a href = "market.html">market</a></li>
      <li>This little pig stayed
          <a href = "home.html">home</a>.</li>
      <li>This little pig had
          <a href = "roastBeef.html">roast beef</a></li>
      <li>This little pig had
          <a href = "none.html">none</a>.</li>
      <li>This little pig went
          <a href = "wee.html">'wee wee wee'</a>
          all the way home.</li>
    </ul>
  </body>
</html>
```

Most of the code is completely familiar. The only thing surprising is what's *not* there. Take a closer look at one of the links:

```
<a href = "market.html">home</a>.</li>
```

There's no protocol (the `http://` part) and no address at all, just a file-name. This is a *relative reference.* Relative references work by assuming the address of the current page. When the user clicks `market.html`, the browser sees no protocol, so it assumes that market.html is in the same directory on the same server as `pigs.html`.

Relative references work like directions. For example, if you're in my lab and ask where the water fountain is, I'd say, "Go out into the hallway, turn left, and turn left again at the end of the next hallway." Those directions get you to the water fountain if you start in the right place. If you're somewhere else and you follow the same directions, you don't really know where you'll end up.

Relative references work well when you have a bunch of interconnected web pages. If you create a lot of pages about the same topic and put them in the same directory, you can use relative references between the pages. If you decide to move your pages to another server, all the links still work correctly.

In Book VIII, you discover how to set up a permanent web server. It's often most convenient to create and modify your pages on the local machine and then ship them to the web server for the world to see. If you use relative references, it's easy to move a group of pages together and know the links will still work.

If you're referring to a page on somebody else's site, you have to use an absolute reference. If you're linking to another page on your site, you typically use a relative reference.

Chapter 6: Adding Images, Sound, and Video

In This Chapter

✔ **Understanding the main uses of images**

✔ **Choosing an image format**

✔ **Creating inline images**

✔ **Using IrfanView and other image software**

✔ **Changing image sizes**

✔ **Adding audio clips**

✔ **Working with video**

*Y*ou have the basics of text, but pages with nothing but text are... well, a little boring. Pictures do a lot for a web page, and they're pretty easy to work with. Today's web is really a multimedia environment, and HTML5 finally offers great support for audio and video. Find out how to add all these great features to your web pages.

Adding Images to Your Pages

Every time you explore the web, you're bound to run into tons of pictures on just about every page you visit. Typically, images are used in four ways on web pages:

✦ **External link:** The page has text with a link embedded in it. When the user clicks the link, the image replaces the page in the web browser. To make an externally linked image, just make an ordinary link (as I describe in Chapter 5 of this minibook), but point toward an image file, rather than an HTML (HyperText Markup Language) file.

✦ **Embedded images:** The image is embedded into the page. The text of the page usually flows around the image. This is the most common type of image used on the web.

✦ **Background images:** An image can be used as a background for the entire page or for a specific part of the page. Images usually require some special manipulation to make them suitable for background use.

✦ **Custom bullets:** With CSS, you can assign a small image to be a bullet for an ordered or unordered list. This allows you to make any kind of customized list markers you can draw.

The techniques you read about in this chapter apply to all type of images, but a couple of specific applications (such as backgrounds and bullets) use CSS. For details on using images in CSS, see Book II, Chapter 4.

Linking to an image

The easiest way to incorporate images is to link to them. Figure 6-1 shows the externalImage.html page.

The page's code isn't much more than a simple link:

```
<!DOCTYPE html>
<html lang = "en-US">
  <head>
    <meta charset = "UTF-8">
    <title>externalImage.html</title>
  </head>
  <body>
    <h1>Linking to an External Image</h1>
    <p>
      <a href = "shipStandard.jpg">
        Susan B. Constant
      </a>
    </p>
  </body>
</html>
```

The `href` points to an image file, not an HTML page. You can point to any type of file you want in an anchor tag. If the browser knows the file type (for example, HTML and standard image formats), the browser displays the file. If the browser doesn't know the file format, the user's computer tries to display the file using whatever program it normally uses to open that type of file.

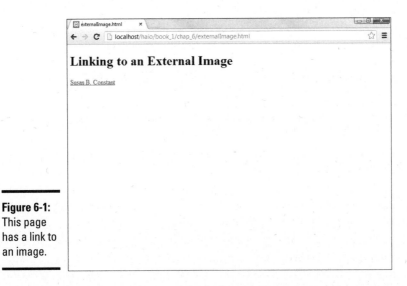

Figure 6-1:
This page
has a link to
an image.

See Chapter 5 of this minibook for a discussion of anchor tags if you need a refresher.

This works fine for most images because the image is displayed directly in the browser.

You can use this anchor trick with any kind of file, but the results can be very unpredictable. If you use the link trick to point to some odd file format, there's no guarantee the user has the appropriate software to view it. Generally, save this trick for very common formats, like GIF and JPG. (If these formats are unfamiliar to you, they are described later in this chapter.)

Most browsers automatically resize the image to fit the browser size. This means a large image may appear to be smaller than it really is, but the user still has to wait for the entire image to download.

Because this is a relative reference, the indicated image must be in the same directory as the HTML file. When the user clicks the link, the page is replaced by the image, as shown in Figure 6-2.

Figure 6-2:
The image appears in place of the page.

External links are easy to create, but they have some problems:

✦ **They don't preview the image.** The user has only the text description to figure out what the picture might be.

✦ **They interrupt the flow.** If the page contains a series of images, the user has to keep leaving the page to view images.

✦ **The user must back up to return to the main page.** The image looks like a web page, but it isn't. No link or other explanatory text in the image indicates how to get back to the web page. Most users know to click the browser's Back button, but don't assume all users know what to do.

Adding inline images using the <img> tag

The alternative to providing links to images is to embed your images into the page. Figure 6-3 displays an example of this technique.

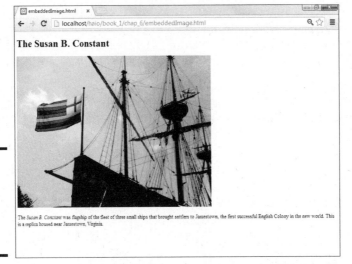

Figure 6-3:
The ship image is embedded into the page.

The code shows how this image was included into the page:

```
<!DOCTYPE html>
<html lang = "en-US">
  <head>
    <meta charset = "UTF-8">
    <title>embeddedImage.html</title>
  </head>
  <body>
    <h1>The Susan B. Constant</h1>
    <p>
      <img src = "shipStandard.jpg"
           height = "480"
           width = "640"
           alt = "Susan B. Constant" />
    </p>
    <p>
      The <em>Susan B. Constant</em> was flagship of the
      fleet of three small ships that brought settlers to Jamestown, the first
      successful English Colony in the new world.  This is a replica housed
      near Jamestown, Virginia.
    </p>
  <body>
</html>
```

The image (img) tag is the star of this page. This tag allows you to grab an image file and incorporate it into the page directly. The image tag is a one-shot tag. It doesn't end with </img>. Instead, use the /> characters at the end of the img definition to indicate that this tag doesn't have content.

You might have noticed that I italicized *Susan B. Constant* in the page, and I used the <em> tag to get this effect. <em> stands for *emphasis,* and <strong> means *strong emphasis.* By default, any text within an <em></em> pair is italicized, and <strong></strong> text is boldfaced. Of course, you can change this behavior with CSS.

The image tag has a number of important attributes, which I discuss in the following sections.

src (source)

The src attribute allows you to indicate the URL (Uniform Resource Locator) of the image. This can be an absolute or relative reference. Linking to an image in your own directory structure is generally best because you can't be sure an external image will still be there when the user gets to the page. (For more on reference types, turn to Chapter 5 of this minibook.)

height and width

The height and width attributes are used to indicate the size of the image. The browser uses this information to indicate how much space to reserve on the page.

The height and width attributes should *describe* the size of an image. You can use these attributes to actually change the size of an image, but it's a bad idea. Change the image size with your image editor (I show you how later in this chapter). If you use the height and width attributes, the user has to wait for the full image, even if she'll see a smaller version. Don't make the user wait for information she won't see. If you use these attributes to make the image larger than its default size, the resulting image has poor resolution. Find the image's actual size by looking at it in your image tool and use these values. If you leave out height and width, the browser determines the size automatically, but you aren't guaranteed to see the text until all the images have downloaded. Adding these attributes lets the browser format the page without waiting for the images.

alt (alternate text)

The alt attribute gives you an opportunity to specify alternate text describing the image. Alternate text information is used when the user has images turned off and by screen-readers. Information in alt tags is also used in image-searching software like Google Images.

The alt attribute is required on all images.

Additionally, the <img> tag is an inline tag, so it needs to be embedded inside a block-level tag, like a <p> or <li>.

Choosing an Image Manipulation Tool

You can't just grab any old picture off your digital camera and expect it to work on a web page. The picture might work, but it could cause problems for your viewers. It's important to understand that *digital images* (any kind of images you see on a computer or similar device) are different from the kind of images you see on paper.

An image is worth 3.4 million words

Digital cameras and scanners are amazing these days. Even moderately priced cameras can now approach the resolution of old-school analog cameras. Scanners are also capable of taking traditional images and converting them into digital formats that computers use. In both cases, though, the default image can be in a format that causes problems. Digital images are stored as a series of dots, or *pixels.* In print, the dots are very close together, but computer screens have larger dots. Figure 6-4 shows how the ship image looks straight from the digital camera.

Figure 6-4: Wow. That doesn't look like much.

My picture (taken on an older digital camera) registers at 6 megapixels (MP). That's a pretty good resolution, but modern digital cameras are much higher. If I print that picture on paper, all those dots are very tiny, and I get a nice picture. If I try to show the same picture on the computer screen, I see only one corner. This actual picture came out at 2,816 pixels wide by 2,112 pixels tall. You only see a small corner of the image because the screen shots for this book are taken at 1024×768 pixels. Less than a quarter of the image is visible.

When you look at a large image in most browsers, it's automatically resized to fit the page. The cursor usually turns into some kind of magnifying glass, and if you click the image, you can see it in its full size or the smaller size.

WARNING!

Some image viewers take very large images and automatically resize them so they fit the screen. (This is the default behavior of Windows' default image viewer and most browsers.) The image may appear to be a reasonable size because of this feature, but it'll be huge and difficult to download in an actual web page. Make sure you know the actual size of an image before you use it.

Although shrinking an image so that it can be seen in its entirety is obviously beneficial, there's an even more compelling reason to do so. Each pixel on the screen requires 3 bytes of computer memory. (A *byte* is the basic unit of memory in a computer.) For comparison purposes, one character of text requires roughly 1 byte. The uncompressed image of the ship weighs a whopping 17 megabytes (MB). If you think of a word as five characters long, one picture straight from the digital camera takes up the same amount of storage space and transmission time as roughly 3,400,000 words. This image requires nearly three minutes to download on a 56K modem!

In a web page, small images are often shown at about 320×240 pixels, and larger images are often 640×480 pixels. If I use software to resample the image to the size I actually need and use an appropriate compression algorithm, I can get the image to look like Figure 6-5.

Figure 6-5:
The resized image is a lot more manageable.

The new version of the image is the size and file format I need, it looks just as good, and it weighs a much more reasonable 88 kilobytes. That's 2 percent of the original image size.

 Although this picture is a lot smaller than the original image, it still takes up a lot more memory than text. Even this smaller image takes up as much transmission time and storage space as 1,600 words! It still takes 10 seconds to download without a broadband connection. Use images wisely.

Images are great, but keep some things in mind when you use them:

✦ **Make sure the images are worth displaying.** Don't use a picture without some good reason because each picture makes your page dramatically slower to access.

✦ **Use software to resize your image.** Later in this chapter, I show you how to use free software to change the image to exactly the size you need.

✦ **Use a compressed format.** Images are almost never used in their native format on the web because they're just too large. Several formats have emerged that are useful for working with various types of images. I describe these formats in the section "Choosing an Image Format," later in this chapter.

Introducing IrfanView

IrfanView, by Irfan Skiljan, is a freeware program that can handle your basic image manipulation needs and quite a bit more. I used it for all the screenshots in this book, and I use it as my primary image viewer when I'm using Windows. You can get a copy at www.irfanview.net. Of course, you can use any software you want, but if something's really good and free, it's a great place to start. In the rest of this chapter, I show you how to do the main image-processing jobs with IrfanView, but you can use any image editor you want.

A web developer needs to have an image manipulation program to help with all these chores. Like other web development tools, you can pay quite a bit for an image manipulation tool, but you don't have to. Your image tool should have at least the following capabilities:

✦ **Resizing:** Web pages require smaller images than printing on paper. You need a tool that allows you to resize your image to a specific size for web display.

✦ **Saving to different formats:** There's a dizzying number of image formats available, but only a few formats work reliably on the web (which I discuss in the next section). You need a tool that can take images in a wide variety of formats and reliably switch it to a web-friendly format.

✦ **Cropping:** You may want only a small part of the original picture. A crop-ping tool allows you to extract a rectangular region from an image.

✦ **Filters:** You may find it necessary to modify your image in some way. You may want to reduce red-eye, lighten or darken your image, or adjust the colors. Sometimes, images can be improved with sharpen or blur filters, or more artistic filters, such as canvas or oil-painting tools.

✦ **Batch processing:** You may have a number of images you want to work with at one time. A batch processing utility can perform an operation on a large number of images at once, as you see later in this chapter.

You may want some other capabilities, too, such as the ability to make composite images, images with transparency, and more powerful effects. You can use commercial tools or the excellent open-source program Gimp. I use IrfanView for basic processing, and I use Gimp when I need a little more power. See Book VIII, Chapter 4 for a more complete discussion of Gimp.

IrfanView is my favorite, but it's only available for Windows. Here are a few free alternatives if you want to try some other great software:

✦ **XnView:** Similar to IrfanView, XnView allows you to preview and modify pictures in hundreds of formats, create thumbnails, and more. It's avail-able for Mac and Linux.

✦ **Pixia:** Pixia is a full-blown Windows-only graphic editor from Japan. Very powerful.

✦ **GimpShop:** This is a version of Gimp modified to have menus like Photoshop.

✦ **Paint.NET:** This is a powerful Windows-only Paint program.

Use Google or another search engine to locate any of these programs.

Choosing an Image Format

Almost nobody uses raw images on the web because they're just too big and unwieldy. Usually, web images are compressed to take up less space. All the types of image files you see in the computer world (BMP, JPG, GIF, and so on) are essentially different ways to make an image file smaller. Not all the for-mats work on the web, and they have different characteristics, so it's good to know a little more about them.

BMP

The BMP format is Microsoft's standard image format. Although it's com-pressed sometimes, usually it isn't. The BMP format creates very detailed images with little to no compression, and the file is often too large to use on the web. Many web browsers can handle BMP images, but you shouldn't use them. Convert to one of the other formats, instead.

JPG/JPEG

The JPG format (also called JPEG) is a relatively old format designed by the Joint Photographic Experts Group. (Get it? JPEG!) It works by throwing away data that's less important to human perception. Every time you save an image in the JPG format, you lose a little information. This sounds terrible, but it really isn't. The same image that came up as 13MB in its raw format is squeezed down to 1.5MB when stored as a JPG. Most people can't tell the difference between the compressed and non-compressed version of the image by looking at them.

The JPG algorithm focuses on the parts of the image that are important to perception (brightness and contrast, for example) and throws away data that isn't as important. (Actually, much of the color data is thrown away, but the colors are re-created in an elaborate optical illusion.)

JPG works best on photographic-style images with a lot of color and detail. Many digital cameras save images directly as JPGs.

One part of the JPG process allows you to determine the amount of compression. When you save an image as a JPG, you can often determine the quality on a scale between accuracy and compression.

The JPG compression scheme causes particular problems with text. JPG is not good at preserving sharp areas of high contrast (such as letters on a background). JPG is not the best format for banner images or other images with text on them. Use GIF or PNG instead. A JPG with text will show characteristic square artifacts.

Even if you choose 100 percent accuracy, the file is still greatly compressed. The adjustable compression operates only on a small part of the process. Compressing the file too much can cause visible square shadows, or *artifacts*. Experiment with your images to see how much compression they can take and still look like the original.

Keep a high-quality original around when you're making JPG versions of an image because each copy loses some detail. If you make a JPG from a JPG that came from another JPG, the loss of detail starts to add up, and the picture loses some visual quality.

GIF

The GIF format was developed originally for CompuServe, way before the web was invented. This format was a breakthrough in its time and still has some great characteristics.

GIF is a *lossless* algorithm so, potentially, no data is lost when converting an image to GIF (compare that to the *lossy* JPG format). GIF does its magic with a *color palette* trick and a *run-length encoding* trick.

The color palette works like a paint-by-number set where an image has a series of numbers printed on it, and each of the paint colors has a corresponding number. What happens in a GIF image is similar. GIF images have a list of 256 colors, automatically chosen from the image. Each of the colors is given a number. A *raw* (uncompressed) image requires 3 bytes of information for each pixel (1 each to determine the amount of red, green, and blue). In a GIF image, all that information is stored one time in the color palette. The image itself contains a bunch of references to the color palette.

For example, if blue is stored as color 1 in the palette, a strip of blue might look like this:

1, 1, 1, 1, 1, 1, 1, 1, 1, 1

GIF uses its other trick — run-length encoding — when it sees a list of identical colors. Rather than store the above value as 1, 1, 1, 1, 1, 1, 1, 1, 1, 1, the GIF format can specify a list of 10 ones. That's the general idea of run-length encoding. The ship image in this example weighs 2.92MB as a full-size GIF image.

The GIF format works best for images with a relatively small number of colors and large areas of the same color. Most drawings you make in a drawing program convert very well to the GIF format. Photos aren't ideal because they usually have more than 256 colors in them, and the subtle changes in color mean there are very few solid blotches of color to take advantage of run-length encoding.

GIF does have a couple of great advantages that keep it popular. First, a GIF image can have a transparent color defined. Typically, you'll choose some awful color not found in nature (kind of like choosing bridesmaid dresses) to be the transparent color. Then, when the GIF encounters a pixel that color, it displays whatever is underneath instead. This is a crude but effective form of transparency. Figure 6-6 shows an image with transparency.

Whenever you see an image on a web page that doesn't appear to be rectangular, there's a good chance the image is a GIF. The image is still a rectangle, but it has transparency to make it look more organic. Typically, whatever color you set as the background color when you save a GIF becomes the transparent color.

Creating a complex transparent background, like the statue, requires a more complex tool than IrfanView. I used Gimp, but any high-end graphics tool can do the job. IrfanView is more suited to operations that work on the entire image.

Another interesting feature of GIF is the ability to create animations. Animated GIFs are a series of images stored in the same file. You can embed information, determining the interval between images. You can create animated GIFs with Gimp.

Figure 6-6:
This statue
is a GIF
with trans-
parency.

Animated GIFs were overused in the early days of the web, and many now consider them the mark of an amateur. Nobody really thinks that animated mailbox is cute anymore. Look ahead to Book IV, Chapter 7 for the more flexible modern way to add animation to your pages.

For a while, there were some legal encumbrances regarding a part of the GIF scheme. The owners of this algorithm tried to impose a license fee. This was passed on to people using commercial software, but became a big problem for free software creators.

Fortunately, it appears that the legal complications have been resolved for now. Still, you'll see a lot of open-software advocates avoiding the GIF algorithm altogether because of this problem.

PNG

Open-source software advocates created a new image format that combines some of the best features of both JPG and GIF, with no legal problems. The resulting format is *Portable Network Graphics,* or *PNG.* This format has a number of interesting features, such as

+ **Lossless compression:** Like GIF, PNG stores data without losing any information.

+ **Dynamic color palette:** PNG supports as many colors as you want. You aren't limited to 256 colors as you are with GIF.

✦ **No software patents:** The underlying technology of PNG is completely open source, with no worries about whether somebody will try to enforce a copyright down the road.

✦ **True alpha transparency:** The PNG format has a more sophisticated form of transparency than GIF. Each pixel can be stored with an alpha value. *Alpha* refers to the amount of transparency. The alpha can be adjusted from completely transparent to completely opaque.

With all these advantages, it's not surprising that PNG is one of the most popular formats on the web. At one point, browser support for PNG was inconsistent, but now browsers can manage PNG pretty well. The only disadvantage of PNG is the inability to create animations. This is not a major issue, as you'll see in Book IV, Chapter 7.

SVG

All of the previously-mentioned formats store information pixel-by-pixel. This mechanism is called *raster-based* image formats. However, this is not the only approach to images. A format called "Scalable Vector Graphics (SVG)" is relatively new to web development. SVG graphics are stored as a series of instructions in a format much like HTML. For example, a circle in SVG is stored like this:

```
<circle cx="50" cy="50" r="30"
            style="stroke:#0000ff; stroke-width: 5px; fill:#ff0000;"/>
```

Although it's possible to write SVG code by hand, it's more common to use an editor like Inkscape. SVG graphics have some nice advantages:

✦ **The image can be resized without loss of quality.** The biggest advantage of SVG is the ability to change the image size. With raster-based images, any change of image size will involve a loss of image quality. SVG images can change size arbitrarily without a loss of quality.

✦ **File sizes can be extremely small.** The file size of a vector-based image is based on the complexity of the image rather than its visual size. So simple images that can be described as a series of shapes can result in tiny files, even if they take up an entire page.

✦ **Vector images are easy to edit.** You can edit a vector image by moving and manipulating the various shapes that make up an image. This makes vector-images like SVG quite easy to edit.

Vector images were not practical in previous versions of HTML. This is one reason Flash (which is primarily a vector format) was so popular. SVG is one of the most interesting new features of HTML5. An SVG image can be embedded like any other sort of image, or it can be manipulated directly though

JavaScript code. You can find a great number of free-to-use SVG images at `http://openclipart.org/`.

Summary of web image formats

All these formats may seem overwhelming, but choosing an image format is easy because each format has its own advantages and disadvantages:

✦ **GIF** is best when you need transparency or animation. Avoid using GIF on photos, as you won't get optimal compression, and you'll lose color data.

✦ **JPG** is most useful for photographic images, which are best suited for the JPG compression technique. However, keep in mind that JPG isn't suitable for images that require transparency. Text in JPG images tends to become difficult to read because of the lossy compression technique.

✦ **PNG** is useful in most situations. Older browsers may have trouble with this format.

✦ **SVG** is useful for images which need to be re-sized without a loss of image quality or when the image is relatively simple.

✦ **BMP and other formats** should be avoided entirely. Although you can make other formats work in certain circumstances, there's no good reason to use any other image formats most of the time.

Manipulating Your Images

All this talk of compression algorithms and resizing images may be dandy, but how do you do it?

Fortunately, IrfanView can do nearly anything you need for free. IrfanView has nice features for all the main types of image manipulation you need.

Changing formats in IrfanView

Changing image formats with IrfanView is really easy. For example, find an image file on your computer and follow these steps:

1. **Load the image into IrfanView by dragging the image into IrfanView or using the File ⇨ Open menu command.**

2. **Make any changes you may want to the image before saving.**

3. **Use the File ⇨ Save As command to save the file.**

4. **Pick the image format from the Save Picture As dialog box, as shown in Figure 6-7.**

5. **Save the file with a new filename.** Keep the original file and save any changes in a new file. That way, you don't overwrite the original file. This is especially important if you're converting to JPG because each successive save of a JPG causes some image loss.

Figure 6-7:
IrfanView
can save
in all these
formats.

Don't use spaces in your filenames. Your files may move to other computers on the Internet, and some computers have trouble with spaces. It's best to avoid spaces and punctuation (except the underscore character) on any files that will be used on the Internet. Also, be very careful about capitalization. It's likely that your image will end up on a Linux server someday, and the capitalization makes a big difference there.

Resizing your images

All the other image-manipulation tricks may be optional, but you should *really* resize your images. Although high-speed connections may have no trouble with a huge image, nothing makes a web page inaccessible to users with weaker connectivity faster than bloated image sizes.

To resize an image with IrfanView, perform the following steps:

1. **Load the image into IrfanView.** You can do this by dragging the image onto the IrfanView icon, dragging into an open instance of IrfanView, or using the menus within IrfanView.

2. **From the Image menu, choose Resize/Resample.** You can also use Ctrl+R for this step. Figure 6-8 shows the resulting dialog box.

3. **Determine the new image size.** A number of standard image sizes are available. 800×600 pixels will create a large image in most browsers. If you want the image smaller, you need to enter a size in the text boxes. Images embedded in web pages are often 320 pixels wide by 240 pixels tall. That's a very good starting point. Anything smaller will be hard to see, and anything larger might take up too much screen space.

4. **Preserve the aspect ratio using the provided check box.** This makes sure the ratio between height and width is maintained. Otherwise, the image may be distorted.

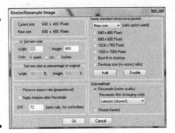

Figure 6-8:
IrfanView's
Resize/
Resample
Image
dialog box.

5. **Save the resulting image as a new file.** When you make an image smaller, you lose data. That's perfectly fine for the version you put on the web, but you should hang on to the original large image in case you want to resize again.

6. **Resample, rather than resize.** *Resampling* is a slower but more accurate technique for changing the image size. This is IrfanView's default behavior, so leave it alone. It's still quite fast on a modern computer. The default (Lanczos) filter is fine, although you can experiment with other filters to get a faster conversion, if you want.

Enhancing image colors

Sometimes, you can make improvements to an image by modifying the colors. The Color corrections dialog box on the Images menu gives you a wide range of options, as shown in Figure 6-9.

You can do a surprising number of helpful operations on an image with this tool:

✦ **Brightness:** When adjusted to a higher value, the image becomes closer to white. When adjusted to a negative value, the image becomes closer to black. This is useful when you want to make an image lighter or darker for use as a background image.

Figure 6-9:
You can
change
several
options in
the Color
Corrections
dialog box.

If your image is too dark or too bright, you may be tempted to use the Brightness feature to fix it. The Gamma Correction feature described later in this section is more useful for this task.

✦ **Contrast:** You usually use the Contrast feature in conjunction with the Brightness feature to adjust an image. Sometimes, an image can be improved with small amounts of contrast adjustments.

✦ **Color Balance:** Sometimes, an image has poor color balance (for example, indoor lighting sometimes creates a bluish cast). You can adjust the amount of red, green, and blue with a series of sliders. The easiest way to manage color balance is to look at a part of the image that's supposed to be white and play with the slider until it looks truly white.

✦ **Gamma Correction:** This is used to correct an image that is too dark or too light. Unlike the Brightness adjustment, Gamma Correction automatically adjusts the contrast. Small adjustments to this slider can sometimes fix images that are a little too dark or too light.

✦ **Saturation:** When saturation is at its smallest value, the image becomes black and white. At its largest value, the colors are enhanced. Use this control to create a grayscale image or to enhance colors for artistic effect.

Using built-in effects

IrfanView has a few other effects available that can sometimes be extremely useful. These effects can be found individually on the Image menu or with the Image Effects browser on the Image menu. The Image Effects browser (as shown in Figure 6-10) is often a better choice because it gives you a little more control of most effects and provides interactive feedback on what the effect will do. Sometimes, effects are called *filters* because they pass the original image through a math function, which acts like a filter or processor to create the modified output.

Figure 6-10:
The Image
Effects
browser lets
you choose
special
effects.

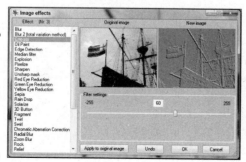

Here's a rundown of some of the effects, including when you would use them:

✦ **None:** Just for comparison purposes, Figure 6-11 shows the ship image without any filters turned on.

I've exaggerated the effects for illustration purposes, but it may still be difficult to see the full effect of these filters on the printed page. The grayscale images in this book are a poor representation of the actual color images. Use the images in this chapter as a starting point, but to understand these filters, you really need to experiment with your own images in IrfanView or a similar tool. I've also added all these images to this book's companion website so you can see them there. For more on the companion website, see this book's Introduction.

✦ **Blur:** This filter reduces contrast between adjacent pixels. (Really, we could go over the math, but let's leave that for another day, huh?) You might wonder why you'd make an image blurry on purpose. Sometimes, the Blur filter can fix graininess in an image. You can also use Blur in conjunction with Sharpen (which I cover in just a moment) to fix small flaws in an image. I applied the Blur filter to the standard ship image in Figure 6-12.

✦ **Sharpen:** The opposite of Blur, the Sharpen filter enhances the contrast between adjacent pixels. When used carefully, it can sometimes improve an image. The Sharpen filter is most effective in conjunction with the Blur filter to remove small artifacts. Figure 6-13 shows the ship image with the Sharpen filter applied.

Figure 6-11:
Here's the standard ship image, at full-screen resolution.

Figure 6-12:
The Blur
filter
reduces
contrast.

Figure 6-13:
The
Sharpen
filter
increases
contrast.

If you believe crime shows on TV, you can take a blurry image and keep applying a sharpen filter to read a license plate on a blurry image from a security camera a mile away. However, it just doesn't usually work that way. You can't make detail emerge from junk, but sometimes, you can make small improvements.

✦ **Emboss:** This filter creates a grayscale image that looks like embossed metal, as shown in Figure 6-14. Sometimes, embossing can convert an image into a useful background image because embossed images have low contrast. You can use the Enhance Colors dialog box to change the gray embossed image to a more appealing color.

✦ **Oil Paint:** This filter applies a texture reminiscent of an oil painting to an image, as shown in Figure 6-15. It can sometimes clean up a picture and give it a more artistic appearance. The higher settings make the painting more abstract.

Figure 6-14: Embossing creates a low-contrast 3D effect.

Figure 6-15: Oil Paint makes an image slightly more abstract.

Figure 6-16:
The image appears to stick up from the page like a button.

✦ **3D Button:** This feature can be used to create an image, similar to Figure 6-16, that appears to be a button on the page. This will be useful later when you figure out how to use CSS or JavaScript to swap images for virtual buttons. You can set the apparent height of the image in the filter. Normally, you apply this filter to smaller images that you intend to make into buttons the user can click.

✦ **Red Eye Reduction:** You use this filter to fix a common problem with flash photography. Sometimes, a person's eyes appear to have a reddish tinge to them. Unlike the other filters, this one is easier to access from the Image menu. Use the mouse to select the red portion of the image and then apply the filter to turn the red areas black. It's best not to perform this filter on the entire image because you may inadvertently turn other red things black.

Other effects you can use

Many more effects and filters are available. IrfanView has a few more built in that you can experiment with. You can also download a huge number of effects in the Adobe Photoshop 8BF format. These effects filters can often be used in IrfanView and other image-manipulation programs.

Some effects allow you to explode the image, add sparkles, map images onto 3D shapes, create old-time sepia effects, and much more.

If you want to do even more image manipulation, consider a full-blown image editor. Adobe Photoshop is the industry standard, but Gimp is an open-source alternative that does almost as much. See Book VIII, Chapter 4 for more about using Gimp for image processing.

Batch processing

Often, you'll have a lot of images to modify at one time. IrfanView has a wonderful *batch-processing* tool that allows you to work on several images at once. I frequently use this tool to take all the images I want to use on a page and convert them to a particular size and format. The process seems a little complicated, but after you get used to it, you can modify a large number of images quickly and easily.

If you want to convert a large number of images at the same time, follow these steps:

1. **Identify the original images and place them in one directory.** I find it easiest to gather all the images into one directory, whether they come from a digital camera, scanner, or other device.

2. **Open the Batch Conversion dialog box by choosing File ⇨ Batch Conversion — Rename.** This Batch Conversion dialog box appears, as shown in Figure 6-17.

3. **Find your original images by navigating the directory window in the Batch Conversion dialog box.**

4. **Copy your images to the Input Files workspace by clicking the Add button.** Select the images you want to modify and press the Add button. The selected image names are copied to the Input Files workspace.

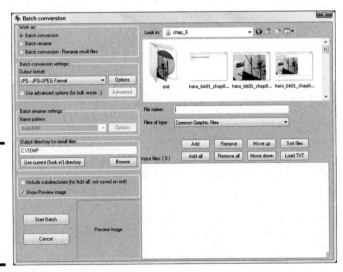

Figure 6-17: IrfanView has a powerful batch conversion tool.

5. **Specify the output directory.** If you want to put the new images in the same directory as the input files, click the Use This Directory as Output button. If not, choose the directory where you want the new images to go.

6. **In the Work As box, choose Batch Conversion — Rename Result Files.** You can use this setting to rename your files, to do other conversions, or both. Generally, I recommend both.

7. **Set the output format to the format you want.** For photos, you probably want JPG format.

8. **Change renaming settings in the Batch Rename Settings area if you want to specify some other naming convention for your images.** By default, each image is called *image*### where ### is a three-digit number. They are numbered according to the listing in the Input Files workspace. You can use the Move Up and Move Down buttons to change the order images appear in this listing.

9. **Click the Set Advanced Options button to change the image size.** This displays the Set for All Images dialog box, as shown in Figure 6-18.

10. **Specify the new size of the image in the Resize area.** Several common sizes are preset. If you want another size, use the given options. I set my size to 320×240.

11. **Close the Set for All Images dialog box and then, in the Batch Conversion dialog box, click the Start button.** In a few seconds, the new images are created.

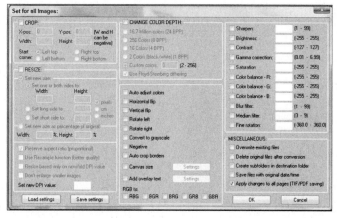

Figure 6-18:
Use the
Set for All
Images
dialog box
to resize
images in
batch mode.

Working with Audio

HTML has supported images for a long time, but now it works just as well with audio files. This is a major breakthrough, as audio previously required external programs like Flash.

Figure 6-19 demonstrates a page with a simple audio file.

Figure 6-19:
This page
has a song
embedded
in it.

It's quite easy to add audio to a web page in HTML5 with the new `<audio>` tag. Here's the code for creating this page:

```
<!doctype html>
<html lang="en">
<head>
  <meta charset="UTF-8">
  <title>audio.html</title>
</head>
<body>
  <h1>Audio Demo</h1>
  <audio controls = "controls">
    <source src = "Allemande.mp3" type = "audio/mpeg">
    <source src = "Allemande.ogg" type = "audio/ogg">
      Your browser does not support HTML5 Audio
      Please use this link instead:
      <a href = "Allemande.mp3">Allemande.mp3</a>
  </audio>
  <p>
    Music: J.S. Bach "Allemande" Partita for Violin #2
  </p>
</body>
</html>
```

Although nearly every current browser supports the `<audio>` tag, they still can't agree on which format to support. Some browsers support MP3 files, some support a newer standard called Ogg, and some support WAV.

The best way to be sure the sound plays is to supply two different formats. I've found that including both Ogg and MP3 formats ensures my audio will play on all major browsers.

To add an audio file to your page, follow these steps:

1. **Add the audio tag to your page.** The `<audio>` tag indicates where an audio file will be placed. Where you place the tag in the code corresponds to where the controls will appear.

2. **Turn on controls.** You can specify a control panel with the `controls = "controls"` attribute. This causes a small control like the one in Figure 6-19 to appear. If you leave this directive out, there will be no control panel, which means the user will not be able to play the clip.

3. **Create a `<source>` element or two.** Inside the `<audio></audio>` pair, add one or more `<source>` elements. Each source element indicates a file you will link to.

4. **Set the `src` attribute to indicate the file.** The `src` attribute of the `<source>` tag (could we please have one more thing with almost the same name here?) is used to indicate the file name of the audio file you wish to play.

5. **Add alternate code for older browsers.** Any additional HTML code between the `<sound>` and `<sound>` tags will be interpreted only by browsers that do not understand the sound tag. You can add an ordinary anchor to download the sound effect if you wish. This way, even those with older browsers can hear what they're missing.

Adding Video

The `<video>` tag is very similar to the `<audio>` tag, and it works in exactly the same way. You can use this tag to add a video to your web page, and the video plays directly in the browser without requiring a plugin like Flash. The ability to play videos through HTML is a major breakthrough, and it's not difficult to implement.

Of course, it isn't perfect. There are a number of competing video standards, and the browsers (imagine this) cannot agree on which standard to accept. The most important standards are called H.264 and Ogg. Some browsers prefer one; some prefer the other. To make things more complicated, the file extension for a video doesn't always indicate the underlying coding mechanism. This means video encoding requires some experimentation. If your video file is not in the format you want, you may need to convert it. FFmpeg and VLC are outstanding free tools you can use to convert video to whatever format you need.

As with any intellectual property, be sure you have the permission of the file's original owner. Just because you *can* embed a video into your web page doesn't mean you *should* do so.

Figure 6-20 shows a page with a simple video embedded in it.

Figure 6-20:
This page
has a video.

The code for this page shows how much the `<video>` tag is like `<audio>`:

```
<!DOCTYPE html>
<html lang="en">
  <head>
    <title>videoDemo</title>
  </head>
  <body>
    <h1>Video Demo</h1>
    <video src = "bigBuck.ogv"
        controls = "controls">
    Your browser does not support embedded video
    through HTML 5.
    </video>
    <p>
    This video is a trailer for the incredible short movie
    "Big Buck Bunny."  This experiment proves that talented
    volunteers can produce a high-quality professional video
    using only open-source tools.
    Go to <a href = "http://www.bigbuckbunny.org">
    http://www.bigbuckbunny.org</a> to see the entire video.
    </p>
  </body>
</html>
```

Video files are extremely large, and they can make your website seem much slower to users. They also are cumbersome to move to a web server. For this reason, many web developers prefer to upload videos to a service like YouTube and simply link to the video on another server. If you right-click a YouTube video, you can select Copy Embed Code from the menu that appears. This gives you code you can use on your own site.

Chapter 7: Creating Forms

In This Chapter

✔ Adding forms to your pages

✔ Creating input and password text boxes

✔ Building multi-line text inputs

✔ Making list boxes and check boxes

✔ Building groups of radio buttons

✔ Using HTML5 form elements

✔ Creating buttons

*H*TML gives you the ability to describe web pages, but today's web isn't a one-way affair. Users want to communicate through web pages, by typing in information, making selections from drop-down lists, and interacting, rather than simply reading. In this chapter, you learn how to build these interactive elements in your pages.

You Have Great Form

There's one more aspect to HTML that you need to understand — the ability to make forms. *Forms* are the parts of the page that allow user interaction. Figure 7-1 shows a page with all the primary form elements in place.

The form demo (or formDemo.html on this book's web site, if you're playing along at home) exemplifies the main form elements in HTML. In this chapter, you discover how to build all these elements. For more on this book's website, see the Introduction.

You can create forms with ordinary HTML, but to make them *do* something, you need a programming language. Book IV explains how to use JavaScript to interact with your forms, and Book V describes the PHP language. Use this chapter to figure out how to build the forms and then jump to another minibook to figure out how to make them do stuff. If you aren't ready for full-blown programming yet, feel free to skip this chapter for now and move on to CSS in Books II and III. Come back here when you're ready to make forms to use with JavaScript or PHP.

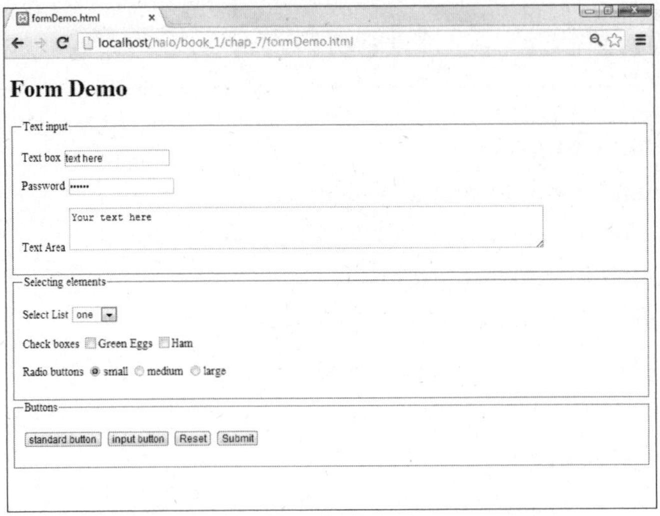

Figure 7-1:
Form
elements
allow user
interaction.

The formDemo.html page shows the following elements:

✦ **A form:** A container for form elements. Although the form element itself isn't usually a visible part of the page (like the body tag), it could be with appropriate CSS.

✦ **Text boxes:** These standard form elements allow the user to type text into a one-line element.

✦ **Password boxes:** These boxes are like text boxes, except they automatically obscure the text to discourage snooping.

✦ **Text areas:** These multi-line text boxes accommodate more text than the other types of text boxes. You can specify the size of the text area the user can type into.

✦ **Select lists:** These list boxes give the user a number of options. The user can select one element from the list. You can specify the number of rows to show or make the list drop down when activated.

✦ **Check boxes:** These non-text boxes can be checked or not. Check boxes act *independently* — more than one can be selected at a time (unlike radio buttons).

✦ **Radio buttons:** Usually found in a group of options, only one radio button in a group can be selected at a time. Selecting one radio button deselects the others in its group.

✦ **Buttons:** These elements let the user begin some kind of process. The Input button is used in JavaScript coding (which I describe in Book IV), whereas the Submit buttons are used for server-side programming (see Book V). The Reset button is special because it automatically resets all the form elements to their default configurations.

✦ **Labels:** Many form elements have a small text label associated with them. Although labels are not required, they can make a form easier to style with CSS and easier for the user.

✦ **Fieldsets and legends:** These set off parts of the form. They're optional, but they can add a lot of visual appeal to a form.

Now that you have an overview of form elements, it's time to start building some forms!

Forms must have some form

All the form elements must be embedded inside a `<form></form>` pair. The code for basicForm.html illustrates the simplest possible form:

```
<!DOCTYPE html>
<html lang = "en-US">

  <head>
    <meta charset = "UTF-8">
    <title>basicForm.html</title>
  </head>

  <body>
    <h1>A basic form</h1>
    <form action = "">
      <h2>Form elements go here</h2>
      <h3>Other HTML is fine, too.</h3>
    </form>
    <p>
      <input type = "text"
             value = "googoo" />
    </p>
  </body>
</html>
```

The `<form></form>` pair indicates a piece of the page that may contain form elements. All the other form doohickeys and doodads (buttons, `select` objects, and so on) must be inside a `<form>` pair.

The `action` attribute indicates what should happen when the form is submitted. This requires a programming language, so a full description of the `action` attribute is in Book IV. Still, you must indicate an action to validate, so for now just leave the `action` attribute null with a pair of quotes (`""`).

Organizing a form with fieldsets and labels

Forms can contain many components, but the most important are the *input elements* (text boxes, buttons, drop-down lists, and the like) and the *text labels* that describe the elements. Traditionally, web developers used tables to set up forms, but this isn't really the best way to go because forms aren't tabular information. HTML includes some great features to help you describe the various parts of a form. Figure 7-2 shows a page with fieldsets, layouts, and basic input.

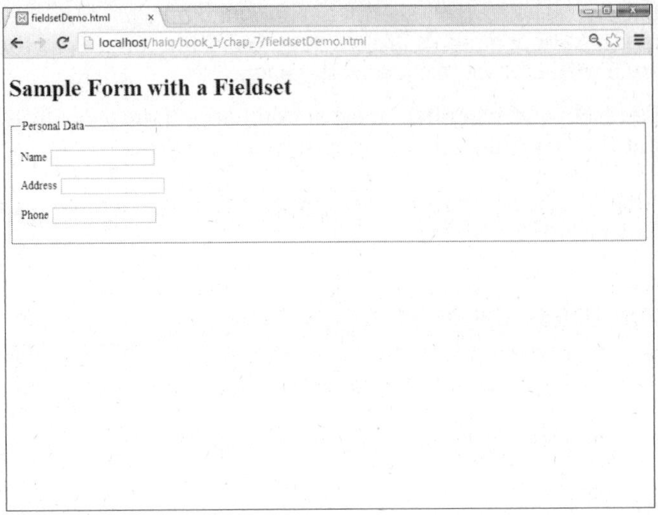

Figure 7-2:
This form
has a
legend and
labels.

A *fieldset* is a special element used to supply a visual grouping to a set of form elements.

The form still doesn't look very good, I admit, but that's not the point. Like all HTML tags, the form elements aren't about describing how the form looks; they're about what all the main elements mean. (Here I go again. . . .) You use CSS to make the form look the way you want. The HTML tags describe the parts of the form, so you have something to hook your CSS to. It all makes sense very soon, I promise.

Here's the code for the fieldset demo (fieldsetDemo.html on this book's website):

```
<!DOCTYPE html>
<html lang = "en-US">

  <head>
    <meta charset = "UTF-8">
    <title>fieldsetDemo.html</title>
  </head>
  <body>
    <h1>Sample Form with a Fieldset</h1>
    <form action = "">
      <fieldset>
        <legend>Personal Data</legend>
        <p>
          <label>Name</label>
          <input type = "text" />
        </p>
        <p>
          <label>Address</label>
          <input type = "text" />
        </p>
```

```
    <p>
      <label>Phone</label>
      <input type = "text" />
    </p>
  </fieldset>
  </form>
 </body>
</html>
```

The form has these elements:

✦ **The `<form>` and `</form>` tags:** These define the form as a part of the page. Don't forget the null `action` attribute.

✦ **The `<fieldset>` pair:** This pair describes the included elements as a set of fields. This element isn't necessary, but it does give you some nice organization and layout options later when you use CSS. You can think of the fieldset as a blank canvas for adding visual design to your forms. By default, the fieldset places a border around all the contained elements.

✦ **The `<legend>` tag:** A part of the fieldset, this tag allows you to specify a legend for the entire fieldset. The legend is visible to the user.

✦ **The paragraphs:** I sometimes place each label and its corresponding input element in a paragraph. This provides some nice formatting capabilities and keeps each pair together.

✦ **The `<label>` tag:** This tag allows you to specify a particular chunk of text as a label. No formatting is done by default, but you can add formatting later with CSS. The label also has an optional `for` attribute that allows you to connect the label with a specific input element. This can help to organize your form just a little more.

✦ **The `<input>` elements:** The user types data into these elements. For now, I'm just using very basic text inputs so the form has some kind of input. In the next section, I explain how to build more complete text inputs.

Building Text-Style Inputs

Most of the form elements are variations of the same tag. The `<input>` tag can create single-line text boxes, password boxes, buttons, and even invisible content (such as hidden fields). Most of these objects share the same basic attributes, although the outward appearance can be different.

Making a standard text field

Figure 7-3 shows the most common form of the input element — a *plain text field*.

To make a basic text input, you need a form and an input element. Adding a label so that the user knows what he's supposed to enter into the text box is also common. Here's the code:

```
<!DOCTYPE html>
<html lang = "en-US">

  <head>
    <meta charset = "UTF-8">
    <title>textbox.html</title>
  </head>
  <body>
    <form action = "">
      <p>
        <label>Name</label>
        <input type = "text"
             id = "txtName"
             . value = "Jonas"/>
      </p>
    </form>
  </body>
</html>
```

An input element has three common attributes:

✦ **`type`:** The `type` attribute indicates the type of input element this is. This first example sets `type` to `text` , creating a standard text box. Other types throughout this chapter create passwords, hidden fields, check boxes, and buttons.

✦ **`id`:** The `id` attribute creates an identifier for the field. When you use a programming language to extract data from this element, use `id` to specify which field you're referring to. An `id` field often begins with a hint phrase to indicate the type of object it is (for instance, `txt` indicates a text box).

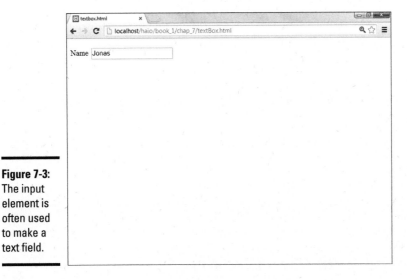

Figure 7-3:
The input element is often used to make a text field.

✦ `value`: This attribute determines the default value of the text box. If you leave this attribute out, the text field begins empty.

Text fields can also have other attributes, which aren't used as often, such as

✦ `size`: This attribute determines the number of characters that are displayed.

✦ `maxlength`: Use this attribute to set the largest number of characters that are allowed.

There is no `</input>` tag. Input tags are a holdover from the days when many tags did not have ending tags. You just end the original tag with a slash character (/), as shown in the preceding sample code.

You might wonder why I added the `<label>` tag if it doesn't have any effect on the appearance or behavior of the form. In this particular example, the `<label>` tag doesn't have an effect, but like everything else in HTML, you can do amazing style things with it in CSS. Even though labels don't typically have a default style, they are still useful.

Building a password field

Passwords are just like text boxes, except the text isn't displayed. Instead, a series of asterisks appears. Figure 7-4 shows a basic password field.

The following code reveals that passwords are almost identical to ordinary text fields:

```
<!DOCTYPE html>
<html lang = "en-US">

  <head>
    <meta charset = "UTF-8">
    <title>password.html</title>
  </head>
  <body>
    <form action = "">
      <fieldset>
        <legend>Enter a password</legend>
        <p>
          <label>Type password here</label>
          <input type = "password"
                  id = "pwd"
                  value = "secret" />
        </p>
      </fieldset>
    </form>
  </body>
</html>
```

In this example, I've created a password field with the ID `pwd`. The default value of this field is `secret`. The term *secret* won't actually appear in the field; it will be replaced with six asterisk characters.

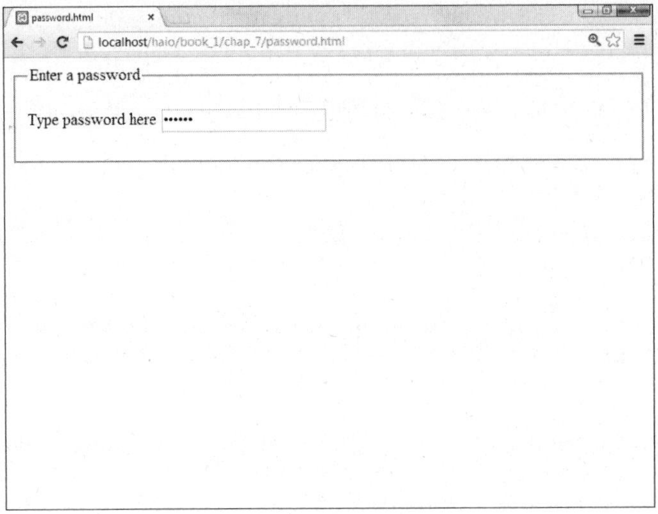

Figure 7-4:
Enter the
secret pass-
word. . . .

The password field offers virtually no meaningful security. It protects the user from spy satellites glancing over his shoulder to read a password, but that's about it. The open standards of HTML and the programming languages mean passwords are often passed in the open. There are solutions — such as the SSL (Secure Socket Layer) technology — but for now, just be aware that the password field isn't suitable for protecting the recipe of your secret sauce.

This example doesn't really do anything with the password, but you'll use other technologies for that.

Making multi-line text input

The single-line text field is a powerful feature, but sometimes, you want something with a bit more space. The essay.html program, as shown in Figure 7-5, demonstrates how you might create a page for an essay question.

The star of this program is a new tag — <textarea>:

```
<!DOCTYPE html>
<html lang = "en-US">

  <head>
    <meta charset = "UTF-8">
    <title>essay.html</title>
  </head>
  <body>
    <form action = "">
      <fieldset>
        <legend>Quiz</legend>
        <p>
          <label>Name</label>
          <input type = "text"
                 id = "txtName" />
```

```
      </p>
      <p>
        <label>
          Please enter the sum total of
          Western thought. Be brief.
        </label>
      </p>
      <p>
        <textarea id = "txtAnswer"
                  rows = "10"
                  cols = "40"></textarea>
      </p>
    </fieldset>
  </form>
 </body>
</html>
```

Here are a few things to keep in mind when using the `<textarea>` tag:

✦ **It needs an `id` attribute, just like an input element.**

✦ **You can specify the size with `rows` and `cols` attributes.**

✦ **The content goes between the tags.** The text area can contain a lot more information than the ordinary `<input>` tags, so rather than placing the data in the `value` attribute, the content of the text goes between the `<textarea>` and `</textarea>` tags.

Anything placed between `<textarea>` and `</textarea>` in the code ends up in the output, too. This includes spaces and carriage returns. If you don't want any blank spaces in the text area, place the ending tag right next to the beginning tag, as I did in the essay example.

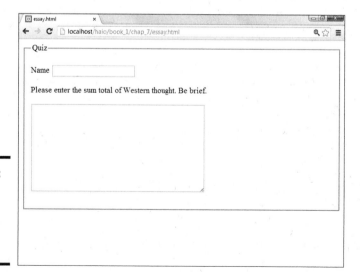

Figure 7-5:
This quiz
might
require a
multi-line
response.

Creating Multiple Selection Elements

Sometimes, you want to present the user with a list of choices and then have the user pick one of these elements. HTML has a number of interesting ways to do this.

Making selections

The drop-down list is a favorite selection tool of web developers for the following reasons:

✦ **It saves screen space.** Only the current selection is showing. When the user clicks the list, a series of choices drop down and then disappear again after the selection is made.

✦ **It limits input.** The only things the user can choose are things you've put in the list. This makes it much easier to handle the potential inputs because you don't have to worry about typing errors.

✦ **The value can be different from what the user sees.** This seems like an odd advantage, but it does turn out to be very useful sometimes. I show an example when I describe color values later in this chapter.

Figure 7-6 shows a simple drop-down list in action.

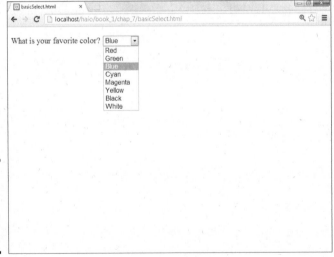

Figure 7-6:
The user can choose from a list of colors.

The code for this simple drop-down list follows:

```
<!DOCTYPE html>
<html lang = "en-US">
```

```
<head>
  <meta charset = "UTF-8">
  <title>basicSelect.html</title>
</head>
<body>
  <form action = "">
    <p>
      <label>What is your favorite color?</label>
      <select id = "selColor">
        <option value = "#ff0000">Red</option>
        <option value = "#00ff00">Green</option>
        <option value = "#0000ff">Blue</option>
        <option value = "#00ffff">Cyan</option>
        <option value = "#ff00ff">Magenta</option>
        <option value = "#ffff00">Yellow</option>
        <option value = "#000000">Black</option>
        <option value = "#ffffff">White</option>
      </select>
    </p>
  </form>
</body>
</html>
```

The `select` object is a bit different from some of the other input elements
you're used to, such as

✦ **It's surrounded by a `<select></select>` pair.** These tags indicate the
entire list.

✦ **The `select` object has an `id` attribute.** Although the `select` object has
many other tags inside, typically only the `select` object itself has an `id`
attribute.

✦ **It contains a series of `<option></option>` pairs.** Each individual
selection is housed in an `<option></option>` set.

✦ **Each `<option>` tag has a value associated with it.** The value is used by
code. The value isn't necessarily what the user sees. (See the sidebar
"What are those funky #ff00ff things?" for an example.)

✦ **The content between `<option></option>` is visible to the user.** The
content is what the user actually sees.

What are those funky #ff00ff things?

If you look carefully at the code for `basic
Select.html`, you see that the values are
all strange text with pound signs and weird
characters. These are *hex codes,* and they're
a good way to describe colors for computers.
I explain all about how these work in Book
II, Chapter 1. This coding mechanism is not
nearly as hard to understand as it seems. For
now though, this code with both color names
and hex values is a good example of wanting
to show the user one thing (the name of a color
in English) and send some other value (the hex
code) to a program. You see this code again in
Book IV, Chapter 5, where I use a list box just
like this to change the background color of the
page with JavaScript.

Select boxes don't require the drop-down behavior. If you want, you can specify the number of rows to display with the `size` attribute. In this case, the number of rows you specify will always be visible on the screen.

Building check boxes

Check boxes are used when you want the user to turn a particular choice on or off. For example, look at Figure 7-7.

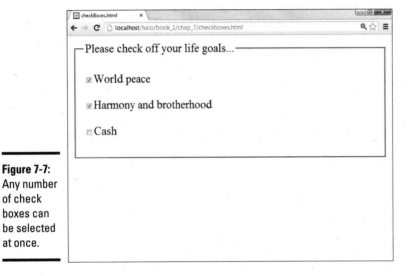

Figure 7-7:
Any number
of check
boxes can
be selected
at once.

Each check box represents a true or false value that can be selected or not selected, and the status of each check box is completely independent from the others. The user can check none of the options, all of them, or any combination.

This code shows that check boxes use your old friend the `<input>` tag:

This all seems inconsistent

Sometimes, the value of a form element is visible to users, and sometimes it's hidden. Sometimes, the text the user sees is inside the tag, and sometimes it isn't. It's a little confusing. The standards evolved over time, and they honestly could have been a little more consistent. Still, this is the set of elements you have, and they're not really that hard to understand. Write forms a few times, and you'll remember. You can always start by looking over my code and borrowing it as a starting place.

```
<!DOCTYPE html>
<html lang = "en-US">

  <head>
    <meta charset = "UTF-8">
    <title>checkBoxes.html</title>
  </head>
  <body>
    <form action = "">
      <fieldset>
        <legend>Please check off your life goals   </legend>
        <p>
          <input type = "checkbox"
                 id = "chkPeace"
                 value = "peace" />World peace
        </p>
        <p>
          <input type = "checkbox"
                 id = "chkHarmony"
                 value = "harmony" />Harmony and brotherhood
        </p>
        <p>
          <input type = "checkbox"
                 id = "chkCash"
                 value = "cash" />Cash
        </p>
      </fieldset>
    </form>
  </body>
</html>
```

You're using the same attributes of the `<input>` tag, but they work a bit differently than the way they do in a plain old text box:

✦ **The `type` is `checkbox`.** That's how the browser knows to make a check box, rather than a text field.

✦ **The checkbox still requires an ID.** If you'll be writing programming code to work with this thing (and you will, eventually), you'll need an ID for reference.

✦ **The value is hidden from the user.** The user doesn't see the actual value. That's for the programmer (like the `select` object). Any text following the check box only *appears* to be the text associated with it.

Creating radio buttons

Radio buttons are used when you want to let the user pick only one option from a group. Figure 7-8 shows an example of a radio button group in action.

Radio buttons might seem similar to check boxes, but they have some important differences:

✦ **Only one can be checked at a time.** The term *radio button* came from the old-style car radios. When you pushed the button for one station, all the other buttons popped out. Even my car isn't that old any more, but the name has stuck.

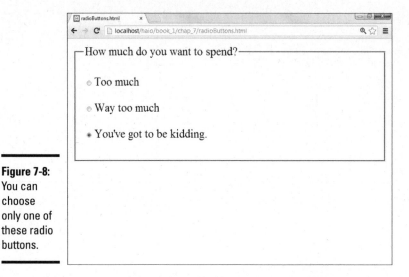

Figure 7-8:
You can
choose
only one of
these radio
buttons.

✦ **They have to be in a group.** Radio buttons make sense only in a group context. The point of a radio button is to interact with its group.

✦ **They all have the same name!** Each radio button has its own ID (like other input elements), but they also have a `name` attribute. The `name` attribute indicates the *group* a radio button is in.

✦ **You can have more than one group on a page.** Just use a different `name` attribute for each group.

✦ **One of them has to be selected.** The group should always have one value and only one. Some browsers check the first element in a group by default, but just in case, you should select the element you want selected. Add the `checked = "checked"` attribute (developed by the Department of Redundancy Department) to the element you want selected when the page appears. In this example, I preselected the most expensive option, all in the name of good capitalistic suggestive selling.

Here's some code that explains it all:

```
<!DOCTYPE html>
<html lang = "en-US">

  <head>
    <meta charset = "UTF-8">
    <title>radioButtons.html</title>
  </head>
  <body>
    <form action = "">
      <fieldset>
        <legend>How much do you want to spend?</legend>
        <p>
          <input type = "radio"
                 name = "radPrice"
                 id = "rad100"
```

```
                          value = "100" />Too much
          </p>
          <p>
            <input type = "radio"
                   name = "radPrice"
                   id = "rad200"
                   value = "200" />Way too much
          </p>
          <p>
            <input type = "radio"
                   name = "radPrice"
                   id = "rad5000"
                   value = "5000"
                   checked = "checked" />You've got to be kidding.
          </p>
        </fieldset>
      </form>
    </body>
</html>
```

Pressing Your Buttons

HTML5 also comes with several types of buttons. You use these guys to make something actually happen. Generally, the user sets up some kind of input by typing in text boxes and then selecting from lists, options, or check boxes. Then, the user clicks a button to trigger a response. Figure 7-9 demonstrates four types of buttons.

Figure 7-9:
HTML5
supports
several
types of
buttons.

The code for this button example is shown here:

```
<!DOCTYPE html>
<html lang = "en-US">
```

```
<head>
  <meta charset = "UTF-8">
  <title>buttons.html</title>
</head>
<body>
  <h1>Button Demo</h1>
  <form action = "">
    <fieldset>
      <legend>
        input-style buttons
      </legend>
      <input type = "button"
             value = "input type = button" />
      <input type = "submit" />
      <input type = "reset" />
    </fieldset>
    <fieldset>
      <legend>button tag buttons</legend>
      <button type = "button">
        button tag
      </button>
      <button>
        <img src = "clickMe.gif"
             alt = "click me" />
      </button>
    </fieldset>
  </form>
</body>
</html>
```

Each button type is described in this section.

Making input-style buttons

The most common form of button is just another form of your old friend, the
`<input>` tag. If you set the input's `type` attribute to `"button"`, you generate a basic button:

```
<input type = "button"
       value = "input type = button" />
```

The ordinary Input button has a few key features:

+ **The `input type` is set to `"button"`.** This makes an ordinary button.

+ **The `value` attribute sets the button's caption.** Change the `value`
  attribute to make a new caption. This button's caption shows how the
  button was made: `input type = "button"`.

+ **This type of button doesn't imply a link.** Although the button appears
  to depress when it's clicked, it doesn't do anything. You have to write
  some JavaScript code to make it work.

+ **Later, you'll add event-handling to the button.** After you discover
  JavaScript in Book IV, you use a special attribute to connect the button
  to code.

✦ **This type of button is for client-side programming.** This type of code resides on the user's computer. I discuss client-side programming with JavaScript in Book IV.

Building a Submit button

Submit buttons are usually used in server-side programming. In this form of programming, the code is on the web server. In Book V, you use PHP to create server-side code. The `<input>` tag is used to make a Submit button, too!

```
<input type = "submit" />
```

Although they look the same, the Submit button is different than the ordinary button in a couple subtle ways:

✦ **The `value` attribute is optional.** If you leave it out, the button displays Submit Query. Of course, you can change the `value` to anything you want, and this becomes the caption of the Submit button.

✦ **Clicking it causes a link.** This type of button is meant for server-side programming. When you click the button, all the information in the form is gathered and sent to some other page on the web.

✦ **Right now, it goes nowhere.** When you set the form's `action` attribute to null (`""`), you told the Submit button to just reload the current page. When you figure out real server-side programming, you change the form's `action` attribute to a program that works with the data.

✦ **Submit buttons aren't for client-side.** Although you can attach an event to the Submit button (just like the regular Input button), the linking behavior often causes problems. Use regular Input buttons for client-side and Submit buttons for server-side.

It's a do-over: The Reset button

Yet another form of the versatile `<input>` tag creates the Reset button:

```
<input type = "reset" />
```

This button has a very specific purpose. When clicked, it resets all the elements of its form to their default values. Like the Submit button, it has a default value (`"reset"`), and it doesn't require any code.

Introducing the <button> tag

The button has been a useful part of the web for a long time, but it's a bit boring. HTML 4.0 introduced the `<button>` tag, which works like this:

```
<button type = "button">
  button tag
</button>
```

The `<button>` tag acts more like a standard HTML tag, but it can also act like a Submit button. Here are the highlights:

✦ **The `type` attribute determines the style.** You can set the button to `ordinary` (by setting its type to `button`), `submit`, or `reset`. If you don't specify the type, buttons use the Submit style. The button's `type` indicates its behavior, just like the Input-style buttons.

✦ **The caption goes between the `<button></button>` pair.** There's no `value` attribute. Instead, just put the intended caption inside the `<button>` pair.

✦ **You can incorporate other elements.** Unlike the Input button, you can place images or styled text inside a button. This gives you some other capabilities. The second button in the buttons.html example uses a small GIF image to create a more colorful button.

New Form Input Types

HTML forms are centered around the humble but flexible `input` element. HTML5 adds a number of very useful forms of input, which help build more modern and flexible interfaces.

Although support for these tags is not universal, it is safe to begin using them now. Any browser (even IE6) which does not understand the advanced input types will revert to `input type = "text"`, which will still work exactly as expected (although not with the validation and user interface improvements of the newer tags).

Note that the standard indicates that the various types will be supported, but the exact way the elements are supported will vary from browser to browser. For example, the e-mail field will likely look just like an ordinary text field to a user with a standard desktop machine, but the virtual keyboard on a mobile device might change to include the @ when it encounters an e-mail field.

Figure 7-10 illustrates many of these form elements in action using Google Chrome, which supports all of these features.

date

Setting the input type to `date` indicates that you wish the user to enter a date value. Some browsers (Firefox 3.5) still display a text field, and others (Opera 10) display a special calendar control, allowing for much more accurate and easier date selection. Still other browsers (Chrome) include both text and a pop-up calendar. If the date is entered by text, it must be entered in a yyyy-mm-dd format.

```
<input type="date"
       id = "date" />
```

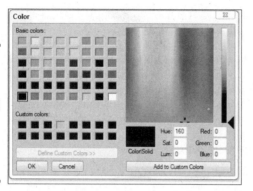

Figure 7-10:
Newer browsers have special inputs — here I'm picking a color.

You can restrict the dates allowed to a specific range by applying the min and max attributes to the element.

time

The purpose of the time input type is to allow the user to enter a time. Time is stored in hh:mm format, where hh is the hour (in 24-hour format) and mm is the minutes. Some browsers include a colon directly in the field, and some modify the virtual keyboard with numbers and the colon character. It is also possible that a browser will pop up some sort of custom time selector, but this is not yet supported in any major browsers.

```
<input type = "time"
       id = "time" />
```

datetime

The datetime element combines date and time into a single element. It also includes a mechanism for entering the time zone.

```
<input type="datetime"
       id = "datetime" />
```

Some browsers pop up a calendar control for the date and a formatted input for the time. Others may modify virtual keyboards for date and time input.

datetime-local

The datetime-local element is just like the datetime element except it does not include a time zone indicator.

```
<input type="datetime-local"
       id = "datetimeLocal" />
```

Managing date and time data

The official full date and time format returned from the various date and time elements is a specialized code:

```
yyyy-mm-ddThh:mm+ff:gg
```

Each of the characters in the code describe a part of the date and time:

- ✔ **yyyy:** Four digits for the year.

- ✔ **- (dash):** Must be placed between year and month. Another dash is placed between the month and the day.

- ✔ **mm:** Two digits for the month.

- ✔ **dd:** Two digits for the day.

- ✔ **T:** Capital "T" indicates the beginning of the time part of the code.

- ✔ **hh:** Two digits for the hour, in 24-hour format.

- ✔ **:(colon):** The colon character between the hour and minutes. Another colon will appear between the hour and minutes of the time zone offset.

- ✔ **mm:** Two digits for the minutes.

- ✔ **+/-/Z:** The time zone offset is indicated by a capital Z (if the time is Zulu or GMT time) or the + or - symbol if time is in another time zone.

- ✔ **ff:** If the time zone is not Zulu time, indicate the number of hours offset from GMT.

- ✔ **gg:** Number of minutes offset from Zulu time. Typically this is 00, but it is possible that the time zone will be offset by 15, 30, or 45 minutes.

For example, 5:30 PM on October 11, 2010, in New York City will be indicated like this:

```
2010-10-11T17:30-05:00
```

If the user is using a browser that validates a `datetime` field, the date and time will need to be in this format to be considered valid. The value of a `datetime` field will be in this format, which is relatively easy for computer programs to parse and manage.

The `datetime-local` input type expects and returns a date and time in the same format as the standard `datetime` element, except `datetime-local` does not include a time zone offset.

week

The `week` field is used to pick a week from a calendar control. It returns a value in the following format:

```
yyyy-Wnn
```

- ✦ **yyyy** represents a four-digit year
- ✦ **-** is the dash character
- ✦ **W** is the capital W character
- ✦ **nn** is the week as a two-digit number

Some browsers pop up the standard calendar control. When the user selects a date (or a week), only the year and week will be returned. Other browsers will simply validate for the proper format:

```
<input type = "week"
       id = "week" />
```

month

The month input type generates a four-digit year followed by a two-digit month. It frequently pops up the same calendar control as other date pickers, but only the year and month (yyyy-mm format) are returned.

```
<input type = "month"
       id = "month" />
```

color

The color tool allows the user to choose a color using standard web formats: recognized color names (yellow) and hex values preceded by a # symbol (#ff0033.) The browser may display a color-picking tool like the ones found in word processors and paint programs. At the moment, some browsers simply display a text box and indicate whether the current content is a valid color name or value.

```
<input type = "color"
       id = "color" />
```

number

The number field allows the input of numerical data. This often consists of a text field followed by some kind of selector (say up and down arrows), or it might change the virtual keypad of a portable device to handle only numeric input.

```
<input type = "number"
       id = "number"
       max = "10"
       min = "0" />
```

The number input type supports several special attributes:

✦ **min:** This is the minimum value allowed. If there is an on-screen input element, it will not allow a value less than the min value. The field will also not validate if the value of the field is less than the min value.

✦ **max:** This is the maximum allowed value. If there is an on-screen input element, it will not allow a value larger than the max value. The field will not validate if the value of the field is larger than the max value.

✦ **step:** This value indicates how much the visual interface tools (typically small up and down arrows) will change the value when activated.

✦ **value:** This is the numeric value of the element.

All values can be integer or floating point. However, current browsers which support this tag (Opera and Chrome) do not seem to validate as well with floating-point values as they do with integer values. For more control of numeric input, consider the range input type, described in the following section.

range

The range input type is a long-anticipated addition to the HTML toolbox. User interface experts have known for years that user input of integer values is very difficult to get right. Most user interface toolkits have some sort of slider or scrollbar mechanism that makes it easy for users to enter a numeric value visually. The <input type = "range"> construct finally adds this functionality to HTML forms.

```
<input type = "range"
       id = "range"
       min = "0"
       max = "255"
       value = "128" />
```

The range input takes the attributes number, min, max, value, and step. If the browser supports this tag, the user will see a scroller. If not, a plain-text input type will appear. When this element becomes widespread, its use will be encouraged because it is much easier to restrict the users input to a valid range (especially when the mechanism for doing so is visual and easy) than it is to check the user's input after the fact.

However, the range type does not display the exact value, and it can be harder to get precise results than with the number input type. One solution is to pair an output tag to the range, and use JavaScript to update the output when the range is changed. See rangeOutput.html on the book's website to see this in action. (You may need to review JavaScript coding in Book IV to completely follow this example.)

search

The search input type is used to retrieve text that's intended to be used as part of a search (either internally or through some searching service like Google). On most browsers, it is displayed like an ordinary text field. It does sometimes have some special behavior. On Safari, the search field has a small X that clears the contents of the search. On Chrome, the auto-completion features of the main search bar (which is also the URL input element in Chrome) are automatically applied to the search box.

```
<input type="search"
       id = "search" />
```

Like the other new input types, there is no penalty for using the `search` element in browsers that do not support it. The fall-back is a plain text input.

Note that the `search` element doesn't actually do any searching. If you want to actually search for the value, you'll still need to write some code. The `search` element does give you an interface consistent with the browser's integrated search tools, but the actual behavior is still up to the programmer.

email

The `email` element generally looks like a plain text field, but it validates on an e-mail address. Also, it is possible that the browser will modify the user experience in other ways. For example, mobile browsers may modify the virtual keyboard to include the @ symbol, which is always present in e-mail addresses:

```
<input type="email"
       id = "txtEmail" />
```

tel

The `tel` field is used to input a telephone number. It expects three digits followed by a dash and four digits. You may need to play with the `pattern` attribute if you want to allow an area code or extensions to validate.

```
<input type = "tel"
       id = "tel"  />
```

url

Use this input type to indicate a web address. Browsers that support this element will check for the `http://` prefix. Mobile browsers may also adapt the virtual keyboard to include characters commonly found in URLs: the colon (:), forward slash (/), and tilde (~).

```
<input type = "url"
       id = "url"  />
```

Part II
Styling with CSS

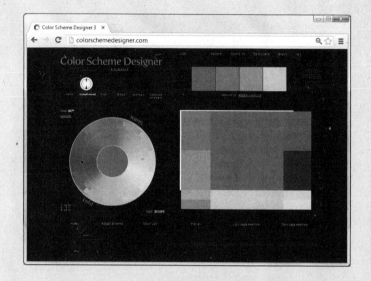

Visit www.dummies.com/extras/html5css3aio for more on using HTML entities.

Contents at a Glance

Chapter 1: Coloring Your World

In This Chapter

- ✔ Introducing the style element
- ✔ Adding styles to tags
- ✔ Modifying your page dynamically
- ✔ Specifying foreground and background colors
- ✔ Understanding hex colors
- ✔ Appreciating HSL colors
- ✔ Developing a color scheme

HTML does a good job of setting up the basic design of a page, but face it: The pages it makes are pretty ugly. In the old days, developers added a lot of other tags to HTML to make it prettier, but changing the design with HTML code was a haphazard affair. Now, HTML disallows all the tags that made pages more attractive. That sounds bad, but it isn't really a loss. Today, HTML is almost always written in concert with CSS (Cascading Style Sheets). It's amazing how much you can do with CSS to beautify your HTML pages.

CSS allows you to change the color of any image on the page, add backgrounds and borders, change the visual appearance of elements (like lists and links), as well as customize the entire layout of your page. Additionally, CSS allows you to keep your HTML simple because all the formatting is stored in the CSS. CSS is efficient, too, because it allows you to reuse a style across multiple elements and pages. If HTML gives your pages structure, CSS gives them beauty.

This chapter gets you started by describing how to add color to your pages.

Now You Have an Element of Style

The secret to CSS is the *style sheet,* a set of rules for describing how various objects will display. For example, look at basicColors.html in Figure 1-1.

As always, don't take my word for it. This chapter is about color, and you need to look at these pages from the companion website to see what I'm talking about. See this book's Introduction for more on the companion website.

Figure 1-1:
This page is
in color!

Nothing in the HTML code provides color information. What makes this page different from plain HTML pages is a new section that I've stashed in the header. Take a gander at the code to see what's going on (interesting part is in bold):

```
<!DOCTYPE html>
<html lang = "en-US">

  <head>
    <meta charset = "UTF-8">
    <title>basicColors.html</title>
    <style type = "text/css">
      body {
        color: yellow;
        background-color: red;
      }
      h1 {
        color: red;
        background-color: yellow;
      }
    </style>
  </head>
  <body>
    <h1>Red text on a yellow background</h1>
    <p>
      Yellow text on a red background
    </p>
  </body>
</html>
```

As you can see, nothing is dramatically different in the HTML code. The body simply contains an `h1` and a `p`. Although the text mentions the colors, nothing in the HTML code makes the colors really happen.

The secret is the new `<style></style>` pair I put in the header area:

```
<style type = "text/css">
  body {
    color: yellow;
    background-color: red;
  }

  h1 {
    color: red;
    background-color: yellow;
  }
</style>
```

The `<style>` tag is an HTML tag, but what it does is special: It switches languages! Inside the style elements, you're not writing HTML anymore. You're in a whole new language — CSS. CSS has a different job than HTML, but they're made to work well together.

It may seem that the CSS code is still part of HTML because it's inside the HTML page, but it's best to think of HTML and CSS as two distinct (if related) languages. HTML describes the content, and CSS describes the layout. CSS (as you soon see) has a different syntax and style than HTML and isn't always embedded in the web page.

Setting up a style sheet

Style sheets describe presentation rules for HTML elements. If you look at the preceding style sheet (the code inside the `<style>` tags), you can see that I've described presentation rules for two elements: the `<body>` and `<h1>` tags. Whenever the browser encounters one of these tags, it attempts to use these style rules to change that tag's visual appearance.

Styles are simply a list of *selectors* (places in the page that you want to modify). For now, I use tag names (`body` and `h1`) as selectors. However, in Chapter 3 of this minibook, I show many more selectors that you can use.

Each selector can have a number of style *rules*. Each rule describes some attribute of the selector. To set up a style, keep the following in mind:

✦ **Begin with the style tags.** The type of style you'll be working with for now is embedded into the page. You should describe your style in the header area.

✦ **Include the style type in the header area.** The style type is always `"text/css"`. The beginning `<style>` tag always looks like this:

```
<style type = "text/css">
```

✦ **Define an element.** Use the element name (the tag name alone) to begin the definition of a particular element's style. You can define styles for all the HTML elements (and other things, too, but not today). The selector for the body is designated like this:

```
body {
```

✦ **Use braces ({ }) to enclose the style rules.** Each style's rules are enclosed in a set of braces. Similar to many programming languages, braces mark off special sections of code. It's traditional to indent inside the braces.

✦ **Give a rule name.** In this chapter, I'm working with two very simple rules: `color` and `background-color`. Throughout this minibook, you can read about many more CSS rules (sometimes called attributes) that you can modify. A colon (`:`) character always follows the rule name.

✦ **Enter the rule's value.** Different rules take different values. The attribute value is followed by a semicolon. Traditionally, each name-value pair is on one line, like this:

```
body {
  color: yellow;
  background-color: red;
}
```

Changing the colors

In this very simple example, I just changed some colors around. Here are the two primary color attributes in CSS:

✦ `color:` This refers to the foreground color of any text in the element.

✦ `background-color:` The background color of the element. (The hyphen is a formal part of the name. If you leave it out, the browser won't know what you're talking about.)

With these two elements, you can specify the color of any element. For example, if you want all your paragraphs to have white text on a blue background, add the following text to your style:

```
p {
  color: white;
  background-color: blue;
}
```

CSS is case-sensitive. CSS styles should be written entirely in lowercase.

You'll figure out many more style elements in your travels, but they all follow the same principles illustrated by the color attributes.

Specifying Colors in CSS

Here are the two main ways to define colors in CSS. You can use color names, such as `pink` and `fuchsia`, or you can use *hex values*. (Later in this chapter, in the section "Creating Your Own Color Scheme," you find out how to use special numeric designators to choose colors.) Each approach has its advantages.

Using color names

Color names seem like the easiest solution, and, for basic colors like red and yellow, they work fine. However, here are some problems with color names that make them troublesome for web developers:

✦ **Only 16 color names will validate.** Although most browsers accept hundreds of color names, only 16 are guaranteed to validate in CSS and HTML validators. See Table 1-1 for a list of those 16 colors.

✦ **Color names are somewhat subjective.** You'll find different opinions on what exactly constitutes any particular color, especially when you get to the more obscure colors. (I personally wasn't aware that PeachPuff and PapayaWhip are colors. They sound more like dessert recipes to me.)

✦ **It can be difficult to modify a color.** For example, what color is a tad bluer than Gainsboro? (Yeah, that's a color name, too. I had no idea how extensive my color disability really was.)

✦ **They're hard to match.** Say you're building an online shrine to your cat and you want the text to match your cat's eye color. It'll be hard to figure out exactly what color name corresponds to your cat's eyes. I guess you could ask the cat.

Hex color values can be indicated in uppercase or lowercase. The mysterious hex codes are included in this table for completeness. It's okay if you don't understand what they're about. All is revealed in the next section.

**Book II
Chapter 1**

Coloring Your World

Table 1-1	Legal Color Names and Hex Equivalents
Color	*Hex Value*
Black	#000000
Silver	#C0C0C0
Gray	#808080
White	#FFFFFF
Maroon	#800000
Red	#FF0000
Purple	#800080
Fuchsia	#FF00FF
Green	#008800
Lime	#00FF00

(continued)

Table 1-1 *(continued)*

Color	Hex Value
Olive	#808000
Yellow	#FFFF00
Navy	#000080
Blue	#0000FF
Teal	#008080
Aqua	#00FFFF

Obviously, I can't show you actual colors in this black-and-white book, so I added a simple page to this book's companion website that displays all the named colors. Check namedColors.html to see the actual colors, and see this book's Introduction for information on how to access the website.

Putting a hex on your colors

Colors in HTML are a strange thing. The "easy" way (with color names) turns out to have many problems. The method most web developers *really* use sounds a lot harder, but it isn't as bad as it may seem at first. The *hex color* scheme uses a seemingly bizarre combination of numbers and letters to determine color values. #00FFFF is aqua. #FFFF00 is yellow. It's a scheme only a computer scientist could love. Yet, after you get used to it, you'll find the system has its own geeky charm. (And isn't geeky charm the best kind?)

Hex colors work by describing exactly what the computer is doing, so you have to know a little more about how computers work with color. Each dot (or *pixel*) on the screen is actually composed of three tiny beams of light (or LCD diodes or something similar). Each pixel has tiny red, green, and blue beams.

The light beams work kind of like stage lights. Imagine a black stage with three spotlights (red, green, and blue) trained on the same spot. If all the lights are off, the stage is completely dark. If you turn on only the red light, you see red. You can turn on combinations to get new colors. For example, turning on red and green creates a spot of yellow light. Turning on all three lights makes white.

Coloring by number

In a computer system, each of the little lights can be adjusted to various levels of brightness. These values measure from 0 (all the way off) to 255 (all the way on). Therefore, you could describe red as `rgb(255, 0, 0)` and yellow as `rgb(255, 255, 0)`.

The 0 to 255 range of values seems strange because you're probably used to base 10 mathematics. The computer actually stores values in binary notation. The way a computer sees it, yellow is actually

11111111111111111100000000. Ack! There has to be an easier way to handle all those binary values. That's why we use *hexadecimal notation*. Read on. . . .

Figure 1-2 shows a page which allows you to pick colors with red, green, and blue sliders. Each slider shows its value in base 10 as well as in hexadecimal.

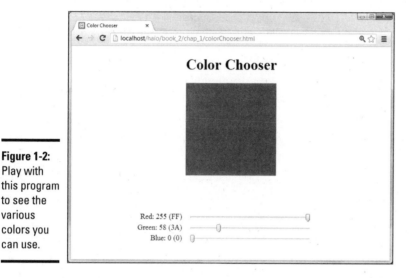

Figure 1-2: Play with this program to see the various colors you can use.

The colorChooser program shown in Figure 1-2 uses technology that will be described in Book IV. Any page that interacts with the user will tend to use a programming language (in this case, JavaScript). Feel free to look over the code, but don't worry if you're not yet ready to add programming to your sites. You'll get there soon enough, I promise.

Hex education

All those 1s and 0s get tedious. Programmers like to convert to another format that's easier to work with. Believe it or not, it's easier to convert binary numbers to base 16 than base 10, so that's what programmers do. You can survive just fine without understanding base 16 (also called *hexadecimal* or *hex*) conversion, but you should understand a few key features, such as:

✦ **Each hex digit is shorthand for four digits of binary.** The whole reason programmers use hex is to simplify working with binary.

✦ **Each digit represents a value between 0 and 15.** Four digits of binary represent a value between 0 and 15.

✦ **We have to invent some digits.** The whole reason hex looks so weird is the inclusion of characters. This is for a simple reason: There aren't enough numeric digits to go around! Table 1-2 illustrates the basic problem.

Table 1-2	Hex Representation of Base Ten Numbers
Decimal (Base 10)	*Hex (Base 16)*
0	0
1	1
2	2
3	3
4	4
5	5
6	6
7	7
8	8
9	9
10	A
11	B
12	C
13	D
14	E
15	F

The ordinary digits 0–9 are the same in hex as they are in base 10, but the values from 10–15 (base ten) are represented by alphabetic characters in hexadecimal.

You're very used to seeing the value 10 as equal to the number of fingers on both hands, but that's not always the case when you start messing around with numbering systems like we're doing here. The number 10 simply means one of the current base. Until now, you may have never used any base but base ten, but all that changes today. The numeral 10 is ten in base ten, but in base two, 10 means two. In base eight, 10 means eight, and in base sixteen, 10 means sixteen. This is important because when you want to talk about the number of digits on your hands in hex, you can't use the familiar notation 10 because in hex 10 means sixteen. We need a single-digit value to represent ten, so computer scientists legislated themselves out of this mess by borrowing letters. 10 is A, 11 is B, and 15 is F.

If all this math theory is making you dizzy, don't worry. I show in the next section some shortcuts for creating great colors using this scheme. For now, though, here's what you need to understand to use hex colors:

✦ **A color requires six digits of hex.** A pixel requires three colors, and each color uses eight digits of binary. Two digits of hex cover each color. Two digits represent red, two for green, and finally two for blue.

✦ **Hex color values usually begin with a pound sign.** To warn the browser that a value will be in hexadecimal, the value is usually preceded with a pound sign (#). So, yellow is #FFFF00.

Working with colors in hex may seem really crazy and difficult, but it has some important advantages:

✦ **Precision:** Using this system gives you a huge number of colors to work with (over 16 million, if you really want to know). There's no way you could come up with that many color names on your own. Well, you could, but you'd be very, very old by the time you were done.

✦ **Objectivity:** Hex values aren't a matter of opinion. There could be some argument about which color is burnt sienna, but hex value #666600 is unambiguous.

✦ **Portability:** Most graphic editing software uses the hex system, so you can pick any color of an image and get its hex value immediately. This would make it easy to find your cat's eye color for that online shrine.

✦ **Predictability:** After you understand how it works, you can take any hex color and convert it to a value that's a little darker, a little brighter, or that has a little more blue in it. This is difficult to do with named colors.

✦ **Ease of use:** This one may seem like a stretch, but after you understand the web-safe palette, which I describe in the next section, it's very easy to get a rough idea of a color and then tweak it to make exactly the form you're looking for.

Using the web-safe color palette

A long time ago, browsers couldn't even agree on what colors they'd display reliably. Web developers responded by working within a predefined palette of colors that worked pretty much the same on every browser. Today's browsers have no problems showing lots of colors, but the so-called *web-safe color palette* is still sometimes used because it's an easy starting point.

The basic idea of the web-safe palette (shown in Table 1-3) is this: Each color can have only one of the following values: 00, 33, 66, 99, CC, or FF. 00 is the darkest value for each color, and FF is the brightest. The primary colors are all made of 0s and Fs: #FF0000 is red (all red, no green, no blue). A web-safe color uses any combination of these values, so #33CC00 is web-safe, but #112233 is not.

Table 1-3	Web-Safe Color Values		
Description	*Red*	*Green*	*Blue*
Very bright	FF	FF	FF
	CC	CC	CC

(continued)

Table 1-3 *(continued)*

Description	Red	Green	Blue
	99	99	99
	66	66	66
	33	33	33
Very dark	00	00	00

To pick a web-safe value from this chart, determine how much of each color you want. A bright red will have red turned on all the way (FF) with no green (00) and no blue (00), making #FF0000. If you want a darker red, you might turn the red down a little. The next darker web-safe red is #CC0000. If that isn't dark enough, you might try #990000. Say you like that, but you want it a little purple. Simply add a notch or two of blue: #990033 or #990066.

Figure 1-3 is a simple tool that allows you to experiment with the web-safe color palette.

Figure 1-3:
Use this tool
to explore
web-safe
colors.

 The original problem web-safe colors were designed to alleviate is long resolved, but they're still popular as a starting point. Web-safe colors give you a dispersed and easily understood subset of colors you can start with. You don't have to stay there, but it's a great place to start.

Choosing Your Colors

Colors can seem overwhelming, but with a little bit of practice, you'll be managing colors with style.

Starting with web-safe colors

The webSafe.html program works by letting you quickly enter a web-safe value. To make red, press the FF button in the red column. The blue and green values have the default value of 00, so the background is red.

The web-safe colors give you a lot of room to play, and they're very easy to work with. In fact, they're so common that you can use a shortcut. Because the web-safe colors are all repeated, you can write a repeated digit (FF) as a single digit (F). You can specify magenta as either #FF00FF or as #F0F and the browser understands, giving you a headache-inducing magenta.

To make a darker red, change the FF to the next smallest value, making #CC0000. If you want it darker yet, try #990000. Experiment with all the red values and see how easy it is to get several different types of red. If you want a variation of pink, raise the green and blue values together. #FF6666 is a dusty pink color; #FF9999 is a bit brighter; and #FFCCCC is a very white pink.

Modifying your colors

The web-safe palette is convenient, but it gives you a relatively small number of colors (216, if you're counting). Two hundred and sixteen crayons in the box are pretty nice, but you might need more. Generally, I start with web-safe colors and then adjust as I go. If you want a lighter pink than #FFCCCC, you can jump off the web-safe bandwagon and use #FFEEEE or any other color you wish!

In the webSafe.html program, you can use the top and bottom button in each row to fine-tune the adjustments to your color.

Doing it on your own pages

Of course, it doesn't really matter how the colors look on *my* page. The point is to make things look good on *your* pages. To add color to your pages, do the following:

1. **Define the HTML as normal.**

   The HTML shouldn't have any relationship to the colors. Add the color strictly in CSS.

2. **Add a `<style>` tag to the page in the header area.**

   Don't forget to set the `type = "text/css"` attribute.

3. **Add a selector for each tag you want to modify.**

   You can modify any HTML tag, so if you want to change all the paragraphs, add a p { } selector. Use the tag name without the angle braces, so `<h1>` becomes h1{ }.

4. **Add `color` and `background-color` attributes.**

You'll discover many more CSS elements you can modify throughout Books II and III but for now, stick to `color` and `background-color`.

5. **Specify the color values with color names or hex color values.**

Changing CSS on the fly

The Chrome web browser has an especially cool trick when it comes to CSS coding. You can look at the CSS of any element on a web page and change it, seeing the results in real time!

Here's how it works:

1. **Build the page in the normal way.**

   Use your text editor to build the basic page.

2. **Add CSS selectors.**

   Specify the CSS for the elements you intend to change. The emptyCSS. html page on the website shows a very simple example. You can put any values you want in the CSS, or you can simply leave the CSS blank for now. If you want to experiment, take a look at emptyCSS.html on the website. It has empty selectors for the three elements described on the page (`body`, `h1`, and `p`).

3. **Load your page in Chrome.**

   The other browsers are starting to develop tools like Chrome, but it's clearly the leader, so start with Chrome.

4. **Inspect an element.**

   Right-click any element and choose Inspect element from the resulting pop-up menu.

5. **Gasp in wonderment at the awesome developer tools.**

   Figure 1-4 shows the developer tools that pop up when you inspect an element. Keep it in the Elements tab for now.

6. **Change the HTML code!**

   You can double-click the code in the code viewer and modify the contents. This is fun, but not permanent or especially helpful.

7. **You can also modify the CSS.**

   If a style selector has been defined, it appears under the Styles tab in the Matched CSS Rules section. You can add new style rules or change the existing ones, and you'll be able to see the results on the fly.

8. **You can even use a fancy color selector.**

   When a color rule has been defined, you'll see a little color swatch. Click on that color to get a nice color selector you can use.

9. **Select different parts of the page to modify other rules.**

You can modify the CSS of any element as long as some sort of rule has been saved.

10. **Copy and paste any style rules you want to keep.**

    Modifications made in the web developer toolbar are not permanent. If you find colors or other style rules you like, you can copy them from the developer window and paste them into your code.

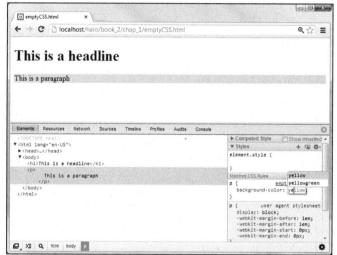

Figure 1-4:
The Chrome developer tools allow you to change CSS on the fly.

Creating Your Own Color Scheme

The technical side of setting colors isn't too difficult, but deciding *what* colors to use can be a challenge. Entire books have been written about how to determine a color scheme. A little bit of subjectivity is in the process, but a few tools and rules can get you started.

Understanding hue, saturation, and lightness

The RGB color model is useful because it relates directly to how computers generate color, but it's not perfect. It's a bit difficult to visualize variations of a color in RGB. For that reason, other color schemes are often used. The most common variation is *Hue, Saturation, and Lightness,* or *HSL.* The HSL system organizes colors in a way more closely related to the color wheel.

Sometimes you'll run across the HSB or HSV color schemes, which are very similar to HSL. In all these color modes, you begin with a Hue, and then use saturation to indicate how far the color is from a grayscale. Brightness, value and lightness, do basically the same thing (determine the general amount of energy in the color) but using different models.

To describe a color using HSL, you specify three characteristics of a color using numeric values:

✦ **Hue:** The basic color. The color wheel is broken into a series of hues. These are generally middle of the road colors that can be made *brighter* (closer to white) and *darker* (closer to black).

✦ **Saturation:** How pervasive the color is. A high saturation is very bright. A low saturation has very little color. If you reduce all the saturation in an image, the image is *grayscale,* with no color at all.

✦ **Lightness:** The amount of light in the color. The easiest way to view value is to think about how the image would look when reduced to grayscale (by pulling down the saturation). All the brighter colors will be closer to white, and the darker colors will be nearly black.

The HSL model is useful because it allows you to pick colors that go well together. Use the hue property to pick the basic colors. Because there's a mathematical relationship between the various color values, it becomes easy to predict which colors work well together. After you have all the hues worked out, you can change the saturation and value to modify the overall tone of the page. Generally, all the colors in a particular scheme have similar saturation and values.

You can use the HSL color model to pick colors if you prefer. Figure 1-5 shows a color picker that lets you design colors based on the HSL model.

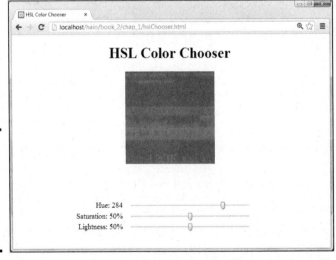

Figure 1-5: The HSL model provides another way to view colors.

Using HSL colors in your pages

You can assign an HSL value wherever you use colors in your CSS. As an example, look at HSLcolors.html on the companion website. (I do not show it here because the color differences are too subtle to display in a black and white book.) The code for HSLcolors.html shows how the HSL scheme can be used:

```
<!DOCTYPE html>
<html lang = "en-US">

  <head>
    <meta charset = "UTF-8">
    <title>HSLcolors.html</title>
    <style type = "text/css">
      body {
        background-color: HSL(180, 75%, 75%);
      }
      h1 {
        color: HSL(180, 75%, 25%);
        background-color: HSL(180, 75%, 90%);
      }
      p {
        color: HSL(0, 75%, 25%);
      }
    </style>
  </head>
  <body>
    <h1>This is a headline</h1>
    <p>
      This is a paragraph
    </p>
  </body>
</html>
```

To specify a color using the HSL scheme, do this:

1. **Set up your selectors as usual**.

   In the CSS, set up a selector for each element you wish to color.

2. **Add the color rule.**

   In this chapter you learn two color rules: `color` and `background-color`. Apply one or both to each selector.

3. **Use the HSL function.**

   Using HSL followed by parentheses indicates you wish to calculate the color using the HSL technique.

4. **Indicate the hue.**

   Imagine a color wheel with red at the top. The hue is the angle (in degrees) of the color you want to pick. Hue should have a value between 0 and 360.

5. **Determine the saturation.**

   Saturation is measured as a percentage. Saturation of 0% indicates a grayscale (somewhere between black and white) whereas Saturation of 100% is a fully saturated color with no grayscale. You need to include the percent sign as part of the saturation value.

6. **Specify the lightness.**

   Lightness is also indicated as a percentage, with 0% being completely black and 100% being completely white. A lightness value of 50% will determine a balanced color between white and black. Lightness values should also include the percent sign.

The HSL model is a relatively recent addition to CSS, so it may not work with older browsers, but it can be extremely helpful. HSL makes it easier to predict whether colors will look good together. If you keep any two of the HSL values the same and change the third, the two colors are likely to fit together well.

Using the Color Scheme Designer

Some people have great color sense. Others (like me) struggle a little bit because it all seems a little subjective. If you're already confident with colors, you may not need this section — although, you still might find it interesting validation of what you already know. On the other hand, if you get perplexed in a paint store, you might find it helpful to know that some really useful tools are available.

One great way to get started is with a free tool: the Color Scheme Designer, shown in Figure 1-6. This tool, created by Petr Stanicek, uses a variation of the HSV model to help you pick color schemes. You can find this program at `http://colorschemedesigner.com`.

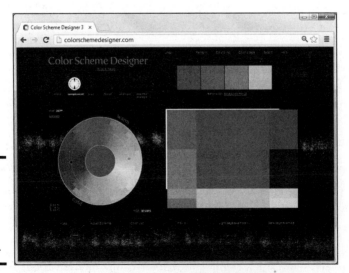

Figure 1-6:
The Color Scheme Designer helps you pick colors.

The Color Scheme Designer has several features, such as

✦ **The color wheel:** This tool may bring back fond memories of your elementary school art class. The wheel arranges the colors in a way familiar to artists. You can click the color wheel to pick a primary color for your page.

✦ **The color scheme selector:** You can pick from a number of color schemes. I describe these schemes a little later in this section.

✦ **A preview area:** This area displays the selected colors in action so you can see how the various colors work together.

✦ **Hex values:** The hex values for the selected colors display on the page so you can copy them to your own application.

✦ **Variations:** You can look at variations of the selected scheme. These variations are often useful because they show differences in the saturation and value without you doing the math.

✦ **Color-blindness simulation:** This very handy tool lets you see your color scheme as it appears to people with various types of color-blindness.

This won't make sense without experimentation. Be sure to play with this tool and see how easy it is to create colors that work well together.

**Book II
Chapter 1**

Coloring Your World

Selecting a base hue

The Color Scheme Designer works by letting you pick one main hue and then uses one of a number of schemes for picking other hues that work well with the base one. To choose the base hue you want for your page, click a color on the color wheel.

The color wheel is arranged according to the traditional artist's color scheme based on HSV rather than the RGB scheme used for computer graphics. When you select a color, the closest RGB representation is returned. This is nice because it allows you to apply traditional (HSV-style) color theory to the slightly different RGB model.

When you pick a color on the color wheel, you're actually picking a hue. If you want any type of red, you can pick the red that appears on the wheel. You can then adjust the variations to modify the saturation and value of all the colors in the scheme together.

To pick a color using this scheme, follow these steps:

1. **Pick a hue.**

   The colors on the color wheel represent hues in the HSV model. Find a primary color you want to use as the foundation of your page.

2. **Determine a scheme.**

   The scheme indicates which other colors you will use and how they relate to the primary hue. More information on the various schemes is available in the next section.

3. **Adjust your scheme.**

   The main schemes are picked using default settings for saturation and value. The Adjust Scheme tab allows you to modify the saturation and value settings to get much more control of your color scheme. You can also adjust the level of contrast to get very interesting effects.

4. **Preview the scheme.**

   The Designer has several options for previewing your color scheme, including the ability to create quick web pages using the scheme. You might also look at the color blindness simulators to see how your page appears to people with different kinds of color blindness.

5. **Export the color settings.**

   If you want, you can export the color settings to a number of formats, including a very nice HTML/CSS format. You can also save the colors to a special file for importing into GIMP or Photoshop, so the exact colors used in your page will be available to your image editor, too.

Picking a color scheme

The various color schemes use mathematical relationships around the color wheel to predict colors that work well with the primary color. Here are the basic schemes, including what they do:

✦ **Mono (monochromatic):** Takes the base hue and offers a number of variations in saturation and value. This scheme is nice when you really want to emphasize one particular color (for example, if you're doing a website about rain forests and want a lot of greens). Be sure to use high contrast between the foreground and background colors so your text is readable.

✦ **Complement:** Uses the base hue and the *complementary* (opposite) color. Generally, this scheme uses several variations of the base hue and a splash of the complementary hue for contrast.

✦ **Triad:** Selects the base hue and two opposite hues. When you select the Triad scheme, you can also choose the angular distance between the opposite colors. If this distance is zero, you have the complementary color scheme. When the angle increases, you have a *split complementary* system, which uses the base hue and two hues equidistant from the contrast. Such schemes can be jarring at full contrast, but when adjusted for saturation and value, you can create some very nice color schemes.

✦ **Tetrad:** Generates four hues. As with the Triad scheme, when you add more hues, keeping your page unified becomes more difficult unless you adjust the variations for lower contrast.

✦ **Analogic:** Schemes use the base hue and its two neighbors.

✦ **Accented Analogic:** Just like the Analogic scheme, but with the addition of the complementary color.

Chapter 2: Styling Text

In This Chapter

✓ **Introducing fonts and typefaces**

✓ **Specifying the font family**

✓ **Determining font size**

✓ **Understanding CSS measurement units**

✓ **Managing other font characteristics**

✓ **Using the font rule to simplify font styles**

Web pages are still primarily a text-based media, so you'll want to add some formatting capabilities. HTML doesn't do any meaningful text formatting on its own, but CSS adds a wide range of tools for choosing the typeface, font size, decorations, alignment, and much more. In this chapter, you discover how to manage text the CSS way.

A bit of semantics is in order. The thing most people dub a *font* is more properly a *typeface*. Technically, a font is a particular typeface at a particular size with a specific set of decorations (underlining, italic, and so on). The distinction is honestly not that important in a digital setting. You don't explicitly set the font in CSS. You determine the *font family* (which is essentially a typeface), and then you modify its characteristics (creating a font as purists would think of it). Still, when I'm referring to the thing that most people call a font (a file in the operating system that describes the appearance of an alphabet set), I use the familiar term *font*.

Setting the Font Family

To assign a font family to part of your page, use some new CSS. Figure 2-1 illustrates a page with the heading set to Comic Sans MS.

If this page is viewed on a Windows machine, it generally displays the font correctly because Comic Sans MS is installed with most versions of Windows. If you're on another type of machine, you may get something else. More on that in a moment, but for now, look at the simple case.

Here's the code:

```
<!DOCTYPE html>
<html lang = "en-US">
```

```
<head>
  <meta charset = "UTF-8">
  <title>comicHead.html</title>
  <style type = "text/css">
    h1 {
       font-family: "Comic Sans MS";
    }
  </style>
</head>
<body>
  <h1>This is a heading</h1>
  <p>
    This is ordinary text.
  </p>
</body>
</html>
```

Applying the font-family style attribute

The secret to this page is the CSS `font-family` attribute. Like most CSS elements, this can be applied to any HTML tag on your page. In this particular case, I applied it to my level one heading.

```
h1 {
   font-family: "Comic Sans MS";
}
```

You can then attach any font name you wish, and the browser attempts to use that font to display the element.

Even though a font may work perfectly fine on your computer, it may not work if that font isn't installed on the user's machine.

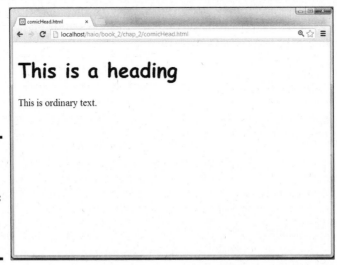

Figure 2-1:
The headline is in the Comic Sans font (most of the time).

If you run exactly the same page on an iPad, you might see the result shown in Figure 2-2.

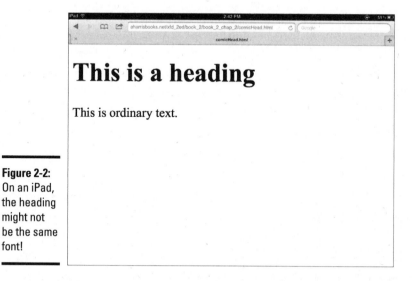

This is a heading

This is ordinary text.

Figure 2-2:
On an iPad, the heading might not be the same font!

The specific font Comic Sans MS is installed on Windows machines, but the *MS* stands for Microsoft. This font isn't always installed on Linux or Mac. (Sometimes it's there, and sometimes it isn't.) You can't count on users having any particular fonts installed.

The Comic Sans font is fine for an example, but it has been heavily over-used in web development. Serious web developers avoid using it in real applications because it tends to make your page look amateurish.

Using generic fonts

It's a little depressing. Even though it's easy to use fonts, you can't use them freely because you don't know if the user has them. Fortunately, you can do a few things that at least increase the odds in your favor. The first trick is to use *generic font names.* These are *virtual* font names that every compliant browser agrees to support. Figure 2-3 shows a page with all the generic fonts.

I used browser controls to make the fonts larger than normal so you can see the details in this figure. Both the programmer and the user should be able to change the font size. Later, I describe how to change the font size through code. If you want to see how your browser handles these fonts, take a look at fontFamilyDemo.html on the companion website. For more on the companion website, see this book's Introduction.

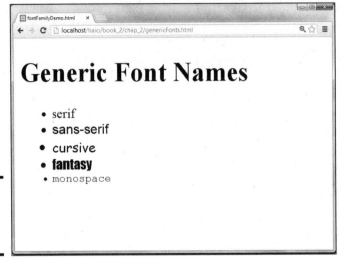

Figure 2-3:
Here are all
the generic
fonts.

The generic fonts really are families of fonts:

+ **Serif:** These fonts have those little serifs (the tiny cross strokes that enhance readability). Print text (like the paragraph you're reading now) tends to use serif fonts, and they're the default font for most browsers. The most common serif typeface is Times New Roman or Times.

+ **Sans Serif:** Sans serif fonts don't have the little feet. Generally, they're used for headlines or other emphasis. Sometimes, they're seen as more modern and cleaner than serif fonts, so sometimes they're used for body text. Arial is the most common sans serif font. In this book, the figure captions use a sans serif font.

+ **Cursive:** These fonts look a little like handwriting. In Windows, the script font is usually Comic Sans MS. Script fonts are used when you want a less formal look. *For Dummies* books use script fonts all over the place for section and chapter headings.

+ **Fantasy:** Fantasy fonts are decorative. Just about any theme you can think of is represented by a fantasy font, from Klingon to Tolkien. You can also find fonts that evoke a certain culture, making English text appear to be Persian or Chinese. Fantasy fonts are best used sparingly, for emphasis, as they often trade readability for visual appeal.

+ **Monospace:** Monospace fonts produce a fixed-width font like typewritten text. Monospace fonts are frequently used to display code. Courier is a common monospace font. All code listings in this book use a monospaced font.

Because the generic fonts are available on all standards-compliant browsers, you'd think you could use them confidently. Well, you can be sure they'll appear, but you still might be surprised at the result. Figure 2-4 shows the same page as Figure 2-3 (in Windows) but on an iPad.

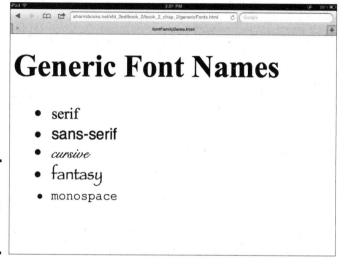

Figure 2-4:
Windows
and the iPad
disagree on
fantasy.

Macs display yet another variation because the fonts listed here aren't *actual* fonts. Instead, they're *virtual* fonts. A standards-compliant browser promises to select an appropriate stand in. For example, if you choose sans serif, one browser may choose to use Arial. Another may choose Chicago. You can always use these generic font names and know the browser can find something close, but there's no guarantee exactly what font the browser will choose. Still, it's better than nothing. When you use these fonts, you're assured something in the right neighborhood, if not exactly what you intended.

Making a list of fonts

This uncertainty is frustrating, but you can take some control. You can specify an entire list of font names if you want. The browser tries each font in turn. If it can't find the specified font, it goes to the next font and on down the line.

You might choose a font that you know is installed on all Windows machines, a font found on Macs, and finally one found on all Linux machines. The last font on your list should be one of the generic fonts, so you'll have some control over the worst-case scenario.

Table 2-1 shows a list of fonts commonly installed on Windows, Mac, and Linux machines.

Table 2-1	Font Equivalents	
Windows	*Mac*	*Linux*
Arial	Arial	Nimbus Sans L
Arial Black	Arial Black	

(continued)

Table 2-1 *(continued)*

Windows	Mac	Linux
Comic Sans MS	Comic Sans MS	TSCu_Comic
Courier New	Courier New	Nimbus Mono L
Georgia	Georgia	Nimbus Roman No9 L
Lucida Console	Monaco	
Palatino	Palatino	FreeSerif
Tahoma	Geneva	Kalimati
Times New Roman	Times	FreeSerif
Trebuchet MS	Helvetica	FreeSans
Verdana	Verdana	Kalimati

You can use this chart to derive a list of fonts to try. For example, look at the following style:

```
p {
    font-family: "Trebuchet MS", Helvetica, FreeSans, sans-serif;
}
```

This style has a whole smorgasbord of options. First, the browser tries to load Trebuchet MS. If it's a Windows machine, this font is available, so that one displays. If that doesn't work, the browser tries Helvetica (a default Mac font). If that doesn't work, it tries FreeSans, a font frequently installed on Linux machines. If this doesn't work, it defaults to the old faithful sans serif, which simply picks a sans serif font.

Note that font names of more than one word must be encased in quotes, and commas separate the list of font names.

 Don't get too stressed about Linux fonts. It's true that the equivalencies are harder to find, but Linux users tend to fall into two camps: They either don't care if the fonts are exact, or they do care and they've installed equivalent fonts that recognize the common names. In either case, you can focus on Mac and Windows people for the most part, and, as long as you've used a generic font name, things work okay on a Linux box. Truth is, I mainly use Linux, and I've installed all the fonts I need.

The Curse of Web-Based Fonts

Fonts seem pretty easy at first, but some big problems arise with actually using them.

Understanding the problem

The problem with fonts is this: Font resources are installed in each operating system. They aren't downloaded with the rest of the page. Your web page

The death of the font tag

There used to be a tag in old-school HTML called the `<font>` tag. You could use this tag to change the size, color, and font family. There were also specific tags for italic (`<i>`), bold-face (`<b>`), and centering (`<center>`). These tags were very easy to use, but they caused some major problems. To use them well, you ended up littering your page with all kinds of tags trying to describe the markup, rather than the meaning. There was no easy way to reuse font information, so you often had to repeat things many times throughout the page, making it difficult to change. Web developers are now discouraged from using `<font>`, `<i>`, `<b>`, or `<center>` tags. The CSS elements I show in this chapter more than compensate for this loss. You now have a more flexible, more powerful alternative.

can call for a specific font, but that font isn't displayed unless it's already installed on the user's computer.

Say I have a cool font called Happygeek. (I just made that up. If you're a font designer, feel free to make a font called that. Just send me a copy. I can't wait.) It's installed on my computer, and when I choose a font in my word processor, it shows up in the list. I can create a word-processing document with it, and everything will work great.

If I send a printout of a document using Happygeek to my grandma, everything's great because the paper doesn't need the actual font. It's just ink. If I send her the digital file and tell her to open it on her computer, we'll have a problem. See, she's not that hip and doesn't have Happygeek installed. Her computer will pick some other font.

This isn't a big problem in word processing because people don't generally send around digital copies of documents with elaborate fonts in them. However, web pages are passed around *only* in digital form. To know which fonts you can use, you have to know what fonts are installed on the user's machine, and that's impossible.

Part of the concern is technical (figuring out how to transfer the font information to the browser), but the real issue is digital rights management. If you've purchased a font for your own use, does that give you the right to transfer it to others, so now they can use it without paying?

Using embedded fonts

Although a web developer can suggest any font for a web page, the font files are traditionally a client-level asset. If the client doesn't have the font installed, she won't see it. Fortunately, CSS3 supports a sensible solution for providing downloadable fonts, called `@font-face`. Figure 2-5 shows a page with a couple of embedded fonts.

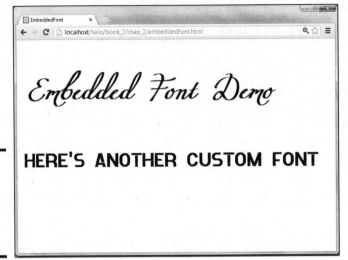

Figure 2-5:
This page
includes a
couple of
embedded
fonts.

The `@font-face` style does not work like most CSS elements. It doesn't apply markup to some part of the page. Instead, it defines a new CSS value that can be used in other markup. Specifically, it allows you to place a font file on your server and define a font family using that font.

```
@font-face {
  font-family: "Miama";
  src: url("Miama.otf");
}
```

The `font-family` attribute indicates the name you will be giving this font in the rest of your CSS code. Typically it is similar to the font file name, but this is not required. The `src` attribute is the URL of the actual font file as it is found on the server. After a font-face has been defined, it can be used in an ordinary `font-family` attribute in the rest of your CSS code:

```
h1 {
  font-family: Miama;
}
```

Here's the code for the custom font example:

```
<!DOCTYPE html>
  <head>
   <title>EmbeddedFont</title>
   <style type = "text/css">
     @font-face {
       font-family: "Miama";
       src: url("Miama.otf");
     }
     @font-face {
       font-family: "spray";
       src: url("ideoma_SPRAY.otf");
     }
```

```
     h1 {
       font-family: Miama;
       font-size: 300%;
     }

     h2 {
       font-family: spray;
     }
   </style>
 </head>

 <body>
   <h1>Embedded Font Demo</h1>
   <h2>Here's another custom font</h2>
 </body>
</html>
```

Although all modern browsers support the `@font-face` feature, the actual file types supported vary from browser to browser. Here are the primary font types:

✦ **TTF:** The standard TrueType format is well-supported, but not by all browsers. Many open-source fonts are available in this format.

✦ **OTF:** This is similar to TTF, but is a truly open standard, so it is preferred by those who are interested in open standards. It is supported by most browsers except IE.

✦ **WOFF:** WOFF is a proposed standard format currently supported by Firefox. Microsoft has hinted at supporting this format in IE.

✦ **EOT:** This is Microsoft's proprietary embedded font format. It only works in IE, but to be fair, Microsoft has had embedded font support for many years.

You can use a font conversion tool like `http://onlinefontconverter.com/` to convert to whatever font format you prefer.

It's possible to supply multiple `src` attributes. This way, you can include both an EOT and OTF version of a font so that it will work on a wide variety of browsers.

When you use this technique, you need to have a copy of the font file locally. For now, it should be in the same directory as your web page (just as you do with images.) When you begin hosting on a web server, you'll want to move your font file to the server along with all the other resources your web page needs. Just because you can include a font doesn't mean you should. Think carefully about readability. Also, be respectful of intellectual property. Fortunately there are many excellent free open-source fonts available. Begin by looking at Open Font Library (`http://openfontlibrary.org/`). Google Fonts (`www.google.com/fonts/`) is another great resource for free fonts. With the Google Font tool, you can select a font embedded on Google's servers, and you can copy code that makes the font available without downloading.

Using images for headlines

Generally, you should use standard fonts for the page's main content, so having a limited array of fonts isn't such a big problem. Sometimes, though, you want to use fonts in your headlines. You can use a graphical editor, like GIMP, to create text-based images and then incorporate them into your pages. Figure 2-6 shows an example of this technique.

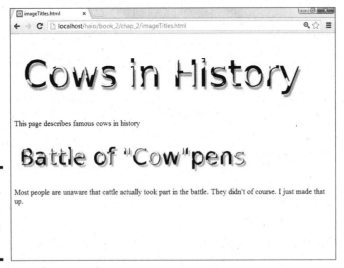

Figure 2-6:
The font shows up because it's an image.

In this case, I want to use my special cow font. (I *love* my cow font.)

Here's the process:

1. **Plan your page.**

   When you use graphics, you lose a little flexibility. You need to know exactly what the headlines should be. You also need to know what headline will display at what level. Rather than relying on the browser to display your headlines, you're creating graphics in your graphic tool (I'm using GIMP) and placing them directly in the page.

2. **Create your images.**

   I used the wonderful Logos feature in GIMP (choose Xtns ⇨ Script-fu ⇨ logos) to create my cow text. I built an image for each headline with the *Bovination* tool. I'm just happy to have a Bovination tool. It's something I've always wanted. If only it could be converted to a weapon.

3. **Specify font sizes directly.**

   In the image, it makes sense to specify font sizes in pixels because here you're really talking about a specific number of pixels. You're creating "virtual text" in your graphic editor, so make the text whatever size you want it to be in the finished page.

4. **Use any font you want.**

   You don't have to worry about whether the user has the font because you're not sending the font, just an image composed with the font.

5. **Create a separate image for each headline.**

   This particular exercise has two images — a level 1 heading and a level 2. Because I'm creating images directly, it's up to me to keep track of how the image will communicate its headline level.

6. **Consider the headline level.**

   Be sure to make headline level 2 values look a little smaller or less emphasized than level 1. That is, if you have images that will be used in a heading 1 setting, they should use a larger font than images that will be used in a less emphasized heading level. Usually, this is done by adjusting the font size in your images.

7. **Build the page the way you normally would.**

   After you create these specialty images, build a regular web page. Put `<h1>` and `<h2>` tags in exactly the same places you usually do.

8. **Put `<img>` tags inside the headings.**

   Rather than ordinary text, place image tags inside the `<h1>` and `<h2>` tags. See the upcoming code imageTitles.html if you're a little confused.

9. **Put headline text in the `alt` attribute.**

   The `alt` attribute is especially important here because if the user has graphics turned off, the text still appears as an appropriately styled heading. People with slow connections see the text before the images load, and people using text readers can still read the image's alt text.

Here's the code used to generate the image-based headers:

```
<!DOCTYPE html>
<html lang = "en-US">

  <head>
    <meta charset = "UTF-8">
    <title>imageTitles.html</title>
  </head>
  <body>
    <h1>
      <img src = "cowsHistory.png"
           alt = "Cows in History" />
    </h1>
    <p>
      This page describes famous cows in history
    </p>
    <h2>
      <img src = "cowpens.png"
           alt = "Battle of Cowpens" />
    </h2>
    <p>
      Most people are unaware that cattle actually took
      part in the battle. They didn't of course. I just
      made that up.
```

```
      </p>
   </body>
</html>
```

This technique is a nice compromise between custom graphics and ordinary HTML as follows:

✦ **You have great control of your images.** If you're skilled with your graphics tool, you can make any type of image you want act as a headline. There's literally no limit except your skill and creativity.

✦ **The page retains its structure.** You still have heading tags in place, so it's easy to see that you mean for a particular image to act as a headline. You can still see the page organization in the HTML code.

✦ **You have fallback text.** The alt attributes will activate if the images can't be displayed.

✦ **The semantic meaning of image headlines is preserved.** The alt tags provide another great feature. If they replicate the image text, this text is still available to screen readers and search engines, so the text isn't buried in the image.

This technique is great for headlines or other areas, but notice that I was careful to repeat the headline text in the `<alt>` tag. This is important because I don't want to lose the text. Search engine tools and screen readers need the text.

Don't be tempted to use this technique for larger amounts of body text. Doing so causes some problems:

✦ **The text is no longer searchable.** Search engines can't find text if it's buried in images.

✦ **The text is harder to change.** You can't update your page with a text editor. Instead, you have to download the image, modify it, and upload it again.

✦ **Images require a lot more bandwidth than text.** Don't use images if they don't substantially add to your page. You can make the case for a few heading images, but it's harder to justify having your entire page stored as an image just to use a particular font.

Specifying the Font Size

Like font names, font sizes are easy to change in CSS, but there are some hidden traps.

Size is only a suggestion!

In print media, after you determine the size of the text, it pretty much stays there. The user can't change the font size in print easily. By comparison, web browsers frequently change the size of text. A cellphone-based browser displays text differently than one on a high-resolution LCD panel. Further, most browsers allow the user to change the size of all the text on the screen. Use Ctrl++ (plus sign) and Ctrl+− (minus sign) to make the text larger or smaller. In older versions of IE (prior to IE7), choose the Text Size option from the Page menu to change the text size.

The user should really have the ability to adjust the font size in the browser. When I display a web page on a projector, I often adjust the font size so students in the back can read. Some pages have the font size set way too small for me to read. (It's probably my high-tech monitor. It couldn't possibly have anything to do with my age.)

Determining font sizes precisely is counter to the spirit of the web. If you declare that your text will be exactly 12 points, for example, one of two things could happen:

✦ **The browser might enforce the 12-point rule literally.** This takes control from the user, so users who need larger fonts are out of luck. Older versions of IE do this.

✦ **The user might still change the size.** If this is how the browser behaves (and it usually is), 12 points doesn't always mean 12 points. If the user can change font sizes, the literal size selection is meaningless.

The web developer should set up font sizes, but only in *relative* terms. Don't bother using absolute measurements (in most cases) because they don't really mean what you think. Let the user determine the base font size and specify relative changes to that size.

Using the font-size style attribute

The basic idea of font size is pretty easy to grasp in CSS. Take a look at font Size.html in Figure 2-7.

This page obviously shows a number of different font sizes. The line "Font Sizes" is an ordinary h1 element. All the other lines are paragraph tags. They appear in different sizes because they have different styles applied to them.

Font sizes are changed with the (cleverly named) font-size attribute:

```
p {
  font-size: small;
}
```

Simply indicate the font-size rule, and, well, the size of the font. In this example, I used the special value small, but there are many other ways to specify sizes in CSS.

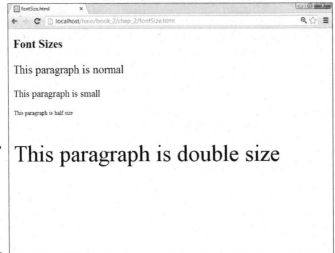

Figure 2-7:
You can easily modify font sizes in your pages.

Absolute measurement units

Many times, you need to specify the size of something in CSS. Of course, font size is one of these cases. The different types of measurement have different implications. It's important to know there are two distinct kinds of units in CSS. *Absolute measurements* attempt to describe a particular size, as in the real world. *Relative measurements* are about changes to some default value. Generally, web developers are moving toward relative measurement for font sizes.

Points (pt)

In word processing, you're probably familiar with *points* as a measurement of font size. You can use the abbreviation `pt` to indicate you're measuring in points, for example:

```
p {
  font-size: 12pt;
}
```

There is no space between `12` and `pt`.

Unfortunately, points aren't an effective unit of measure for web pages. Points are an absolute scale, useful for print, but they aren't reliable on the web because you don't know what resolution the user's screen has. A 12-point font might look larger or smaller on different monitors.

In some versions of IE, after you specify a font size in points, the user can no longer change the size of the characters. This is unacceptable from a usability standpoint. Relative size schemes (which I describe later in this chapter) prevent this problem.

Pixels (px)

Pixels refer to the small dots on the screen. You can specify a font size in pixels, although that's not the way it's usually done. For one thing, different monitors make pixels in different sizes. You can't really be sure how big a pixel will be in relationship to the overall screen size. Different letters are different sizes, so the pixel size is a rough measurement of the width and height of the average character. Use the px abbreviation to measure fonts in pixels:

```
p {
   font-size: 20px;
}
```

Traditional measurements (in, cm)

You can also use inches (in) and centimeters (cm) to measure fonts, but this is completely impractical. Imagine you have a web page displayed on both your screen and a projection system. One inch on your own monitor may look like ten inches on the projector. Real-life measurement units aren't meaningful for the web. The only time you might use them is if you'll be printing something and you have complete knowledge of how the printer is configured. If that's the case, you're better off using a print-oriented layout tool (like a word processor) rather than HTML.

Relative measurement units

Relative measurement is a wiser choice in web development. Use these schemes to change sizes in relationship to the standard size.

Named sizes

CSS has a number of font size names built in:

xx-small	large
x-small	x-large
small	xx-large
medium	

It may bother you that there's nothing more specific about these sizes: How big is large? Well, it's bigger than medium. That sounds like a flip answer, but it's the truth. The user sets the default font size in the browser (or leaves it alone), and all other font sizes should be in relation to this preset size. The medium size is the default size of paragraph text on your page. For comparison purposes, <h1> tags are usually xx-large.

**Book II
Chapter 2**

Styling Text

Percentage (%)

The percentage unit is a relative measurement used to specify the font in relationship to its normal size. Use 50% to make a font half the size it would normally appear and 200% to make it twice the normal size. Use the % symbol to indicate percentage, as shown here:

```
p {
  font-size: 150%;
}
```

Percentages are based on the default size of ordinary text, so an <h1> tag at 100% is the same size as text in an ordinary paragraph.

Em (em)

In traditional typesetting, the em is a unit of measurement equivalent to the width of the "m" character in that font. In actual web use, it's really another way of specifying the relative size of a font. For instance, 0.5 ems is half the normal size, and 3 ems is three times the normal size. The term em is used to specify this measurement.

```
p {
  font-size: 1.5em;
}
```

Here are the best strategies for font size:

+ **Don't change sizes without a good reason.** Most of the time, the browser default sizes are perfectly fine, but there may be some times when you want to adjust fonts a little more.

+ **Define an overall size for the page.** If you want to define a font size for the entire page, do so in the <body> tag. Use a named size, percentage, or ems to avoid the side effects of absolute sizing. The size defined in the body is applied to every element in the body automatically.

+ **Modify any other elements.** You might want your links a little larger than ordinary text, for example. You can do this by applying a font-size attribute to an element. Use relative measurement if possible.

Determining Other Font Characteristics

In addition to size and color (see Chapter 1 of this minibook), you can change fonts in a number of other ways.

Figure 2-8 shows a number of common text modifications you can make.

The various paragraphs in this page are modified in different ways. You can change the alignment of the text as well as add italic, bold, underline, or strikethrough to the text.

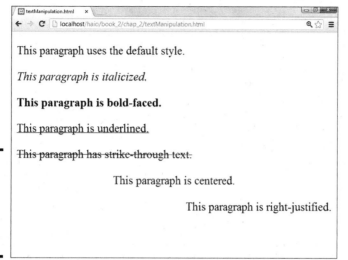

Figure 2-8:
Here are a few of the things you can do to modify text.

CSS uses a potentially confusing set of rules for the various font manipulation tools. One rule determines the font style, and another determines boldness.

I describe these techniques in the following sections for clarity.

I used a trick I haven't shown yet to produce this comparison page. I have multiple paragraphs, each with their own style. Look to Chapter 3 of this minibook to see how to have more than one paragraph style in a particular page.

Using font-style for italics

The `font-style` attribute allows you to make italic text, as shown in Figure 2-9.

Here's some code illustrating how to add italic formatting:

```
<!DOCTYPE html>
<html lang = "en-US">

  <head>
    <meta charset = "UTF-8">
    <title>italics.html</title>
    <style type = "text/css">
      p {
        font-style: italic;
      }
    </style>
  </head>
  <body>
    <h1>Italics</h1>
    <p>This paragraph is in italic form.</p>
  </body>
</html>
```

Figure 2-9:
You can make italic text with the font-style attribute.

The `font-style` values can be `italic`, `normal`, or `oblique` (tilted toward the left).

If you want to set a particular segment to be set to italic, normal, or oblique style, use the `font-style` attribute.

Using font-weight for bold

You can make your font bold by using the `font-weight` CSS attribute, as shown in Figure 2-10.

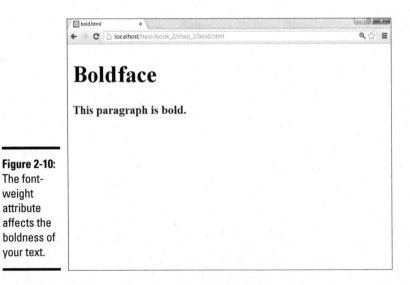

Figure 2-10:
The font-weight attribute affects the boldness of your text.

If you want to make some of your text bold, use the font-weight CSS attribute, like this:

```
<!DOCTYPE html>
<html lang = "en-US">

  <head>
    <meta charset = "UTF-8">
    <title>bold.html</title>
    <style type = "text/css">
      p {
        font-weight: bold;
      }
    </style>
  </head>
  <body>
    <h1>Boldface</h1>
    <p>
      This paragraph is bold.
    </p>
  </body>
</html>
```

Font weight can be defined a couple ways. Normally, you simply indicate bold in the font-weight rule, as I did in this code. You can also use a numeric value from 100 (exceptionally light) to 900 (dark bold).

Using text-decoration

Text-decoration can be used to add a couple other interesting formats to your text, including underline, strikethrough, overline, and blink.

For example, the following code produces an underlined paragraph:

```
<!DOCTYPE html>
<html lang = "en-US">

  <head>
    <meta charset = "UTF-8">
    <title>underline.html</title>
    <style type = "text/css">
      p {
        text-decoration: underline;
      }
    </style>
  </head>
  <body>
    <h1>Underline</h1>
    <p>
      This paragraph is underlined.
    </p>
  </body>
</html>
```

Be careful using underline in web pages. Users have been trained that underlined text is a link, so they may click your underlined text expecting it to take them somewhere.

The underline.html code produces a page similar to Figure 2-11.

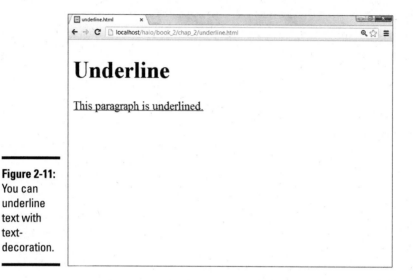

Figure 2-11:
You can
underline
text with
text-
decoration.

You can also use `text-decoration` for other effects, such as strikethrough (called "line-through" in CSS), as shown in the following code:

```
<!DOCTYPE html>
<html lang = "en-US">

  <head>
    <meta charset = "UTF-8">
    <title>strikethrough.html</title>
    <style type = "text/css">
      p {
        text-decoration: line-through;
      }
    </style>
  </head>
  <body>
    <h1>Strikethrough</h1>
    <p>
      This paragraph has strikethrough text.
    </p>
  </body>
</html>
```

The strikethrough.html code produces a page similar to Figure 2-12.

`Text-decoration` has a few other rarely used options, such as

✦ **Overline:** The `overline` attribute places a line over the text. Except for a few math and chemistry applications (which would be better done in an equation editor and imported as images), I can't see when this might be used.

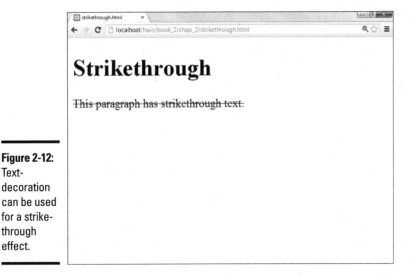

Figure 2-12:
Text-
decoration
can be used
for a strike-
through
effect.

✦ **Blink:** The `blink` attribute is a distant cousin of the legendary `<blink>` tag in Netscape and causes the text to blink on the page. The `<blink>` tag (along with gratuitous animated GIFs) has long been derided as the mark of the amateur. Avoid blinking text at all costs.

There's an old joke among Internet developers: The only legitimate place to use the `<blink>` tag is in this sentence: Schrodinger's cat is `<blink>not </blink>` dead. Nothing is funnier than quantum mechanics illustrated in HTML.

Using text-align for basic alignment

You can use the `text-align` attribute to center, left-align, or right-align text, as shown in the following code:

```
<!DOCTYPE html>
<html lang = "en-US">

  <head>
    <meta charset = "UTF-8">
    <title>center.html</title>
    <style type = "text/css">
      p {
        text-align: center;
      }
    </style>
  </head>
  <body>
    <h1>Centered</h1>
    <p>This paragraph is centered.</p>
  </body>
</html>
```

You can also use the `text-align` attribute to right- or left-justify your text. The page shown in Figure 2-13 illustrates the `text-align` attribute.

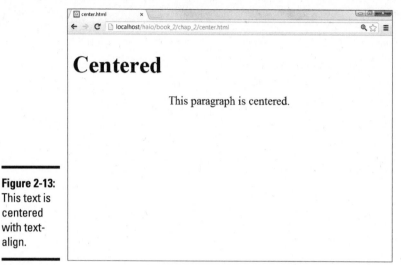

Figure 2-13:
This text is
centered
with text-
align.

You can apply the `text-align` attribute only to text. The old `<center>` tag could be used to center nearly anything (a table, some text, or images), which was pretty easy but caused problems. Book III explains how to position elements in all kinds of powerful ways, including centering anything. Use `text-align` to center text inside its own element (whether that's a heading, a paragraph, a table cell, or whatever).

Other text attributes

CSS offers a few other text manipulation tools, but they're rarely used:

✦ **Font-variant:** Can be set to `small-caps` to make your text use only capital letters. Lowercase letters are shown in a smaller font size.

✦ **Letter-spacing:** Adjusts the spacing between letters. It's usually measured in ems. (See the section "Relative measurement units" earlier in the chapter for more on ems.) Fonts are so unpredictable on the web that if you're trying to micromanage this much, you're bound to be disappointed by the results.

✦ **Word-spacing:** Allows you to adjust the spacing between words.

✦ **Text-indent:** Lets you adjust the indentation of the first line of an element. This value uses the normal units of measurement. Indentation can be set to a negative value, causing an outdent if you prefer.

✦ **Vertical-align:** Used when you have an element with a lot of vertical space (often a table cell). You can specify how the text behaves in this situation.

✦ **Text-transform:** Helps you convert text into uppercase, lowercase, or capitalized (first letter uppercase) forms.

✦ **Line-height:** Indicates the vertical spacing between lines in the element. As with letter and word spacing, you'll probably be disappointed if you're this concerned about exactly how things are displayed.

Using the font shortcut

It can be tedious to recall all the various font attributes and their possible values. Aptana and other dedicated CSS editors make it a lot easier, but there's another technique often used by the pros. The font rule provides an easy shortcut to a number of useful font attributes. The following code shows you how to use the font rule:

```
<!DOCTYPE html>
<html lang = "en-US">

  <head>
    <meta charset = "UTF-8">
    <title>fontTag.html</title>
    <style type = "text/css">
      p {
        font: bold italic 150% "Dadhand", cursive;
      }
    </style>
  </head>
  <body>
    <h1>Using Font shortcut</h1>
    <p>
      This paragraph has many settings.
    </p>
  </body>
</html>
```

Figure 2-14 illustrates the powerful font rule in action.

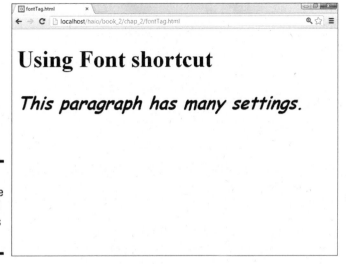

Figure 2-14: The font rule can change many things at once.

The great thing about the `font` rule is how it combines many of the other font-related rules for a simpler way to handle most text-formatting needs.

The `font` attribute is extremely handy. Essentially, it allows you to roll all the other font attributes into one. Here's how it works:

+ **Specify the `font` rule in the CSS.**

+ **List any `font-style` attributes.** You can mention any attributes normally used in the `font-style` rule (`italic` or `oblique`). If you don't want either, just move on.

+ **List any `font-variant` attributes.** If you want small caps, you can indicate it here. If you don't, just leave this part blank.

+ **List any `font-weight` values.** This can be "bold" or a font-weight number (100–900).

+ **Specify the font-size value in whatever measurement system you want (but ems or percentages are preferred).** Don't forget the measurement unit symbol (em or %) because that's how the `font` rule recognizes that this is a size value.

+ **Indicate a font-family list last.** The last element is a list of font families you want the browser to try. This list must be last, or the browser may not interpret the `font` attribute correctly. (Dadhand is a custom font I own; cursive will be used if Dadhand is not available.)

The `font` rule is great, but it doesn't do everything. You still may need separate CSS rules to define your text colors and alignment. These attributes aren't included in the font shortcut.

Don't use commas to separate values in the `font` attribute list. Use commas only to separate values in the list of font-family declarations.

You can skip any values you want as long as the order is correct. For example,

```
font: italic "Comic Sans MS", cursive;
```

is completely acceptable, as is

```
font: 70% sans-serif;
```

Working with subscripts and superscripts

Occasionally, you'll need *superscripts* (characters that appear a little bit higher than normal text, like exponents and footnotes) or *subscripts* (characters that appear lower, often used in mathematical notation). Figure 2-15 demonstrates a page with these techniques.

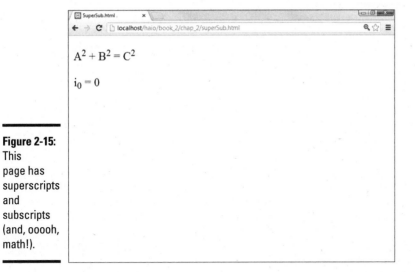

Figure 2-15:
This
page has
superscripts
and
subscripts
(and, ooooh,
math!).

Surprisingly, you don't need CSS to produce superscripts and subscripts. These properties are managed through HTML tags. You can still style them the way you can any other HTML tag.

```
<!DOCTYPE html>
<html lang = "en-US">

  <head>
    <meta charset = "UTF-8">
    <title>SuperSub.html</title>
  </head>
  <body>
    <p>
      A<sup>2</sup> + B<sup>2</sup> = C<sup>2</sup>
    </p>
    <p>
      i<sub>0</sub> = 0
    </p>
  </body>
</html>
```

Chapter 3: Selectors: Coding with Class and Style

In This Chapter

✔ Modifying specific named elements

✔ Adding and modifying emphasis and strong emphasis

✔ Creating classes

✔ Introducing `span` and `div`

✔ Using pseudo-classes and the `link` tag

✔ Selecting specific contexts

✔ Defining multiple styles

You know how to use CSS to change all the instances of a particular tag, but what if you want to be more selective? For example, you might want to change the background color of only one paragraph, or you might want to define some special new type of paragraph. Maybe you want to specify a different paragraph color for part of your page, or you want visited links to appear differently from unselected links. The part of the CSS style that indicates what element you want to style is a *selector*. In this chapter, you discover powerful new ways to select elements on the page.

Selecting Particular Segments

Figure 3-1 illustrates how you should refer to someone who doesn't appreciate your web development prowess.

Defining more than one kind of paragraph

Apart from its cultural merit, this page is interesting because it has three different paragraph styles. The introductory paragraph is normal. The quote is set in italicized font, and the attribution is monospaced and right-aligned.

The quote in the following code was generated by one of my favorite sites on the Internet: the Shakespearean insult generator. Nothing is more satisfying than telling somebody off in iambic pentameter (www.pangloss.com/seidel/Shaker/index.html.)

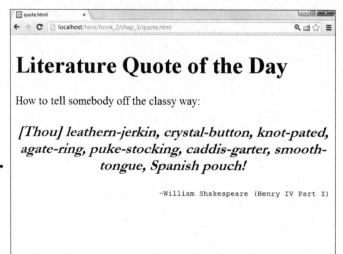

Figure 3-1:
This page
has three
kinds of
paragraphs.

```
<!DOCTYPE html>
<html lang = "en-US">

  <head>
    <meta charset = "UTF-8">
    <title>quote.html</title>
    <style type = "text/css">
      #quote {
        font: bold italic 130% Garamond, Comic Sans MS, fantasy;
        text-align: center;
      }
      #attribution {
        font: 80% monospace;
        text-align: right;
      }
    </style>
  </head>
  <body>
    <h1>Literature Quote of the Day</h1>
    <p>
      How to tell somebody off the classy way:
    </p>
    <p id = "quote">
      [Thou] leathern-jerkin, crystal-button, knot-pated,
      agate-ring, puke-stocking, caddis-garter, smooth-tongue, Spanish pouch!
    </p>
    <p id = "attribution">
      -William Shakespeare (Henry IV Part I)
    </p>
  </body>
</html>
```

Styling identified paragraphs

Until now, you've used CSS to apply a particular style to an element all
across the page. For example, you can add a style to the <p> tag, and that
style applies to all the paragraphs on the page.

Sometimes (as in the Shakespeare insult page), you want to give one element more than one style. You can do this by naming each element and using the name in the CSS style sheet. Here's how it works:

1. **Add an `id` attribute to each HTML element you want to modify.**

   For example, the paragraph with the attribution now has an `id` attribute with the value `attribution`.

   ```
   <p id = "attribution">
   ```

2. **Make a style in CSS.**

   Use a pound sign followed by the element's ID in CSS to specify you're not talking about a tag type any more, but a specific element: For example, the CSS code contains the selector `#attribution`, meaning, "Apply this style to an element with the attribution id."

   ```
   #attribution {
   ```

3. **Add the style.**

   Create a style for displaying your named element. In this case, I want the paragraph with the `attribution` ID right-aligned, monospace, and a little smaller than normal. This style will be attached only to the specific element.

   ```
   #attribution {
      font: 80% monospace;
      text-align: right;
   }
   ```

The ID trick works great on any named element. IDs have to be *unique* (you can't repeat the same ID on one page), so this technique is best when you have a style you want to apply to only one element on the page. It doesn't matter what HTML element it is (it could be a heading 1, a paragraph, a table cell, or whatever). If it has the ID `quote`, the `#quote` style is applied to it. You can have both ID selectors and ordinary (element) selectors in the same style sheet.

Using Emphasis and Strong Emphasis

You may be shocked to know that HTML doesn't allow italics or bold. Old-style HTML had the `<i>` tag for italics and the `<b>` tag for bold. These seem easy to use and understand. Unfortunately, they can trap you. In your HTML5, you shouldn't specify *how* something should be styled. You should specify instead the *purpose* of the styling. The `<i>` and `<b>` tags in XHTML Strict are removed in HTML5 and replaced with `<em>` and `<strong>`.

The `<em>` tag means *emphasized*. By default, em italicizes your text. The `<strong>` tag stands for *strong emphasis*. It defaults to bold.

Figure 3-2 illustrates a page with the default styles for em and strong.

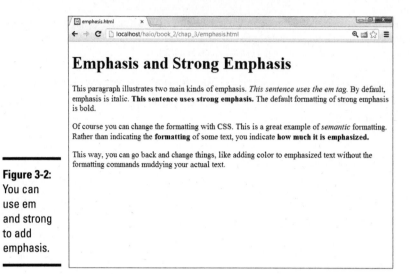

Figure 3-2:
You can
use em
and strong
to add
emphasis.

The code for the `emphasis.html` page is pretty straightforward. It has no CSS at all:

```
<!DOCTYPE html>
<html lang = "en-US">

  <head>
    <meta charset = "UTF-8">
    <title>emphasis.html</title>
  </head>
  <body>
    <h1>Emphasis and Strong Emphasis</h1>
    <p>
      This paragraph illustrates two main kinds of emphasis.
      <em>This sentence uses the em tag.</em>
      By default, emphasis is italic.
      <strong>This sentence uses strong emphasis.</strong>
      The default formatting of strong emphasis is bold.
    </p>
    <p>
      Of course you can change the formatting with CSS.
      This is a great example of <em>semantic</em> formatting.
      Rather than indicating the <strong>formatting</strong>
      of some text, you indicate <strong>how much it is emphasized.</strong>
    </p>
    <p>
      This way, you can go back and change things, like adding color
      to emphasized text without the formatting commands
      muddying your actual text.
    </p>
  </body>
</html>
```

It'd be improper to think that em is just another way to say *italic* and strong is another way to say *bold*. In the old scheme, after you define something as italic, you're pretty much stuck with that. The HTML way describes the meaning, and you can define it how you want.

Modifying the Display of em and strong

Figure 3-3 shows how you might modify the levels of emphasis. I used yellow highlighting (without italics) for `em` and a larger red font for `strong`.

The HTML code for `emphasisStyle.html` (as shown in Figure 3-3) is *identical* to the code for `emphasis.html` (as shown in Figure 3-2). The only difference is the addition of a style sheet. The style sheet is embedded in the web page between style tags. Check out Chapter 1 of this minibook for a refresher on how to incorporate CSS styles in your web pages.

**Book II
Chapter 3**

**Selectors: Coding
with Class and Style**

```
<style type = "text/css">
  em {
    font-style: normal;
    background-color: yellow;
  }

  strong {
    color: red;
    font-size: 110%;
  }
</style>
```

The style is used to modify the HTML. The meaning in the HTML stays the same — only the style changes.

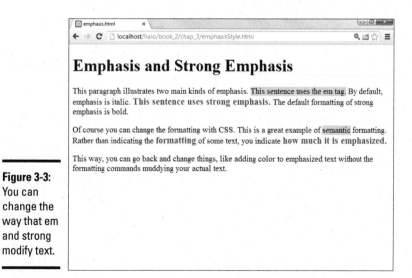

Figure 3-3:
You can change the way that em and strong modify text.

The semantic markups are more useful than the older (more literal) tags because they still tell the truth even if the style has been changed. (In the HTML code, the important thing is whether the text is emphasized, not what it means to emphasize the text. That job belongs to CSS.)

What's funny about the following sentence?

<strong> is always bold.

Get it? *That's a bold-faced lie!* Sometimes I crack myself up.

Defining Classes

You can easily apply a style to all the elements of a particular type in a page, but sometimes you might want to have tighter control of your styles. For example, you might want to have more than one paragraph style. As an example, look at the classes.html page featured in Figure 3-4.

Once again, multiple formats are on this page:

✦ **Questions have a large italic sans serif font.** There's more than one question.

✦ **Answers are smaller, blue, and in a cursive font.** There's more than one answer, too.

Figure 3-4:
Each joke has a question and an answer.

Questions and answers are all paragraphs, so you can't simply style the paragraph because you need two distinct styles. There's more than one question and more than one answer, so the ID trick would be problematic. Two different elements can't have the same ID. This is where the notion of classes comes into play. Every ID belongs to a single element, but many elements (even of different types) can share the same class.

Adding classes to the page

CSS allows you to define classes in your HTML and make style definitions that are applied across a class. It works like this:

1. **Add the `class` attribute to your HTML questions.**

   Unlike ID, several elements can share the same class. All my questions are defined with this variation of the `<p>` tag. Setting the class to `question` indicates these paragraphs will be styled as questions:

   ```
   <p class = "question">
     What kind of cow lives in the Arctic?
   </p>
   ```

2. **Add similar class attributes to the answers by setting the class of the answers to `answer`:**

   ```
   <p class = "answer">
     An Eskimoo!
   </p>
   ```

   Now you have two different subclasses of paragraph: `question` and `answer`.

3. **Create a class style for the questions.**

   The class style is defined in CSS. Specify a class with the period (`.`) before the class name. Classes are defined in CSS like this:

   ```
   <style type = "text/css">
     .question {
       font: italic 150% arial, sans-serif;
       text-align: left;
     }
   ```

   In this situation, the `question` class is defined as a large sans serif font aligned to the left.

4. **Define the look of the answers.**

   The `answer` class uses a right-justified cursive font.

   ```
   .answer {
     font: 120% "Comic Sans MS", cursive;
     text-align: right;
     color: #00F;
   }
   </style>
   ```

Using classes

Here's the code for the `classes.html` page, showing how to use CSS classes:

```html
<!DOCTYPE html>
<html lang = "en-US">

  <head>
    <meta charset = "UTF-8">
    <title>classes.html</title>
    <style type = "text/css">
      .question {
        font: italic 150% arial, sans-serif;
        text-align: left;
      }
      .answer {
        font: 120% "Comic Sans MS", cursive;
        text-align: right;
        color: #00F;
      }
    </style>
  </head>
  <body>
    <h1>Favorite Jokes</h1>
    <p class = "question">
      What kind of cow lives in the Arctic?
    </p>
    <p class = "answer">
      An Eskimoo!
    </p>
    <p class = "question">
      What goes on top of a dog house?
    </p>
    <p class = "answer">
      The woof!
    </p>
  </body>
</html>
```

Sometimes you see selectors, like

`p.fancy`

that include both an element and a class name. This style is applied only to paragraphs with the `fancy` class attached. Generally, I like classes because they can be applied to all kinds of things, so I usually leave the element name out to make the style as reusable as possible.

Combining classes

One element can use more than one class. Figure 3-5 shows an example of this phenomenon.

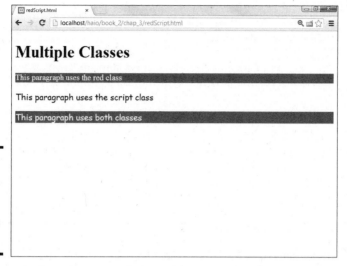

Figure 3-5:
There's red, there's script, and then there's both.

The paragraphs in Figure 3-5 appear to be in three different styles, but only red and script are defined. The third paragraph uses both classes. Here's the code:

```
<!DOCTYPE html>
<html lang = "en-US">

  <head>
    <meta charset = "UTF-8">
    <title>redScript.html</title>
    <style type = "text/css">
      .red {
        color: white;
        background-color: red;
      }
      .script {
        font-family: cursive;
      }
    </style>
  </head>
  <body>
    <h1>Multiple Classes</h1>
    <p class = "red">
      This paragraph uses the red class
    </p>
    <p class = "script">
      This paragraph uses the script class
    </p>
    <p class = "red script">
      This paragraph uses both classes
    </p>
  </body>
</html>
```

The style sheet introduces two classes. The `red` class makes the paragraph red (well, white text with a red background), and the `script` class applies a cursive font to the element.

The first two paragraphs each have a class, and the classes act as you'd expect. The interesting part is the third paragraph because it has two classes.

```
<p class = "red script">
```

This assigns both the `red` and `script` classes to the paragraph. Both styles will be applied to the element in the order they are written. Note that both class names occur inside quotes and no commas are needed (or allowed). You can apply more than two classes to an element if you wish. If the classes have conflicting rules (say one makes the element green and the next makes it blue), the latest class in the list will overwrite earlier values.

An element can also have an ID. The ID style, the element style, and all the class styles are taken into account when the browser tries to display the object.

Normally, I don't like to use colors or other specific formatting instructions as class names. Usually, it's best to name classes based on their meaning (like mainBackgroundColor). You might decide that green is better than red, so you either have to change the class name or you have to have a `red` class that colored things green. That'd be weird.

Introducing div and span

So far, I've applied CSS styles primarily to paragraphs (with the `<p>` tag), but you can really use any element you want. In fact, you may want to invent your own elements. Perhaps you want a particular style, but it's not quite a paragraph. Maybe you want a particular style inside a paragraph. HTML has two very useful elements that are designed as *generic* elements. They don't have any predefined meaning, so they're ideal candidates for modification with the `id` and `class` attributes.

✦ `div`: A block-level element (like the p element). It acts just like a paragraph. A `div` usually has carriage returns before and after it. Generally, you use `div` to group a series of paragraphs.

✦ `span`: An inline element. It doesn't usually cause carriage returns because it's meant to be embedded into some other block-level element (usually a paragraph or a div). Usually, a `span` is used to add some type of special formatting to an element that's contained inside a block-level element.

Organizing the page by meaning

To see why div and span are useful, take a look at Figure 3-6.

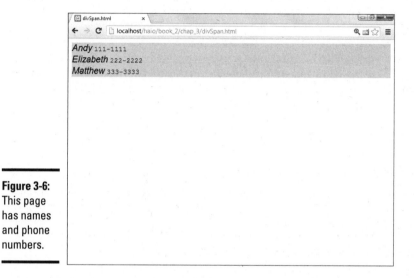

Figure 3-6:
This page
has names
and phone
numbers.

The formatting of the page isn't complete (read about positioning CSS in Book III), but some formatting is in place. Each name and phone number pair is clearly a group of things. Names and phone numbers are formatted differently. The interesting thing about this page is the code:

```
<!DOCTYPE html>
<html lang = "en-US">

  <head>
    <meta charset = "UTF-8">
    <title>divSpan.html</title>
    <style type = "text/css">
      .contact {
        background-color: #CCCCFF;
      }
      .name {
        font: italic 110% arial, sans-serif;
      }
      .phone {
        font: 100% monospace;
      }
    </style>
  </head>
  <body>
    <div class = "contact">
      <span class = "name">Andy</span>
      <span class = "phone">111-1111</span>
    </div>
    <div class = "contact">
      <span class = "name">Elizabeth</span>
```

```
        <span class = "phone">222-2222</span>
      </div>
      <div class = "contact">
        <span class = "name">Matthew</span>
        <span class = "phone">333-3333</span>
      </div>
    </body>
</html>
```

What's exciting about this code is its clarity. When you look at the HTML, it's very clear what type of data you're talking about because the structure describes the data. Each `div` represents a contact. A contact has a name and a phone number.

The HTML doesn't specify how the data displays, just what it means.

Why not make a table?

This is where experienced web people shake their heads in disbelief. This page seems like a table, so why not make it one? What matters here isn't that the information is in a table, but that names and phone numbers are part of contacts. There's no need to bring in artificial table elements if you can describe the data perfectly well without them.

If you still want to make the data *look* like a table, that's completely possible, as shown in Figure 3-7. See Book III to see exactly how some of the styling code works. Of course, you're welcome to look at the source code for this styled version (dubbed `divSpanStyled.html` on the companion website) if you want a preview. See this book's Introduction for more on the companion website.

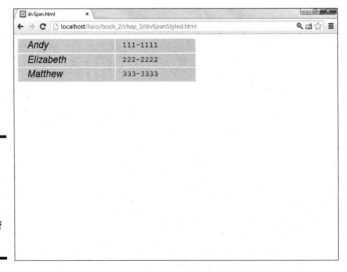

Figure 3-7:
After you define the data, you can style it as a table if you want.

The point is this: After you define the data, you can control it as much as you want. Using `span` and `div` to define your data gives you far more control than tables and leaves your HTML code much cleaner.

`div` and `span` aren't simply a replacement for tables. They're tools for organizing your page into segments based on *meaning*. After you have them in place, you can use CSS to apply all kinds of interesting styles to the segments.

Using Pseudo-Classes to Style Links

Now that you have some style going in your web pages, you may be a bit concerned about how ugly links are. The default link styles are useful, but they may not fit with your color scheme.

Styling a standard link

Adding a style to a link is easy. After all, `<a>` (the tag that defines links) is just an HTML tag, and you can add a style to any tag. Here's an example, where I make my links black with a yellow background:

```
a {
  color: black;
  background-color: yellow;
}
```

That works fine, but links are a little more complex than some other elements. Links actually have three *states:*

+ **Normal:** This is the standard state. With no CSS added, most browsers display unvisited links as blue underlined text.

+ **Visited:** This state is enabled when the user visits a link and returns to the current page. Most browsers use a purple underlined style to indicate that a link has been visited.

+ **Hover:** The hover state is enabled when the user's mouse is lingering over the element. Most browsers don't use the hover state in their default settings.

If you apply a style to the `<a>` tags in a page, the style is applied to all the states of all the anchors.

Styling the link states

You can apply a different style to each state, as illustrated by Figure 3-8. In this example, I make ordinary links black on a white background. A visited link is black on yellow; and, if the mouse is hovering over a link, the link is white with a black background.

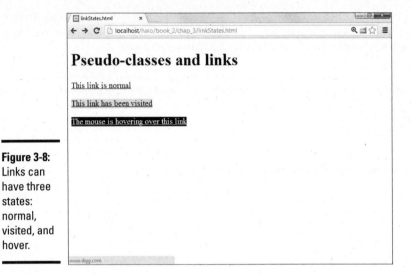

Figure 3-8:
Links can
have three
states:
normal,
visited, and
hover.

Take a look at the code and see how it's done:

```
<!DOCTYPE html>
<html lang = "en-US">

  <head>
    <meta charset = "UTF-8">
    <title>linkStates.html</title>
    <style type = "text/css">
      a {
        color: black;
        background-color: white;
      }
      a:visited {
        color: black;
        background-color: #FFFF33;
      }
      a:hover {
        color: white;
        background-color: black;
      }
    </style>
  </head>
  <body>
    <h1>Pseudo-classes and links</h1>
    <p>
      <a href = "http://www.google.com">This link is normal</a>
    </p>
    <p>
      <a href = "http://www.reddit.com">This link has been visited</a>
    </p>
    <p>
      <a href = "http://www.digg.com">The mouse is hovering over this link</a>
    </p>
  </body>
</html>
```

Nothing is special about the links in the HTML part of the code. The links change their state dynamically while the user interacts with the page. The style sheet determines what happens in the various states. Here's how you approach putting the code together:

1. Determine the ordinary link style first by making a style for the `<a>` tag.

   If you don't define any other pseudo-classes, all links will follow the ordinary link style.

2. Make a style for visited links.

   A link will use this style after that site is visited during the current browser session. The `a:visited` selector indicates links that have been visited.

3. Make a style for hovered links.

   The `a:hover` style is applied to the link only when the mouse is hovering over the link. As soon as the mouse leaves the link, the style reverts to the standard or visited style, as appropriate.

Best link practices

Link styles have some special characteristics. You need to be a little bit careful how you apply styles to links. Consider the following issues when applying styles to links:

+ **The order is important.** Be sure to define the ordinary anchor first. The pseudo-classes are based on the standard anchor style.

+ **Make sure they still look like links.** It's important that users know something is intended to be a link. If you take away the underlining and the color that normally indicates a link, your users might be confused. Generally, you can change colors without trouble, but links should be either underlined text or something that clearly looks like a button.

+ **Test visited links.** Testing visited links is a little tricky because, after you visit a link, it stays visited. Most browsers allow you to delete the browser history, which should also clear the link states to `unvisited`.

+ **Don't change font size in a hover state.** Unlike most styles, hover changes the page in real time. A hover style with a different font size than the ordinary link can cause problems. The page is automatically reformatted to accept the larger (or smaller) font, which can move a large amount of text on the screen rapidly. This can be frustrating and disconcerting for users. It's safest to change colors or borders on hover but not the font family or font size.

Selecting in Context

CSS allows some other nifty selection tricks. Take a look at Figure 3-9 and you see a page with two kinds of paragraphs in it.

The code for the context-style.html page is deceptively simple:

```
<!DOCTYPE html>
<html lang = "en-US">

  <head>
    <meta charset = "UTF-8">
    <title>context-style</title>
    <style type = "text/css">
      #special p {
        text-align: right;
      }
    </style>
  </head>
  <body>
    <h1>Selecting By Context</h1>
    <div>
      <p>This paragraph is left-justified.</p>
      <p>This paragraph is left-justified.</p>
      <p>This paragraph is left-justified.</p>
    </div>
    <div id = "special">
      <p>The paragraphs in this div are different.</p>
      <p>The paragraphs in this div are different.</p>
      <p>The paragraphs in this div are different.</p>
    </div>
  </body>
</html>
```

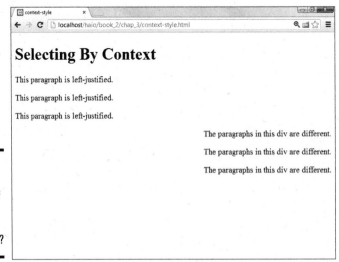

Figure 3-9:
Obviously
two kinds of
paragraphs
are here —
or are there?

If you look at the code for context-style.html, you see some interesting things:

✦ **The page has two `divs`.** One `div` is anonymous, and the other is `special`.

✦ **None of the paragraphs has an ID or class.** The paragraphs in this page don't have names or classes defined, yet they clearly have two different types of behavior. The first three paragraphs are aligned to the left, and the last three are aligned to the right.

✦ **The style rule affects paragraphs inside the `special` div.** Take another look at the style:

```
#special p {
```

This style rule means, "Apply this style to any paragraph appearing inside something called `special`." You can also define a rule that could apply to an image inside a list item or emphasized items inside a particular class. When you include a list of style selectors without commas, you're indicating a nested style.

✦ **Paragraphs defined outside `special` aren't affected.** This nested selection technique can help you create very complex style combinations. It becomes especially handy when you start building positioned elements, like menus and columns.

Defining Styles for Multiple Elements

Sometimes, you want a number of elements to share similar styles. As an example, look at Figure 3-10.

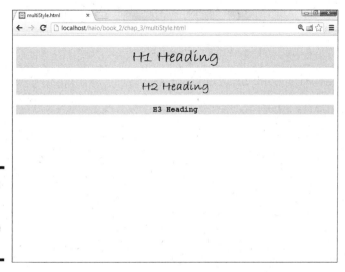

Figure 3-10: H1, H2, and H3 have similar style rules.

As shown in Figure 3-10, the top three headings all have very similar styles. Creating three different styles would be tedious, so CSS includes a shortcut:

```html
<!DOCTYPE html>
<html lang = "en-US">

  <head>
    <meta charset = "UTF-8">
    <title>multiStyle.html</title>
    <style type = "text/css">
      h1, h2, h3 {
        text-align: center;
        font-family: "Bradley Hand ITC", cursive;
        background-color: yellow;
      }
      h3 {
        font-family: monospace;
      }
    </style>
  </head>
  <body>
    <h1>H1 Heading</h1>
    <h2>H2 Heading</h2>
    <h3>H3 Heading</h3>
  </body>
</html>
```

One style element (the one that begins h1, h2, h3) provides all the information for all three heading types. If you include more than one element in a style selector separated by commas, the style applies to all the elements in the list. In this example, the centered cursive font with a yellow background is applied to heading levels 1, 2, and 3 all in the same style.

If you want to make modifications, you can do so. I created a second h3 rule, changing the font-family attribute to monospace. Style rules are applied in order, so you can always start with the general rule and then modify specific elements later in the style if you wish.

If you have multiple elements in a selector rule, it makes a huge difference whether you use commas. If you separate elements with spaces (but no commas), CSS looks for an element nested within another element. If you include commas, CSS applies the rule to all the listed elements.

It's possible to get even more specific about selectors with punctuation. For example, the + selector describes sibling relationship. For example, look at the following rule:

h1+p

This targets only the paragraph that immediately follows a level-one headline. All other paragraphs will be ignored. There are other selectors as well, but the ones mentioned here will suffice for most applications.

You might wonder why we need so many different kinds of selectors. You can use the tag name for most elements, and just apply a class or ID to any element that requires special attention. That's true, but one goal of CSS is to keep your HTML code as clean as possible. As much as possible, you want to use the structure of the page itself to help you determine the style.

Using New CSS3 Selectors

CSS3 supports several new selectors with interesting new capabilities.

Attribute selection

You can now apply a style to any element with a specific attribute value. For example, the `input` tag takes many different forms, all determined by the `type` attribute. If you apply a single style to the `input` element, that style gets applied to many different kinds of elements: check boxes, text fields, and radio buttons. By using the new attribute syntax, you can apply a style to any particular type of input element:

```
input[type="text"]{
  background-color: #CCCCFF;
}
```

You can apply the style with or without a tag type, but it is possible to have unexpected side effects if you choose an extremely common attribute.

Figure 3-11 illustrates the input selector in operation.

**Book II
Chapter 3**

**Selectors: Coding
with Class and Style**

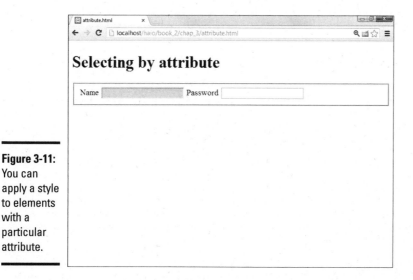

Figure 3-11:
You can
apply a style
to elements
with a
particular
attribute.

not

There are times you want an inverse selection. For example, imagine you wanted to apply a style to all the paragraphs that are not members of the special class:

```
p:not(.special) {
   border: 1px solid red;
}
```

nth-child

The nth-child selector allows you to select one or more elements in a group. The basic version uses a numeric input:

```
#myList>li:nth-child(1){
   border: 1px solid blue;
}
```

This allows you to apply a style to the first of a group of elements. In my example, I have a list with four items. The style is applied to the list items, not the list. (It seems to me the list items are children of the list, so it should be the nth-child of the list, but nobody asked me.)

The numeric value can actually be a formula, like an+b. If you love algebra (and who doesn't?), you can select all the even-numbered elements like this:

```
#myList>li:nth-child(2n){
   border: 1px solid blue;
}
```

A similar formula can be used to pick the odd-numbered children.

```
#myList>li:nth-child(2n+1){
   border: 1px solid blue;
}
```

You could use this formula system to get all kinds of groupings (every third element with 3n, for example), but most people simply need a particular element, or all the even or odd rows. CSS3 supplies shortcut keywords, even and odd, so you don't have to do it using math:

```
#myList>li:nth-child(even){
   color: white;
   background-color: red;
}
```

The last keyword allows you to pick the last element from a group. There are a few more variations of this selection technique:

✦ :nth-last-child(N) : Works just like nth-child, excepts counts from the end of the group of elements rather than the beginning.

✦ `:nth-of-type(N)`: This selector works just like `nth-child`, except it filters to a specific type and ignores any elements that are not of exactly the same type of element.

✦ `last-child`: This (naturally enough) selects the last child element.

✦ `last-nth-of-type(N)`: Works like `nth-of-type`, but from the end of the group.

✦ `first-child`: Grabs the first element (technically this was available in CSS2, but it was rarely used).

These selection tools are fully-supported in all the recent browsers. However, as they are generally used simply to improve readability, it should be safe to use them. Older browsers simply skip the style.

Figure 3-12 shows a number of variations of the `nth-child` selector.

Figure 3-12:
You can select specific elements in a group.

Other new pseudo-classes

Pseudo-classes allow you to specify styles based on the state of an element. Modern CSS supports a number of new pseudo-classes:

✦ `:hover`: The `:hover` pseudo-class has been a part of CSS from the beginning, but it was officially defined only for the `<a>` tag. Now the `:hover` pseudo-class can be applied to any element. If the mouse (or other pointing device) is over an element, that element has the `hover` state activated. Note that mobile devices don't always support `hover` because the position of the pointing device (the stylus or finger) isn't known until the item is activated. Mobile devices may have some sort of tabbing mechanism to indicate which item is being hovered over.

✦ `:focus`: The `:focus` pseudo-class is activated when an element is ready to receive keyboard input.

✦ `:active`: A form element is active when it is currently being used: for example, when a button has been pressed but not yet released. Mobile devices often skip directly to active mode without going through `hover` mode. This can be an important design consideration when using state for styling.

The state pseudo-classes are fully supported by all modern browsers except the IE family of browsers. There is limited but buggy support in even early versions of IE.

Chapter 4: Borders and Backgrounds

In This Chapter

✔ Creating borders

✔ Managing border size, style, and color

✔ Using the border shortcut style

✔ Understanding the box model

✔ Setting padding and margin

✔ Creating background and low-contrast images

✔ Changing background image settings

✔ Adding images to list items

CSS offers some great features for making your elements more colorful, including a flexible and powerful system for adding borders to your elements. You can also add background images to all or part of your page. This chapter describes how to use borders and backgrounds for maximum effect.

Joining the Border Patrol

You can use CSS to draw borders around any HTML element. You have some freedom in the border size, style, and color. Here are two ways to define border properties: using individual border attributes, and using a shortcut. Borders don't actually change the layout, but they do add visual separation that can be appealing, especially when your layouts are more complex.

Using the border attributes

Figure 4-1 illustrates a page with a simple border drawn around the heading.

Figure 4-1:
This page
features a
double red
border.

The code for the borderProps.html page demonstrates the basic principles of borders in CSS:

```
<!DOCTYPE html>
<html lang = "en-US">

  <head>
    <meta charset = "UTF-8">
    <title>borderProps.html</title>
    <style type = "text/css">
     h1 {
        border-color: red;
        border-width: .25em;
        border-style: double;
      }
    </style>
  </head>
  <body>
    <h1>This has a border</h1>
  </body>
</html>
```

Each element can have a border defined. Borders require three attributes:

✦ `width`: The width of the border. This can be measured in any CSS unit, but border width is normally described in pixels (px) or ems. (***Remember:*** An *em* is roughly the width of the capital letter "M" in the current font.)

✦ `color`: The color used to display the border. The color can be defined like any other color in CSS, with color names or hex values.

✦ `style`: CSS supports a number of border styles. For the example, in the following section, I chose a double border. This draws a border with two thinner lines around the element.

You must define all three attributes if you want borders to appear properly. You can't rely on the default values to work in all browsers.

Defining border styles

CSS has a predetermined list of border styles you can choose from. Figure 4-2 shows a page with all the primary border styles displayed.

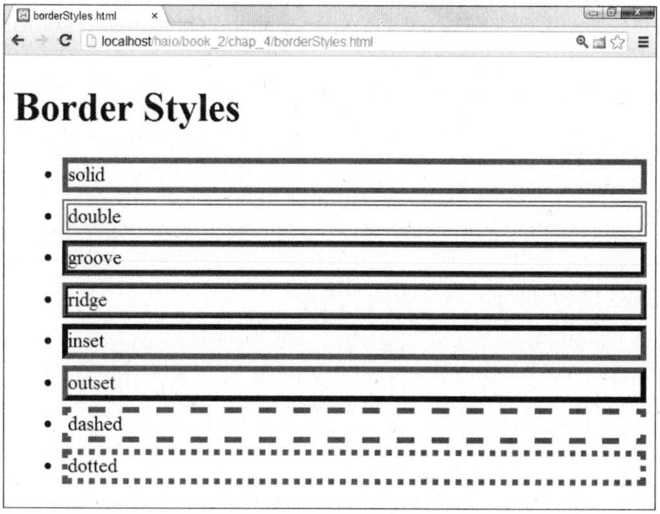

Figure 4-2: This page shows the main border styles.

> **Border Styles**
>
> - solid
> - double
> - groove
> - ridge
> - inset
> - outset
> - dashed
> - dotted

You can choose any of these styles for any border:

✦ **Solid:** A single solid line around the element.

✦ **Double:** Two lines around the element with a gap between them. The border width is the combined width of both lines and the gap.

✦ **Groove:** Uses shading to simulate a groove etched in the page.

✦ **Ridge:** Uses shading to simulate a ridge drawn on the page.

✦ **Inset:** Uses shading to simulate a pressed-in button.

✦ **Outset:** Uses shading to simulate a button *sticking out* from the page.

✦ **Dashed:** A dashed line around the element.

✦ **Dotted:** A dotted line around the element.

I didn't reprint the source of `borderStyles.html` here, but it's included on the companion website if you want to look it over. (See this book's Introduction for more on the companion website.) I added a small margin to each list item to make the borders easier to distinguish. Margins are discussed later in this chapter in the "Border, margin, and padding" section.

Shades of danger

Several border styles rely on shading to produce special effects. Here are a couple things to keep in mind when using these shaded styles:

✔ **You need a wide border.** The shading effects are typically difficult to see if the border is very thin.

✔ **Browsers shade differently.** All the shading tricks modify the *base* color (the color you indicate with the `border-color` attribute) to simulate depth. Unfortunately, the browsers don't all do this in the same way. I show a technique to define different color schemes for each browser in Chapter 5 of this minibook. For now, avoid shaded styles if this bothers you.

✔ **Black shading doesn't work in IE.** IE makes colors darker to get shading effects. If your base color is black, IE can't make anything darker, so you don't see the shading effects at all. Likewise, white shading doesn't work well on Firefox.

Using the border shortcut

Defining three different CSS attributes for each border is a bit tedious. Fortunately, CSS includes a handy border shortcut that makes borders a lot easier to define, as Figure 4-3 demonstrates.

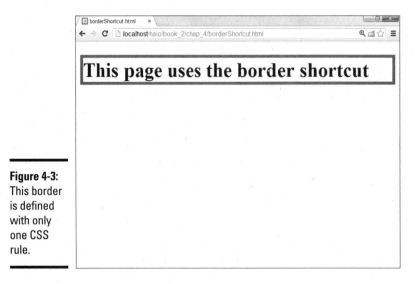

Figure 4-3:
This border is defined with only one CSS rule.

You can't tell the difference from the output, but the code for borderShortcut.html is extremely simple:

```
<!DOCTYPE html>
<html lang = "en-US">

  <head>
    <meta charset = "UTF-8">
    <title>borderShortcut.html</title>
    <style type = "text/css">
      h1 {
         border: red 5px solid;
      }
    </style>
  </head>
  <body>
    <h1>This page uses the border shortcut</h1>
  </body>
</html>
```

The order in which you describe border attributes doesn't matter. Just specify a color, a size, and a border style.

Creating partial borders

If you want, you can have more precise control of each side of a border. There are a number of specialized border shortcuts for each of the sub-borders. Figure 4-4 shows how you can add borders to the top, bottom, or sides of your element.

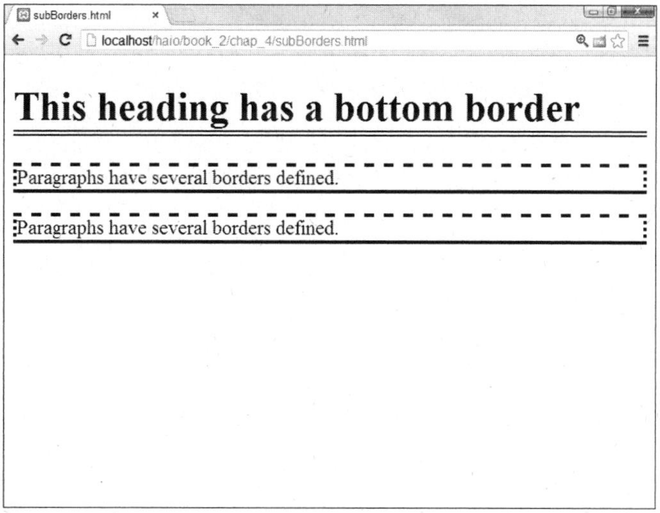

Figure 4-4: You can specify parts of your border if you want.

Figure 4-4 applies a border style to the bottom of the heading as well as different borders above, below, and to the sides of the paragraphs. Partial borders are pretty easy to build, as you can see from the code listing:

```
<!DOCTYPE html>
<html lang = "en-US">

  <head>
    <meta charset = "UTF-8">
    <title>subBorders.html</title>
    <style type = "text/css">
      h1 {
        border-bottom: 5px black double;
      }
      p {
        border-left:3px black dotted;
        border-right: 3px black dotted;
        border-top: 3px black dashed;
        border-bottom: 3px black groove;
      }
    </style>
  </head>
  <body>
    <h1>This heading has a bottom border</h1>
    <p>
      Paragraphs have several borders defined.
    </p>
    <p>
      Paragraphs have several borders defined.
    </p>
  </body>
</html>
```

Notice the border styles. CSS has style rules for each side of the border: `border-top`, `border-bottom`, `border-left`, and `border-right`. Each of these styles acts like the border shortcut, but it only acts on one side of the border.

 There are also specific border attributes for each side (bottom-border-width adjusts the width of the bottom border, for example), but they're almost never used because the shortcut version is so much easier.

Introducing the Box Model

XHTML and CSS use a specific type of formatting called the *box model*. Understanding how this layout technique works is important. If you don't understand some of the nuances, you'll be surprised by the way your pages flow.

The box model relies on two types of elements: inline and block-level. Block-level elements include `<div>` tags, paragraphs, and all headings (h1– h6), whereas `strong`, `a`, and `image` are examples of inline elements.

The main difference between inline and block-level elements is this: Block-level elements always describe their own space on the screen, whereas inline elements are allowed only within the context of a block-level element.

Your overall page is defined in block-level elements, which contain inline elements for detail.

Each block-level element (at least in the default setting) takes up the entire width of the parent element. The next block-level element goes directly underneath the last element defined.

Inline elements flow differently. They tend to go immediately to the right of the previous element. If there's no room left on the current line, an inline element drops down to the next line and goes to the far left.

Border, margin, and padding

Each block-level element has several layers of space around it, such as

✦ **Padding:** The space between the content and the border.

✦ **Border:** Goes around the padding.

✦ **Margin:** Space outside the border between the border and the parent element.

Figure 4-5 shows the relationship among margin, padding, and border.

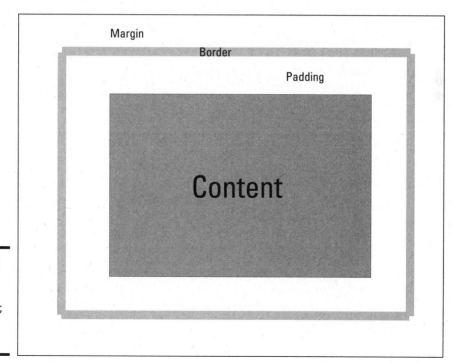

Figure 4-5: Margin is outside the border; padding is inside.

You can change settings for the margin, border, and padding to adjust the space around your elements. The `margin` and `padding` CSS rules are used to set the sizes of these elements, as shown in Figure 4-6.

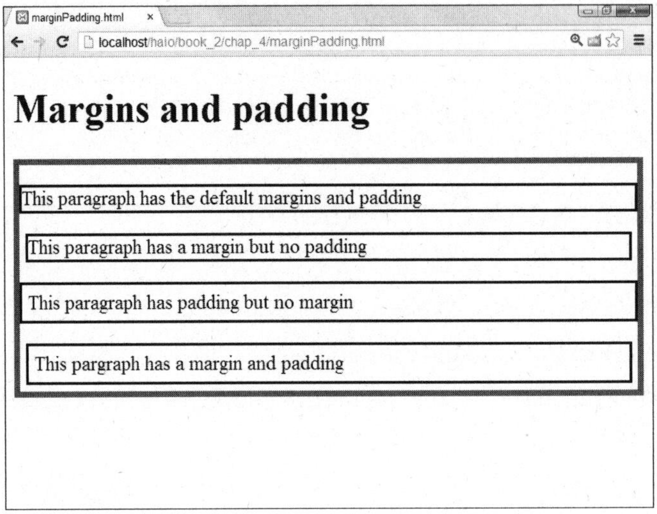

Figure 4-6: Margins and padding affect the positioning of an element.

In Figure 4-6, I applied different combinations of `margin` and `padding` to a series of paragraphs. To make things easier to visualize, I drew a border around the `<div>` containing all the paragraphs and each individual paragraph element. You can see how the spacing is affected.

```
<!DOCTYPE html>
<html lang = "en-US">

  <head>
    <meta charset = "UTF-8">
    <title>marginPadding.html</title>
    <style type = "text/css">
      div {
        border: red 5px solid;
      }
      p {
        border: black 2px solid;
      }
      #margin {
        margin: 5px;
      }
      #padding {
        padding: 5px;
      }
      #both {
        margin: 5px;
        padding: 5px;
      }
    </style>
```

```
  </head>
  <body>
    <h1>Margins and padding</h1>
    <div id = "main">
      <p>This paragraph has the default margins and padding</p>
      <p id = "margin">This paragraph has a margin but no padding</p>
      <p id = "padding">This paragraph has padding but no margin</p>
      <p id = "both">This paragraph has a margin and padding</p>
    </div>
  </body>
</html>
```

You can determine margin and padding using any of the standard CSS measurement units, but the most common are pixels and ems.

Positioning elements with margins and padding

As with borders, you can use variations of the `margin` and `padding` rules to affect spacing on a particular side of the element. One particularly important form of this trick is *centering*.

In old-style HTML, you could center any element or text with the `<center>` tag. This was pretty easy, but it violated the principle of separating content from style. The `text-align:center` rule is a nice alternative, but it only works on the contents of an element. If you want to center an entire block-level element, you need another trick, as you can see in Figure 4-7.

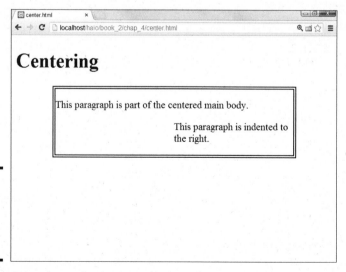

Figure 4-7:
Using
margins
to adjust
positioning.

This page illustrates a few interesting ideas:

✦ **You can adjust the width of a block.** The main `div` that contains all the paragraphs has its width set to 75 percent of the page body width.

✦ **Center an element by setting `margin-left` and `margin-right` to `auto`.** Set both the left and right margins to `auto` to make an element center inside its parent element. This trick is most frequently used to center `div`s and tables.

✦ **Use `margin-left` to indent an entire paragraph.** You can use `margin-left` or `margin-right` to give extra space between the border and the contents.

✦ **Percentages refer to percent of the parent element.** When you use percentages as the unit measurement for margins and padding, you're referring to the percentage of the parent element; so a `margin-left` of 50 percent leaves the left half of the element blank.

✦ **Borders help you see what's happening.** I added a border to the `main-Body` `div` to help you see that the `div` is centered.

✦ **Setting the margins to `auto` doesn't center the *text*.** It centers the *div* (or other block-level element). Use `text-align: center` to center text inside the `div`.

The code that demonstrates these ideas is shown here:

```
<!DOCTYPE html>
<html lang = "en-US">

 <head>
    <meta charset = "UTF-8">
    <title>center.html</title>
    <style type = "text/css">
      #mainBody {
        border: 5px double black;
        width: 75%;
        margin-left: auto;
        margin-right: auto;
      }
        .indented {
        margin-left: 50%;
      }
    </style>
  </head>
  <body>
    <h1>Centering</h1>
    <div id = "mainBody">
      <p>
        This paragraph is part of the centered main body.
      </p>
      <p class = "indented">
        This paragraph is indented to the right.
      </p>
    </div>
  </body>
</html>
```

New CSS3 Border Techniques

Borders have been a part of CSS from the beginning, but CSS3 adds some really exciting new options. Modern browsers now support borders made from an image as well as rounded corners and box shadows. These techniques promise to add exciting new capabilities to your designs.

Image borders

CSS3 allows you to use an image for an element border. The mechanism is quite powerful because it detects the edges of an image and "slices" it to create the edges and corners of the border from the edges and corners of the image.

For example, look at the simple picture frame image in Figure 4-8.

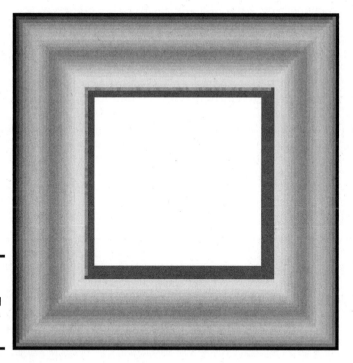

Figure 4-8:
This image
will be used
as a border
image.

The frame image is stored as frame.png in the same directory as the HTML file. It has a transparent center. Apply the following code to add an image border around all h2 elements on the page:

```
h2 {
    border-width: 15px;
    border-image: url("frame.png") 25% repeat;
    -webkit-border-image: url("frame.png") 25% repeat;
    -moz-border-image: url("frame.png") 25% repeat;
}
```

Here's how you add a border image:

1. **Acquire your image.**

   The image should already be designed as some sort of border. Typically it will be a shape around the edges, with either a solid-color center or a transparent center. I typically make the image 100×100 pixels, so the math is easier to figure later.

2. **Specify the border width.**

   You'll need to indicate the border width directly. The border of the frame image is scaled to fit whatever size you want.

3. **Calculate how much of the image's border you want.**

   I want to use the outer 25% of my frame image as the border, so specify 25%. If you leave off the percent sign, the value calculates in pixels. You can add four values if you prefer to use different amounts of the original image for each boundary.

4. **Indicate the behavior you want.**

   The original image is almost never the same size as the element you're wanting to surround, so you can supply a tip to explain how the browser should handle elements larger than the original. The most common choices are `repeat` (repeat the original image) or `stretch` (stretch the image to take up the entire space). With a simple image like the frame.png used in this example, the results will be the same.

What's up with the -moz and -webkit stuff?

As you look over the code for the image border demo, you'll see three versions of the border-image rule: `border-image`, `-webkit-border-image`, and `-moz-border-image`. This is a pattern you'll see on many of the newer CSS elements. While an element is still being finalized, some of the browser manufacturers will define a test version of the rule using a special browser-specific prefix. `-webkit` is the rendering image used in Chrome and Safari, and `-moz` is used by Firefox. Sometimes you'll also see the `-o` prefix to indicate Opera, and `-ms` to represent Internet Explorer. You can always try the generic rule name, but for newer rules like image border, it's also safe to include the vendor-specific versions. As acceptance of these newer rules becomes more widespread, the vendor prefixes will no longer be needed.

Figure 4-9 shows the image being used as a border around my headline.

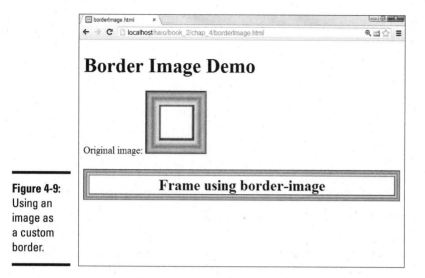

Figure 4-9:
Using an
image as
a custom
border.

Adding Rounded Corners

Older CSS was known for being very rectangular, so web designers tried to soften their designs by adding rounded corners. This was a difficult effect to achieve. CSS3 greatly simplifies the creation of rounded corners with the `border-radius` rule.

Figure 4-10 demonstrates a simple page with a rounded border.

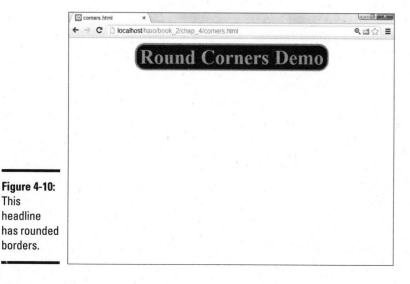

Figure 4-10:
This
headline
has rounded
borders.

It's pretty easy to get rounded corners on those browsers that support the tag:

```
<!DOCTYPE HTML>
<html lang = "en">

 <head>
  <title>corners.html</title>
  <meta charset = "UTF-8" />
  <style type = "text/css">
    h1 {
      width: 60%;
      background-color: #000066;
      color: #9999ff;
      border: #9999ff 3px groove;
      margin: auto;
      text-align: center;
      border-radius: .5em;
    }
  </style>
 </head>
 <body>
  <h1>Round Corners Demo</h1>

 </body>
</html>
```

The `border-radius` rule works by cutting an arc from each corner of the element. The arc has the specified radius, so for sharp corners, you'll want a small radius. You can measure the radius in any of the common measurements, but pixels (px) and character width (em) are the most commonly used.

The border is not visible unless the element has the `background-color` or `border` defined. Note that there are variations of each tag to support specific corners: `border-top-left-radius` and so on. This can be useful if you do not wish to apply the same radius to all four corners of your element. The most recent browsers now support the generic `border-radius` rule. You can pick up a number of the previous-generation browsers by using the vendor-specific prefix. If your browser does not understand the border-radius rule, it will simply create the ordinary squared corners.

Adding a box shadow

Box shadows are often added to elements to create the illusion of depth. Figure 4-11 displays a page with a simple box shadow.

The box shadow effect is not difficult to achieve, but it is normally done as part of a class definition so it can be re-used throughout the page. Here's some sample code:

```
<!DOCTYPE HTML>
<html lang = "en">
<head>
  <title>boxShadow.html</title>
  <meta charset = "UTF-8" />
  <style type = "text/css">
```

```
    .shadow {
box-shadow: 10px 10px 10px #000000;

    height: 200px;
    width: 200px;
    padding: 1em;
    border: 1px solid black;
    border-radius: 5px;

    background-color: #EEEEEE;
    }
  </style>
</head>
<body>
  <h1>Box Shadow Demo</h1>
  <div class = "shadow">
  This box has a shadow
    </div>
</body>
</html>
```

Figure 4-11:
Adding a
box shadow.

Adding a box shadow is much easier in CSS3 than it once was. Here are the
steps:

1. **Define a class.**

   Often you'll want to apply the same settings to a number of elements
   on a page, so the box shadow is often combined with other elements
   like background-color and border in a CSS class that can be reused
   throughout the page.

2. **Add the box-shadow rule.**

   The latest browsers support the standard box-shadow rule, but you may
   also want to include browser prefixes to accommodate older browses.

3. **Specify the offset.**

   A shadow is typically offset from the rectangle it belongs to. The first two values indicate the horizontal and vertical offset. Measure using any of the standard CSS measurements (normally pixels or ems).

4. **Determine the blur and spread distances.**

   You can further modify the behavior of the shadow by specifying how quickly the shadow blurs and how far it spreads. These are optional parameters.

5. **Indicate the shadow color.**

   You can make the shadow any color you wish. Black and gray are common, but you can get interesting effects by picking other colors.

Many other shadow effects are possible. You can add multiple shadows, and you can also use the `inset` keyword to produce an interior shadow to make it look like part of the page is cut out.

There is a similar rule called `text-shadow`. It has the same general behavior as `box-shadow`, but it's designed to work on text. It's possible to get some really nice effects with this tool, but be careful not to impede readability.

Changing the Background Image

You can use the `img` tag to add an image to your page, but sometimes you want to use images as a background for a specific element or for the entire page.

You can the `background-image` CSS rule to apply a background image to a page or elements on a page. Figure 4-12 shows a page with this feature.

Figure 4-12:
This page has a background image for the body and another for the heading.

Background images are easy to apply. The code for backgroundImage.html shows how:

```
<!DOCTYPE html>
<html lang = "en-US">

  <head>
    <meta charset = "UTF-8">
    <title>backgroundImage.html</title>
    <style type = "text/css">
      body {
        background-image: url("ropeBG.jpg");
      }
      h1 {
        background-image: url("ropeBGLight.jpg");
      }
      p {
        background-color: white;
        background-color: rgba(255, 255, 255, .85);
      }
    </style>
  </head>
  <body>
    <h1>Using Background Images</h1>
    <p>
      The heading uses a lighter version of the background,
      and the paragraph uses a solid color background with
      light transparency.
    </p>
    <p>
      The heading uses a lighter version of the background,
      and the paragraph uses a solid color background with
      light transparency.
    </p>
  </body>
</html>
```

Attaching the background image to an element through CSS isn't difficult. Here are the general steps:

1. **Find or create an appropriate image and place it in the same directory as the page so it's easy to find.**

2. **Attach the `background-image` style rule to the page you want to apply the image to.**

   If you want to apply the image to the entire page, use the `body` element.

3. **Tell CSS where `background-image` is by adding a `url` identifier.**

   Use the keyword `url()` to indicate that the next thing is an address.

4. **Enter the address of the image.**

   It's easiest if the image is in the same directory as the page. If that's the case, you can simply type the image name. Make sure you surround the URL with quotes.

5. **Test your background image by viewing the web page in your browser.**

   A lot can go wrong with background images. The image may not be in the right directory, you might have misspelled its name, or you may have forgotten the `url()` bit. (I do all those things sometimes.)

Getting a background check

It's pretty easy to add backgrounds, but background images aren't perfect. Figure 4-13 demonstrates a page with a nice background. Unfortunately, the text is difficult to read.

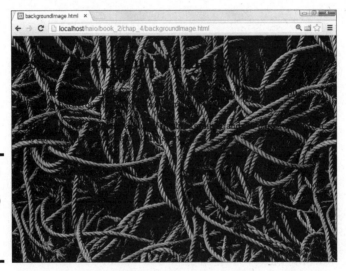

Figure 4-13: The text is very hard to read. Don't do this to your users!

Background images can add a lot of *zing* to your pages, but they can introduce some problems, such as

+ **Background images can add to the file size.** Images are very large, so a big background image can make your page much larger and harder to download.

+ **Some images can make your page harder to read.** An image in the background can interfere with the text, so the page can be much harder to read.

+ **Good images don't make good backgrounds.** A good picture draws the eye and calls attention to it. The job of a background image is to fade into the background. If you want people to look at a picture, embed it. Background images shouldn't jump into the foreground.

+ **Backgrounds need to be low contrast.** If your background image is dark, you can make light text viewable. If the background image is light, dark text shows up. If your image has areas of light and dark (like nearly all good images), it'll be impossible to find a text color that looks good against it.

Solutions to the background conundrum

Web developers have come up with a number of solutions to background image issues over the years. I used several of these solutions in the backgroundImage.html page (the readable one shown in Figure 4-12).

Using a tiled image

If you try to create an image the size of an entire web page, the image will be so large that dial-up users will almost never see it. Even with compression techniques, a page-sized image is too large for quick or convenient loading.

Fortunately, you can use a much smaller image and fool the user into thinking it takes up the entire screen. Figure 4-14 shows the ropeBG.jpg that I used to cover the entire page.

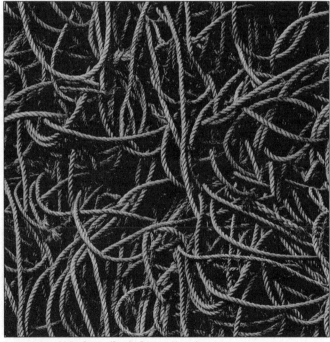

Figure 4-14:
The image is only 500×500 pixels.

Image courtesy of Julian Burgess (Creative Commons License)

I used a specially created image for the background. Even though it's only 500 pixels wide by 500 pixels tall, it's been carefully designed to repeat so you can't see the seams. If you look carefully, you can tell that the image repeats, but you can't tell exactly where one copy ends and the next one begins.

This type of image is a *tiled background* or sometimes a *seamless texture*.

Getting a tiled image

If you want an image that repeats seamlessly, you have two main options:

✦ **Find an image online.** A number of sites online have free seamless backgrounds for you to use on your site. Try a search and see what you come up with.

✦ **Make your own image.** If you can't find a pre-made image that does what you want, you can always make your own. All the main image editing tools have seamless background tools. In GIMP, choose Filters ➪ Map ➪ Make Seamless. Check Book VIII, Chapter 4 for a technique to build your own tiled backgrounds in GIMP.

By default, a background image repeats as many times as necessary in both the horizontal and vertical dimensions to fill up the entire page. This fills the entire page with your background, but you only have to download a small image.

Setting background colors

Background colors can be a great tool for improving readability. If you set the background color of a specific element, that background color appears on top of the underlying element's background image. For the backgroundImage.html example, I set the background color of all p objects to white, so the text appears on white regardless of the complex background. This is a useful technique for body text (like <p> tags) because text tends to be smaller and readability is especially important. If you want, you can set a background color that's similar to the background image. Just be sure the foreground color contrasts with the background color so the text is easy to read.

Setting a semi-transparent background color

In modern browsers, you will be able to see the background through the paragraph. I achieved this trick by setting the background color twice. The first `background-color` rule sets the background to white. This always works (but it won't produce any transparency). The second `background-color` rule uses a newer form of the color rule called `rgba`. This trick allows you to supply a color value with transparency. This rule takes four parameters. The first few are the RGB values (in base 10, so white is 255, 255, 255). The fourth parameter is the *alpha* value, which represents transparency. Alpha is specified by a value between 0 and 1, where 0 is fully transparent and 1 is fully opaque. To make your text readable, you should set alpha quite high. I used .85 for this example.

There is also an HSLA color rule that allows you to add alpha to a color defined with the HSL mechanism described in Chapter 1 of this mini-book. Like RGBA, it simply takes a fourth 0-1 parameter to indicate the amount of alpha.

When you use a dark background image with light text, be sure to also set the `background-color` to a dark color. This way the text is readable. Images take longer to load than colors and may be broken. Make sure the user can read the text immediately.

Reducing the contrast

In backgroundImage.html, the heading text is pretty dark, which won't show up well against the dark background image. I used a different trick for the `h1` heading. The heading uses a different version of the ropes image; this one is adjusted to be much brighter. The image is shown in Figure 4-15.

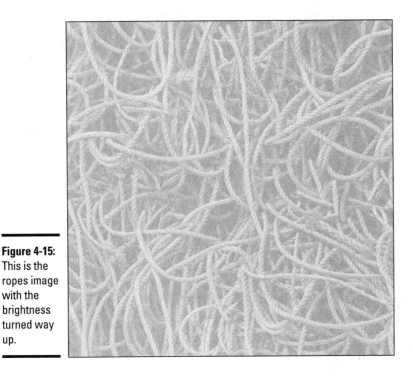

Book II Chapter 4

Styling with CSS

Figure 4-15: This is the ropes image with the brightness turned way up.

With this element, I kept the ropes image, but I made a much brighter background so the dark text would show up well underneath. This technique allows you to use the background image even underneath text, but here are a few things to keep in mind if you use it:

✦ **Make the image very dark or very light.** Use the Adjust Colors command in IrfanView or your favorite image editor to make your image dark or light. Don't be shy. If you're creating a lighter version, make it *very* light. (See Book I, Chapter 6 for details on color manipulation in IrfanView and Book VIII, Chapter 4 for how to change colors in GIMP.)

✦ **Set the foreground to a color that contrasts with the background.** If you have a very light version of the background image, you can use dark text on it. A dark background requires light text. Adjust the text color with your CSS code.

✦ **Set a background color.** Make the background color representative of the image. Background images can take some time to appear, but the background color appears immediately because it is defined in CSS. This is especially important for light text because white text on the default white background is invisible. After the background image appears, it overrides the background color. Be sure the text color contrasts with the background, whether that background is an image or a solid color.

✦ **Use this trick for large text.** Headlines are usually larger than body text, and they can be easier to read, even if they have a background behind them. Try to avoid putting background images behind smaller body text. This can make the text much harder to read.

Manipulating Background Images

After you place your background image, you might not be completely pleased with the way it appears. Don't worry. You still have some control. You can specify how the image repeats and how it's positioned.

Turning off the repeat

Background images repeat both horizontally and vertically by default. You may not want a background image to repeat, though. Figure 4-16 is a page with the ropes image set to not repeat at all.

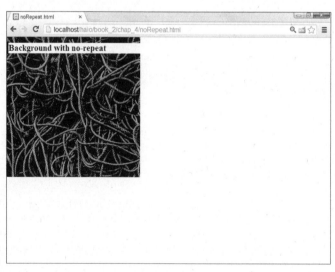

Figure 4-16:
The background doesn't repeat at all.

The code uses the `background-repeat` attribute to turn off the automatic repetition.

```
<!DOCTYPE html>
<html lang = "en-US">

    <head>
```

```
  <meta charset = "UTF-8">
  <title>noRepeat.html</title>
  <style type = "text/css">
    body {
      background-image: url("ropeBG.jpg");
      background-repeat: no-repeat;
    }
    h1 {
      background-color: white;
    }
  </style>
</head>
<body>
  <h1>Background with no-repeat</h1>
</body>
</html>
```

The `background-repeat` attribute can be set to one of four values:

✦ `repeat`: The default value; the image is repeated indefinitely in both *x*- and *y*-axes.

✦ `no-repeat`: Displays the image one time; no repeat in *x*- or *y*-axis.

✦ `repeat-x`: Repeats the image horizontally but not vertically.

✦ `repeat-y`: Repeats the image vertically but not horizontally.

Using CSS3 Gradients

A gradient (which is a blend between two or more colors) can be a nice background. Previously, developers would create a gradient by building a thin gradient strip in an image editor, and then using the repeat-x or repeat-y rules to make that smaller image replicate across the page. This was a nice technique, but it was not terribly flexible because the image size was still fixed, and only relatively simple linear gradients were possible.

CSS3 has added a remarkable gradient rule that makes gradients natively through CSS. When this technique is fully adopted, it makes gradients much easier to work with.

Figure 4-17 demonstrates a number of examples of CSS3 gradients in action:

CSS3 supports two major types of gradients: linear and radial. A linear gradient changes colors along a straight line, and a radial gradient radiates outward from a center point.

The gradient mechanism has been one of the slower parts of CSS to be standardized and adopted, so it's still changing, but it looks like the browsers are finally setting on a standard. Unfortunately, the vendor-specific prefixes are necessary for the time being, making this technique a bit tedious.

Up until very recently, the gradient syntax was even more messy than it is now, with WebKit (Chrome and Safari) using an entirely different gradient syntax than Mozilla, and Microsoft refusing to add any implementation at all.

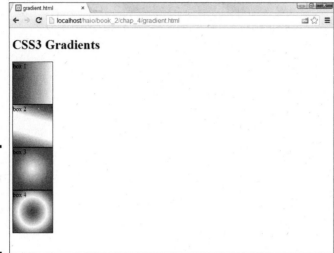

Figure 4-17:
CSS3 allows
a number of
interesting
gradient
types.

Now it looks like everybody's settling on the Mozilla-style implementation, which is pretty easy to use and the one demonstrated here. If you search on the web, you will see some other syntaxes, especially for WebKit-based browsers, but the mechanism described here looks to be the standard.

Building a simple gradient

The simplest gradient is demonstrated in box 1 of Figure 4-17. It varies from left to right, starting at red and ending with white. (of course, you'll need to see this in color to fully appreciate it). Check `gradient.html` on the book's companion site to see this example in its multicolor glory.

```
#box1 {
  background-image: linear-gradient(left, red, white);
  background-image: -moz-linear-gradient(left, red, white);
  background-image: -webkit-linear-gradient(left, red, white);
}
```

Here's how you build a simple linear gradient:

1. **Define the selector.**

   A gradient is defined in CSS, and you'll need to use any of your standard CSS selectors to determine which element you'll be adding the gradient to. See Chapter 3 of this mini-book if you need more details on CSS selectors.

2. **Use the background-image rule.**

   A gradient is a special form of image. You can use the background-image rule to apply a gradient to the background of any element, including the entire body of the page.

3. **Invoke the `linear-gradient` function.**

   A few CSS elements such as `url()` and `rgba()` require parentheses because technically they are functions. The distinction doesn't matter right now, but you need to incorporate the parentheses when you use this type of value. The `linear-gradient` technique is a function. (You'll write your own functions in JavaScript in Book IV and in PHP in Book V.)

4. **Determine the direction the gradient will flow.**

   You can make a gradient flow in any direction you want inside the element. Indicating `left` causes the element to flow from left to right. You can use `top` to flow from top to bottom, or `top left` to go from top left to bottom right. Use any combination of `top`, `left`, `bottom`, and `right`. You can also specify an angle in degrees, as demonstrated in the next example.

5. **Indicate a starting color.**

   Use any of the standard color tools (color names, hex colors, `rgb()`/`rgba()`, or `hsl()`) to determine the beginning color.

6. **Indicate an ending color.**

   The last color indicated will be the ending color of the gradient. The gradient flows from the beginning to ending color evenly.

7. **Repeat with browser extensions.**

   By the time you read this, it's possible that the browsers will all use the standard `linear-gradient` mechanism, and browser-specific rules will no longer be necessary. For the moment, though, you'll need to add variants for the specific browsers. You'll need to make a new version of the `background-image` rule for each major vendor.

Making a more interesting gradient

As you look at box 2 of Figure 4-17, you'll see a more complex gradient showing multiple colors and an interesting angle.

```
#box2 {
  background-image:
    linear-gradient(75deg, red, white 33%, white 66%, blue);
  background-image:
    -moz-linear-gradient(75deg, red, white 33%, white 66%, blue);
  background-image:
    -webkit-linear-gradient(75deg, red, white 33%, white 66%, blue);
}
```

Here's how you add more pizazz to your gradients.

1. **Use an angle for direction.**

   Rather than specifying your gradient direction with the standard `top/ left` keywords, you can specify a starting angle. Angles are measured mathematically in degrees, with 0 coming from the right and 90 coming from top-down. You must specify the degree measurement with `deg`, so 75 degrees is written as `75deg`.

2. **Add as many colors as you wish.**

   A gradient can have any number of colors in it. Each change in colors is called a *color stop*. My example shows three different colors.

3. **Determine where the color stops happen.**

   By default, the colors are evenly distributed along the gradient. If you want, you can move any color to appear anywhere on the gradient you wish. The color stop locations are indicated by percentages. It is not necessary to add a location for the first and last color stop, as they are presumed to be 0% and 100%.

4. **Create a band of color by providing two stops of the same color.**

   Box 2 features a band of white. To get this effect, I produced two color stops with white, one appearing at 33%, and the other at 66%. This breaks my gradient roughly into thirds.

5. **Put two colors at the same location for an abrupt color change.**

   If you want an abrupt color change, simply put two different colors at the same percentage.

6. **Repeat for all browsers.**

   Again, you'll need to consider the various browsers until this technique becomes more standardized.

Building a radial gradient

CSS3 supports a second gradient type called the *radial gradient*. The basic idea is the same, except rather than following a straight line like a linear gradient, a radial gradient appears to flow from a central spot in the element and radiate outwards.

The basic radial gradient shown in box 3 is created with this CSS code:

```
#box3 {
  background-image: radial-gradient(white, blue);
  background-image: -moz-radial-gradient(white, blue);
  background-image: -webkit-radial-gradient(white, blue);
}
```

As you can see, the basic radial gradient is created much like a linear gradient, except it uses the `radial-gradient` function instead of the `linear-gradient` function.

Radial gradients have many options, which makes them quite promising, but the browser support for these various standards is quite spotty. Box 4 has a radial gradient with three colors:

```
#box4 {
    background-image:
      radial-gradient(red, white, blue);
    background-image:
      -moz-radial-gradient(red, white, blue);
    background-image:
      -webkit-radial-gradient(red, white, blue);
}
```

It's also possible to change the shape of the gradient from circle to ellipse, to change the center of the gradient to a different point inside the element, and to specify color stops. You'll need to check the current specifications to see how these things are done, as they are still quite experimental.

Using Images in Lists

It's not quite a background, but you can also use images for list items. Sometimes, you might want some type of special bullet for your lists, as shown in Figure 4-18.

Figure 4-18:
I can't get enough of those Arrivivi Gusanos.

On this page, I've listed some of my (many) favorite varieties of peppers. For this kind of list, a custom pepper bullet is just the thing. Of course, CSS is the answer:

```
<!DOCTYPE html>

<html lang = "en-US">
 <head>
    <meta charset = "UTF-8">
    <title>listImages.html</title>
    <style type = "text/css">
      li {
        list-style-image: url("pepper.gif");
      }
    </style>
  </head>
  <body>
    <h1>My Favorite Peppers</h1>
    <ul>
      <li>Green</li>
      <li>Habenero</li>
      <li>Arrivivi Gusano</li>
    </ul>
  </body>
</html>
```

The `list-style-image` attribute allows you to attach an image to a list item. To create custom bullets:

1. **Begin with a custom image.**

   Bullet images should be small, so you may have to make something little. I took a little pepper image and resized it to 25×25 pixels. The image will be trimmed to an appropriate width, but it will have all the height of the original image, so make it small.

2. **Specify the `list-style-image` with a `url` attribute.**

   You can set the image as the `list-style-image`, and all the bullets will be replaced with that image.

3. **Test the list in your browser.**

   Be sure everything is working correctly. Check to see that the browser can find the image, that the size is right, and that everything looks like you expect.

If you don't want to use an image, CSS has a number of other styles you can apply to your list items. Use the `list-style-type` rule to set your list to one of many styles. Look at official CSS documentation for a complete list, but the most commonly used style types are `disc`, `circle`, `square`, `decimal`, `upper-roman`, `lower-roman`, `upper-latin`, and `lower-latin`. Note that you can apply a numeric styling to a list item in an ordered or unordered list, so the distinction between these list types is less important than it used to be.

Chapter 5: Levels of CSS

In This Chapter

✔ **Building element-level styles**

✔ **Creating external style sheets**

✔ **Creating a multipage style**

✔ **Managing cascading styles**

✔ **Working with a CSS reset style**

✔ **Using conditional comments**

CSS is a great tool for setting up the visual display of your pages. When you first write CSS code, you're encouraged to place all your CSS rules in a `style` element at the top of the page. CSS also allows you to define style rules inside the body of the HTML and in a separate document. In this chapter, you read about these alternative methods of applying style rules, when to use them, and how various style rules interact with each other.

Managing Levels of Style

Styles can be applied to your pages at three levels:

✦ **Local styles:** Defined by specifying a style within an HTML element's attributes.

✦ **Page-level styles:** Defined in the page's header area. This is the type of style used in Chapters 1 through 4 of this minibook.

✦ **External styles:** Defined on a separate document and linked to the page.

Using local styles

A style can be defined directly in the HTML body. Figure 5-1 is an example of this type of code. A local style is also sometimes called an *element-level* style because it modifies a particular instance of an element on the page.

You can't see the difference from Figure 5-1, but if you look over the code, you'll see it's not like the style code you see in the other chapters in this minibook:

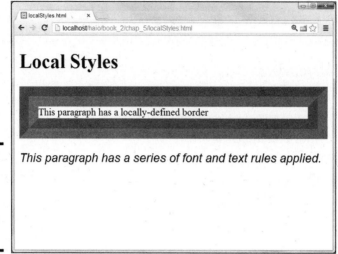

Figure 5-1:
This page
has styles,
but they're
defined in a
new way.

```
<!DOCTYPE html>
<html lang = "en-US">

  <head>
    <meta charset = "UTF-8">
    <title>localStyles.html</title>
  </head>
  <body>
    <h1>Local Styles</h1>
    <p style = "border: 2em #FF00FF groove">
      This paragraph has a locally-defined border
    </p>
    <p style = "font-family: sans-serif;
                font-size: 1.2em;
                font-style: italic">
      This paragraph has a series of font and text rules applied.
    </p>
  </body>
</html>
```

As you look over this code, a couple things should become evident:

✦ **No `<style>` element is in the header.** Normally, you use a `<style>` section in the page header to define all your styles. This page doesn't have such a segment.

✦ **Paragraphs have their own style attributes.** I added a `style` attribute to each paragraph in the HTML body. All HTML elements support the `style` attribute.

✦ **The entire style code goes in a single pair of quotes.** For each styled element, the entire style goes into a pair of quotes because it's one HTML attribute. You can use indentation and white space (as I did) to make things easier to understand.

When to use local styles

Local styles should not be your first choice, but they can be useful in some circumstances.

If you're writing a program to translate from a word processor or other tool, local styles are often the easiest way to make the translation work. If you use a word processor to create a page and you tell it to save the page as HTML, it will often use local styles because word processors often use this technique in their own proprietary format. Usually when you see an HTML page with a lot of local styles, it's because an automatic translation tool made the page.

Sometimes, you see local styles used in code examples. For example, the following code could be used to demonstrate different border styles:

```
<!DOCTYPE html>
<html lang = "en-US">

  <head>
    <meta charset = "UTF-8">
    <title>localBorders.html</title>
  </head>
  <body>
    <h1>Inline Borders</h1>
    <p style = "border: 5px solid black">
      This paragraph has a solid black border
    </p>
    <p style = "border: 5px double black">
      This paragraph has a double black border
    </p>
  </body>
</html>
```

For example purposes, it's helpful to see the style right next to the element. This code would be fine for demonstration or testing purposes (if you just want to get a quick look at some border styles), but it wouldn't be a good idea for production code.

Local styles have very high priority, so anything you apply in a local style overrides the other style rules. This can be a useful workaround if things aren't working like you expect, but it's better to get your styles working correctly than to rely on a workaround.

The drawbacks of local styles

It's pretty easy to apply a local style, but for the most part, the technique isn't usually recommended because it has some problems, such as

✦ **Inefficiency:** If you define styles at the element level with the `style` attribute, you're defining only the particular instance. If you want to set paragraph colors for your whole page this way, you'll end up writing a lot of style rules.

✦ **Readability:** If style information is interspersed throughout the page, it's much more difficult to find and modify than if it's centrally located in the header (or in an external document, as you'll see shortly).

✦ **Lack of separation:** Placing the styles at the element level defeats the goal of separating content from style. It becomes much more difficult to make changes, and the mixing of style and content makes your code harder to read and modify.

✦ **Awkwardness:** An entire batch of CSS rules has to be stuffed into a single HTML attribute with a pair of quotes. This can be tricky to read because you have CSS integrated directly into the flow of HTML.

✦ **Quote problems:** The HTML attribute requires quotes, and some CSS elements also require quotes (font families with spaces in them, for example). Having multiple levels of quotes in a single element is a recipe for trouble.

Using an external style sheet

CSS supports another way to use styles, called *external style sheets*. This technique allows you to define a style sheet as a separate document and import it into your web pages. To see why this might be attractive, take a look at the following figure.

Figure 5-2 shows a page with a distinctive style.

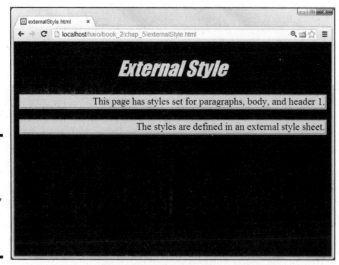

Figure 5-2:
This page has styles for the body, h1, and paragraph tags.

When you look at the code for externalStyle.html, you might be surprised to see no obvious style information at all!

```
<!DOCTYPE html>
<html lang = "en-US">

  <head>
    <meta charset = "UTF-8">
    <title>externalStyle.html</title>
    <link rel = "stylesheet"
          type = "text/css"
          href = "myStyle.css" />
  </head>
  <body>
    <h1>External Style</h1>
    <p>
      This page has styles set for paragraphs, body, and header 1.
    </p>
    <p>
      The styles are defined in an external style sheet.
    </p>
  </body>
</html>
```

Where you normally see style tags (in the header), there is no style. Instead, you see a `<link>` tag. This special tag is used to connect the current document with another document.

Defining the external style

When you use an external style, the style elements aren't embedded in the page header but in an entirely separate document.

In this case, the page is connected to a special file called myStyle.css. This file contains all the CSS rules:

```
/* myStyle.css */

body {
  background-color: #333300;
  color: #FFFFFF;
}

h1 {
  color: #FFFF33;
  text-align: center;
  font: italic 200% fantasy;
}

p {
  background-color: #FFFF33;
  color: #333300;
  text-align: right;
  border: 3px groove #FFFF33;
}
```

The style sheet looks just like a page-level style, except for a few key differences:

✦ **The style sheet rules are contained in a separate file.** The style is no longer part of the HTML page but is an entirely separate file stored on the server. CSS files usually end with the `.css` extension.

✦ **There are no `<style></style>` tags.** These aren't needed because the style is no longer embedded in HTML.

✦ **The code begins with a comment.** The `/* */` pair indicates a comment in CSS. Truthfully, you can put comments in CSS in the page level just like I did in this external file. External CSS files frequently have comments in them.

✦ **The style document has no HTML.** CSS documents contain nothing but CSS. This comes closer to the goal of separating style (in the CSS document) and content (in the HTML document).

✦ **The document isn't tied to any particular page.** The great advantage of external CSS is reuse. The CSS document isn't part of any particular page, but any page can use it.

Reusing an external CSS style

External style sheets are really fun when you have more than one page that needs the same style. Most websites today use multiple pages, and they should share a common style sheet to keep consistency. Figure 5-3 shows a second page using the same myStyle.css style sheet.

Figure 5-3:
Another page using exactly the same style.

The code shows how easily this is done:

```
<!DOCTYPE html>
<html lang = "en-US">

  <head>
    <meta charset = "UTF-8">
    <title>SecondPage.html</title>
    <link rel = "stylesheet"
          type = "text/css"
          href = "myStyle.css" />
  </head>
  <body>
    <h1>Second Page</h1>
    <p>
      This page uses the same style as
      <a href = "externalStyle.html">externalStyle.html</a>.
    </p>
  </body>
</html>
```

External style sheets have some tremendous advantages:

✦ **One style sheet can control many pages:** Generally, you have a large number of different pages in a website that all share the same general style. You can define the style sheet in one document and have all the HTML files refer to the CSS file.

✦ **Global changes are easier:** Say you have a site with a dozen pages, and you decide you want some kind of chartreuse background (I don't know why — go with me here). If each page has its own page-level style definition, you have to make the change 12 times. If you're using external styles, you make the change in one place and it's automatically propagated to all the pages in the system.

✦ **Separation of content and design:** With external CSS, all the design is housed in the CSS, and the data is in HTML.

✦ **Easy upgrades:** Because the design parameters of the entire site are defined in one file, you can easily change the site without having to mess around with individual HTML files.

Understanding the link tag

The <link> tag is the key to adding a CSS reference to an HTML document. The <link> tag has the following characteristics:

✦ **The <link> tag is part of the HTML page.** Use a <link> tag in your HTML document to specify which CSS document will be used by the HTML page.

✦ **The <link> tag only occurs in the header.** Unlike the <a> tag, the <link> tag can occur only in the header.

✦ **The tag has no visual presence.** The user can't see the `<link>` tag, only its effects.

✦ **The `<link>` tag is used to relate the document with another document.** You use the `<link>` tag to describe the relationship between documents.

✦ **The `<link>` tag has a `rel` attribute, which defines the type of relationship.** For now, the only relationship you'll use is the `stylesheet` attribute.

✦ **The `<link>` tag also has an `href` attribute, which describes the location of the other document.**

Link tags are often used to connect a page to an externally defined style document (more on them in the next section).

Most people refer to the hyperlinks created by the anchor (`<a>`) tag as hyperlinks or links. This can lead to some confusion because, in this sense, the link tag doesn't create that type of link. If it were up to me, the `<a>` tag would have been called the `<link>` tag, and the tag now called `link` would have been called `import` or something. Maybe Tim Berners-Lee meant to call me the day he named these elements, and he just forgot. That's what I'm thinking.

Specifying an external link

To use the `<link>` tag to specify an external style sheet, follow these steps:

1. **Define the style sheet.**

   External style sheets are very similar to the ones you already know. Just put all the styles in a separate text document without the `<style>` and `</style>` tags. In my example, I created a new text file called myStyle.css.

2. **Create a `link` element in the HTML page's head area to define the link between the HTML and CSS pages.**

   My link element looks like this:

   ```
   <link rel = "stylesheet"
         type = "text/css"
         href = "myStyle.css" />
   ```

3. **Set the `link` 's relationship by setting the `rel = "stylesheet"` attribute.**

   Honestly, `stylesheet` is almost the only relationship you'll ever use, so this should become automatic.

4. **Specify the type of style by setting `type = "text/css"` (just like you do with page-level styles).**

5. **Determine the location of the style sheet with the `href` attribute.**

Understanding the Cascading Part of Cascading Style Sheets

The *C* in CSS stands for *cascading,* which is an elegant term for an equally elegant and important idea. Styles cascade or flow among levels. An element's visual display may be affected by rules in another element or even another document.

Inheriting styles

When you apply a style to an element, you change the appearance of that element. If the element contains other elements, the style is often passed on to those containers. Take a look at Figure 5-4 for an illustration.

Figure 5-4 shows several paragraphs, all with different font styles. Each paragraph is white with a black background. All the paragraphs use a fantasy font. Two of the paragraphs are italicized, and one is also bold. Look at the code to see how the CSS is defined.

Figure 5-4:
The last paragraph inherits several style rules.

```
<!DOCTYPE html>
<html lang = "en-US">
  <head>
    <meta charset = "UTF-8">
    <title>CascadingStyles</title>
    <style type = "text/css">
      body {
        color: white;
        background-color: black;
      }
```

```
      p {
        font-family: comic sans ms, fantasy;
      }
      .italicized {
        font-style: italic;
      }
      #bold {
        font-weight: bold;
      }
    </style>
  </head>
  <body>
    <h1>Cascading Styles</h1>
    <p>This is an ordinary paragraph</p>
    <p class = "italicized">
      This paragraph is part of a special class
    </p>
    <p class = "italicized"
       id = "bold">
      This paragraph has a class and an ID
    </p>
  </body>
</html>
```

Take a look at the page, and you'll notice some interesting things:

✦ **Everything is white on a black background.** These styles were defined in the body. Paragraphs without specific colors will inherit the colors of the parent element (in this case, the `body`). There's no need to specify the paragraph colors because the `body` takes care of them.

✦ **Paragraphs all use the fantasy font.** I set the paragraph's `font-family` attribute to `fantasy`. All paragraphs without an explicit `font-family` attribute will use this rule.

✦ **A class is used to define italics.** The second paragraph is a member of the `italicized` class, which gives it italics. Because it's also a paragraph, it gets the paragraph font, and it inherits the color rules from the `body`.

✦ **The `bold` ID only identifies font weight.** The third paragraph has all kinds of styles associated with it. This paragraph displays all the styles of the second, plus the added attributes of its own ID.

In the cascadingStyles.html example, the final paragraph inherits the font from the generic p definition, italics from its class, and boldfacing from its ID. Any element can attain style characteristics from any of these definitions.

Hierarchy of styles

An element will display any style rules you define for it, but certain rules are also passed on from other places. Generally, this is how style rules cascade through the page:

✦ **The body defines overall styles for the page.** Any style rules that you want the entire page to share should be defined in the body. Any element in the body begins with the style of the page. This makes it easy to define an overall page style.

✦ **A block-level element passes its style to its children.** If you define a `div` with a particular style, any elements inside that `div` will inherit the `div`'s style attributes. Likewise, defining a list will also define the list items.

✦ **You can always override inherited styles.** Of course, if you don't want paragraphs to have a particular style inherited from the body, you can just change them.

Not all style rules are passed on to child elements. The text formatting and color styles are inherited, but border and positioning rules are not. This actually makes sense. Just because you define a border around a `div` doesn't mean you want the same border around the paragraphs inside that `div`.

Book II
Chapter 5

Levels of CSS

Overriding styles

The other side of inherited style is the ability to override an inherited style rule. For example, take a look at this code:

```
<!DOCTYPE html>
<html lang = "en-US">

  <head>
    <meta charset = "UTF-8">
    <title>overRide.html</title>
    <style type = "text/css">
      body { color: red; }
      p {color: green; }
      .myClass { color: blue; }
      #whatColor { color: purple; }
    </style>
  </head>
  <body>
    <div>
      This div has only the style from the body.
    </div>
    <p>
      This is a regular paragraph with paragraph styling
    </p>
    <p class = "myClass">
      This paragraph is a member of a class
    </p>
    <p class = "myClass" id = "whatColor">
      This paragraph is a member of a class and has an ID,
      both with style rules.
    </p>
  </body>
</html>
```

The code listing has a different indentation scheme than I've used in the rest of the chapter. Because all the styles had one rule, I chose not to indent to save space.

The question is this: What color will the `whatColor` element display? It's a member of the body, so it should be red. It's also a paragraph, and paragraphs are green. It's also a member of the `myClass` class, so it should be blue. Finally, it's named `whatColor`, and elements with this ID should be purple.

Four seemingly conflicting color rules are all dropped on this poor element. What color will it be?

CSS has a clear ranking system for handling this type of situation. In general, more specific rules trump more general rules. Here's the precedence (from highest to lowest precedence):

1. **User preference:** The user always has the final choice about what styles are used. Users aren't required to use any styles at all and can always change the style sheet for their own local copy of the page. If a user needs to apply a special style (for example, high contrast for people with visual disabilities), he should always have that option.

2. **Local style:** A local style (defined with the `style` attribute in the HTML) has the highest precedence of developer-defined styles. It overrules any other styles.

3. `id`: A style attached to an element `id` has a great deal of weight because it overrides any other styles defined in the style sheet.

4. **Class:** Styles attached to a class override the style of the object's element. So, if you have a paragraph with a color green that belongs to a class colored blue, the element will be blue because class styles outrank element styles.

5. **Element:** The element style takes precedence over any of its containers. For example, if a paragraph is inside a `div`, the paragraph style has the potential to override both the `div` and the body.

6. **Container element:** `div`s, tables, lists, and other elements used as containers pass their styles on. If an element is inside one or more of these containers, it can inherit style attributes from them.

7. **Body:** Anything defined in the body style is an overall page default, but it will be overridden by any other styles.

In the overRide.html example, the `id` rule takes precedence, so the paragraph displays in purple.

If you want to see a more complete example, look at cascadingStyles.html on the companion website. It extends the `whatColor` example with other paragraphs that demonstrate the various levels of the hierarchy.

Precedence of style definitions

When you have styles defined in various places (locally, page level, or externally), the placement of the style rule also has a ranking. Generally, an external style has the weakest rank. You can write a page-level style rule to override an external style.

You might do this if you decide all your paragraphs will be blue, but you have one page where you want the paragraphs green. Define paragraphs as green in the page-level style sheet, and your page will have the green paragraphs without interfering with the other pages' styles.

Page-level styles (defined in the header) have medium weight. They can override external styles but are overridden by local styles.

Locally defined styles (using the HTML style attribute) have the highest precedence, but they should be avoided as much as possible. Use classes or IDs if you need to override the page-level default styles.

In general, a style defined later in the page takes precedence over one defined earlier.

Managing Browser Incompatibility

While we're messing around with style sheets, there's one more thing you should know. Although all the modern browsers manage CSS pretty well these days, Internet Explorer (especially the earlier versions) is well known for doing things in non-standard ways.

Most of what you know works equally well in any browser. I've focused on the established standards, which work very well on most browsers. Unfortunately, Internet Explorer (especially before version 7) is notorious for not following the standards exactly. Internet Explorer (IE) doesn't do everything exactly right. When IE had unquestioned dominance, everybody just made things work for IE. Now you have a bigger problem. You need to make your code work for standards-compliant browsers, and sometimes you need to make a few changes to make sure that IE displays things correctly.

Coping with incompatibility

This has been a problem since the beginning of web development, and a number of solutions have been proposed over the years, such as

✦ **"Best viewed with" disclaimers:** One common technique is to code for one browser or another and then ask users to agree with your choice by putting up this disclaimer. This isn't a good technique because the user shouldn't have to adapt to you. Besides, sometimes the choice is out of the user's hands. More and more custom devices (such as gaming consoles, tablets and cellphones) have browsers built in, which are difficult to change. IE isn't available on Linux machines, and not everyone can install a new browser.

✦ **Parallel pages:** You might be tempted to create two versions of your page, one for IE and one for the standards-compliant browsers (Firefox, Netscape Navigator, Opera, Safari, and so on). This is also a bad solution because it's twice (or more) as much work. You'll have a lot of trouble keeping track of changes in two different pages. They'll inevitably fall out of synch.

✦ **JavaScript-based browser detection:** In Book IV, you see that JavaScript has features for checking on the browser. This is good, but it still doesn't quite handle the differences in style sheet implementation between the browsers.

✦ **CSS hacks:** The CSS community has frequently relied on a series of hacks (unofficial workarounds) to handle CSS compatibility problems. This approach works by exploiting certain flaws in IE to overcome others. The biggest problem with this is that when Microsoft fixes some flaws (as they've done with IE 10), many of the flaws you relied on to fix a problem may be gone, but the original problem is still there.

✦ **Conditional comments:** Although IE has bugs, it also has some innovative features. One of these features, *conditional comments,* lets you write code that displays only in IE. Because the other browsers don't support this feature, the IE-specific code is ignored in any browser not based on IE. This is the technique currently preferred by coders who adhere to web standards.

Making Internet Explorer–specific code

It's a little easier for you to see how conditional comments work if I show you a simple example and then show you how to use the conditional comment trick to fix CSS incompatibility problems.

Figure 5-5 shows a simple page with Firefox. Figure 5-6 shows the exact same page displayed in IE 7.

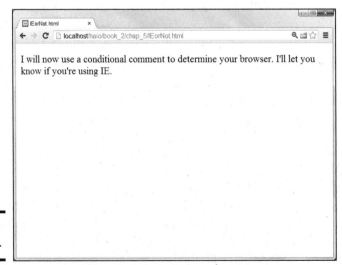

Figure 5-5:
This isn't IE.

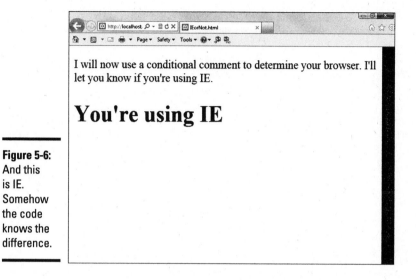

Figure 5-6:
And this
is IE.
Somehow
the code
knows the
difference.

Take a look at the code for IEorNot.html and see how it works.

```
<!DOCTYPE html>
<html lang = "en-US">

  <head>
    <meta charset = "UTF-8">
    <title>IEorNot.html</title>
  </head>
  <body>
    <p>
      I will now use a conditional comment to determine your
      browser. I'll let you know if you're using IE.
    </p>
    <[!--if IE]
      <h1>You're using IE</h1>
    <![endif]-->
  </body>
</html>
```

The only part that's new is the strange comments:

```
<!--[if IE]>
  <h1>You're using IE</h1>
<![endif]-->
```

Conditional comments are a special feature available only in Internet
Explorer. They allow you to apply a test to your browser. You can place any
HTML code you wish between `<!-- [if IE] >` and `<![endif]-->` , but that
code is rendered only by versions of Internet Explorer. Any other browser
reads the entire block as a comment and ignores it completely.

So, when you look at IEorNot.html in IE, it sees the conditional comment, says
to itself, "Why yes, I'm Internet Explorer," and displays the "Using IE" headline.
If you look at the same page with Firefox, the browser doesn't understand the

conditional comment but sees an HTML comment (which begins with < ! -- and ends with -->). HTML comments are ignored, so the browser does nothing.

Using a conditional comment with CSS

Conditional comments on their own aren't that interesting, but they can be a very useful tool for creating compatible CSS. You can use conditional comments to create two different style sheets, one that works for IE and one that works with everything else. Figures 5-7 and 5-8 illustrate a simple example of this technique:

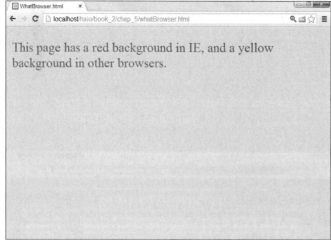

Figure 5-7: This page has a yellow background in most browsers.

Most browsers will read a standard style sheet that creates a yellow background.

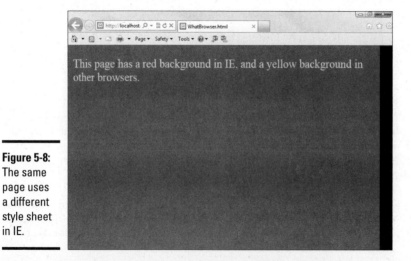

Figure 5-8: The same page uses a different style sheet in IE.

If the page is rendered in IE, it uses a second style sheet.

Look at the code, and you'll see it's very similar to the IEorNot.html page.

```
<!DOCTYPE html>
<html lang = "en-US">

  <head>
    <meta charset = "UTF-8">
    <title>WhatBrowser.html</title>
    <!-- default style -->
    <style type = "text/css">
      body {
        background-color: yellow;
        color: blue;
      }
    </style>
    <!-- IE only style overrides default -->
    <!--[if IE]>
      <style type = "text/css">
        body {
          background-color: red;
          color: yellow;
        }
      </style>
    <![endif]-->
  </head>
  <body>
    <p>
      This page has a red background in IE, and a yellow
      background in other browsers.
    </p>
  </body>
</html>
```

If you want a page to use different styles in IE and other browsers, do the following:

1. **Define the default style first.**

   Begin by creating the style that will work in most browsers. Most of the time, this style will also work in IE. You can create the style at the page level (with the `<style></style>` pair) or externally (with the `<link>` tag).

2. **Create a conditional comment in the header.**

   Create a conditional comment *after* the primary style, as shown in this code snippet.

   ```
   <!-- default style -->
   <style type = "text/css">
     body {
       background-color: yellow;
       color: blue;
     }
   </style>

   <!-- IE only style overrides default -->
   ```

```
<!--[if IE]>

<![endif]-->
```

3. **Build a new IE-specific style inside the comment.**

   The style inside the comment will be applied only to IE browsers, such as in the following lines:

   ```
   <!--[if IE]>
     <style type = "text/css">
       body {
         background-color: red;
         color: yellow;
       }
     </style>
   <![endif]-->
   ```

4. **The commented style can be page level or external.**

   Like the default style, you can use the `<style></style>` pair to make a page-level style, or you can use the `<link>` tag to pull in an externally defined style sheet.

5. **Only place code that solves IE issues in the conditional style.**

   IE will read the code in both styles, so there's no need to repeat everything. Use the conditional style for only those areas where IE doesn't do what you expect.

6. **Don't forget to end the conditional comment.**

   If you leave off the end of your conditional comment (or any comment, for that matter), most of your page won't appear. That could be bad.

Checking the Internet Explorer version

So far, you haven't encountered many situations that require conditional comments, but they're handy when you need them. One more trick can be useful. You can specify which version of IE you're using. This is important when you read about positionable CSS in Book III because IE versions 7 and later work pretty well with standards-compliant code, but the earlier versions do not. You can use this variation to specify code only for IE 6 and earlier.

```
<!--[if lte IE 6]>
...
<[endif]-->
```

The `lte` signifies *less than or equal to,* so code inside this condition will run only on early versions of IE. If you know the user is using IE version 10 or later, most of the concepts described in this book will work fine. For earlier versions of IE, you may have to rely on conditional comments to make everything work.

Using a CSS reset

Even when browsers agree on which CSS elements to incorporate, they sometimes differ on the actual details. For example, they may choose different margins and paddings for list elements. Web developers often use a special CSS style called a *css reset*. This is simply an external CSS file that explicitly determines the details of every single element. When you use a CSS reset, you're less likely to be surprised by differences between browsers. A number of great resets are available to use for free from www.cssreset.com. For HTML5 use, I prefer the HTML5 Doctor CSS reset available from that page.

Although page resets are a godsend for designers, they do slow down the page load and rendering time a bit (as they reset every single element whether it is used in the page or not). You should never use a page reset as the only CSS, but modify it to suit your specific needs. Also, you'll find that resets aren't critical until you're concerned that things work exactly the same on every browser (which is not likely to happen anyway).

For these reasons, I do not use CSS resets in this book, but they are frequently used in web frameworks and CMS systems as described in Book VIII.

Chapter 6: CSS Special Effects

In This Chapter

✔ **Adding reflections**

✔ **Working with opacity**

✔ **Manipulating text with strokes and shadows**

✔ **Adding transformations to elements**

✔ **Animating with transitions**

CSS is great for adding visual interest to websites. Newer implementations of CSS go even further, adding new capabilities to web pages that once required hours of work in an image editor or programming language. In this chapter, you discover what you need to know to make your page elements pop out, reflect, turn, move, and even respond to basic input, all with CSS.

Image Effects

CSS allows you to apply some interesting special effects to your pages. These effects can be applied to any element, but they generally are applied to images and headlines. Note that these are still considered experimental, so the browser implementations vary.

Transparency

CSS3 has complete support for adjustable opacity. This is reflected in a couple of ways. First, any element has an `opacity` attribute that can be set from 0 (fully transparent) to 1 (fully opaque).

Figure 6-1 shows a `div` with partial transparency superimposed on an image.

Figure 6-1:
The box
and text
are partially
transparent.

The complete code for this page is easy to follow:

```
<!DOCTYPE HTML>
<html lang = "en">
  <head>
    <title>opacity.html</title>
    <meta charset = "UTF-8" />
    <style type = "text/css">
    body {
     background-image: url("apoyo.jpg");
     background-repeat: no-repeat;
    }
    h1 {
     color: rgba(0, 0, 0, .3);
    }

    #box {
     position: absolute;
     top: 350px;
     left: 100px;
     height: 100px;
     width: 100px;
     border: 1px solid red;
     background-color: white;
     opacity: .3;
    }
    </style>
  </head>
  <body>
    <h1>Opacity Demo</h1>
    <div id = "box"></div>
  </body>
</html>
```

All of the code is common HTML and CSS2 stuff, except the last attribute. The `opacity` attribute takes a single floating point value between 0 and 1. Zero (0) is completely transparent and one (1) is completely opaque.

Note that Figure 6-1 also illustrates the other main form of transparency supported by CSS — the headline uses the RGBA model to add alpha transparency to a color. Take a look at Chapter 4 of this mini-book for more on the rgba and hsla color models. In general, use alpha when you want to add partial transparency to an individual color. Opacity can be used for an entire element, even something complex like an image or a video.

All of the recent browser versions support opacity without requiring vendor-specific prefixes. Older browsers simply display the element as fully opaque, so anything under a partially transparent element may be invisible to older browsers.

Reflections

Reflection is another one of those visual elements that adds quite a bit to a page when done well. Although it's not a formal part of the CSS3 specification, it is a promising technology. Currently only the WebKit-based browsers (that is, Safari, iPhone/iPad, and Chrome) support this capability. However, it shows such promise that some form of this capability is likely to appear in the other browsers at some point.

Figure 6-2 shows a reflected headline and image.

**Book II
Chapter 6**

CSS Special Effects

Figure 6-2:
Using the
reflection
attribute on
text and an
image.

Apply the following CSS to make any element with the `reflect` class have a nice-looking reflection in the supported browsers:

```
-webkit-box-reflect: below 2px;
```

Basic reflections are quite simple:

1. **Apply the `-webkit-box-reflect` attribute.**

   Unfortunately, there is no generic version, nor has the `reflect` attribute been duplicated by other browsers.

2. **Specify where the reflection is to be placed.**

   Normally the reflection goes below the primary element, but it can also be `above`, `left`, or `right`.

3. **Indicate a gap width.**

   The reflection can be placed right next to the original element, but often it looks better with a small gap. The gap is normally measured in pixels.

This will produce a very nice reflection.

However, reflections aren't usually pixel-perfect duplications. They tend to fade out over distance. WebKit allows you to add a gradient to a reflection. In this case, the gradient goes from completely opaque (white) to completely transparent (transparent).

```
.reflect {
 -webkit-box-reflect: below 2px
 -webkit-linear-gradient(bottom, white, transparent 40%, transparent);    }
```

The standard part of the reflection is just like the previous example, but it includes a gradient that fades the reflection to transparency.

1. **Build a linear gradient.**

   The gradient for a reflection is nearly linear. Note that the gradient is NOT a new CSS rule, but simply a parameter in the existing reflection rule.

2. **Make the gradient move from bottom to top.**

   Use `top` to indicate the gradient starts at the top, and `bottom` to indicate the gradient starts at the bottom. These values represent the top and bottom of the *original* image, not the reflection (which will, of course, be reversed). Normally, your gradient starts at the bottom of the original image (which is at the top of the reflected image).

3. **Begin with complete opacity.**

   The bottom of the original image is the top of the reflected image, and the top of the reflected image should be completely opaque. This gradient isn't really about color, but about which parts of the reflection are visible. Setting the initial color to `white` makes the top of the reflection completely opaque. (Of course, you can use `rgba()` to set any other transparency value you want, but only the alpha part is important in this context.)

4. **Finish at complete opacity.**

   The top of the original image (the bottom of the reflection) should be completely transparent, so end the gradient with the special color keyword `transparent` (which is equivalent to `rgba(255, 255, 255, 0)`).

5. **Add a color-stop to adjust the fade.**

   Add a color stop to indicate where in the reflection you want the image to begin fading. I want the picture to begin fading around 40%, so I added an internal transparent color stop at 40%.

If you need a refresher on how gradients work, please check Chapter 4 of this mini-book.

Note that the reflected image is not calculated as a separate element for page layout purposes, so text and other content will flow right on top of your reflection.

Reflections are commonly applied to images, but they can be applied to any element, even video!

It's possible to get a reflection effect in other browsers with clever use of the transformation and gradient attributes. For now, though, it's probably safest to reserve this effect for situations where you know the user will be using a supported browser or when the reflected effect is not absolutely necessary.

Text Effects

The most significant improvement to text in CSS is the `@font` mechanism described in Chapter 2 of this minibook. This technique allows you to define your own fonts and package them with your website. CSS3 has other text-formatting tricks available, too. The `text-stroke` and `text-shadow` rules allow you to make interesting transformations on text in your pages.

Both of these rules are used to decorate text, but they can impact readability, so you should use them carefully. They're more appropriate for larger text (like headlines) than the main content of your site.

Text stroke

With CSS3, you can specify a stroke color for your text. This defines an outline around the letter. You can specify the stroke color (using any of the standard CSS color values) as well as a stroke width (using the normal size attributes).

Figure 6-3 shows a page with stroked text.

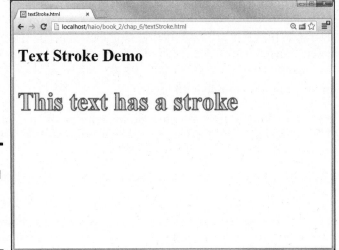

Figure 6-3:
You can add
an outline
to text for
interesting
effects.

The `text-stroke` rule applies this effect. You can see it used in the code:

```
<!DOCTYPE HTML>
<html lang = "en">
  <head>
    <title>textStroke.html</title>
    <meta charset = "UTF-8" />
    <style type = "text/css">
      h2 {
        color: yellow;
        -webkit-text-stroke: 2px red;
        font-size: 300%;
        }
    </style>

  </head>

  <body>
    <h1>Text Stroke Demo</h1>

    <h2>This text has a stroke</h2>
  </body>
</html>
```

Currently no browsers support the `text-stroke` attribute directly, but WebKit-based browsers (Chrome and Safari) support the vendor-specific `-webkit-` version. A browser that does not support the rule will simply ignore it, so this should not be a significant part of your design until support is more complete.

Text-shadow

Shadows are another common feature of modern web designs. Shadows add an element of depth to a page, but they can also enhance readability (if used properly) to lift a headline from the page. The text-shadow attribute was technically part of CSS2, but it has only recently been supported by major browsers. Figure 6-4 illustrates text-shadow in action:

```
<!DOCTYPE HTML>
<html lang = "en">
  <head>
    <title>textShadow.html</title>
    <meta charset = "UTF-8" />
    <style type = "text/css">
    h2 {
        font-size: 300%;
        text-shadow: 5px 5px 2px #cccccc;
      }
    </style>
  </head>

  <body>
    <h1>Text Shadow Demo</h1>

    <h2>This text has a shadow</h2>

  </body>
</html>
```

Book II
Chapter 6

CSS Special Effects

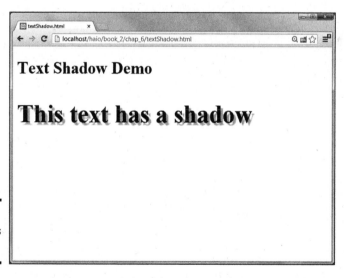

Figure 6-4:
This text has a shadow.

The text-shadow attribute has four parameters:

✦ **offset-x:** Determines how far in the x (left-right) axis the shadow will be from the original text. A positive value moves the shadow to the right, and a negative value moves to the left.

✦ **offset-y:** Determines how far in the y (up-down) axis the shadow will be from the original text. A positive value moves the shadow down, and a negative value moves the shadow up.

✦ **blur:** Specifies the blur radius of the shadow. If the value is 0px, there is no blur, and the shadow looks just like the original text. Generally, you'll want the blur value to be near the longest of your offsets. This allows the shadow to be recognizable as a shadow of the text without becoming a distraction.

✦ **color:** Defines the shadow color. Generally a dark gray is preferred, but you can also try other colors for special effects. Note that blurring tends to lighten the shadow color. If there is a great deal of blur applied, the shadow color can be the same color as the text. If the shadow will not be blurred much, you may need to lighten the shadow color for readability.

The size of the shadow is determined indirectly with a combination of offsets and blurs. You may have to experiment to get the shadow you're looking for. Shadow effects are best when they are subtle because they can affect readability. For Figure 6-4, I made the shadow darker than I would in a normal web page to ensure that the shadow is visible in the screen shot. Normally, I'd make the shadow even lighter to give an almost subconscious indication of depth.

A special case of text shadowing can be used to help text stand out against a background image. Apply a small shadow of a contrasting color. This technique is frequently used when you need to have text on a background because each letter produces its own high-contrast background. Again, be sure not to sacrifice readability for sake of design ethic.

All latest-model browsers support the text-shadow feature. No special prefixes are necessary.

Transformations and Transitions

One of the most consistent criticisms of early HTML was the limitations on how elements are displayed on the screen. An entire mini-book (Book III) is dedicated to screen layout, but CSS3 incorporates a significant new set of tools for modifying the position, size, and orientation of any element.

The transformation mechanism allows you to apply classic transformations (rotation, translation, or scale) on any element. The transition mechanism allows you to perform these changes over time. Together, these two techniques allow a relatively simple and powerful form of animation that once required sophisticated programming techniques or an external plug-in like Flash.

Transformations

CSS3 includes the ability to apply geometric transformations onto any element. This provides a remarkable level of visual control not previously available to web developers.

The `transform` attribute allows you to apply a mathematical transformation to any `div`. When you apply `transform` to an element, you need to apply one or more of the following parameters to describe the type of transformation:

✦ `translate`: Moves the object from its default position. Translation requires two parameters, an X measurement and a Y measurement. Use the standard CSS measurement units.

✦ `rotate`: Rotates the image around its center value. Takes one parameter, an angle measurement in degrees. (For example, 30 degrees is `30deg`.)

✦ `scale`: Changes the size of the object. The standard version changes both the horizontal and vertical size uniformly. The `scalex` and `scaley` attributes can be used to adjust the scale along an individual axis. Scale is measured in the standard CSS measurement units. If scale is larger than 1, the object is larger than the original. A scale between zero and one makes the item smaller than it was. Zero or negative scale values are not defined.

✦ `skew`: This allows you to tilt the element by some angle. The `skew` parameter requires an angle measurement in degrees. The `skewx` and `skewy` variations allow for more complete control of the transformation.

**Book II
Chapter 6**

CSS Special Effects

You can combine multiple parameters by listing them after the transform attribute separated by spaces.

To illustrate, imagine the following HTML snippet:

```
<div id = "box1">box 1</div> <div id = "box2">box 2</div> <div id = "box3">box
    3</div> <div id = "box4">box 4</div> <div id = "box5">box 5</div>
```

The code shows five identical `divs`. For illustration purposes, all the `divs` share the same common CSS:

```
#box1, #box2, #box3, #box4, #box5{  width: 100px;   height: 80px;   border: 3px
    solid black;   background-color: yellow;  }
```

Apply variations of the `transform` attribute to each element to see how the transformations work.

```
#box2 {   transform: translate(100px, 0px);  } #box3 {   transform:
    rotate(45deg);  }   #box4 {   transform: scale(2) translate(100px, 0px);  }
    #box5 {   transform: skew(3);  }
```

This code is illustrated in Figure 6-5.

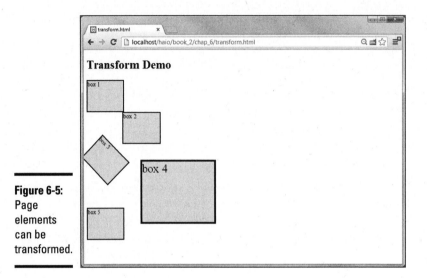

Figure 6-5:
Page
elements
can be
transformed.

Note that browser support is changing on this element. Chrome and Safari still expect the -webkit prefix, but Firefox and Opera support the non-prefixed version. IE 10 theoretically works with the standard version, but version 9 requires the -ms- prefix, and earlier versions of IE simply ignore transformations altogether. If you view the actual source code of the transform.html site, you'll see multiple versions of each rule to handle the various browsers:

```
#box2 {
  transform: translate(100px, 0px);
  -webkit-transform: translate(100px, 0px);
  -ms-transform: translate(100px, 0px);
}
```

Eventually, common sense will break out and vendor-specific prefixes will no longer be necessary, but for the time being, it's safest to put them all in place. If you want to catch older versions of Firefox and Opera, you can also include these (-moz- and -o-) prefixes as well.

Three-dimensional transformations

As browsers become more powerful, interesting new capabilities are emerging. One of the more exciting developments is the formation of 3D transformations. A 3D transform is similar to the traditional transformations, but it allows for a virtual third axis.

Ordinary, 2D animations utilize the 2D coordinate system, with an X axis going side-to-side and a Y axis traversing top-to-bottom. Even in 2D transformations, there is a tacit acknowledgment of a Z axis. The Z axis goes through the center of the object and points directly to the viewer's eyes and back into infinity behind the screen. 2D rotations are around this imaginary Z axis. You can determine which elements overlap other elements through the CSS z-index property, so although all screen elements are the same actual distance from the user, they appear to have some form of depth.

3D transformations have the same general operations as 2D (translate, rotate, and scale), but you can apply the transformation along one of the three axes: X, Y, or Z. This might seem confusing, so take a look at Figure 6-6 for some clarification:

In Figure 6-6, you see five boxes with nearly identical styles. Each box has a different 3D transformation applied:

✦ **Box 1 has default behavior:** Box 1 uses ordinary layout with no 3D transformation applied at all.

✦ **Box 2 is rotated 45 degrees around x:** Box 2 appears to be truncated, but it's actually rotated around the horizontal (X) axis. Note that both the box itself and the text inside the box are shortened.

✦ **Box 3 is nearly invisible:** Box 3 has also been rotated around the X axis, but this one is rotated nearly 90 degrees, so it's almost invisible. (Had I rotated 90 degrees, it *would* be invisible because the element has no depth.)

**Book II
Chapter 6**

CSS Special Effects

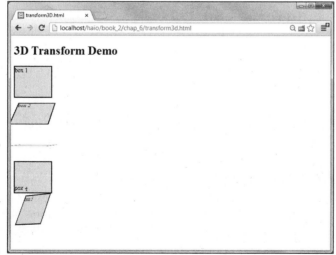

Figure 6-6:
These boxes are transformed in three dimensions.

✦ **Box 4 is upside-down:** I rotated box 4 180 degrees around the X axis, flipping it completely. Note that rotating around the Y axis would also flip the box, but the text would remain at the top, and would be reversed along the vertical axis.

✦ **Box 5 is doing all kinds of crazy things:** Box 5 has two transformations applied at the same time. It is rotated 45 degrees around x and -45 degrees along y.

Take a look at the code to see exactly what is happening here.

```
<!DOCTYPE HTML>
<html lang = "en">
   <head>
     <title>transform3D.html</title>
     <meta charset = "UTF-8" />
     <style type = "text/css">
     body {
     perspective: 1000;
     -webkit-perspective: 1000;
     }

     #box1, #box2, #box3, #box4, #box5{
     width: 100px;
     height: 80px;
     border: 3px solid black;
     background-color: yellow;
     }

     #box2 {
      transform: rotateX(45deg);
      -webkit-transform: rotateX(45deg);
     }

     #box3 {
      transform: rotateX(89deg);
      -webkit-transform: rotateX(89deg);
     }

     #box4 {
      transform: rotateX(180deg);
      -webkit-transform: rotateX(180deg);
     }

     #box5 {
      transform: rotate3D(1, 2, 0, 45deg);
      -webkit-transform: rotate3D(1, -1, 0, 45deg);
     }

   </style>
   </head>

<body>
 <h1>3D Transform Demo</h1>

 <div id = "box1">box 1</div>
 <div id = "box1">box 2</div>
 <div id = "box1">box 3</div>
```

```
<div id = "box1">box 4</div>
<div id = "box1">box 5</div>

</body>
</html>
```

The first new rule is `perspective`. Change the perspective of the parent element that will contain your transformed elements. This gives you the ability to determine how the elements appear to be displayed. The perspective indicates how close the camera appears to be to the elements. I applied a perspective of 1,000 to my example, which gives a decent illusion.

Boxes 2 through 4 all use the same transformation rule: `rotateX()`. This mechanism is much like the 2D `rotate()` function, but it rotates along the X axis. There are also `rotateY()` and `rotateZ()` functions, but `rotateZ()` is infrequently used because it's just like the 2D `rotate()` technique.

If you want to apply more than one rotation, you can use the `rotate3d()` function. This function takes four parameters. The first three are modifiers for the three axes, and the fourth is an angle. Looking at box 5, I've rotated 45 degrees in the X and Y axes.

CSS3 also supports the `translateX`, `translateY()`, and `trans-lateZ()` functions. These mechanisms allow you to specify a translation along a specific axis. (They are not used frequently because the 2D `translate()` method encapsulates both `translateX` and `translateY`, and `z-index` is a well-established way to translate along the z axis.) The `translate3d()` function allows you to translate along multiple axes at the same time.

CSS3 includes `scaleX`, `scaleY`, and `scaleZ` functions, but again these are not always used because they act similar to the 2D scaling function. There is also a `scale3d()` function for use with multiple scales.

Support for the 3D transformations is growing but not complete. At the moment, the `-webkit` and no-prefix versions will support most browsers. The IE family of browsers has limited support for 3D transformations.

Transition animation

It's already possible to change CSS properties on the fly through pseudo-classes (like hover) or with JavaScript code. Prior to CSS3, all CSS state changes happened instantly. With the new `transition` attribute, you can cause transitions to happen over time.

Figure 6-7 demonstrates transitions, but as it involves movement, you really need to see this example in your browser.

Book II
Chapter 6

CSS Special Effects

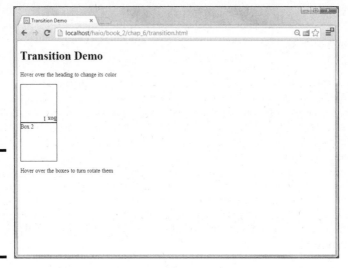

Figure 6-7:
As you hover over elements, they change!

Look at a simple h1 heading:

```
<h1>Transition Demo</h1>
```

The CSS code is mainly quite straightforward:

```
h1 {   color: black    font-size: 300%;   transition:color 1s ease-in;  }

h1:hover {   color: red;  }
```

Begin by ignoring the `transition` attribute. If you look at the rest of the code, it's easy to see what it does. In the normal state, the heading is black. In the hover state, the color is red. Typically, the heading turns red as soon as the mouse hovers over it, and will instantly turn black when the mouse leaves. However, when the `transition` attribute is added, the color change is not immediate, but takes a second. The color gradually changes from black to red and back.

Transitions are even more interesting when you pair them with transformations. Imagine a very simple `div`:

```
<div id = "box">Box 1</div>
```

Apply a little CSS3 magic and when the user hovers over the `div`, it rotates smoothly until it is upside-down. When the user leaves the `div`, it smoothly rotates back to its original position:

```
#box {   transition: all 1s ease-in;   height: 100px;   width: 100px;   border:
  1px solid black;   }

#box:hover {    transform: rotate(180deg);   }
```

The `transform` is defined in the: `hover` pseudo-class. The only new element is the transition specified in the class' standard style.

The `transition` attribute takes several parameters:

✦   `animation property`: The type of animation defined by this tag. The default value is `all`, but other types are expected to work, including `color`, `length`, `width`, `percentage`, `opacity`, and `number`. If in doubt, use the standard `all`.

✦   `duration`: The length of the animation in seconds. One second is `1s`.

✦   `timing function`: If you want the animation to occur at a constant speed, use `linear`. If you want a more natural motion that gradually speeds up and slows down at the ends of the animation, use one of the following: `ease`, `ease-in`, `ease-out`, `ease- in-out`.

✦   `delay`: If you include a second time value, this will be considered a delay. The animation will not begin until after the delay.

If you prefer, you can use individual properties for the various parts of the animation, but most developer prefer the one-line shortcut (like the one used for borders).

Not all CSS attributes can be animated, but many can be. It may require some experimentation to determine which CSS attributes can be animated with the `transition` attribute.

Unfortunately, the stock `transition` attribute is not supported by any major browsers, but there are vendor-specific versions for Mozilla (`-moz-`), WebKit (`-webkit-`), and Opera (`-o-`). Your best bet until support is widespread is to include all vendor-specific versions in addition to the standard version.

Animations

The `transform` behavior is pretty cool, but CSS3 promises an even more exciting form of animation called the (wait for it) `animation` mechanism.

Figure 6-8 illustrates an animation of a box moving around the screen.

Of course, it doesn't make sense to view an animation in a book. You'll need to see this on the website.

**Book II
Chapter 6**

CSS Special Effects

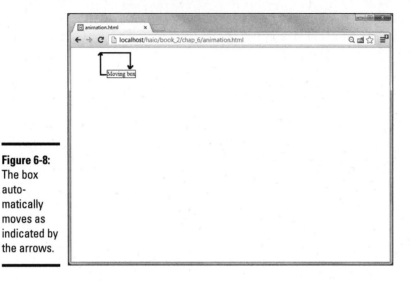

Figure 6-8:
The box auto-matically moves as indicated by the arrows.

Here's the basic strategy for building a CSS animation:

1. **Generate a set of keyframes.**

   Animations are based on the notion of keyframes. Each keyframe speci-fies the state of an object, and the browser attempts to smoothly transi-tion between keyframes.

2. **Provide a percentage for each keyframe.**

   The keyframe starts with a percentage, indicating where in the animation the keyframe will happen. The first keyframe should be 0% (the beginning of the animation) and the last should be 100% (the end of the animation). You can indicate as many intermediate keyframes as you want.

3. **Add a mini style sheet for each keyframe.**

   Place any styles you want modified in a little style sheet. At the indicated place in the timeline, an element following this animation will display the given style behavior. You can place any style information you want here.

4. **Apply the animation to your elements.**

   The `animation` rule allows you to apply a keyframe to an element. You can reuse the same keyframes among many different elements if you want.

5. **Modify the animation.**

   You can apply many of the same characteristics to an animation as you do a transition. There are a number of parameters, but the most com-monly used elements are keyframe, time, and repeat.

Take a look at the code for animation.html to see it all in action:

```
<!doctype html>
<html lang="en">
   <head> <meta charset="UTF-8"> <title>animation.html</title>

      <style type = "text/css"> @keyframes anim {  0%  {left: 0px;  top: 0px;}  25%
      {left: 100px; top: 0px;}  50% {left: 100px; top: 100px;}  75% {left: 0px;
      top: 100px;}  100% {left: 0px;  top: 0px;} }  @-webkit-keyframes anim {  0%
      {left: 0px;  top: 0px;}  25% {left: 100px; top: 0px;}  50% {left: 100px;
      top: 100px;}  75% {left: 0px;  top: 100px;}  100% {left: 0px;  top: 0px;}
      }  @-moz-keyframes anim {  0%  {left: 0px;  top: 0px;}  25% {left: 100px;
      top: 0px;}  50% {left: 100px; top: 100px;}  75% {left: 0px;  top: 100px;}
      100% {left: 0px;  top: 0px;} }  @-o-keyframes anim {  0%  {left: 0px;  top:
      0px;}  25% {left: 100px; top: 0px;}  50% {left: 100px; top: 100px;}  75%
      {left: 0px;  top: 100px;}  100% {left: 0px;  top: 0px;} }  #box {  position:
      absolute;  border: 1px solid black;  -webkit-animation: anim 5s linear
      infinite;   -moz-animation:  anim 5s linear infinite;   -o-animation:   anim
      5s linear infinite;  animation:     anim 5s linear infinite;  }

      </style>
   </head>
   <body>  <div id = "box">Moving box</div>
   </body>
</html>
```

There are a number of things to note about this example:

+ **Create a keyframes set called `anim`:** The `@keyframes` rule (much like
  the `@font-family` rule described in Chapter 2 of this mini-book) is
  used to create a page-level resource that can be used in the rest of the
  CSS. In this case, it's used to generate a keyframe set.

+ **Build browser-specific versions:** Unfortunately, the animation mechanism still requires browser-specific prefixes. It's usually easiest to target
  one browser (I usually start with WebKit) and then copy for the other
  browsers when the basic behavior is working.

+ **This example moves an element in a square pattern:** For this particular
  example, I intend to make a `div` move in a square motion. As you look at
  the keyframes, you'll see that I simply change the left and top position of
  the `div` throughout time.

+ **Make beginning and end the same:** Because I plan to run this animation
  continuously, I want the beginning and ending places to be the same.

+ **Apply the `anim` keyframe set to the `box` element:** Apply the `anim` keyframe set by using the `animation` rule.

+ **Indicate the length of the animation:** Animations are about changes
  over time, so the `animation` tag also requires a duration, measured in
  seconds (s) or milliseconds (ms).

+ **Determine the easing:** Easing is how the animation acts at the beginning and end of an animation segment. The `linear` rule used here keeps

the animation at a constant speed. You can also use `ease-in-out` (the default behavior) to make the element move at a variable rate.

✦ **Determine the number of repetitions:** You can specify a number of times to repeat the animation. If you leave this part out, the animation will happen only once when the page first loads. You can specify infinite (as I did in the example) to make the animation repeat as long as the page is in memory.

Note there are many other parameters you can set, such as `easing` (described in the "Transition animation" section of this chapter) and `delay`. These can be set through the `animation` rule or with individual rules. For now, I tend to keep my animations as simple as possible, at least until the browsers can all manage animations without vendor prefixes.

You learn much more sophisticated animation techniques with JavaScript programming in Book IV.

Part III
Building Layouts with CSS

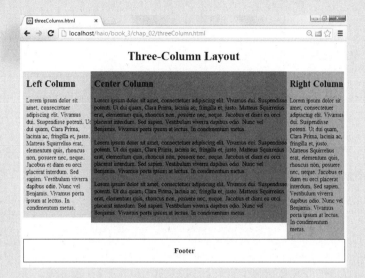

Contents at a Glance

Chapter 1: Fun with the Fabulous Float

In This Chapter

✔ **Understanding the pitfalls of traditional layout tools**

✔ **Using float with images and block-level tags**

✔ **Setting the width and margins of floated elements**

✔ **Creating attractive forms with float**

✔ **Using the clear attribute with float**

*O*ne of the big criticisms against HTML is that it lacks real layout tools. You can do a lot with your page, but it's still basically a list of elements arranged vertically on the screen. As the web matures and screen resolutions improve, people want web pages to look more like print matter, with columns, good-looking forms, and more layout options. CSS provides several great tools for building nice layouts. After you get used to them, you can build just about any layout you can imagine. This chapter describes the amazing `float` attribute and how it can be used as the foundation of great page layouts.

Avoiding Old-School Layout Pitfalls

Back in the prehistoric (well, pre-CSS) days, no good option was built into HTML for creating a layout that worked well. Clever web developers and designers found some ways to make things work, but these proposed solutions all had problems.

Problems with frames

Frames were a feature of the early versions of HTML. They allowed you to break a page into several segments. Each segment was filled with a different page from the server. You could change pages independently of each other, to make a very flexible system. You could also specify the width and height of each frame.

At first glance, frames sound like an ideal solution to layout problems. In practice, they had a lot of disadvantages, such as

✦ **Complexity:** If you had a master page with four segments, you had to keep track of five web pages. A *master* page kept track of the relative positions of each section, but had no content of its own. Each of the other pages had content but no built-in awareness of the other pages.

✦ **Linking issues:** The default link action caused content to pop up in the same frame as the original link, which isn't usually what you want. Often, you'd put a menu in one frame and have the results of that menu pop up in another frame. This meant most anchors had to be modified to make them act properly.

✦ **Backup nightmares:** If the user navigated to a page with frames and then caused one of the frames to change, what should the backup button do? Should it return to the previous state (with only the one segment returned to its previous state) or was the user's intent to move entirely off the master page to what came before? There are good arguments for either and no good way to determine the user's intention. Nobody ever came up with a reasonable compromise for this problem.

✦ **Ugliness:** Although it's possible to make frames harder to see, they did become obvious when the user changed the screen size and scroll bars would automatically pop up.

✦ **Search engine problems:** Search engines had a lot of problems with frame-based pages. The search engine might only index part of a frame-based site, and the visitor might get incomplete websites missing navigation or sidebars.

For all these reasons, frames are no longer supported in HTML5. The layout techniques you read about in this chapter more than compensate for the loss of frames as layout tools.

HTML5 does allow one limited type of frame called the iFrame, but even it is not necessary. Read how to integrate content from other pages on the server with AJAX in Book VII, Chapter 6.

Problems with tables

When it became clear that frames weren't the answer, web designers turned to tables. HTML has a flexible and powerful table tool, and it's possible to do all kinds of creative things with that tool to create layouts. A few web developers still do this, but you'll see that flow-based layout is cleaner and easier. Tables are meant for tabular data, not as a layout tool. When you use tables to set up the visual layout of your site, you'll encounter these problems:

✦ **Complexity:** Although table syntax isn't that difficult, a lot of nested tags are in a typical table definition. To get exactly the look you want, you probably won't use an ordinary table but tricks, like `rowspan` and `colspan`, special spacer images, and tables inside tables. It doesn't take long for the code to become bulky and confusing.

✦ **Content and display merging:** Using a table for layout violates the principle of separating content from display. If your content is buried inside a complicated mess of table tags, it'll be difficult to move and update.

✦ **Inflexibility:** If you create a table-based layout and then decide you don't like it, you basically have to redesign the entire page from scratch. It's no simple matter to move a menu from the left to the top in a table-based design, for example.

Tables are great for displaying tabular data. Avoid using them for layout because you have better tools available.

Problems with huge images

Some designers skip HTML altogether and create web pages as huge images. Tools, like Photoshop, include features for creating links in a large image. Again, this seems ideal because a skilled artist can have control over exactly what is displayed. Like the other techniques, this has some major drawbacks, such as

✦ **Size and shape limitations:** When your page is based on a large image, you're committed to the size and shape of that image for your page. If a person wants to view your page on a cellphone or PDA, it's unlikely to work well, if at all.

✦ **Content issues:** If you create all the text in your graphic editor, it isn't really stored to the web page as text. In fact, the web page will have no text at all. This means that search engines can't index your page, and screen-readers for people with disabilities won't work.

✦ **Difficult updating:** If you find an error on your page, you have to modify the image, not just a piece of text. This makes updating your page more challenging than it would be with a plain HTML document.

✦ **File size issues:** An image large enough to fill a modern browser window will be extremely large and slow to download. Using this technique will all but eliminate users with slower access from using your site.

Problems with Flash

Another tool that's gained great popularity is the Flash animation tool from Adobe. This tool allows great flexibility in how you position things on a page and supports techniques that were once difficult or impossible in ordinary HTML, such as sound and video integration, automatic motion tweening, and path-based animation. Flash certainly had an important place in web development (especially for embedded games — check out my earlier book, *Beginning Flash Game Programming For Dummies,* published by John Wiley & Sons). Even though Flash has historic significance, you should avoid using it for ordinary web development for the following reasons:

+ **Cost:** The Flash editor isn't cheap, and it doesn't look like it'll get cheaper. The tool is great, but if free or low-cost alternatives work just as well, it's hard to justify the cost.

+ **Binary encoding:** All text in a Flash web page is stored in the Flash file itself. It's not visible to the browser. Flash pages (like image-based pages) don't work in web searches and aren't useful for people with screen-readers.

+ **Updating issues:** If you need to change your Flash-based page, you need the Flash editor installed. This can make it more difficult to keep your page up-to-date.

+ **No separation of content:** As far as the browser is concerned, there's no content but the Flash element, so there's absolutely no separation of content and layout. If you want to make a change, you have to change the Flash application.

+ **Search engine problems:** Code written in Flash can't always be read by search engines (though Google is working on the problem).

+ **Technical issues:** Flash is not integrated directly into the browser, which leads to a number of small complications. The Forward and Back buttons don't work as expected, printing can be problematic, and support is not universal.

+ **Limited mobile access:** Flash is not supported on iPhones and iPads, and support is limited on other mobile platforms. As the mobile platform becomes more and more important, it's hard to justify working with a system that is not supported on these platforms.

+ **It's no longer necessary:** HTML5, CSS3, and JavaScript have now addressed many of the shortcomings that once made Flash such a compelling alternative. You no longer need a plug-in to play audio and video, or to program games. (In fact, I now do all my web-based game programming in HTML5 — see another of my books, *HTML5 Game Programming For Dummies,* published by John Wiley & Sons).

Introducing the Floating Layout Mechanism

CSS supplies a couple techniques for layout. The preferred technique for most applications is a *floating layout.* The basic idea of this technique is to leave the HTML layout as simple as possible, but to provide style hints that tell the various elements how to interact with each other on the screen.

In a floating layout, you don't legislate exactly where everything will go. Instead, you provide hints and let the browser manage things for you. This ensures flexibility because the browser will try to follow your intentions, no matter what size or shape the browser window becomes. If the user resizes the browser, the page will flex to fit to the new size and shape, if possible.

Floating layouts typically involve less code than other kinds of layouts because only a few elements need specialized CSS. In most of the other layout techniques, you need to provide CSS for every single element to make things work as you expect.

Using float with images

The most common place to use the `float` attribute is with images. Figure 1-1 has a paragraph with an image embedded inside.

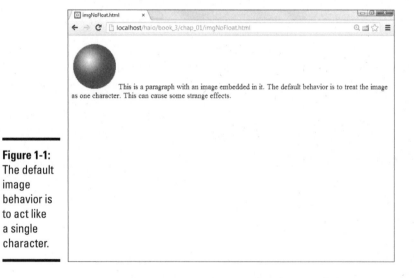

Figure 1-1:
The default image behavior is to act like a single character.

It's more likely that you want the image to take up the entire left part of the paragraph. The text should flow around the paragraph, similar to Figure 1-2.

When you add a `float:left` attribute to the `img` element, the image tends to move to the left, pushing other content to the right. Now, the text flows around the image. The image is actually removed from the normal flow of the page layout, so the paragraph takes up all the space. Inside the paragraph, the text avoids overwriting the image.

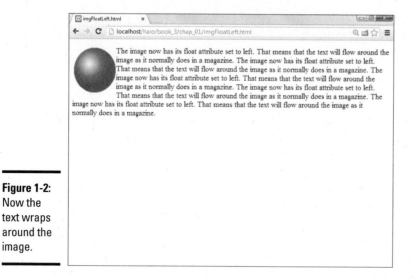

Figure 1-2:
Now the
text wraps
around the
image.

Adding the float property

The code for adding the `float` property is pretty simple:

```
<!DOCTYPE html>
<html lang = "en-US">

  <head>
    <meta charset = "UTF-8">
    <title>imgFloatLeft.html</title>
    <style type = "text/css">
      img {
        float: left;
      }
    </style>
  </head>
  <body>
    <p>
      <img src = "ball.gif"
           alt = "ball" />
      The image now has its float attribute set to left. That means
      that the text will flow around the image as it normally does
      in a magazine.
      The image now has its float attribute set to left. That means
      that the text will flow around the image as it normally does
      in a magazine.
      The image now has its float attribute set to left. That means
      that the text will flow around the image as it normally does
      in a magazine.
      The image now has its float attribute set to left. That means
      that the text will flow around the image as it normally does
      in a magazine.
      The image now has its float attribute set to left. That means
      that the text will flow around the image as it normally does
      in a magazine.
    </p>
  </body>
</html>
```

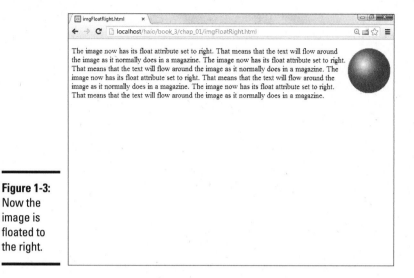

Figure 1-3:
Now the
image is
floated to
the right.

The only new element in the code is the CSS `float` attribute. The `img` object has a `float:left` attribute. It isn't necessary to change any other attributes of the paragraph because the paragraph text knows to float around the image.

Of course, you don't have to simply float to the left. Figure 1-3 shows the same page with the image's `float` attribute set to the right.

Using Float with Block-Level Elements

The `float` attribute isn't only for images. You can also use it with any element (typically `p` or `div`) to create new layouts. Using the `float` attribute to set the page layout is easy after you understand how things really work.

Floating a paragraph

Paragraphs and other block-level elements have a well-defined default behavior. They take the entire width of the page, and the next element appears below. When you apply the `float` element to a paragraph, the behavior of that paragraph doesn't change much, but the behavior of *succeeding* paragraphs is altered.

To illustrate, I take you all the way through the process of building two side-by-side paragraphs.

Begin by looking at a page with three paragraphs. Paragraph 2 has its `float` property set to `left`. Figure 1-4 illustrates such a page.

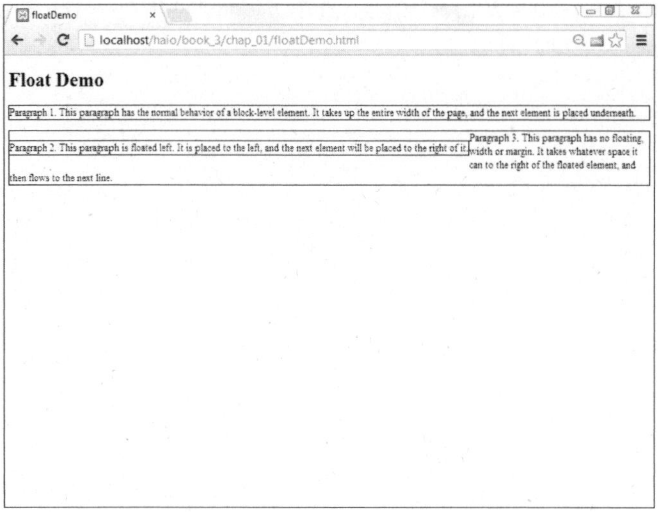

Figure 1-4:
Paragraphs
2 and 3
are acting
strangely.

As you can see, some strange formatting is going on here. I improve on things later to make the beginnings of a two-column layout, but for now, just take a look at what's going on:

✦ **I've added borders to the paragraphs.** As you'll see, the width of an element isn't always obvious by looking at its contents. When I'm messing around with `float`, I often put temporary borders on key elements so I can see what's going on. You can always remove the borders when you have it working right.

✦ **The first paragraph acts normally.** The first paragraph has the same behavior you see in all block-style elements. It takes the entire width of the page, and the next element will be placed below it.

✦ **The second paragraph is pretty normal.** The second paragraph has its `float` attribute set to `left`. This means that the paragraph will be placed in its normal position, but that other text will be placed to the right of this element.

✦ **The third paragraph seems skinny.** The third paragraph seems to surround the second, but the text is pushed to the right. The `float` parameter in the previous paragraph causes this one to be placed in any remaining space (which currently isn't much). The remaining space is on the right and eventually underneath the second paragraph.

The code to produce this is simple HTML with equally simple CSS markup:

```
<!DOCTYPE html>
<html lang = "en-US">

  <head>
    <meta charset = "UTF-8">
    <title>floatDemo</title>
    <style type = "text/css">
      p {
        border: 2px black solid;
      }
      .floated {
        float: left;
      }
    </style>
  </head>
  <body>
    <h1>Float Demo</h1>
    <p>
      Paragraph 1.
      This paragraph has the normal behavior of a block-level element.
      It takes up the entire width of the page, and the next element
      is placed underneath.
      </p>
    <p class = "floated">
      Paragraph 2.
      This paragraph is floated left. It is placed to the left, and the
      next element will be placed to the right of it.
    </p>
    <p>
      Paragraph 3.
      This paragraph has no floating, width or margin. It takes whatever
      space it can to the right of the floated element, and then flows
      to the next line.
    </p>
  </body>
</html>
```

As you can see from the code, I have a simple class called `floated` with the `float` property set to `left`. The paragraphs are defined in the ordinary way. Even though paragraph 2 seems to be embedded inside paragraph 3 in the screen shot, the code clearly shows that this isn't the case. The two paragraphs are completely separate.

I added a black border to each paragraph so you can see that the size of the element isn't always what you'd expect.

Adjusting the width

When you float an element, the behavior of succeeding elements is highly dependent on the width of the first element. This leads to a primary principle of float-based layout:

> If you float an element, you must also define its width.

The exception to this rule is elements with a predefined width, such as images and many form elements. These elements already have an implicit width, so you don't need to define width in the CSS. If in doubt, try setting the width at various values until you get the layout you're looking for.

Figure 1-5 shows the page after I adjusted the width of the floated paragraph to 50 percent of the page width.

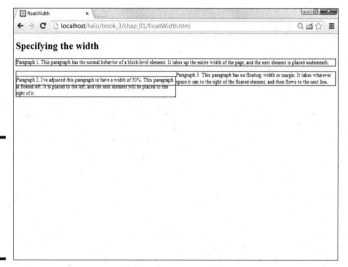

Figure 1-5:
The floated paragraph has a width of 50 percent of the page.

Things look better in Figure 1-5, but paragraph 2 still seems to be embedded inside paragraph 3. The only significant change is in the CSS style:

```
<style type = "text/css">
  p {
    border: 2px black solid;
  }
  .floated {
    float: left;
    width: 50%;
  }
</style>
```

I've added a `width` property to the floated element.

Elements that have the `float` attribute enabled generally also have a width defined, except for images or other elements with an inherent width.

When you use a percentage value in the context of width, you're expressing a percentage of the *parent* element (in this case, the body because the paragraph is embedded in the document body). Setting the `width` to 50% means I want this paragraph to span half the width of the document body.

Setting the next margin

Things still don't look quite right. I added the borders around each paragraph so you can see an important characteristic of floating elements. Even though the text of paragraph 3 wraps to the right of paragraph 2, the actual paragraph element still extends all the way to the left side of the page. The *element* doesn't necessarily flow around the floated element, but its *contents* do. The background color and border of paragraph 3 still take as much space as they normally would if paragraph 2 didn't exist.

This is because a floated element is removed from the normal flow of the page. Paragraph 3 has access to the space once occupied by paragraph 2, but the text in paragraph 3 will try to find its own space without stepping on text from paragraph 2.

Somehow, you need to tell paragraph 3 to move away from the paragraph 2 space. This isn't a difficult problem to solve after you recognize it. Figure 1-6 shows a solution.

Book III
Chapter 1

Fun with the
Fabulous Float

```
floatWidthMargin.html     ×
←  →  C    localhost/haio/book_3/chap_01/floatWidthMargin.html

Specifying the width

Paragraph 1. This paragraph has the normal behavior of a block-level element. It takes up the entire width of the page, and the next element is placed underneath.

Paragraph 2. This paragraph is floated left. The next element will be placed to the     Paragraph 3. This paragraph now has a margin-left so it is separated from the
right of it. Now this has a width of 50%.                                              previous paragraph. Its width is still automatically determined.
```

Figure 1-6:
The left
margin of
paragraph
3 is set
to give a
two-column
effect.

The `margin-left` property of paragraph 3 is set to 52 percent. Because the width of paragraph 2 is 50 percent, this provides a little gap between the columns. Take a look at the code to see what's going on here:

```
<!DOCTYPE html>
<html lang = "en-US">

  <head>
    <meta charset = "UTF-8">
    <title>floatWidthMargin.html</title>
    <style type = "text/css">
      p {
        border: 2px black solid;
      }
      .floated {
        float: left;
        width: 50%;
      }
      .right {
        margin-left: 52%;
      }
    </style>
  </head>
  <body>
    <h1>Specifying the width</h1>
    <p>
      Paragraph 1.
      This paragraph has the normal behavior of a block-level element.
      It takes up the entire width of the page, and the next element
      is placed underneath.
    </p>
    <p class = "floated">
      Paragraph 2.
      This paragraph is floated left. The
      next element will be placed to the right of it. Now this has a width
      of 50%.
    </p>
    <p class = "right">
      Paragraph 3.
      This paragraph now has a margin-left so it is separated from the
      previous paragraph. Its width is still automatically
      determined.
    </p>
  </body>
</html>
```

Using Float to Style Forms

Many page layout problems appear to require tables. Some clever use of the CSS float can help elements with multiple columns without the overhead of tables.

Forms cause a particular headache because a form often involves labels in a left column followed by input elements in the right column. You'd probably be tempted to put such a form in a table. Adding table tags makes the HTML much more complex and isn't required. It's much better to use CSS to manage the layout.

You can float elements to create attractive forms without requiring tables. Figure 1-7 shows a form with float used to line up the various elements.

As page design gets more involved, it makes more sense to think of the HTML and the CSS separately. The HTML will give you a sense of the overall intent of the page, and the CSS can be modified separately. Using external CSS is a natural extension of this philosophy. Begin by looking at floatForm. html and concentrate on the HTML structure before worrying about style:

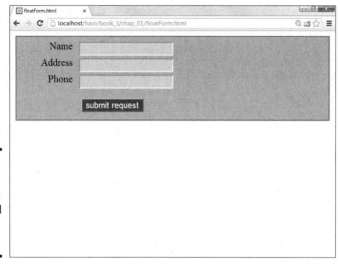

Figure 1-7:
This is a nice-looking form defined without a table.

**Book III
Chapter 1**

**Fun with the
Fabulous Float**

```
<!DOCTYPE html>
<html lang = "en-US">

  <head>
    <meta charset = "UTF-8">
    <title>floatForm.html</title>
    <link rel = "stylesheet"
          type = "text/css"
          href = "floatForm.css" />
  </head>
  <body>
    <form action = "">
      <fieldset>
        <label>Name</label>
        <input type = "text"
               id = "txtName" />
        <label>Address</label>
        <input type = "text"
               id = "txtAddress" />
        <label>Phone</label>
        <input type = "text"
               id = "txtPhone" />
        <button type = "button">
          submit request
        </button>
      </fieldset>
    </form>
  </body>
</html>
```

While you look over this code, note several interesting things about how the page is designed:

✦ **The CSS is external.** CSS is defined in an external document. This makes it easy to change the style and helps you to focus on the HTML document in isolation.

✦ **The HTML code is minimal.** The code is very clean. It includes a form with a `fieldset`. The `fieldset` contains labels, `input` elements, and a `button`.

✦ **There isn't a table.** There's no need to add a table as an artificial organization scheme. A table wouldn't add to the clarity of the page. The form elements themselves provide enough structure to allow all the formatting you need.

✦ **Labels are part of the design.** I used the `label` element throughout the form, giving me an element that can be styled however I wish.

✦ **Everything is selectable.** I'll want to apply one CSS style to labels, another to `input` elements, and a third style to the `button`. I've set up the HTML so I can use CSS selectors without requiring any `id` or `class` attributes.

✦ **There's a `button`.** I used a `button` element instead of `<input type = "button">` on purpose. This way, I can apply one style to all the `input` elements and a different style to the `button` element.

Designing a page like this one so its internal structure provides all the selectors you need is wonderful. This keeps the page very clean and easy to read. Still, don't be afraid to add classes or IDs if you need them.

Figure 1-8 demonstrates how the page looks with no CSS.

It's often a good idea to look at your page with straight HTML before you start messing around with CSS.

Figure 1-8: The plain HTML is a start, but some CSS would help a lot.

If you have a page with styles and you want to see how it will look without the style rules, use Chrome developer tools or Firebug. You can temporarily disable some or all CSS style rules to see the default content underneath. This can sometimes be extremely handy.

Using float to beautify the form

It'd be very nice to give the form a tabular feel, with each row containing a label and its associated input element. My first attempt at a CSS file for this page looked like this:

```
/* floatNoClear.css
   CSS file to go with float form
   Demonstrates use of float, width, margin
   Code looks fine but the output is horrible.
*/

fieldset {
  background-color: #AAAAFF;
}
label {
  float: left;
  width: 5em;
  text-align: right;
  margin-right: .5em;
}
input {
  background-color: #CCCCFF;
  float: left;
}
button {
  float: left;
  width: 10em;
  margin-left: 7em;
  margin-top: 1em;
  background-color: #0000CC;
  color: #FFFFFF;
}
```

**Book III
Chapter 1**

**Fun with the
Fabulous Float**

This CSS looks reasonable, but you'll find it doesn't quite work right. (I show the problem and how to fix it later in this chapter.) Here are the steps to build the CSS:

1. **Add colors to each element.**

   Colors are a great first step. For one thing, they ensure that your selectors are working correctly so that everything's where you think it is. This color scheme has a nice modern feel to it, with a lot of blues.

2. **Float the labels to the left.**

   Labels are all floated to the left, meaning they should move as far left as possible, and other things should be placed to the right of them.

3. **Set the label width to** 5em.

   This gives you plenty of space for the text the labels will contain.

4. **Set the labels to be right-aligned.**

   Right-aligning the labels makes the text snug up to the input elements but gives them a little margin-right so the text isn't too close.

5. **Set the** input's float **to** left.

   This tells each input element to go as far to the left (toward its label) as it can. The input element goes next to the label if possible and on the next line, if necessary. Like images, input elements have a default width, so it isn't absolutely necessary to define the width in CSS.

6. **Float the** button, **too, but give the** button **a little top margin so it has a respectable space at the top. Set the width to** 10em.

This seems to be a pretty good CSS file. It follows all the rules, but if you apply it to floatNoClear.html, you'll be surprised by the results shown in Figure 1-9.

After all that talk about how nice float-based layout is, you're probably expecting something a bit neater. If you play around with the page in your browser, you'll find that everything works well when the browser is narrow, but when you expand the width of the browser, it gets ugly. Figure 1-10 shows the form when the page is really skinny.

Figure 1-9:
This form is ... well ... ugly.

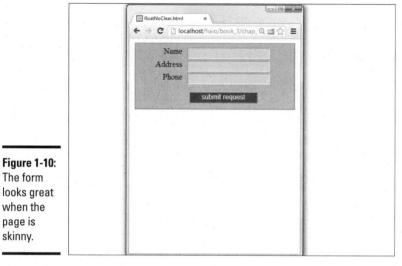

Figure 1-10:
The form looks great when the page is skinny.

Things get worse when the page is a little wider, as you can see in Figure 1-11.

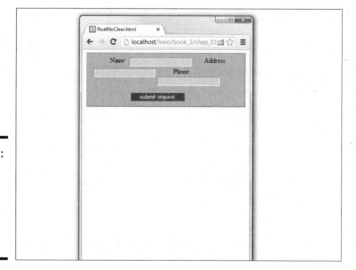

Figure 1-11:
With a slightly wider browser, things get strange.

If you make the page as wide as possible, you'll get a sense of what the browser was trying to accomplish in Figure 1-12.

Figure 1-12:
The browser
is trying to
put all the
inputs on
the same
line.

When CSS doesn't do what you want, it's usually acting on some false assumptions, which is the case here. Floating left causes an element to go as far to the left as possible and on the next line, if necessary. However, that's not really what you want on this page. The inputs should float next to the labels, but each label should begin its own line. The labels should float all the way to the left margin with the inputs floating left next to the labels.

Adjusting the fieldset width

One approach is to consider how well the page behaves when it's skinny because the new label and input combination will simply wrap down to the next line. You can always make a container narrow enough to force the behavior you're expecting. Because all the field elements are inside the `fieldset`, you can simply make it narrower to get a nice layout, as shown in Figure 1-13.

When you want to test changes in CSS, nothing beats the CSS editor in the Chrome developer tools. I made Figure 1-13 by editing the CSS on the fly with this tool.

Setting the width of the `fieldset` to `15em` does the job. Because the widths of the other elements are already determined, forcing them into a `15em`-wide box makes everything line up nicely with the normal wrapping behavior of the `float` attribute. If you don't want the width change to be so obvious, you can apply it to the `form` element, which doesn't have any visible attributes (unless you add them, such as `color` or `border`).

Figure 1-13:
With a
narrower
fieldset,
all the
elements
look much
nicer.

Unfortunately, this doesn't always work because the user may adjust the font size and mess up all your careful design.

Using the clear attribute to control page layout

Adjusting the width of the container is a suitable solution, but it does feel like a bit of a hack. There should be some way to make the form work right, regardless of the container's width. There is exactly such a mechanism.

The `clear` attribute is used on elements with a `float` attribute. The `clear` attribute can be set to `left`, `right`, or `both`. Setting the `clear` attribute to `left` means you want nothing to the left of this element. In other words, the element should be on the left margin of its container. That's exactly what you want here. Each label should begin its own line, so set its `clear` attribute to `left`.

To force the button onto its own line, set its `clear` attribute to `both`. This means that the button should have no elements to the left or the right. It should occupy a line all its own.

If you want an element to start a new line, set both its `float` and `clear` attributes to `left`. If you want an element to be on a line alone, set `float` to `left` and `clear` to `both`.

Using the `clear` attribute allows you to have a flexible-width container and still maintain reasonable control of the form design. Figure 1-14 shows that the form can be the same width as the page and still work correctly. This version works, no matter the width of the page.

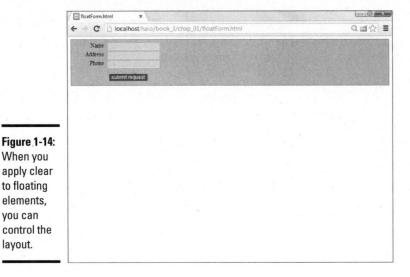

Figure 1-14:
When you
apply clear
to floating
elements,
you can
control the
layout.

Here's the final CSS code, including `clear` attributes in the labels and button:

```
/* floatForm.css
   CSS file to go with float form
   Demonstrates use of float, width, margin, and clear
*/

fieldset {
  background-color: #AAAAFF;
}

label {
  clear: left;
  float: left;
  width: 5em;
  text-align: right;
  margin-right: .5em;
}

input {
 float: left;
 background-color: #CCCCFF;
}

button {
  float: left;
  clear: both;
  margin-left: 7em;
  margin-top: 1em;
  background-color: #0000CC;
  color: #FFFFFF;
}
```

You now have the basic tools in place to use flow layout. Look to Chapter 2 of this minibook to see how these tools are put together to build a complete page layout.

Chapter 2: Building Floating Page Layouts

In This Chapter

✔ Creating a classic two-column page

✔ Creating a page-design diagram

✔ Using temporary background colors

✔ Creating fluid layouts and three-column layouts

✔ Working with and centering fixed-width layouts

The floating layout technique provides a good alternative to tables, frames, and other layout tricks formerly used. You can build many elegant multi-column page layouts with ordinary HTML and CSS styles.

Creating a Basic Two-Column Design

Many pages today use a two-column design with a header and footer. Such a page is quite easy to build with the techniques you read about in this chapter.

Designing the page

It's best to do your basic design work on paper, not on the computer. Here's my original sketch in Figure 2-1.

Draw the sketch first so you have some idea what you're aiming for. Your sketch should include the following information:

✦ **Overall page flow:** How many columns do you want? Will it have a header and footer?

✦ **Section names:** Each section needs an ID, which will be used in both the HTML and the CSS.

✦ **Width indicators:** How wide will each column be? (Of course, these widths should add up to 100 percent or less.)

✦ **Fixed or percentage widths:** Are the widths measured in percentages (of the browser size) or in a fixed measurement (pixels)? This has important implications. For this example, I'm using a dynamic width with percentage measurements.

✦ **Font considerations:** Do any of the sections require any specific font styles, faces, or colors?

```
+----------------------------------------------------------+
|              Header - centered text                      |
+----------+-----------------------------------------------+
| Left     |  Right                                        |
|          |                                               |
| 20%      |  80% wide                                     |
| wide     |  Newspaper style -                            |
|          |  all grayscale, single and                    |
|          |  double borders                               |
|          |                                               |
|          |                                               |
|          |                                               |
+----------+-----------------------------------------------+
|              Footer - centered text                      |
+----------------------------------------------------------+
```

Figure 2-1:
This is
a very
standard
two-column
style.

◆ **Color scheme:** What are the main colors of your site? What will be the color and background color of each section?

This particular sketch (in Figure 2-1) is very simple because the page will use default colors and fonts. For a more complex job, you need a much more detailed sketch. The point of the sketch is to separate design decisions from coding problems. Solve as much of the design stuff as possible first so you can concentrate on building the design with HTML and CSS.

A note to perfectionists

If you're really into detail and control, you'll find this chapter frustrating. People accustomed to having complete control of a design (as you often do in the print world) tend to get really stressed when they realize how little actual control they have over the appearance of a web page.

Really, it's okay. This is a good thing. When you design for the web, you give up absolute control, but you gain unbelievable flexibility. Use the ideas outlined in this chapter to get your page looking right on a standards-compliant browser. Take a deep breath and look at it on something else (like Internet Explorer 6 if you want to suffer a heart attack!). Everything you positioned so carefully is all messed up. Take another deep breath and use conditional comments to fix the offending code without changing how it works in those browsers that do things correctly. It is now becoming reasonable to expect most users to have a browser that is at least partially HTML5-compliant.

Building the HTML

After you have a basic design in place, you're ready to start building the HTML code that will be the framework. Start with basic CSS, but create a `div` for each section that will be in your final work. You can put a placeholder for the CSS, but don't add any CSS yet. Here's my basic code. I removed some of the redundant text to save space:

```
<!DOCTYPE html>
<html lang = "en-US">

  <head>
    <meta charset = "UTF-8">
    <title>twoColumn.html</title>
    <link rel = "stylesheet"
          type = "text/css"
          href = "twoCol.css" />
  </head>
  <body>
    <div id = "head">
      <h1>Two Columns with Float</h1>
    </div>
    <div id = "left">
      <h2>Left Column</h2>
      <p>
        Lorem ipsum dolor sit amet, consectetuer adipiscing elit. Vivamus dui.
      </p>
    </div>
    <div id = "right">
      <h2>Right Column</h2>
      <p>
        Lorem ipsum dolor sit amet, consectetuer adipiscing elit. Vivamus dui.
      </p>
    </div>
    <div id = "footer">
      <h3>Footer</h3>
    </div>
  </body>
</html>
```

Nothing at all is remarkable about this HTML code, but it has a few important features, such as

✦ **It's standards-compliant.** It's good to check and make sure the basic HTML code is well formed before you do a lot of CSS work with it. Sloppy HTML can cause you major headaches later.

✦ **It contains four divs.** The parts of the page that will be moved later are all encased in `div` elements.

✦ **Each `div` has an ID.** All the divs have an ID determined from the sketch.

✦ **No formatting is in the HTML.** The HTML code contains no formatting at all. That's left to the CSS.

✦ **It has no style yet.** Although a `<link>` tag is pointing to a style sheet, the style is currently empty.

Figure 2-2 shows what the page looks like before you add any CSS to it.

What's up with the Latin?

The flexible layouts built throughout this chapter require some kind of text so the browser knows how big to make things. The actual text isn't important, but something needs to be there.

Typesetters have a long tradition of using phony Latin phrases as filler text. Traditionally, this text has begun with the words "Lorem Ipsum," so it's called *Lorem Ipsum* text.

This particular version is semi-randomly generated from a database of Latin words.

If you want, you can also use Lorem Ipsum in your page layout exercises. Conduct a search

for Lorem Ipsum generators on the web to get as much fake text as you want for your mockup pages.

Although Lorem Ipsum text is useful in the screen shots, it adds nothing to the code listings. Throughout this chapter, I remove the Lorem Ipsum text from the code listings to save space. See the original files on the website for the full pages in all their Caesarean goodness. This book's Introduction explains how to access the companion website.

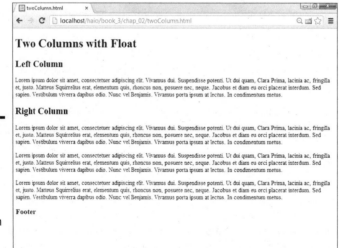

Figure 2-2:
The plain HTML is plain indeed; some CSS will come in handy.

Using temporary background colors

And now for one of my favorite CSS tricks... Before doing anything else, create a selector for each of the named divs and add a temporary background color to each div. Make each div a different color. The CSS might look like this:

```
#head {
  background-color: lightblue;
}
```

```
#left {
  background-color: yellow;
}

#right {
  background-color: green;
}

#footer {
  background-color: orange;
}
```

You won't keep these background colors, but they provide some very useful cues while you're working with the layout:

✦ **Testing the selectors:** While you change the background of each selector, you can see whether you've remembered the selector's name correctly. It's amazing how many times I've written code that I thought was broken just because I didn't write the selector properly.

✦ **Identifying the divs:** If you make each div a different color, it'll be easier to see which div is which when they are not acting the way you want.

✦ **Specifying the size of each div:** The text inside a div isn't always a good indicator of the actual size. The background color tells you what's really going on.

Of course, you won't leave these colors in place. They're just helpful tools for seeing what's going on during the design process. Look at bg.html and bg.css on the website to see the full code.

Figure 2-3 displays how the page looks with the background colors turned on.

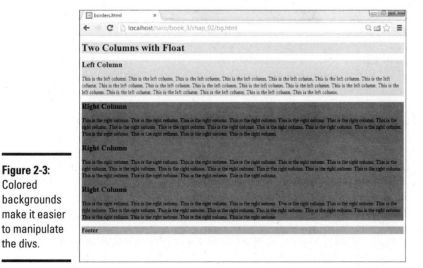

Figure 2-3:
Colored
backgrounds
make it easier
to manipulate
the divs.

It's fine that you can't see the actual colors in the black-and-white image in Figure 2-3. Just appreciate that when you see the page in its full-color splendor, the various colors will help you see what's going on.

Setting up the floating columns

This particular layout doesn't require major transformation. A few CSS rules will do the trick:

```
#head {
  border: 3px black solid;
}

#left {
  border: 3px red solid;
  float: left;
  width: 20%;
}

#right {
  border: 3px blue solid;
  float: left;
  width: 75%
}

#footer {
  border: 3px green solid;
  clear: both;
}
```

I made the following changes to the CSS:

✦ **Float the #left div.** Set the #left div's float property to left so other divs (specifically the #right div) are moved to the right of it.

✦ **Set the #left width.** When you float a div, you must also set its width. I've set the left div width to 20 percent of the page width as a starting point.

✦ **Float the #right div, too.** The right div can also be floated left, and it'll end up snug to the left div. Don't forget to add a width. I set the width of #right to 75 percent, leaving another 5 percent available for padding, margins, and borders.

✦ **Clear the footer.** The footer should take up the entire width of the page, so set its clear property to both.

Figure 2-4 shows how the page looks with this style sheet in place (see floated.html and floated.css on the website for complete code).

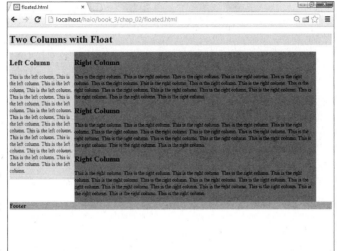

Figure 2-4:
Now, the left
column is
floated.

Tuning up the borders

The colored backgrounds in Figure 2-4 point out some important features of this layout scheme. For instance, the two columns are not the same height. This can have important implications.

You can change the borders to make the page look more like a column layout. I'm going for a newspaper-style look, so I use simple double borders. I put a black border under the header, a gray border to the left of the right column, and a gray border on top of the bottom segment. Tweaking the padding and centering the footer complete the look. Here's the complete CSS:

```
#head {
  border-bottom: 3px double black;
}
#left {
  float: left;
  width: 20%;
}
#right {
  float: left;
  width: 75%;
  border-left: 3px double gray;
}
#footer {
  clear: both;
  text-align: center;
  border-top: 3px double gray;
}
```

The final effect is shown in Figure 2-5.

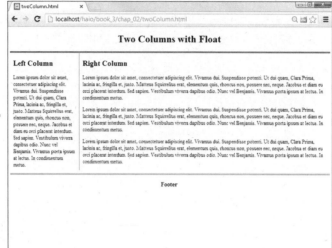

Figure 2-5:
This is a decent design, which adjusts with the page width.

Advantages of a fluid layout

This type of layout scheme (with floats and variable widths) is often called a *fluid* layout because it has columns but the sizes of the columns are dependent on the browser width. This is an important issue because, unlike layout in the print world, you really have no idea what size the browser window that displays your page will be. Even if the user has a widescreen monitor, the browser may be in a much smaller window. Fluid layouts can adapt to this situation quite well.

Fluid layouts (and indeed all other float-based layouts) have another great advantage. If the user turns off CSS or can't use it, the page still displays. The elements will simply be printed in order vertically, rather than in the intended layout. This can be especially handy for screen readers or devices with exceptionally small screens, like phones.

Using semantic tags

As web developers began using floating layout techniques, they almost always created divs called `nav`, `header`, and `footer`. The developers of HTML5 decided to create new elements with these names. Take a look at the following code to see the semantic tags in action.

```
<!DOCTYPE HTML>
<html lang="en">
<head>
```

```
<title>semantic</title>
<meta charset="UTF-8">
<style type = "text/css">
header {
  border-bottom: 5px double black;
}

nav {
  float: left;
  width: 20%;
  clear: left;
  min-height: 400px;
  border-right: 1px solid black;
}

section {
  float: left;
  width: 75%;
  padding-left: 1em;
}

article {
  float: left;
  width: 75%;
  padding-left: 1em;
}

footer {
  clear: both;
  border-top: 5px double black;
  text-align: center;
}

  </style>
</head>
<body>
  <header>
    <h1>This is my header</h1>
  </header>

  <nav>
    <h2>Navigation</h2>
    <ul>
      <li><a href="#">link a</a></li>
      <li><a href="#">link b</a></li>
      <li><a href="#">link c</a></li>
      <li><a href="#">link d</a></li>
      <li><a href="#">link e</a></li>
    </ul>
  </nav>

  <section id = "1">
    <h2>Section 1</h2>
    <p>Section body...</p>
  </section>

  <section id = "2">
    <h2>Section 2</h2>
    <p>Section body...</p>
  </section>
```

```
<article>
   <h2>Article</h2>
   <p>Article body...</p>
</article>

<footer>
   <h2>Footer</h2>
   <address>
     Andy Harris <br />
     <a href = "mailto:andy@aharrisbooks.net">
     andy@aharrisbooks.net</a>
   </address>
</footer>

</body>
</html>
```

As you can see, there are a number of new semantic markup tags in HTML5:

✦ **header:** This is not the same as the h1-h6 tags. It denotes a chunk of the page that will contain a header for the page. Often the header will fill up the page width, and will have some sort of banner image. It frequently contains h1 content.

✦ **nav:** This tag indicates some kind of navigation section. It has no particular style of its own, but it is frequently used as either a horizontal or vertical menu for site navigation.

✦ **section:** A section is used to specify a generic part of the page. You can have multiple sections on the same page.

✦ **article:** An article is like a section, but it's intended for use with external resources. Many pages are built automatically by software, and when these pages integrate content from other sources, it's intended to use the article tag to integrate this content.

✦ **footer:** A footer is intended to display footer contents at the bottom of a page. Typically a footer covers the bottom of a page, although this is not the default behavior.

Note that none of these elements have any specific formatting. It's up to you to provide formatting through CSS code. Each of the elements can be formatted directly as an HTML element (because that's what it is). All latest-version browsers support the semantic markup tags, but if you want to support older browsers (especially IE before version 8), you'll still need to use divs.

More fun with semantic tags

HTML5 introduced a number of other semantic tags. Most of them have no specific formatting. Still, you will run across them, so here are a few that seem likely to make the cut:

- ✔ `address`: Holds contact information.

- ✔ `aside`: Indicates a page fragment that is related to but separate from the main content.

- ✔ `menu/command`: Eventually, will allow a pop-up menu or toolbar. to be defined in the page, and commands will be embedded inside that menu. Not supported yet.

- ✔ `figure`: Incorporates an image and a caption.

- ✔ `figcaption`: Describes an image, normally enclosed in a figure tag.

- ✔ `time`: Display dates or times.

- ✔ `summary/detail`: A summary is visible at all times, and when it is clicked on, the detail appears. Not supported yet.

- ✔ `svg`: Allows you to use the SVG language to describe a vector image through code.

- ✔ `meter`: Indicates a numeric value falling within a specific range.

- ✔ `output`: Intended for output in interactive applications.

- ✔ `progress`: Should indicate progress of a task (but it doesn't look like a progress bar yet).

Building a Three-Column Design

Sometimes, you'll prefer a three-column design. It's a simple variation of the two-column approach. Figure 2-6 shows a simple three-column layout.

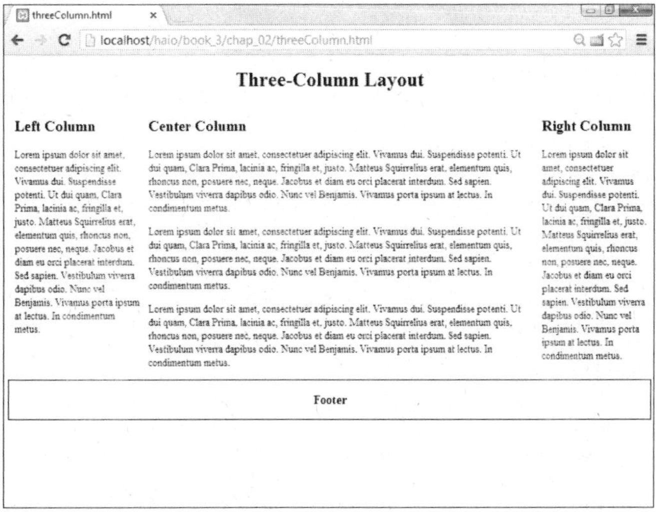

Figure 2-6:
This is
a three-
column
floating
layout.

This design uses very basic CSS with five named divs. Here's the code (with the dummy paragraph text removed for space):

```html
<!DOCTYPE html>
<html lang = "en-US">

  <head>
    <meta charset = "UTF-8">
    <title>threeColumn.html</title>
    <link rel = "stylesheet"
          type = "text/css"
          href = "threeColumn.css" />
  </head>
  <body>
    <div id = "head">
      <h1>Three-Column Layout</h1>
    </div>
    <div id = "left">
      <h2>Left Column</h2>
      <p>
        Lorem ipsum dolor sit amet, consectetuer adipiscing elit. Vivamus dui.
      </p>
    </div>
    <div id = "center">
      <h2>Center Column</h2>
      <p>
        Lorem ipsum dolor sit amet, consectetuer adipiscing elit. Vivamus dui.
      </p>
    </div>
    <div id = "right">
      <h2>Right Column</h2>
      <p>
        Lorem ipsum dolor sit amet, consectetuer adipiscing elit. Vivamus dui.
      </p>
    </div>
    <div id = "footer">
      <h3>Footer</h3>
    </div>
  </body>
</html>
```

Styling the three-column page

As you can see from the HTML, there isn't really much to this page. It has five named divs, and that's about it. All the really exciting stuff happens in the CSS:

```css
#head {
  text-align: center;
}

#left {
  float: left;
  width: 20%;
  padding-left: 1%;
}

#center {
  float: left;
```

```
    width: 60%;
    padding-left: 1%;
}

#right {
    float: left;
    width: 17%;
    padding-left: 1%;
}

#footer {
    border: 1px black solid;
    float: left;
    width: 100%;
    clear: both;
    text-align: center;
}
```

Each element (except the head) is floated with an appropriate width. The process for generating this page is similar to the two-column layout:

1. **Diagram the layout.**

   Begin with a general sense of how the page will look and the relative width of the columns. Include the names of all segments in this diagram.

2. **Create the HTML framework.**

   Create all the necessary divs, including `id` attributes. Add representative text so you can see the overall texture of the page.

3. **Add temporary background colors.**

   Add a temporary background color to each element so you can see what's going on when you start messing with `float` attributes. This also ensures you have all the selectors spelled properly.

4. **Float the leftmost element.**

   Add the `float` attribute to the leftmost column. Don't forget to specify a width (in percentage).

5. **Check your work.**

   Frequently save your work and view it in a browser. Use the browser's F5 key for a quick reload after you've saved the page.

6. **Float the center element.**

   Add `float` and `width` attributes to the center element.

7. **Float the right-most element.**

   Incorporate `float` and `width` in the right element.

8. **Ensure the widths total around 95 percent.**

   You want the sum of the widths to be nearly 100 percent but not quite. Generally, you need a little space for margins and padding. Final adjustments come later, but you certainly don't want to take up more than 100 percent of the available real estate.

9. **Float and clear the footer.**

   To get the footer acting right, you need to float it and clear it on both margins. Set its width to 100 percent, if you want.

10. **Tune up.**

    Remove the temporary borders, adjust the margins and padding, and set alignment as desired. Use percentages for margins and padding, and then adjust so all percentages equal 100 percent.

Early versions of Internet Explorer (6 and earlier) have a well-documented problem with margins and padding. According to the standards, the width of an element is supposed to be the width of the *content,* with borders, margins, and padding outside. A properly behaved browser won't shrink your content when you add borders and margins. The early versions of Internet Explorer (IE) counted the width as *including* all borders, padding, and margin, effectively shrinking the content when you added these elements. If your page layout is looking a little off with IE, this may be the problem. Use the conditional comment technique described in Chapter 5 of Book II to make a variant style for IE if this bothers you.

Problems with the floating layout

The floating layout solution is very elegant, but it does have one drawback. Figure 2-7 shows the three-column page with the background colors for each element.

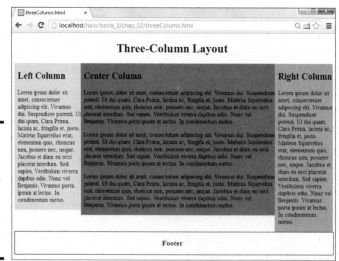

Figure 2-7: The columns aren't really columns; each is a different height.

Figure 2-7 shows an important aspect of this type of layout. The columns are actually blocks, and each is a different height. Typically, I think of a column as stretching the entire height of a page, but this isn't how CSS does it. If you want to give each column a different background color, for example, you'll want each column to be the same height. This can be done with a CSS trick (at least, for the compliant browsers).

Specifying a min-height

The standards-compliant browsers (all versions of Firefox and Opera, and IE 7+) support a `min-height` property. This specifies a minimum height for an element. You can use this property to force all columns to the same height. Figure 2-8 illustrates this effect.

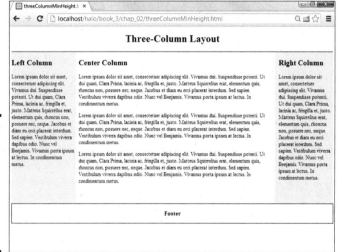

Figure 2-8: The min-height attribute forces all columns to be the same height.

The CSS code simply adds the `min-height` attribute to all the column elements:

```
#head {
  text-align: center;
  border-bottom: 3px double gray;
}

#left {
  float: left;
  width: 20%;
  min-height: 30em;
  background-color: #EEEEEE;
}

#center {
  float: left;
```

```
      width: 60%;
      padding-left: 1%;
      padding-right: 1%;
      min-height: 30em;
    }

    #right {
      float: left;
      width: 17%;
      padding-left: 1%;
      min-height: 30em;
      background-color: #EEEEEE;
    }

    #footer {
      border: 1px black solid;
      float: left;
      width: 100%;
      clear: both;
      text-align: center;
    }
```

Some guesswork is involved still. You have to experiment a bit to determine what the min-height should be. If you guess too short, one column will be longer than the min-height, and the columns won't appear correctly. If you guess too tall, you'll have a lot of empty space at the bottom of the screen.

All modern browsers support min-height, but a few of the older browsers may not support this attribute.

Using height and overflow

The min-height trick is ideal if you know the size of your content, but modern web development is all about multiple screen sizes. It's hard to predict how your page will look on a smart phone or other smaller browser. If you use min-height and the text is too large to fit the screen, you can use another strategy. You can set the height of each element if you wish using the height rule. Like all CSS, the height is a suggestion. The question is what to do when content that fits fine in a large browser is forced to fit in a smaller space. The answer is a range of techniques popularly called *responsive design*. The basic idea of responsive design is to design a page so it naturally adjusts to a good view regardless of the device it's on. One very basic approach to responsive design is to specify both width and height for a page element, but then allow the browser to manage overflow conditions. Figure 2-9 illustrates a page that is shrunk below the minimum size needed to display the text. See Book VII chapter 7 for more information on responsive web design and mobile web development.

Figure 2-9:
The page
is too small
to hold the
text. Note
the scroll
bar.

If you set the height and width to a specific percentage of the page width,
there is a danger the text will not fit. You can resolve this by adding an
`overflow` rule in your CSS.

Take a look at the CSS code used in overflow.html:

```
#head {
  text-align: center;
  border-bottom: 3px double gray;
}

#left {
  float: left;
  width: 20%;
  height: 30em;
  overflow: auto;
  background-color: #EEEEEE;
}

#center {
  float: left;
  width: 60%;
  padding-left: 1%;
  padding-right: 1%;
  height: 30em;
  overflow: auto;
}

#right {
  float: left;
  width: 17%;
  padding-left: 1%;
  height: 30em;
  overflow: auto;
  background-color: #EEEEEE;
}
```

```
#footer {
  border: 1px black solid;
  float: left;
  width: 100%;
  clear: both;
  text-align: center;
}
```

Setting the overflow property tells the browser what to do if it cannot place the text in the indicated space. Use `overflow: auto` to place scrollbars only when necessary. Other options for the `overflow` rule are `visible` (text flows outside the box — the default value), `hidden` (overflow is not shown), and `scroll` (always place a scrollbar). I prefer `auto`.

Building a Fixed-Width Layout

Fluid layouts are terrific. They're very flexible, and they're not hard to build. Sometimes, though, it's nice to use a fixed-width layout, particularly if you want your layout to conform to a particular background image.

The primary attribute of a fixed-width layout is the use of a fixed measurement (almost always pixels), rather than the percentage measurements used in a fluid layout.

Figure 2-10 shows a two-column page.

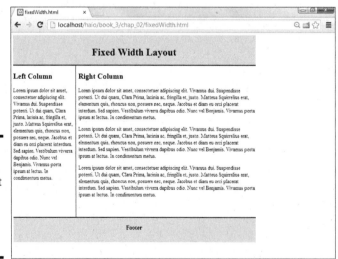

Figure 2-10: A fixed-width layout can work well but looks off-center.

The next examples will look off-center. Follow along to see what's going on, and see how to center a floated layout in the "Building a Centered Fixed-width Layout" section later in this chapter.

Setting up the HTML

As usual, the HTML code is minimal. It contains a few named divs. (Like usual, I've removed filler text for space reasons.)

```
<!DOCTYPE html>
<html lang = "en-US">

  <head>
    <meta charset = "UTF-8">
    <title>fixedWidth.html</title>
    <link rel = "stylesheet"
          type = "text/css"
          href = "fixedWidth.css" />
  </head>
  <body>
    <div id = "header">
      <h1>Fixed Width Layout</h1>
    </div>
    <div id = "left">
      <h2>Left Column</h2>
    </div>
    <div id = "right">
      <h2>Right Column</h2>
    </div>
    <div id = "footer">
      <h3>Footer</h3>
    </div>
  </body>
</html>
```

Fixing the width with CSS

After the HTML is set up, you can use CSS to enforce the two-column scheme.

Here's the CSS code:

```
#header {
  background-color: #e2e393;
  border-bottom: 3px solid black;
  text-align: center;
  width: 800px;
  padding-top: 1em;
}

#left {
  float: left;
  width: 200px;
  clear: left;
  border-right: 1px solid black;
  height: 30em;
  overflow: auto;
  padding-right: .5em;
}

#right {
  float: left;
  width: 570px;
```

```
    height: 30em;
    overflow: auto;
    padding-left: .5em;
}

#footer {
    width: 800px;
    text-align: center;
    background-color: #e2e393;
    border-top: 3px double black;
    clear: both;
}
```

It's all pretty straightforward:

1. **Color each element to see what's happening.**

   Begin by giving each div a different background color so you can see what is happening.

2. **Determine the overall width of the layout.**

   Pick a target width for the entire layout. I chose 800 pixels because it's a reasonably standard width.

3. **Adjust the widths of the page-wide elements.**

   It's often easiest to start with elements like the header and footer that often take up the entire width of the design.

4. **Float the columns.**

   The columns are floated as described throughout this chapter. Float each column to the left.

5. **Set the column widths.**

   Begin by making the column widths add up to the width of the entire design (in my case, 800 pixels). Later you'll adjust a bit for margins and borders.

6. **Clear the left column.**

   Ensure the left column has the clear: left rule applied.

7. **Set column heights.**

   Give each column the same height. This makes things look right if you add borders or background colors to the columns.

8. **Adjust borders and padding.**

   Use borders, padding, and margin to adjust your page to get the look you want. In my case, I added a border to the left column to separate the columns, and I added padding to keep the text from sitting right on the border.

9. **Adjust widths again.**

Adding borders, padding, and margin can change the widths of the existing elements. After you've modified these attributes, take a careful look at your layout to be sure it didn't get messed up, and modify the various widths if necessary.

Building a Centered Fixed-Width Layout

Fixed-width layouts are common, but they look a little strange if the browser isn't the width specified in the CSS. If the browser is too narrow, the layout won't work, and the second column will (usually) drop down to the next line.

If the browser is too wide, the page appears to be scrunched onto the left margin with a great deal of white space on the right.

The natural solution is to make a relatively narrow fixed-width design that's centered inside the entire page. Figure 2-11 illustrates a page with this technique.

Figure 2-11: Now the fixed-width layout is centered in the browser.

Some have called this type of design (fixed-width floating centered in the browser) a *jello* layout because it's not quite fluid and not quite fixed.

Making a surrogate body with an all div

In any case, the HTML requires only one new element, an `all` div that encases everything else inside the body (as usual, I removed the placeholder text):

```
<!DOCTYPE html>
<html lang = "en-US">

  <head>
    <meta charset = "UTF-8">
    <title>fixedWidthCentered.html</title>
    <link rel = "stylesheet"
          type = "text/css"
          href = "fixedWidthCentered.css" />
  </head>
  <body>
    <div id = "all">
      <div id = "header">
        <h1>Fixed Width Centered Layout</h1>
      </div>
      <div id = "left">
        <h2>Left Column</h2>
      </div>
      <div id = "right">
        <h2>Right Column</h2>
      </div>
      <div id = "footer">
        <h3>Footer</h3>
      </div>
    </div>
  </body>
</html>
```

The entire page contents are now encapsulated in a special `all` div. This div will be resized to a standard width (typically 640 or 800 pixels). The `all` element will be centered in the body, and the other elements will be placed inside `all` as if it were the body:

```
#all {
  width: 800px;
  height: 600px;
  margin-left: auto;
  margin-right: auto;
  border: 1px solid gray;
}

#header {
  background-color: #e2e393;
  border-bottom: 3px solid black;
  text-align: center;
  width: 800px;
  height: 100px;
  padding-top: 1em;
}
```

```
#left {
  float: left;
  width: 200px;
  clear: left;
  border-right: 1px solid black;
  height: 400px;
  padding-right: .5em;
}

#right {
  float: left;
  width: 580px;
  height: 400px;
  padding-left: .5em;
}

#footer {
  width: 800px;
  height: 60px;
  text-align: center;
  background-color: #e2e393;
  border-top: 3px double black;
  padding-bottom: 1em;
  clear: both;
}
```

How the jello layout works

This code is very similar to the `fixedWidth.css` style, but it has some important new features:

✦ **The `all` element has a fixed width.** This element's width will determine the width of the fixed part of the page.

✦ `all` **also needs a fixed height.** If you don't specify a height, `all` will be 0 pixels tall because all the elements inside it are floated.

✦ **Center `all`.** Remember, to center divs (or any other block-level elements) you set `margin-left` and `margin-right` both to `auto`.

✦ **Do *not* float `all`.** The `margin: auto` trick doesn't work on floated elements. `all` shouldn't have a `float` attribute set.

✦ **Ensure the interior widths add up to `all`'s width.** If `all` has a width of 800 pixels, be sure that the widths, borders, and margins of all the elements inside `all` add up to exactly 800 pixels. If you go even one pixel over, something will spill over and mess up the effect. You may have to fiddle with the widths to make everything work.

✦ **Adjust the heights:** If your design has a fixed height, you'll also need to fiddle with the heights to get everything to look exactly right. Calculations will get you close, but you'll usually need to spend some quality time fiddling with exact measurements to get everything just right.

**Book III
Chapter 2**

**Building Floating
Page Layouts**

Limitations of the jello layout

Jello layouts represent a compromise between fixed and fluid layouts, but they aren't perfect:

✦ **Implicit minimum width:** Very narrow browsers (like cellphones) can't render the layout the way you want. Fortunately, the content will still be visible, but not in exactly the format you wanted.

✦ **Wasted screen space:** If you make the rendered part of the page narrow, a lot of space isn't being used in higher-resolution browsers. This can be frustrating.

✦ **Complexity:** Although this layout technique is far simpler than table-based layouts, it's still a bit involved. You do have to plan your divs to make this type of layout work.

You can investigate a number of other layout techniques in Chapter 4 of this mini-book.

Doesn't CSS3 support columns?

If you've been looking through the CSS3 specifications (and what better bedtime reading is there?), you may have discovered the new column rule. I was pretty excited when I found support for columns because it seemed like the answer to the complexities of floating layouts. Unfortunately, the column mechanism isn't really useful for page layout. The columns are all exactly the same width, and there's no way to determine exactly which content is displayed in which column. It's useful if you want to have a magazine-style layout with text that flows in columns, but for page layout, CSS3 has a better new tool, the flexible box layout model (described in Chapter 4 of this mini-book). If you want to experiment with columns, take a look at this example from one of my other books: www.aharrisbooks.net/h5qr/part6/columns.html.

Chapter 3: Styling Lists and Menus

In This Chapter

✔ Using CSS styles with lists

✔ Building buttons from lists of links

✔ Dynamically displaying sublists

✔ Managing vertical and horizontal lists

✔ Building CSS-based menus

*M*ost pages consist of content and navigation tools. Almost all pages have a list of links somewhere on the page. Navigation menus are lists of links, but lists of links in plain HTML are ugly. There has to be a way to make 'em prettier.

It's remarkably easy to build solid navigation tools with CSS alone (at least, in the modern browsers that support CSS properly). In this chapter, you rescue your lists from the boring 1990s sensibility, turning them into dynamic buttons, horizontal lists, and even dynamically cascading menus.

Revisiting List Styles

HTML does provide some default list styling, but it's pretty dull. You often want to improve the appearance of a list of data. Most site navigation is essentially a list of links. One easy trick is to make your links appear as a set of buttons, as shown in Figure 3-1.

The buttons in Figure 3-1 are pretty nice. They have a 3D effect with shadows. They also act like buttons, with each button *depressing* when the mouse hovers over it. When you click one of these buttons, it acts like a link, taking you to another page, but they aren't really buttons at all, but a list, cleverly disguised to look and act like buttons.

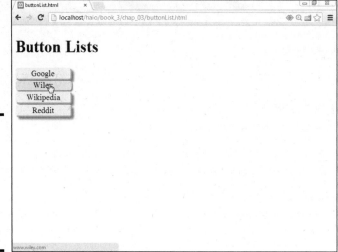

Figure 3-1:
These
buttons are
actually a
list. Note
that one
button is
depressed.

Defining navigation as a list of links

If you look at the HTML, you'll be astonished at its simplicity:

```
<!DOCTYPE html>
<html lang = "en-US">

  <head>
    <meta charset = "UTF-8">
    <title>buttonList.html</title>
    <link rel = "stylesheet"
          type = "text/css"
          href = "buttonList.css" />
  </head>
  <body>
    <h1>Button Lists</h1>
    <div id = "menu">
      <ul>
        <li><a href = "http://www.google.com">Google</a></li>
        <li><a href = "http://www.wiley.com">Wiley</a></li>
        <li><a href = "http://www.wikipedia.org">Wikipedia</a></li>
        <li><a href = "http://www.reddit.com">Reddit</a></li>
      </ul>
    </div>
  </body>
</html>
```

Turning links into buttons

As far as the HTML code is concerned, it's simply a list of links. There's nothing special here that makes this act like a group of buttons, except the creation of a div called `menu`. All the real work is done in CSS:

```
#menu li {
  list-style-type: none;
  width: 7em;
```

```
  text-align: center;
  margin-left: -2.5em;
}

#menu a {
  text-decoration: none;
  color: black;
  display: block;
  background-color: #EEEEFF;
  box-shadow: 5px 5px 5px gray;
  margin-bottom: 2px;
}

#menu a:hover {
  background-color: #DDDDEE;
  box-shadow: 3px 3px 3px gray;
  border: none;
}
```

The process for turning an ordinary list of links into a button group like this is simply an application of CSS tricks:

1. **Begin with an ordinary list that will validate properly.**

   It doesn't matter if you use an unordered or ordered list. Typically, the list will contain anchors to other pages. In this example, I'm using this list of links to some popular websites:

   ```
   <div id = "menu">
     <ul>
       <li><a href = "http://www.google.com">Google</a></li>
       <li><a href = "http://www.wiley.com">Wiley</a></li>
       <li><a href = "http://www.wikipedia.org">Wikipedia</a></li>
       <li><a href = "http://www.reddit.com">Reddit</a></li>
     </ul>
   </div>
   ```

2. **Enclose the list in a named div.**

   Typically, you still have ordinary links on a page. To indicate that these menu links should be handled differently, put them in a div named `menu`. All the CSS-style tricks described here refer to lists and anchors only when they're inside a `menu` div.

3. **Remove the bullets by setting the `list-style-type` to `none`.**

   This removes the bullets or numbers that usually appear in a list because these features distract from the effect you're aiming for (a group of buttons). Use CSS to specify how list items should be formatted when they appear in the context of the `menu` ID:

   ```
   #menu li {
     list-style-type: none;
     width: 5em;
     text-align: center;
     margin-left: -2.5em;
   }
   ```

TIP

4. **Specify the width of each button:**

```
width: 5em;
```

A group of buttons looks best if they're all the same size. Use the CSS width attribute to set each li to 5em.

5. **Remove the margin by using a negative margin-left value, as shown here:**

```
margin-left: -2.5em;
```

Lists have a default indentation of about 2.5em to make room for the bullets or numbers. Because this list won't have bullets, it doesn't need the indentations. Overwrite the default indenting behavior by setting margin-left to a negative value.

6. **Clean up the anchor by setting text-decoration to none and setting the anchor's color to something static, such as black text on light blue in this example:**

```
#menu a {
    text-decoration: none;
    color: black;
    display: block;
    background-color: #EEEEFF;
    box-shadow: 5px 5px 5px gray;
    margin-bottom: 2px;
}
```

The button's appearance will make it clear that users can click it, so this is one place you can remove the underlining that normally goes with links.

7. **Give each button a box shadow, as shown in the following:**

```
box-shadow: 5px 5px 5px gray;
```

The shadow makes it look like a 3D button sticking out from the page. This is best attached to the anchor, so you can swap the border when the mouse is hovering over the button.

8. **Set the anchor's display to block.**

This is a sneaky trick. Block display normally makes an element act like a block-level element inside its container. In the case of an anchor, the entire button becomes clickable, not just the text. This makes your page easier to use because the mouse has a much bigger target to aim for:

```
display: block;
```

9. **Provide a small gap to separate each element.**

Use the margin-bottom rule to separate each button. This will enhance the 3D effect by making the shadows more obvious.

```
margin-bottom: 2px;
```

10. **Provide a border radius for rounded corners.**

Use of the border-radius property gives the corners a nice rounded effect, enhancing the button feel.

11. **Use an outset border for a little more dimension.**

Setting the border to outset can give the buttons just a bit more 3D appeal.

12. Make the button depress when the mouse hovers on an anchor:

```
#menu a:hover {
  background-color: #DDDDEE;
  box-shadow: 3px 3px 3px gray;
  border: none;
}
```

When the mouse hovers on the button, the shadow is smaller, and the background color of the element is darker. I also removed the border, making the button feel flat. These techniques together give a convincing illusion of the button being depressed.

This list makes an ideal navigation menu, especially when placed inside one column of a multicolumn floating layout.

The shadow trick is easy, but there are many variations. If you prefer, you can build two empty button images (one up and one down) in your image editor and simply swap the background images rather than changing the shadows. Some variations also involve changing the border.

Building horizontal lists

Sometimes, you want horizontal button bars. Because HTML lists tend to be vertical, you might be tempted to think that a horizontal list is impossible. In fact, CSS provides all you need to convert exactly the same HTML to a horizontal list. Figure 3-2 shows such a page.

**Book 3
Chapter 3**

**Styling Lists
and Menus**

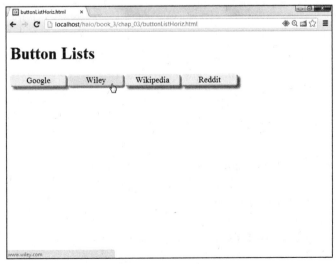

Figure 3-2:
This list
uses the
same HTML
but different
CSS.

There's no need to show the HTML again because it hasn't changed at all. (Ain't CSS grand?) Even the CSS hasn't changed much:

```
#menu ul {
  margin-left: -2.5em;
}

#menu li {
  list-style-type: none;
  width: 7em;
  text-align: center;
  float: left;
}

#menu a {
  text-decoration: none;
  color: black;
  display: block;
  background-color: #EEEEFF;
  box-shadow: 5px 5px 5px gray;
  margin-bottom: 2px;
  margin-right: 2px;
  border-radius: 5px;
  border: 3px outset #EEEEFF;
}

#menu a:hover {
  background-color: #DDDDEE;
  box-shadow: 3px 3px 3px gray;
  border: none;
}
```

The modifications are incredibly simple:

1. **Float each list item by giving each `li` a `float:left` value:**

   ```
   #menu li {
     list-style-type: none;
     float: left;
     width: 5em;
     text-align: center;
   }
   ```

2. **Move the `margin-left` of the entire `ul` by taking the `margin-left` formatting from the `li` elements and transferring it to the `ul`:**

   ```
   #menu ul {
     margin-left: -2.5em;
   }
   ```

3. **Add a right margin.**

   Now that the button bar is horizontal, add a little space to the right of each button so they don't look so crowded together:

   ```
   margin-right: 2px;
   ```

Creating Dynamic Lists

A simple list of buttons can look better than ordinary HTML links, but sometimes, your page needs to have a more complex navigation scheme. For example, you may want to create a menu system to help the user see the structure of your site.

When you think of a complex hierarchical organization (which is how most multipage websites end up), the easiest way to describe the structure is in a set of *nested* lists. HTML lists can contain other lists, and this can be a great way to organize data.

Nested lists are a great way to organize a lot of information, but they can be complicated. You can use some special tricks to make parts of your list appear and disappear when needed. In the sections "Hiding the inner lists" and "Getting the inner lists to appear on cue," later in this chapter, you expand this technique to build a menu system for your pages.

Building a nested list

Begin by creating a system of nested lists without any CSS at all. Figure 3-3 shows a page with a basic nested list.

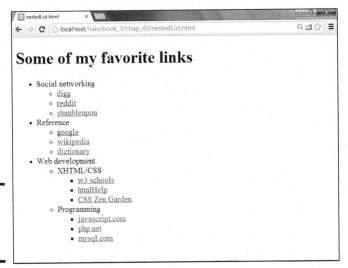

Figure 3-3:
This nested list has no styles yet.

No CSS styling is in place yet, but the list has its own complexities:

✦ **The primary list has three entries.** This is actually a multilayer list. The top level indicates categories, not necessarily links.

✦ **Each element in the top list has its own sublist.** A second layer of links has various links in most elements.

✦ **The Web Development element has another layer of sublists.** The general layout of this list entry corresponds to a complex hierarchy of information — like most complex websites.

✦ **The list validates to the HTML Strict standard.** It's especially important to validate your code before adding CSS when it involves somewhat complex HTML code, like the multilevel list. A small problem in the

HTML structure that may go unnoticed in a plain HTML document can cause all kinds of strange problems in your CSS.

Here is the code for the nested list in plain HTML:

```
<!DOCTYPE html>
<html lang = "en-US">

  <head>
    <meta charset = "UTF-8">
    <title>nestedList.html</title>
  </head>
  <body>
    <h1>Some of my favorite links</h1>
    <ul>
      <li>Social networking
        <ul>
          <li><a href = "http://www.digg.com">digg</a></li>
          <li><a href = "http://www.reddit.com">reddit</a></li>
          <li><a href = "http://www.stumbleupon.com">stumbleupon</a></li>
        </ul>
      </li>
      <li>Reference
        <ul>
          <li><a href = "http://www.google.com">google</a></li>
          <li><a href = "http://wikipedia.org">wikipedia</a></li>
          <li><a href = "http://dictionary.com">dictionary</a></li>
        </ul>
      </li>
      <li>Web development
        <ul>
          <li>XHTML/CSS
            <ul>
              <li><a href = "http://www.w3schools.com">w3 schools</a></li>
              <li><a href = "http://htmlhelp.com">htmlHelp</a></li>
              <li><a href = "http://www.csszengarden.com">CSS Zen Garden</a></li>
            </ul>
          </li>
          <li>Programming
            <ul>
              <li><a href = "http://javascript.com">javascript.com</a></li>
              <li><a href = "http://php.net">php.net</a></li>
              <li><a href = "http://www.mysql.com">mysql.com</a></li>
            </ul>
          </li>
        </ul>
      </li>
    </ul>
  </body>
</html>
```

Take special care with your indentation when making a complex nested list like this one. Without proper indentation, it becomes very difficult to establish the structure of the page. Also, a list item can contain text and another list. Any other arrangement (putting text between list items, for example) will cause a validation error and big headaches when you try to apply CSS.

Hiding the inner lists

The first step of creating a dynamic menu system is to hide any lists that are embedded in a list item. Add the following CSS style to your page:

```
li ul {
  display: none;
}
```

In reality, you usually apply this technique only to a specially marked div, like a menu system. Don't worry about that for now. Later in this chapter, I show you how to combine this technique with a variation of the button technique for complex menu systems.

Your page will undergo a startling transformation, as shown in Figure 3-4.

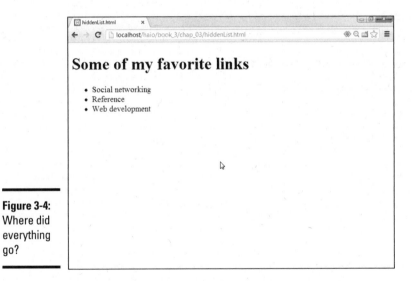

Figure 3-4:
Where did everything go?

Book 3
Chapter 3

Styling Lists and Menus

That tiny little snippet of CSS code is a real powerhouse. It does some fascinating things, such as

+ **Operating on unordered lists that appear inside list items:** What this really means is the topmost list won't be affected, but any unordered list that appears inside a list item will have the style applied.

+ **Using `display:none` to make text disappear:** Setting the `display` attribute to `none` tells the HTML page to hide the given data altogether.

This code works well on almost all browsers. It's pretty easy to make text disappear. Unfortunately, it's a little trickier to make all the browsers bring it back.

Getting the inner lists to appear on cue

The fun part is getting the interior lists to pop up when the mouse is over the parent element. A second CSS style can make this happen:

```
li ul {
  display: none;
}

li:hover ul {
  display: block;
}
```

The new code is pretty interesting. When the page initially loads, it appears the same as what's shown in Figure 3-4, but see the effect of holding the mouse over the Social Networking element in Figure 3-5.

Figure 3-5:
Holding the mouse over a list item causes its children to appear.

This code doesn't work on all browsers! Internet Explorer 6 (IE6) and earlier versions don't support the:hover pseudo-class on any element except a. Provide a conditional comment with an alternative style for early versions of IE. All modern browsers (including IE 7 and later) work fine.

Here's how the list-reappearing code works:

✦ **All lists inside lists are hidden.** The first style rule hides any list that's inside a list element.

✦ `li:hover` **refers to a list item that's being hovered on.** That is, if the mouse is situated on top of a list item, this rule pertains to it.

✦ `li:hover ul` **refers to an unordered list inside a hovered list item.** In other words, if some content is an unordered list that rests inside a list that currently has the mouse hovering over it, apply this rule. *(Whew!)*

✦ **Display the list as a block.** `display:block` overrides the previous `display:none` instruction and displays the particular element as a block. The text reappears magically.

This hide-and-seek trick isn't all that great on its own. It's actually quite annoying to have the contents pop up and go away like that. There's another more annoying problem. Look at Figure 3-6 to see what can go wrong.

Figure 3-6: If the mouse hovers on Web development, *both* submenus appear.

Book III
Chapter 3

Styling Lists and Menus

To see why this happens, take another look at the CSS code that causes the segment to reappear:

```
li:hover ul {
  display: block;
}
```

This code means set `display` to `block` for any `ul` that's a child of a hovered `li`. The problem is that the Web Development `li` contains a `ul` that contains *two more* `ul`s. All the lists under Web Development appear, not just the immediate child.

One more modification of the CSS fixes this problem:

```
li ul {
  display: none;
}

li:hover > ul {
  display: block;
}
```

The greater than symbol (>) is a special selector tool. It indicates a direct relationship. In other words, the `ul` must be a direct child of the hovered `li`, not a grandchild or great-grandchild. With this indicator in place, the page acts correctly, as shown in Figure 3-7.

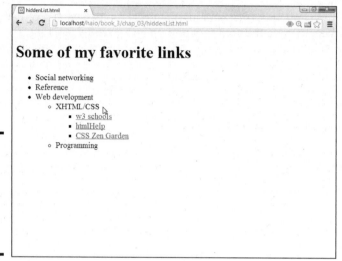

Figure 3-7:
Now, only the next menu level shows up on a mouse hover.

This trick allows you to create nested lists as deeply as you wish and to open any segment by hovering on its parent.

My current code has a list with three levels of nesting, but you can add as many nested lists as you want and use this code to make it act as a dynamic menu.

Figure 3-8 illustrates how to open the next section of the list.

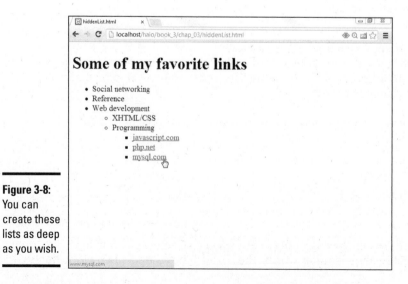

Figure 3-8:
You can create these lists as deep as you wish.

I'm not suggesting that this type of menu is a good idea. Having stuff pop around like this is actually pretty distracting. With a little more formatting, you can use these ideas to make a functional menu system. I'm just starting here so you can see the hide-and-seek behavior in a simpler system before adding more details.

Building a Basic Menu System

You can combine the techniques of buttons and collapsing lists to build a menu system entirely with CSS. Figure 3-9 shows a page with a vertically arranged menu.

Figure 3-9:
Only the top-level elements are visible by default.

**Book 3
Chapter 3**

**Styling Lists
and Menus**

When the user hovers over a part of the menu, the related sub-elements appear, as shown in Figure 3-10.

This type of menu has a couple interesting advantages, such as

✦ **It's written entirely with CSS.** You don't need any other code or programming language.

✦ **The menus are simply nested lists.** The HTML is simply a set of nested lists. If the CSS turns off, the page is displayed as a set of nested lists, and the links still function normally.

✦ **The relationships between elements are illustrated.** When you select an element, you can see its parent and sibling relationships easily.

Nice as this type of menu system is, it isn't perfect. Because it relies on the `li:hover` trick, it doesn't work in versions of Internet Explorer (IE) prior to 7.0. You need alternate CSS for these users.

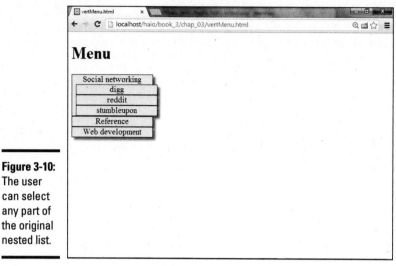

Figure 3-10:
The user
can select
any part of
the original
nested list.

Building a vertical menu with CSS

The vertical menu system works with exactly the same HTML as the `hiddenList` example — only the CSS changed. Here's the new CSS file:

```css
/* vertMenu.css */
/* unindent entire list */
#menu ul {
  margin-left: -2.5em;
}

/* set li as buttons */
#menu li {
  list-style-type: none;
  border: 1px black solid;;
  width: 10em;
  background-color: #cccccc;
  text-align: center;
}

/* display anchors as buttons */
#menu a {
  color: black;
  text-decoration: none;
  display: block;
}

/* flash white on anchor hover */
#menu a:hover {
  background-color: white;
}

/* collapse menus */
#menu li ul {
  display: none;
}
```

```
/* show submenus on hover */
#menu li:hover > ul {
  display: block;
  margin-left: -2em;
}
```

Of course, the CSS uses a few tricks, but there's really nothing new. It's just a combination of techniques you already know:

1. **Un-indent the entire list by setting the ul's margin-left to a negative value to compensate for the typical indentation. 2.5em is about the right amount.**

   Because you're removing the list-style types, the normal indentation of list items will become a problem.

2. **Format the li tags.**

   Each li tag inside the menu structure should look something like a button. Use CSS to accomplish this task:

   ```
   /* set li as buttons */
   #menu li {
     list-style-type: none;
     border: 1px black solid;
     width: 10em;
     background-color: #cccccc;
     text-align: center;
   }
   ```

   a. *Set list-style-type to none.*

   b. *Set a border with the border attribute.*

   c. *Center the text by setting text-align to center.*

   d. *Add a background color or image, or you'll get some strange border bleed-through later when the buttons overlap.*

3. **Format the anchors as follows:**

   ```
   /* display anchors as buttons */
   #menu a {
     color: black;
     text-decoration: none;
     display: block;
   }
   ```

   a. *Take out the underline with text-decoration: none.*

   b. *Give the anchor a consistent color.*

   c. *Set display to block (so the entire area will be clickable, not just the text).*

4. **Give some indication it's an anchor by changing the background when the user hovers on the element:**

   ```
   /* flash white on anchor hover */
   #menu a:hover {
     background-color: white;
   }
   ```

Book 3
Chapter 3

Styling Lists and Menus

Because the anchors no longer look like anchors, you have to do something else to indicate there's something special about these elements. When the user moves the mouse over any anchor tag in the menu div, that anchor's background color will switch to white.

5. **Collapse the menus using the hidden menus trick (discussed in the section "Hiding the inner lists," earlier in this chapter) to hide all the sublists:**

```
/* collapse menus */
#menu li ul {
  display: none;
}
```

6. **Display the hidden menus when the mouse hovers on the parent element by adding the code described in the "Getting the inner lists to appear on cue" section:**

```
/* show submenus on hover */
#menu li:hover > ul {
  display: block;
  margin-left: -2em;
}
```

Building a horizontal menu

You can make a variation of the menu structure that will work along the top of a page. Figure 3-11 shows how this might look.

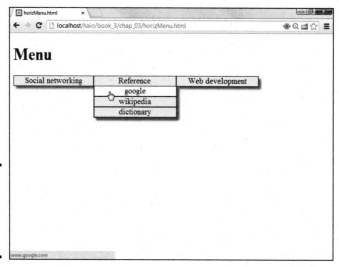

Figure 3-11:
The same list is now a horizontal menu.

The submenus come straight down from their parent elements. I find a little bit of indentation helpful for deeply nested lists, as shown in Figure 3-12.

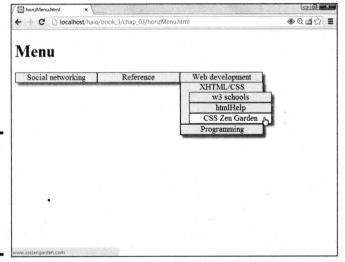

**Book 3
Chapter 3**

Styling Lists and Menus

Figure 3-12:
For the multilevel menus, a little bit of indentation is helpful.

Again, the HTML is identical. The CSS for a horizontal menu is surprisingly close to the vertical menu. The primary difference is floating the list items:

```
/* vertMenu.css */
/* unindent each unordered list */

#menu ul {
  margin-left: -2.5em;
}

/* turn each list item into a solid gray block */
#menu li {
  list-style-type: none;
  border: black solid 1px;
  float: left;
  width: 10em;
  background-color: #CCCCCC;
  text-align: center;
}

/* set anchors to act like buttons */
#menu a {
  display: block;
  color: black;
  text-decoration: none;
}

/* flash anchor white when hovered */
#menu a:hover {
  background-color: white;
}

/* collapse nested lists */
#menu li ul {
  display: none;
}
```

```
/* display sublists on hover */
#menu li:hover > ul {
  display: block;
}

/* indent third-generation lists */
#menu li li li{
  margin-left: 1em;
}
```

The CSS code has just a few variations from the vertical menu CSS:

✦ Float each list item by adding `float` and `width` attributes.

```
/* turn each list item into a solid gray block */
#menu li {
  list-style-type: none;
  border: black solid 1px;
  float: left;
  width: 10em;
  background-color: #CCCCCC;
  text-align: center;
}
```

This causes the list items to appear next to each other in the same line.

✦ Give each list item a width. In this case, `10em` seems about right.

✦ Indent a deeply nested list by having the first-order sublists appear directly below the parent.

A list nested deeper than its parent is hard to read. A little indentation helps a lot with clarity.

✦ Use `#menu li li li` to indent nested list items, as shown here:

```
/* indent third-generation lists */
#menu li li li{
  margin-left: 1em;
}
```

This selector is active on an element which has #menu and three list items in its family tree. It will work only on list items three levels deep. This special formatting isn't needed at the other levels but is helpful to offset the third-level list items.

These tricks are just the beginning of what you can do with some creativity and the amazing power of CSS and HTML. You can adopt the simple examples presented here to create your own marvels of navigation.

These menu systems work pretty well, but if they're used in a standard layout system, the rest of the page can shift around to fit the changing shape of the menus. To avoid this, place the menu using the fixed mechanisms described in Chapter 4 of this minibook.

Chapter 4: Using Alternative Positioning

In This Chapter

✔ **Setting position to absolute**

✔ **Managing z-index**

✔ **Creating fixed and flexible layouts**

✔ **Working with fixed and relative positioning**

✔ **Using the new flexbox model**

*F*loating layouts (described in Chapter 2 of this minibook) are the preferred way to set up page layouts today but, sometimes, other alternatives are useful. You can use *absolute, relative,* or *fixed positioning* techniques to put all your page elements exactly where you want them. Well, *almost* exactly. It's still web development, where nothing's exact. Because none of these alternatives are completely satisfying, the W3C (web standards body) has introduced a very promising new layout model called the *flexbox model.*

The techniques described in this chapter will give you even more capabilities when it comes to setting up great-looking websites.

Working with Absolute Positioning

Begin by considering the default layout mechanism. Figure 4-1 shows a page with two paragraphs on it.

I used CSS to give each paragraph a different color (to aid in discussion later) and to set a specific height and width. The positioning is left to the default layout manager, which positions the second (black) paragraph directly below the first (blue) one.

Setting up the HTML

The code is unsurprising:

```
<!DOCTYPE html>
<html lang = "en-US">
 <head>
    <meta charset = "UTF-8">
```

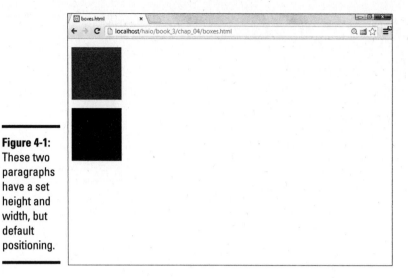

Figure 4-1:
These two
paragraphs
have a set
height and
width, but
default
positioning.

```
<title>boxes.html</title>
<style type = "text/css">
  #blueBox {
     background-color: blue;
     width: 100px;
     height: 100px;
  }
  #blackBox {
     background-color: black;
     width: 100px;
     height: 100px;
  }
</style>
</head>
<body>
  <p id = "blueBox"></p>
  <p id = "blackBox"></p>
</body>
</html>
```

If you provide no further guidance, paragraphs (like other block-level elements) tend to provide carriage returns before and after themselves, stacking on top of each other. The default layout techniques ensure that nothing ever overlaps.

Adding position guidelines

Figure 4-2 shows something new: The paragraphs are overlapping!

This feat is accomplished through some new CSS attributes:

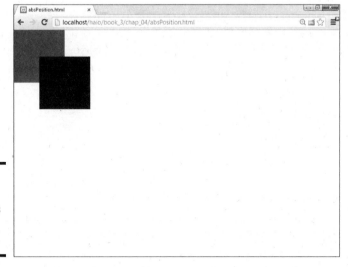

Figure 4-2:
Now the paragraphs overlap each other.

```
<!DOCTYPE html>
<html lang = "en-US">

  <head>
    <meta charset = "UTF-8">
    <title>absPosition.html</title>
    <style type = "text/css">
      #blueBox {
        background-color: blue;
        width: 100px;
        height: 100px;
        position: absolute;
        left: 0px;
        top: 0px;
        margin: 0px;
      }
      #blackBox {
        background-color: black;
        width: 100px;
        height: 100px;
        position: absolute;
        left: 50px;
        top: 50px;
        margin: 0px;
      }
    </style>
  </head>
  <body>
    <p id = "blueBox"></p>
    <p id = "blackBox"></p>
  </body>
</html>
```

**Book III
Chapter 4**

**Using
Alternative
Positioning**

So, why do I care if the boxes overlap? Well, you might not care, but the interesting part is this: You can have much more precise control over where elements live and what size they are. You can even override the browser's normal tendency to keep elements from overlapping, which gives you some interesting options.

Making absolute positioning work

A few new parts of CSS allow this more direct control of the size and position of these elements. Here's the CSS for one of the boxes:

```
#blueBox {
  background-color: blue;
  width: 100px;
  height: 100px;
  position: absolute;
  left: 0px;
  top: 0px;
  margin: 0px;
}
```

1. **Set the `position` attribute to `absolute`.**

   Absolute positioning can be used to determine exactly (more or less) where the element will be placed on the screen:

   ```
   position: absolute;
   ```

2. **Specify a `left` position in the CSS.**

   After you determine that an element will have `absolute` position, it's removed from the normal flow, so you're obligated to fix its position. The `left` attribute determines where the left edge of the element will go. This can be specified with any of the measurement units, but it's typically measured in pixels:

   ```
   left: 0px;
   ```

3. **Specify a `top` position with CSS.**

   The `top` attribute indicates where the top of the element will go. Again, this is usually specified in pixels:

   ```
   top: 0px;
   ```

4. **Use the `height` and `width` attributes to determine the size.**

   Normally, when you specify a position, you also want to determine the size:

   ```
   width: 100px;
   height: 100px;
   ```

5. **Set the margins to 0.**

   When you're using absolute positioning, you're exercising quite a bit of control. Because browsers don't treat margins identically, you're better off setting margins to 0 and controlling the spacing between elements manually:

   ```
   margin: 0px;
   ```

 Generally, you use absolute positioning only on named elements, rather than classes or general element types. For example, you won't want all the paragraphs on a page to have the same size and position, or you couldn't see them all. Absolute positioning works on only one element at a time.

Managing z-index

When you use absolute positioning, you can determine exactly where things are placed, so it's possible for them to overlap. By default, elements described later in HTML are positioned on top of elements described earlier. This is why the black box appears over the top of the blue box in Figure 4-2.

Handling depth

You can use a special CSS attribute called z-index to change this default behavior. The z-axis refers to how close an element appears to be to the viewer. Figure 4-3 demonstrates how this works.

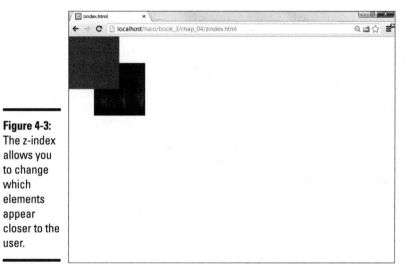

Figure 4-3: The z-index allows you to change which elements appear closer to the user.

The z-index attribute requires a numeric value. Higher numbers mean the element is closer to the user (or on *top*). Any value for z-index places the element higher than elements with the default z-index. This can be very useful when you have elements that you want to appear over the top of other elements (for example, menus that temporarily appear on top of other text).

Here's the code illustrating the z-index effect:

```
<!DOCTYPE html>
<html lang = "en-US">

  <head>
    <meta charset = "UTF-8">
    <title>zindex.html</title>
    <style type = "text/css">
      #blueBox {
        background-color: blue;
        width: 100px;
        height: 100px;
        position: absolute;
```

```
      left: 0px;
      top: 0px;
      margin: 0px;
      z-index: 1;
   }
   #blackBox {
      background-color: black;
      width: 100px;
      height: 100px;
      position: absolute;
      left: 50px;
      top: 50px;
      margin: 0px;
   }
  </style>
 </head>
 <body>
  <p id = "blueBox"></p>
  <p id = "blackBox"></p>
 </body>
</html>
```

Working with z-index

The only change in this code is the addition of the z-index property. The higher a z-index value is, the closer that object appears to be to the user. Here are a couple things to keep in mind when using z-index:

✦ **One element can totally conceal another.** When you start positioning things absolutely, one element can seem to disappear because it's completely covered by another. The z-index attribute is a good way to check for this situation.

✦ **Negative z-index can be problematic.** The value for z-index should be positive. Although negative values are supported, some browsers (notably older versions of Firefox) do not handle them well and may cause your element to disappear.

✦ **It may be best to give all values a z-index.** If you define the z-index for some elements and leave the z-index undefined for others, you have no guarantee exactly what will happen. If in doubt, just give every value its own z-index, and you'll know exactly what should overlap what.

✦ **Don't give two elements the same z-index.** The point of the z-index is to clearly define which element should appear closer. Don't defeat this purpose by assigning the same z-index value to two different elements on the same page.

Building a Page Layout with Absolute Positioning

You can use absolute positioning to create a page layout. This process involves some trade-offs. You tend to get better control of your page with absolute positioning (compared to floating techniques), but absolute layout requires more planning and more attention to detail. Figure 4-4 shows a page layout created with absolute positioning techniques.

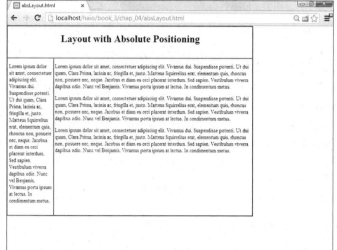

Book III
Chapter 4

Using
Alternative
Positioning

Figure 4-4:
This layout
was created
with
absolute
positioning.

The technique for creating an absolutely positioned layout is similar to the floating technique (in the general sense).

Overview of absolute layout

Before you begin putting your page together with absolute positioning, it's good to plan the entire process. Here's an example of how the process should go:

1. **Plan the site.**

   Having a drawing that specifies how your site layout will look is really important. In absolute positioning, your planning is even more important than the floating designs because you'll need to specify the size and position of every element.

2. **Specify an overall size.**

   This particular type of layout has a fixed size. Create an `all` div housing all the other elements and specify the size of this div (in a fixed unit for now, usually `px` or `em`).

3. **Create the HTML.**

   The HTML page should have a named div for each part of the page (so if you have headers, columns, and footers, you need a div for each).

4. **Build a CSS style sheet.**

   The CSS styles can be internal or linked, but because absolute positioning tends to require a little more markup than floating, external styles are preferred.

5. **Identify each element.**

   It's easier to see what's going on if you assign a different colored border to each element.

6. **Make each element absolutely positioned.**

   Set `position: absolute` in the CSS for each element in the layout.

7. **Specify the size of each element.**

   Set the `height` and `width` of each element according to your diagram. (You *did* make a diagram, right?)

8. **Determine the position of each element.**

   Use the `left` and `top` attributes to determine where each element goes in the layout.

9. **Tune-up your layout.**

   You'll probably want to adjust margins and borders. You may need to do some adjustments to make it all work. For example, the menu is `150px` wide, but I added `padding-left` and `padding-right` of `5px` each. This means the width of the menu needs to be adjusted to `140px` to make everything still fit.

Writing the HTML

The HTML code is pretty straightforward:

```
<!DOCTYPE html>
<html lang = "en-US">

  <head>
    <meta charset = "UTF-8">
    <title>absLayout.html</title>
    <link rel = "stylesheet"
          type = "text/css"
          href = "absLayout.css" />
  </head>
  <body>
    <div id = "all">
      <div id = "head">
        <h1>Layout with Absolute Positioning</h1>
      </div>

      <div id = "menu">
      </div>

      <div id = "content">
      </div>

    </div>
  </body>
</html>
```

(As typical with layout examples, I have removed the lorem text from this code listing for clarity.)

The HTML file calls an external style sheet called absLayout.css.

Adding the CSS

The CSS code is a bit lengthy but not too difficult:

```
/* absLayout.css */
#all {
  border: 1px solid black;
  width: 800px;
  height: 600px;
  position: absolute;
  left: 0px;
  top: 0px;
}

#head {
  border: 1px solid green;
  position: absolute;
  width: 800px;
  height: 100px;
  top: 0px;
  left: 0px;
  text-align: center;
}

#menu {
  border: 1px solid red;
  position: absolute;
  width: 140px;
  height: 500px;
  top: 100px;
  left: 0px;
  padding-left: 5px;
  padding-right: 5px;
}

#content{
  border: 1px solid blue;
  position: absolute;
  width: 645px;
  height: 500px;
  top: 100px;
  left: 150px;
  padding-left: 5px;
}
```

Book III
Chapter 4

Using
Alternative
Positioning

A static layout created with absolute positioning has a few important features to keep in mind:

✦ **You're committed to position everything.** After you start using absolute positioning, you need to use it throughout your site. All the main page elements require absolute positioning because the normal flow mechanism is no longer in place.

You can still use floating layout *inside* an element with absolute position, but all your main elements (heading, columns, and footing) need to have absolute position if one of them does.

✦ **You should specify size and position.** With a floating layout, you're still encouraging a certain amount of fluidity. Absolute positioning means you're taking the responsibility for both the shape and size of *each* element in the layout.

✦ **Absolute positioning is less adaptable.** With this technique, you're pretty much bound to a specific screen width and height. You'll have trouble adapting to tablets and cellphones. (A more flexible alternative is shown in the next section.)

✦ **All the widths and the heights have to add up.** When you determine the size of your display, all the heights, widths, margins, padding, and borders have to add up, or you'll get some strange results. When you use absolute positioning, you're also likely to spend some quality time with your calculator, figuring out all the widths and the heights.

Creating a More Flexible Layout

You can build a layout with absolute positioning and some flexibility. Figure 4-5 illustrates such a design.

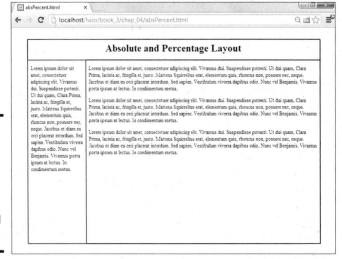

Figure 4-5: This page uses absolute layout, but it doesn't have a fixed size.

The size of this layout is attached to the size of the browser screen. It attempts to adjust to the browser while it's resized. You can see this effect in Figure 4-6.

Figure 4-6:
The layout resizes in proportion to the browser window.

The page simply takes up a fixed percentage of the browser screen. The proportions are all maintained, no matter what the screen size is.

Having the page resize with the browser works, but it's not a complete solution. When the browser window is small enough, the text will no longer fit without some ugly bleed-over effects. You can fix this with the overflow attribute, but then you will have scrollbars in your smaller elements.

Designing with percentages

This *absolute but flexible* trick is achieved by using percentage measurements. The position is still set to absolute, but rather than defining size and position with pixels, use percentages instead. Here's the CSS:

```
/* absPercent.css */

#all {
  border: 1px black solid;
  position: absolute;
  left: 5%;
  top: 5%;
  width: 90%;
  height: 90%;
}
```

```
#head {
  border: 1px black solid;
  position: absolute;
  left: 0%;
  top: 0%;
  width: 100%;
  height: 10%;
  text-align: center;
}

#head h1 {
  margin-top: 1%;
}

#menu {
  border: 1px green solid;
  position: absolute;
  left: 0%;
  top: 10%;
  width: 18%;
  height: 90%;
  padding-left: 1%;
  padding-right: 1%;
  overflow: auto;
}

#content {
  border: 1px black solid;
  position: absolute;
  left: 20%;
  top: 10%;
  width: 78%;
  height: 90%;
  padding-left: 1%;
  padding-right: 1%;
  overflow: auto;
}
```

The key to any absolute positioning (even this flexible kind) is math. When you just look at the code, it isn't clear where all those numbers come from. Look at the diagram for the page in Figure 4-7 to see how all the values are derived.

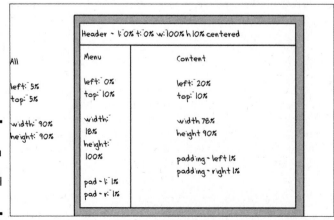

Figure 4-7:
The diagram is the key to a successful layout.

Building the layout

Here's how the layout works:

1. **Create an `all` container by building a div with the `all` ID.**

   The `all` container will hold *all* the contents of the page. It isn't absolutely necessary in this type of layout, but it does allow for a centering effect.

2. **Specify the size and position of `all`.**

   I want the content of the page to be centered in the browser window, so I set its height and width to 90 percent, and its `margin-left` and `margin-top` to 5 percent. In effect, this sets the `margin-right` and `margin-bottom` to 5 percent also. These percentages refer to the `all` div's container element, which is the body, with the same size as the browser window.

3. **Other percentages are in relationship to the `all` container.**

   Because all the other elements are placed inside `all`, the percentage values are no longer referring to the entire browser window. The widths and heights for the menu and content areas are calculated as percentages of their container, which is `all`.

4. **Determine the heights.**

   Height is usually pretty straightforward because you don't usually have to change the margins. Remember, though, that the head accounts for 10 percent of the page space, so the height of both the menu and content needs to be 90 percent.

5. **Figure the general widths.**

   In principle, the width of the menu column is 20 percent, and the content column is 80 percent. This isn't entirely accurate, though.

6. **Compensate for margins.**

   You probably want some margins, or the text looks cramped. If you want 1 percent `margin-left` and 1 percent `margin-right` on the menu column, you have to set the menu's width to 18 percent to compensate for the margins. Likewise, set the content width to 78 percent to compensate for margins.

As if this weren't complex enough, remember that Internet Explorer 6 (IE6) and earlier browsers calculate margins differently! In these browsers, the margin happens *inside* the content, so you don't have to compensate for them (but you have to remember that they make the useable content area smaller). You'll probably have to make a conditional comment style sheet to handle IE6 if you use absolute positioning.

Exploring Other Types of Positioning

If you use the position attribute, you're most likely to use `absolute`. However, here are other positioning techniques that can be handy in certain circumstances:

✦ **Relative:** Set `position: relative` when you want to move an element from its default position. For example, if you set position to `relative` and `top: -10px`, the element would be placed 10 pixels higher on the screen than normal.

✦ **Fixed:** Use fixed position when you want an element to stay in the same place, even when the page is scrolled. This is sometimes used to keep a menu on the screen when the contents are longer than the screen width. If you use fixed positioning, be sure you're not overwriting something already on the screen.

The real trick is to use appropriate combinations of positioning schemes to solve interesting problems.

Creating a fixed menu system

Figure 4-8 illustrates a very common type of web page — one with a menu on the left and a number of stories or topics in the main area.

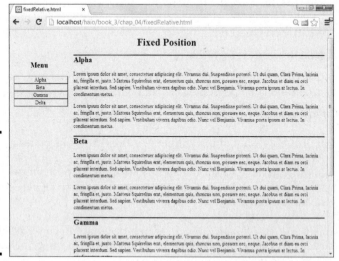

Figure 4-8: At first glance, this is yet another two-column layout.

Something is interesting about this particular design. The button list on the left refers to specific segments of the page. When you click one of these buttons (say, the Gamma button), the appropriate part of the page is called up, as shown in Figure 4-9.

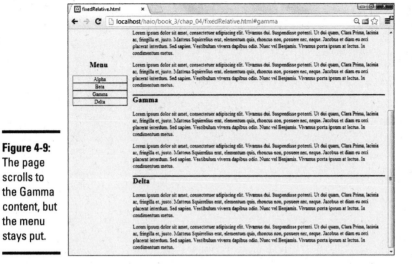

Book III
Chapter 4

Using
Alternative
Positioning

Figure 4-9:
The page
scrolls to
the Gamma
content, but
the menu
stays put.

Normally, when you scroll down the page, things on the top of the page (like the menu) disappear. In this case, the menu stays on the screen, even though the part of the page where it was originally placed is now off the screen.

Gamma isn't necessarily moved to the top of the page. Linking to an element ensures that it's visible but doesn't guarantee where it will appear.

You can achieve this effect using a combination of positioning techniques.

Setting up the HTML

The HTML for the fixed menu page is simple (as you'd expect by now):

```
<!DOCTYPE html>
<html lang = "en-US">

  <head>
    <meta charset = "UTF-8">
    <title>fixedRelative.html</title>
    <link rel = "stylesheet"
          type = "text/css"
          href = "fixedRelative.css" />
  </head>
  <body>
    <h1>Fixed Position</h1>
    <div id = "menu">
      <h2>Menu</h2>
      <ul>
        <li><a href = "#alpha">Alpha</a></li>
        <li><a href = "#beta">Beta</a></li>
        <li><a href = "#gamma">Gamma</a></li>
        <li><a href = "#delta">Delta</a></li>
      </ul>
```

```
      </div>

      <div class = "content"
          id = "alpha">
          <h2>Alpha</h2>
      </div>

      <div class = "content"
          id = "beta">
          <h2>Beta</h2>
      </div>

      <div class = "content"
          id = "gamma">
          <h2>Gamma</h2>
      </div>

      <div class = "content"
          id = "delta">
          <h2>Delta</h2>
      </div>
    </body>
</html>
```

The HTML has only a few noteworthy characteristics:

✦ **It has a menu.** The div named menu contains a list of links (like most menus).

✦ **The menu has internal links.** A menu can contain links to external documents or (like this one) links inside the current document. The `<a href = "#alpha">Alpha</a>` code means create a link to the element in this page with the ID alpha.

✦ **The page has a series of content divs.** Most of the page's content appears in one of the several divs with the content class. This class indicates all these divs will share some formatting.

✦ **The content divs have separate IDs.** Although all the content divs are part of the same class, each has its own ID. This allows the menu to select individual items (and would also allow individual styling, if desired).

As normal for this type of code, I left out the filler paragraphs from the code listing.

Setting the CSS values

The interesting work happens in CSS. Here's an overview of the code:

```
/* fixedRelative.css */

body {
  background-color: #fff9bf;
}
```

```
h1 {
 text-align: center;
}

#menu {
  position: fixed;
  width: 18%;
}

#menu li {
  list-style-type: none;
  margin-left: -2em;
  text-align: center;
}

#menu a{
  display: block;
  border: 2px gray outset;
  text-decoration: none;
  color: black;
}

#menu a:hover{
  color: white;
  background-color: black;
  border: 2px gray inset;
}

#menu h2 {
  text-align: center;
}

.content {
  position: relative;
  left: 20%;
  width: 80%;
}

.content h2 {
  border-top: 3px black double;
}
```

Most of the CSS is familiar if you've looked over the other chapters in this minibook. I changed the menu list to make it look like a set of buttons, and I added some basic formatting to the headings and borders. The interesting thing here is how I positioned various elements.

Here's how you build a fixed menu:

1. **Set the menu position to** `fixed` **by setting the** `position` **attribute to** `fixed`**.**

   The `menu` div should stay on the same spot, even while the rest of the page scrolls. Fixed positioning causes the menu to stay put, no matter what else happens on the page.

2. **Give the menu a width with the** `width` **attribute.**

   It's important that the width of the menu be predictable, both for aesthetic reasons and to make sure the content isn't overwritten by the menu. In this example, I set the menu width to 18 percent of the page width (20 percent minus some margin space).

3. **Consider the menu position by explicitly setting the `top` and `left` attributes.**

   When you specify a fixed position, you can determine where the element is placed on the screen with the `left` and `top` attributes. I felt that the default position was fine, so I didn't change it.

4. **Set `content` position to `relative`.**

   By default, all members of the `content` class will fill out the entire page width. Because the menu needs the leftmost 20 percent of the page, set the `content` class position to `relative`.

5. **Change `content`'s `left` attribute to 20 percent.**

   Because `content` has `relative` positioning, setting the left to 20 percent will add 20 percent of the parent element to each `content`'s `left` value. This will ensure that there's room for the menu to the left of all the content panes.

6. **Give `content` a `width` property.**

   If you don't define the width, `content` panels may bleed off the right side of the page. Use the `width` property to ensure this doesn't happen.

 In reality, I rarely use absolute positioning for page layout. It's just too difficult to get working and too inflexible for the range of modern browsers. However, it is still used in certain specialty situations like web game development where the programmer is deliberately subverting normal layout schemes for more control of the visual interface.

Flexible Box Layout Model

Page layout has been a constant concern in web development. There have been many different approaches to page layout, and all have weaknesses. The current standard is the floating mechanism. While this works quite well, it has two major weaknesses.

✦ **It can be hard to understand:** The various parts of the float specification can be difficult to follow, and the behavior is not intuitive. The relationship between `width`, `clear`, and `float` attributes can be difficult to follow.

✦ **The page order matters:** One goal of semantic layout is to completely divorce the way the page is created from how it is displayed. With the floating layout, the order in which various elements are written in the HTML document influences how they are placed. An ideal layout solution would allow any kind of placement through CSS, even after the HTML is finished.

Absolute positioning seems great at first, but it has its own problems:

✦ **It's a lot more detail-oriented:** Absolute positioning is a commitment. You often end up having to directly control the size and position of every element on the screen, which is tedious and difficult.

✦ **It's not as flexible:** With responsive design (creating a page that can adapt to the many different devices available) all the rage today, the absolute position scheme simply doesn't deliver the flexibility needed in modern web development.

There are some other layout mechanisms (tables and frames) that have already been rejected as viable layout options, which seems to leave web programmers without an ideal solution.

Creating a flexible box layout

CSS3 proposes a new layout mechanism which aims to solve a lot of the layout problems that have plagued web development. The flexible box layout scheme (sometimes called *flexbox*) shows a lot of promise. Here's essentially how it works (I'm deliberately leaving out details here for clarity. Read on for specific implementation):

Book III
Chapter 4

**Using
Alternative
Positioning**

1. **Designate a page segment as a box**.

   The `display` attribute of most elements can be set to various types. CSS3 introduces a new display type: `box`. Setting the display of an element to `box` makes it capable of holding other elements with the flexible box mechanism.

2. **Determine the orientation of child elements.**

   Use a new attribute called `box-orient` to determine if the child elements of the current element will be placed vertically or horizontally inside the main element.

3. **Specify the weight of child elements.**

   Each child element can be given a numeric weight. The weight determines how much space that element takes up. If the weight is zero, the element takes as little space as possible. If the weight of all the elements is one, they all take up the same amount of space. If one element has a weight of two and the others all have a weight of one, the larger element has twice the size of the others, and so on. Weight is determined through the `box-flex` attribute.

4. **Nest another box inside the first.**

   You can nest flexboxes inside each other. Simply apply the `box` display type to inner elements that will show the display.

5. **Modify the order in which elements appear.**

   Normally elements appear in the order in which they were placed on the page, but you can use the `box-ordinal-group` attribute to adjust the placement order.

Viewing a flexible box layout

As an example, take a look at the following HTML code:

```
<div id = "a">
  <div id = "b">b</div>
  <div id = "c">c</div>
  <div id = "d">
    <div id = "e">e</div>
    <div id = "f">f</div>
  </div>
</div>
```

Although this is a clearly made-up example, it shows a complex structure that could be difficult to style using standard layout techniques. Figure 4-10 illustrates a complex nested style that would be difficult to achieve through traditional layout techniques:

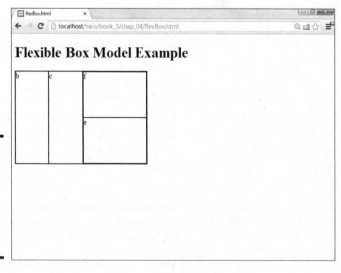

Figure 4-10: This structure would not be easy to build with CSS2.

The following style sheet is used to apply a flex grid style to this page:

```css
div {
  border: 1px solid black;
}

#a {
  width: 300px;
  height: 200px;

  display: box;
  box-orient: horizontal;
}

#b {
  box-flex: 1;
}

#c {
  box-flex: 1;
}

#d {
  display: box;
  box-orient: vertical;
  box-flex: 2;
}

#e {
  box-flex: 1;
    box-ordinal-group: 2;
}

#f {
  box-flex: 1;
}
```

The CSS looks complex, but there are only four new CSS elements. Here's how this specific example works:

1. **Set up a to be the primary container.**

   The a div is the primary container, so give it a height and width. It will contain flex boxes, so set the `display` attribute to `box`. Determine how you want the children of this box to be lined up by setting the `box-orient` attribute to `vertical` or `horizontal`.

2. **Specify the weights of b, c, and d.**

   In my example, I want elements b and c to take up half the space, and d to fill up the remainder of the space. To get this behavior, set the `box-flex` value of b and c to 1, and the box-flex value of d to 2.

3. **Set up d as another container.**

   The d element will contain e and f. Use `display: box` to make d a flex container, and `box-orient` to `vertical` to make the elements line up vertically. (Normally nested elements will switch between horizontal and vertical.)

4. **Elements e and f should each take half of d.**

   Use the `box-flex` attribute to give these elements equal weight.

5. **Change the ordinal group of e so it appears after f.**

   The `box-ordinal-group` attribute indicates the order in which an element will be displayed inside its group. Normally, all items have a default value of 1, so they appear in the order they are written. You can demote an element by setting its `box-ordinal-group` value to a higher number, causing that element to be displayed later than normal. I set e to ordinal group 2, so it is displayed after element f.

... And now for a little reality

The flexbox system seems perfect. It's much more sensible than the Byzantine layout techniques that are currently in use. However, the flexible box system is not ready for common use yet. Right now, not a single browser implements the flexbox attributes directly. However, there are special vendor-specific versions available. WebKit-based browsers (primarily Safari and Chrome) use variations that begin with `-webkit-` and Gecko-based browsers (Firefox and Mozilla) use the `-moz-` prefix. Microsoft finally supports flexbox, but it requires the `-ms-`. To make the example in this chapter work in modern browsers, you need to include `-ms-`, `-webkit-` and `-moz-` versions of all the attributes, like this:

```
#a {
  width: 300px;
  height: 200px;

  box-orient: horizontal;
  display: box;

  -moz-box-orient: horizontal;
  display: -moz-box;

  -webkit-box-orient: horizontal;
  display: -webkit-box;

  -ms-box-orient: horizontal;
  display: -ms-box;
}

#b {
  box-flex: 1;
  -moz-box-flex: 1;
  -webkit-box-flex: 1;
  -ms-box-flex: 1;
}
```

None of the browsers currently support the vanilla version, but I put it in anyway because hopefully in the near future only that version will be necessary. This technique is worth learning about because it may well become the preferred layout technique in the future.

For a complete example, take a look at Figure 4-11, which shows a standard two-column page.

Figure 4-11:
This
standard
layout uses
flexbox.

Though you can't tell from the screen shot, this page uses HTML5 through-out, including the new semantic tags (See the sidebar for a discussion of semantic tags) and a flexbox layout model.

Although the CSS code may look complex, it's actually quite simple, but repeated four times to handle all the various browser prefixes:

```
<!DOCTYPE HTML>
    <html lang = "en">
    <head>
      <title>flexTwoCol.html</title>
      <meta charset = "UTF-8" />
      <style type = "text/css">
        #all {
            display: box;
            display: -moz-box;
            display: -wekbit-box;
            display: -ms-box;

            box-orient: vertical;
            -moz-box-orient: vertical;
            -webkit-box-orient: vertical;
            -ms-box-orient: vertical;

            height: 400px;
            width: 600px;
            margin-right: auto;
            margin-left: auto;
        }

        #main {
            display: box;
            display: -moz-box;
            display: -webkit-box;
            display: -ms-box;
```

```
      box-orient: horizontal;
      -moz-box-orient: horizontal;
      -webkit-box-orient: horizontal;
      -ms-box-orient: horizontal;
    }

    #nav {
      box-flex: 1;
      -moz-box-flex: 1;
      -webkit-box-flex: 1;
      -ms-box-flex: 1;
    }

    #article {
      box-flex: 6;
      -moz-box-flex: 6;
      -webkit-box-flex: 6;
      -ms-box-flex: 6;
    }

    header, footer {
      display:block;
      text-align: center;
    }
  </style>
</head>

<body>
  <div id = "all">
    <header>
      <hgroup>
        <h1>Two Column Demo</h1>
        <h2>Using flexbox layout</h2>
      </hgroup>
    </header>

    <div id = "main">

      <div id = "nav">
        <h2>Navigation List</h2>
        <ul>
          <li><a href = "#">one</a></li>
          <li><a href = "#">two</a></li>
          <li><a href = "#">three</a></li>
          <li><a href = "#">four</a></li>
          <li><a href = "#">five</a></li>
        </ul>
      </div>

      <div id = "article">
        <h2>Main content</h2>
      </div>
    </div>

    <footer>
      <h2>Andy Harris</h2>
      <a href = "http://www.aharrisbooks.net">
         http://www.aharrisbooks.net</a>
    </footer>
  </div>
</body>
</html>
```

Introducing Semantic Layout Tags

Web developers have embraced the idea of semantic markup, which is all about labeling things based on their *meaning*. Soon enough, nearly every page had a number of divs with the same name: div id = "header", div id = "navigation", div id = "footer", and so on.

HTML5 finally released a set of semantic markup elements to describe the standard page elements. Here's a list of the most important ones:

<header> - describes the header area of your page

<nav> - navigation element, often contains some sort of menu system

<section> - contains a section of content

<article> - contains an article – typically generated from an external source

<footer> - contains the footer elements

The semantic elements are useful because they simplify markup. Unfortunately, all the browsers do not yet recognize these elements. They will render just fine, but it may be a while before CSS can be used with these elements with any confidence.

The flexbox approach is really promising. When you get used to it, flexbox is less mysterious than the `float` approach, and far more flexible than absolute positioning. Essentially, my page uses a fixed width div and places a flexbox inside it. There's no need to worry about `float`, `clear`, or any specific measurements except the one for the all div. The only downside is the need to code the CSS for all the browser prefixes. For now, I fix that with macros in my text editor.

Determining Your Layout Scheme

All these layout options might just make your head spin. What's the right strategy? Well, that depends.

The most important thing is to find a technique you're comfortable with that gives you all the flexibility you need.

Floating layouts are generally your best bet, but it's good to know how absolute positioning works. Every once in a while, you find a situation where absolute positioning is a good idea, but generally it's more difficult to pull off than the floating mechanism.

Absolute positioning seems very attractive at first because it promises so much control. The truth is, it's pretty complicated to pull off well, it isn't quite as flexible as the floating layout techniques, and it's hard to make it work right in older browsers.

Sometimes, fixed and relative positioning schemes are handy, as in the example introduced in the fixed menu example described in this chapter.

The flexbox approach seems very promising, but it's currently tedious to write as you'll need to repeat your code for all the browser prefixes. When it can be used without prefixes, it will probably become the dominant scheme.

Sometimes, you'll find it's best to combine schemes. (It's difficult to combine absolute positioning with another scheme, but you can safely combine floating, fixed, and relative positioning techniques most of the time.)

The main point is to understand the various options available to you so you can make a good choice for whatever project you're currently working on.

Part IV
Client-Side Programming with JavaScript

Visit www.dummies.com/extras/html5css3aio for more on JavaScript Libraries.

Contents at a Glance

Chapter 1: Getting Started with JavaScript

In This Chapter

✔ Adding JavaScript code to your pages

✔ Setting up your environment for JavaScript

✔ Creating variables

✔ Inputting and outputting with modal dialogs

✔ Using concatenation to build text data

✔ Understanding data types

✔ Using string methods and properties

✔ Using conversion functions

Web pages are defined by the HTML code and fleshed out by CSS. But to make them move and breathe, sing, and dance, you need to add a programming language or two. If you thought building web pages was cool, you're going to love what you can do with a little programming. Programming is what makes pages interact with the user. Interactivity is the "new" in "new media" (if you ask me, anyway). Learn to program, and your pages come alive.

Sometimes people are nervous about programming. It seems difficult and mysterious, and only super-geeks do it. That's a bunch of nonsense. Programming is no more difficult than HTML and CSS. It's a natural extension, and you're going to like it.

In this chapter, you discover how to add code to your web pages. You use a language called JavaScript, which is already built into most web browsers. You don't need to buy any special software, compilers, or special tools because you build JavaScript just like HTML and CSS — in an ordinary text editor or a specialty editor such as Aptana.

Working in JavaScript

JavaScript is a programming language first developed by Netscape Communications. It is now standard on nearly every browser. You should know a few things about JavaScript right away:

+ **It's a real programming language.** Don't let anybody tell you otherwise. Sure, JavaScript doesn't have all the same features as a monster, such as C++ or VB.NET, but it still has all the hallmarks of a complete programming language.

+ **It's not Java.** Sun Microsystems developed a language called Java, which is also sometimes used in web programming. Despite the similar names, Java and JavaScript are completely different languages. The original plan was for JavaScript to be a simpler language for controlling more complex Java applets, but that never really panned out.

Don't go telling people you're programming in Java. Java people love to act all superior and condescending when JavaScript programmers make this mistake. If you're not sure, ask a question on my web page. I can help you with either language.

+ **It's a scripting language.** As programming languages go, JavaScript's pretty friendly. It's not quite as strict or wordy as some other languages. It also doesn't require any special steps (such as compilation), so it's pretty easy to use. These things make JavaScript a great first language.

Choosing a JavaScript editor

Even though JavaScript is a programming language, it is still basically text. Because it's normally embedded in a web page, you can work in the same text editor you're using for HTML and CSS. I'm a big fan of Komodo because the same general features you've been enjoying in HTML and CSS are even more important when you're writing code in a more formal programming language:

+ **Syntax highlighting:** Like it does with HTML and CSS, Komodo automatically adjusts code colors to help you see what's going on in your program. As you see in the later sidebar "Concatenation and your editor," this adjustment can be a big benefit when things get complicated.

+ **Code completion:** When you type the name of an object, Komodo provides you with a list of possible completions. This shortcut can be really helpful because you don't have to memorize all the details of the various functions and commands.

+ **Pop-up help:** As you enter a function that Komodo recognizes, it automatically pops up a help menu explaining what the function does and what parameters could be placed there.

Picking your test browser

In addition to your editor, you should think again about your browser when you're testing JavaScript code. All the major browsers support JavaScript, and the support for JavaScript is relatively similar across the browsers (at least for the stuff in this chapter). However, browsers aren't equal when it comes to testing your code.

Things will go wrong when you write JavaScript code, and the browser is responsible for telling you what went wrong. Chrome is by far the favorite browser for JavaScript programmers today because it has extremely powerful editing tools. The Firebug plug-in adds many of the same features to other browsers, but it's probably best to start with Chrome because everything you need is already built-in. See Chapter 3 of this mini-book for much more on debugging JavaScript code.

Writing Your First JavaScript Program

The foundation of any JavaScript program is a standard web page like the ones featured in the first three minibooks.

To create your first JavaScript program, you need to add JavaScript code to your pages. Figure 1-1 shows the classic first program in any language.

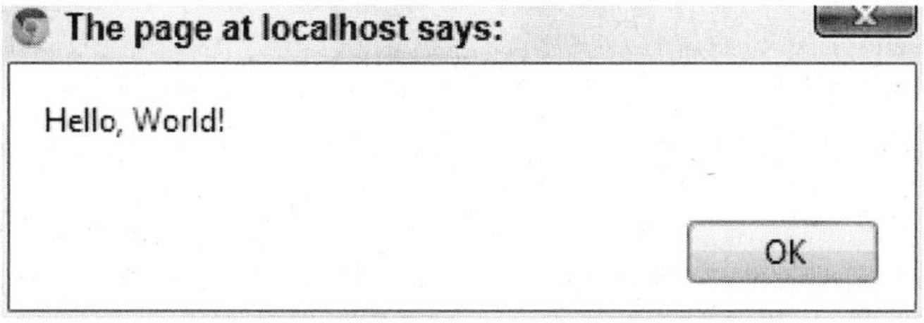

Figure 1-1:
A JavaScript program caused this little dialog box to pop up!

> The page at localhost says:
>
> Hello, World!
>
> OK

This page has a very simple JavaScript program in it that pops up the phrase "Hello, World!" in a special element called a dialog box. It's pretty cool.

Hello World?

There's a long tradition in programming languages that your first program in any language should simply say, "Hello, World!" and do nothing else. There's actually a very good practical reason for this habit. Hello World is the simplest possible program you can write that you can prove works. Hello World programs are used to help you figure out the mechanics of the programming environment — how the program is written, what special steps you have to do to make the code run, and how it works. There's no point in making a more complicated program until you know you can get code to pop up and say hi.

Here's an overview of the code:

```
<!DOCTYPE html>
<html lang = "en-US">

  <head>
    <meta charset = "UTF-8">
    <title>HelloWorld.html</title>
    <script type = "text/javascript">
       // Hello, world!
        alert("Hello, World!");
    </script>
  </head>
  <body>
  </body>
</html>
```

As you can see, this page contains nothing in the HTML body. You can incorporate JavaScript with HTML content. For now, though, you can simply place JavaScript code in the head area in a special tag and make it work.

Embedding your JavaScript code

JavaScript code is placed in your web page via the <script> tag. JavaScript code is placed inside the <script></script> pair. The <script> tag has one required attribute, type, which will usually be text/javascript. (Other types are possible, but they're rarely used.)

Creating comments

Just like HTML and CSS, comments are important. Because programming code can be more difficult to decipher than HTML or CSS, it's even more important to comment your code in JavaScript than it is in these environments. The comment character in JavaScript is two slashes (//).The browser ignores everything from the two slashes to the end of the line. You can also use a multi-line comment (/* */) just like the one in CSS.

Using the alert () method for output

You can output data in JavaScript in a number of ways. In this chapter, I focus on the simplest to implement and understand — the alert().

This technique pops up a small dialog box containing text for the user to read. The alert box is an example of a *modal dialog*. Modal dialogs interrupt the flow of the program until the user pays attention to them. Nothing else will happen in the program until the user acknowledges the dialog by clicking the OK button. The user can't interact with the page until he clicks the button.

Modal dialogs may seem a bit rude. In fact, you probably won't use them much after you discover other input and output techniques. The fact that the dialog box demands attention makes it a very easy tool to use when you start programming. I use it (and one of its cousins) throughout this chapter because it's easy to understand and use. Also, note that the dialog will be slightly different from browser to browser and between operating systems. There isn't really a way to control more precisely how dialogs work, but they're easy. You'll learn much more sophisticated means of interacting with the user in the next few chapters.

Adding the semicolon

Each command in JavaScript ends with a semicolon (;) character. The semicolon in most computer languages acts like the period in English. It indicates the end of a logical thought. Usually, each line of code is also one line in the editor.

To tell the truth, JavaScript will usually work fine if you leave out the semicolons. However, you should add them anyway because they help clarify your meaning. Besides, many other languages, including PHP (see Book V), require semicolons. You may as well start a good habit now.

Introducing Variables

Computer programs get their power by working with information. Figure 1-2 shows a program that gets user data from the user to include in a customized greeting.

Figure 1-2: First, the program asks the user for a name.

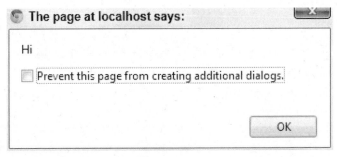

This program introduces a new kind of dialog that allows the user to enter some data. The information is stored in the program for later use. After the user enters her name, she gets a greeting, as shown in Figure 1-3.

Figure 1-3: The beginning of the greeting. Press the button for the rest.

The rest of the greeting happens in a second dialog box, shown in Figure 1-4. It incorporates the username supplied in the first dialog box.

Your browser might or might not have the 'prevent this page from creating additional dialogs' checkbox. This is actually a nice debugging feature in Chrome. It will be possible to create programs that get out of control. Chrome noticed two dialogs popping up in a row and thinks we might be in one of those dangerous situations, called an *endless loop*. (More on loops, endless and otherwise, in Chapter 3 of this mini-book.) For now, just press the OK button because this program is acting as intended. Soon enough, we'll stop using dialogs because they're just too annoying.

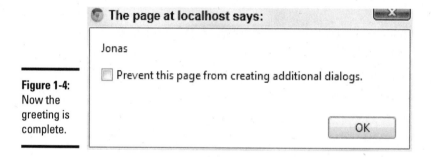

Figure 1-4:
Now the greeting is complete.

The output may not seem that incredible, but take a look at the source code to see what's happening:

```
<!DOCTYPE html>
<html lang = "en-US">

  <head>
    <meta charset = "UTF-8">
    <title>prompt.html</title>
    <script type = "text/javascript">
      // from prompt.html
      var person = "";
      person = prompt("What is your name?");
      alert("Hi");
      alert(person);
    </script>
  </head>
  <body>
  </body>
</html>
```

Creating a variable for data storage

This program is interesting because it allows user interaction. The user can enter a name, which is stored in the computer and then returned in a greeting. The key to this program is a special element called a *variable*.

Variables are simply places in memory for holding data. Any time you want a computer program to "remember" something, you can create a variable and store your information in it.

Variables typically have the following characteristics:

+ **The var statement:** You can indicate that you're creating a variable with the var command.

+ **A name:** When you create a variable, you're required to give it a name.

+ **An initial value:** It's useful to give each variable a value immediately.

+ **A data type:** JavaScript automatically determines the type of data in a variable (more on this in the upcoming "Understanding Variable Types" section), but you should still be clear in your mind what type of data you expect a variable to contain.

Asking the user for information

The prompt statement does several interesting things:

+ **Pops up a dialog box.** This modal dialog box is much like the one the alert() method creates.

+ **Asks a question.** The prompt() command expects you to ask the user a question.

+ **Provides space for a response.** The dialog box contains a space for the user to type a response and buttons for the user to click when he's finished or wants to cancel the operation.

+ **Passes the information to a variable.** The purpose of a prompt() command is to get data from the user, so prompts are nearly always connected to a variable. When the code is finished, the variable contains the indicated value.

Responding to the user

This program uses the alert() statement to begin a greeting to the user. The first alert works just like the one from the helloWorld program, described earlier in this chapter in the "Writing Your First JavaScript Program" section:

```
alert("Hi");
```

The content of the parentheses is the text you want the user to see. In this case, you want the user to see the literal value "Hi".

The second alert() statement is a little bit different:

```
alert(person);
```

This `alert()` statement has a parameter with no quotes. Because the parameter has no quotes, JavaScript understands that you don't really want to say the text *person*. Instead, it looks for a variable named `person` and returns the value of that variable.

The variable can take any name, store it, and return a customized greeting.

Using Concatenation to Build Better Greetings

To have a greeting and a person's name on two different dialogs seems a little awkward. Figure 1-5 shows a better solution.

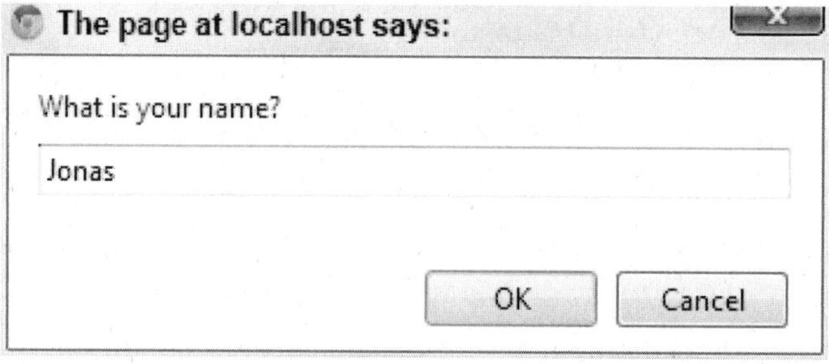

Figure 1-5:
Once again, I ask the user for a name.

The program asks for a name again and stores it in a variable. This time, the greeting is combined into one alert (see Figure 1-6), which looks a lot better.

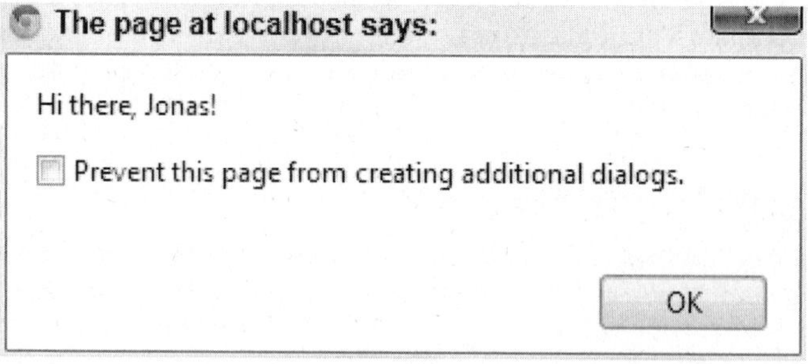

Figure 1-6:
Now the user's name is integrated into the greeting.

The secret to Figure 1-6 is one of those wonderful gems of the computing world: a really simple idea with a really complicated name. The term *concatenation* is a delightfully complicated word for a basic process. Look at the following code, and you see that combining variables with text is not all that complicated:

```
<script type = "text/javascript">
  //from concat.html
```

```
    var person = "";
    person = prompt("What is your name?");
    alert("Hi there, " + person + "!");
</script>
```

For the sake of brevity, I include only the script tag and its contents throughout this chapter. The rest of this page is a standard blank HTML page. You can see the complete document on the website. I do include a comment in each JavaScript snippet that indicates where you can get the entire file on the companion website.

Comparing literals and variables

The program concat.html contains two kinds of text. `"Hi there, "` is a *literal* text value. That is, you really mean to say "Hi there, " (including the comma and the space). `person` is a variable. (For more on variables, see the section "Introducing Variables," earlier in this chapter.)

You can combine literal values and variables in one phrase if you want:

```
    alert("Hi there, " + person + "!");
```

The secret to this code is to follow the quotes. `"Hi there, "` is a literal value because it is in quotes. On the other hand, `person` is a variable name because it is *not* in quotes; `"!"` is a literal value. You can combine any number of text snippets together with the plus sign.

Using the plus sign to combine text is called *concatenation*. (I told you it was a complicated word for a simple idea.)

Concatenation and your editor

The hard part about concatenation is figuring out which part of your text is a literal value and which part is a string. It won't take long before you go cross-eyed trying to understand where the quotes go.

Modern text editors (like Komodo) have a wonderful feature that can help you here. They color different kinds of text. By default, Komodo makes JavaScript keywords purple, text blue,

and variables black. This can be really helpful, especially when you do something goofy like forget to close a quote.

If these color differences are too subtle for you, most editors that have syntax highlighting allow you to change settings to fit your needs. Don't be afraid to use these tools to help you program better.

**Book IV
Chapter 1**

**Getting Started
with JavaScript**

Including spaces in your concatenated phrases

You may be curious about the extra space between the comma and the quote in the output line:

```
alert("Hi there, " + person + "!");
```

This extra space is important because you want the output to look like a normal sentence. If you don't have the space, the computer doesn't add one, and the output looks like this:

```
Hi there,Rachael!
```

You need to construct the output as it should look, including spaces and punctuation.

Understanding the String Object

The `person` variable used in the previous program is designed to hold text. Programmers (being programmers) devised their own mysterious term to refer to text. In programming, text is referred to as *string* data.

The term *string* comes from the way text is stored in computer memory. Each character is stored in its own cell in memory, and all the characters in a word or phrase reminded the early programmers of beads on a string. Surprisingly poetic for a bunch of geeks, huh?

Introducing object-based programming (and cows)

JavaScript (and many other modern programming languages) uses a powerful model called *object-oriented programming (OOP)*. This style of programming has a number of advantages. Most important for beginners, it allows you access to some very powerful objects that do interesting things out of the box.

Objects are used to describe complicated things that can have a lot of characteristics — like a cow. You can't really put an adequate description of a cow in an integer variable.

In many object-oriented environments, objects can have the following characteristics. (Imagine a cow object for the examples.)

✦ **Properties:** Characteristics about the object, such as `breed` and `age`

✦ **Methods:** Things the objects can do, such as `moo()` and `giveMilk()`

✦ **Events:** Stimuli the object responds to, such as `onTip`

I describe each of these ideas throughout this minibook because not all objects support all these characteristics.

If you have a variable of type `cow`, it describes a pretty complicated thing. This thing might have properties, methods, and events, all of which can be used together to build a good representation of a cow. (Believe it or not, I've built cow programming constructs more than once in my life — and you thought programming was dull!)

Most variable types in Java are actually objects, and most JavaScript objects have a full complement of properties and methods; many even have event handlers. Master how these things work and you've got a powerful and compelling programming environment.

Okay, before you send me any angry e-mails, I know debate abounds about whether JavaScript is a *truly* object-oriented language. I'm not going to get into the (frankly boring and not terribly important) details in this beginner book. We're going to call JavaScript object-oriented for now because it's close enough for beginners. If that bothers you, you can refer to JavaScript as an object-based language. Nearly everyone agrees with that. You can find out more information on this topic throughout this minibook while you discover how to make your own objects in Chapter 4 and use HTML elements as objects in Chapter 2.

Investigating the length of a string

When you assign text to a variable, JavaScript automatically treats the variable as a string object. The object instantly takes on the characteristics of a string object. Strings have a couple of properties and a bunch of methods. The one interesting property (at least for beginners) is `length`. Look at the example in Figure 1-7 to see the `length` property in action.

Figure 1-7:
This program reports the length of any text.

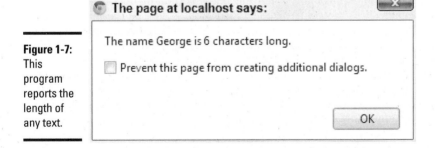

That's kind of cool how the program can figure out the length of a phrase. The cooler part is the way it works. As soon as you assign a text value to a variable, JavaScript treats that variable as a string, and because it's a string, it now has a `length` property. This property returns the length of the string in characters. Here's how it's done in the code.

```
<script type = "text/javascript">
 //from nameLength.html

 var person = prompt("Please enter your name.");
 var length = person.length;

 alert("Hi, " + person + "!");
 alert("The name " + person + " is " + length + " characters long.");
</script>
```

A property is used like a special subvariable. For example, `person` is a variable in the previous example. `person.length` is the `length` property of the `person` variable. In JavaScript, an object and a variable are connected by a period (with no spaces).

The `string` object in JavaScript has only two other properties (`constructor` and `prototype`). Both of these properties are needed only for advanced programming, so I skip them for now.

Using string methods to manipulate text

The `length` property is kind of cool, but the string object has a lot more up its sleeve. Objects also have *methods* (things the object can do). Strings in JavaScript have all kinds of methods. Here are a few of my favorites:

✦ `toUpperCase()` makes an entirely uppercase copy of the string.

✦ `toLowerCase()` makes an entirely lowercase copy of the string.

✦ `substring()` returns a specific part of the string.

✦ `indexOf()` determines whether one string occurs within another.

The string object has many other methods, but I'm highlighting the preceding because they're useful for beginners. Many string methods, such as `big()` and `fontColor()`, simply add HTML code to text. They aren't used very often because they produce HTML code that won't validate, and they don't really save a lot of effort anyway. Some other methods, such as `search()`, `replace()`, and `slice()`, use advanced constructs like arrays and regular expressions that aren't necessary for beginners. (To find out more about working with arrays, see Chapter 4 of this minibook. You can find out more about regular expressions in Chapter 5.)

Don't take my word for it. Look up the JavaScript string object (in one of the many online JavaScript references) and see what properties and methods it has.

Like properties, methods are attached to an object by the period. Methods are distinguished by a pair of parentheses, which sometimes contain special information called *parameters*.

The best way to see how methods work is to look at some in action. Look at the code for stringMethods.html:

```
<script type = "text/javascript">
  //from stringMethods.html

  var text = new String;
  text = prompt("Please enter some text.");

  alert("I'll shout it out:");
  alert(text.toUpperCase());

  alert("Now in lowercase...");
  alert(text.toLowerCase());

  alert("The first 'a' is at letter...");
  alert(text.indexOf("a"));

  alert("The first three letters are ...");
  alert(text.substring(0, 3));

</script>
```

Figure 1-8 displays the output produced by this program.

Figure 1-8: String methods can be fun.

In this example, I explicitly defined text as a string variable by saying

```
var text = new String;
```

JavaScript does not require you to explicitly determine the type of a variable, but you can do so, and this is sometimes helpful.

Here's another cool thing about Komodo Edit. When you type `text`, Komodo understands that you're talking about a string variable and automatically pops up a list of all the possible properties and methods of the string object. I wish I had that when I started doing this stuff!

You can see from the preceding code that methods are pretty easy to use. When you have a string variable, you can invoke the variable name followed by a period and the method name. Some methods require more information to do their job. Here are the specifics:

✦ `toUpperCase()` and `toLowerCase()` take the value of the variable and convert it entirely to the given case. This method is often used when you aren't concerned about the capitalization of a variable.

✦ `indexOf(substring)` returns the character position of the substring within the variable. If the variable doesn't contain the substring, it returns the value –1.

✦ `substring(begin, end)` returns the substring of the variable from the beginning character value to the end.

Understanding Variable Types

JavaScript isn't too fussy about whether a variable contains text or a number, but the distinction is still important because it can cause some surprising problems. To illustrate, take a look at a program that adds two numbers together, and then see what happens when you try to get numbers from the user to add.

Adding numbers

First, take a look at the following program:

```
<script type = "text/javascript">
  //from addNumbers.html

  var x = 5;
  var y = 3;
  var sum = x + y;

  alert(x + " plus " + y + " equals " + sum);
</script>
```

(As usual for this chapter, I'm only showing the script part because the rest of the page is blank.)

This program features three variables. I've assigned the value 5 to x and 3 to y. I then add x + y and assign the result to a third variable, sum. The last line prints the results, which are also shown in Figure 1-9.

Figure 1-9:
This program (correctly) adds two numbers together.

The page at localhost says:

5 plus 3 equals 8

OK

Note a few important things from this example:

- ✦ **You can assign values to variables.** It's best to read the equal sign as "gets" so that the first assignment is read as "variable x gets the value 5."

  ```
  var x = 5;
  ```

- ✦ **Numeric values aren't enclosed in quotes.** When you refer to a text literal value, it's always enclosed in quotes. Numeric data, such as the value 5, isn't placed in quotes.

- ✦ **You can add numeric values.** Because x and y both contain numeric values, you can add them together.

- ✦ **You can replace the results of an operation in a variable.** The result of the calculation x + y is placed in a variable called sum.

✦ **Everything works as expected.** The behavior of this program works as expected. That's important because it's not always true. (You can see an example of this behavior in the next section — I love writing code that blows up on purpose!)

Adding the user's numbers

The natural extension of the addNumbers.html program is a feature that allows the user to input two values and then returns the sum. This program can be the basis for a simple adding machine. Here's the JavaScript code:

```
<script type = "text/javascript">
  //from addInputWrong.html

  var x = prompt("first number:");
  var y = prompt("second number:");
  var sum = x + y;

  alert(x + " plus " + y + " equals " + sum);
</script>
```

This code seems reasonable enough. It asks for each value and stores them in variables. It then adds the variables and returns the results, right? Well, look at Figure 1-10 to see a surprise.

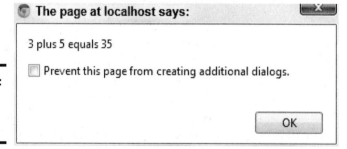

Figure 1-10: Wait a minute... 3 + 5 = 35?

Something's obviously not right here. To understand the problem, you need to see how JavaScript makes guesses about data types (see the next section).

The trouble with dynamic data

Ultimately, all the information stored in a computer, from music videos to e-mails, is stored as a bunch of ones and zeroes. The same value 01000001 can mean all kinds of things: It may mean the number 65 or the character A. (In fact, it does mean both those things in the right context.) The same binary value may mean something entirely different if it's interpreted as a real number, a color, or a part of a sound file.

The theory isn't critical here, but one point is really important: Somehow the computer has to know what kind of data is stored in a specific variable.

Many languages, such as C and Java, have all kinds of rules about defining data. If you create a variable in one of these languages, you have to define exactly what kind of data will go in the variable, and you can't change it.

JavaScript is much more easygoing about variable types. When you make a variable, you can put any kind of data in it that you want. In fact, the data type can change. A variable can contain an integer at one point, and the same variable may contain text in another part of the program.

JavaScript uses the context to determine how to interpret the data in a particular variable. When you assign a value to a variable, JavaScript puts the data in one of the following categories:

✦ *Integers* are whole numbers (no decimal part). They can be positive or negative values.

✦ A *floating point number* has a decimal point — for example, 3.14. You can also express floating point values in scientific notation, such as 6.02e23 (Avogadro's number –6.02 times 10 to the 23rd). Floating point numbers can also be negative.

✦ A *Boolean* value can only be true or false.

✦ Text is usually referred to as *string* data in programming languages. String values are usually enclosed in quotes.

✦ *Arrays* and *objects* are more complex data types that you can ignore for now.

Most of the time, when you make a variable, JavaScript guesses right, and you have no problems. But sometimes, JavaScript makes some faulty assumptions, and things go wrong.

The pesky plus sign

I use the plus sign in two ways throughout this chapter. The following code uses the plus sign in one way (concatenating two string values):

```
var x = "Hi, ";
var y = "there!";

result = x + y;
alert(result);
```

In this code, x and y are text variables. The `result = x + y` line is interpreted as "concatenate x and y," and the result is `"Hi, there!"`

Here's the strange thing: The following code is almost identical.

```
var x = 3;
var y = 5;

result = x + y;
alert(result);
```

Strangely, the behavior of the plus sign is different here, even though the statement `result = x + y` is identical in the two code snippets.

In this second case, `x` and `y` are numbers. The plus operator has two entirely different jobs. If it's surrounded by numbers, it adds. If it's surrounded by text, it concatenates.

That's what happened to the first adding machine program. When the user enters data in prompt dialogs, JavaScript assumes that the data is text. When I try to add `x` and `y`, it "helpfully" concatenates instead.

There's a fancy computer science word for this phenomenon (an operator doing different things in different circumstances). Those Who Care about Such Things call this mechanism an *overloaded operator*. Smart people sometimes have bitter arguments about whether overloaded operators are a good idea because they can cause problems like this one, but they can also make things easier in other contexts. I'm not going to enter into that debate here. It's not really a big deal, as long as you can see the problem and fix it.

Changing Variables to the Desired Type

If JavaScript is having a hard time figuring out what type of data is in a variable, you can give it a friendly push in the right direction with some handy conversion functions, as shown in Table 1-1.

Table 1-1		Variable Conversion Functions		
Function	*From*	*To*	*Example*	*Result*
parseInt()	String	Integer	parseInt("23")	23
parseFloat()	String	Floating point	parse-Float("21.5")	21.5
toString()	Any variable	String	myVar.toString()	*varies*
eval()	Expression	Result	eval("5 + 3")	8
Math.ceil()	Floating point	Integer	Math.ceil(5.2)	6
Math.floor()	Floating point	Integer	Math.floor(5.2)	5
Math.round()	Floating point	Integer	Math.round(5.2)	5

Using variable conversion tools

The conversion functions are incredibly powerful, but you only need them if the automatic conversion causes you problems. Here's how they work:

✦ `parseInt()` is used to convert text to an integer. If you put a text value inside the parentheses, the function returns an integer value. If the string has a floating-point representation ("4.3" for example), an integer value (4) is returned.

✦ `parseFloat()` converts text to a floating-point value.

✦ `toString()` takes any variable type and creates a string representation. Usually, using this function isn't necessary to use because it's invoked automatically when needed.

✦ `eval()` is a special method that accepts a string as input. It then attempts to evaluate the string as JavaScript code and return the output. You can use this method for variable conversion or as a simple calculator — `eval("5 + 3")` returns the integer 8.

✦ `Math.ceil()` is one of several methods of converting a floating-point number to an integer. This technique always rounds *upward,* so `Math.ceil(1.2)` is 2, and `Math.ceil(1.8)` is also 2.

✦ `Math.floor()` is similar to `Math.ceil()`, except it always rounds *downward*, so `Math.floor(1.2)` and `Math.floor(1.8)` will both evaluate to 1.

✦ `Math.round()` works like the standard rounding technique used in grade school. Any fractional value less than .5 rounds down, and greater than or equal to .5 rounds up, so `Math.round(1.2)` is 1, and `Math.round(1.8)` is 2.

Fixing the addInput code

With all this conversion knowledge in place, it's pretty easy to fix up the `addInput` program so that it works correctly. Just use `parseFloat()` to force both inputs into floating-point values before adding them. You don't have to explicitly convert the result to a string. That's automatically done when you invoke the `alert()` method.

```
// from addInput.html

var x = prompt("first number:");
var y = prompt("second number:");
var sum = parseFloat(x) + parseFloat(y);

alert(x + " plus " + y + " equals " + sum);
```

You can see the program works correctly in Figure 1-11.

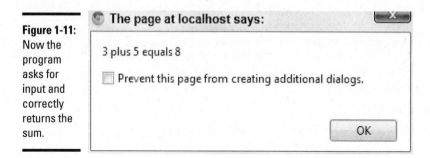

Figure 1-11: Now the program asks for input and correctly returns the sum.

Conversion methods allow you to ensure that the data is in exactly the format you want.

Chapter 2: Talking to the Page

In This Chapter

✔ **Introducing the Document Object Model**

✔ **Responding to form events**

✔ **Connecting a button to a function**

✔ **Retrieving data from text fields**

✔ **Changing text in text fields**

✔ **Sending data to the page**

✔ **Working with other text-related form elements**

*J*avaScript is fun and all, but it lives in web browsers for a reason: to let you change web pages. The best thing about JavaScript is how it helps you control the page. You can use JavaScript to read useful information from the user and to change the page on the fly.

Understanding the Document Object Model

JavaScript programs usually live in the context of a web page. The contents of the page are available to the JavaScript programs through a mechanism called the *Document Object Model* (DOM).

The DOM is a special set of complex variables that encapsulates the entire contents of the web page. You can use JavaScript to read from the DOM and determine the status of an element. You can also modify a DOM variable and change the page from within JavaScript code.

Previewing the DOM

The easiest way to get a feel for the DOM is to load a page in Chrome and play around in the console. Follow these steps to get a feel for the DOM:

1. **Use the Chrome browser.**

   Most browsers have something like the web developer console used in this example, but Chrome's is very easy to use and comes built-in, so you should begin with that one.

2. **Load any page you want.**

   It's probably easiest to start with a page that's relatively simple, so you can get a sense of what's happening.

3. **Turn on the web developer toolbar.**

   Use the F12 key, View ⇨ Developer ⇨ Developer Tools or Tools ⇨ Developer Tools from the menu. (It may vary based on your version of Chrome or your operating system.)

4. **Go to the Console tab.**

   The Developer Tools window has many tabs, but the console tab is the one we need for now (and it will continue to be useful as you get more advanced).

5. **Type** document .

   Don't forget the period at the end. When you type a period, Chrome's auto-complete describes all the various elements related to the document. document is a very fancy variable (called an *object*) that contains a ton of sub-variables. You can scroll through this list to see all the things related to document.

6. **Change the page's background color.**

   Try typing this in the console:

   ```
   document.body.style.backgroundColor = "green"
   ```

   You can use this trick to (temporarily) change all kinds of features.

7. **Play around with the document tree a bit more.**

   It's fine if you don't know exactly what's going on yet, but use this technique to get a general feel for the complexity of the page and all the interesting things you can do with it.

Figure 2-1 illustrates a simple web page being dynamically modified through the console tab.

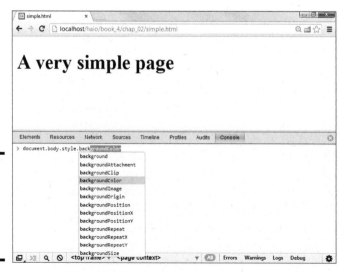

Figure 2-1:
Even a
very simple
page has
a complex
DOM.

The Console tab is far more involved and powerful than I'm letting on here. Chapter 3 of this mini-book goes into all kinds of details about how to use this powerful tool to figure out what's going on in your page.

When you look over the DOM of a simple page, you can easily get overwhelmed. You'll see a lot of variables listed. Technically, these variables are all elements of a special object called `window`. The `window` object has a huge number of subobjects, all listed in the DOM view. Table 1 describes a few important `window` variables.

Table 1		Primary DOM Objects
Variable	*Description*	*Notes*
document	Represents HTML page	Most commonly scripted element
location	Describes current URL	Change location.href to move to a new page
history	A list of recently visited pages	Access this to view previous pages
status	The browser status bar	Change this to set a message in the status bar

Getting the blues, JavaScript-style

It all gets fun when you start to write JavaScript code to access the DOM. Take a look at blue.html in Figure 2-2.

Figure 2-2: This page is blue. But where's the CSS?

The page has white text on a blue background, but there's no CSS! Instead, it has a small script that changes the DOM directly, controlling the page colors through code.

```html
<!DOCTYPE html>
<html lang = "en-US">

  <head>
    <meta charset = "UTF-8">
    <title>blue.html</title>
  </head>
  <body>
    <h1>I've got the JavaScript Blues</h1>
    <script type = "text/javascript">
      // use javascript to set the colors
      document.body.style.color = "white";
      document.body.style.backgroundColor = "blue";
    </script>
  </body>
</html>
```

Writing JavaScript code to change colors

The page shown in Figure 2-3 is pretty simple, but it has a few unique features.

Figure 2-3:
The page is white. It has two buttons on it. I've gotta click Blue.

✦ **It has no CSS.** A form of CSS is dynamically created through the code.

✦ **The script is in the body.** I can't place this particular script in the header because it refers to the body.

When the browser first sees the script, there must be a body for the text to change. If I put the script in the head, no body exists when the browser reads the code, so it gets confused. If I place the script in the body, there is a body, so the script can change it. (It's really okay if you

Shouldn't it be background-color?

If you've dug through the DOM style elements, you'll notice some interesting things. Many of the element names are familiar but not quite identical. `background-color` becomes `backgroundColor` and `font-weight` becomes `fontWeight`. CSS uses dashes to indicate word breaks, and the DOM combines words and uses capitalization for clarity. You'll find all your old favorite CSS elements, but the names change according to this very predictable formula. Still, if you're ever confused, just use the console to look over various style elements.

don't get this discussion. This example is probably the only time you'll see this trick because I show a better way in the next example.)

✦ **Use a DOM reference to change the style colors.** That long "trail of breadcrumbs" syntax (`document.body.style.color`) takes you all the way from the document through the body to the style and finally the color. It's tedious but thorough.

✦ **Set the foreground color to white.** You can change the color property to any valid CSS color value (a color name or a hex value). It's just like CSS because you are affecting the CSS.

✦ **Set the background color to blue.** Again, this adjustment is just like setting CSS.

Managing Button Events

Of course, there's no good reason to write code like `blue.html`. You will find that it's just as easy to build CSS as it is to write JavaScript. The advantage comes when you use the DOM dynamically to change the page's behavior after it has finished loading.

Figure 2-3 shows a page called backgroundColors.html.

The page is set up with the default white background color. It has two buttons on it, which should change the body's background color. Click the Blue button, and you see that it works, as verified in Figure 2-4.

Some really exciting things just happened.

✦ **The page has a form.** For more information on form elements, refer to Book I, Chapter 7.

✦ **The buttons do something.** Plain-old HTML forms don't really do anything. You've got to write some kind of programming code to accomplish a task. This program does it. Twice. All for free.

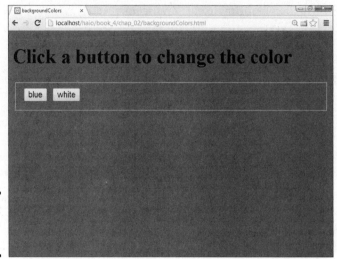

Figure 2-4: It turned blue! Joy!

✦ **Each button has a special attribute called `onclick`:** The `onclick` attribute is an *event handler*. This is special because it allows you to apply some sort of action to the button press. The action (a single line of JavaScript code) assigned to `onclick` will happen each time the button is clicked.

✦ **Each button changes the background to a different color:** The Blue button makes the background blue and the White one — well, you get it. I simply used the code from the console example to change the background colors.

✦ **The code is integrated directly into the buttons:** You can attach one line of JavaScript code to a button's `onclick` event. I use that line to change the background colors.

Here's the code:

```
<!DOCTYPE html>
<html lang = "en-US">

  <head>
    <meta charset = "UTF-8">
    <title>backgroundColors</title>
  </head>
  <body>
    <h1>Click a button to change the color</h1>
    <form action = "">
      <fieldset>
        <input type = "button"
               value = "blue"
               onclick = "document.body.style.backgroundColor = 'blue'"/>
        <input type = "button"
               value = "white"
               onclick = "document.body.style.backgroundColor = 'white'" />
```

```
        </fieldset>
      </form>
    </body>
  </html>
```

Adding a function for more ... functionality

The buttons work, but the program seems quite inefficient. First, buttons can only have one line of code attached to the `onclick` event handler. Secondly, the code is almost exactly the same in both buttons. There must be a more efficient way. Most of the time, JavaScript code is not done one line at a time. Instead, it is packaged into a special element called a *function*. Functions are simply a collection of code lines with a name. Functions can also be sent an optional parameter, and they can return output. You learn much more about functions in Chapter 4 of this minibook, but look at this basic version for now.

```
<!DOCTYPE html>
<html lang = "en-US">

  <head>
    <meta charset = "UTF-8">
    <title>backgroundColors</title>
    <script type = "text/javascript">
      // from backgroundColors
      function makeBlue(){
        document.body.style.backgroundColor = "blue";
      } // end changeColor

      function makeWhite(){
        document.body.style.backgroundColor = "white";
      }
    </script>
  </head>
  <body>
    <h1>Click a button to change the color</h1>
    <form action = "">
      <fieldset>
        <input type = "button"
               value = "blue"
               onclick = "makeBlue()"/>
        <input type = "button"
               value = "white"
               onclick = "makeWhite()" />
      </fieldset>
    </form>
  </body>
</html>
```

This program looks and acts exactly like the program in Figures 2-3 and 2-4, so I don't provide a screenshot here. The important thing is how I've improved the code underneath the visible part of the page.

Something interesting is happening here. Take a look at how this program has changed from the first one.

1. **There's a function called `makeBlue()` in the script area.**

   The `function` keyword allows you to collect one or more commands and give them a name. In this case, I'm giving that nasty `document.body.style` nonsense a much more sensible name — `makeBlue()`.

2. **The parentheses are necessary.**

   Whenever you define a function, you have to include parentheses, but sometimes (as in this simple example), they're empty. You see how to add something to the parentheses in the next example.

3. **One or more lines of code go inside the function.**

   Mark a function with squiggle braces ({ }). This example has only one line of code in the function, but you can have as many code lines as you want.

4. **The function name describes what the function does.**

   Functions are used to simplify code, so it's really important that a function name describes what the function does.

5. **Another function makes the background white.**

   One button makes the background blue, and the other makes it white, so I'll make a function to go with each button.

6. **Attach the functions to the buttons.**

   Now the buttons each call a function rather than doing the work directly.

You might wonder if all this business of making a function is worth the effort — after all, these programs seem exactly the same — but the new one is a bit more work. In this very simple example, the functions are a little more work but clarify the code a smidge. As your programs get more complex, there's no doubt that functions improve things, especially as you learn more about how functions work.

Making a more flexible function

The version of the code that uses functions doesn't seem a lot easier than adding the code directly, and it isn't. But functions are much more powerful than simply renaming a line of code. If you think about the two functions in that example, you quickly realize they're almost exactly the same. It would be awesome if you could write one simple function and have it change the background to any color you want. That's exactly what happens in the next example (backgroundColorFunction.html). Here's the code:

```
<!DOCTYPE html>
<html lang = "en-US">

  <head>
    <meta charset = "UTF-8">
    <title>backgroundColors</title>
    <script type = "text/javascript">
      // from backgroundColors
      function changeColor(color){
```

```
        document.body.style.backgroundColor = color;
      } // end changeColor
    </script>
  </head>
  <body>
    <h1>Click a button to change the color</h1>
    <form action = "">
      <fieldset>
        <input type = "button"
               value = "blue"
               onclick = "changeColor('blue')"/>
        <input type = "button"
               value = "white"
               onclick = "changeColor('white')" />
      </fieldset>
  </form>
  </body>
</html>
```

Once again, this program will seem to the casual user to be exactly like the programs in Figures 2-3 and 2-4, so I'm not including a screen shot. This is an important part of computer programming. Often the most important changes are not visible to the user. If you've ever hired a programmer, you're no doubt aware of this issue.

✦ **The page has a single `changeColor()` function.** The page has only one function called `changeColor()` defined in the header.

✦ **The `changeColor()` function includes a color parameter.** This time, there's a value inside the parentheses:

```
function changeColor(color){
```

The term `color` inside the parentheses is called a *parameter*. A parameter is a value sent to a function. Inside the function, `color` is available as a variable. When you call a function, you can send a value to it, like this:

```
changeColor('white');
```

This sends the text value `'white'` to the function, where it becomes the value of the `color` variable.

You'll sometimes see the terms *argument* and *parameter* used interchangeably to reference the stuff passed to a function, but these terms are not exactly the same. Technically, the parameter is the variable name (`color`) and the argument is the value of that variable (`'white'`).

You can design a function with as many parameters as you wish, but you need to name each one. After a function is designed with parameters, you must supply an argument for each parameter when you call the function.

✦ **Both buttons pass information to `changeColor`:** Both of the buttons call the `changeColor()` function, but they each pass a different color value. This is one of the most useful characteristics of functions. They allow you to repeat code that's similar but not identical. That makes it possible to build very powerful functions that can be reused easily.

Embedding quotes within quotes

Take a careful look at the `onclick` lines in the code in the preceding section. You may not have noticed one important issue:

`onclick` is an HTML parameter, and its value must be encased in quotes. The parameter happens to be a function call, which sends a string value. String values must also be in quotes. This setup can become confusing if you use double quotes everywhere because the browser has no way to know the quotes are nested. Look at this incorrect line of code:

```
onclick = "changeColor("white")" />
```

HTML thinks the `onclick` parameter contains the value `"changeColor("` and it will have no idea what `white")"` is.

Fortunately, JavaScript has an easy fix for this problem. If you want to embed a quote inside another quote, just switch to single quotes. The line is written with the parameter inside single quotes:

```
onclick = "changeColor('white')" />
```

Writing the changeColor function

The `changeColor()` function is pretty easy to write.

```
<script type = "text/javascript">
  // from backgroundColors

  function changeColor(color){
    document.body.style.backgroundColor = color;
  } // end changeColor
  //
</script>
```

It goes in the header area as normal. It's simply a function accepting one parameter called `color`. The body's `backgroundColor` property is set to `color`.

I can write JavaScript in the header that refers to the body because the header code is all in a function. The function is read before the body is in place, but it isn't activated until the user clicks the button. By the time the user activates the code by clicking on the button, there is a body, and there's no problem.

Managing Text Input and Output

Perhaps the most intriguing application of the DOM is the ability to let the user communicate with the program through the web page, without all those annoying dialog boxes. Figure 2-5 shows a page with a web form containing two textboxes and a button.

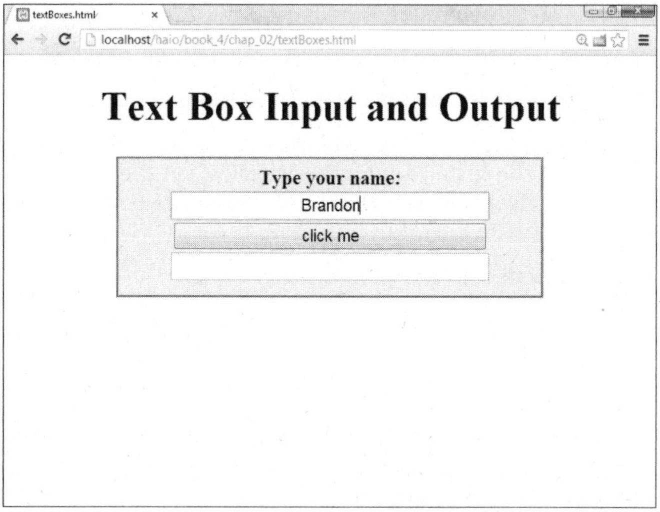

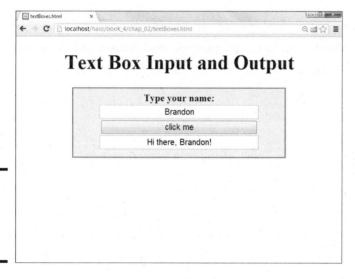

Figure 2-5:
I've typed
a name
into the top
textbox.

When you click the button, something exciting happens, demonstrated by
Figure 2-6.

Figure 2-6:
I got a
greeting!
With no
alert box!

Clearly, form-based input and output is preferable to the constant interruption of dialog boxes.

Introducing event-driven programming

Graphic user interfaces usually use a technique called *event-driven programming*. The idea is simple.

1. **Create a user interface.**

   In web pages, the user interface is usually built of HTML and CSS.

2. **Identify events the program should respond to.**

   If you have a button, users will click it. (If you want to guarantee they click it, put the text "Launch the Missiles" on the button. I don't know why, but it always works.) Buttons almost always have events. Some other elements do, too.

3. **Write a function to respond to each event.**

   For each event you want to test, write a function that does whatever needs to happen.

4. **Get information from form elements.**

   Now you're accessing the contents of form elements to get information from the user. You need a mechanism for getting information from a text field and other form elements.

5. **Use form elements for output.**

   For this simple example, I also use form elements for output. The output goes in a second textbox, even though I don't intend the user to type any text there.

Creating the HTML form

The first step in building a program that can manage text input and output is to create the HTML framework. Here's the HTML code:

```
<!DOCTYPE html>
<html lang = "en-US">

  <head>
    <meta charset = "UTF-8">
    <title>textBoxes.html</title>
    <script type = "text/javascript">
      // from textBoxes.html
      function sayHi(){
        var txtName = document.getElementById("txtName");
        var txtOutput = document.getElementById("txtOutput");
        var name = txtName.value;
        txtOutput.value = "Hi there, " + name + "!"
      } // end sayHi
    </script>
    <link rel = "stylesheet"
          type = "text/css"
          href = "textBoxes.css" />
  </head>
  <body>
    <h1>Text Box Input and Output</h1>
    <form action = "">
      <fieldset>
        <label>Type your name: </label>
        <input type = "text"
               id = "txtName" />
        <input type = "button"
               value = "click me"
```

```
              onclick = "sayHi()"/>
        <input type = "text"
               id = "txtOutput" />
      </fieldset>
    </form>
  </body>
</html>
```

As you look over the code, note a few important ideas:

+ **The page uses external CSS.** The CSS style is nice, but it's not important in the discussion here. It stays safely encapsulated in its own file. Of course, you're welcome to look it over or change it.

+ **Most of the page is a form.** All form elements must be inside a form.

+ **A `fieldset` is used to contain form elements.** input elements need to be inside some sort of block-level element, and a `fieldset` is a natural choice.

+ **There's a text field named `txtName`.** This text field contains the name. I begin with the phrase `txt` to remind myself that this field is a textbox.

+ **The second element is a button.** You don't need to give the button an ID (as it won't be referred to in code), but it does have an `onclick()` event.

+ **The button's `onclick` event refers to a (yet undefined) function.** In this example, it's named "`sayHi()`".

+ **A second textbox contains the greeting.** This second textbox is called `txtOutput` because it's the text field meant for output.

After you set up the HTML page, the function becomes pretty easy to write because you've already identified all the major constructs. You know you need a function called `sayHi()`, and this function reads text from the `txt-Name` field and writes to the `txtOutput` field.

Using getElementById to get access to the page

HTML is one thing, and JavaScript is another. You need some way to turn an HTML form element into something JavaScript can read. The magical `getElementById()` method does exactly that. First, look at the first two lines of the `sayHi()` function (defined in the header as usual).

```
function sayHi(){
    var txtName = document.getElementById("txtName");
    var txtOutput = document.getElementById("txtOutput");
```

You can extract every element created in your web page by digging through the DOM. In the old days, this approach is how we used to access form elements. It was ugly and tedious. Modern browsers have the wonderful `getElementById()` function instead. This beauty searches through the DOM and returns a reference to an object with the requested ID.

A *reference* is simply an indicator where the specified object is in memory. You can store a reference in a variable. Manipulating this variable manipulates the object it represents. If you want, you can think of it as making the textbox into a variable.

Note that I call the variable `txtName`, just like the original textbox. This variable refers to the text field from the form, not the value of that text field. After I have a reference to the text field object, I can use its methods and properties to extract data from it and send new values to it.

Manipulating the text fields

After you have access to the text fields, you can manipulate the values of these fields with the `value` property:

```
var name = txtName.value;
txtOutput.value = "Hi there, " + name + "!"
```

Text fields (and, in fact, all input fields) have a `value` property. You can read this value as an ordinary string variable. You can also write to this property, and the text field will be updated on the fly.

This code handles the data input and output:

1. **Create a variable for the name.**

    This is an ordinary string variable.

2. **Copy the value of the textbox into the variable.**

    Now that you have a variable representing the textbox, you can access its `value` property to get the value typed in by the user.

3. **Create a message for the user.**

    Use ordinary string concatenation.

4. **Send the message to the `output` textbox.**

    You can also write text to the `value` property, which changes the contents of the text field on the screen.

Text fields always return string values (like prompts do). If you want to pull a numeric value from a text field, you may have to convert it with the `parseInt()` or `parseFloat()` functions.

Writing to the Document

Form elements are great for getting input from the user, but they're not ideal for output. Placing the output in an editable field really doesn't make much sense. Changing the web document is a much better approach.

The DOM supports exactly such a technique. Most HTML elements feature an `innerHTML` property. This property describes the HTML code inside the element. In most cases, it can be read from and written to.

So what are the exceptions? Single-element tags (like `<img>` and `<input>`) don't contain any HTML, so obviously reading or changing their inner HTML doesn't make sense. Table elements can often be read from but not changed directly.

Figure 2-7 shows a program with a basic form.

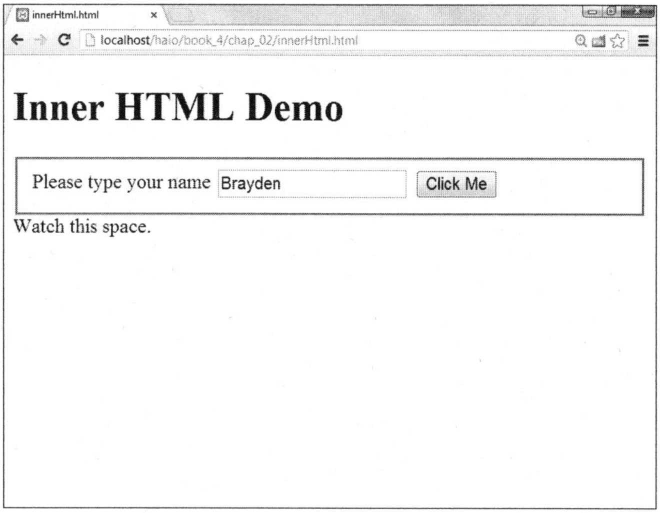

Figure 2-7:
Wait, there's no output text field!

This form doesn't have a form element for the output. Enter a name and click the button, and you see the results in Figure 2-8.

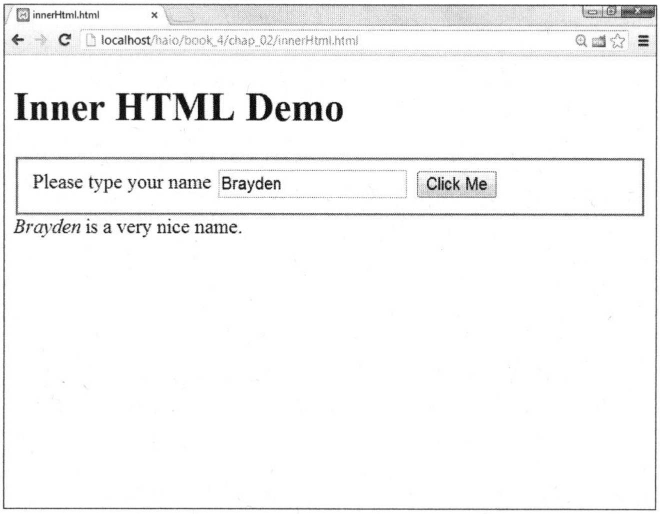

Figure 2-8:
The page has changed itself.

Amazingly enough, this page can make changes to itself dynamically. It isn't simply changing the values of form fields, but changing the HTML.

Preparing the HTML framework

To see how the page changes itself dynamically, begin by looking at the HTML body for innerHTML.html:

```
<body>
  <h1>Inner HTML Demo</h1>
  <form action = "">
    <fieldset>
      <label>Please type your name</label><p>
      <input type = "text"
             id = "txtName" />
      <button type = "button"
              onclick = "sayHi()">
        Click Me
      </button>
    </fieldset>
  </form>

  <div id = "divOutput">
    Watch this space.
  </div>
</body>
```

The code body has a couple of interesting features:

✦ **The program has a form.** The form is pretty standard. It has a text field for input and a button, but no output elements.

✦ **The button will call a `sayHi()` function.** The page requires a function with this name. Presumably, it says hi somehow.

✦ **There's a div for output.** A `div` element in the main body is designated for output.

✦ **The div has an ID.** The `id` attribute is often used for CSS styling, but the DOM can also use it. Any HTML elements that will be dynamically scripted should have an `id` field.

Writing the JavaScript

The JavaScript code for modifying `innerHTML` isn't very hard:

```
<script type = "text/javascript">
  //from innerHTML.html

  function sayHi(){
    txtName = document.getElementById("txtName");
    divOutput = document.getElementById("divOutput");

    name = txtName.value;

    divOutput.innerHTML = "<em>" + name +  "</em>";
    divOutput.innerHTML += " is a very nice name.";
  }
</script>
```

The first step (as usual with web forms) is to extract data from the input elements. Note that I can create a variable representation of any DOM element, not just form elements. The `divOutput` variable is a JavaScript representation of the DOM div.

Finding your innerHTML

Like form elements, divs have other interesting properties you can modify. The `innerHTML` property allows you to change the HTML code displayed by the div. You can put any valid HTML code you want inside the `innerHTML` property, even HTML tags. Be sure that you still follow the HTML rules so that your code will be valid.

Working with Other Text Elements

When you know how to work with text fields, you've mastered about half of the form elements. Several other form elements work exactly like text fields, including these:

✦ **Password fields** obscure the user's input with asterisks, but preserve the text.

✦ **Hidden fields** allow you to store information in a page without revealing it to the user. (They're used a little bit in client-side coding, but almost never in JavaScript.)

✦ **Text areas** are a special variation of textboxes designed to handle multiple lines of input.

Figure 2-9 is a page with all these elements available on the same form.

Figure 2-9:
Passwords, hidden fields, and text areas all look the same to JavaScript.

When the user clicks the button, the contents of all the fields (even the password and hidden fields) appear on the bottom of the page, as shown in Figure 2-10.

Figure 2-10:
Now you
can see
what was in
everything.

Building the form

Here's the HTML (otherText.html) that generates the form shown in Figures 2-9 and 2-10:

```
<body>
  <h1>Text Input Devices</h1>
  <form action = "">
    <fieldset>
      <label>Normal Text field</label>
      <input type = "text"
             id = "txtNormal" />
      <label>Password field</label>
      <input type = "password"
             id = "pwd" />
      <label>Hidden</label>
      <input type = "hidden"
             id = "hidden"
             value = "I can't tell you" />
      <textarea id = "txtArea"
                rows = "10"
                cols = "40">
This is a big text area.
It can hold a lot of text.
      </textarea>
      <button type = "button"
              onclick = "processForm()">
        Click Me
      </button>
    </fieldset>
  </form>
```

```
<div id = "output">

</div>
</body>
```

The code may be familiar to you if you read about form elements in Book I, Chapter 7. A few things are worth noting for this example:

✦ **An ordinary text field appears, just for comparison purposes.** It has an `id` so that it can be identified in the JavaScript.

✦ **The next field is a password field.** Passwords display asterisks, but store the actual text that was entered. This password has an `id` of `pwd`.

✦ **The hidden field is a bit strange.** You can use hidden fields to store information on the page without displaying that information to the user. Unlike the other kinds of text fields, the user can't modify a hidden field. (She usually doesn't even know it's there.) This hidden field has an `id` of `secret` and a value ("I can't tell you").

✦ **The text area has a different format.** The `input` elements are all single-tag elements, but the `textarea` is designed to contain a large amount of text, so it has beginning and end tags. The text area's `id` is `txtArea`.

✦ **A button starts all the fun.** As usual, most of the elements just sit there gathering data, but the button has an `onclick` event associated with it, which calls a function.

✦ **External CSS gussies it all up.** The page has some minimal CSS to clean it up. The CSS isn't central to this discussion, so I don't reproduce it. Note that the page will potentially have a `dl` on it, so I have a CSS style for it, even though it doesn't appear by default.

The password and hidden fields seem secure, but they aren't. Anybody who views the page source will be able to read the value of a hidden field, and passwords transmit their information in the clear. You really shouldn't be using web technology (especially this kind) to transport nuclear launch codes or the secret to your special sauce. (Hmmm, maybe the secret sauce recipe *is* the launch code — sounds like a bad spy movie.)

When I create a text field, I often suspend my rules on indentation because the text field preserves everything inside it, including any indentation.

Writing the function

After you build the form, all you need is a function. Here's the good news: JavaScript treats all these elements in exactly the same way! The way you handle a password, hidden field, or text area is identical to the technique for a regular text field (described under "Managing Text Input and Output," earlier in this chapter). Here's the code:

```
// from otherText.html
function processForm(){
  //grab input from form
  var txtNormal = document.getElementById("txtNormal");
  var pwd = document.getElementById("pwd");
  var hidden = document.getElementById("hidden");
  var txtArea = document.getElementById("txtArea");

  var normal = txtNormal.value;
  var password = pwd.value;
  var secret = hidden.value;
  var bigText = txtArea.value;

  //create output
  var result = ""
  result += "<dl> \n";
  result += "  <dt>normal</dt> \n";
  result += "  <dd>" + normal + "</dd> \n";
  result += " \n";
  result += "  <dt>password</dt> \n";
  result += "  <dd>" + password + "</dd> \n";
  result += " \n";
  result += "  <dt>secret</dt> \n";
  result += "  <dd>" + secret + "</dt> \n";
  result += "   \n";
  result += "  <dt>big text</dt> \n";
  result += "  <dd>" + bigText + "</dt> \n";
  result += "</dl> \n";

  var output = document.getElementById("output");
  output.innerHTML = result;

} // end function
```

The function is a bit longer than the others in this chapter, but it follows exactly the same pattern: It extracts data from the fields, constructs a string for output, and writes that output to the `innerHTML` attribute of a div in the page.

The code has nothing new, but it still has a few features you should consider:

✦ **Create a variable for each form element.** Use the `document.getElementById` mechanism.

✦ **Create a string variable containing the contents of each element.** Don't forget: The `getElementById` trick returns an object. You need to extract the `value` property to see what's inside the object.

✦ **Make a big string variable to manage the output.** When output gets long and messy like this one, concatenate a big variable and then just output it in one swoop.

✦ **HTML is your friend.** This output is a bit complex, but `innerHTML` is HTML, so you can use any HTML styles you want to format your code. The `return` string is actually a complete definition list. Whatever is inside the textbox is (in this case) reproduced as HTML text, so if I want carriage returns or formatting, I have to add them with code.

✦ **Newline characters (\n) clean up the output.** If I were writing an ordinary definition list in HTML, I'd put each line on a new line. I try to make my programs write code just like I do, so I add newline characters everywhere I'd add a carriage return if I were writing the HTML by hand.

Understanding generated source

When you run the program in the preceding section, your JavaScript code actually changes the page it lives on. The code that doesn't come from your server (but is created by your program) is sometimes called *generated source*. The generated code technique is powerful, but it can have a significant problem. Try this experiment to see what I mean:

1. **Reload the page.**

   You want to view it without the form contents showing so that you can view the source. Everything will be as expected; the source code shows exactly what you wrote.

2. **Click the Click Me button.**

   Your function runs, and the page changes. You clearly added HTML to the `output` div because you can see the output right on the screen.

3. **View the source again.**

   You'll be amazed. The `output` div is empty, even though you can clearly see that it has changed.

4. **Check generated code.**

   Using the HTML validator extension or the W3 validator (described in Book I, Chapter 2) doesn't check for errors in your generated code. You have to check it yourself, but it's hard to see the code!

Figure 2-11 illustrates this problem.

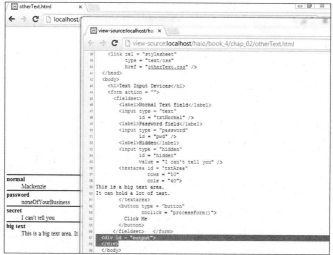

Figure 2-11: The ordinary view source command isn't showing the contents of the div!

Here's what's going on: The `view source` command (on most browsers) doesn't actually view the source of the page as it currently stands. It goes back to the server and retrieves the page, but displays it as source rather than rendered output. As a result, the `view source` command isn't useful for telling you how the page has changed dynamically. Likewise, the page validators check the page as it occurs on the server without taking into account things that may have happened dynamically.

When you build regular web pages, this approach isn't a problem because regular web pages don't change. Dynamically generated pages can change on the fly, and the view source tool doesn't expect that. If you made a mistake in the dynamically-generated HTML, you can't simply view the source to see what you did wrong. Fortunately, Chrome gives you a pretty easy solution.

The Chrome developer tools (available with the F12 or Cmd+shift+I on Mac — have I mentioned how awesome this tool is?) can show you exactly what the browser is currently displaying.

Here's how you can use it:

1. **Run the page and put it through its paces.**

   Click the buttons and do what the page does to modify itself.

2. **Inspect the page.**

   Right-click anywhere on the page and choose `inspect element` from the popup menu. The developer tools will pop up and you'll be in a special outline view.

3. **Select the code to see the corresponding page element.**

   Select a piece of code in the `elements` view and the corresponding part of the page is highlighted.

4. **Select an element to see its code.**

   When you're in inspect mode, you can click on any visible element of the page and the corresponding code will be highlighted.

5. **The displayed code is what's currently being displayed.**

   Unlike the `view source` results, the element inspector shows what's currently on the screen rather than what's on the server.

6. **You can even change the content here.**

   You can double-click on content in the Elements tab and change it, and the page changes alongside it. (Hmm … does this mean you could change the headlines of an online newspaper and make it look totally real? That seems mischievous. I hope nobody ever does that.) Don't worry. None of the changes are permanent.

7. **The "trail of breadcrumbs" shows where you are.**

   You can see exactly what tags are active by looking at the bottom of the developer screen.

8. **You can also see which CSS files are currently active.**

   As described in Book II, you can also modify the CSS on this screen to see how the page will look if the CSS is changed. This is an ideal way to experiment with the page.

These tools keep you sane when you're trying to figure out why your generated code isn't acting right. (I wish I'd had them years ago....)

Figure 2-12 shows the Chrome developer tools with the dynamically generated contents showing.

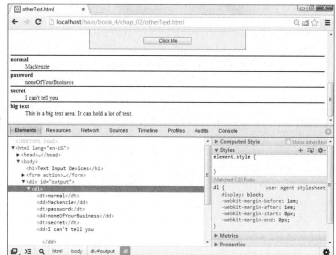

Figure 2-12: Chrome shows the current status of dynamically-modified pages

What if you're not in Chrome?

If you're using another browser, the Firebug extension does most of the same things as the Chrome developer tools. Firebug performs best on Firefox, but there is a light version which works on any browser.

If none of these tools is available, there's another cool trick you can do. Type the following into the address bar:

```
javascript:alert(document.body.innerHTML)
```

This very sneaky trick uses JavaScript to generate the source code of the page as it currently stands:

1. **Begin with the `javascript:` identifier.**

   When you begin an address with `javascript`, the browser immediately renders the rest of the address as a JavaScript instruction rather than an address. Cool, huh? (Try `javascript: alert(2+5)` to turn your browser into a calculator. Whoa.)

2. **Use `alert` to produce quick output.**

   You want to look at the source of whatever page is currently loaded, so use the `alert` mechanism to print the code in a pop-up and leave the original page in place.

3. **Print the current page's source code.**

   The `document.body.innerHTML` trick returns all the HTML code inside the `body` tag. This doesn't show your header or `doctype` information, but it does display the page as it currently sits in memory, even if it has been changed dynamically through code. That's usually enough to figure out what's going wrong in a pinch.

Chapter 3: Decisions and Debugging

In This Chapter

✔ Making decisions with conditions

✔ Working with nested if statements and switch

✔ Repeating with for loops

✔ Repeating with while loops

✔ Understanding the difference between bugs and crashes

✔ Using the debugger console

✔ Debugging your programs

Computer programs are complex. They involve information. Variables (described in Chapter 1 of this mini-book) are the foundation of information (although you'll learn about some more complex and interesting data types in later chapters). The other key component of programming is *control* — that is, managing the instructions needed to solve interesting complex problems. In this chapter, you learn the key control structures — if statements and looping structures. With increased control comes increased opportunity for error, so you also learn how to manage problems in your code.

Making Choices with if

Sometimes you'll need your code to make decisions. For example, if somebody famous typed their name in your website, you might want to create a custom greeting for them. (I know this is a goofy example, but stay with me.) Take a look at the ifElse.html site in Figures 3-1 and 3-2.

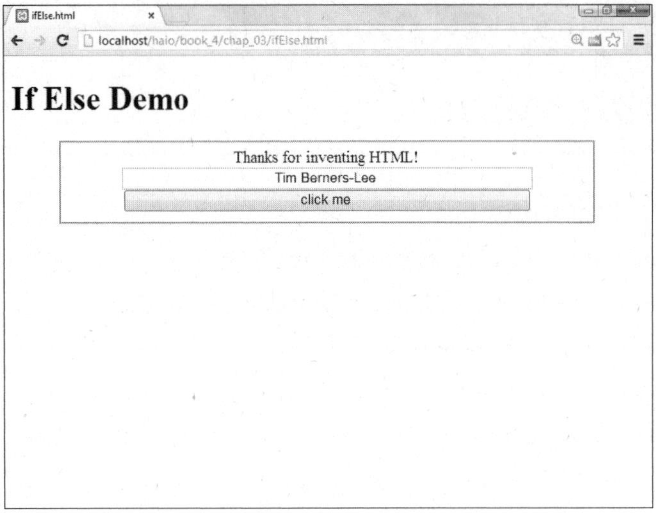

Figure 3-1:
Tim
Berners-
Lee gets
a special
greeting.

Figure 3-2:
Apparently,
this guy
isn't famous
enough.

This program (and the next few) uses a basic HTML set up to take information from a text field, respond to a button click, and print output in a designated area. Here's the HTML part of the code:

```
<body>
  <h1>If Demo</h1>

  <form action = "">
    <fieldset>
      <label id = "lblOutput">Please enter your name</label>
      <input type = "text"
```

```
            id = "txtInput"
            value = "Tim Berners-Lee" />
      <button type = "button"
              onclick = "checkName()">
        click me
      </button>
    </fieldset>
  </form>
</body>
</html>
```

As you can see, the program looks at the input in the text box and changes behavior based on the value of the text field. Here's the `checkName()` function called in ifElse.html:

```
function checkName(){
  // from ifElse.html
  lblOutput = document.getElementById("lblOutput");
  txtInput = document.getElementById("txtInput");

  userName = txtInput.value;
  if (userName == "Tim Berners-Lee"){
    lblOutput.innerHTML = "Thanks for inventing HTML!";
  } else {
    lblOutput.innerHTML = "Do I know you?";
  } // end if
} // end function
```

Changing the greeting with if

This code uses an important idea called a *condition* inside a construct called an `if` statement. Here's how to do it:

1. **Set up the web page as usual.**

   The HTML code has elements called `lblOutput` and `txtInput`. It also has a button that calls `checkName()` when it is clicked.

2. **Create variables for important page elements.**

   You're getting data from `txtInput` and changing the HTML code in `lblOutput`, so create variables for these two elements.

3. **Get `userName` from txtInput.**

   Use the `txtInput.value` trick to get the value of the input element called `txtInput` and place it in the variable `userName`.

4. **Set up a condition.**

   The key to this program is a special element called a *condition* — an expression that can be evaluated as true or false. Conditions are often (as in this case) comparisons. Note that the double equals sign (`==`) is used to represent equality. In this example, I'm asking whether the `userName` variable equals the value "Tim Berners-Lee".

5. **Place the condition in an `if` structure.**

   The `if` statement is one of a number of programming constructs which use conditions. It contains the keyword `if` followed by a condition (in parentheses). If the condition is true, all of the code in the following set of braces is executed.

6. Write code to execute if the condition is true.

Create a set of squiggly braces after the condition. Any code inside these braces will execute if the condition is true. Be sure to indent your code, and use the right squiggle brace (}) to end the block of code. In this example, I give a special greeting to Tim Berners-Lee (because he *is* just that awesome).

7. Build an `else` clause.

You can build an `if` statement with a single code block, but often you want the code to do something else if the condition was `false`. Use the `else` construct to indicate you will have a second code block that will execute only if the condition is `false`.

8. Write the code to happen when the condition is false.

The code block following the `else` clause will execute only if the condition is false. In this particular example, I have a greeting for everyone except Berners-Lee.

The different flavors of if

If statements are extremely powerful, and there are a number of variations. You can actually have one, two, or any number of branches. You can write code like this:

```
if (userName == "Tim Berners-Lee"){
  lblOutput.innerHTML = "Thanks for inventing HTML"
} // end if
```

With this structure, the greeting will occur if `userName` is "Tim Berners-Lee" and nothing will happen if the `userName` is anything else. You can also use the `if-else` structure (this is the form used in the actual code):

```
if (userName == "Tim Berners-Lee"){
  lblOutput.innerHTML = "Thanks for inventing HTML!";
} else {
  lblOutput.innerHTML = "Do I know you?";
} // end if
```

One more alternative lets you compare as many results as you wish by adding new conditions:

```
if (userName == "Tim Berners-Lee"){
  lblOutput.innerHTML = "Thanks for inventing HTML!";
} else if (userName == "Al Gore") {
  lblOutput.innerHTML = "Thanks for inventing the Internet";
} else if (userName == "Hakon Wium Lie") {
  lblOutput.innerHTML = "Thanks for inventing CSS";
```

```
} else {
  lblOutput.innerHTML = "Do I know you?";
} // end if
```

I don't repeat all the HTML code for these examples to save space. Please look on the book's website to see the appropriate HTML code that uses these examples. (Find out how to access this book's website in the Introduction.) You'll find if.html, ifElse.html, and ifElseIf.html available on the site. Be sure to view the source to see how the HTML and the JavaScript code interact. Also, review Chapter 2 of this mini-book if you want to remember how to have JavaScript code interact directly with the web page.

Conditional operators

The == operator checks to see if two values are identical, but JavaScript supports a number of other operators as well:

Operator	Meaning
a == b	a is equal to b
a < b	a is less than b
a > b	a is greater than b
a <= b	a is less than or equal to b
a >= b	a is greater than or equal to b
a != b	a is not equal to b

If you're coming from another programming language like Java, C++, or PHP you might wonder how string comparisons work because they require different operators in these languages. JavaScript uses exactly the same comparison operators for types of data, so there's no need to learn different operators. Yeah, JavaScript!

Nesting your if statements

There are a few other variations of the if structure you'll sometimes run across. One variation is the *nested* if statement. This simply means you can put if statements inside each other for more complex options. For example, look at the following code:

```
function checkTemp(){
  //from nestedIf.html
  var temp = prompt("What temperature is it outside?");
  temp = parseInt(temp);

  if (temp < 60){
    //less than 60
    if (temp < 32){
```

```
        //less than 32
        alert("It's freezing!");
      } else {
        //between 32 and 60
        alert("It's cold.");
      } // end 'freezing if'
    } else {
      //We're over 60
      if (temp < 75){
        //between 60 and 75
        alert("It's cool.");
      } else {
        //temp is higher than 75
        if (temp > 90){
          //over 90
          alert("It's really hot.");
        } else {
          //between 75 and 90
          alert("It's warm.");
        } // end 'over 90' if
      } // end 'over 75' if
    } // end 'over 60' if
} // end function
```

This code looks complicated, but it really isn't. It simply takes in a temperature and looks for a range of values. Here's what's happening:

1. **Get a temperature value from the user.**

   Ask the user for a temperature. I'm using the simple prompt statement here, but you could also grab the value from a form field. See Chapter 2 of this mini-book if you need help on that process.

2. **Convert the temperature to a numeric type.**

   Recall that computers are fussy about data types, and sometimes you need to nudge a variable to the right type. The parseInt() function forces any value into an integer, which is perfect for our needs.

3. **Use an if statement to chop the possibilities in half.**

   The outer (most encompassing) if statement separates all the cooler temperatures from the warmer ones.

4. **Use an inner if statement to clarify more if needed.**

   Within the cool (less than 60 degree) temperatures, you might want to know if it's cold or below freezing, so place a second condition to determine the temperatures.

5. **The upper bound is determined by the outer if statement.**

   The first else clause in the code is triggered when the temperature is between 32 and 60 degrees because it's inside two if statements: temp < 60 is true, and temp < 32 is false, so the temperature is between 32 and 60 degrees.

6. Indentation and comments are not optional.

As the code becomes more complex, indentation and comment characters become more critical. Make sure your indentation accurately reflects the beginning and end of each if statement, and the code is clearly commented so you know what will happen (or what you expect will happen — the truth may be different).

7. You can nest as deeply as you wish.

As you can see in this structure, there are three different possibilities for temperatures higher than 60 degrees. Simply add more if statements to get the behavior you wish.

8. Test your code.

When you build this kind of structure, you need to run your program several times to ensure it does what you expect.

Making decisions with switch

JavaScript, like a number of languages, supports another decision-making structure called switch. This is a useful alternative when you have a number of discrete values you want to compare against a single variable. Take a look at this variation of the name program from earlier in this chapter:

```
function checkName(){
    //from switch.html
    var name = prompt("What is your name?");

    switch(name){
      case "Bill Gates":
        alert("Thanks for MS Bob!");
        break;
      case "Steve Jobs":
        alert("The Newton is awesome!");
        break;
      default:
        alert("do I know you?");
    } // end
} // end checkName
```

The switch code is similar to an if-elseif structure in its behavior, but it uses a different syntax:

1. Indicate a variable in the switch statement.

In the switch statement's parentheses, place a variable or other expression. The switch statement is followed by a code block encased in squiggly braces ({ }).

2. Use the case statement to indicate a case.

The case statement is followed by a potential value of the variable, followed by a colon. It's up to the programmer to ensure the value type matches the variable type.

3. **End each case with the `break` statement.**

   End each case with the `break` statement. This indicates that you're done thinking about cases, and it's time to pop out of this data structure. If you don't explicitly include the `break` statement, you'll get strange behavior (all the subsequent cases will evaluate true as well).

4. **Define a `default` case to catch other behavior.**

   Just like you normally add a default `else` to an `if-elseif` structure to catch any unanticipated values, the `default` keyword traps for any values of the variable that were not explicitly caught.

Useful as the `switch` structure seems to be, I'm personally not a big fan of it, for the following reasons:

✦ **There are better options:** The `switch` behavior can be built with the `if-else` structure, and can often be improved by using arrays or functions. (Arrays and functions are both described in chapter 4 of this mini-book.)

✦ **Switches are not good with inequalities:** The `switch` structure works fine when there are discrete values to compare (like names) but are much more awkward when you're comparing a range of values (like temperatures).

✦ **The syntax is anachronistic:** The syntax of the `switch` statement harkens back to the C language, developed in the early days of programming. The colons and break statements combine awkwardly with the braces used elsewhere to contain code fragments.

✦ **Use of the `break` keyword is discouraged:** Normally the `break` keyword indicates you want to break the normal flow of your program. This is often used as a shortcut by sloppy programmers who can't come up with a more elegant way to write code. Because use of the `break` keyword is discouraged elsewhere in programming, it's weird to have a structure that requires its use.

✦ **Modern languages don't even have it:** A number of the newer languages (like Python) don't support `switch` at all, so at some point you're likely to be in a language that cannot do `switch`. You might as well learn alternatives now.

For these reasons, I rarely use `switch` in my own programming.

Managing Repetition with for Loops

Computers are well-known for repetitive behavior. It's pretty easy to get a computer to do something many times. The main way to get this behavior is to use a mechanism called a `loop`. The `for` loop is a standard kind of loop that is used when you know how often something will happen. Figure 3-3 shows the most basic form of the `for` loop:

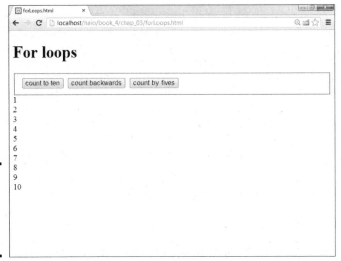

Figure 3-3:
This
program
counts from
one to ten.

Setting up the web page

The same web page is used to demonstrate three different kinds of `for` loops. As usual, the HTML code sets everything up. Here's the HTML code that creates the basic framework:

```
<body onload = "init()">
  <h1>For loops</h1>
  <form action = "">
    <fieldset>
      <button type = "button"
              onclick = "count()">
        count to ten
      </button>

      <button type = "button"
              onclick = "back()">
        count backwards
      </button>

      <button type = "button"
              onclick = "byFive()">
        count by fives
      </button>

    </fieldset>
  </form>

  <div id = "output">Click a button to see some counting...</div>
</body>
```

While the HTML is pretty straightforward, it does have some important features:

1. **The body calls an initialization function.**

   Often you'll want some code to happen when the page first loads. One common way to do this is to attach a function call to the `onload` attribute of the `body` element. In this example, I call the `init()` function as soon as the body is finished loading. The contents of the `init()` function will be described in the next section.

2. **The page is mostly an HTML form.**

   The most important part of this page is the form with three buttons on it. Each button calls a different JavaScript function.

3. **A special div is created for output.**

   It's a good idea to put some default text in the div so you can see where the output should go and so you can ensure the div is actually changing when it's supposed to.

From this example, it's easy to see why it's a good idea to write the HTML first. The HTML code gives me a solid base for the program, and it also provides a good outline of what JavaScript code I'll need. Clearly this page calls for four JavaScript functions, `init()`, `count()`, `back()`, and `byFive()`. The names of all the functions are pretty self-explanatory, so it's pretty easy to see what each one is supposed to do. It's also clear that the div named `output` is intended as an output area. When you design the HTML page well, the JavaScript code becomes very easy to start.

Initializing the output

This program illustrates a situation that frequently comes up in JavaScript programming: All three of the main functions will refer to the same output area. It seems a waste to create a variable for `output` three different times. Instead, I make a single global `output` variable available to all functions, and attach the variable to that element once when the page loads.

In order to understand why this is necessary, it's important to discuss an idea called *variable scope*. Generally, variables are created inside functions. As long as the function is running, the variable still exists. However, when a function is done running, all the variables created inside that function are instantly destroyed. This prevents functions from accidentally changing the variables in other functions. Practically, it means you can think of each function as a separate program.

However, sometimes you want a variable to live in more than one function. The `output` variable in the forLoop.html page is a great example because all of the functions will need it. One solution is to create the variable *outside* any functions. Then all the functions will have access to it.

You can create the `output` variable without being in a function, but you can't attach it to the actual div in the web page until the web page has finished forming. The init () function is called when the body loads. Inside that function, I assign a value to the global output variable. Here's how the main JavaScript and the init () method code looks:

```
var output;

function init(){
  output = document.getElementById("output");
} // end init
```

This code creates output as a global variable, and then attaches it to the output div after the page has finished loading.

Creating the basic for loop

The standard for loop counts the values between 1 and 10. The "count to ten" button triggers the count () function. Here's the code for count ():

```
function count(){
  output.innerHTML = "";
  for (i = 1; i <= 10; i++){
    output.innerHTML += i + "<br />";
  } // end for loop
} // end count
```

Although the count () function clearly prints ten lines, it only has one line that modifies the output div. The main code repeats many times to create the long output.

1. **You can use the output var immediately.**

   Because output is a global variable and it has already been created, you can use it instantly. There's no need to initialize it in the function.

2. **Clear the output.**

   Set output.value to the empty string ("") to clear the output. This will destroy whatever text is currently in the div.

3. **Start a for loop.**

   The for loop is a special loop used to repeat something a certain number of times. For loops have three components: initialization, comparison, and update.

4. **Initialize your counting variable.**

   A for loop works by changing the value of an integer many times. The first part of a for loop initializes this variable (often called i) to a starting value (usually 0 or 1).

5. **Specify a condition for staying in the loop.**

   The second part of a for statement is a condition. As long as the condition is true, the loop will continue. As soon as the condition is evaluated as false, the loop will exit.

6. **Change the variable.**

   The third part of a `for` statement somehow changes the counting variable. The most common way to change the variable is to add one to it. The `i++` syntax is a shortcut for "add one to i."

7. **Build a code block for repeated code.**

   Use braces and indentation to indicate which code repeats. All code inside the braces repeats.

8. **Inside the loop, write to the output.**

   On each iteration of the loop, add the current value of `i` to the output div's `innerHTML`. Also add a break (`<br />`) to make the output look better. When you add to an `innerHTML` property, you're writing HTML code, so if you want the output to occur on different lines, you need to write the HTML to make this happen. (See the section "Introducing shortcut operators" in this chapter for an explanation of the `+=` statement.)

9. **Close the loop.**

   Don't forget to end the loop, or your program will not run correctly.

Introducing shortcut operators

You might have noticed a couple of new operators in the code for forLoops. html. These are some shortcut tools that allow you to express common ideas more compactly. For example, consider the following code:

```
i = i + 1;
```

This means, "Add one to `i`, and store the result back in `i`." It's a pretty standard statement, even if it does drive algebra teachers bananas. The statement is so common that it is often abbreviated, like this:

```
i += 1;
```

This statement means exactly the same as the last one; add one to `i`. You can use this to add any amount to the variable `i`.Because the `+` sign is used to concatenate (combine) strings, you can use the `+=` shortcut with string manipulation, so consider this variation:

```
var userName = "Andy";
userName += ", Benevolent Dictator for Life";
```

The second statement appends my official (I wish) title to the end of my name.

You can also use the `-=` operator to subtract from a variable. It's even possible to use `*=` and `/=`, but they are not commonly used.

Moving back to numbers — because adding one is extremely common, there's another shortcut that's even more brief:

```
i++;
```

This statement also means, "Add one to `i`." In the standard `for` loop, I use that variation because it's very easy.

When programmers decided to make a new variation of C, they called the new language C++. Get it? It's one better than C! Those guys are a hoot!

Counting backwards

After you understand basic `for` loops, it's not difficult to make a loop that counts backwards. Here's the `back()` function (called by the Count Backwards button):

```
function back(){
  output.innerHTML = "";
  for (i = 10; i > 0; i--){
    output.innerHTML += i + "<br />";
  } // end for loop
} // end back
```

When the user activates this function, she gets the result shown in Figure 3-4.

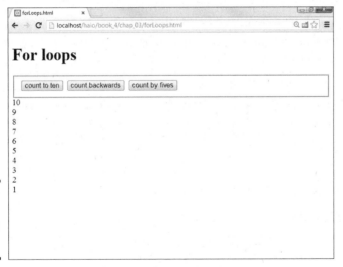

Figure 3-4:
Now the page counts backwards.

Book IV
Chapter 3

Decisions and
Debugging

This code is almost exactly like the first loop, but look carefully at how the loop is created:

1. **Initialize `i` to a high value.**

   This time I want to count backwards from 10 to 1, so start `i` with the value `10`.

2. **Keep going as long as `i` is *greater than* 0.**

   It's important to note that the logic changes here. If `i` is greater than 0, the loop should continue. If `i` becomes 0 or less, the loop exits.

3. **Subtract 1 from i on each pass.**

   The - - operator works much like ++, but it subtracts 1 from the variable.

Counting by fives

Counting by fives (or any other value) is pretty trivial after you know how for loops work. Here's the byFive() code called by the Count by Five button:

```
function byFive(){
  output.innerHTML = "";
  for (i = 5; i <= 25; i += 5){
    output.innerHTML += i + "<br />";
  } // end for loop
} // end byFive
```

It is remarkably similar to the other looping code you've seen.

1. **Initialize i to 5.**

   The first value I want is 5, so that is the initial value for i.

2. **Continue as long as i is less than or equal to 25.**

   Because I want the value 25 to appear, I set the condition to be less than or equal to 25.

3. **Add 5 to i on each pass.**

   Each time through the loop, I add 5 to i using the += operator.

The Count by Five code is shown in action in Figure 3-5.

Figure 3-5:
Now the page counts by fives.

Understanding the Zen of for loops

For loops might seem complex, but they really aren't. The key to making a good for loop is understanding that the for statement has three parts. All three parts of the statement refer to the same variable. Sometimes the variable used in a loop is called a *sentry variable.* If you don't have a better name for the sentry variable, it's traditional to use i. To make a good loop, you need to know three things about the sentry variable:

✦ **How does it start?** The first part of the for loop indicates the starting value of the sentry variable. If you're counting up, you'll usually begin the sentry variable at 0 or 1. If you're counting down, you'll usually begin the sentry value with a larger number. Regardless, you have to indicate some starting value.

✦ **How does it end?** The middle part of the for loop indicates a condition. As long as the condition remains true, the loop continues. As soon as the condition is evaluated as false, the loop ends.

✦ **How does it change?** There must be some mechanism for moving the sentry from its starting position to the final position. In a for loop, this is normally some kind of addition or subtraction. Whatever you do here, you need to ensure that it's possible for the sentry to move from the starting position to the ending position, or the loop will never end.

Building while Loops

For loops are useful when you know how often a loop will continue, but sometimes you need a more flexible type of loop. The while loop is based on a simple idea. It contains a condition. When the condition is true, the loop continues; if the condition is evaluated as false, the loop exits.

Making a basic while loop

Figure 3-6 shows a dialog box asking for a password. The program keeps asking for a password until the user enters the correct password.

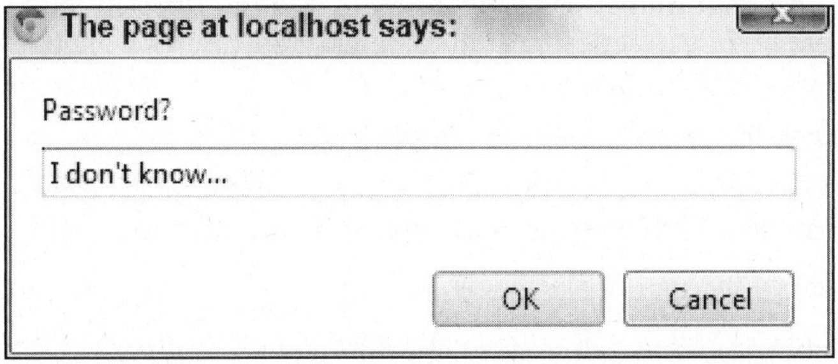

Figure 3-6:
This program keeps asking for the password until the user gets it right.

Here's the HTML code used for two different `while` examples:

```html
<body>
  <h1>While Loop Demo</h1>
  <p>The password is 'HTML5'</p>
  <form action = "">
    <fieldset>
      <button type = "button"
              onclick = "getPassword()">
        guess the password
      </button>

      <button type = "button"
              onclick = "threeTries()">
        guess the password in three tries
      </button>
    </fieldset>
  </form>
</body>
```

The version shown in Figure 3-6 keeps popping up a dialog box until the user gets the answer correct.

```javascript
function getPassword(){
  //from while.html
  var correct = "HTML5";
  var guess = "";
  while (guess != correct){
    guess = prompt("Password?");
  } // end while
  alert("You may proceed");
} // end getPassword
```

A `while` loop for passwords is not hard to build:

1. **Store the correct password in a variable.**

   Variable names are important because they can make your code easier to follow. I use the names `correct` and `guess` to differentiate the two types of password. Beginners often call one of these variables `password`, but that can be confusing because there are actually *two* passwords (the correct password and the guessed password) in play here. The best way to design variable names is to anticipate the conditions they will be used in. This function is based on the condition `guess == correct`. This is a really nice condition because it's really easy to determine what we're trying to figure out (whether the guess is correct). It takes some practice to anticipate variable names well, but it's a habit well worth forming.

2. **Initialize the `guess` to an empty value.**

   The key variable for this loop is `guess`. It starts as an empty string. It's critical to initialize the key variable before the loop begins.

3. **Set up the `while` statement.**

   The `while` statement has extremely simple syntax: the keyword `while` followed by a condition, followed by a block of code.

4. **Build the condition.**

   The condition is the heart of a `while` loop. The condition must be constructed so the loop happens at least once (ensure this by comparing
   the condition to the variable initialization). When the condition is true,
   the loop continues. When the condition is evaluated to false, the loop
   will exit. This condition compares `guess` to `correct`. If `guess` is not
   equal to `correct`, the code will continue.

5. **Write the code block.**

   Use braces and indentation to indicate the block of code that will be
   repeated in the loop. The only code in this particular loop asks the user
   for a password.

6. **Add code to change the key variable inside the loop.**

   Somewhere inside the loop, you need code that changes the value of the
   key variable. In this example, the prompt statement changes the password. As long as the user eventually gets the right password, the loop
   ends.

Getting your loops to behave

While loops can be dangerous. It's quite easy to write a `while` loop that
works incorrectly, and these can be an exceptionally difficult kind of bug
to find and fix. If a `while` loop is incorrectly designed, it can refuse to
ever run or run forever. These *endless loops* are especially troubling in
JavaScript because they can crash the entire browser. If a JavaScript program gets into an endless loop, often the only solution is to use the operating system task manager (Ctrl+Alt+Delete on Windows) to shut down the
entire browser.

The easy way to make sure your loop works is to remember that `while`
loops need all the same features as `for` loops. (These ideas are built into
the structure of a `for` loop. You're responsible for them yourself in a `while`
loop.) If your loop doesn't work, check that you've followed these steps:

+ **Identify a key variable:** A `while` loop is normally based on a condition,
  which is usually a comparison (although it might also be a variable or
  function that returns a Boolean value). In a `for` loop, the key variable
  is almost always an integer. While loops can be based on any type of
  variable.

+ **Initialize the variable before the loop:** Before the loop begins, set up
  the initial value of the key variable to ensure the loop happens at least
  once. (How does the variable start?)

+ **Identify the condition for the loop:** A `while` loop is based on a condition. Define the condition so the loop continues while the condition is
  `true`, and exits when the condition is evaluated to `false`. (How does
  the variable end?)

✦ **Change the condition inside the loop:** Somewhere inside the loop code, you need to have statements that will eventually make the condition `false`. If you forget this part, your loop will never end. (How does the variable change?)

This example is a good example of a `while` loop, but a terrible way to handle security. The password is shown in the clear, and anybody could view the source code to see the correct password. There are far better ways to handle security, but this is the cleanest example of a `while` loop I could think of.

Managing more complex loops

It won't take long before you find situations where the standard `for` or `while` loops do not seem adequate. For example, consider the password example again. This time, you want to ask for a password until the user gets the password correct or guesses incorrectly three times. Think about how you would build that code. There are a number of ways to do it, but here's the cleanest approach:

```
function threeTries(){
  //continues until user is correct or has three
  //incorrect guesses
  //from while.html

  var correct = "HTML5";
  var guess = "";
  var keepGoing = true;
  var tries = 0;

  while (keepGoing){
    guess = prompt("Password?");
    if (guess == correct){
      alert("You may proceed");
      keepGoing = false;
    } else {
      tries++;
      if (tries >= 3){
        alert("Too many tries. Launching missiles...");
        keepGoing = false;
      } // end if
    } // end if
  } // end while
} // end threetries
```

This code is a little more complex, but it uses a nice technique to greatly simplify loops:

1. **Initialize `correct` and `guess`.**

   As in the previous example, initialize the `correct` and `guess` passwords.

2. **Build a counter to indicate the number of tries.**

   The `tries` variable will count how many attempts have been made.

3. **Build a Boolean sentry variable.**

   The keepGoing variable is special. Its entire job is to indicate whether the loop should continue or not. It is a Boolean variable, meaning it will only contain the values true or false.

4. **Use keepGoing as the condition.**

   A condition doesn't have to be a comparison. It just has to be true or false. Use the Boolean variable as the condition! As long as keepGoing has the value true, the loop will continue. Any time you want to exit the loop, set keepGoing to false.

5. **Ask for the password.**

   You still need the password, so get this information from the user.

6. **Check to see if the password is correct.**

   Use an if statement to see if the password is correct.

7. **If the password is correct, provide feedback to the user and set keepGoing to false.**

   The next time the while statement is executed, the loop ends. (Remember, you want the loop to end when the password is correct.)

8. **If the password is incorrect, if the (guess == correct) condition is false, that means the user did not get the password right.**

   In this case, add one to the number of tries.

9. **Check the number of tries.**

   Build another if statement to check the number of tries.

10. **If it's been three turns, provide feedback (threatening global annihilation is always fun) and set keepGoing to false.**

The basic idea of this strategy is quite straightforward: Create a special Boolean variable with the singular job of indicating whether the loop continues. Any time you want the loop to exit, change the value of that variable.

If you change most of your while loops to this format (using a Boolean variable as the condition), you'll generally eliminate most while loop issues. When your code gets complicated, it gets tempting to use and (&&) and or (||) operators to make more complex conditions. These Boolean operators are very confusing for beginners and are generally not necessary. (My rule of thumb is this: If you can explain DeMorgan's law, you can use Boolean operators in your conditions.) Most beginners (like me, and I've been doing this for thirty years) make their loops *way* too complicated. Using a Boolean variable in your loop can eliminate the need for Boolean operators and solve a lot of logic problems.

**Book IV
Chapter 3**

**Decisions and
Debugging**

Managing Errors with a Debugger

By the time you're writing loops and conditions, things can go pretty badly in your code. Sometimes it's very hard to tell what exactly is going on. Fortunately, modern browsers have some nice tools that help you look at your code more carefully.

A *debugger* is a special tool that allows you to run a program in "slow motion," moving one line at a time so you can see exactly what is happening. Google Chrome has a built-in debugger, so I begin with that one.

To see how a debugger works, follow these steps.

1. **Load a page into Chrome.**

   You can add a debugger to most browsers, but Chrome has one built in, so start with that one. I'm loading the forLoops.html page because loops are a common source of bugs.

2. **Open the Developer Tools window.**

   If you right-click anywhere on the page and choose Inspect Element (or press the F12 key), you'll get a wonderful debugging tool that looks like Figure 3-7.

3. **Inspect the page with the Elements tab.**

   The default tab shows you the page in an outline view, letting you see the structure of your page. If you click any element in the outline, you can see what styles are associated with that element. The actual element is also highlighted on the main page so you can see exactly where everything is. This can be very useful for checking your HTML and CSS.

4. **Move to the Sources tab.**

   The Developer Tools window has a separate tab for working with JavaScript code. Select the Sources tab to see your entire code at once. There's a small menu button that lets you select from all the source pages your program uses. If your page pulls in external JavaScript files, you'll be able to select them here as well. (Note some older versions of Chrome called this the Scripts tab.)

5. **Set a breakpoint.**

   Typically you let the program begin at normal speed and slow down right before you get to a trouble spot. In this case, I'm interested in the count() function, so click on the first line (16) of that function in the code window. (It's more reliable to click on the first line of the function than the line that declares it, so use line 16 instead of line 15.) Click the line number of the line you want to pause, and the line number will highlight, indicating it is now a break point.

6. **Refresh the page.**

   In the main browser, use the refresh button or F5 key to refresh the page. The page may initially be blank. That's fine — it means the program has paused when it encountered the function.

7. **Your page is now running.**

   If you look back over the main page, you should see it is now up and running. Nothing is happening yet because you haven't activated any of the buttons.

8. **Click the Count button.**

   The Count button should activate the code in the count function. Click this button to see if that happens.

9. **Code should now be paused on line 17.**

   Back in the code window, line 17 is now highlighted. That means the browser is paused, and when you activate the step button, the highlighted code will happen.

10. **Step into the next line.**

    In the Developer Tool window is a series of buttons on top of the right column. Step into the next line looks like a down arrow with a dot under it. You can also use the F11 key to activate the command.

11. **Step a few times.**

    Use the F11 key or the step button to step forward a few times. Watch how the highlight moves around so you can actually see the loop happening. This is very useful when your code is not behaving properly because it allows you to see exactly how the processor is moving through your code.

12. **Hover over the variable i in your code.**

    When you are in debug mode, you can hover the mouse over any variable in the code window and you'll see what the current value of that variable is. Often when your code is performing badly, it's because a variable isn't doing what you think it is.

13. **Add a watch expression to simplify looking at variables.**

    If you think the loop is not behaving, you can add a *watch expression* to make debugging easier. Right under the step buttons you'll see a tab called Watch Expressions. Click the plus sign to add a new expression. Type in i and enter.

14. **Continue stepping through the code.**

    Now you can continue to step through the code and see what is happening to the variable. This is incredibly useful when your code is not performing like you want it to.

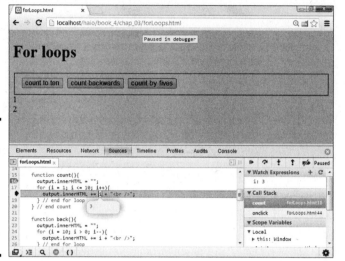

Figure 3-7:
The Chrome
debugger
makes it
easy to
figure out
what's
happening.

I personally think the debugger built into Chrome is one of the best out there, but it's not the only choice. If you're using Firefox, the excellent Firebug extension adds the same functionality to Firefox (`http://get firebug.com/`). Safari has a similar Web Inspector tool built in, and even IE finally has a decent debugger called `F12`. All work in roughly the same way. Usually, however, a JavaScript error will crash on all browsers, so pick one you like for initial testing, and then use other browser-specific tools only when necessary.

Debugging with the interactive console

The Developer Tools window has another really wonderful tool called the *console*. I introduced it briefly in Chapter 2 of this mini-book, but there's much more you can do with this wonderful tool. Try this exercise to see some of the great ways you can use the console:

1. **Begin with the forLoops.html page.**

   You can debug any page, but forLoops.html is especially helpful for debugging.

2. **Place a breakpoint.**

   For this demonstration, put a breakpoint in the `count()` function (line 16 if you're using my version of the code).

3. **Step through a few lines.**

   Use the `step` button or F11 key to step through a few lines of code.

4. **Switch to the console tab.**

    The Console tab switches to console mode. This is particularly interesting when the program is paused, as you can investigate and change the nature of the page in real time.

5. **Change a style.**

    Try typing `document.body.style.backgroundColor = light Green` in the console. This modifies the background color of the page in real time. This is fun but not seriously useful.

6. **Examine the `document.body`.**

    Type `document.body` in the console and press Enter. You'll see plenty of information about the body. `Document.body` is actually a JavaScript variable containing the current document body. It's very powerful and allows you to understand a lot about what's going on.

7. **Examine the body's innerHTML.**

    Like any HTML element, `document.body` has an innerHTML property. You can examine this in the console: `document.body.innerHTML`.

8. **Look at the variable `i`.**

    You can examine the current value of any variable as long as that variable currently has a meaning. Type `i` (then press enter) to see the current value of the variable `i`. If the `count()` function isn't currently running, you may get a strange value here.

9. **Check the type of `i`.**

    As you may recall from Chapter 2 of this minibook, all variables have a specific type defined by JavaScript, and sometimes that data type is not what you expected. You can ask the browser what type of data any variable contains: `typeof(i)` returns "number." You may also see "string" or "object."

10. **See if your output variable is defined correctly.**

    Like many interactive programs, this page has a div called `div` that contains the output. If this is not defined correctly, it won't work. Try `output` in the console to see if the `output` variable is correctly defined and in scope. You can view the contents of `output` with `output.innerHTML`, or you can even change the value of `output` like this: `output.innerHTML = "Hi Mom!"`.

11. **Check your functions.**

    You can check to see if the functions are what you think they are in the console. Try typing `count` (with no parentheses) to see the contents of count.

12. **Print to the console from your programs.**

    You can even have your programs print information to the console. Use the code `console.log("hi there")` anywhere in your code to have the code print a value to the console. Normally you'll do this only when your code is not functioning properly to see what's going on. You might use something like this: `console.log("current value of i" + i)`. The user typically doesn't know there is a console, so she won't see any results of `console.log()`. You should remove all calls to `console.log()` before releasing the final version of your code.

The console was not available in earlier browser versions, so it isn't always taught as a part of JavaScript programming. Now that it's a commonly available tool, you should definitely consider using it.

Debugging strategies

It's a fact of life — when you write code, you will have bugs. Every programmer needs to know how to diagnose and fix code when it goes wrong.

The first thing to understand is that crashes and bugs are not the same. A *crash* is a problem with your code that prevents the program from running at all. These sound bad, but they're actually easier to resolve than *bugs*, which are caused by technically correct code doing the wrong thing.

Resolving syntax errors

The most common type of error is a *crash* or *syntax error*, usually meaning you misspelled a command or used a function incorrectly. From the user's point of view, browsers don't usually tell you directly when a syntax error occurs, but simply sit there and pout. The best way to discover what's going wrong is to call up the debugging console. As soon as you discover a page not acting correctly, go to the debugging console and look at the Console tab. You'll see error messages there, and you can often click on an error message to see the problem. As an example, take a look at the following code from syntaxError.html:

```
function getPassword(){
    var correct "HTML5";
    var guess = "";
    while (guess != correct){
        guess = prompt("Password?");
    } // end while
    alert("You may proceed");
} // end getPassword
```

This code might look just like the `getPassword()` function from `while.html`, but I introduced a subtle error that's difficult to find with the naked eye. Run the program in your browser, click the Guess the Password button, and the browser will seem to do nothing but glare at you insolently. However, if you activate the Debugging console, you'll realize it's telling you what it thinks is wrong. Figure 3-8 illustrates the Debugging console trying to help.

Figure 3-8:
The
debugging
console
has useful
information
here!

It would be great if the debugger told you exactly what is wrong, but normally there's a bit of detective work involved in deciphering error messages. It appears in this case that there are two errors, but they're really the same thing. Click the link to the right of the first error and you'll be taken to the Sources view with the offending line highlighted, as you see in Figure 3-9.

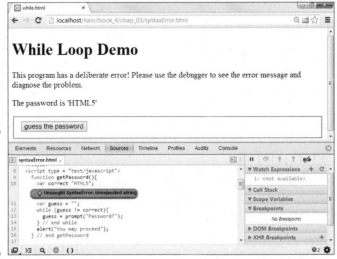

**Book IV
Chapter 3**

**Decisions and
Debugging**

Figure 3-9:
Here's
where the
browser
thinks
something
went wrong.

The error messages aren't always as clear as they could be, but they are usually helpful in their own way. The error message here is "unexpected string." That means the browser encountered a string value when it expected something else. That's somewhat helpful, but the real strategy is to know that *something* is probably wrong with this line, and you need to look it over carefully. At some point, you'll probably realize that line 10 should have a single equals sign. Rather than `var correct "HTML5"`, it should read `var correct = "HTML5"`. This was (as are most syntax errors) a problem caused by sloppy typing. Like most syntax errors, it's kind of difficult to find (but much easier with the debugger). After you find the error, it's usually pretty easy to fix. Change the code in your editor and reload in the browser (with the F5 key) to see if your change fixes things.

Note that fixing the "unexpected string" error automatically resolves the "function not defined" error. This is pretty common because often one error cascades and causes other error messages. Generally you only need to worry about the topmost error on the list because resolving it may solve the other errors with no further work. (Of course, resolving one error may unmask other heretofore hidden errors, but this is less common.)

Squashing logic bugs

Syntax errors seem bad because they cause the whole program to crash, but they're actually pretty easy to resolve. There's another type of problem called *logic errors* that are much more troublesome. In fact, they're nearly impossible to resolve without some sort of debugging tool. However, like a syntax error, when you can find a logic error, it's usually quite easy to repair. Take a look at logicError.html to see a typical logic problem in the `getPassword()` function:

```
function getPassword(){
  var correct = "HTML5";
  var guess = "";
  while (guess == correct){
    guess = prompt("Password?");
  } // end while
  alert("You may proceed");
} // end getPassword
```

Just looking at the code, it's very difficult to see the problem. Worse, when you run the program in your browser, it won't report an error. It won't work correctly, but the code is all technically correct. Rather than telling it to do something illegal (which would result in a syntax error), I have told the program to do something that's completely legal but not logical. Logic errors are called *bugs*, and they're much more interesting (but subtle) to resolve than syntax errors (normally called *crashes*).

To resolve a logic error, there's a few steps:

1. **Understand what you're trying to accomplish.**

    Whenever you write a program, be sure you review what you're trying to accomplish before you run the program. If you don't know what you expect, you won't know if your program got there. It's often good to write down what you expect so you'll know if you got there. (Professional programmers are usually required to list expectations before they write a single line of code.) For this example, when the user clicks the Guess the Password button, the user should get a prompt allowing them to guess the password.

2. **Understand what your code did.**

   Run the logicError.html page yourself to see what actually happens. With a logic error, the behavior is unpredictable. A loop may never happen, it may never end, or it might sometimes work right and sometimes not. The key to finding logic errors is to predict why the code is doing what it's doing and why it's not doing what you want. In this example, when I press the Guess the Password button, the You May Proceed dialog box immediately appears, never giving me the chance to guess a password.

3. **Form a hypothesis or two *before* looking at code.**

   Think about what is wrong before you look over the code. Try to describe in plain English (not technical jargon) what is going wrong. In this case, I think something is preventing the prompt from appearing. Maybe the statement causing the prompt is written incorrectly, or maybe the code is never getting there. Those are the two most likely possibilities, so they're what I'll look for. Decide this before you look at code because the moment you see code, you'll start worrying about details rather than thinking about the big picture. Logic errors are almost always about logic, and no amount of staring at code will show you logic errors, nor will a debugger spot them for you.

4. **Resolve syntax errors**.

   Go to the console and see if there are any syntax errors. If so, resolve them. Logic errors will not appear until you've resolved all syntax errors. If your code shows no syntax errors but still doesn't work correctly, you've got a logic error.

5. **Start the debugger.**

   Interactive debugging is incredibly helpful with logic errors. Begin with your English definitions of what you think should happen and what you know is happening. Find the function you think is the problem and set a breakpoint at that function.

6. **Identify key variables or conditions.**

   Most logic errors are centered around a condition that's not working right, and conditions are usually based on variables. Begin by taking a careful look at the conditions that control the behavior you're worried about. In this case, I've got a loop that doesn't seem to be happening — ever. This means I should take a careful look at that loop statement and any variables used in that statement.

7. **Step to your suspicious code.**

If you're worried about a condition (which is very common), use the debugger tools to step to that condition, but don't run it yet. (In most debuggers, a highlighted line is *about* to be run.)

8. **Look at the relevant variables.**

Before running the condition line, think about what you think any variables used in that condition should contain. Use the Watch tools or hover over the variable names to ensure you know the current values and they're what you think they should be. In this example, I'm concerned about line 12 (`while guess == correct`), so I want to see what those variables contain.

9. **Predict what the suspicious line should do.**

If you're worried about a condition, you're generally expecting it to do something it isn't doing. In this case, the condition should trigger the prompt command on line 13 when the function is called, but it appears that we're never getting to line 13 (or we are getting there and line 13 isn't doing what we think it's doing). The goal of debugging is to identify which possible problems could be happening and isolate which of these problems are actually occurring. Make sure you know what you're looking for before you start looking for it.

10. **Compare your expectations with reality**.

As you step through the `getPassword()` function in the debugger (with the `step into` button or F11 key), you might see the problem. The `while` loop begun in line 12 *never* executes, meaning line 13 never happens, but it should *always* happen on the first pass. Now you know exactly what the program is doing, but you don't know why yet.

11. **Think about your logic.**

Logic errors aren't about getting the commands right (those are syntax errors). Logic errors are about telling the computer to do the wrong thing. Think hard about the logic you've applied here. In this case, it appears my condition is backwards. You told the computer to continue looping as long as the guess is correct. You probably meant to continue as long as the guess is incorrect. The guess starts out incorrect because of the way you (appropriately) initialized both variables. Thus the condition is automatically skipped and the prompt never happens.

12. **Fix it.**

Fixing code is easy when you know what's wrong. In this case, my condition was legal but illogical. Replace `guess == correct` with `guess != correct` and your code will work correctly.

Don't worry if you find debugging difficult. Programming is both an art and a science, and debugging logic errors falls much more along the art side of the equation. It does get much easier with practice and experience.

Couldn't we make this automatic?

If a debugger can find syntax errors, wouldn't it be awesome if debuggers could find logic errors too? This issue turns out to be one of the big unsolved problems of computer science. Researchers are still trying to discover a technique for mathematically determining whether a program is logically correct without having to run it, and such efforts are called *proofs of program correctness*. If you study formal computer science, you'll encounter these problems as part of a programming languages class. Who knows? You might be the person who solves this problem, and makes programming easier for everybody!

Book IV
Chapter 3

Decisions and
Debugging

Chapter 4: Functions, Arrays, and Objects

In This Chapter

↙ **Passing parameters into functions**

↙ **Returning values from functions**

↙ **Functions and variable scope**

↙ **Producing basic arrays**

↙ **Retrieving data from arrays**

↙ **Building a multidimensional array**

↙ **Creating objects**

↙ **Building object constructors**

↙ **Introducing JSON notation**

It doesn't take long for your code to become complex. Soon enough, you find yourself wanting to write more sophisticated programs. When things get larger, you need new kinds of organizational structures to handle the added complexity.

You can bundle several lines of code into one container and give this new chunk of code a name: a *function*. You can also take a whole bunch of variables, put them into a container, and give it a name. That's called an *array*. If you combine functions and data, you get another interesting structure called an *object*.

You may have encountered variables and functions in their simplest forms elsewhere in this book (variables were first introduced in Chapter 1 of this minibook, and functions made their appearance in Chapter 2). This chapter is about how to work with more code and more data without going crazy.

Breaking Code into Functions

Functions come in handy when you're making complex code easier to handle — a useful tool for controlling complexity. You can take a large, complicated program and break it into several smaller pieces. Each piece stands alone and solves a specific part of the overall problem.

You can think of each function as a miniature program. You can define variables in functions, put loops and branches in there, and do anything else you can do with a program. A program using functions is basically a program full of subprograms.

After you define your functions, they're just like new JavaScript commands. In a sense, when you add functions, you're adding to JavaScript.

To explain functions better, think back to an old campfire song, "The Ants Go Marching." Figure 4-1 re-creates this classic song for you in JavaScript format. (You may want to roast a marshmallow while you view this program.)

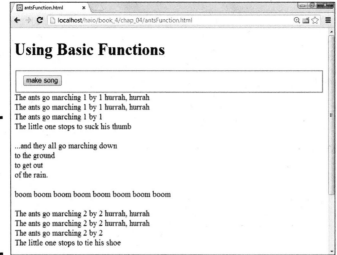

Figure 4-1: Nothing reminds me of functions like a classic campfire song.

If you're unfamiliar with this song, it simply recounts the story of a bunch of ants. The littlest one apparently has some sort of attention issues. During each verse, the little one gets distracted by something that rhymes with the verse number. The song typically has ten verses, but I'm just doing two for the demo.

Thinking about structure

Before you look at the code, think about the structure of the song, "The Ants Go Marching." Like many songs, it has two parts. The *chorus* is a phrase repeated many times throughout the song. The song has several *verses*, which are similar to each other, but not quite identical.

Think about the song sheet passed around the campfire. (I'm getting hungry for a s'more.) The chorus is usually listed only one time, and each verse is listed. Sometimes, you have a section somewhere on the song sheet that looks like the following:

```
Verse 1
Chorus
Verse 2
Chorus
```

Musicians call this a *road map,* and that's a great name for it. A road map is a high-level view of how you progress through the song. In the road map, you don't worry about the details of the particular verse or chorus. The road map shows the big picture, and you can look at each verse or chorus for the details.

Building the antsFunction.html program

Take a look at the code for antsFunction.html and see how it reminds you of the song sheet for "The Ants Go Marching":

```
<!DOCTYPE html>
<html lang = "en-US">

  <head>
    <meta charset = "UTF-8">
    <title>antsFunction.html</title>
    <script type = "text/javascript">
      //from antsFunction.html

      var output;

      function chorus() {
        var text = "...and they all go marching down <br />";
        text += "to the ground <br />";
        text += "to get out <br />";
        text += "of the rain. <br />";
        text += " <br />";
        text += "boom boom boom boom boom boom boom boom <br /><br />";
        output.innerHTML += text;
      } // end chorus

      function verse1(){
        var text = "The ants go marching 1 by 1 hurrah, hurrah <br />";
        text += "The ants go marching 1 by 1 hurrah, hurrah <br />";
        text += "The ants go marching 1 by 1 <br />";
        text += " The little one stops to suck his thumb <br /><br />";
        output.innerHTML += text;
      } // end verse1

      function verse2(){
        var text = "The ants go marching 2 by 2 hurrah, hurrah <br />";
        text += "The ants go marching 2 by 2 hurrah, hurrah <br />";
        text += "The ants go marching 2 by 2 <br />";
        text += " The little one stops to tie his shoe <br /><br />";
        output.innerHTML += text;
      } // end verse2

      function makeSong(){
        output = document.getElementById("output");
        output.innerHTML = "";
        verse1();
        chorus();
        verse2();
        chorus();
      } // end makeSong

    </script>

  </head>
```

```
<body>
  <h1>Using Basic Functions</h1>
  <form action = "">
    <fieldset>
      <button type = "button"
              onclick = "makeSong()">
        make song
      </button>
    </fieldset>
  </form>

  <div id = "output">
    The song will appear here...
  </div>

</body>
</html>
```

The program code breaks the parts of the song into the same pieces a song sheet does. Here are some interesting features of antsFunction.html:

✦ **I created a function called** `chorus()`**.** Functions are simply collections of code lines with a name.

✦ **All the code for the chorus goes into this function.** Anything I want as part of printing the chorus goes into the `chorus()` function. Later, when I want to print the chorus, I can just call the `chorus()` function and it will perform the code I stored there.

✦ **Each verse has a function, too.** I broke the code for each verse into its own function.

✦ **The** `makeSong` **function is a road map.** When all the details are delegated to the functions, the main part of the code just controls the order in which the functions are called. In this case, the `makeSong()` function is called by the button press, which runs all the other functions.

✦ **Details are hidden in the functions.** The `makeSong` code handles the big picture. The details (how to print the chorus or verses) are hidden inside the functions.

✦ **I'm using standard form-based output.** Each of the functions creates its own part of the song and adds it to the output as needed.

Passing Data to and from Functions

Functions are logically separated from each other. This separation is a good thing because it prevents certain kinds of errors. However, sometimes you want to send information to a function. You may also want a function to return some type of value. The antsParam.html page rewrites the "The Ants Go Marching" song in a way that takes advantage of function input and output.

```
<!DOCTYPE HTML>
<html lang = "en">
<head>
  <title>param.html</title>
  <meta charset = "UTF-8" />
  <style type = "text/css">
  </style>
  <script type = "text/javascript">
  //Ants to marching in using functions with parameters

  function makeSong(){
    //create output variable
    var output = document.getElementById("output");

    output.innerHTML = "";

    output.innerHTML += verse(1);
    output.innerHTML += chorus();
    output.innerHTML += verse(2);
    output.innerHTML += chorus();
  } // end makeSong

  function chorus(){
    var result = "-and they all go marching down, <br />";
    result += "to the ground, to get out, of the rain. <br />";
    result += "boom boom boom boom <br />";
    result += "boom boom boom boom <br />";
    result += "<br />";
    return result;
  } // end chorus

  function verse(verseNumber){
    var distraction = "";
    if (verseNumber == 1){
      distraction = "suck his thumb";
    } else if (verseNumber == 2){
      distraction = "tie his shoe";
    } else {
      distraction = "there's a problem here...";
    } // end if

    var result = "The ants go marching ";
    result += verseNumber + " by " + verseNumber + ", ";
    result += "hurrah, hurrah <br />";
    result += "The ants go marching ";
    result += verseNumber + " by " + verseNumber + ", ";
    result += "hurrah, hurrah <br />";
    result += "The ants go marching ";
    result += verseNumber + " by " + verseNumber + "<br />";
    result += "The little one stops to ";
    result += distraction + "<br /> <br />";

    return result;
  } // end verse

  </script>
```

I don't provide a figure of this program because it looks just like antsFunction.html to the user. One advantage of functions is that I can improve the underlying behavior of a program without imposing a change in the user's experience.

This code incorporates a couple of important new ideas. (The following list is just the overview; the specifics are coming in the following sections.)

+ **These functions return a value.** The functions no longer do their own `alerts`. Instead, they create a value and return it to the main program.

+ **Only one verse function exists.** Because the verses are all pretty similar, using only one verse function makes sense. This improved function needs to know what verse it's working on to handle the differences.

Examining the makeSong code

The `makeSong` code has been changed in one significant way. In the last program, the `makeSong` code called the functions, which did all the work. This time, the functions don't actually output anything themselves. Instead, they collect information and pass it back to the main program. Inside the `make-Song` code, each function is treated like a variable.

You've seen this behavior before. The `prompt()` method returns a value. Now the `chorus()` and `verse()` methods return values. You can do anything you want to this value, including storing it to a variable, printing it, or comparing it to some other value.

If you have one function that controls all the action, often that function is called `main()`. Some languages require you to have a function called `main()`, but JavaScript isn't that picky. For this example, I went with `makeSong()` because that name is more descriptive than `main()`. Still, the `makeSong()` function is a `main` function because it controls the rest of the program.

Separating the creation of data from its use as I've done here is a good idea. That way, you have more flexibility. After a function creates some information, you can print it to the screen, store it on a web page, put it in a database, or whatever.

Looking at the chorus

The chorus of "The Ants Go Marching" song program has been changed to return a value. Take another look at the `chorus()` function to see what I mean.

```
function chorus(){
    var result = "-and they all came marching down, <br />";
    result += "to the ground, to get out, of the rain. <br />";
    result += "boom boom boom boom <br />";
    result += "boom boom boom boom <br />";
    result += "<br />";
    return result;
} // end chorus
```

Here's what changed:

✦ **The purpose of the function has changed.** The function is no longer designed to output some value to the screen. Instead, it now provides text to the main program, which can do whatever it wants with the results.

✦ **There's a variable called `text`.** This variable contains all the text to be sent to the main program. (It contained all the text in the last program, but it's even more important now.)

✦ **The `text` variable is concatenated over several lines.** I used string concatenation to build a complex value. Note the use of break tags (`<br />`) to force carriage returns in the HTML output.

✦ **The `return` statement sends `text` to the main program.** When you want a function to return some value, simply use `return` followed by a value or variable. Note that `return` should be the last line of the function.

Handling the verses

The `verse()` function is quite interesting:

✦ It can print more than one verse.

✦ It takes input to determine which verse to print.

✦ It modifies the verse based on the input.

✦ It returns a value, just like `chorus()`.

To make the verse so versatile (get it? verse-atile!), it must take input from the primary program and return output.

Passing data to the verse () function

The `verse()` function is always called with a value inside the parentheses. For example, the main program sets `verse(1)` to call the first verse, and `verse(2)` to invoke the second. The value inside the parentheses is called an *argument*.

The verse function must be designed to accept an argument (because I call it using values inside the parentheses). Look at the first line to see how.

```
function verse(verseNumber){
```

In the function definition, I include a variable name. Inside the function, this variable is known as a *parameter*. (Don't get hung up on the terminology. People often use the terms parameter and argument interchangeably.) The important idea is that whenever the `verse()` function is called, it automatically has a variable called `verseNumber`. Whatever argument you send to

**Book IV
Chapter 4**

Functions, Arrays, and Objects

the `verse()` function from the main program will become the value of the variable `verseNumber` inside the function.

You can define a function with as many parameters as you want. Each parameter gives you the opportunity to send a piece of information to the function.

Determining the distraction

If you know the verse number, you can determine what distracts "the little one" in the song. You can determine the distraction in a couple ways, but a simple `if-elseif` structure is sufficient for this example.

```
var distraction = "";
if (verseNumber == 1){
  distraction = "suck his thumb.";
} else if (verseNumber == 2){
  distraction = "tie his shoe.";
} else {
  distraction = "I have no idea.";
}
```

I initialized the variable `distraction` to be empty. If `verseNum` is 1, set `distraction` to `"suck his thumb"`. If `verseNumber` is 2, `distraction` should be `"tie his shoe"`. Any other value for `verseNumber` is treated as an error by the `else` clause.

If you're an experienced coder, you may be yelling at this code. It still isn't optimal. Fortunately, in the section "Building a Basic Array" later in this chapter, I show an even better solution for handling this particular situation with arrays.

By the time this code segment is complete, `verseNumber` and `distraction` both contain a legitimate value.

Creating the text

When you know these variables, it's pretty easy to construct the output text:

```
var result = "The ants go marching ";
 result += verseNumber + " by " + verseNumber + ", ";
 result += "hurrah, hurrah <br />";
 result += "The ants go marching ";
 result += verseNumber + " by " + verseNumber + ", ";
 result += "hurrah, hurrah <br />";
 result += "The ants go marching ";
 result += verseNumber + " by " + verseNumber + "<br />";
 result += "The little one stops to ";
 result += distraction + "<br /> <br />";

 return result;
} // end verse
```

A whole lotta concatenating is going on, but it's essentially the same code as the original `verse()` function. This one's just a lot more flexible because it can handle any verse. (Well, if the function has been preloaded to understand how to handle the `verseNumber`.)

Managing Scope

A function is much like an independent mini-program. Any variable you create inside a function has meaning only inside that function. When the function is finished executing, its variables disappear! This setup is actually a really good thing. A major program will have hundreds of variables, and they can be difficult to keep track of. You can reuse a variable name without knowing it or have a value changed inadvertently. When you break your code into functions, each function has its own independent set of variables. You don't have to worry about whether the variables will cause problems elsewhere.

Introducing local and global variables

You can also define variables at the main (script) level. These variables are *global* variables. A global variable is available at the main level and inside each function. A *local* variable (one defined inside a function) has meaning only inside the function. The concept of local versus global functions is sometimes referred to as *scope*.

Local variables are kind of like local police. Local police have a limited geographical jurisdiction, but they're very useful within that space. They know the neighborhood. Sometimes, you encounter situations that cross local jurisdictions. This situation is the kind that requires a state trooper or the FBI. Local variables are local cops, and global variables are the FBI.

Generally, try to make as many of your variables local as possible. The only time you really need a global variable is when you want some information to be used in multiple functions.

Book IV
Chapter 4

Functions, Arrays, and Objects

Examining variable scope

To understand the implications of variable scope, take a look at scope.html:

```
<script type = "text/javascript">
  //from scope.html
  var globalVar = "I'm global!";

  function myFunction(){
    var localVar = "I'm local";
    console.log(localVar);
  }

  myFunction();
</script>
```

This program defines two variables. In the main code, `globalVar` is defined, and `localVar` is defined inside a function. If you run the program in debug mode while watching the variables, you can see how they behave. Figure 4-2 shows what the program looks like early in the run.

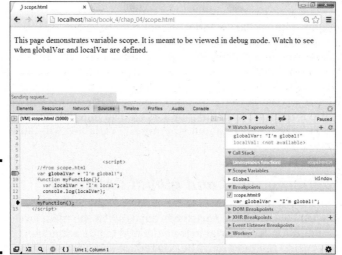

Figure 4-2: globalVar is defined, but localVar is not.

`localVar` doesn't have meaning until the function is called, so it remains undefined until the computer gets to that part of the code. Step ahead a few lines, and you see that `localVar` has a value, as shown in Figure 4-3.

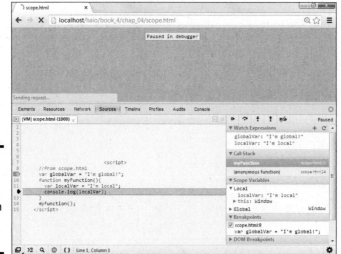

Figure 4-3: localVar has a value because I'm inside the function.

Be sure to use Step Into (down arrow) rather than Step Over (up arrow) on the "remote control" toolbar for this example. When Step Over encounters a function, it runs the entire function as one line rather than looking at the function code line by line. If you want to look into the function and see what's happening inside it (as you do here), use Step Into. Use Step Over when you know a function is working fine and you want to treat it as a single instruction. If in doubt, always use Step Into to see exactly what's happening in your code. (I added watch expressions to clarify the content of the variables.)

`globalVar` still has a value (it's an FBI agent), and so does `localVar` because it's inside the function.

If you move a few more steps, `localVar` no longer has a value when the function ends (see Figure 4-4).

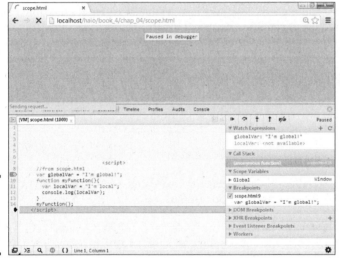

Figure 4-4: Once again, localVar has no meaning.

Variable scope is a good thing because it means you have to keep track of only global variables and the variables defined inside your current function. The other advantage of scope is the ability to reuse a variable name. You can have ten different functions all using the same variable name, and they won't interfere with each other because they're entirely different variables.

Building a Basic Array

If functions are groups of code lines with a name, *arrays* are groups of variables with a name. Arrays are similar to functions because they're used to manage complexity. An array is a special kind of variable. Use an array whenever you want to work with a list of similar data types.

The following code shows a basic demonstration of arrays:

```
<script type = "text/javascript">
  //from genres.html

  //creating an empty array
  var genre = new Array(5);

  //storing data in the array
  genre[0] = "flight simulation";
  genre[1] = "first-person shooters";
  genre[2] = "driving";
  genre[3] = "action";
  genre[4] = "strategy";

  //returning data from the array
  alert ("I like " + genre[4] + " games.");
  //]]
</script>
```

The variable `genre` is a special variable because it contains many values. Essentially, it's a list of genres. The `new Array(5)` construct creates space in memory for five variables, all named `genre`.

Accessing array data

After you specify an array, you can work with the individual elements using square-bracket syntax. An integer identifies each element of the array. The index usually begins with.

```
genre[0] = "flight simulation";
```

The preceding code assigns the text value "`flight simulation`" to the `genre` array variable at position 0.

Most languages require all array elements to be the same type. JavaScript is very forgiving. You can combine all kinds of stuff in a JavaScript array. This flexibility can sometimes be useful, but be aware that this trick doesn't work in all languages. Generally, I try to keep all the members of an array the same type.

After you store the data in the array, you can use the same square-bracket syntax to read the information.

The line

```
alert ("I like " + genre[4] + " games.");
```

finds element 4 of the `genre` array and includes it in an output message.

Figure 4-5 shows a run of genres.html.

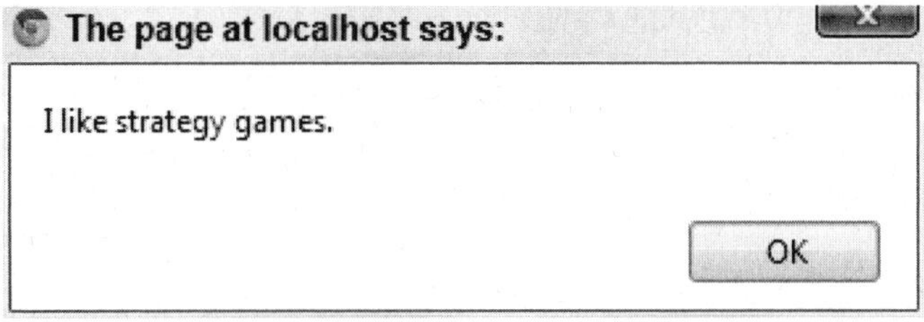

Figure 4-5:
This data came from an array.

The page at localhost says:

I like strategy games.

OK

Using arrays with for loops

The main reason to use arrays is convenience. When you have a lot of information in an array, you can write code to work with the data quickly. Whenever you have an array of data, you commonly want to do something with each element in the array. Take a look at `games.html` to see how you can do so:

```
<script type = "text/javascript">
  //from games.html

  //pre-loading an array
  var gameList = new Array("Flight Gear", "Sauerbraten", "Future Pinball",
      "Racer", "TORCS", "Orbiter", "Step Mania", "NetHack",
      "Marathon", "Crimson Fields");

  var text = "";
  for (i = 0; i < gameList.length; i++){
    text += "I love " + gameList[i] + "\n";
  } // end for loop
  alert(text);
</script>
```

Notice several things in this code:

✦ **The array called `gameList`.** This array contains the names of some of my favorite freeware games.

✦ **The array is preloaded with values.** If you provide a list of values when creating an array, JavaScript simply preloads the array with the values you indicate. You don't need to specify the size of the array if you preload it.

✦ **A `for` loop steps through the array.** Arrays and `for` loops are natural companions. The `for` loop steps through each element of the array.

✦ **The array's length is used in the `for` loop condition.** Rather than specifying the value 10, I used the array's `length` property in my `for` loop. This practice is good because the loop automatically adjusts to the size of the array when I add or remove elements.

✦ **Do something with each element.** Because i goes from 0 to 9 (the array indices), I can easily print each value of the array. In this example, I simply add to an output string.

✦ **Note the newline characters.** The \n combination is a special character that tells JavaScript to add a carriage return, such as you get by pressing the Enter key. Figure 4-6 shows a run of games.html.

The page at localhost says:

I love Flight Gear
I love Sauerbraten
I love Future Pinball
I love Racer
I love TORCS
I love Orbiter
I love Step Mania
I love NetHack
I love Marathon
I love Crimson Fields

OK

Figure 4-6:
Now I
have a list
of games.
Arrays and
loops are
fun!

If you want to completely ruin your productivity, Google some of these game names. They're absolutely incredible, and every one of them is free. It's hard to beat that. See, even if you don't learn how to program in this book, you get something good from it!

Revisiting the ants song

If you read the earlier sections, you probably just got that marching ant song out of your head. Sorry. Take a look at the following variation, which uses arrays and loops to simplify the code even more.

```
<script type = "text/javascript">
    //This old man using functions and arrays

    var distractionList = Array("", "suck his thumb", "tie his shoe",
        "climb a tree", "shut the door");

    function makeSong(){
      //create output variable
      var output = document.getElementById("output");
```

```
        output.innerHTML = "";
        for (verseNumber = 1; verseNumber < distractionList.length; verseNumber++){
          output.innerHTML += verse(verseNumber);
          output.innerHTML += chorus();
        } // end for loop

    } // end makeSong

    function chorus(){
      var result = "-and they all came marching down, <br />";
      result += "to the ground, to get out, of the rain. <br />";
      result += "boom boom boom boom <br />";
      result += "boom boom boom boom <br />";
      result += "<br />";
      return result;
    } // end chorus

    function verse(verseNumber){
      var distraction = distractionList[verseNumber];

      var result = "The ants go marching ";
      result += verseNumber + " by " + verseNumber + ", ";
      result += "hurrah, hurrah <br />";
      result += "The ants go marching ";
      result += verseNumber + " by " + verseNumber + ", ";
      result += "hurrah, hurrah <br />";
      result += "The ants go marching ";
      result += verseNumber + " by " + verseNumber + "<br />";
      result += "The little one stops to ";
      result += distraction + "<br /> <br />";

      return result;
    } // end verse

    </script>
```

This code is just a little different from the antsParam program shown in the section of this chapter called "Passing Data to and from Functions."

✦ **It has an array called `distractionList`.** This array is (despite the misleading name) a list of distractions. I made the first one (element zero) blank so that the verse numbers would line up properly. (Remember, computers normally count beginning with zero.)

✦ **The `verse()` function looks up a distraction.** Because distractions are now in an array, you can use the `verseNumber` as an index to loop up a particular distraction. Compare this function to the `verse()` function in `antsParam`. This program can be found in the section "Passing data to and from Functions." Although arrays require a little more planning than code structures, they can highly improve the readability of your code.

✦ **The makeSong() function is a loop.** I step through each element of the `distractionList` array, printing the appropriate verse and chorus.

✦ **The `chorus()` function remains unchanged.** You don't need to change `chorus()`.

Working with Two-Dimension Arrays

Arrays are useful when working with lists of data. Sometimes, you encounter data that's best imagined in a table. For example, what if you want to build a distance calculator that determines the distance between two cities? The original data might look like Table 4-1.

Table 4-1	Distance between Major Cities			
	0) *Indianapolis*	*1)* *New York*	*2)* *Tokyo*	*3)* *London*
0) Indianapolis	0	648	6476	4000
1) New York	648	0	6760	3470
2) Tokyo	6476	6760	0	5956
3) London	4000	3470	5956	0

Think about how you would use Table 4-1 to figure out a distance. If you wanted to travel from New York to London, for example, you'd pick the New York row and the London column and figure out where they intersect. The data in that cell is the distance (3,470 miles).

When you look up information in any kind of a table, you're actually working with a *two-dimensional data structure* — a fancy term, but it just means table. If you want to look something up in a table, you need two indices, one to determine the row and another to determine the column.

If this concept is difficult to grasp, think of the old game Battleship. The playing field is a grid of squares. You announce I-5, meaning column I, row 5, and the opponent looks in that grid to discover that you've sunk his battleship. In programming, you typically use integers for both indices, but otherwise, it's exactly the same as Battleship. Any time you have two-dimensional data, you access it with two indices.

Often, we call the indices *row* and *column* to help you think of the structure as a table. Sometimes, other names more clearly describe how the behavior works. Take a look at Figure 4-7, and you see that the distance. html program asks for two cities and returns a distance according to the data table.

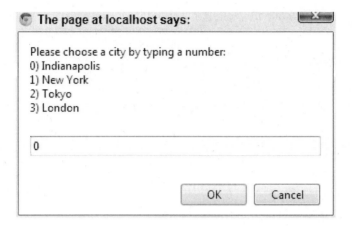

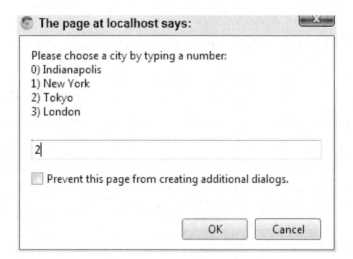

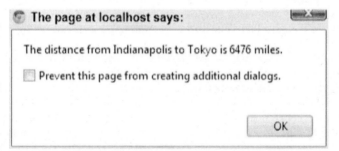

Figure 4-7:
It's a Tale of
Two Cities.
You even get
the distance
between
them!

Yep, you can have three, four, or more dimension arrays in programming, but don't worry about that yet. (It may make your head explode.) Most of the time, one or two dimensions are all you need.

This program is a touch longer than some of the others, so I break it into parts in the following sections for easy digestion. Be sure to look at the program in its entirety on the website.

Setting up the arrays

The key to this program is the data organization. The first step is to set up two arrays.

```
<script type = "text/javascript">
  //from distance.html

  //cityName has the names of the cities
  cityName = new Array("Indianapolis", "New York", "Tokyo", "London");

  //create a 2-dimension array of distances
  distance = new Array (
    new Array (0, 648, 6476, 4000),
    new Array (648, 0, 6760, 3470),
    new Array (6476, 6760, 0, 5956),
    new Array (4000, 3470, 5956, 0)
  );
```

The first array is an ordinary single-dimension array of city names. I've been careful to always keep the cities in the same order, so whenever I refer to city 0, I'm talking about Indianapolis (my hometown), New York is always going to be at position 1, and so on.

You have to be careful in your data design that you always keep things in the same order. Be sure to organize your data on paper before you type it into the computer, so you'll understand what value goes where.

The `cityNames` array has two jobs. First, it reminds me what order all the cities will be in, and, second, it gives me an easy way to get a city name when I know an index. For example, I know that `cityName [2]` will always be "Tokyo".

The `distance` array is very interesting. If you squint at it a little bit, it looks a lot like Table 4-1, shown earlier in this chapter. That's because it *is* Table 4-1, just in a slightly different format.

`distance` is an array. JavaScript arrays can hold just about everything, including other arrays! That's what `distance` does. It holds an array of rows. Each element of the `distance` array is another (unnamed) array holding all the data for that row. If you want to extract information from the array, you need two pieces of information. First, you need the row. Then because the row is an array, you need the column number within that array. So, `distance[1][3]` means go to row 1 ("New York") of `distance`. Within that row go to element 3 ("London") and return the resulting value (3470). Cool, huh?

A beginning programmer would typically solve this problem with a huge number of `if` statements. That solution will work, but it becomes unwieldy in a hurry. With four cities, you'll have four conditions to determine which city you're coming from, and each of these will need three conditions to determine where we're going. That's doable, but by the time you have ten cities, you'll have somewhere near one hundred conditions, and with one hundred cities, you'll have roughly ten thousand conditions. When you use an array like I'm demonstrating here, the code doesn't get more complex when the number of elements increases. For computer science majors out there, this problem has a complexity of Big $O(n^2)$, meaning as the number of elements increases, the complexity increases by the square. Using an array tames that complexity and makes the program much more efficient and extensible. Experienced programmers tend to aim for simpler code structure by using more complex data structures.

Getting a city

The program requires that you ask for two cities. You want the user to enter a city number, not a name, and you want to ask this question twice. Sounds like a good time for a function.

```
function getCity(){
    // presents a list of cities and gets a number corresponding to
    // the city name
    var theCity = "";   //will hold the city number

    var cityMenu = "Please choose a city by typing a number: \n";
    cityMenu += "0) Indianapolis \n";
    cityMenu += "1) New York \n";
    cityMenu += "2) Tokyo \n";
    cityMenu += "3) London \n";

    theCity = prompt(cityMenu);
    return theCity;
} // end getCity
```

The `getCity()` function prints a little menu of city choices and asks for some input. It then returns that input.

You can improve `getCity()` in all kinds of ways. For one thing, maybe it should repeat until you get a valid number so that users can't type the city name or do something else crazy. I'll leave it simple for now. If you want to find out how user interface elements help the user submit only valid input, skip ahead to Chapter 5 of this minibook.

Creating a main ( ) function

The `main()` function handles most of the code for the program.

```
function main(){
  var output = "";
  var from = getCity();
  var to = getCity();
  var result = distance[from][to];
  output = "The distance from " + cityName[from];
  output += " to " + cityName[to];
  output += " is " + result + " miles.";
  alert(output);
} // end main

main();
```

The `main()` function controls traffic. Here's what you do:

1. **Create an `output` variable.**

   The point of this function is to create some text output describing the distance. I begin by creating a variable called `output` and setting its initial value to empty.

2. **Get the city of origin.**

   Fortunately, you have a great function called `getCity()` that handles all the details of getting a city in the right format. Call this function and assign its value to the new variable `from`.

3. **Get the destination city.**

   That `getCity()` function sure is handy. Use it again to get the city number you'll call `to`.

4. **Get the distance.**

   Because you know two indices, and you know they're in the right format, you can simply look them up in the table. Look up `distance[from][to]` and store it in the variable `result`.

5. **Output the response.**

   Use concatenation to build a suitable response string and send it to the user.

6. **Get city names from the `cityNames` array.**

   The program uses numeric indices for the cities, but they don't mean anything to the user. Use the `cityNames` array to retrieve the two city names for the output.

7. **Run the `main()` function.**

   Only one line of code doesn't appear in a function. That line calls the `main()` function and starts the whole thing.

I didn't actually write the program in the order I showed it to you in the preceding steps. Sometimes it makes more sense to go "inside out." I actually created the data structure first (as an ordinary table on paper) and then constructed the `main()` function. This approach made it obvious that I needed a `getCity()` function and gave me some clues about how `getCity` should work. (In other words, it should present a list of cities and prompt for a numerical input.)

Creating Your Own Objects

So far you've used a lot of wonderful objects in JavaScript, like the `document` object and the `array` object. However, that's just the beginning. It turns out you can build your own objects too, and these objects can be very powerful and flexible. Objects typically have two important components: *properties* and *methods*. A *property* is like a variable associated with an object. The properties taken together describe the object. A method is like a function associated with an object. The methods describe things the object can do. If functions allow you to put code segments together and arrays allow you to put variables together, objects allow you to put both code segments and variables (and functions and arrays) in the same large construct.

Building a basic object

JavaScript makes it trivially easy to build an object. Because a variable can contain any value, you can simply start treating a variable like an object and it becomes one.

Figure 4-8 shows a critter that has a property.

Book IV
Chapter 4

Functions, Arrays, and Objects

Figure 4-8: This alert box is actually using an object.

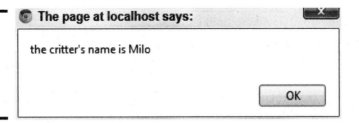

Take a look at the following code:

```
//from basicObject.html
//create the critter
var critter = new Object();

//add some properties
critter.name = "Milo";
critter.age = 5;
```

```
//view property values
alert("the critter's name is " + critter.name);
```

The way it works is not difficult to follow:

1. **Create a new `Object`.**

   JavaScript has a built-in object called `Object`. Make a variable with the `new Object()` syntax, and you'll build yourself a shiny, new standard object.

2. **Add properties to the object.**

   A property is a subvariable. It's nothing more than a variable attached to a specific object. When you assign a value to `critter.name`, for example, you're specifying that `critter` has a property called `name` and you're also giving it a starting value.

3. **An object can have any number of properties.**

   Just keep adding properties. This allows you to group a number of variables into one larger object.

4. **Each property can contain any type of data.**

   Unlike arrays where it's common for all the elements to contain exactly the same type of data, each property can have a different type.

5. **Use the dot syntax to view or change a property.**

   If the `critter` object has a name property, you can use `critter.name` as a variable. Like other variables, you can change the value by assigning a new value to `critter.name` or you can read the content of the property.

If you're used to a stricter object-oriented language, such as Java, you'll find JavaScript's easy-going attitude quite strange and maybe a bit sloppy. Other languages do have a lot more rules about how objects are made and used, but JavaScript's approach has its charms. Don't get too tied up in the differences. The way JavaScript handles objects is powerful and refreshing.

Adding methods to an object

Objects have other characteristics besides properties. They can also have *methods*. A method is simply a function attached to an object. To see what I'm talking about, take a look at this example:

```
//create the critter
//from addingMethods.html
var critter = new Object();

//add some properties
critter.name = "Milo";
critter.age = 5;
```

```
//create a method
critter.talk = function(){
  msg = "Hi! My name is " + this.name;
  msg += " and I'm " + this.age;
  alert(msg);
} // end method

// call the talk method
critter.talk();
```

This example extends the `critter` object described in the last section. In addition to properties, the new critter has a `talk()` method. If a property describes a characteristic of an object, a method describes something the object can do. Figure 4-9 illustrates the critter showing off its `talk()` method:

Figure 4-9: Now the critter can talk!

The page at localhost says:

Hi! My name is Alpha and I'm 1

OK

Here's how it works:

1. **Build an object with whatever properties you need.**

   Begin by building an object and giving it some properties.

2. **Define a method much like a property.**

   In fact, methods *are* properties in JavaScript, but don't worry too much about that; it'll make your head explode.

3. **You can assign a prebuilt function to a method.**

   If you created a function that you want to use as a method, you can simply assign it.

4. **You can also create an anonymous function.**

   More often, you'll want to create your method right there as you define the object. You can create a function immediately with the `function()` `{` syntax.

5. **The `this` keyword refers to the current object.**

   Inside the function, you may want to access the properties of the object. `this.name` refers to the `name` property of the current object.

6. **You can then refer to the method directly.**

    After you define an object with a method, you can invoke it. For exam-
    ple, if the `critter` object has a `talk` method, use `critter.talk()` to
    invoke this method.

Building a reusable object

These objects are nice, but what if you want to build several objects with
the same definition? JavaScript supports an idea called a *constructor,* which
allows you to define an object pattern and reuse it.

Here's an example:

```
//building a constructor
//from constructor.html
function Critter(lName, lAge){
  this.name = lName;
  this.age = lAge;
  this.talk = function(){
    msg = "Hi! My name is " + this.name;
    msg += " and I'm " + this.age;
    alert(msg);
  } // end talk method
} // end Critter class def

function main(){
  //build two critters
  critterA = new Critter("Alpha", 1);

  critterB = new Critter("Beta", 2);
  critterB.name = "Charlie";
  critterB.age = 3;

  //have 'em talk
  critterA.talk();
  critterB.talk();

} // end main
main();
```

This example involves creating a *class* (a pattern for generating objects) and
reusing that definition to build two different critters. First, look over how the
class definition works:

✦ **Build an ordinary function:** JavaScript classes are defined as exten-
    sions of a function. The function name will also be the class name. Note
    that the name of a class function normally begins with an uppercase
    letter. When a function is used in this way to describe an object, the
    function is called the object's *constructor.* The constructor can take
    parameters if you wish, but it normally does not return any values. In my
    particular example, I add parameters for name and age.

✦ **Use this to define properties:** Add any properties you want to include,
    including default values. Note that you can change the values of these

later if you wish. Each property should begin with `this` and a period. If you want your object to have a color property, you'd say something like `this.color = "blue"`. My example uses the local parameters to define the properties. This is a very common practice because it's an easy way to preload important properties.

✦ **Use `this` to define any methods you want:** If you want your object to have methods, define them using the `this` operator followed by the `function(){` keyword. You can add as many functions as you wish.

The way JavaScript defines and uses objects is easy but a little nonstandard. Most other languages that support object-oriented programming (OOP) do it in a different way than the technique described here. Some would argue that JavaScript is not a true OOP language, as it doesn't support a feature called *inheritance*, but instead uses a feature called *prototyping*. The difference isn't all that critical because most uses of OOP in JavaScript are very simple objects like the ones described here. Just appreciate that this introduction to object-oriented programming is very cursory, but enough to get you started.

Using your shiny new objects

After you define a class, you can reuse it. Look again at the main function to see how I use my newly minted `Critter` class:

```
function main(){
  //build two critters

  critterA = new Critter("Alpha", 1);

  critterB = new Critter("Beta", 2);
  critterB.name = "Charlie";
  critterB.age = 3;

  //have 'em talk
  critterA.talk();
  critterB.talk();

} // end main
main();
```

After you define a class, you can use it as a new data type. This is a very powerful capability. Here's how it works:

✦ **Be sure you have access to the class:** A class isn't useful unless JavaScript knows about it. In this example, the class is defined within the code.

✦ **Create an instance of the class with the `new` keyword:** The new keyword means you want to make a particular critter based on the definition. Normally, you assign your new object to a variable. My constructor expects the name and age to be supplied, so it automatically creates a critter with the given name and age.

✦ **Modify the class properties as you wish:** You can change the values of any of the class properties. In my example, I change the name and age of the second critter just to show how it's done.

✦ **Call class methods:** Because the `critter` class has a `talk()` method, you can use it whenever you want the critter to talk.

Introducing JSON

JavaScript objects and arrays are incredibly flexible. In fact, they are so well known for their power and ease of use that a special data format called JavaScript Object Notation (JSON) has been adopted by many other languages.

JSON is mainly used as a way to store complex data (especially multidimensional arrays) and pass the data from program to program. JSON is essentially another way of describing complex data in a JavaScript object format. When you describe data in JSON, you generally do not need a constructor because the data is used to determine the structure of the class.

JSON data is becoming a very important part of web programming because it allows an easy mechanism for transporting data between programs and programming languages.

Storing data in JSON format

To see how JSON works, look at this simple code fragment:

```
var critter = {
  "name": "George",
  "age": 10
};
```

This code describes a critter. The critter has two properties, a name and an age. The critter looks much like an array, but rather than using a numeric index like most arrays, the critter has string values to serve as indices. It is in fact an object.

You can refer to the individual elements with a variation of array syntax, like this:

```
alert(critter["name"]);
```

You can also use what's called *dot* notation (as used in objects) like this:

```
alert(critter.age);
```

Both notations work the same way. Most of the built-in JavaScript objects use dot notation, but either is acceptable.

The reason JavaScript arrays are so useful is that they are in fact objects. When you create an array in JavaScript, you are building an object with numeric property names. This is why you can use either array or object syntax for managing JSON object properties.

Look at `jsonDistance.html` on the website to see the code from this section in action. I don't show a screenshot here because all the interesting work happens in the code.

To store data in JSON notation:

1. **Create the variable.**

   You can use the `var` statement like you do any variable.

2. **Contain the content within braces ({ }).**

   This is the same mechanism you use to create a preloaded array (as described earlier in this chapter).

3. **Designate a key.**

   For the critter, I want the properties to be named "name" and "age" rather than numeric indices. For each property, I begin with the property name. The key can be a string or an integer.

4. **Follow the key with a colon (:).**

5. **Create the value associated with that key.**

   You can then associate any type of value you want with the key. In this case, I associate the value `George` with the key `name`.

6. **Separate each name/value pair with a comma (,).**

   You can add as many name/value pairs as you wish.

If you're familiar with other languages, you might think a JSON structure similar to a hash table or associative array. JavaScript does use JSON structures the way these other structures are used, but it isn't quite accurate to say JSON is either a hash or an associative array. It's simply an object. However, if you want to think of it as one of these things, I won't tell anybody.

Building a more complex JSON structure

JSON is convenient because it can be used to handle quite complex data structures. For example, look at the following (oddly familiar) data structure written in JSON format:

```
var distance = {
  "Indianapolis" :
    { "Indianapolis": 0,
      "New York": 648,
      "Tokyo": 6476,
      "London": 4000 },
```

```
    "New York" :
      { "Indianapolis": 648,
        "New York": 0,
        "Tokyo": 6760,
        "London": 3470 },

    "Tokyo" :
      { "Indianapolis": 6476,
        "New York": 6760,
        "Tokyo": 0,
        "London": 5956 },

    "London" :
      { "Indianapolis": 4000,
        "New York": 3470,
        "Tokyo": 5956,
        "London": 0 },
  };
```

This data structure is another way of representing the distance data used to describe two-dimension arrays. This is another two-dimension array, but it is a little different than the one previously described.

+ **`distance` is a JSON object:** The entire data structure is stored in a single variable. This variable is a JSON object with name/value pairs.

+ **The `distance` object has four keys:** These correspond to the four rows of the original chart.

+ **The keys are city names:** The original 2D array used numeric indices, which are convenient but a bit artificial. In the JSON structure, the indices are actual city names.

+ **The value of each entry is another JSON object:** The value of a JSON element can be anything, including another JSON object. Very complex relationships can be summarized in a single variable.

+ **Each row is summarized as a JSON object:** For example, the value associated with "Indianapolis" is a list of distances from Indianapolis to the various cities.

+ **The entire declaration is one "line" of code:** Although it is placed on several lines in the editor (for clarity) the entire definition is really just one line of code.

Setting up the data in this way seems a bit tedious, but it's very easy to work with. The city names are used directly to extract data, so you can find the distance between two cities with array-like syntax:

```
alert(distance["Indianapolis"]["London"]);
```

If you prefer, you can use the dot syntax:

```
alert(distance.Indianapolis.Tokyo);
```

You can even go with some kind of hybrid:

```
alert(distance["London"].Tokyo);
```

JSON has a number of important advantages as a data format:

✦ **Self-documenting:** Even if you see the data structure on its own without any code around it, you can tell what it means.

✦ **The use of strings as indices makes the code more readable:** It's much easier to understand `distance["Indianapolis"]["London"]` than `distance[0][3]`.

✦ **JSON data can be stored and transported as text:** This turns out to have profound implications for web programming, especially in AJAX (the techniques described in Book VII).

✦ **JSON can describe complex relationships:** The example shown here is a simple two-dimension array, but the JSON format can be used to describe much more complex relationships including complete databases.

✦ **Many languages support JSON format:** Many web languages now offer direct support for JSON. The most important of these is PHP, which is frequently used with JavaScript in AJAX applications.

✦ **JSON is more compact than XML:** Another data format called XML is frequently used to transmit complex data. However, JSON is more compact and less "wordy" than XML.

✦ **JavaScript can read JSON natively:** Some kinds of data need to be translated before they can be used. As soon as your JavaScript program has access to JSON data, it can be used directly.

You might wonder whether you can embed methods in JSON objects. The answer is yes, but this isn't usually done when you're using JSON to transport information. In Book VII about AJAX, you see that methods are often added to JSON objects to serve as *callback functions*, but that usage won't make sense until you learn more about events.

Chapter 5: Getting Valid Input

In This Chapter

✔ **Extracting data from drop-down lists**

✔ **Working with multiple-selection lists**

✔ **Getting data from check boxes and radio groups**

✔ **Validating input with regular expressions**

✔ **Using character, boundary, and repetition operators**

✔ **Using pattern memory**

Getting input from the user is always nice, but sometimes users make mistakes. Whenever you can, you want to make the user's job easier and prevent certain kinds of mistakes.

Fortunately, you can take advantage of several tools designed exactly for that purpose. In this chapter, you discover two main strategies for improving user input: specialized input elements and pattern-matching. Together, these tools can help ensure that the data the user enters is useful and valid.

Getting Input from a Drop-Down List

The most obvious way to ensure that the user enters something valid is to supply him with valid choices. The drop-down list is an obvious and easy way to do this, as you can see from Figure 5-1.

The list-box approach has a lot of advantages over text field input:

✦ The user can input with the mouse, which is faster and easier than typing.

✦ You shouldn't have any spelling errors because the user didn't type the response.

✦ The user knows all the answers available because they're listed.

✦ You can be sure the user gives you a valid answer because you supplied the possible responses.

✦ User responses can be mapped to more complex values — for example, you can show the user Red and have the list box return the hex value `#FF0000`.

If you want to know how to build a list box with the HTML `select` object, refer to Book I, Chapter 7.

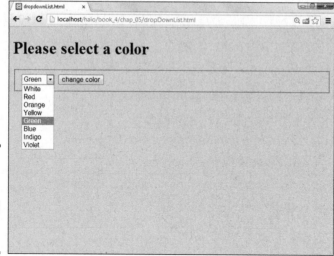

Figure 5-1:
The user
selects from
a predefined
list of valid
choices.

Building the form

When you're creating a predefined list of choices, create the HTML form first because it defines all the elements you'll need for the function. The code is a standard form:

```html
<body>
  <form action = "">
    <h1>Please select a color</h1>
    <fieldset>
      <select id = "selColor">
        <option value = "#FFFFFF">White</option>
        <option value = "#FF0000">Red</option>
        <option value = "#FFCC00">Orange</option>
        <option value = "#FFFF00">Yellow</option>
        <option value = "#00FF00">Green</option>
        <option value = "#0000FF">Blue</option>
        <option value = "#663366">Indigo</option>
        <option value = "#FF00FF">Violet</option>
      </select>

      <input type = "button"
             value = "change color"
             onclick = "changeColor()" />
    </fieldset>
  </form>

</body>
</html>
```

The `select` object's default behavior is to provide a drop-down list. The first element on the list is displayed, but when the user clicks the list, the other options appear.

A `select` object that the code refers to should have an `id` field.

In this and most examples in this chapter, I add CSS styling to clean up each form. Be sure to look over the styles if you want to see how I did it. Note also that I'm only showing the HTML right now. The entire code listing also includes JavaScript code, which I describe in the next section.

The other element in the form is a button. When the user clicks the button, the `changeColor()` function is triggered.

Because the only element in this form is the `select` object, you may want to change the background color immediately without requiring a button click. You can do so by adding an event handler directly onto the `select` object:

```
<select id = "selColor"
        onchange = "changeColor()">
```

The event handler causes the `changeColor()` function to be triggered as soon as the user changes the `select` object's value. Typically, you'll forego the user clicking a button only when the `select` is the only element in the form. If the form includes several elements, processing doesn't usually happen until the user signals she's ready by clicking a button.

Reading the list box

Fortunately, standard drop-down lists are quite easy to read. Here's the JavaScript code:

```
<script type = "text/javascript">
  // from dropdownList.html

  function changeColor(){
    var selColor = document.getElementById("selColor");
    var color = selColor.value;
    document.body.style.backgroundColor = color;
  } // end function
</script>
```

As you can see, the process for reading the `select` object is much like working with a text-style field:

✦ **Create a variable to represent the `select` object.** The `document.getElementById()` trick works here just like it does for text fields.

✦ **Extract the `value` property of the `select` object.** The `value` property of the `select` object reflects the `value` of the currently selected `option`. So, if the user has chosen Yellow, the `value` of `selColor` is `"#FFFF00"`.

✦ **Set the document's background color.** Use the DOM mechanism to set the body's background color to the chosen value.

Managing Multiple Selections

You can use the `select` object in a more powerful way than the method I describe in the preceding section. Figure 5-2 shows a page with a multiple-selection list box.

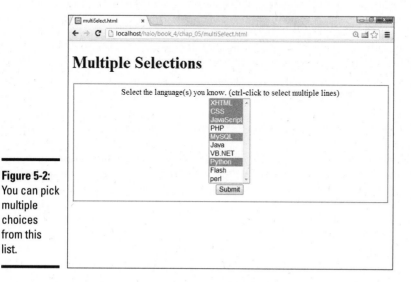

Figure 5-2: You can pick multiple choices from this list.

To make multiple selection work, you have to make a few changes to both the HTML and the JavaScript code.

Coding a multiple selection select object

You modify the `select` code in two ways to make multiple selections:

✦ **Indicate multiple selections are allowed.** By default, `select` boxes have only one value. You'll need to set a switch to tell the browser to allow more than one item to be selected.

✦ **Make the mode a multiline select.** The standard drop-down behavior doesn't make sense when you want multiple selections because the user needs to see all the options at once. Most browsers automatically switch into a multiline mode, but you should control the process directly.

The HTML code for `multiSelect.html` is similar to the `dropdownList` page, described in the preceding section, but note a couple of changes.

```
<body>
  <h1>Multiple Selections</h1>
  <form action = "">
    <fieldset>
```

```
          <label>
            Select the language(s) you know.
            (ctrl-click to select multiple lines)
          </label>
          <select id = "selLanguage"
                  multiple = "multiple"
                  size = "10">
            <option value = "HTML">HTML</option>
            <option value = "CSS">CSS</option>
            <option value = "JavaScript">JavaScript</option>
            <option value = "PHP">PHP</option>
            <option value = "MySQL">MySQL</option>
            <option value = "Java">Java</option>
            <option value = "VB.NET">VB.NET</option>
            <option value = "Python">Python</option>
            <option value = "Flash">Flash</option>
            <option value = "Perl">perl</option>
          </select>
          <button type = "button"
                  onclick = "showChoices()">
            Submit
          </button>
        </fieldset>
      </form>

      <div id = "output">

      </div>
    </body>
  </html>
```

The code isn't shocking, but it does have some important features:

✦ **Call the `select` object `selLanguage`.** As usual, the form elements need an `id` attribute so that you can read it in the JavaScript.

✦ **Add the `multiple` attribute to your `select` object.** This attribute tells the browser to accept multiple inputs using Shift+click (for contiguous selections) or Ctrl+click (for more precise selection).

✦ **Set the `size` to 10.** The size indicates the number of lines to be displayed. I set the size to 10 because my list has ten options.

✦ **Make a button.** With multiple selection, you probably won't want to trigger the action until the user has finished making selections. A separate button is the easiest way to make sure the code is triggered when you want it to happen.

✦ **Create an `output` div.** This code holds the response.

Writing the JavaScript code

The JavaScript code for reading a multiple-selection list box is a bit different than the standard selection code described in the section "Reading the list box" earlier in this chapter. The `value` property usually returns one value, but a multiple-selection list box often returns more than one result.

The key is to recognize that a list of `option` objects inside a `select` object is really a kind of array, not just one value. You can look more closely at the list of objects to see which ones are selected, which is essentially what the `showChoices()` function does:

```
<script type = "text/javascript">
  //from multi-select.html
  function showChoices(){
    //retrieve data
    var selLanguage = document.getElementById("selLanguage");

    //set up output string
    var result = "<h2>Your Languages<\/h2>";
    result += "<ul> \n";

    //step through options
    for (i = 0; i < selLanguage.length; i++){
      //examine current option
      currentOption = selLanguage[i];

      //print it if it has been selected
      if (currentOption.selected == true){
        result += "  <li>" + currentOption.value + "<\/li> \n";
      } // end if
    } // end for loop

    //finish off the list and print it out
    result += "<\/ul> \n";

    output = document.getElementById("output");
    output.innerHTML = result;
  } // end showChoices
</script>
```

At first, the code seems intimidating, but if you break it down, it's not too tricky.

1. **Create a variable to represent the entire `select` object.**

   The standard `document.getElementById()` technique works fine.

   ```
   var selLanguage = document.getElementById("selLanguage");
   ```

2. **Create a string variable to hold the output.**

   When you're building complex HTML output, working with a string variable is much easier than directly writing code to the element.

   ```
   var result = "<h2>Your Languages<\/h2>";
   ```

3. **Build an unordered list to display the results.**

   An unordered list is a good way to spit out the results, so I create one in my `result` variable.

   ```
   result += "<ul> \n";
   ```

4. **Step through `selLanguage` as if it were an array.**

   Use a `for` loop to examine the list box line by line. Note that `selLanguage` has a `length` property like an array.

   ```
   for (i = 0; i < selLanguage.length; i++){
   ```

5. **Assign the current element to a temporary variable.**

   The `currentOption` variable holds a reference to each `option` element in the original `select` object as the loop progresses.

   ```
   currentOption = selLanguage[i];
   ```

6. **Check to see whether the current element has been selected.**

   The object `currentOption` has a `selected` property that tells you whether the object has been highlighted by the user. `selected` is a Boolean property, so it's either true or false.

   ```
   if (currentOption.selected == true){
   ```

7. **If the element has been selected, add an entry to the output list.**

   If the user has highlighted this object, create an entry in the unordered list housed in the `result` variable.

   ```
   result += "  <li>" + currentOption.value + "<\/li> \n";
   ```

8. **Close up the list.**

   After the loop has finished cycling through all the objects, you can close up the unordered list you've been building.

   ```
   result += "<\/ul> \n";
   ```

9. **Print results to the `output` div.**

   The `output` div's `innerHTML` property is a perfect place to print the unordered list.

   ```
   output = document.getElementById("output");
   output.innerHTML = result;
   ```

Something strange is going on here. The options of a select box act like an array. An unordered list is a lot like an array. Bingo! They *are* arrays, just in different forms. You can think of any listed data as an array. Sometimes you organize the data like a list (for display), sometimes like an array (for storage in memory), and sometimes it's a select group (for user input). Now you're starting to think like a programmer!

Check, Please: Reading Check Boxes

Check boxes fulfill another useful data input function. They're useful any time you have Boolean data. If some value can be true or false, a check box is a good tool. Figure 5-3 illustrates a page that responds to check boxes.

Check boxes are independent of each other. Although they're often found in groups, any check box can be checked or unchecked regardless of the status of its neighbors.

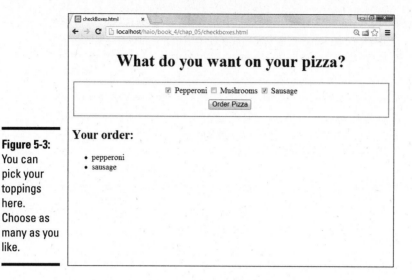

Figure 5-3:
You can
pick your
toppings
here.
Choose as
many as you
like.

Building the check box page

To build the check box page shown in Figure 5-3, start by looking at the HTML:

```
<body>
  <h1>What do you want on your pizza?</h1>
  <form action = "">
    <fieldset>
      <input type = "checkbox"
             id = "chkPepperoni"
             value = "pepperoni" />
      <label for = "chkPepperoni">Pepperoni</label>
      <input type = "checkbox"
             id = "chkMushroom"
             value = "mushrooms" />
      <label for = "chkMushroom">Mushrooms</label>
      <input type = "checkbox"
             id = "chkSausage"
             value = "sausage" />
      <label for = "chkSausage">Sausage</label>
      <button type = "button"
              onclick = "order()">
        Order Pizza
      </button>
    </fieldset>
  </form>
  <h2>Your order:</h2>
  <div id = "output">
  </div>
</body>
```

Each check box is an individual `input` element. Note that check box values aren't displayed. Instead, a label (or similar text) is usually placed after the check box. A button calls an `order()` function.

Note the labels have a `for` attribute which connects each label to the corresponding check box. When you connect a label to a check box in this way, the user can activate the check box by clicking on the box or the label. This provides a larger target for the user, making their life easier. Happy users make fewer mistakes, which makes your life easier.

Responding to the check boxes

Check boxes don't require a lot of care and feeding. After you extract it, the check box has two critical properties:

✦ You can use the `value` property to store a value associated with the check box (just like you do with text fields in Chapter 2 of this minibook).

✦ The `checked` property is a Boolean value, indicating whether the check box is checked or not.

The code for the `order()` function shows how it's done:

```
   //from checkBoxes.html
function order(){
  //get variables
  var chkPepperoni = document.getElementById("chkPepperoni");
  var chkMushroom = document.getElementById("chkMushroom");
  var chkSausage = document.getElementById("chkSausage");
  var output = document.getElementById("output");
  var result = "<ul> \n"
  if (chkPepperoni.checked){
    result += "<li>" + chkPepperoni.value + "</li> \n";
  } // end if
  if (chkMushroom.checked){
    result += "<li>" + chkMushroom.value + "</li> \n";
  } // end if
  if (chkSausage.checked){
    result += "<li>" + chkSausage.value + "</li> \n";
  } // end if
  result += "</ul> \n"
  output.innerHTML = result;
} // end function
```

For each check box,

1. **Determine whether the check box is checked.**

   Use the `checked` property as a condition.

2. **If so, return the `value` property associated with the check box.**

Often, in practice, the `value` property is left out. The important thing is whether the check box is checked. If `chkMushroom` is checked, the user obviously wants mushrooms, so you may not need to explicitly store that data in the check box itself.

Working with Radio Buttons

Radio button groups appear pretty simple, but they're more complex than they seem. Figure 5-4 shows a page using radio button selection.

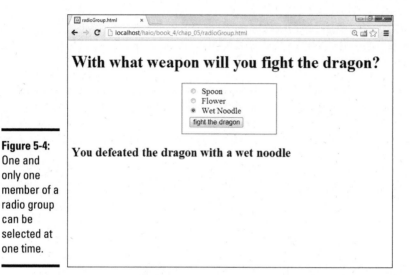

Figure 5-4:
One and only one member of a radio group can be selected at one time.

The most important thing to remember about radio buttons is that, like wildebeests and power-walkers, they must be in groups. Each group of radio buttons has only one button active. The group should be set up so that one button is always active.

You specify the radio button group in the HTML code. Each element of the group can still have a unique `id` (which comes in handy for associating with a label). Look over the code, and you'll notice something interesting. All the radio buttons have the same name!

```
<body>
  <h1>With what weapon will you fight the dragon?</h1>
  <form action = "">
    <fieldset>
      <input type = "radio"
             name = "weapon"
             id = "radSpoon"
             value = "spoon"
             checked = "checked" />
      <label for = "radSpoon">Spoon</label>
      <input type = "radio"
             name = "weapon"
             id = "radFlower"
             value = "flower" />
      <label for = "radFlower">Flower</label>
      <input type = "radio"
```

```
            name = "weapon"
            id = "radNoodle"
            value = "wet noodle" />
        <label for = "radNoodle">Wet Noodle</label>
        <button type = "button"
                onclick = "fight()">
          fight the dragon
        </button>
      </fieldset>
    </form>
    <div id = "output">
    </div>
  </body>
```

Using a `name` attribute when everything else has an `id` seems a little odd, but you do it for a good reason. The `name` attribute is used to indicate the *group* of radio buttons. Because all the buttons in this group have the same name, they're related, and only one of them will be selected. Each button can still have a unique ID (and in fact it does). The ID is still useful for associating a label with the button. Once again, this provides a larger click target so the user can click on either the button or the label associated with that button.

The browser recognizes this behavior and automatically unselects the other buttons in the group whenever one is selected.

I added a label to describe what each radio button means.

You need to preset one of the radio buttons to true with the `checked = "checked"` attribute. If you fail to do so, you have to add code to account for the possibility that there is no answer at all.

Interpreting Radio Buttons

Getting information from a group of radio buttons requires a slightly different technique than most of the form elements. Unlike the `select` object, there is no container object that can return a simple value. You also can't just go through every radio button on the page because you may have more than one group. (Imagine a page with a multiple-choice test.)

This issue is where the `name` attribute comes in. Although `id`s must be unique, multiple elements on a page can have the same `name`. If they do, you can treat these elements as an array.

Look over the code to see how it works:

```
// from radioGroup.html
function fight(){
  var weapon = document.getElementsByName("weapon");
  for (i = 0; i < weapon.length; i++){
    currentWeapon = weapon[i];
```

```
      if (currentWeapon.checked){
        var selectedWeapon = currentWeapon.value;
      } // end if
    } // end for
    var output = document.getElementById("output");
    var response = "<h2>You defeated the dragon with a ";
    response += selectedWeapon + "</h2> \n";
    output.innerHTML = response;
  } // end function
```

This code looks much like all the other code in this chapter, but it has a sneaky difference:

✦ **It uses** `getElementsByName` **to retrieve an array of elements with this name.** Now that you're comfortable with `getElementById`, I throw a monkey wrench in the works. Note that it's plural — `getElements-ByName` — because this tool is used to extract an array of elements. It returns an array of elements. (In this case, all the radio buttons in the weapon group.)

✦ **It treats the result as an array.** The resulting variable (`weapon` in this example) is an array. As usual, the most common thing to do with arrays is process them with loops. Use a `for` loop to step through each element in the array.

✦ **Assign each element of the array to** `currentWeapon`. This variable holds a reference to the current radio button.

✦ **Check to see whether the current weapon is checked.** The `checked` property indicates whether any radio button is checked.

✦ **If so, retain the value of the radio button.** If a radio button is checked, its value is the current value of the group, so store it in a variable for later use.

✦ **Output the results.** You can now process the results as you would with data from any other resource.

Working with Regular Expressions

Having the right kinds of form elements can be helpful, but things can still go wrong. Sometimes, you have to let the user type things, and that information must be in a particular format. As an example, take a look at Figure 5-5.

A mechanism that checks whether input from a form is in the correct format would be great. This program implements such a feature, checking whether there is content in every field and ensuring the e-mail address and phone number are formatted correctly. You can create this kind of testing feature with string functions, but it can be really messy. Imagine how many `if` statements and string methods it would take to enforce the following rules on this page:

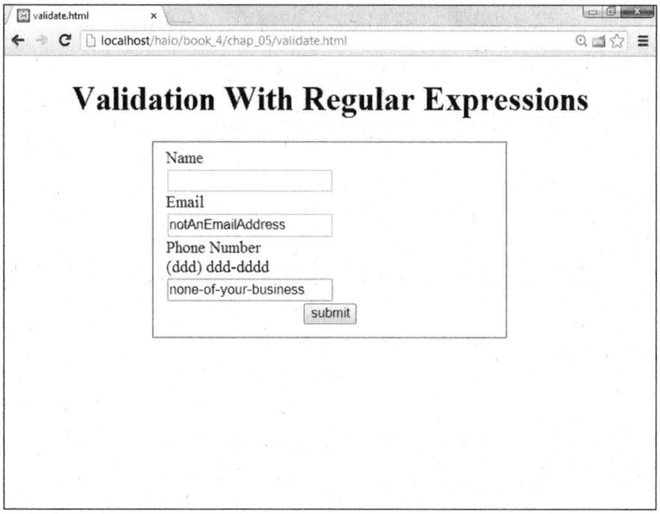

Figure 5-5:
This page is
a mess. No
username,
plus an
invalid
e-mail and
phone
number.

✦ **An entry must appear in each field.** This one is reasonably easy — just check for non-null values.

✦ **The e-mail must be in a valid format.** That is, it must consist of a few characters, an "at" sign (@), a few more characters, a period, and a domain name of two to four characters. That format would be a real pain to check for.

✦ **The phone number must also be in a valid format.** Phone numbers can appear in multiple formats, but assume that you require an area code in parentheses, followed by an optional space, followed by three digits, a dash, and four digits. All digits must be numeric.

Although you can enforce these rules, it would be extremely difficult to do so using ordinary string manipulation tools.

JavaScript strings have a `match` method, which helps find a substring inside a larger string. This tool is good, but we're not simply looking for specific text, but patterns of text. For example, we want to know whether something's an e-mail address (text, an @, more text, a period, and two to four more characters).

Imagine how difficult that code would be to write, and then take a look at the code for the `validate.html` page:

```
<script type = "text/javascript">
  function validate(){
    // get inputs
    name = document.getElementById("txtName").value;
    email = document.getElementById("txtEmail").value;
    phone = document.getElementById("txtPhone").value;
```

```
//create an empty error message
errors = "";

//check name - It simply needs to exist
if (name == ""){
  errors += "please supply a name \n";
} // end if

//check email
emailRE = /^.+@.+\..{2,4}$/;
if (email.match(emailRE)){
  //console.log("email match");
  //do nothing.
} else {
  //console.log("email not a match");
  errors += "please check email address \n";
} // end if

//check phone number
phoneRE = /^\(\d{3}\) *\d{3}-\d{4}$/;
if (phone.match(phoneRE)){
  //console.log("phone matches");
  //do nothing
} else {
  //console.log("phone problem");
  errors += "please check phone #\n";
} // end phone if

//check for errors
if (errors == ""){
  alert ("now processing data");
  //process the form
} else {
  alert(errors);
} // end if

} // end function
```

I only show the JavaScript code here to save space. Look on the website to see how the HTML and CSS are written.

The code isn't really all that difficult!

✦ **It extracts data from the form.** It does so in the usual way.

✦ **The validation is a series of nested if statements.** Look at the overall structure. The if statements go three layers deep.

✦ **The name check is very simple.** The only way it can go wrong is to have no name.

✦ **Don't check anything else if the name is wrong.** If the name isn't right, you don't need to check the other things.

✦ **Build a regular expression.** This verification seems pretty simple until you look at the line that contains the emailRE = /^.+@.+\.. {2,4}$/; business. That line looks like a cursing cartoonist. The weird-looking text is a *regular expression* and the key to this program. For now, just accept it as a magic incantation. I explain it in a moment, but focus on the big picture here.

✦ **Match the regular expression against the e-mail address.** The next line checks to see whether the e-mail address is a match to the regular expression. The result is true if the expression matches an e-mail address or null if it doesn't.

✦ **Check the phone number.** Once again, the phone number check is simple except the match business, which is just as mysterious: `/^\(\d{3}\) *\d{3}-\d{4}$/` (seriously, who makes this stuff up?). That's another regular expression.

✦ **If everything worked, process the form.** Usually, at this point, you call some sort of function to finish handling the form processing.

Frequently, you do validation in JavaScript before you pass information to a program on the server. This way, your server program already knows the data is valid by the time it gets there. Look ahead to AJAX in Book VII, Chapter 1 to see how this is done.

Introducing regular expressions

Of course, the secret of this program is to decode the mystical expressions used in the `match` statements. They aren't really strings at all, but very powerful text-manipulation techniques called *regular expression parsing*. Regular expressions have migrated from the Unix world into many programming languages, including JavaScript.

A *regular expression* is a powerful mini-language for searching and replacing text patterns. Essentially, what it does is allow you to search for complex patterns and expressions. It's a weird-looking language, but it has a certain charm once you know how to read the arcane-looking expressions.

Regular expressions are normally used with the string `match()` method in JavaScript, but you can also use them with the `replace()` method and a few other places.

Table 5-1 summarizes the main operators in JavaScript regular expressions.

Table 5-1	Regular Expression Operators in JavaScript			
Operator	*Description*	*Sample Pattern*	*Matches*	*Doesn't Match*
. (period)	Any single character except new-line	.	e	\n
^	Beginning of string	^a	apple	banana

(continued)

Table 5-1 *(continued)*

Operator	Description	Sample Pattern	Matches	Doesn't Match
`$`	End of string	`a$`	Banana	apple
`[characters]`	Any of a list of characters in braces	`[abcABC]`	A	D
`[char range]`	Any character in the range	`[a-zA-Z]`	F	9
`\d`	Any single numerical digit	`\d\d\d-` `\d\d\d\d`	123-4567	The-thing
`\b`	A word boundary	`\bthe\b`	the	theater
`+`	One or more occurrences of the previous character	`\d+`	1234	text
`*`	Zero or more occurrences of the previous character	`[a-zA-Z]\d*`	B17, g	7
`{digit}`	Repeat preceding character *digit* times	`\d{3}-` `\d{4}`	123-4567	999-99-9999
`{min, max}`	Repeat preceding character at least *min* but not more than *max* times	`^.{2,4}$`	ca, com, info	water-melon
`(pattern segment)`	Store results in pattern memory returned with code	`^(.).*\1$`	gig, wallow	Bobby

Don't memorize this table! I explain in the rest of this chapter exactly how regular expressions work. Keep Table 5-1 handy as a reference.

To see how regular expressions work, take a look at `regex.html` in Figure 5-6.

Figure 5-6:
This tool
allows
you to test
regular
expressions.

The top textbox accepts a regular expression, and the second text field contains text to examine. You can practice the examples in the following sections to see how regular expressions work. They're really quite useful after you get the hang of them. While you walk through the examples, try them out in this tester. (I include it on the website for you, but I don't reproduce the code here. Of course you're always welcome to view the source code.)

Using characters in regular expressions

The main thing you do with a regular expression is search for text. Say that you work for the bigCorp company, and you ask for employee e-mail addresses. You can make a form that accepts only e-mail addresses with the term *bigCorp* in them by using the following code:

```
if (email.match(/bigCorp/)){
  alert("match");
} else {
  alert("no match");
} // end if
```

The text in the `match()` method is enclosed in slashes (/) rather than quote symbols because the expression isn't technically a string; it's a regular expression. The slashes help the interpreter realize this special kind of text requires additional processing.

If you forget and enclose a regular expression inside quotes, it will still work most of the time. JavaScript tries to convert string values into regular expressions when it needs to. However, if you've ever watched a science fiction movie, you know it's generally not best to trust computers. Use the slash characters to explicitly coerce the text into regular expression format. I'm not saying your computer will take over the world if you don't, but you never can tell. . . .

This match is the simplest type. I'm simply looking for the existence of the needle (bigCorp) in a haystack (the e-mail address stored in `email`). If *big-Corp* is found anywhere in the text, the match is true, and I can do what I want (usually process the form on the server). More often, you want to trap for an error and remind the user what needs to be fixed.

Marking the beginning and end of the line

You may want to improve the search because what you really want are addresses that end with `bigCorp.com`. You can put a special character inside the match string to indicate where the end of the line should be:

```
if (email.match(/bigCorp.com$/)){
  alert("match");
} else {
  alert("no match");
} // end if
```

The dollar sign at the end of the match string indicates that this part of the text should occur at the end of the search string, so *andy@bigCorp.com* is a match, but not *bigCorp.com announces a new Website*.

If you're an ace with regular expressions, you know this example has a minor problem, but it's pretty picky. I explain it in the upcoming "Working with special characters" section. For now, just appreciate that you can include the end of the string as a search parameter.

Likewise, you can use the caret character (^) to indicate the beginning of a string.

If you want to ensure that a text field contains only the phrase *oogie boogie* (and why wouldn't you?), you can tack on the beginning and ending markers. The code `/^oogie boogie$/` is a true match only if nothing else appears in the phrase.

Working with special characters

In addition to ordinary text, you can use a bunch of special character symbols for more flexible matching:

+ **Matching a character with the period:** The most powerful character is the period (`.`), which represents a single character. Any single character except the newline (`\n`) matches against the period. A character that matches any character may seem silly, but it's actually quite powerful. The expression `/b.g/` matches *big, bag,* and *bug*. In fact, it matches any phrase that contains *b* followed by any single character and then *g*, so *bxg, b g,* and *b9g* are also matches.

+ **Using a character class:** You can specify a list of characters in square braces, and JavaScript matches if any one of those characters matches.

This list of characters is sometimes called a *character class*. For example, /b[aeiou]g/ matches on *bag, beg, big, bog,* or *bug*. This method is a really quick way to check a lot of potential matches.

You can also specify a character class with a range. [a-zA-Z] checks all the letters.

✦ **Specifying digits:** One of the most common tricks is to look for numbers. The special character \d represents a number (0–9). You can check for a U.S. phone number (without the area code — yet) using a pattern that looks for three digits, a dash, and four digits: /\d\d\d-\d\d\d\d/.

✦ **Marking punctuation characters:** You can tell that regular expressions use a lot of funky characters, such as periods and braces. What if you're searching for one of these characters? Just use a backslash to indicate that you're looking for the actual character and not using it as a modifier. For example, the e-mail address would be better searched with bigCorp\.com because it specifies there must be a period. If you don't use the backslash, the regular expression tool interprets the period as "any character" and allows something like *bigCorpucom*. Use the backslash trick for most punctuation, such as parentheses, braces, periods, and slashes.

If you want to include an area code with parentheses, just use backslashes to indicate the parentheses: /\(\d\d\d\) \d\d\d-\d\d\d\d/. And if you want to ensure the only thing in the sample is the phone number, just add the boundary characters: /^\(\d\d\d\) \d\d\d \d\d\d\d$/.

✦ **Finding word boundaries:** Sometimes you want to know whether something is a word. Say that you're searching for *the,* but you don't want a false positive on *breathe* or *theater*. The \b character means "the edge of a word," so /\bthe\b/ matches *the* but not words containing "the" inside them.

Conducting repetition operations

All the character modifiers refer to one particular character at a time, but sometimes you want to deal with several characters at once. Several operators can help you with this process.

✦ **Finding one or more elements:** The plus sign (+) indicates "one or more" of the preceding character, so the pattern /ab+c/ matches on *abc, abbbbbbc,* or *abbbbbbbc,* but not on *ac* (there must be at least one b) or on *afc* (it's gotta be b).

✦ **Matching zero or more elements:** The asterisk means "zero or more" of the preceding character. So /I'm .* happy/ matches on *I'm happy* (zero occurrences of any character between *I'm* and *happy*). It also matches on *I'm not happy* (because characters appear in between).

The .* combination is especially useful, because you can use it to improve matches like e-mail addresses: /^.*@bigCorp\.com$/ does a pretty good job of matching e-mail addresses in a fictional company.

✦ **Specifying the number of matches:** You can use braces ({}) to indicate the specific number of times the preceding character should be repeated. For example, you can rewrite a phone number pattern as /\(\d{3}\) *\d{3}-\d{4}/. This structure means "three digits in parentheses, followed by any number of spaces (zero or more), and then three digits, a dash, and four digits. Using this pattern, you can tell whether the user has entered the phone number in a valid format.

You can also specify a minimum and maximum number of matches, so /[aeiou]{1, 3}/ means "at least one and no more than three vowels."

Now you can improve the e-mail pattern so that it includes any number of characters, an @ sign, and ends with a period and two to four letters: /^.+@.+\..{2,4}$/.

A regular expression can check to see if an e-mail address matches the right pattern, but it can't tell if it's a valid address that really exists on the Internet. You actually have to try to send an e-mail to see if it's valid, which is beyond the scope of JavaScript. (I show how to send e-mails through PHP in Book V.)

Working with pattern memory

Sometimes you want to remember a piece of your pattern and reuse it. You can use parentheses to group a chunk of the pattern and remember it. For example, /(foo){2}/ doesn't match on *foo*, but it does on *foofoo*. It's the entire segment that's repeated twice.

You can also refer to a stored pattern later in the expression. The pattern /^(.).*\1$/ matches any word or phrase that begins and ends with the same character. The \1 symbol represents the first pattern in the string; \2 represents the second, and so on.

After you've finished a pattern match, the remembered patterns are still available in special variables. The variable $1 is the first pattern stored; $2 is the second, and so on. You can use this trick to look for HTML tags and report what tag was found: Match ^<(.*)>.*<\/\1>$ and then print $1 to see what the tag was.

There's much more to discover about regular expressions, but this basic overview should give you enough to write some powerful and useful patterns.

New HTML5/CSS3 Tricks for Validation

HTML5 and CSS3 add a few more tricks to simplify validation, and they are absolutely wonderful.

While you can always use JavaScript and regular expressions to validate your pages (as described in this chapter), HTML5 promises a much easier solution. When you use the special-purpose input elements (described in Book I, Chapter 7), the browser will automatically check the form field to ensure it is in a proper format. If the entry is not valid, the form will (generally) not submit, and the special `:invalid` CSS pseudo-class will be associated with the invalid field. Simply supply CSS to your page handling the `:invalid` state:

```
:invalid {
   background-color: red;
}
```

When this CSS state is active, any invalid fields will have the `:invalid` styling. For example, if you have an `email` field defined and the content of that field is not a valid e-mail address, the `invalid` style will be applied. As soon as the address is in the right format, the `invalid` style will be removed.

The developer doesn't need to add any other code to the form. Simply add CSS to display invalid entries, and the browser will do the rest. You don't even need to specify the regular expression for e-mail addresses or any other specialty input fields — the appropriate regular expression for each field type is already built in.

Note that if a field is required (with the `required` attribute), it will be considered invalid until it contains some value.

It is possible that the browser will refuse to process a form until all fields are validated, but this behavior does not yet seem to be universal among HTML5-compliant browsers.

If you wish, you can turn off the validation for any field by adding the `novalidate` attribute to that element.

Figure 5-7 shows the `newElements.html` page from Book I, Chapter 7 modified with a nice style sheet and the validation modifiers in place. Note that the name field is required and the e-mail address is invalid, so these fields show the red background I specified for invalid fields.

**Book IV
Chapter 5**

Getting Valid Input

Figure 5-7:
The new
HTML5 form
elements
have
automatic
validation.

Please look over the code for `html5validation.html` on the website — the
code hasn't changed substantially from Book I, Chapter 7.
The CSS code is new, so I reproduce that here:

```
<style type = "text/css">
        fieldset {
            width: 600px;
            background-color: #EEEEEE;
            margin-left: auto;
            margin-right: auto;
            box-shadow: 5px 5px 5px gray;
        }
        label {
            float: left;
            clear: left;
            width: 250px;
            text-align: right;
            padding-right: 1em;
        }

        input {
            float: left;
        }

        :required {
            border: 1px solid red;
        }

        :invalid {
            color: white;
            background-color: red;
        }

        button {
            display: block;
            margin-left: auto;
            margin-right: auto;
            clear: both;
        }
</style>
```

Adding a pattern

The `pattern` attribute allows you to specify a regular expression used to validate the form. If the content matches the regular expression, the field will be considered valid. (See the "Working with Regular Expressions" section of this chapter for more details.) The `pattern` attribute should be used only when the standard validation techniques are not sufficient (that is, you're using an ordinary input element that doesn't have an automatic pattern) because it can be difficult to debug regular expressions.

```
<input type = "text"
       id = "txtPhone"
       pattern = "\(\d{3}\) +\d{3}-\d{4}"
       title = "(ddd) ddd-dddd" />
```

When you specify a pattern, you should also include a `title` attribute. The title should indicate what the pattern is. The browser can use this as a tip for the user. It may also be useful to add pattern information as placeholder text. (See the `placeholder` attribute later.)

Marking a field as required

The `required` attribute allows you to specify a particular field as required. Supporting browsers will mark all required fields (perhaps by highlighting them in red) if they are not filled in. Some browsers will also send a warning if the user tries to submit a form with empty required fields.

```
<input type = "text"
       required />
```

The special `:required` pseudo-class allows you to apply a CSS style to all required elements in your form (giving them a border or background-color, for example). Here's an example of a CSS style for marking required elements with a red border:

```
:required {
  border: 1px solid red;
}
```

If you have a required field and it has no content, that field will trigger the `invalid` style.

Adding placeholder text

The `placeholder` attribute allows you to add a special placeholder value in your text fields. This placeholder acts as a temporary label showing the purpose of the field without requiring a label tag. As soon as the user activates the field, the placeholder text disappears.

```
<input type = "text"
       placeholder = "Name" />
```

Not all browsers support placeholder text. Other browsers will simply ignore the `placeholder` attribute. Likewise, if the field is already filled in, the placeholder will not be visible. For these reasons, it is still preferred to add a label so users know what to type in each text area. Placeholder text is especially helpful when it is used to indicate how the input should be formatted (especially if this will be enforced by validation or a pattern).

Chapter 6: Drawing on the Canvas

In This Chapter

↙ **Adding a canvas to your HTML page**

↙ **Using colors, patterns, and gradients**

↙ **Drawing paths and geometric shapes**

↙ **Working with images**

↙ **Pixel manipulation**

The canvas element is one of the most interesting new developments in HTML5. Although the <canvas> tag is an HTML tag, it really isn't interesting without JavaScript programming. The <canvas> tag provides a *graphics context*, which is an area of the page that can be drawn upon with JavaScript commands.

The <canvas> tag supplies a rich toolkit of drawing operations that may very well revolutionize the web. Innovations in the <canvas> tag along with advances in the speed of JavaScript engines may very well lead to new uses of the web. A number of developers have developed games with the <canvas> tag and JavaScript that would have required Flash or Java just a few years ago. Also, the flexibility of <canvas> could lead to entirely new visual tools and widgets that are not based on HTML, which could have profound implications on usability and user interfaces.

The <canvas> tag is supported by all current browsers.

Although many of the features of the <canvas> element (shadows, transformations, and images) are available through other parts of the HTML5 universe, the implementation of the various <canvas> elements is identical on all browsers that support the platform. This universal support makes the canvas ideal for animation applications.

Canvas Basics

Begin with a simple demonstration of the <canvas> tag. The canvas variation of "Hello World" creates a simple canvas and draws a rectangle on it.

Setting up the canvas

To use the `<canvas>` tag, build a web page with a `<canvas>` element in it. Typically you'll provide `width`, `height`, and `id` parameters:

```
<canvas id = "drawing"
        width = "200"
        height = "200">
  <p>Your browser does not support the canvas tag...</p>
</canvas>
```

Inside the `<canvas>` tag, you can put any HTML code you wish. This code will appear if the browser does not support the `<canvas>` tag. Typically, you'll just put some sort of message letting the user know what she's missing.

Nothing interesting happens in a canvas without some kind of JavaScript code. Often you'll use a function to draw on the screen. Here's my `draw()` function, which is called by the `body onload` event:

```
function draw(){
  //from basicCanvas.html
  var canvas = document.getElementById("surface");
  if (canvas.getContext){
    var con = canvas.getContext('2d');
    con.fillStyle = "rgb(255,255,0)";
    con.fillRect(40,140,150,50);
  } // end if
} // end draw
```

Figure 6-1 illustrates the page created with this code:

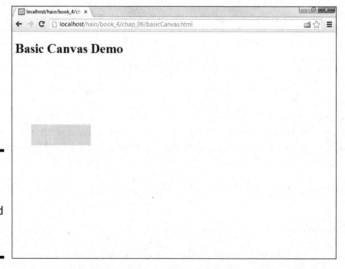

Figure 6-1:
This
rectangle
was created
through
code.

The draw() function illustrates all of the main ideas of working with the canvas tag. Here's how you build a basic drawing:

✦ **Create a variable reference to the canvas:** Use the standard getElementById() mechanism to create a variable referring to the canvas.

✦ **Extract the graphics context from the canvas:** Canvas elements have a *graphics context,* which is a special object that encapsulates all the drawing methods the canvas can perform. Most browsers support a 2D context now, but 3D contexts are beginning to appear as well.

✦ **Set the context's fillStyle:** The fillStyle indicates how you will color filled-in areas (like rectangles). The basic approach is to supply a CSS color value. See the section "Fill and Stroke Styles" for information on how to fill with colors, gradients, or image patterns.

✦ **Create a filled-in rectangle:** The graphics context has a few built-in shapes. The rectangle shape is pretty easy to build. It expects four parameters: x, y, width, and height. The x and y parameters indicate the position of the rectangle's top left corner, and the width and height parameters indicate the size of the rectangle. All measurements are in pixels. See the "Drawing Essential Shapes" section for more information on the various types of primitive shapes you can build.

How <canvas> works

I go into detail throughout this chapter, but it's helpful to begin with an overview of the way <canvas> works and what it does in general.

There are really only two main drawing functions in <canvas>: fill and stroke. Most drawing is done as a two-step process. First you define some sort of shape (a rectangle, an arc, a series of lines) and then you tell the canvas to draw with a *stroke* or a *fill.* A stroke simply draws a line, so if you stroke a rectangle, you'll see the outline of the rectangle, but it will not be filled in. The fill draws the filled-in shape, so a filled rectangle will show the interior of the rectangle.

You can specify a fillStyle, which specifies the color and pattern of subsequent fill commands. You can also indicate a strokeStyle, which determines how subsequent stroke commands will be drawn.

More complex shapes are drawn with a mechanism called *paths,* which are a series of line-drawing instructions. You can use paths to create strokes or filled-in shapes.

You can draw images onto a canvas. You can draw an entire image, or part of an image onto the canvas.

You can also draw text directly onto the canvas in various fonts and colors. You can add shadow effects to your text elements, or even images.

The canvas object gives you access to the underlying data of an image. This allows you to perform any kind of transformation you wish on image data, including color balancing, adjusting brightness, and so on.

It's possible to add *transformations* to any of your objects. Transformations allow you to move, resize, or rotate any element (text, drawing, image) you place on the canvas.

Finally, you can use JavaScript's animation and user interface tools to build your own animations that move an element around in real time or under user control.

Fill and Stroke Styles

Nearly every operation in the canvas implements a fill or stroke style. To get the most out of canvas, you need to understand how they work. There are three primary types of styles that can be used on fills and strokes: colors, gradients, and patterns.

Colors

There are a number of places where you can indicate a color value in the canvas API. In general, you can use the same color tools you use in CSS and HTML:

✦ **Six-digit hex values:** The most common way to manage colors is with the same six-digit hexadecimal scheme commonly used in CSS, with two digits each for red, green, and blue. The value begins with a pound sign. For example, #FF0000 is red, and #FFFF00 is yellow.

✦ **Three-digit hex values:** Hex color values often use repeating values, so you can abbreviate these values as three-digit numbers. In this scheme, red is #F00 and yellow is #FF0

✦ **Color names:** You can often use color names, like "red" or "yellow." Common color names usually work, but not all browsers support the same list of color names, so "papaya whip" is not likely to be supported. (It sounds more like a dessert recipe than a color to me anyway.)

✦ **rgb and rgba values:** You can use the rgb() function to create colors using integers (0–255) or percentages (0%–100%). Red would be rgb(255, 0, 0), and yellow is rgb(100%, 100%, 0%). Note that the `rgb` function must go in quotes like any other color value. If you want to include alpha, add a fourth parameter that is a 0–1 value. Transparent red would be `rgba(255, 0, 0, 0.5)`.

✦ **`hsl` and `hsla`:** The new `hsl` and `hsla` color formats are supposed to be supported by the `<canvas>` element, but so far the support for these features varies by browser.

Note that the various values for a color are always enclosed in quotes. The color parameter is a string that can be interpreted as a CSS color.

Gradients

You can also fill a shape with a gradient. Canvas gradients are defined in two steps:

✦ **Create a gradient object:** There are two methods built into the context object for this. One builds linear gradients, and the other builds radial gradients.

✦ **Add color stops:** A *color stop* is a special element that indicates a color to be added to the gradient. You can add as many colors as you wish, and you can also specify where along the gradient pattern the color will appear.

The following code builds a radial gradient and a linear gradient on a canvas.

```
function draw(){
  //from gradient.html
  var drawing = document.getElementById("drawing");
  var con = drawing.getContext("2d");

  //build a linear gradient
  lGrad = con.createLinearGradient(0,0,100,200);

  lGrad.addColorStop(0, "#FF0000");
  lGrad.addColorStop(.5, "#00FF00");
  lGrad.addColorStop(1, "#0000FF");

  con.fillStyle = lGrad;
  con.fillRect(0, 0, 100, 200);

  //build a radial gradient
  rGrad = con.createRadialGradient(150, 100,
          0, 150, 100, 100);
  rGrad.addColorStop(0, "#FF0000");
  rGrad.addColorStop(.5, "#00FF00");
  rGrad.addColorStop(1, "#0000FF");

  con.fillStyle = rGrad;
  con.fillRect(100,0, 200, 200);

} // end draw
```

The output of this code is shown in Figure 6-2.

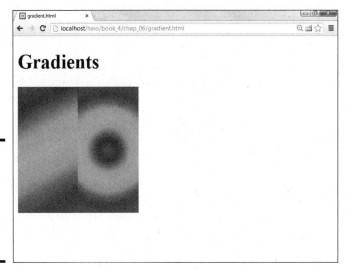

Figure 6-2: These gradient patterns were created by code.

A *linear* gradient is a pattern of colors that blend into each other along a straight-line path. To define a linear gradient:

✦ **Create a variable to hold the gradient:** Gradients are a little more complex than simple colors, so they are stored in variables so they can be re-used.

✦ **Build the gradient:** Use the createLinearGradient() method of the context object to build a linear gradient.

✦ **Define the gradient path:** The createLinearGradient() method expects four parameters. These define a line (x1, y1, x2, y2). The colors are perpendicular to this line, so if you want horizontal color bands, draw a vertical line. If you want vertical color bands, draw a horizontal line. In my example, I drew a diagonal line for diagonal colors. The line typically takes up the entire width or height of the element, but it does not have to. If the line is smaller than the image, the excess area is automatically assigned a color from the nearest end of the gradient.

✦ **Add color stops:** Gradients aren't much fun without colors. The addColorStop() method of the gradient object allows you to add a color to the gradient. Each color stop has two parameters: position and color. The position is a 0–1 value indicating where on the gradient line the color should be positioned. 0 is the beginning, 1 is the end, and intermediate values are in the middle. The color parameter is a text value that can be evaluated as a CSS color. You can use any of the mechanisms described in the color section of this part. At a minimum, you should define two color stops, one for the beginning, and one for the end.

✦ **Apply the gradient as a fill pattern:** If you want to use the gradient as a fill pattern, set the context's `fillStyle` to the gradient variable you just created. All subsequent fills will be done using the gradient pattern until the `fillStyle` is changed to something else.

Radial gradients are similar. Rather than drawing a gradient in a straight line, they draw a series of circular color bands. The first color is the center of the circle, and the last color defines an outer radius. Building a radial gradient is very similar to building a linear gradient. The only difference is the `create` command.

Use the console object's `createRadialGradient()` method to build a radial gradient. This command actually takes six parameters:

✦ **beginX:** The X position of the starting point. This is often in the center of your shape.

✦ **beginY:** Along with `centerX`, this determines the beginning position of your gradient.

✦ **beginRadius:** The radius of your center circle. Usually this is 0, but you can make it larger if you want to emphasize the center color more.

✦ **endX:** Describes the X position of the ending circle. Typically this is the same as `beginX`.

✦ **endY:** Along with `endX`, `endY` defines the position of the ending circle. If the beginning and ending circles have the same positions, you'll get a circular gradient. Change the ending position to make the gradient stretch in a particular direction.

✦ **endRadius:** The ending radius defines where the last color gradient will be placed. Smaller values for this radius will lead to a tightly grouped gradient, and larger values will spread the gradient along a larger area. After the gradient is defined, the `addColorStops()` method works exactly like it does for linear gradients. The variable created through the `addRadialGradient()` command is usually stored in a variable, where it can be used for subsequent `fillStyle()` requests.

Patterns

A pattern is used to define an image to be used as a fill or stroke. You can use any image as a pattern, but it's generally best to find or create an image that is designed to be tiled. (See Book VIII, Chapter 4 for complete information on how to build tiled patterns using free software.) Many sources of tiled patterns exist on the web as well. After you've got an image you want to use as a fill pattern, here's how to implement it in the `<canvas>` tag:

```
function draw(){
  //from pattern.html
  var drawing = document.getElementById("drawing");
  var con = drawing.getContext("2d");
  var texture = document.getElementById("texture");

  pFill = con.createPattern(texture, "repeat");
  con.fillStyle = pFill;

  con.fillRect(10,150,190,150);

  con.font = "40px sans-serif";
  con.fillText("Pattern!", 20, 80);

  con.strokeStyle = pFill;
  con.lineWidth = 5;
  con.strokeRect(10, 10, 180, 100);

} // end draw
```

You can see the results of this code in Figure 6-3.

Figure 6-3:
An image pattern can be applied to text and other shapes.

A pattern is simply an image. Building a pattern is relatively straightforward:

1. **Get access to an image.**

    You'll need a JavaScript image object to serve as the basis of your pattern. There's a number of ways to do this, but the easiest is to create the image somewhere in your HTML, hide it with the `display:none` style, and use the standard `document.getElementById()` technique to get access to your image. (See "Drawing an image on the canvas" toward the end of this chapter for alternate ways to load images.)

2. **Create a variable for the pattern.**

    Like gradients, pattern fills can be reused, so store the pattern in a variable for later reuse.

3. **Build the pattern.**

    The context's `createPattern()` method creates a pattern from an image.

4. **Specify the pattern's repeat parameter.**

    The second parameter indicates how the pattern will repeat. The default value is `repeat`, which repeats the pattern in both the X and Y axis indefinitely. If your pattern is not tiled, you will see a visible seam where the pattern repeats. You can also set the repeat value to `repeat-x`, `repeat-y`, and `no-repeat`.

5. **Apply the pattern variable to the `fillStyle` or `strokeStyle`.**

    Assign the pattern variable to the context's `fillStyle` and then perform any fill operation to draw in the pattern.

Drawing Essential Shapes

A few primitive shapes can be drawn directly onto the graphics context. The most common shapes are rectangles and text.

Rectangle functions

You can draw three different types of rectangles:

✦ `clearRect(x, y, w, h)`: Erases a rectangle with the upper-left corner (x, y) and size (w, h). Generally, erasing draws in the background color.

✦ `fillRect(x, y, w, h)`: Draws a box with upper-left corner (x, y) and size (w, h). The rectangle is filled in with the currently-defined `fillStyle`.

✦ **strokeRect(x, y, w, h):** Draws a box with upper-left corner (x, y) and size (w, h). The box is not filled in, but the outline is drawn in the currently-defined `strokeStyle` and using the current `lineWidth`.

Figure 6-4 illustrates a couple of rectangles.

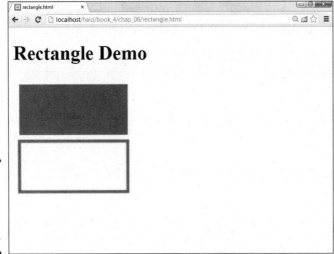

Figure 6-4:
You can easily draw rectangles on a canvas.

Here's the code that generates Figure 6-4:

```
function draw(){
  //from rectangle.html
  var drawing = document.getElementById("drawing");
  var con = drawing.getContext("2d");

  con.fillStyle = "red";
  con.strokeStyle = "green";
  con.lineWidth = "5";

  con.fillRect(10, 10, 180, 80);
  con.strokeRect(10, 100, 180, 80);

} // end draw
```

Drawing text

The `<canvas>` tag has complete support for text. You can add text anywhere on the canvas, using whichever font style and size you wish.

Figure 6-5 shows a canvas with embedded text.

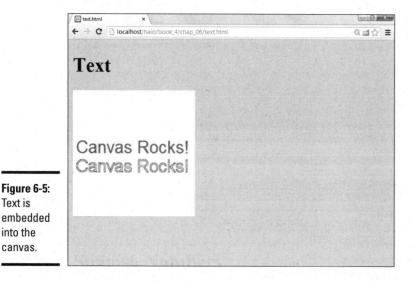

Figure 6-5:
Text is
embedded
into the
canvas.

Text is drawn onto canvas much like a rectangle. The first step is to pick the desired font. Canvas fonts are created by assigning a font to the context's `font` attribute. Fonts are defined like the single-string font assignment in CSS. You can specify all of the font characteristics in the same order you do when using the font shortcut: style, variant, weight, size, and family.

When you're ready to display actual text on the screen, use the `fillText()` method, which accepts three parameters. The first parameter is the text to display. The last two parameters are the X and Y position of the left-hand side of the text. The following code is used to produce the result shown in Figure 6-5. When the strokeStyle is not explicitly set, the stroke is black by default.

```
function draw(){
   //from text.html
   var drawing = document.getElementById("drawing");
   var con = drawing.getContext("2d");

   //clear background
   con.fillStyle = "white";
   con.fillRect(0,0, 200, 200);

   // draw font in red
   con.fillStyle = "red";
   con.font = "20pt sans-serif";
   con.fillText("Canvas Rocks!", 5, 100);
   con.strokeText("Canvas Rocks!", 5, 130);

} // end draw
```

**Book IV
Chapter 6**

**Drawing on the
Canvas**

Adding shadows

You can add shadows to anything you draw on the canvas. Shadows are quite easy to build. They require a number of methods of the context object:

✦ **shadowOffsetX:** Determines how much the shadow will be moved along the X axis. Normally this will be a value between 0 and 5. A positive value moves the shadow to the right of an object. Change this value and the shadowOffsetY value to alter where the light source appears to be.

✦ **shadowOffsetY:** Determines how far the shadow is moved along the Y axis. A positive value moves the shadow below the object. In general, all shadows on a page should have the same X and Y offsets to indicate consistent lighting. The size of the offset values implies how high the element is "lifted" off the page.

✦ **shadowColor:** The shadow color indicates the color of the shadow. Normally this is defined as black, but the color can be changed to other values if you wish.

✦ **shadowBlur:** The shadowBlur effect determines how much the shadow is softened. If this is set to 0, the shadow is extremely crisp and sharp. A value of 5 leads to a much softer shadow. Shadow blur generally lightens the shadow color.

If you apply a shadow to text, be sure that the text is still readable. Large simple fonts are preferred, and you may need to adjust the shadow color or blur to ensure the main text is still readable. After you've applied shadow characteristics, all subsequent drawing commands will incorporate the shadow. If you want to turn shadows off, set the shadowColor to a transparent color using RGBA.

Here's the code to produce text with a shadow:

```
<!DOCTYPE HTML>
<html lang = "en">
<head>
  <title>shadow.html</title>
  <meta charset = "UTF-8" />
  <style type = "text/css">
    body {
      background-color: #cccccc;
    }
  </style>
  <script type = "text/javascript">
    function draw(){
      //from shadow.html
      var drawing = document.getElementById("drawing");
      var con = drawing.getContext("2d");
```

```
        //clear background
        con.fillStyle = "white";
        con.fillRect(0,0, 200, 200);

        // draw font in red
        con.fillStyle = "red";
        con.font = "18pt sans-serif";

        //add shadows
        con.shadowOffsetX = 3;
        con.shadowOffsetY = 3;
        con.shadowColor = "gray";
        con.shadowBlur = 5;
        con.fillText("Canvas Rocks!", 5, 100);

      } // end draw

    </script>
  </head>

<body onload = "draw()">
  <h1>Shadows</h1>

  <canvas id = "drawing"
          height = "200"
          width = "200">
    <p>Canvas not supported!</p>
  </canvas>

</body>
</html>
```

An example of a shadow inside a `<canvas>` is shown in Figure 6-6.

Figure 6-6:
You can apply a shadow to any canvas drawing, including text.

Working with Paths

More complex shapes are created using the path mechanism. A path is simply a series of commands "played back" by the graphics context. You can think of it as a recording of pen motions. Here's an example that draws a blue triangle with a red border:

```
function draw(){
  //from pathDemo.html
  var drawing = document.getElementById("drawing");
  var con = drawing.getContext("2d");

  con.strokeStyle = "red";
  con.fillStyle = "blue";
  con.lineWidth = "5";

  con.beginPath();
    con.moveTo(100, 100);
    con.lineTo(200, 200);
    con.lineTo(200, 100);
    con.lineTo(100, 100);
  con.closePath();
  con.stroke();
  con.fill();
} // end draw
```

The code shown here generates the output displayed in Figure 6-7.

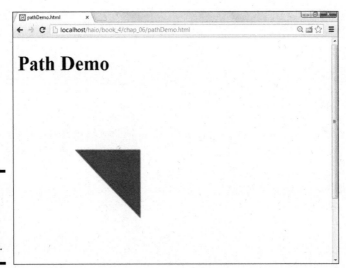

Figure 6-7:
A path can be used to draw multi-line shapes.

The technique for drawing a path is not terribly complicated, but it does involve new steps:

1. **Generate the graphics context.**

   All `<canvas>` programs begin by creating a variable for the canvas and another variable for the graphics context.

2. **Set the `strokeStyle` and `fillStyle`.**

   `strokeStyle` indicates the color of lines. The `lineWidth` attribute describes how wide the line will be (in pixels), and `fillStyle` indicates the color that enclosed shapes will have.

3. **Begin the path.**

   A path is a series of drawing commands. Use the `beginPath()` method to start your path definition.

4. **Move the pen.**

   The `moveTo(x,y)` command moves the pen to a particular point on the screen without drawing.

5. **Draw lines.**

   The `lineTo(x, y)` command draws a line from the current pen position to the indicated `(x, y)` coordinates. See the "Drawing Essential Shapes" section for information on other drawing commands for building arcs, circles, and more complex curves. (Note that the line will still not be visible. See Step 7.)

6. **Close the path.**

   When you're finished with a path, use the `closePath()` function to indicate you are finished defining the path.

7. **Stroke or fill the path.**

   When you define a path, it is not immediately displayed! The `stroke()` command draws a line using the current stroke style and line width along the path. If you prefer, use the `fill()` command to draw a filled-in shape defined by the path. If the path did not define a closed shape, the `fill()` command draws a line from the ending point to the beginning point. The `fill()` command fills in the path with the color, gradient, or pattern designated with `fillStyle()`.

Note that the `closePath()` function draws a connecting line between the first point of the path and the last point. This creates closed shapes. If you want a path to remain open, use the `stroke()` command before the `close-Path()` command. It is still necessary to call `closePath()` before creating a new path.

**Book IV
Chapter 6**

**Drawing on the
Canvas**

TIP

Remember, the `lineTo()` method doesn't actually draw a line! It simply indicates your path. The path is not visible until you execute a `stroke()`, `closePath()`, or `fill()` command.

Line-drawing options

Whenever you are using stroke commands, you can modify the line width and style with a number of interesting options. Figure 6-8 shows a few of these choices.

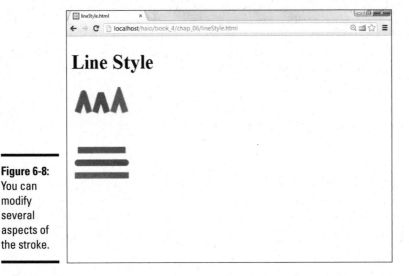

Figure 6-8:
You can modify several aspects of the stroke.

The code used to create Figure 6-8 is here:

```
function draw(){
  //from lineStyle.html
  var drawing = document.getElementById("drawing");
  var con = drawing.getContext("2d");

  //change line width and color
  con.strokeStyle = "red";
  con.lineWidth = 10;

  con.lineJoin = "round"
  con.beginPath();
  con.moveTo(10, 40);
  con.lineTo(20, 10);
  con.lineTo(30, 40);
  con.stroke();
  con.closePath();

  con.strokeStyle = "blue";
  con.lineJoin = "bevel"
  con.beginPath();
  con.moveTo(40, 40);
```

```
con.lineTo(50, 10);
con.lineTo(60, 40);
con.stroke();
con.closePath();

con.lineJoin = "miter";
con.strokeStyle = "green"
con.beginPath();
con.moveTo(70, 40);
con.lineTo(80, 10);
con.lineTo(90, 40);
con.stroke();
con.closePath();

//line caps
con.lineCap = "butt";
con.strokeStyle = "red"
con.beginPath();
con.moveTo(10, 100);
con.lineTo(90, 100);
con.stroke();
con.closePath();

con.lineCap = "round";
con.strokeStyle = "blue"
con.beginPath();
con.moveTo(10, 120);
con.lineTo(90, 120);
con.stroke();
con.closePath();

con.lineCap = "square";
con.strokeStyle = "green"
con.beginPath();
con.moveTo(10, 140);
con.lineTo(90, 140);
con.stroke();
con.closePath();

} // end draw
```

While the code listing is long, it is quite repetitive. There are only a few new elements:

- ✦ **strokeStyle:** Use any of the style options (color, gradient, or pattern) to specify how your line will be drawn.

- ✦ **linewidth:** Specify the width of your line in pixels.

- ✦ **lineJoin:** The lineJoin property indicates how corners are rendered in your paths. The default form is miter, which produces sharp corners. You can also choose round, which gives rounded corners, and bevel, which squares off the corners.

- ✦ **lineCap:** You can also determine how the ends of the lines are rendered. Use round to produce rounded edges, square to produce squared-off edges, and butt to produce edges that are cut off exactly at the line width. Square and butt look almost identical, but square adds a small length to each line, and butt cuts off the line immediately.

Drawing arcs and circles

Arcs and circles are part of the `path` mechanism. They are created much like lines, as they are executed as part of a path. After the path is complete, use the `stroke()` or `fill()` command to actually draw the arc or circle.

Arcs and circles are both created with the `arc()` method.

To draw an arc or a circle:

1. **Set the stroke or fill style.**

   Like all path-drawing commands, you'll need to specify the fill or stroke style before drawing the arc.

2. **Begin a path.**

   Arcs, like lines, must be drawn as part of a path. Arcs can be combined with lines if you wish.

3. **Specify the center of the circle.**

   An arc is simply a partial circle, so you begin defining an arc by determining the center of a circle. The first two parameters of the `arc()` method are the center of the circle.

4. **Indicate the radius of the circle.**

   The third parameter is the radius of the circle that describes the arc.

5. **Define beginning and ending points.**

   An arc is a part of a circle. To indicate which part of the circle you want to draw, indicate the beginning and ending angles. These measurements are the fourth and fifth parameters of the `arc()` method. Note that angles are defined in radians.

6. **Indicate the direction to draw.**

   The last parameter determines the drawing direction. Use `true` for counter-clockwise, and `false` for clockwise.

The arc drawing functions are used in the following code:

```
function draw(){
  //from arcCirc.html
  var drawing = document.getElementById("drawing");
  var con = drawing.getContext("2d");

  con.strokeStyle = "green";
  con.fillStyle = "rgba(255,0,0,0.5)";
  con.lineWidth = "5";

  //half-circle stroked
  con.beginPath();
  con.arc(220, 140, 50, 0, Math.PI, false);
```

```
con.closePath();
con.stroke();

//full circle filled
con.beginPath();
con.arc(220, 220, 50, 0, Math.PI*2, true);
con.closePath();
con.fill();
}
```

This code generates the image shown in Figure 6-9.

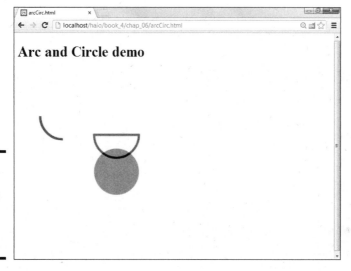

Figure 6-9:
Draw
circles and
arcs with
the arc()
command.

The angle measurements of the `arc()` command use *radians* as the unit
of angle measurement. Radians are frequently used in mathematics rather
than degrees. A radian is simply the angle described when you stretch the
radius of a circle around the circumference of that same circle. Radians are
normally expressed using the constant π, so there are $2 * \pi$ radians in a full
circle. JavaScript has the built-in constant `Math.PI` to simplify working with
pi. You can use Table 6-1 to determine the main angles. (See Table 6-1.)

Table 6-1	Angle Measurements in Radians
Direction	*Angle*
North	`3 * Math.PI/2`
West	`Math.PI`
South	`Math.PI/2`
East	`0`

If you're familiar with radian measurement, you might think the angles are upside down (typically, $\pi/2$ is north and $3*\pi/2$ is south). The angles are reversed because Y increases downwards in computer systems.

Drawing quadratic curves

The canvas element also supports two elegant curve-drawing mechanisms. A *quadratic curve* is a special curve with a start and ending point. However, the line between the beginning and ending point is influenced by a *control point*. As an example, look at Figure 6-10. It shows a simple curve with a control point.

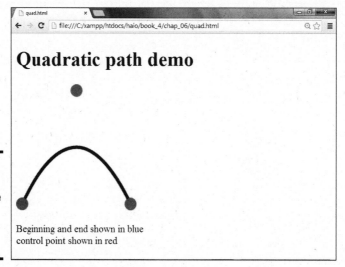

Figure 6-10: Quadratic curves have a single control point.

If you examine the code for the quadratic curve, you'll see it works much like drawing lines and arcs:

```
function draw(){
  //from quad.html
  drawing = document.getElementById("drawing");
  con = drawing.getContext("2d");

  con.strokeStyle = "black";
  con.lineWidth = "5";
  con.beginPath();
  con.moveTo(10,190);
  con.quadraticCurveTo(100, 10, 190, 190);
  con.stroke();
  con.closePath();

  //mark beginning and end with blue
  drawDot(10, 190, "blue");
```

```
drawDot(190, 190, "blue");

//mark control points with red
drawDot(100, 10, "red");

} // end draw
    function drawDot(x, y, color){
        con.fillStyle = color;
        con.beginPath();
        con.arc(x, y, 10, 0, 2 * Math.PI, true);
        con.fill();
        con.closePath();
    } // end drawDot
```

The beginning and ending points of a quadratic curve are described explicitly, and the line begins and ends on these points. However, the control point doesn't usually lie on the curve. Instead, it *influences* the curve.

Here's how to build a quadratic curve:

1. **Begin a path.**

   Curves, like most drawing features, act in the context of a path.

2. **Move to the starting position.**

   Use the `moveTo()` command to move to where you want the curve to begin.

3. **Use the `quadraticCurveTo()` method to draw the curve**.

   This method takes four parameters: the X and Y position of the control point and the X and Y position of the end point.

4. **Draw another curve if you wish.**

   Like most of the drawing commands, you can chain a series of `quadraticCurveTo()` calls together to build a more complex shape.

Note that for this example I called a custom function called `drawDot` to draw the various points on the screen. See the complete code on my website. (For more information on the website, see this book's Introduction.)

**Book IV
Chapter 6**

**Drawing on the
Canvas**

Building a Bézier curve

The *Bézier curve* is another curve-drawing tool. It is similar to the quadratic curve, except it requires two control points. Figure 6-11 illustrates a Bézier curve.

Building a Bézier curve is almost exactly like building a quadratic curve. The `bezierCurveTo` function takes six parameters, the X and Y position of control point one, control point two, and the ending point. Here's the code for the Bézier path shown in Figure 6-11.

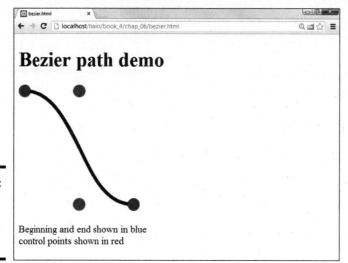

Figure 6-11:
The Bézier
curve uses
two control
points.

```
function draw(){

    //from bezier.html
    drawing = document.getElementById("drawing");
    con = drawing.getContext("2d");

    con.strokeStyle = "black";
    con.lineWidth = "5";
    con.beginPath();
    con.moveTo(10,10);
    con.bezierCurveTo(100, 10, 100, 190, 190, 190);
    con.stroke();
    con.closePath();

    //mark beginning and end with blue
    drawDot(10, 10, "blue");
    drawDot(190, 190, "blue");

    //mark control points with red
    drawDot(100, 10, "red");
    drawDot(100, 190, "red");

} // end draw

function drawDot(x, y, color){
    con.fillStyle = color;
    con.beginPath();
    con.arc(x, y, 10, 0, 2 * Math.PI, true);
    con.fill();
    con.closePath();
} // end drawDot
```

Like the quadratic curve example, I used a custom `drawDot()` function to
draw circles for the control point. See the section "Drawing arcs and circles"
for information on how to draw these dots.

Images

Although HTML has long had support for images, the canvas interface adds new life to web images. Images can be displayed inside a canvas, where they can be integrated with the vector-drawing techniques of the canvas API. You can also select a portion of an image to display and apply the various transformations to your image to create interesting compositions and animations.

Figure 6-12 shows a basic version of this technique, with an image drawn twice on a canvas element.

Figure 6-12: The canvas element has flexible options for drawing images.

Drawing an image on the canvas

The easiest way to use an image in a `<canvas>` element is to use an image that is already available on the web page. You can put an image on the page with the ordinary `<img>` tag and use the CSS `display: none` rule to make the image invisible. An alternate approach is to create an `Image` object in JavaScript and apply the `src` attribute to connect that image to a specific image file. For examples of both techniques, consider the following HTML code:

```
<img class = "hidden"
     id = "goofyPic"
     src = "andyGoofy.gif"
     alt = "Goofy pic of me" />

<canvas id = "drawing"
        height = "400"
        width = "400">
   <p>Canvas not supported</p>
```

The following JavaScript code displays the image in the canvas:

```
function draw(){
    //from image.html
    var drawing = document.getElementById("drawing");
    var con = drawing.getContext("2d");
    var goofyPic = document.getElementById("goofyPic");
    con.drawImage(goofyPic, 0, 0, 50, 50);

    var image2 = new Image();
    image2.src = "andyGoofy.gif";
    con.drawImage(image2, 100, 100, 70, 50);
} // end draw
```

Here's how it's done:

1. **Create the image in the main page.**

   The easiest way to access an image is to use ordinary HTML to embed the image in the main page. If you wish, you can hide the `<img>` tag with CSS code (`display: none`) so that only the version in the canvas is visible.

2. **Create a JavaScript variable for the image.**

   Use the ordinary `document.getElementByID()` mechanism to create a variable referring to the image.

3. **Draw the image on the canvas.**

   The `drawImage()` function takes five parameters. The first is the name of an image object (It must be the name of a JavaScript image object, not just the filename of an image.) The next two parameters are the X and Y values of the top-left corner of the image, and the last two parameters are the size of the image (width and height.)

4. **Create a JavaScript `Image` object.**

   If you don't want to embed an image in the page, you can use JavaScript to create an image dynamically. Use the `new Image()` constructor to build a new image.

5. **Change the image's `src` property.**

   If you create a JavaScript image, you must specify the `src` attribute to indicate the file associated with the image. It might take some time for the image to load.

The image won't display until it has loaded from the server. In most cases, this won't be a problem, but sometimes you'll find you need to delay your program until the image has finished loading. The image object has an `onload` property that accepts a callback function. Use this technique to wait until your drawing finishes.

```
image.onload = finishDrawing;
function finishDrawing(){
 //rest of drawing code goes here
}
```

Drawing part of an image

Sometimes you'll want to draw a small part of the original image.
Figure 6-13 illustrates a program focusing in on the center of the
goofy face:

Figure 6-13:
This
image is a
zoomed-in
section of
the previous
image.

It's quite easy to draw part of an image. Use the same `drawImage()` command, but this time use a version with nine parameters:

```
con.drawImage(goofyPic, 60, 70, 90, 90, 0, 0, 150, 150);
```

Here's what all these parameters mean:

✦ **Image name:** The first parameter is the name of the image (not the filename, but the name of the JavaScript `Image` object).

✦ **Top left corner of source:** The first job is to choose the part of the original picture that will be displayed. The next two parameters indicate the
   top left corner of a selection on the original picture. (You might use an
   image editor like Gimp or IrfanView to determine the selection position
   and size.)

✦ **Height and width of source:** The next two parameters indicate the
   height and width of the source selection.

✦ **Position of destination:** The next two parameters are the position of the
   picture's top left corner on the canvas.

✦ **Size of destination:** The last two parameters describe the size of the
destination image on the canvas.

The "draw only part of an image" technique described here is quite useful
because it allows you to combine several images into a single image (sometimes called a *sprite sheet*). This decreases the overhead for delivering the
image (one large image is faster to deliver than several small ones). It's also
frequently used in games and animations where one entity might have several images displayed in sequence to suggest walking or attacking.

Manipulating Pixels

The `<canvas>` tag has one more incredible trick up its sleeve. You can
extract the data of a `<canvas>` tag into the underlying pixel data. If you
know how to manipulate this data, you can have very extensive control of
your image in real time. You can use this data for color balancing, as well as
experimenting with your own blurs, sharpens, and chroma-key effects.

In order to understand how to have this much control of your images, you
need to have some knowledge of how pictures are stored in memory. No
matter what format an image is stored in on the file system, it is displayed
as a list of pixels. Each pixel is represented (in the standard 32-bit system,
anyway) by four integers: RGBA. The R value represents how much red is in
the current dot. G stands for green, and B stands for blue. The A stands for
alpha, which is a measure of the transparency of the image. Each of these
values can vary from 0 to 255. When you convert an image to the `image-
Data`, you get a huge array of integers. Each group of four integers repre-
sents a single pixel of color data.

Here's an example that changes the color balance of an image:

```
function draw(){
 //from pixel.html
 var drawing = document.getElementById("drawing");
 var con = drawing.getContext("2d");
 var original = document.getElementById("original");

 CANV_WIDTH = 200;
 CANV_HEIGHT = 200;

 //draw the original on the canvas
 con.drawImage(original, 0, 0);

 //get the image data
 imgData = con.getImageData(0, 0, 200, 200);

 //loop through image data
 for (row = 0; row < CANV_HEIGHT; row++){
   for (col = 0; col < CANV_WIDTH; col++){
     //find current pixel
     index = (col + (row * imgData.width)) * 4;

     //separate into color values
```

```
r = imgData.data[index];
g = imgData.data[index + 1];
b = imgData.data[index + 2];
a = imgData.data[index + 3];

//manipulate color values
r -= 20;
g += 50;
b -= 30;
a = a;

//manage boundary conditions
if (r > 255){
  r = 255;
}
if (r < 0){
  r = 0;
}
if (g > 255){
  g = 255;
}
if (g < 0){
  g = 0;
}
if (b > 255){
  r = 255;
}
if (b < 0){
  b = 0;
}
if (a > 255){
  a = 255;
}
if (a < 0){
  a = 0;
}

//return new values to data
imgData.data[index] = r;
imgData.data[index+1] = g;
imgData.data[index+2] = b;
imgData.data[index+3] = a;
} // end col for loop
} // end row for loop

//draw new image onto canvas
con.putImageData(imgData, 0, 0);

} // end function
```

Although the code listing seems quite long, it really isn't too difficult to follow:

1. **Draw an original image.**

   The technique you'll use extracts data from a `<canvas>` element, so to modify an image, first you need to draw it onto a canvas. I drew my goofy face image on the canvas first with the ordinary `drawImage()` method.

2. **Extract the image data.**

   The `getImageData()` method gets the picture displayed by the current canvas and places it in a huge array of integers.

3. **Make a loop to handle the rows.**

   Image data is broken into rows and columns. Each row goes from 0 to the height of the canvas, so make a `for` loop to iterate through the rows.

4. **Make another loop to handle the columns.**

   Inside each row is data from 0 to the width of the canvas, so make a second for loop inside the first. It's very common to use a pair of nested `for` loops to step through two-dimensional data like image information.

5. **Find the index in `imageData` for the current row and column.**

   The `imageData` array contains four integers for each pixel, so we have to do a little math to figure out where the first integer for each pixel is. The easiest formula is to multiply the row number by the width of the canvas, add that to the column number, and multiply the entire result by four.

6. **Pull the corresponding color values from the index.**

   The index also represents the red value of the current pixel. The next int holds the green value, followed by the blue value, and finally the alpha value.

7. **Manipulate the color values as you wish.**

   If you're going to do a color-balancing app (as I'm doing), you can simply add or subtract values to change the overall color balance. In my example, I add a bit to green and subtract a bit from red and blue. I chose to leave the alpha alone. Of course, this is where you can do much more elaborate work if you want to play around with pixel-level image manipulation.

8. **Check for boundaries.**

   A pixel value cannot be lower than 0 or higher than 255, so check for both of these boundaries and adjust all pixel values to be within legal limits.

9. **Return manipulated values back to the `imgData` array.**

   You can copy values back to the array, and you should do so, to make the changes visible.

10. **Draw the `imageData` back to the canvas.**

    The `putImageData()` function draws the current image data back to the canvas as an ordinary image. The new version of the image will reflect the changes. In my case, I have a decidedly ill-looking image.

Color-balancing is too subtle an effect to display accurately in a black-and-white screen shot, so please visit the book's companion website to see this program in its full glory. See the book's Introduction for more on the website.

Chapter 7: Animation with the Canvas

In This Chapter

✔ **Working with images**

✔ **Managing transformations**

✔ **Handling keyboard input**

✔ **Building basic animations**

The <canvas> tag (introduced in Chapter 6 of this minibook) adds some long-needed graphical support to HTML. In this chapter, you see how to extend these ideas to create interesting animations and even user interaction.

Transformations

Transformations are math operations that can be applied to any drawing or image to change the appearance. There are three major transformations:

✦ translation: Move a particular amount in X and Y

✦ rotation: Rotate around a particular point

✦ scale: Change the size of the drawing in X and Y

The <canvas> element allows all these operations on any type of drawing. However, the way the <canvas> element does this gets a little closer to math than you may have gotten before. Transformations in the canvas element can be hard to understand until you understand a little about how they really work.

In math, you don't really transform *objects*. Instead, you modify the *coordinate system,* and draw your image in the newly transformed coordinate system. It's common in a vector-drawing application to have several hidden coordinate systems working at once. That's important because it's the way canvas transformations work. Essentially when you want to perform transformations on an object, you'll do the following:

1. **Announce the beginning of a temporary coordinate system.**

   The main image already has its own coordinate system that won't change. Before you can transform anything, you need to build a new coordinate system to hold those changes. The (poorly named) save() command indicates the beginning of a new coordinate system definition.

2. **Move the center with `translate()`.**

   The origin (0, 0) starts in the upper-left corner of the canvas by default. Normally you'll build your transformed objects on the (new) origin and move the origin to place the object. If you `translate` (`50, 50`) and then draw an image at (0, 0), the image is drawn at the origin of the temporary coordinate system, which is at (50, 50) in the main canvas.

3. **Rotate the coordinate system with `rotate()`.**

   The `rotate()` command rotates the new coordinate system around its origin. The rotation parameter is a degree in radians.

4. **Scale the coordinate system in X and Y.**

   You can also alter the new coordinate system by applying X and Y scale values. This allows you to create stretched and squashed images.

5. **Create elements in the new coordinate system.**

   After you've applied all the transformations you want, you can use all the ordinary canvas drawing techniques. However, these drawings will be drawn in the "virtual" coordinate system you just made, not in the canvas's main coordinate system.

6. **Close the temporary coordinate system.**

   Generally you'll want to apply different transformations to different parts of your canvas. When you're finished with a particular transformation, use the `restore()` command to close out the new coordinate system. All subsequent drawing commands will use the default coordinate system of the `<canvas>` object.

Building a transformed image

A real example is easier to follow, so look at the code below:

```
function draw(){
  //from transform.html
  var drawing = document.getElementById("drawing");
  var con = drawing.getContext("2d");
  var goofyPic = document.getElementById("goofyPic");

  con.save();
  con.translate(100, 100);
  con.rotate(Math.PI / 4);
  con.scale(3.0, 1.5);
  con.drawImage(goofyPic, -25, -25, 50, 50);
  con.restore();

  //draw a rectangle using the ordinary coordinate system
  con.strokeStyle = "red";
  con.lineWidth = 5;
  con.strokeRect(0, 0, 200, 200);

} // end draw
```

This program creates a new coordinate system containing a translation, rotation, and scale. It draws an image in the new coordinate system. It then reverts to the standard coordinate system and draws a rectangular frame.

This program will display like Figure 7-1.

Here's how to build this type of image:

1. **Get access to an image object.**

   Load the image from the main site as explained in Chapter 6 of this mini-book.

2. **Start the transformation with the `save()` method.**

   The `save()` method has (if you ask me) a very confusing name. This method *does not* save the canvas to a file. Instead, it saves the current coordinate system settings in memory and allows you to define a new coordinate system. I would have called this method `beginTransform()`.

3. **Apply any translations you wish.**

   Remember, translations move the entire coordinate system. If you translate the coordinate system by (100, 100) as I did in this example, that means any subsequent drawings at (0, 0) will actually appear in the center of my 200×200 canvas.

4. **Rotate the coordinate system if you wish.**

   You can apply a rotation to the coordinate system if you prefer. The system will rotate around its origin. Typically, to get the behavior you want, design your images so they are centered on the origin, and translate the origin to move the image. Rotation angles are defined in radians.

Figure 7-1: This canvas features several transformations.

If you're more comfortable with degrees, you can use this formula to convert: `radians = degrees * (Math.PI / 180)`.

5. **Scale the coordinate system by X and Y.**

   You can change the apparent width and height of your new coordinate system by indicating new scale values. Scaling is a multiplication operation. If the scale is one, the element stays the same size. If the scale is 2, the element is double the original size, and .5 is half the original size. You can even scale by a negative number to invert the image.

6. **Draw your image.**

   Draw on the canvas after you've applied all the transformations. You can use any canvas-drawing techniques you want: paths, rectangles, images, text, or whatever. The drawing will be modified by the indicated transformations.

7. **End the transformation.**

   The `restore()` method should be called `endTransform()`. (If you're listening, W3C, I'm available to help you come up with better names for things. Let me know when the meetings are scheduled.) Regardless, this method indicates that you're done thinking about all the transformations that have been declared in this transform, and you're ready to return to the default coordinate system. The term *restore* really means "return to the coordinate state that was saved with the `save` command that was called to begin this transformation."

8. **Subsequent drawings will use the default coordinates.**

   In my example, I draw an ordinary rectangle around the image. This rectangle should use the regular coordinates of the canvas — I don't want it rotated or scaled like the image. Because these drawing commands exist outside the context of the `save()`/`restore()` pair, they use the regular coordinate system.

A few thoughts about transformations

Transformations are an incredibly powerful tool set, and they're among the most anticipated features of HTML5. However, they do hide a certain amount of math. You can use them without understanding linear algebra (the underlying mathematical theory), but there's still a few key ideas to keep in mind:

✦ **Each transformation is stored as a matrix:** There's an underlying structure called a *matrix* (that's even cooler than the movie) that stores all the translations, rotations, and scales in a single mathematical structure. You can work with the transformation matrix directly if you prefer, with the context objects' `transform()` method.

✦ **The order of transformations makes a difference:** Try this experiment. Stand in the center of the room. Now go forward five steps and turn left 90 degrees. Look at where you are. Now go back to the same starting point. This time, turn left 90 degrees and then go forward five steps. Are you in the same place? You might need to experiment a bit to get things working the way you expect.

✦ **Transform the system then draw on the origin:** Most of the drawing commands in canvas allow you to draw things anywhere on the canvas. If you're not using transformations, you can use this mechanism to place things wherever you wish. However, if you're using a transformation, it's much easier to transform the entire coordinate system and then draw your elements at the origin (0, 0). Otherwise you'll get some very strange results (especially with combined rotations and translations).

Animation

Of course, the big question about the HTML5 canvas tag is whether it can replace Flash as a mechanism for implementing games and animations in the browser. The answer is absolutely. I wrote a whole book about it: *HTML5 Game Development For Dummies* (published by John Wiley & Sons). Check it out for much more on how to build games and animations including user input collision-checking and instructions on building many types of games.

The key to games and animations is to use the animation features already built into the browser.

Overview of the animation loop

An animation generally requires a special organization called an *animation loop*. The basic structure of the animation loop works the same in any language:

1. Initialization.

   Create the assets, including the background and any of the objects you will be using. Objects that will be manipulated in real time are normally called *sprites*. Generally this is done when the program first runs, to save time during the main execution. You may also set constants for image size, display size, frame rate, and other values that will not change during the execution of the game.

2. Determining a frame rate.

   Animations and games work by calling a function repeatedly at a prescribed rate. In general, you'll have some sort of function that is called repeatedly. In JavaScript, you typically use the `setInterval()` function to specify a function that will be called repeatedly. The frame rate indicates how often the specified function will be called. Games and animations typically run at frame rates between 10 and 30 frames per second. A faster frame rate is smoother, but may not be maintainable with some hardware.

3. Evaluating the current state.

   Each sprite is really a data element. During every frame, determine if anything important has happened: Did the user press a key? Is an element supposed to move? Did a sprite leave the screen? Did two sprites conk into each other?

4. Modifying sprite data.

   Each sprite generally has position or rotation data that can be modified during each frame. Usually this is done through transformations (translation, rotation, and scale), although sometimes you may switch between images instead.

5. Clearing the background.

   An animation is really a series of images drawn rapidly in the same place. Usually you'll need to clear the background at the beginning of each frame to clear out the last frame's image.

6. Redrawing all sprites.

   Each sprite is redrawn using its new data. The sprites appear to move because they're drawn in a new location or orientation.

Typically I would display a screen shot here, but a still image of an animation won't be fun to look at in this book. Please look at autoRotate.html on this book's companion website to see the program running in real time. While you're at it, check out all the other great stuff I've got on that site for you. You can find out more about the book's companion website in the Introduction.

Setting up the constants

As an example, build a program that rotates an image inside a canvas. The complete code is in several parts. I'll use a basic image as a sprite. The first job is to set up the various variables and constants that describe the problem. The following code is created outside any functions because it describes values that will be shared among functions:

```
var drawing;
var con;
var goofyPic;
var angle = 0;
CANV_HEIGHT = 200;
CANV_WIDTH = 200;
SPR_HEIGHT = 50;
SPR_WIDTH = 40;
```

The `drawing` variable will refer to the `canvas` element. The `con` variable will be the drawing context, `goofyPic` is the image to be rotated, and `angle` will be used to determine how much the image is currently rotated. The other values are constants used to describe the height and width of the canvas as well as the sprite.

Initializing the animation

As usual, the `body onload` mechanism will be used to start up some code as soon as the page has finished loading. However, the page now has two functions. The `init()` function handles initialization, and the `draw()` function is called repeatedly to handle the actual animation. Here's the code in the `init()` function:

```
function init(){
  drawing = document.getElementById("drawing");
  con = drawing.getContext("2d");
  goofyPic = document.getElementById("goofyPic");
  setInterval(draw, 100);
} // end init
```

The job of the `init()` function is to initialize things. In this particular example, I load up the various elements (the canvas, the context, and the image) into JavaScript variables and set up the animation. The `setInterval()` function is used to set up the main animation loop. It takes two parameters:

+ **A repeatable function:** The first parameter is the name of a function which will be called repeatedly. In this case, I will be calling the `draw` function many times.

+ **A delay value:** The second parameter indicates how often the function should be called in milliseconds (one-thousandths of a second.) A delay of `100` will create a frame rate of 10 frames per second. A delay of `50` will cause a frame rate of 20 frames per second, and so on.

Animate the current frame

The `draw()` function will be called many times in succession. In general, its task is to clear the frame, calculate new sprite states, and redraw the sprite. Here's the code:

```
function draw(){

  //clear background
  con.fillStyle = "white";
  con.fillRect(0, 0, CANV_HEIGHT, CANV_WIDTH);

  //draw border
  con.strokeStyle = "red";
  con.lineWidth = "5";
  con.strokeRect(0, 0, CANV_WIDTH, CANV_HEIGHT);

  //change the rotation angle
  angle += .25;
  if (angle > Math.PI * 2){
    angle = 0;
  }

  //start a new transformation system
  con.save();
  con.translate(100, 100);
  con.rotate(angle);
```

```
    //draw the image
    con.drawImage(goofyPic,
        SPR_WIDTH/-2, SPR_HEIGHT/-2,
        SPR_WIDTH, SPR_HEIGHT);
    con.restore();
} // end draw
```

Although the code may seem a little involved, it doesn't do really do anything new. Here's what it does, step by step:

1. **Clears the background.**

   Remember that animation is repeated drawing. If you don't clear the background at the beginning of every frame, you'll see the previous frame drawings. Use the context's `clearRect()` function to draw a fresh background, or one of the other drawing tools to use a more complex background image. You must clear the background first, so subsequent drawings will happen on a fresh palette.

2. **Draws any non-sprite content.**

   In this example, I want a red border around the frame. Just use ordinary canvas elements for this. I used `strokeStyle`, `lineWidth`, and `strokeRect()` to build a red rectangular frame around my canvas. Note that I used the `CANV_HEIGHT` and `CANV_WIDTH` constants to refer to the current canvas size.

3. **Modifies sprite state.**

   In this example, I want to modify the rotation angle of the image. I already created a variable called `angle` outside the function. (It's important that `angle` was created outside the function context so it can retain its value between calls to the function.) I add a small amount to angle every frame. Whenever you change a variable (especially in a virtually endless loop like an animation), you should check for boundary conditions. In this example, I'm changing angles. The largest permissible angle value (in radians) is $2 * \pi$. If the angle gets larger than $2 * \pi$, it is reset to zero.

4. **Builds a transformation.**

   Many animations are really modifications of a transformation. That's the case here. I'm actually not changing the image at all, but the transformation which contains the image. Set up a new transformation with the `save()` method, and use the `rotate()` and `translate()` functions to transform a temporary coordinate system. (See the section called "Transformations" at the beginning of this chapter for how transformations relate to temporary coordinate systems.)

5. **Draws the image at the center of the new transformation.**

   Remember, the `drawImage()` command draws the image based on the top left corner of an image. If you draw the image at (0, 0) of the new transformation, the image appears to rotate around its top left corner. Usually you'll want an image to rotate around its center point. Simply draw the image so its center is at the origin. Set X to zero minus half the image's width, and Y to zero minus half the image's height.

6. **Closes the transformation.**

Use the restore() method to finish defining the temporary coordinate system.

Moving an element

Often you'll prefer to move an element. This process is actually very similar to the rotation mechanism. Here's some code that moves an image and wraps it to the other side when it leaves the canvas.

```
//from wrap.html
var drawing;
var con;
var goofyPic;
CANV_HEIGHT = 200;
CANV_WIDTH = 200;
SPR_HEIGHT = 50;
SPR_WIDTH = 40;

var x = 0;
var y = 100;
var dx = 10;
var dy = 7;

function init(){
  drawing = document.getElementById("drawing");
  con = drawing.getContext("2d");
  goofyPic = document.getElementById("goofyPic");
  setInterval(draw, 100);
}

function draw(){
  //clear background
  con.clearRect(0, 0, 200, 200);

  //move the element
  x += dx;
  y += dy;

  //check for boundaries
  wrap();

  //draw the image
  con.drawImage(goofyPic, x, y, SPR_WIDTH, SPR_HEIGHT);

  //draw a rectangle
  con.strokeStyle = "red";
  con.lineWidth = 5;
  con.strokeRect(0, 0, CANV_WIDTH, CANV_HEIGHT);

} // end draw

function wrap(){
  if (x > CANV_WIDTH){
    x = 0;
  }
```

```
if (x < 0){
  x = CANV_WIDTH;
}
if (y > CANV_HEIGHT){
  y = 0;
} // end if
if (y < 0){
  y = CANV_HEIGHT;
}
} // end wrap
```

The `wrap` code is very similar to the rotation program. It has a few different features. Here's what it does:

1. **Keeps track of the sprite position.**

   The sprite's position will change now, so the important variables are X and Y, used to track where the sprite is.

2. **Contains variables for the sprite's motion.**

   The `dx` variable stands for *difference in x,* and it is used to show how much the `x` value changes each frame. Likewise, `dy` is used to show how much the `y` value changes in each frame. `x`, `y`, `dx`, and `dy` are all created outside the function context.

3. **Moves the element values.**

   In every frame (in the `draw()` function), add `dx` to `x` and add `dy` to `y`.

4. **Checks for boundaries.**

   I created a new function called `wrap()` to check for boundary conditions.

The code is pretty straightforward. If the sprite's `x` value exceeds the width of the canvas (meaning it has moved to the right border of the canvas), reset the `x` value to `0` (moving it to the left). Use a similar calculation to check the other borders and reset the image to the opposite side. A still image won't do justice to this animation. Please look at wrap.html on the companion website to see an example. The bounce.html page shows the following example.

Bouncing off the walls

If you prefer to have your sprite bounce off the walls, just replace the `wrap()` function with a `bounce()` function that works like this:

```
function bounce(){
//from bounce.html
if (x > CANV_WIDTH - SPR_WIDTH){
  dx *= -1;
}
if (x < 0){
  dx *= -1;
}
if (y > CANV_HEIGHT - SPR_HEIGHT){
  dy *= -1;
}
```

```
    if (y < 0){
      dy *= -1;
    }
} // end bounce
```

Reading the Keyboard

The keyboard is a primary input technology, especially for desktop machines. The standard way to read the keyboard is to set up special functions called *event-handlers*. JavaScript has a number of pre-defined event handlers you can implement. The keyDemo.html program illustrates a basic keyboard handler in action.

```
<!DOCTYPE HTML>
<html lang="en-US">
<head>
    <meta charset="UTF-8">
    <title>keyDemo.html</title>
    <script type="text/javascript">

    //var keysDown = new Array(256);
    var output;

    function init(){
      output = document.getElementById("output");
      document.onkeydown = updateKeys;
    } // end init

    updateKeys = function(e){
      //set current key
      currentKey = e.keyCode;
      output.innerHTML = "current key: " + currentKey;
    }

    //keyboard constants simplify working with the keyboard
    K_A = 65; K_B = 66; K_C = 67; K_D = 68; K_E = 69; K_F = 70; K_G = 71;
    K_H = 72; K_I = 73; K_J = 74; K_K = 75; K_L = 76; K_M = 77; K_N = 78;
    K_O = 79; K_P = 80; K_Q = 81; K_R = 82; K_S = 83; K_T = 84; K_U = 85;
    K_V = 86; K_W = 87; K_X = 88; K_Y = 89; K_Z = 90;
    K_LEFT = 37; K_RIGHT = 39; K_UP = 38;K_DOWN = 40; K_SPACE = 32;
    K_ESC = 27; K_PGUP = 33; K_PGDOWN = 34; K_HOME = 36; K_END = 35;
    K_0 = 48; K_1 = 49; K_2 = 50; K_3 = 51; K_4 = 52; K_5 = 53;
    K_6 = 54; K_7 = 55; K_8 = 56; K_9 = 57;
    </script>
</head>
<body onload = "init()">
    <div id = "output">
        Press a key to see its code
    </div>
</body>
</html>
```

Figure 7-2 illustrates basic keyboard input (but it's interactive, so you should really look at it on the companion website).

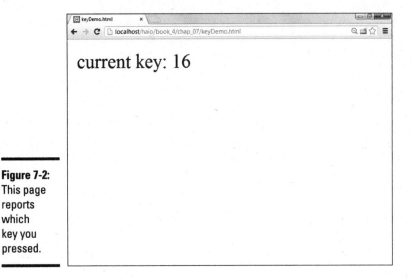

Figure 7-2:
This page reports which key you pressed.

Managing basic keyboard input

This particular example demonstrates basic keyboard-checking as well as the more sophisticated technique used in simpleGame. Here's how the basic version works:

1. Assigns a function to onkeydown.

   The document.onkeydown attribute is a special property. If you assign a function to this property, that function will be automatically called each time the operating system recognizes a key press. In this example, I assign the function updateKeys.

2. Creates the function, including an event parameter.

   The updateKeys() function will automatically be given an event object (normally called e).

3. Determines which key was pressed.

   The e.keyCode property returns a numeric code indicating which key was pressed. In the keyDemo program (as well as simpleGame), the currentKey variable holds this numeric value.

4. Compares the key to one of the keyboard constants.

   It's hard to remember which keys are associated with which numeric values, so keyDemo and simpleGame provide a list of keyboard constants. They are easy to remember: K_A is the A key, and K_SPACE is the space bar. Of course, you can add other keys if there's some key you want to use that isn't available. Although I didn't actually use the keyboard constants in this example, they are useful so you can easily determine which key was pressed.

Moving an image with the keyboard

You can achieve a form of interactivity by having an image move in response to keyboard motion. Figure 7-3 illustrates this technique, but it really isn't satisfying to see in a book. As usual, you need to play with this on the website.

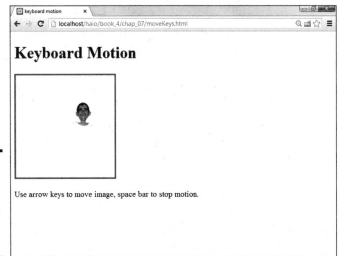

Figure 7-3: Move the image around with the arrow keys.

Essentially moving an image involves combining key ideas from keyDemo. html (for keyboard input) and wrap.html (to set up the canvas and make the object move under timer control). Here's the code:

```
<!DOCTYPE HTML>
<html lang = "en">
<head>
  <title>keyboar motion</title>
  <meta charset = "UTF-8" />
  <style type = "text/css">
    .hidden{
      display: none;
    }
  </style>
  <script type = "text/javascript">
  //move based on keyboard input
  var drawing;
  var con;
  var goofyPic;
  CANV_HEIGHT = 200;
  CANV_WIDTH = 200;
  SPR_HEIGHT = 50;
  SPR_WIDTH = 40;
  var x = 0;
  var y = 100;
  var dx = 0;
  var dy = 0;
  var currentKey;
```

```
function init(){
  drawing = document.getElementById("drawing");
  con = drawing.getContext("2d");
  goofyPic = document.getElementById("goofyPic");
  document.onkeydown = updateKeys;
  setInterval(draw, 100);
}

function updateKeys(e){
  currentKey = e.keyCode;


  if (currentKey == K_LEFT){
    dx = -5;
  }

  if (currentKey == K_RIGHT){
    dx = 5;
  }

  if (currentKey == K_UP){
    dy = -5;
  }

  if (currentKey == K_DOWN){
    dy = 5;
  }


  if (currentKey == K_SPACE){
    dx = 0;
    dy = 0;
  }
} // end updateKeys

function draw(){
  //clear background
  con.clearRect(0, 0, 200, 200);

  currentKey = null;

  //move the element
  x += dx;
  y += dy;

  //check for boundaries
  wrap();

  //draw the image
  con.drawImage(goofyPic, x, y, SPR_WIDTH, SPR_HEIGHT);

  //draw a rectangle
  con.strokeStyle = "red";
  con.lineWidth = 5;
  con.strokeRect(0, 0, CANV_WIDTH, CANV_HEIGHT);

} // end draw

function wrap(){
  if (x > CANV_WIDTH){
    x = 0;
  }
  if (x < 0){
    x = CANV_WIDTH;
```

```
      }
      if (y > CANV_HEIGHT){
        y = 0;
      } // end if
      if (y < 0){
        y = CANV_HEIGHT;
      }
    } // end wrap

    //keyboard constants
    K_LEFT = 37; K_RIGHT = 39; K_UP = 38;K_DOWN = 40; K_SPACE = 32;

    </script>
  </head>

  <body onload = "init()">
    <h1>Keyboard Motion</h1>

    <img class = "hidden"
         id = "goofyPic"
         src = "andyGoofy.gif"
         alt = "Goofy pic of me" />

    <canvas id = "drawing"
            height = "200"
            width = "200">
      <p>Canvas not supported</p>
    </canvas>

    <p>
      Use arrow keys to move image, space bar to stop motion.
    </p>

  </body>
</html>
```

This program is essentially wrap.html with the following changes:

1. **Sets up** `updateKeys()` **as an event handler.**

   Because this program reads the keyboard in real time, you have to assign an event handler.

2. **Determines which key was pressed.**

   Store the last key pressed in a variable called `currentKey`.

3. **Compares** `currentKey` **with keyboard constants.**

   Use constants to compare `currentKey` with whatever keys you're interested in — for now, the arrow keys and space bar.

4. **Changes** `dx` **and** `dy` **based on the current key value.**

   When you know which key is pressed, use this information to modify the `dx` and `dy` values, which determines how the image moves.

5. **The** `draw()` **function still does the drawing.**

   The `draw()` function is called on a regular interval. It's common to separate input (`keyPressed`) from animation (`draw`).

This is a very simple keyboard input mechanism. It's fine for basic user input, but in gaming we use much more sophisticated input techniques including a mechanism called *polling,* which allows multiple keys at a time. In addition, the modern web includes mobile devices, which have interesting new features including touch interface and tilt control. Please see my book *HTML5 Game Development For Dummies* for information on these advanced input techniques. You'll also see other forms of animation including image-swapping and sprite sheet animation.

Part V

Server-Side Programming with PHP

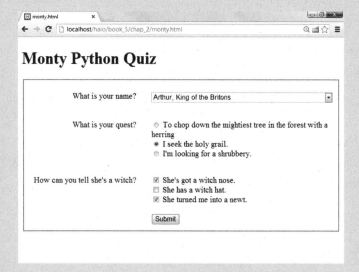

Visit www.dummies.com/extras/html5css3aio for more on using templates with PHP.

Contents at a Glance

Chapter 1: Getting Started on the Server

In This Chapter

✓ **Introducing server-side programming**

✓ **Testing your installation**

✓ **Inspecting** `phpinfo()`

✓ **Writing HTML with embedded PHP**

✓ **Understanding various types of quotation**

✓ **Managing concatenation and interpolation**

✓ **Using heredocs to simplify coding**

*W*elcome to the server-side programming portion of the book. In this minibook, you discover all the basics of PHP and how you can use PHP to make your pages dynamic and relevant in today's Internet.

In this chapter, you read about getting your server set up and ready to go. I walk you through the process as painlessly as possible, and by the end, you'll be up and running, and ready to serve up your own web pages in a test environment. (I talk about making them available to the rest of the world in Book VIII.)

Introducing Server-Side Programming

I begin with an introduction to server-side programming. This is a bit different than the client-side programming you may have done in JavaScript.

Programming on the server

Server-side programming is what you use to create pages dynamically on the server before sending them to the client. Whereas client-side programming is executed on the client's machine, server-side programming all happens on the server before the web page is even sent to the user.

Client-side programming (as done in JavaScript) does most of the work on the individual user's machine. This has advantages because those machines have doohickeys such as mice and graphics cards. Client-side programs can be interactive in real time.

The client has a big problem, though. Programs written on the client usually have a form of forced amnesia (no long-term memory). For security reasons, client-side applications can't store information in files and can't interact with other programs on the computer. Also, you never know exactly what kind of setup the user has, so you can't really be sure whether your program will work.

This is where server-side programming comes in. In a pure server-side programming environment, all the action happens on the web server. The user thinks she's asking for a web page like normal, but the address really goes to a computer program. The program does some magic and produces a web page. The user sees a web page, perhaps never knowing this wasn't a regular web page, but a page that was produced instead by a program.

A program running on a web server has some really nice advantages, such as

✦ **A server-side program can access the local file system.** Asking a server program to load and save files on the server is no problem at all.

✦ **A server-side program can call external programs.** This is a very big deal because many web applications are really about working with data. Database programs are very important to modern web development. See Book VI for much more on this.

✦ **All the user sees is ordinary HTML.** You can set up your program to do whatever you want, but the output is regular HTML. You don't have to worry about what browser the user has, or whether he has a Mac, or what browser version he's using. Any browser that can display HTML can be used with PHP.

Serving your programs

When using a browser to retrieve web pages, you send a request to a server. The server then looks at the extension (.HTML, .php, .js, and so on) of your requested file and decides what to do. If the server sees .HTML or .js, it says, "Cool. Nothing doing here. Just gotta send her back as is." When the server sees .php, it says, "Oh, boy. They need PHP to build something here."

The server takes the page and hollers for PHP to come along and construct the requested web page on the fly. PHP goes through and looks at the programmer's blueprint and then constructs the working page out of HTML.

The server then takes that page from PHP and sends back plain HTML to the client for the browser to display to the user.

When you write PHP programs, a web server must process the form before the browser can see it. To test your PHP programs, you need to have a web server available and place the file in a specific place on your computer for the server to serve it. You can't run a PHP file directly from your desktop. It must be placed in a special place — often, the htdocs or public_html directory under the server.

Picking a language

There are all sorts of different ways to go about dynamically creating web pages with server-side programming. Back in the day when the Internet was still in diapers, people used things like Perl and CGI scripting to handle all their server-side programming. Eventually, people placed more and more demand on their websites, and soon these technologies just weren't enough.

The prevalent languages today are

✦ **ASP.NET:** Microsoft's contender

✦ **Java:** The heavyweight offering from Sun Microsystems

✦ **Python:** Python is becoming a popular alternative, but it has not yet surpassed PHP in popularity as a server-side language.

✦ **PHP:** The popular language described in this minibook

ASP.NET

ASP.NET is event-driven, compiled, and object-oriented. ASP.NET replaced the '90s language ASP in 2002. Microsoft repurposed it for use with the .NET framework to facilitate cross-compatibility with its desktop applications (apps) and integration into Visual Studio (although you can write ASP.NET apps from any text editor). ASP.NET runs on Microsoft's Internet Information Services (IIS) web server, which typically requires more expensive servers than most of the other technologies. Although ASP.NET is an excellent technology, I don't recommend it for cost-conscious users.

Java

Java has been a strong contender for a long time now. The language is indeed named after coffee. If you work for a banking company or insurance company, or need to build the next eBay or Amazon.com, you might want to consider using Java. However, Java can consume a lot of time, and it's hard to figure out. You may have to write up to 16 lines of code to do in Java what could take a mere 4 lines of code in PHP. Java is absolutely free, as is the Apache Tomcat web server that it uses to serve its web components. Java was originally created to write desktop applications and is still very good at doing that. If you're comfortable with C/C++, you'll be very comfortable with Java because it's very similar. It's fully object-oriented and it's compiled. Java is powerful, but it can be challenging for beginners. It'd be a great second language to work with.

Compile versus interpret?

What's the difference between an interpreted language and a compiled language? A *compiled* language is compiled one time into a more computer-friendly format for faster processing when called by the computer. Compiled languages are typically very fast but not very flexible. *Interpreted* languages have to be interpreted on the spot by the server *every time* they're called, which is slower but provides more flexibility. With blazing fast servers these days, interpreted languages can normally stand under the load, and the ability to handle changes without recompiling can be an advantage in the fast-paced world of web development.

Python

The Python language is used in a number of contexts, including server-side programming. Although Python has become much more popular as of late, it still isn't used as frequently as PHP for this purpose.

PHP

PHP was born from a collection of modifications for Perl and has boomed ever since (in a way, replacing Perl, which was once considered the duct tape and bubble gum that held the Internet together).

PHP works great for your server-side web development purposes. *Media Wiki* (the engine that was written to run the popular Internet encyclopedia Wikipedia) runs on PHP, as do many other popular large-, medium-, and small-scale websites. PHP is a solid, easy-to-learn, well-established language (it was introduced in 1994). PHP can be object-oriented or procedural: You can take your pick. PHP is interpreted rather than compiled.

The current stable version of PHP used in this book is PHP5.5. This might confuse you because there are several references to PHP6 on the Internet. There is indeed a PHP6, but it has been discontinued for several years, with the most important improvements moved to the PHP5 engine. Examples in this book will work on any version of PHP past PHP5.3, which is what's most likely to be on your server.

Installing Your Web Server

For PHP to work usefully, you have to have some other things installed on your computer, such as

✦ **A web server:** This special program enables a computer to process files and send them to web browsers. I use Apache because it's free and powerful and works very well with PHP.

✦ **A database backend:** Modern websites rely heavily on data, so a program that can manage your data needs is very important. I use MySQL (a free and powerful tool) for this. Book VI is entirely dedicated to creating data with MySQL and some related tools.

✦ **A programming language:** Server-side programming relies on a language. I use PHP because it works great and it's free.

There are two main ways to work with a web server:

✦ **Install your own, using the free XAMPP software.** Download from www. apachefriends.org/en/xampp.html. Book VIII, Chapter 1 has complete instructions on installing XAMPP.

✦ **Work on a remote server that somebody has already set up.** Most low-cost web servers (and even some free ones) support PHP and MySQL right out of the box.

Please check out Book VIII, Chapter 1 for complete information on both techniques. After you have your machine set up or you have an account somewhere with PHP access, come back here. I'll wait.

Inspecting phpinfo ( )

Using your shiny new server is really quite simple, but a lot of beginners can get confused at this point.

One thing you have to remember is that anything you want the server to serve must be located in the server's file structure. If you have a PHP file on your desktop and you want to view it in your browser, it won't work because it isn't in your server. Although, yes, technically it might be on the same *machine* as your server (if you're using XAMPP), it is not *in* the server.

So, to serve a file from the server, it must be located in the htdocs directory of your server install. If you've installed XAMPP, go to the folder where you installed XAMPP (probably either c:/xampp or c:/Program Files/xampp) and locate the htdocs directory. This is where you'll put all your PHP files. Make note of it now.

If you're using a remote server, you'll need to use your host's file management tools or FTP (both described in Book VIII, Chapter 1) to transfer the file. Often you'll have specially designated folders for placing your web content, usually related to your domain name. You may need to check with your server host to be certain.

To get the hang of placing your files in the correct place and accessing them, create a test file that will display all your PHP, Apache, and MySQL settings.

To test everything, make the PHP version of the famous "Hello World!" program. Follow these steps to make your first PHP program:

1. **Open a text editor to create a new file.**

   PHP files are essentially plain text files, just like HTML and JavaScript. You can use the same editors to create them.

2. **Build a standard web page.**

   Generally, your PHP pages start out as standard web pages, using your basic HTML template. However, start with a simpler example, so you can begin with an empty text file.

3. **Add a PHP reference.**

   Write a tag to indicate PHP. The starting tag looks like `<?php`, and the ending tag looks like `?>`. As far as HTML is concerned, all the PHP code is embedded in a single HTML tag.

4. **Write a single line of PHP code.**

   You'll learn a lot more PHP soon, but one command is especially useful for testing your configuration to see how it works. Type the line `phpinfo();`. This powerful command supplies a huge amount of diagnostic information.

5. **Save the file to your server.**

   A PHP file can't be stored just anywhere. You need to place it under an accessible directory of your web server. If you're running XAMPP, that's the `htdocs` directory of your `xampp` directory. If you're running a remote server, you'll need to move the file to that server, either with your host's file transfer mechanism, an FTP program, or automatically through your editor. (See the nearby sidebar "Picking a PHP editor" for information on remote editing in Komodo.)

6. **Preview your page in the browser.**

   Use your web browser to look at the resulting page. Note that you cannot simply load the file through the file menu or drag it to your browser. If you have XAMPP installed, you need to refer to the file as `http://localhost/fileName.php`. If the file is on a remote server, use the full address of the file on that server: for example, `http://myhost.freehostia.com/fileName.php`.

Your code from Steps 3 and 4 should look like this:

```
<?php
    phpinfo();
?>
```

Hmm. Only three lines of code, and it doesn't seem to do much. There's precious little HTML code there. Run it through the browser, though, and you'll see the page shown in Figure 1-1.

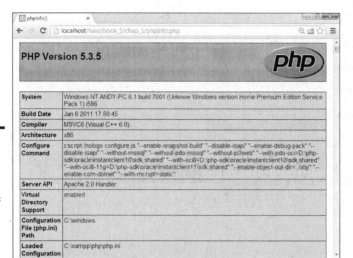

Figure 1-1:
That tiny
PHP pro-
gram sure
puts a lot of
information
on the
screen.

If you see the actual PHP code rather than the results shown in Figure 1-1, you probably didn't refer to the page correctly. Please check the following:

✦ **Is the file in the right place?** Your file must be in htdocs or on a remote server (or in a subdirectory of these places).

✦ **Did you use the .php extension?** The server won't invoke PHP unless the filename has a .php extension.

✦ **Did you refer to the file correctly?** If the URL in the address bar reads file://, you bypassed the server, and PHP was not activated. Your address must begin with http://. Either use http://localhost (for a locally stored file in XAMPP) or the URL of your remote hosting service.

This phpinfo page of Figure 1-1 is critical in inspecting your server configuration. It displays all the different settings for your server, describing what version of PHP is running and what modules are active. This can be very useful information.

You generally should not have a page with all the phpinfo() information running on a live server because it tells the bad guys information they might use to do mischief.

This test.php program shows one of the most interesting things about PHP. The program itself is just a few lines long, but when you run it, the result is a complex web page. Take a look at the source of the web page, and you'll see a lot of code that you didn't write. That's the magic of PHP. You write a program, and it creates a web page for you.

Don't panic if you don't understand anything in the page that gets produced with the phpinfo() command. It contains many details about how PHP is

---

Picking a PHP editor

In the previous edition of this book, I recommend using Aptana for PHP editing. If you already use Aptana for your other web editing, you may also enjoy using it for PHP. However, Aptana has changed, and PHP support is no longer built into the standard version of Aptana.

I honestly prefer using Komodo Edit (also mentioned in Book I, Chapter 3) for all my web editing. It's a little simpler than Aptana, and it still has all the important features like syntax completion and highlighting built in with no plug-ins needed.

Komodo has another feature that can be a lifesaver for PHP programmers. If you're working on a remote web server, you can set up a connection to that server (choose Edit ➪ Preferences ➪ Servers). Then you can use the `Save Remotely` command to save the file to the server directly. That way, you can use all the features of Komodo without a local installation of Apache or PHP, and without having to implement an extra file transfer step.

---

configured on your server, which may not mean much now. If you have trouble with PHP and ask me for help, however, it's the first thing I'll ask you for. An experienced developer can do a lot of troubleshooting by looking over a `phpinfo` so it's a handy skill to know.

The basic flow of PHP programming works like this:

1. You build a standard page, and you include PHP code inside it.

2. When the server recognizes the PHP code, it calls the PHP interpreter and passes that code to it.

PHP programs are almost always designed to create HTML code, which gets passed back to the user. The user will never see PHP code because it will get translated to HTML before it gets to the browser.

By default, Apache will load `index.HTML` or `index.php` automatically if you type a directory path into the web browser. If you're using XAMPP, there's already a program in `htdocs` called `index.php`. Rename it `index.php.off`. Now, if you navigate to `http://localhost/`, you'll see a list of directories and files your server can run, including `test.php`. When you have a live site, you'll typically name one file `index.HTML` or `index.php` so the user doesn't have to type the entire filename. See Book VIII, Chapter 1 for more information on how to set up your server to make it easiest to use.

Building HTML with PHP

In PHP, you aren't actually printing anything to the user. Instead, you're building an HTML document that will be sent to the browser, which will interpret the HTML and then print *that* (the HTML) to the user. Therefore, all your code gets interpreted twice: first on the server to generate the HTML and then on the user's machine to generate the output display.

If you've used HTML, CSS, and JavaScript, you might have been frustrated because all these environments run on the client, and you have no control of the client environment. You don't know what browser the user will have, and thus you don't know exactly how HTML, CSS, and JavaScript will run there. When you program in PHP, you're working on a machine (the server) that you actually control. You know exactly what the server's capabilities are because (in many cases) you configured it yourself.

It's still not a perfect situation, though, because your PHP code will generate HTML/CSS pages (sometimes even with JavaScript), and those pages still have to contend with the wide array of client environments.

The first program you ever write in any language is invariably the "Hello World!" program or some variant thereof. Follow these steps:

1. **Create a new PHP file in your editor.**

   I prefer using Komodo Edit because it has great support for PHP and remote file access.

   If you're using some other text editor, just open a plain text file however you normally do that (often File ➪ New) and be sure to save it under htdocs with a .php extension. If you're using a remote server, transfer your file to that server before testing.

2. **Create your standard HTML page.**

   PHP code is usually embedded into the context of an HTML page. Begin with your standard HTML template. (See Book I, Chapter 2 for a refresher on HTML.)

3. **Enter the following code in the body:**

   ```
   <?php
   print "<h1>Hello World!</h1>";
   ?>
   ```

   Depending on your installation of Apache, you may be able to use the shorter `<? ?>` version of the PHP directive (instead of `<?php ?>`). However, nearly all installations support the `<?php ?>` version, so that's probably the safest way to go.

   Note that you're not just writing text, but creating an HTML tag. PHP creates HTML. That's a really important idea.

4. **Save the file.**

   Remember to save directly into htdocs or a subdirectory of htdocs. If you're using a remote server, save remotely to that server (with Komodo) or save it locally and transfer it to the server to view it.

5. **View the file in a web browser, as shown in Figure 1-2.**

   The address of a web page begins with the `http://` protocol and then the server name. If the page is on the local machine, the server name is localhost, which corresponds directly to your htdocs directory. If you have a file named thing.php in the htdocs directory, the address would be `http://localhost/thing.php`. Likewise, if it's in a subdirectory of htdocs called project, the address would be `http://localhost/project/thing.php`. If the page is on a remote server, the address will include the server's name, like this:

   `http://www.myserver.com/thing.php`

Figure 1-2:
The "Hello World!" program example.

So, what is it that you've done here? You've figured out how to use the `print` statement. This allows you to spit out any text you want to the user.

Note that each line ends with a semicolon (`;`), just like JavaScript code. PHP (unlike JavaScript) is pretty fussy about semicolons, and if you forget, you're likely to get a really strange error that can be hard to figure out.

For all the other examples in this book, you can look at the program running on the companion website and view the source to see what is happening. That won't work with PHP code because the PHP is converted to HTML by the time it gets to the browser. So on my website, I've provided a special source listing for each PHP program so you can see the code before it is passed through the interpreter.

echo or print?

echo is another way to generate your code for the browser. In almost all circumstances, you use echo exactly like you use print. Everyone knows what print does, but echo sounds like I should be making some sort of dolphin noise.

The difference is that print returns a value, and echo doesn't. print can be used as part of a complex expression, and echo can't. It really just comes down to the fact that print is more dynamic, whereas echo is slightly (and I'm talking very slightly here) faster.

I prefer print because there's nothing that echo can do that print can't, and print makes more sense to my simple brain.

Coding with Quotation Marks

There are many different ways to use print. The following are all legal ways to print text, but they have subtle differences:

```
print ("<p>Hello World!</p>");
print ("<p>Hello World!<br />
Hello Computer!</p>");
print '<p><a href="http://www.google.com">Hello Google!</a></p>';
```

Any way you cut it, you have to have some form of quotations around text that you want printed. However, PHP is usually used to write HTML code, and HTML code contains a lot of quote marks itself. All those quotations can lead to headaches.

What if you want to print double quotation marks inside a print statement surrounded by double quotation marks? You *escape* them (you tell PHP to treat them as literal characters, rather than the end of the string) with a backslash, like this:

```
print "<a href=\"link.HTML\">A Link</a>";
```

This can get tedious, so a better solution is discussed in the "Generating output with heredocs" section, later in this chapter.

This backslash technique works only with text encased inside double quotes. Single quotes tell PHP to take everything inside the quotes exactly as is. Double quotes give PHP permission to analyze the text for special characters, like escaped quotes (and variables, which you learn about in the next section of this chapter). Single quotes do not allow for this behavior, which is why they are rarely used in PHP programming.

Escape sequences

Quotation marks aren't the only thing you can escape, though. You can give a whole host of other special escape directives to PHP.

The most common ones are

- ✔ \t: Creates a tab in the resulting HTML
- ✔ \n: Creates a new line in the resulting HTML
- ✔ \$: Creates a dollar sign in the resulting HTML

- ✔ \": Creates a double quote in the resulting HTML
- ✔ \': Creates a single quote in the resulting HTML
- ✔ \\: Creates a backslash in the resulting HTML

PHP can take care of this for you automatically if you're receiving these values from a form. To read more, go to `http://us3.php.net/types.string`.

Working with Variables PHP-Style

Variables are extremely important in any programming language and no less so in PHP.

A variable in PHP always begins with a $.

A PHP variable can be named almost anything. There are some reserved words that you can't name a variable (like `print`, which already has a meaning in PHP), so if your program isn't working and you can't figure out why, try changing some variable names or looking at the reserved words list (in the online help at `www.php.net`) to find out whether your variable name is one of these illegal words.

PHP is very forgiving about the type of data in a variable. When you create a variable, you simply put content in it. PHP automatically makes the variable whatever type it needs. This is called *loose typing*. The same variable can hold numeric data, text, or other more complicated kinds of data. PHP determines the type of data in a variable on the fly by examining the context.

Even though PHP is cavalier about data types, it's important to understand that data is still stored in one of several standard formats based on its type. PHP supports several forms of integers and floating-point numbers. PHP also has great support for text data. Programmers usually don't say "text," but call text data *string* data. This is because the internal data representation of text reminded the early programmers of beads on a string. You rarely have to worry about what type of information you're using in PHP, but you do need to know that PHP is quietly converting data into formats that it can use.

Concatenation

Concatenation is the process of joining smaller strings to form a larger string. (See Book IV, Chapter 1 for a description of concatenation as it's applied in JavaScript.) PHP uses the period (·) symbol to concatenate two string values. The following example code returns the phrase oogieboogie:

```
$word = "oogie ";
$dance = "boogie";

Print $word . $dance
```

If you already know some JavaScript or another language, most of the ideas transfer, but details can trip you up. JavaScript uses the + sign for concatenation, and PHP uses the period. These are annoying details, but with practice, you'll be able to keep it straight.

When PHP sees a period, it treats the values on either side of the period as strings (text) and concatenates (joins) them. If PHP sees a plus sign, it treats the values on either side of the plus sign as numbers and attempts to perform mathematical addition on them. The operation helps PHP figure out what type of data it's working with.

The following program illustrates the difference between concatenation and addition (see Figure 1-3 for the output):

```php
<?php
    //from helloVariable.php
    $output = "World!";
    print "<p>Hello " . $output . "</p>";
    print "<p>" . $output + 5 . "</p>";
?>
```

Figure 1-3:
The difference between addition and concatenation.

The previous code takes the variable `output` with the value `World` and concatenates it to `Hello` when printed. Next, it adds the variable `output` to the number 5. When PHP sees the plus sign, it interprets the values on either side of it as numbers. Because `output` has no logical numerical value, PHP assigns it the value of 0, which it adds to 5, resulting in the output of `<p>5</p>` being sent to the browser.

Interpolating variables into text

If you have a bunch of text to print with variables thrown in, it can get a little tedious to use concatenation to add in the variables. Luckily, you don't have to!

With PHP, you can include the variables as follows (see Figure 1-4 for the output):

```
<!DOCTYPE html>
<html lang = "en-US">

<head>
  <meta charset = "UTF-8" />
  <title>helloInterpolation</title>
</head>
<body>
<?php
  $firstName = "John";
  $lastName = "Doe";
  print "<p>Hello $firstName $lastName!</p>";
?>
</body>
</html>
```

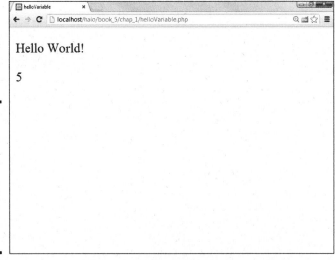

Figure 1-4: The variables are printed without having to do annoying concatenations.

This process is called *interpolation*. Because all PHP variables begin with dollar signs, you can freely put variables right inside your string values, and when PHP sees a variable, it will automatically replace that variable with its value.

Interpolation works only with double-quoted strings because double quotes indicate PHP should process the string before passing it to the user.

Building HTML Output

The output of a PHP program is usually an HTML page. As far as PHP is concerned, HTML is just string data, so your PHP program often has to do a lot of string manipulation. You'll often be writing long chunks of text (HTML code) with several variables (generated by your PHP program) interspersed throughout the code. This type of text (HTML output) will often stretch over several lines, requires carriage returns to be preserved, and often contains special characters like quotes and <> symbols. The ordinary quote symbols are a little tedious if you want to use them to build a web page. Here's an example.

Say you wanted to create a program that could take the value of the $name and $address variables and put them into a table like this:

```
<table style = "border: 1px solid black">
  <tr>
    <td>name</td>
    <td>John</td>
  </tr>
  <tr>
    <td>address</td>
    <td>123 Main St.</td>
  </tr>
</table>
```

There are a few ways to combine the PHP and HTML code as shown in the following sections.

Using double quote interpolation

Using regular double quotes, the code would look something like this:

```
$name = "John";
$address = "123 Main St.";
$output = "";
$output .= "<table style = \"border: 1px solid black\"> \n";
$output .= "   <tr> \n";
$output .= "     <td>name</td> \n";
$output .= "     <td>$name</td> \n";
$output .= "   </tr> \n";
$output .= "   <tr> \n";
$output .= "     <td>address</td> \n";
$output .= "     <td>$address</td> \n";
```

```
$output .= "  </tr> \n";
$output .= "</table> \n";

print $output
```

However, using quotes to generate HTML output is inconvenient for the following reasons:

✦ **The $output variable must be initialized.** Before adding anything to the $output variable, give it an initial null value.

✦ **You must repeatedly concatenate data onto the $output variable.** The .= operator allows me to append something to a string variable.

✦ **All quotes must be escaped.** Because double quotes indicate the end of the string, all internal double quotes must be preceded with the backslash (\).

✦ **Every line must end with a newline (\n) sequence.** PHP creates HTML source code. Your PHP-derived code should look as good as what you write by hand, so you need to preserve carriage returns. This means you need to end each line with a newline.

✦ **The HTML syntax is buried inside PHP syntax.** The example shows PHP code creating HTML code. Each line contains code from two languages interspersed. This can be disconcerting to a beginning programmer.

Generating output with heredocs

PHP uses a clever solution called heredocs to resolve all these issues. A *heredoc* is simply a type of multiline quote, usually beginning and ending with the word HERE.

The best way to understand heredocs is to see one in action, so here's the same example written as a heredoc:

```
<?php
$name = "John";
$address = "123 Main St.";
print <<<HERE
<table style = "border: 1px solid black">
  <tr>
    <td>name</td>
    <td>$name</td>
  </tr>
  <tr>
    <td>address</td>
    <td>$address</td>
  </tr>
</table>
HERE;
?>
```

Figure 1-5 illustrates this code in action.

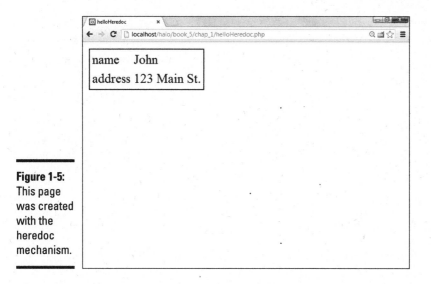

Figure 1-5:
This page
was created
with the
heredoc
mechanism.

Heredocs have some great advantages:

✦ **All carriage returns are preserved.** There's no need to put in any
newline characters. Whatever carriage returns are in the original text
will stay in the output.

✦ **Heredocs preserve quote symbols.** There's also no need to escape your
quotes because the double quote is not the end-of-string character for a
heredoc.

✦ **Variable interpolation is supported.** You can use variable names in a
heredoc, just like you do for an ordinary quoted string.

✦ **The contents of a heredoc feel like ordinary HTML.** When you're working inside a heredoc, you can temporarily put your mind in HTML mode,
but with the ability to interpolate variables.

The following are some things to keep in mind about heredocs:

✦ A heredoc is opened with three less-than symbols (<<<) followed by
a heredoc symbol that will act as a "superquote" (instead of single or
double quotation marks, you make your own custom quotation mark
from any value that you want).

✦ A heredoc symbol can be denoted by almost any text, but HERE is the
most common delimiter (thus, heredoc). You can make absolutely anything you want serve as a heredoc symbol. You probably should just
stick to HERE because that's what other programmers are expecting.

✦ You need only one semicolon for the whole heredoc. Technically, the
entire heredoc counts as one line. That means that the only semicolon
you need is after the closing symbol.

- ✦ A heredoc must be closed with the same word it was opened with.

- ✦ The closing word for the heredoc must be on its own line with no other symbols or spaces, just the word followed by a semicolon.

- ✦ You can't indent the closing word for the heredoc; there can't be any spaces or tabs preceding or following the closing word.

By far, the most common problem with heredocs is indenting the closing token. The HERE (or whatever other symbol you're using) must be flush with the left margin of your editor, or PHP won't recognize it. This usually means PHP interprets the rest of your program as part of a big string and never finishes executing it.

Heredocs have one disadvantage: They tend to mess up your formatting because you have to indent heredocs differently than the rest of the code.

When writing a heredoc, don't put a semicolon after the first <<<HERE. Also, don't forget that the last HERE; can't have any whitespace before it — it must be alone on a new line without any spaces preceding it. An editor that understands the heredoc rules highlights all the code inside the heredoc and saves you lots of grief. Komodo does this automatically, as does Aptana (if you've installed the PHP plug-in). Notepad++ also has this feature.

Switching from PHP to HTML

There's one more way to combine PHP and HTML code. The server treats a PHP document mainly as an HTML document. Any code not inside the `<?php ?>` symbols is treated as HTML, and anything inside the PHP symbols is interpreted as PHP.

This means you can switch in and out of PHP, like the following example:

```
<?php
    $name = "John";
    $address = "123 Main St.";
    // switch 'out' of PHP temporarily
?>
<table style = "border: 1px solid black">
  <tr>
    <td>name</td>
    <td><?php print $name; ?></td>
  </tr>
  <tr>
    <td>address</td>
    <td><?php print $address; ?></td>
  </tr>
</table>
<?php
  //I'm back in PHP
?>
```

Printing shortcut

When switching in and out of PHP, if you have just one variable you want to print, depending upon your server setup, you may be able to print the variable like this:

```
<?= $name ?>
```

You don't have to actually write `print` when using this technique. Note that this trick doesn't work if you have to type **php** after the question mark in the opening PHP tag.

This option (switching back and forth) is generally used when you have a lot of HTML code with only a few simple PHP variables. I prefer the heredoc approach, but feel free to experiment and find out what system works for you.

Chapter 2: PHP and HTML Forms

In This Chapter

✔ Understanding the relationship between HTML and PHP

✔ Using the date( ) function

✔ Formatting date and time information

✔ Creating HTML forms designed to work with PHP

✔ Choosing between get and post data transmission

✔ Retrieving data from your HTML forms

✔ Working with HTML form elements

*P*HP is almost never used on its own. PHP is usually used in tight conjunction with HTML. Many languages have features for creating input forms and user interfaces, but with PHP, the entire user experience is based on HTML. The user never really sees any PHP. Most of the input to PHP programs comes from HTML forms, and the output of a PHP program is an HTML page.

In this chapter, you discover how to integrate PHP and HTML. You explore how PHP code is embedded into HTML pages, how HTML forms can be written so they will send information to a PHP program, how to write a PHP program to read that data, and how to send an HTML response back to the user.

Exploring the Relationship between PHP and HTML

PHP is a different language than HTML, but the two are very closely related. It may be best to think of PHP as an extension that allows you to do things you cannot do easily in HTML. See Figure 2-1 for an example.

Every time you run getTime.php, it generates the current date and time and returns these values to the user. This would not be possible in ordinary HTML because the date and time (by definition) always change. While you could make this page using JavaScript, the PHP approach is useful for demonstrating how PHP works. First, take a look at the PHP code:

```
<!DOCTYPE html>
<html lang = "en-US">

  <head>
    <meta charset = "UTF-8">
    <title>showDate.php</title>
  </head>
  <body>
    <h1>Getting the Time, PHP Style</h1>
```

```php
    <?php
print "<h2>Date: ";
print date("m-d");
print "</h2> \n";
print "    <h2>Time: ";
print date("h:i");
print "</h2>";
    ?>
  </body>
</html>
```

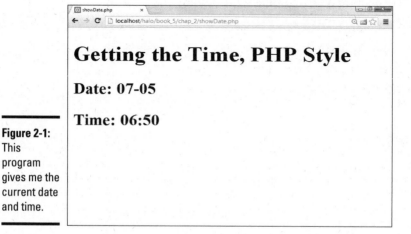

Figure 2-1:
This program gives me the current date and time.

Embedding PHP inside HTML

The PHP code has some interesting characteristics:

+ **It's structured mainly as an HTML document.** The doctype definition, document heading, and initial H1 heading are all ordinary HTML. Begin your page as you do any HTML document. A PHP page can have as much HTML code as you wish. (You might have no PHP at all!) The only thing the PHP designation does is inform the server that PHP code may be embedded into the document.

+ **PHP code is embedded into the page.** You can switch from HTML to PHP with the <?php tag. Signify the end of the PHP code with the ?> symbol.

+ **The PHP code creates HTML.** PHP is usually used to create HTML code. In effect, PHP takes over and prints out the part of the page that can't be created in static HTML. The result of a PHP fragment is usually HTML code.

+ **The date() function returns the current date with a specific format.** The format string indicates how the date should be displayed. (See the sidebar "Exploring the date( ) format function," in this chapter, for more information about date formatting.)

+ **The result of the PHP code will be an HTML document.** When the PHP code is finished, it will be replaced by HTML code.

Viewing the results

If you view `showDate.php` in your browser, you won't see the PHP code. Instead, you'll see an HTML page. It's even more interesting when you use your browser to view the page source. Here's what you'll see:

```
<!DOCTYPE html>
<html lang = "en-US">

  <head>
    <meta charset = "UTF-8">
    <title>showDate.php</title>
  </head>
  <body>
    <h1>Getting the Time, PHP Style</h1>
    <h2>Date: 07-05</h2>
    <h2>Time: 03:50</h2>
  </body>
</html>
```

The remarkable thing is what you don't see. When you look at the source of `showDate.php` in your browser, the PHP is completely gone! This is one of the most important points about PHP: The browser never sees any of the PHP. The PHP code is converted completely to HTML before anything is sent to the browser. This means that you don't need to worry about whether a user's browser understands PHP. Because the user never sees your PHP code (even if he views the HTML source), PHP code works on any browser, and is a touch more secure than client-side code.

Exploring the date() format function

The showDate.php program takes advantage of one of PHP's many interesting and powerful functions to display the date. The PHP `date()` function returns the current date. Generally, you'll pass the `date()` function a special format string that indicates how you want the date to be formatted. Characters in the date string indicate a special code. Here are a few of the characters and their meanings:

✔ d: day of the month (numeric)

✔ D: three character abbreviation of weekday (`Wed`)

✔ m: month (numeric)

✔ M: three-character abbreviation of month (`Feb`)

✔ F: text representation of month (`February`)

✔ y: two-digit representation of the year (`08`)

✔ Y: four-digit representation of the year (`2008`)

✔ h: hour (12 hours)

✔ H: hour (24 hours)

✔ i: minutes

✔ s: seconds

You can embed standard punctuation in the format as well, so `d/m/y` will include the slashes between each part of the date. There are many more symbols available. Check the PHP documentation at `http://us3.php.net/manual/en/function.date.php` for more information about date and time formatting.

Sending Data to a PHP Program

You can send data to a PHP program from an HTML form. For an example of this technique, see askName.html in Figure 2-2.

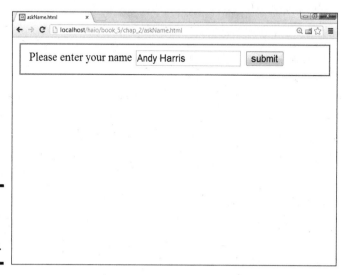

Figure 2-2:
This HTML page has a simple form.

HTML forms (described fully in Book I, Chapter 7) allow the user to enter data onto a web page. However, HTML cannot respond to a form on its own. You need some sort of program to respond to the form. Book IV describes how to use JavaScript to respond to forms, but you can also write PHP code to handle form-based input. When the user submits the form, the askName. html disappears completely from the browser and is replaced with greetUser.php, as shown in Figure 2-3.

The greetUser.php program retrieves the data from the previous page (ask-Name.html, in this case) and returns an appropriate greeting.

Creating a form for PHP processing

The askName.html program is a standard HTML form, but it has a couple of special features which make it suitable for PHP processing. (See Book I, Chapter 7 for more information about how to build HTML forms.) Here is the HTML code:

```
<!DOCTYPE html>
<html lang = "en-US">

  <head>
    <meta charset = "UTF-8">
    <title>askName.html</title>
  </head>
```

```
<body>
  <form action = "greetUser.php"
        method = "get">
    <fieldset>
      <label>Please enter your name</label>
      <input type = "text"
             name = "userName" />
      <button type = "submit">
        submit
      </button>
    </fieldset>
  </form>
</body>
</html>
```

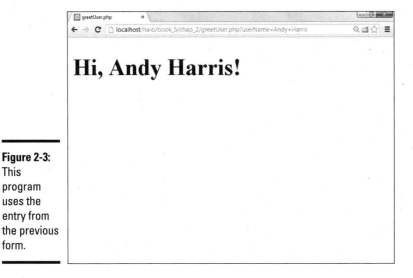

Figure 2-3:
This
program
uses the
entry from
the previous
form.

To build a form designed to work with PHP, there are a few special steps to take:

1. **Write an HTML page as the framework.**

   This page is a regular HTML page. Begin with the same HTML framework you use for building your standard HTML pages. You can use CSS styles, if you wish (but I'm leaving them out of this simple example).

   Normally, you can create an HTML document anywhere you want, but this is not so when your page will be working with PHP. This page is meant to be paired with a PHP document. PHP documents will run only if they are in a server's file space, so you should save your HTML document under htdocs to be sure it will call the PHP form correctly.

2. **Set the form's `action` property to point to a PHP program.**

   The form element has an attribute called `action`. The `action` attribute is used to determine which program should receive the data transmitted by the form. I want this data to be processed by a program called greetUser.php, so I set greetUser.php as the `action`:

```
<form action = "greetUser.php"
     method = "get">
```

3. **Set the form's `method` attribute to `get`.**

The `method` attribute indicates how the form data will be sent to the server. For now, use the `get` method. See the section "Choosing the Method of Your Madness," later in this chapter, for information on the various methods available:

```
<form action = "greetUser.php"
     method = "get">
```

4. **Add any input elements your form needs.**

The point of a form is to get information from the user and send it to a program on the server. Devise a form to ask whatever questions you want from the server. My form is as simple as possible, with one text field, but you can use any HTML form elements you want:

```
<form action = "greetUser.php"
     method = "get">
  <fieldset>
    <label>Please enter your name</label>
    <input type = "text"
           name = "userName" />
    <button type = "submit">
      submit
    </button>
  </fieldset>
```

5. **Give each element a `name` attribute.**

If you want a form element to be passed to the server, you must give it a `name` attribute. ***Note:*** This is a different attribute than `id`, which is used in client-side processing.

```
<input type = "text"
       name = "userName" />
```

The `name` attribute will be used by the PHP program to extract the information from the form.

A form element can have both a name and an ID, if you wish. The `name` attribute will be used primarily by server-side programs, and the `id` attribute is mainly used for CSS and JavaScript. The name and ID can (and usually do) have the same value.

6. **Add a submit button to the page.**

The most important difference between a client-side form and a form destined for processing on the server is the button. A special submit button packages all the data in the form and passes it to the program indicated in the `action` property. Submit buttons can be created in two forms:

```
<input type = "submit" value = "click me"/>
```

or

```
<button type = "submit">click me</button>
```

Specify `submit` as the button's `type` attribute to ensure the button sends the data to the server.

If your form has a submit button and a blank `action` attribute, the current page will be reloaded.

Receiving data in PHP

PHP code is usually a two-step process. First, you create an HTML form, and then you send that form to a PHP program for processing. Be sure to read the previous section on "Creating a form for PHP processing" because now I show you how to read that form with a PHP program.

The HTML form in the last section pointed to a program named greetUser. php. This tells the server to go to the same directory that contained the original HTML document (askName.html) and look for a program named greetUser.php in that directory. Because greetUser is a PHP program, the server passes it through PHP, which will extract data from the form. The program then creates a greeting using data that came from the form. Look over all the code for greetUser.php before I explain it in more detail:

```
<!DOCTYPE html>
<html lang = "en-US">

  <head>
    <meta charset = "UTF-8">
    <title>greetUser.php</title>
  </head>
  <body>
    <?php
    $userName = filter_input(INPUT_GET, "userName");
    print "<h1>Hi, $userName!</h1>";
    ?>
  </body>
</html>
```

greetUser.php is not a complex program, but it shows the most common use of PHP: retrieving data from a form. Here's how you build it:

1. **Build a new PHP program.**

   This program should be in the same directory as askName.html, which should be somewhere the server can find (usually under the htdocs or public_html directory).

2. **Start with ordinary HTML.**

   PHP programs are usually wrapped inside ordinary HTML, so begin the document as if it were plain HTML. Use whatever CSS styling and ordinary

HTML tags you want. (I'm keeping this example as simple as possible, although I'd normally add some CSS styles to make the output less boring.)

3. **Add a PHP segment.**

   Somewhere in the page, you'll need to switch to PHP syntax so that you can extract the data from the form. Use the `<?php` symbol to indicate the beginning of your PHP code:

   ```
   <?php
   $userName = filter_input(INPUT_GET, "userName");
   print "<h1>Hi, $userName!</h1>";
   ?>
   ```

4. **Extract the username variable.**

   All of the data that was sent from the form is stored in a special variable in memory. There are a number of ways to extract that data, but the pre-ferred method is to use the `filter_input()` function as I have done here. This function takes two parameters: The first is a constant deter-mining the type of input (I'm looking for input passed through the GET mechanism here). The second parameter is the `name` associated with the form element. Typically you'll make a PHP variable with the same name as the corresponding form element.

   See the upcoming section "Getting data from the form" for more informa-tion on the `filter_input()` mechanism and some of the other tools that are available for retrieving information.

5. **Print the greeting.**

   Now, your PHP program has a variable containing the user's name, so you can print a greeting to the user. Remember that all output of a PHP program is HTML code, so be sure to embed your output in a suitable HTML tag. I'm putting the greeting inside a level-one heading:

   ```
   print "<h1>Hi, $userName!</h1>";
   ```

The greetUser.php script is not meant to be run directly. It relies on askName.html. If you provide a direct link to greetUser.php, the program will run, but it will not be sent the username, so it will not work as expected. Do not place links to your PHP scripts unless you designed them to work without input. On this book's companion website, you'll find a link to the source code of each of my PHP files, but most of them cannot be run directly, but must be called by an HTML file. See this book's Introduction for more on the website.

Choosing the Method of Your Madness

The key to server-side processing is adding `method` and `action` properties to your HTML form. You have two primary choices for the `method` property:

+ **GET:** The `get` method gathers the information in your form and appends it to the URL. The PHP program extracts form data from the address. The contents of the form are visible for anyone to see.

✦ **POST:** The post method passes the data to the server through a mechanism called *environment variables.* This mechanism makes the form elements slightly more secure because they aren't displayed in public as they are with the get method.

Using get to send data

The get method is easy to understand. View getRequest.php after it has been called from askName.html in Figure 2-4. Pay careful attention to the URL in the address bar.

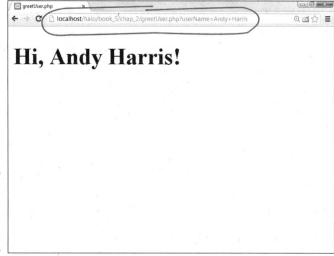

Figure 2-4:
The address has been modified!

The address sent to the PHP program has additional material appended:

```
http://localhost/haio/book_5/chap_2/greetUser.php?userName=Andy+Harris
```

Most of this address is the (admittedly convoluted) address of the page on my test server. The interesting part is the section after greetUser.php:

```
greetUser.php?userName=Andy+Harris
```

This line shows exactly how the get method passes information to the program on the server:

✦ **The URL is extracted from the form action property.** When the submit button is activated, the browser automatically creates a special URL beginning with the action property of the form. The default address is the same directory as the original HTML file.

✦ **A question mark indicates form data is on the way.** The browser appends a question mark to the URL to indicate form data follows.

♦ **Each field/value pair is listed.** The question mark is followed by each field name and its associated value in the following format:

```
URL?field1=value1&field2=value2
```

♦ **An equal sign (=) follows each field name.** Each field name is separated by the value of that field with an equal sign (and no spaces).

♦ **The field value is listed immediately after the equal sign.** The value of each field follows the equal sign.

♦ **Spaces are converted to hexadecimal symbols.** get data is transmitted through the URL, and URLS are not allowed to have spaces or other special characters in them. The browser automatically converts all spaces in field names or values to values it can manage, often converting spaces to special characters. Fortunately, the decoding process removes these special characters, so it's not something you need to worry about.

Sometimes, the spaces are converted to %20 symbols, rather than + signs. It isn't really that important because the conversion is done automatically. Just know that URLs can't contain spaces.

♦ **An ampersand (&) is used to add a new field name/value pair.** This particular example (the URL created by askName.html) has only one name/value pair. If the form had more elements, they would all be separated by ampersands.

You don't have to do any of the URL formatting. It automatically happens when the user clicks the submit button. You'll also never have to decode all this, as PHP will do it for you.

If you understand how the get method works, you can take advantage of it to send data to programs without the original form. For example, take a look at this address:

```
http://www.google.com/search?q=dramatic+chipmunk
```

If you type this code into your browser's location bar, you'll get the Google search results for a classic five-second video. (If you haven't seen this video, it's worth viewing.) If you know a particular server-side program (like Google's search engine) uses the get protocol, and you know which fields are needed (q stands for the query in Google's program), you can send a request to a program as if that request came from a form.

You can also write a link with a preloaded search query in it:

```
<a href = "http://www.google.com/search/q=dramatic+chipmunk">
    Google search for the dramatic chipmunk
</a>
```

If a user clicks the resulting link, he would get the current Google search for the dramatic chipmunk video. (Really, it's a prairie dog, but "dramatic chipmunk" just sounds better.)

How did I know how to write the Google query?

You might wonder how I knew what fields the Google engine expects. If the program uses get, just use the intended form to make a search and look at the resulting URL. Some testing and experience told me that only the q field is absolutely necessary.

This trick (bypassing the form) could be considered rude by some because it circumvents

safety features that may be built into the form. Still, it can be helpful for certain very public features, like preloaded Google searches, or looking up weather data for a particular location through a hard-coded link.

Of course, if you can send requests to a program without using the intended form, others can do the same to you. You can never be 100 percent sure that people are sending requests from your forms. This can cause some problems. Look at the next section for a technique to minimize this problem by reading only data sent via the post method.

Using the post method to transmit form data

The GET method is easy to understand because it sends all data directly in the URL. This makes it easy to see what's going on, but there are some downsides to using get:

✦ **The resulting URL can be very messy.** Addresses on the web can already be difficult without the added details of a get request. A form with several fields can make the URL so long that it's virtually impossible to follow.

✦ **All form information is user-readable.** The get method displays form data in the URL, where it can easily be read by the user. This may not be desired, especially when the form sends potentially sensitive data.

✦ **The amount of information that can be passed is limited.** Some servers won't accept URLs longer than 4,000 characters. If you have a form with many fields or with fields that contain a lot of data, you will easily exceed this limit.

The answer to the limitations of the get method is another form of data transmission: the post method.

Here's how it works:

✦ **You specify that the form's method will be POST.** You create the HTML form in exactly the same way. The only difference is the form method attribute. Set it to post:

```
<form action = "greetUser.php"
      method = "post">
```

✦ **Data is gathered and encoded, just like it is in the `get` method.** When the user clicks the submit button, the data is encoded in a format similar to the `get` request, but it's not attached to the URL.

✦ **The form data is sent directly to the server.** The PHP program can still retrieve the data (usually through a mechanism called *environment variables*) even though the data is not encoded on the URL. Again, you won't be responsible for the details of extracting the data. PHP makes it pretty easy.

The `post` method is often preferable to `get` because

✦ **The URL is not polluted with form data.** The data is no longer passed through the URL, so the resulting URL is a lot cleaner than one generated by the `get` method.

✦ **The data is not visible to the user.** Because the data isn't presented in the URL, it's slightly more secure than `get` data.

✦ **There is no practical size limit.** The size of the URL isn't a limiting factor. If your page will be sending a large amount of data, the `post` method is preferred.

With all these advantages, you might wonder why anybody uses `get` at all. Really, there are two good reasons. The `get` approach allows you to embed requests in URLs (which can't be done with `post`). Also, `get` is sometimes a better choice for debugging because it's easier to see what's being passed to the server.

Getting data from the form

The preferred way to extract data from the form is the `filter_input()` function. This powerful tool not only extracts data from the form, but it also protects against certain kinds of attacks and allows you to sanitize your data before you use it. Filter input requires two or three parameters:

✦ **The input type constant:** The first parameter is a constant describing where the data can be found. Most often, this value is `INPUT_GET` or `INPUT_POST`. A few other values are available (`INPUT_COOKIE` and `INPUT_ENV`) but they are rarely used. A couple of very useful values are not yet implemented (`INPUT_SESSION` and `INPUT_REQUEST`).

✦ **A variable name:** This is the `name` attribute from the form which called this program. If the name is misspelled or does not exist, the results will be unpredictable (see Chapter 3 of this minibook on how to handle this situation). The variable name must have the same case as the HTML form element name, must be encased in quotes, and *does not* include the dollar sign because this is an HTML variable rather than a PHP variable. Typically you'll pass the result of the `filter_input()` function to a PHP variable with the same name as the form element.

✦ **An optional filter:** You can specify one of a number of filters to pass input through before processing. These filters come in two main flavors:

Sanitizing filters all begin with the phrase FILTER_SANITIZE, and they are designed to strip off various types of characters. FILTER_SANITIZE_STRING removes or converts any special characters, and FILTER_SANITIZE_EMAIL removes any character not allowed in an e-mail address. There are filters for all the main data types (int and float) as well as special web-specific filters (e-mail, URL, special HTML characters).

Validation filters do not actually load the value, but check to see that it is in an acceptable format. They all begin with FILTER_VALIDATE and return a Boolean expressing whether the variable passed the validation. Typically you'll validate a variable before you accept it to prevent hackers from passing malicious code to your programs.

If you don't indicate a filter, the FILTER_SANITIZE_STRING filter is automatically applied, which does give you one level of protection. A list of the most commonly used filters is presented in Table 2-1.

Table 2-1	Standard PHP Filters
Filter	*Description*
FILTER_SANITIZE_STRING	Strips tags, encodes or removes special characters.
FILTER_SANITIZE_SPECIAL_CHARS	Converts HTML special characters (<>&) with ASCII equivalents.
FILTER_SANITIZE_EMAIL	Removes any characters not allowed in an e-mail address.
FILTER_SANITIZE_URL	Removes any characters not allowed in a URL.
FILTER_SANITIZE_NUMBER_INT	Removes all characters but numeric digits and sign (+/-) symbols.
FILTER_SANITIZE_NUMBER_INT	Removes all characters but numeric digits, periods, commas, and sign (+/-) symbols.
FILTER_VALIDATE_INT	True if input is an int.
FILTER_VALIDATE_FLOAT	True if input is a floating point value.
FILTER_VALIDATE_BOOLEAN	True if input can be read as a Boolean (true/false, on/off, yes/no, 1/0). Returns NULL if input is non-Boolean.
FILTER_VALIDATE_URL	True if input is a legal URL (doesn't check the address).
FILTER_VALIDATE_EMAIL	True if input is a legal e-mail address (doesn't check the address).
FILTER_VALIDATE_IP	True if input is a valid IP address (doesn't check the address).
FILTER_VALIDATE_REGEXP	True if input matches a given regular expression. (See more about regular expressions in Book IV, Chapter 5.)

There are few more filters, and some have optional parameters, so you may need to look at the online documentation to get all the details. Ninety percent of the time, you'll just stick with the default `FILTER_SANITIZE_STRING` filter.

Kicking it old-school: Form input like Grandma used to do it

The `filter_input` technique described in this chapter is the best way to get form input, but it's relatively new. For many years, other approaches were used.

PHP includes a number of special built-in variables that give you access to loads of information. Each variable is stored as an associative array; see Chapter 4 of this minibook for more on associative arrays. These special variables are available anywhere in your PHP code, so they're called *superglobals*. Here's a few of the most important ones:

- `$_GET`: A list of variables sent to this program through the `get` method

- `$_POST`: A list of variables sent to this program through the `post` method

- `$_REQUEST`: A combination of `$_GET` and `$_POST`

You can use these variables to look up information posted in the form. For example, the askName.html page contains a field called `userName`. When the user views this page, it sends a request to greetUser.php via the `get` method. greetUser.php can then check its `$_GET` variable to see whether a field named `userName` exists:

```
$userName = $_GET["userName"];
```

This line checks all the data sent via `get`, looks for a field named `userName`, and copies the contents of that field to the variable `$user-Name`.

If you want to retrieve a value sent through the `post` method, use this variation:

```
$userName = $_POST["userName"];
```

If you don't care whether the data was sent via `get` or `post`, use `$_REQUEST`:

```
$userName = $_REQUEST["userName"];
```

The `$_REQUEST` superglobal grabs data from both `get` and `post` requests, so it works, no matter how the form was encoded. Many programmers use the `$_REQUEST` technique because then they don't have to worry about the encoding mechanism.

The earliest forms of PHP had a feature called *register_globals* that automatically did the `$_REQUEST` extraction for you. If your program comes from a `userName` field, the program will "magically" just have a `$userName` variable preloaded with the value of that field. Although this was a very convenient option, evildoers soon learned how to take advantage of this behavior to cause all kinds of headaches. Convenient as it may be, the `register_globals` feature is now turned off on most servers and isn't even available on the next version of PHP.

The `filter_input()` mechanism described in this chapter is the preferred way to get input from a form, as it provides a nice level of protection from malicious attackers, but you will still see PHP code floating around that uses the other techniques.

Retrieving Data from Other Form Elements

It's just as easy to get data from drop-down lists and radio buttons as it is to get data from text fields. In PHP (unlike JavaScript), you use exactly the same technique to extract data from any type of form element.

Building a form with complex elements

For an example of a more complex form, look over monty.html in Figure 2-5. This program is a tribute to my favorite movie of all time. (You might just have to rent this movie if you're really going to call yourself a programmer. It's part of the culture.)

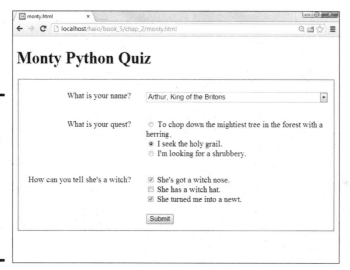

Figure 2-5:
The Monty Python quiz features a drop-down list, radio buttons, and check boxes (and a newt).

The HTML form poses the questions. (Check out Book I, Chapter 7 for a refresher on HTML forms, if you need it.) Here's the code:

```
<!DOCTYPE html>
<html lang = "en-US">

  <head>
    <meta charset = "UTF-8">
    <title>monty.html</title>
    <link rel = "stylesheet"
          type = "text/css"
          href = "monty.css" />
  </head>
  <body>
    <h1>Monty Python Quiz</h1>
    <form action = "monty.php"
          method = "post">
      <fieldset>
```

```
<p>
  <label>What is your name?</label>
  <select name = "name">
    <option value = "Roger">
      Roger the Shrubber
    </option>
    <option value = "Arthur">
      Arthur, King of the Britons
    </option>
    <option value = "Tim">
      Tim the Enchanter
    </option>
  </select>
</p>
<p>
  <label>What is your quest?</label>
  <span>
    <input type = "radio"
           name = "quest"
           value = "herring" />
    To chop down the mightiest tree in the forest
    with a herring
  </span>
  <span>
    <input type = "radio"
           name = "quest"
           value = "grail" />
    I seek the holy grail.
  </span>
  <span>
    <input type = "radio"
           name = "quest"
           value = "shrubbery" />
    I'm looking for a shrubbery.
  </span>
</p>
<p>
  <label>How can you tell she's a witch?</label>
  <span>
    <input type = "checkbox"
           name = "nose"
           value = "nose"/>
    She's got a witch nose.
  </span>
  <span>
    <input type = "checkbox"
           name = "hat"
           value = "hat"/>
    She has a witch hat.
  </span>
  <span>
    <input type = "checkbox"
           name = "newt"
           value = "newt" />
    She turned me into a newt.
  </span>
</p>
<button type = "submit">
  Submit
</button>
      </fieldset>
    </form>
  </body>
</html>
```

There's nothing too crazy about this code. Please note the following features:

✦ **The `action` attribute is set to monty.php.** This page (monty.html) will send data to monty.php, which should be in the same directory on the same server.

✦ **The `method` attribute is set to `post`.** All data on this page will be passed to the server via the `post` method.

✦ **Each form element has a `name` attribute.** The `name` attributes will be used to extract the data in the PHP program.

✦ **All the radio buttons have the same `name` value.** The way you get radio buttons to work together is to give them all the same `name`. And although they all have the same name, each has a different value. When the PHP program receives the request, it will get only the value of the selected radio button.

✦ **Each check box has an individual name.** Check boxes are a little bit different. Each check box has its own name, but the value is sent to the server only if the check box is checked.

I don't cover text areas, passwords fields, or hidden fields here because, to PHP, they are just like text boxes. Retrieve data from these elements just like you do for text fields.

Responding to a complex form

The monty.php program is designed to respond to monty.html. You can see it respond when I submit the form in monty.html, as shown in Figure 2-6.

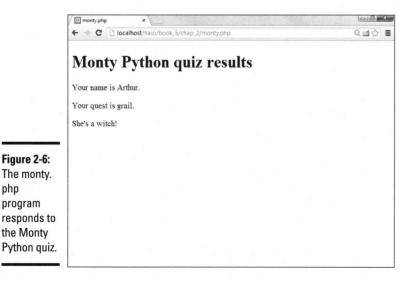

Figure 2-6:
The monty.
php
program
responds to
the Monty
Python quiz.

It's no coincidence that monty.html uses monty.css and calls monty.php. I deliberately gave these files similar names so it will be easy to see how they fit together.

This program works like most PHP programs: It loads data from the form into variables and assembles output based on those variables. Here's the PHP code:

```
<!DOCTYPE html>
<html lang = "en-US">

  <head>
    <meta charset = "UTF-8">
    <title>monty.php</title>
    <!-- Meant to run from monty.html -->
  </head>
  <body>
    <h1>Monty Python quiz results</h1>
    <?php
      //gather the variables
      $name = filter_input(INPUT_POST, "name");
      $quest = filter_input(INPUT_POST, "quest");
      //don't worry about check boxes yet; they may not exist
      //send some output
      $reply = <<< HERE
    <p>
      Your name is $name.
    </p>
    <p>
      Your quest is $quest.
    </p>
HERE;
      print $reply;
      //determine if she's a witch
      $witch = false;
      //See if check boxes exist
      if (filter_has_var(INPUT_POST, "nose")){
        $witch = true;
      }
      if (filter_has_var(INPUT_POST, "hat")){
        $witch = true;
      }
      if (filter_has_var(INPUT_POST, "newt")){
        $witch = true;
      }

      if ($witch == true){
        print "<p>She's a witch!</p> \n";
      } // end if
    ?>
  </body>
</html>
```

If you want to respond to a form with multiple types of data, here's how it's done:

1. **Begin with the HTML form.**

   Be sure you know the names of all the fields in the form because your PHP program will need this information.

2. **Embed your PHP inside an HTML framework.**

   Use your standard HTML framework as the starting point for your PHP documents, too. The results of your PHP code should still be standards-compliant HTML. Use the `<?php` and `?>` symbols to indicate the presence of PHP code.

3. **Create a variable for each form element.**

   Use the `$_REQUEST` technique described in the "Receiving data in PHP" section of this chapter to extract form data and store it in local variables:

   ```
   //gather the variables
   $name = filter_input(INPUT_POST, "name");
   $quest = filter_input(INPUT_POST, "quest");
   ```

   Don't worry about the check boxes yet. Later on, you'll determine whether they exist. You don't really care about their values.

4. **Build your output in a heredoc.**

   PHP programming almost always involves constructing an HTML document influenced by the variables that were extracted from the previous form. The heredoc method (described in Chapter 1 of this minibook) is an ideal method for packaging output:

   ```
   //send some output
   [      $reply = <<< HERE
   [      <p>
            Your name is $name.
          </p>

          <p>
            Your quest is $quest.
          </p>

   [HERE;
   [      print $reply;
   ```

5. **Check for the existence of each check box.**

   Check boxes are the one exception to the "treat all form elements the same way" rule of PHP. The important part of a check box isn't really its value. What you really need to know is whether the check box is checked. Here's how it works: If the check box is checked, a name and value are passed to the PHP program. If the check box is not checked, it's like the variable never existed:

   a. *Create a variable called `$witch` set to `false`.* Assume innocent until proven guilty in *this* witch hunt.

      Each check box, if checked, would be proof that she's a witch. The `filter_has_var()` function is used to determine whether a particular variable exists. This function takes an input type and a variable name (just like `filter_input()`) and returns `true` if the variable exists and `false` if it doesn't.

b. *Check each check box variable.* If it exists, the corresponding check box was checked, so she must be a witch (and she must weigh the same as a duck — you've *really* got to watch this movie).

After testing for the existence of all the check boxes, the $witch variable will still be `false` if none of the check boxes were checked. If any combination of check boxes is checked, $witch will be `true`:

```
//determine if she's a witch
$witch = false;

//See if check boxes exist
if (filter_has_var(INPUT_POST, "nose")){
  $witch = true;
}
if (filter_has_var(INPUT_POST, "hat")){
  $witch = true;
}
if (filter_has_var(INPUT_POST, "newt")){
  $witch = true;
}

if ($witch == true){
  print "<p>She's a witch!</p> \n";
} // end if
```

Before the `filter_has_var()` mechanism became available, programmers used another function called `isset()` to determine if a variable existed. Either is fine, but for this book I stick with the `filter` mechanisms for consistency.

Chapter 3: Using Control Structures

In This Chapter

✔ **Getting used to conditions**

✔ **Using** `if`, `else if`, **and** `else`

✔ **Using** `switch` **structures**

✔ **Working with** `while` **and** `for` **loops**

✔ **Using comparison operators**

omputer programs are most interesting when they appear to make decisions. PHP has many of the same decision-making structures as JavaScript, so if you've already looked over Chapters 2 and 3 of Book IV, you will find this chapter very familiar. In any case, take a look at conditions to see the key to making the computer branch and loop.

Introducing Conditions (Again)

Computer programs make decisions. That's part of what makes them interesting. But all the decisions a computer seems to make were already determined by the programmer. The computer's decision-making power is all based on an idea called a *condition.* This little gem is an expression that can be evaluated as true or false. (That sounds profound. I wonder if it will be on the mid-term?)

Conditions can be comparisons of one variable to another, they can be Boolean (true or false) variables, or they can be functions that return a true or false value.

If this talk of conditions is sounding like déjà vu, you've probably read about conditions in Book IV, Chapters 2 and 3. You'll find a lot of the same ideas here; after all, conditions (and branches and loops, and lots of other stuff) are bigger than one programming language. Even though this mini-book covers a different language, you'll see coverage of the same kinds of things. If you haven't read that minibook already, you might want to look it over first so you can see how programming remains the same even when the language changes.

Building the Classic if Statement

The if statement is the powerhouse of computer programming. Take a look at Figure 3-1 to see it in action. This program might be familiar if you read Book IV already. It rolls a standard six-sided die, and then displays that die on the screen.

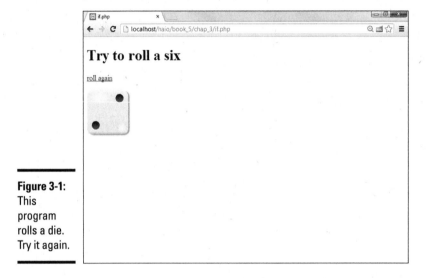

Figure 3-1:
This program rolls a die. Try it again.

When it rolls a six, it displays an elaborate multimedia event, as shown in Figure 3-2. (Okay, it just says *Holy Guacamole! That's a six!* The dancing hippos come later …)

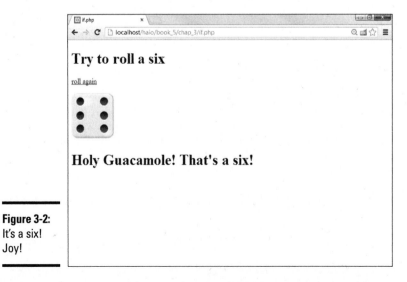

Figure 3-2:
It's a six! Joy!

This program is much like the if.html program in Book IV, Chapter 3. I do all the same things here as in that program. However, PHP and JavaScript are a little different, and that's part of the game of programming. Appreciate the concepts that flow between languages while noting those details that are different.

Rolling dice the PHP way

PHP has a random number generator, which works a little differently than the one in JavaScript. The PHP version is actually easier for dice.

```php
$variable = rand(a, b);
```

This code creates a random integer between a and b (inclusive), so if you want a random 1–6 die, you can use a statement like this:

```php
$die = rand(1,6);
```

It doesn't get a lot easier than that.

Checking your six

The code for the if.php program rolls a die, displays an image, and celebrates the joyous occasion of a six.

```php
<!doctype html>
<html lang="en">
<head>
  <meta charset="UTF-8">
  <title>if.php</title>
</head>
    <title>if.php</title>
    <meta http-equiv="Content-Type" content="text/
    html;charset=UTF-8" />
</head>
<body>
  <h1>Try to roll a six</h1>
  <p>
    <a href = "if.php">roll again</a>
  </p>
  <?php
    //thanks to user rg1024 from openClipart.org for
    //the great dice images
    $roll = rand(1,6);
    print <<<HERE
<p>
    <img src = "images/dado_$roll.png"
        alt = "$roll"
        height = "100px"
        width = "100px" />
</p>
HERE;
    if ($roll == 6){
      print("<h1>Holy Guacamole! That's a six!</h1>\n");
    } // end if
  ?>
</body>
</html>
```

The process is eerily familiar:

1. **Begin with a standard HTML template.**

   As always, PHP is encased in HTML. There's no need to switch to PHP until you get to the part that HTML can't do: that is, rolling dice and responding to the roll.

2. **Add a link to let the user roll again.**

   Add a link that returns to the same page. When the user clicks the link, the server refreshes the page and rolls a new number.

3. **Roll the `rand()` function to roll a die. Put the result in a variable called `$roll`.**

4. **Print out a graphic by creating the appropriate `<img>` tag.**

   I preloaded a bunch of die images into a directory called images. Each image is carefully named `dado_1.png` through `dado_6.png`. (Dado is Spanish for "die" — thanks to user rg1024 from openclipart.org for the great images.) To display an image in PHP, just print out a standard `img` tag. The URL is created by interpolating the variable `$roll` into the image name. Don't forget that HTML requires an `alt` attribute for the `img` tag. I just use the `$roll` value as the `alt`. That way, the die roll will be known even if the image doesn't work.

5. **Check whether the die is a six.**

   This is where the condition comes in. Use the `if` statement to see whether the value of `$roll` is 6. If so, print out a message.

The `==` (two equal sign) means "is equal to." A single equal sign means assignment. If you use the single equal sign in a condition, the code may not crash, but it probably won't do what you intended.

The `else` clause is used when you want to do one thing if a condition is true and something else if the condition is false. The highLow.php program shown in Figure 3-3 handles this kind of situation.

The code is very similar to the if.php program.

The bold code shows the only part of the program that's new.

```
<!doctype html>
<html lang="en">
<head>
  <meta charset="UTF-8">
  <title>highLow.php</title>
</head>
<body>
  <h1>High or low?</h1>
```

```
<p>
  <a href = "highLow.php">roll again</a>
</p>
<?php
  $roll = rand(1,6);
  print <<<HERE
  <p>
      <img src = "images/dado_$roll.png"
           alt = "$roll"
           height = "100px"
           width = "100px" />
  </p>
HERE;
  if ($roll > 3){
    print "<h2>You rolled a high one</h2>\n";
  } else {
    print "<h2>That's pretty low</h2> \n";
  } // end if
  ?>
</body>
</html>
```

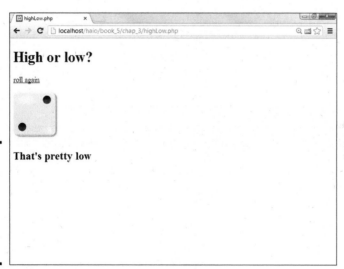

Figure 3-3:
This
program
tells
whether
the roll was
high or low.

Most of the code for this program is the same as the previous code example, but the condition is slightly different:

✦ **Now the condition is an inequality.** I now use the greater-than symbol (>) to compare the roll to the value 3. You can use any of the comparison operators in Table 3-1. If $roll is higher than 3, the condition will evaluate as true, and the first batch of code will run.

Table 3-1	Comparison Operators
Comparison	**Discussion**
A == B	True if A is equal to B
A != B	True if A is not equal to B
A < B	True if A is less than B (if they are numeric) or earlier in the alphabet (for strings)
A > B	True if A is larger than B (numeric) or later in the alphabet (string)
A >= B	A is larger than or equal to B
A<= B	A is less than or equal to B

✦ **Add an `else` clause.**

The `else` clause is special because it handles the situation when the condition is false. All it does is set up another block of code.

✦ **Include code for the false condition.**

The code between `else` and the ending brace for `if` ending brace will run only if the condition is evaluated false.

Understanding comparison operators

PHP uses many of the same comparison operators as JavaScript (and many other languages based on C). Table 3-1 summarizes these operators.

Note that PHP determines the variable type dynamically, so comparisons between numeric and string values may cause problems. It's best to explicitly force variables to the type you want if you're not sure. For example, if you want to ensure that the variable $a is an integer before you compare it to the value 4, you could use this condition:

```
(integer)$a == 4
```

This forces the variable $a to be read as an integer. You can also use this technique (called *typecasting*) to force a variable to other types: `float`, `string`, or `boolean`.

Taking the middle road

Another variation of the `if` structure allows you to check multiple conditions. As an example, look at the highMidLow.php page featured in Figure 3-4.

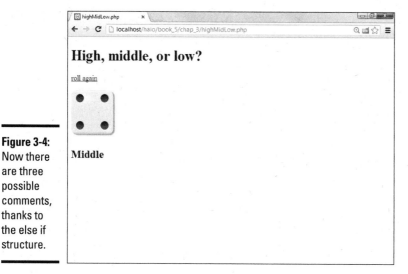

Figure 3-4:
Now there
are three
possible
comments,
thanks to
the else if
structure.

If the roll is 1 or 2, the program reports Low. If the roll is 3 or 4, it says
Middle; and if it's 5 or 6, the result is High. This if has three branches. See
how it works; you can add as many branches as you wish.

```php
<!doctype html>
<html lang="en">
<head>
  <meta charset="UTF-8">
  <title>highMidLow.php</title>
</head>
<body>
  <h1>High, middle, or low?</h1>
  <p>
    <a href = "highMidLow.php">roll again</a>
  </p>
  <?php
$roll = rand(1,6);
print <<<HERE
  <p>
    <img src = "images/dado_$roll.png"
         alt = "$roll"
         height = "100px"
         width = "100px" />
  </p>
HERE;
  if ($roll > 4){
    print "<h2>High!</h2>\n";
  } else if ($roll <= 2){
    print "<h2>Low</h2>\n";
  } else {
    print "<h2>Middle</h2> \n";
  } // end if
  ?>
</body>
</html>
```

The `if` statement is the only part of this program that's new. It's not terribly shocking.

1. **Begin with a standard condition.**

   Check whether the roll is greater than 4. If so, say `High`. If the first condition is true, the computer evaluates the code in the first section and then skips the rest of the `while` loop.

2. **Add a second condition.**

   The `else if` section allows me to add a second condition. This second condition (`roll <= 2`) is evaluated only if the first condition is false. If this condition is true, the code inside this block will be executed (printing the value `Low`). You can add as many `else if` sections as you want. As soon as one is found to be true, the code block associated with that condition executes, and the program leaves the whole `else` system.

3. **Include an `else` clause to catch stragglers.**

   If none of the previous conditions are true, the code associated with the `else` clause operates. In this case, the roll is lower than 4 and higher than 2, so report that it's in the `Middle`.

Building a program that makes its own form

An especially important application of the `if` structure is unique to server-side programming. Up to now, many of your PHP programs required two separate files: an HTML page to get information from the user and a PHP program to respond to that code. Wouldn't it be great if the PHP program could determine whether it had the data or not? If it has data, it will process it. If not, it just produces a form to handle the data. That would be pretty awesome, and that's exactly what you can do with the help of the `if` statement. Figure 3-5 shows the first pass of ownForm.php.

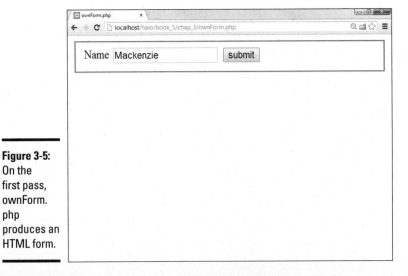

Figure 3-5:
On the first pass, ownForm. php produces an HTML form.

The interesting thing happens when the user submits the form. The program calls itself! This time, though, ownForm recognizes that the user has sent some data and processes that information, giving the result shown in Figure 3-6.

Figure 3-6:
Now the same program processes the data!

This program doesn't really require anything new, just a repurposing of some tools you already know. Take a look at the following code:

```
<!doctype html>
<html lang="en">
<head>
  <meta charset="UTF-8">
  <title>ownForm.php</title>
</head>
<body>
<?php
if (filter_has_var(INPUT_POST, "userName")){
  //the form exists - process it
  $userName = filter_input(INPUT_POST, "userName");
  print "<h1>Hi, $userName</h1>\n";
} else {
  //no form present, so give 'em one
  print <<<HERE
<form action = ""
      method = "post">
    <fieldset>
      <label>Name</label>
      <input type = "text"
             name = "userName">
      <button type = "submit">
        submit
      </button>
```

```
      </fieldset>
    </form>
HERE;
} // end if
?>
</body>
</html>
```

Making a program "do its own stunts" like this is pretty easy. The key is using an `if` statement. However, begin by thinking about the behavior. In this example, the program revolves around the `$userName` variable. If this variable has a value, it can be processed. If the variable has not been set yet, the user needs to see a form so she can enter the data.

1. **Check for the existence of a key variable.**

   Use the `isset()` function to determine whether the variable in question has been set. Check the `$_REQUEST` or one of the other superglobals (`$_POST` or `$_GET`) to determine whether the form has already been submitted. You need to check the existence of only one variable, even if the form has dozens.

2. **If the variable exists, process the form.**

   If the variable exists, extract all the variables from the form and carry on with your processing.

3. **If the variable does not exist, build the form.**

   If the variable does not exist, you need to make the form that will ask the user for that variable (and any others you need). Note that the action attribute of the form element should be null ("". This tells the server to re-call the same program.

If you're using an HTML5 validator, it will complain about the empty action attribute. This is interesting because previous HTML and XHTML implementations required it in this situation. In this particular situation (a PHP program creating a form that will call the PHP program again), many web developers just live with the validator's complaints because the empty attribute explicitly defines what I want to do (call myself) and it does no harm.

Making a switch

Often, you run across a situation where you have one expression that can have many possible values. You can always use the `if-else if` structure to manage this situation, but PHP supplies another interesting option, shown in Figure 3-7.

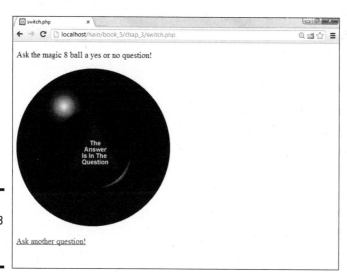

Figure 3-7:
The Magic 8
Ball uses a
switch.

The code for this program uses the `switch` structure. Take a look at how it's done:

```
<!doctype html>
<html lang="en">
<head>
  <meta charset="UTF-8">
  <title>switch.php</title>
</head>
<body>
<p>Ask the magic 8 ball a yes or no question!</p>
<?php
$yourNumber = rand(1,8);
switch($yourNumber){
  case 1:
    print "<p><img src=\"images/8ball1.png\" alt = \"fat chance\"
    /></p>";
    break;
  case 2:
    print "<p><img src=\"images/8ball2.png\" alt = \"Yes\" /></p> ";
    break;
  case 3:
    print "<p><img src=\"images/8ball3.png\" alt = \"PhD\" /></p>";
    break;
  case 4:
    print "<p><img src=\"images/8ball4.png\" alt = \"You didn't say
    please\" /></p>";
    break;
  case 5:
    print "<p><img src=\"images/8ball5.png\" alt = \"tell, then kill\"
    /></p>";
    break;
  case 6:
    print "<p><img src=\"images/8ball6.png\" alt = \"Why trust me?\"
    /></p>";
    break;
```

```
    case 7:
      print "<p><img src=\"images/8ball7.png\" alt = \"Ask your mother\"
      /></p>";
      break;
    case 8:
      print "<p><img src=\"images/8ball8.png\" alt = \"The answer is in
      the question\" /></p>";
      break;
    default:
      print "<p>An error has occurred. Please try again, or contact
      support@somesite.com for assistance. Error code: 8BIC:$yourNumber
      </p>";
}
?>
<p>
  <a href="switch.php">Ask another question!</a>
</p>
</body>
</html>
```

The main (in fact nearly only) feature of this code is the `switch` statement.
Here's how it works:

1. **Begin with the `switch` statement.**

   This indicates that you will be building a `switch` structure.

2. **Put the expression in parentheses.**

   Following the `switch` statement is a pair of parentheses. Put the expression (usually a variable) you wish to evaluate inside the parentheses. In this case, I'm checking the value of the variable $yourNumber.

3. **Encase the entire switch in braces.**

   Use squiggle braces to indicate the entire case. As in most blocking structures, use indentation to help you remember how the structure is organized.

4. **Establish the first case.**

   Put the first value you want to check for. In this situation, I'm looking for the value 1. Note that the type of data matters, so be sure you're comparing against the same type of data you think the variable will contain. Use a colon (:) to indicate the end of the case. This is one of the rare situations where you do not use a semicolon or brace at the end of a line.

5. **Write code that should happen if the expression matches the case.**

   If the expression matches the case (for example, if $yourNumber is equal to 1), the code you write here will execute.

6. **End the code with the `break` statement.**

   When you use an `if-else if` structure to work with multiple conditions, the interpreter jumps out of the system as soon as it encounters the first true condition. Switches work differently. Unless you specify (with the `break` statement), code will continue to evaluate even when one of the expressions is matched. You almost always need the `break` statement.

7. Use the `default` clause to handle any unexpected behavior.

The `default` section of the `switch` structure is used to handle any situation that wasn't covered by one of the previously defined cases. It's a good idea to always include a `default` clause.

It may seem odd to have a `default` clause in this example. After all, I know how the `rand()` function works, and I know that I'll get values only between `1` and `8`. It shouldn't be possible to have a value that isn't covered by one of the cases, yet I have a `default` clause in place for exactly that eventuality. Even though something *shouldn't* ever happen, sometimes it does. At the very least, I want a nice piece of code to explain what happened and send some kind of error message. If it's an important problem, I may have the code quietly e-mail me a message letting me know what went wrong.

You might wonder whether the switch is necessary at all. I could have used the interpolation tricks shown in the dice example to get the necessary images. However, remember that HTML requires all images to have `alt` tags. With dice, the value of the roll is a perfectly acceptable `alt` value. The Magic 8 Ball needs to return text if the image doesn't work properly. I used a switch to ensure that I have the appropriate `alt` text available. (Extra points if you think an array would be an even better way to handle this situation.)

Looping with for

Sometimes you want to repeat something. PHP (like most languages) supports a number of looping constructs. Begin with the humble but lovable `for` loop, as shown in Figure 3-8.

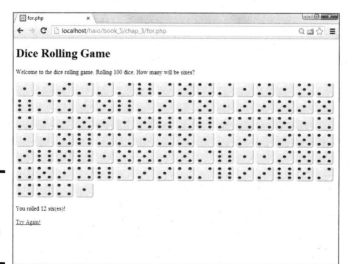

Figure 3-8:
This page prints a lot of dice with a for loop.

As you can see, Figure 3-8 prints a *lot* of dice. In fact, it prints 100 dice. This would be tedious to do by hand, but that's exactly the kind of stuff computers are so good at.

The following code explains all:

```
<!doctype html>
<html lang="en">
<head>
  <meta charset="UTF-8">
  <title>for.php</title>
  <style type="text/css">
    img{
      height: 40px;
      width: 50px;
    }
  </style>
</head>
<body>
  <h1>Dice Rolling Game</h1>
  <p>Welcome to the dice rolling game. Rolling 100 dice. How many
    will be sixes?</p>
  <p>
  <?php
  $sixCount = 0;

  for ($i = 0; $i < 100; $i++){
    $userNumber = rand(1,6);
    print <<< HERE
      <img src="images/dado_$userNumber.png"
          alt = "$userNumber"
          width = "20px"
          height = "20px" />
HERE;

    if($userNumber == 6){
        $sixCount++;
    } // end if
  } // end for

  print "</p><p>You rolled $sixCount six(es)!</p>";
  ?>

  <p><a href="for.php">Try Again!</a></p>

</body>
</html>
```

Most of the code is plain-old HTML. Note the lone `print` statement responsible for printing out dice. That `print` statement (and a few supporting characters) are repeated 100 times. `for` loops are extremely powerful ways to get a lot of work done.

1. **Begin with the `for` keyword.**

   This keyword indicates the beginning of the `for` structure.

   ```
   for ($i = 0; $i < 100; $i++){
   ```

2. **Add an initializer.**

    `for` loops usually center around a specific integer variable, sometimes called the *sentry variable.* The first part of the `for` loop sets up the initial value of that variable. Often, the variable is initialized to 0 or 1.

    ```
    for ($i = 0; $i < 100; $i++){
    ```

3. **Add a condition.**

    The loop continues as long as the condition is true and exits as soon as the condition is evaluated as false. Normally, the condition will check whether the variable is larger than some value.

    ```
    for ($i = 0; $i < 100; $i++){
    ```

4. **Add a modifier.**

    Every time through the loop, you need to do something to change the value of the sentry. Normally, you add 1 to the sentry variable (remember, ++ is a shortcut for "add one").

    ```
    for ($i = 0; $i < 100; $i++){
    ```

5. **Encase the body of the loop in braces.**

    The code that will be repeated is placed inside braces({ }). As usual, indent all code inside braces so you understand that you're inside a structure.

for loops are first described in Book IV, Chapter 3. Please look to that chapter for more details on `for` loops, including how to build a loop that counts backward and counts by fives. I don't repeat that material here because `for` loops work exactly the same in PHP and JavaScript.

This particular program has a few other features that make it suitable for printing out 100 dice.

✦ **It uses $i as a counting variable.** When the sentry variable's name isn't important, $i is often used. $i will vary from 0 to 99, giving 100 iterations of the loop.

✦ **Each time through the loop, roll a die.** The familiar `rand()` function is used to roll a random die value between 1 and 6. Because this code is inside the loop, it is repeated.

```
$userNumber = rand(1,6);
```

✦ **Print out an image related to the die roll.** I use interpolation to determine which image to display. Note that I used code to resize my image files to a smaller size.

```
print <<< HERE
  <img src="images/dado_$userNumber.png"
       alt = "$userNumber"
       width = "20px"
       height = "20px" />
HERE;
```

✦ **Check whether you rolled a 6.** For some strange reason, my obsession
with sixes continues. If the roll is a 6, add 1 to the $sixCount variable.
By the end of the loop, this will contain the total number of sixes rolled.

```
if($userNumber == 6){
    $sixCount++;
} // end if
```

✦ **Print the value of $sixCount.** After the loop is completed, report how
many sixes were rolled.

```
print &#x201C;</p><p>You rolled $sixCount six(es)!</p>&#x201C;;
```

Looping with while

The while loop is the other primary way of repeating code. Figure 3-9 shows
a variation of the dice-rolling game.

Figure 3-9:
This time,
the program
continues
until it gets
a 6.

while loops are much like for loops. They require the same thought:

✦ **A sentry variable:** This special variable controls access to the loop.
Unlike the int usually used in for loops, the sentry of a while loop can
be any type.

✦ **Initialization:** Set the initial value of the sentry variable before the loop
begins. Do not rely on default settings (because you don't know what
they will be). Instead, set this value yourself.

✦ **A condition:** The while statement requires a condition. This condition
controls access to the loop. As long as the condition is true, the loop
continues. As soon as the condition is evaluated as false, the loop exits.

✦ **A modifier:** You must somehow modify the value of the sentry variable. It's important that the modification statement happen somewhere inside the loop. In a `for` loop, you almost always add or subtract to modify a variable. In a `while` loop, any kind of assignment statement can be used to modify the variable.

`for` loops are a little safer than `while` loops because the structure of the `for` loop requires you to think about initialization, condition, and modification. All three features are built into the `for` statement. The `while` statement requires only the condition. This might make you think that you don't need the other parts, but that would be dangerous. In any kind of loop, you need to initialize the sentry variable and modify its value. With the `while` loop, you're responsible for adding these features yourself. Failure to do so will cause endless loops, or loops that never happen. See much more about this in Book IV, Chapter 3.

Take a look at the following code for the while.php program to see how it works:

```
<!doctype html>
<html lang="en">
<head>
  <meta charset="UTF-8">
  <title>while.php</title>
  <style type="text/css">
    img {
      height: 40px;
      width: 50px;
    }
  </style>
</head>
<body>
  <h1>Dice Rolling Game 2</h1>
  <p>Welcome to the dice rolling game. See how many rolls it takes
    to get a six!</p>
  <div id = "output">
  <?php
$userNumber = 999;
$counter = 0;
while ($userNumber != 6){
  $userNumber = rand(1,6);
  print <<< HERE
    <img src = "images/dado_$userNumber.png"
         alt = "$userNumber"
         height = "100px"
         width = "100px" />
HERE;
    $counter++;
  }
    print "<p>It took $counter tries to get a six.</p>";
  ?>
  </div>
  <p><a href="while.php">Try Again!</a></p>
</body>
</html>
```

This example illustrates how subtle `while` loops can be. All the key elements are there, but they don't all *look* like part of the `while` loop.

1. **Initialize `$userNumber`.**

   For this loop, `$userNumber` is the sentry variable. The initialization needs to guarantee that the loop runs exactly once. Because the condition will be (`$userNumber != 6`), I need to give `$userNumber` a value that clearly isn't `6`. `999` will do the job, and it's wild enough to be clearly out of range. Although the initialization step appears in the code before the `while` loop, it's often best to start with your condition and then back up a line to initialize because the initialization step depends on the condition.

2. **Set up the condition.**

   Think about what should cause the loop to continue or quit. Remember that the condition explains when the loop continues. It's often easier to think about what causes the loop to exit. That's fine; just reverse it. For example, I want the loop to quit when `$userNumber` is equal to `6`, so I'll have it continue as long as `$userNumber != 6`.

3. **Modify the sentry.**

   This one is tricky. In this particular example, modify the sentry variable by getting a new random number: `$userNumber = rand(1,6)`. Often in a `while` loop, the modification step is intrinsic to the problem you're solving. Sometimes you get the new value from the user, sometimes you get it from a file or database, or sometimes you just add (just like a `for` loop). The key here is to ensure you have a statement that modifies the sentry variable and that the condition can trigger. For example, using `$userNumber = rand(1,5)` would result in an endless loop because `$userNumber` could never be `6`.

 `while` loops can cause a lot of problems because they may cause logic errors. That is, the *syntax* (structure and spelling of the code) may be fine, but the program still doesn't operate properly. Almost always, the problem can be resolved by thinking about those three parts of a well-behaved loop: Initialize the sentry, create a meaningful condition, and modify the sentry appropriately. See Book IV, Chapter 3 for more on `while` loops.

Can I use a debugger for PHP?

In Book IV, you can see how to use a debugger to check your code. This is especially handy for the logic errors that tend to occur when you're writing `while` loops. It would be great if there was a similar facility for PHP code. Unfortunately, PHP debuggers are relatively rare and can be difficult to install and use. That's because PHP is not an interactive language, but it processes code in batch mode on the server. The Chrome debugger you use in Book IV is a client-side application, and it doesn't ever see the PHP code. The best way to debug PHP is with good-old `print` statements. If something doesn't work correctly, print out the sentry variable before, inside, and after the loop to see whether you can find the pattern. One reason why people are switching to AJAX (see Book VII) is that more of the logic is done on the client side, where it's easier to debug.

Chapter 4: Working with Arrays

In This Chapter

✔ **Creating one-dimensional arrays**

✔ **Making the most of multidimensional arrays**

✔ **Using** `foreach` **loops to simplify array management**

✔ **Breaking a string into an array**

In time, arrays will become one of the most important tools in your toolbox. They can be a bit hard to grasp for beginners, but don't let that stop you. Arrays are awesome because they allow you to quickly apply the same instructions to a large number of items.

In PHP, an *array* is a variable that holds multiple values that are mapped to keys. Think of a golfing scorecard. You have several scores, one for each hole on the golf course. The hole number is the key, and the score for that hole is the value. Keys are usually numeric, but values can be any type. You can have an array of strings, numbers, or even objects. Any time you're thinking about a list of things, an array is the natural way to represent this list.

Using One-Dimensional Arrays

The most basic array is a *one-dimensional array,* which is basically just one container with slots. Each slot has only one variable in it. In this section, you find out how to create this type of array and fill it.

Creating an array

Array creation is pretty simple. First, you need to create a variable and then tell PHP that you want that variable to be an array:

```
$theVar = array();
```

Now, `$theVar` is an array. However, it's an empty array waiting for you to come along and fill it.

Technically, you can skip the variable creation step. It's still a good idea to explicitly define an array because it helps you remember the element is an array, and there are a few special cases (such as passing an array into a function) where the definition really matters.

Filling an array

An array is a container, so it's a lot more fun if you put something in it. You can refer to an array element by adding an *index* (an integer) representing which element of the array you're talking about.

Say I have the following array:

```
$spanish = array();
$spanish[1] = "uno";
$spanish[2] = "dos";
```

What I did here is to add two elements to the array. Essentially, I said that element 1 is uno, and element 2 is dos.

PHP has another interesting trick available. Take a look at the next line:

```
$spanish[] = "tres";
```

This seems a little odd because I didn't specify an index. PHP is pretty helpful. If you don't specify an index, it looks at the largest index already used in the array and places the new value at the next spot. So, the value tres will be placed in element 3 of the array.

PHP is somewhat notorious for its array mechanism. Depending on how you look at it, PHP is far more forgiving or far sloppier than most languages when it comes to arrays. For example, you don't have to specify the length of an array. PHP just makes the array whatever size seems to work. In fact, you don't even have to explicitly create the array. When you start using an array, PHP automatically just makes it if it isn't already there. Although this is pretty easy, I've seen enough science fiction movies to know what can happen when we let computers make all the decisions for us.

Viewing the elements of an array

You can access the elements of an array in exactly the same way you created them. Array elements are just variables; the only difference is the numeric index. Here's one way to print out the elements of the array:

```
print <<< HERE
One: $spanish[1] <br />
Two: $spanish[2] <br />
Three: $spanish[3] <br />

HERE;
```

I can simply print out the array elements like any ordinary variable. Just remember to add the index.

Another great way to print out arrays is particularly useful for debugging. Take a look at this variation:

```
print "<pre> \n";
print_r($spanish);
print "</pre> \n";
```

The `print_r()` function is a special debugging function. It allows you to pass an entire array, and it prints out the array in an easy-to-read format. It's best to put the output of the `print_r()` function inside a `<pre>` element so that the output is preserved.

Of course, the results of the `print_r()` function mean something to you, but your users don't care about arrays. This is only a debugging tool. Typically, you'll use some other techniques for displaying arrays to your users.

To see what all the code in `basicArray.php` looks like, take a look at Figure 4-1.

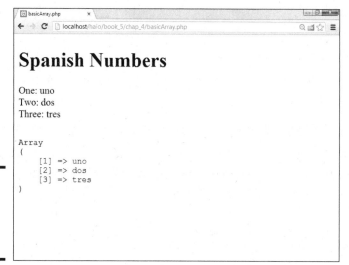

Figure 4-1:
Arrays are pretty easy to use in PHP.

Preloading an array

Sometimes you'll know the elements that go into an array right away. In those cases, you can use a special version of the `array()` function to make this work. Take a look at this code:

```
$english = array("zero", "one", "two", "three");

print "<pre> \n";
print_r($english);
print "<pre> \n";
```

This simple program allows you to load up the value of the array in one swoop. Note that I started with zero. Computers tend to start counting at zero, so if you don't specify indices, the first element will be zero-indexed.

I use the `print_r()` function to quickly see the contents of the array. The preloaded array is shown in Figure 4-2.

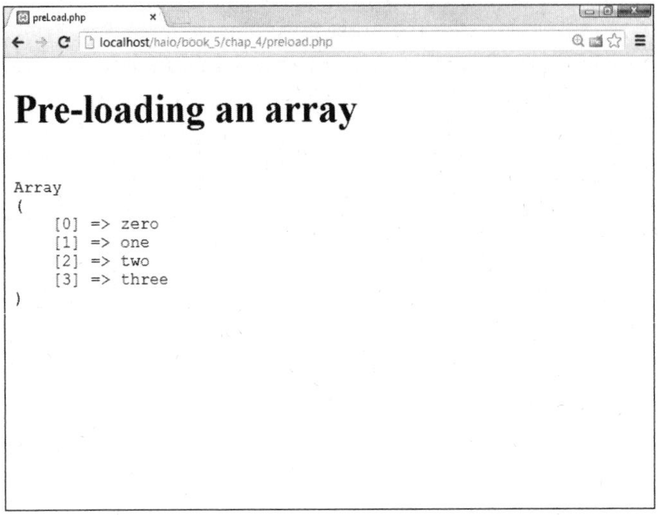

Figure 4-2:
This array was preloaded, but the user can't tell the difference.

Using Loops with Arrays

Arrays and loops are like peanut butter and jelly; they just go together. When you start to use arrays, eventually, you'll want to go through each element in the array and do something with it. The `for` loop is the perfect way to do this.

Look at the `loopingArrays.php` code to see how I step through an array with a couple of variations of the `for` loop:

```
<!doctype html>
<html lang="en">
<head>
  <meta charset="UTF-8">
  <title>loopingArrays.php</title>
</head>

<body>
  <h1>Looping through arrays</h1>
<div>
  <?php
    //first make an array of mini-book names
    $books = array("Creating the HTML Foundation",
                   "Styling with CSS",
                   "Using Positional CSS for Layout",
                   "Client-Side Programming with JavaScript",
                   "Server-Side Programming with PHP",
                   "Databases with MySQL",
                   "Into the Future with AJAX",
                   "Moving From Pages to Web Sites");
```

```
    //just print them out with a loop
    print "<p> \n";
    for ($i = 0; $i < sizeof($books);$i++){
      print $books[$i] . "<br />\n";
    } // end for
    print "</p> \n";

    //use the foreach mechanism to simplify printing out the elements
    print "<p> \n";
    foreach ($books as $book){
      print $book . " <br />\n";
    } // end foreach
    print "</p> \n";
  ?>
</div>
</body>
</html>
```

The relationship between arrays and loops isn't hard to see:

1. **Create your array.**

   This example uses an array of minibook titles in a charming and lovable
   book on web development. Note that I preloaded the array. There's no
   problem with the fact that the array statement (although a single line of
   logic) actually takes up several lines in the editor.

2. **Build a `for` loop to step through the array.**

   The loop needs to happen once for each element in the array; in this
   case, that's eight times. Set up a loop that repeats eight times. It will
   start at 0 and end at 7.

3. **Use the `sizeof()` function to determine the ending point.**

   Because you know that this array has eight elements, you could just set
   the condition to `$i < 8`. The `sizeof()` function is preferred because
   it will work even if the array size changes. Also, it's easier to understand
   what I meant. `sizeof($books)` means "the size of the `$books` array."
   The number 8 could mean anything.

4. **Print out each element.**

   Inside the loop, I simply print out the current element of the array,
   which will be `$books[$i]`. Don't forget to add a `<br />` tag if you want
   a line break in the HTML output. Add the `\n` to keep the HTML source
   code looking nice.

Simplifying loops with foreach

The relationship between loops and arrays is so close that many languages
provide a special version of the `for` loop just for arrays. Take a look at this
code fragment to see how cool it is:

```
    //use the foreach mechanism to simplify printing out the elements
    print "<p> \n";
```

```
foreach ($books as $book){
  print $book . " <br />\n";
} // end foreach
print "</p> \n";
```

The `foreach` loop is a special version of the `for` loop that simplifies working with arrays. Here's how it works:

1. **Use the `foreach` keyword to begin the loop.**

   This tells PHP that you're working with the `foreach` variation.

2. **The first parameter is the array name.**

   The `foreach` loop is designed to work with an array, so the first parameter is the array you want to step through.

3. **Create a variable to hold each element of the array.**

   On each pass through the loop, the `$book` variable will hold the current element of the `$books` array. Most of the time, you use a loop for an array because you want to deal with each element of the array. Using a `foreach` loop makes this easier.

4. **Use the `$book` variable inside the loop.**

   The `$book` variable is ready to go. The nice thing about using `foreach` is you don't have to worry about indices. The `$book` variable always contains the current element of the array.

You can see the results of both of these loops in Figure 4-3. To the user, there's no difference. Both are simply text when it comes to output.

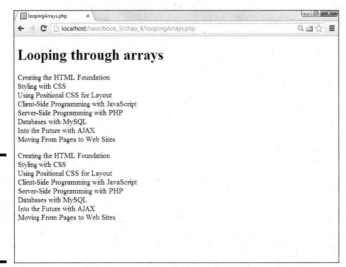

Figure 4-3:
Two kinds
of for loops
are used to
view these
arrays.

Many languages have variations of the `foreach` loop, but they differ greatly in the details. In PHP, the array comes first, then the scalar (non-array) variable. In Python, the order is inverted. In most languages (like PHP), the scalar variable is generated on each pass, but in JavaScript, the key is generated. Feel free to use the `foreach` loop, but be aware that it doesn't translate between languages quite as freely as most operations.

Arrays and HTML

Arrays are great because they're used to hold lists of data in your programming language. Of course, HTML already has other ways of working with lists. The `<ul>` and `<ol>` tags are both used for visual representations of lists, and the `<select>` object is used to let the user choose from a list. It's very common to build these HTML structures from arrays. Figure 4-4 illustrates exactly how this is done.

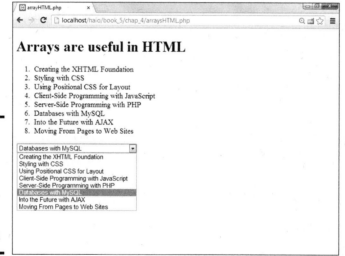

Figure 4-4:
This page features an ordered list and selection, both based on an array.

The code for the page is not too different than the previous examples. It just adds some HTML formatting:

```
<!DOCTYPE html>
<html lang="en">
<head>
  <meta charset="UTF-8">
  <title>arrayHTML.php</title>
</head>
<body>
  <h1>Arrays are useful in HTML</h1>
  <div>
    <?php
      //first make an array of mini-book names
```

```
$books = array("Creating the XHTML Foundation",
               "Styling with CSS",
               "Using Positional CSS for Layout",
               "Client-Side Programming with JavaScript",
               "Server-Side Programming with PHP",
               "Databases with MySQL",
               "Into the Future with AJAX",
               "Moving From Pages to Web Sites");

    //make the array into a numbered list
    print "<ol>\n";
    foreach ($books as $book){
      print "  <li>$book</li> \n";
    } // end foreach
    print "</ol>\n";

    //make the array into a select object
    print "<select name = \"book\"> \n";
    foreach ($books as $book){
      print "  <option value = \"$book\">$book</option> \n";
    } // end foreach
    print "</select> \n";
  ?>
  </div>
</body>
</html>
```

It's a relatively simple matter to build HTML output based on arrays. To create an ordered list or unordered list, just use a `foreach` loop, but add HTML formatting to convert the array to a list formatted in HTML:

```
//make the array into a numbered list
print "<ol>\n";
foreach ($books as $book){
  print "  <li>$book</li> \n";
} // end foreach
print "</ol>\n";
```

Likewise, if you want to allow the user to choose an element from an array, it's pretty easy to set up a `<select>` structure that displays the elements of an array:

```
//make the array into a select object
print "<select name = \"book\"> \n";
foreach ($books as $book){
  print "  <option value = \"$book\">$book</option> \n";
} // end foreach
print "</select> \n";
```

Introducing Associative Arrays

You can use string values as keys. For example, you might create an array like this:

```
$myStuff = array();
$myStuff["name"] = "andy";
```

```
$myStuff["email"] = "andy@aharrisbooks.net";

print $myStuff["name"];
```

Associative arrays are different than normal (numeric-indexed) arrays in some subtle but important ways:

✦ **The order is undefined.** Regular arrays are always sorted based on the numeric index. You don't know what order an associative array will be because the keys aren't numeric.

✦ **You must specify a key.** If you're building a numeric-indexed array, PHP can always guess what key should be next. This isn't possible with an associative array.

✦ **Associative arrays are best for name/value pairs.** Associative arrays are used when you want to work with data that comes in name/value pairs. This comes up a lot in PHP and HTML. HTML attributes are often in this format, as are CSS rules and form input elements.

✦ **Some of PHP's most important values are associative arrays.** The `$_REQUEST` variable (described in Chapter 3 of this minibook) is an important associative array. So are `$_GET`, `$_POST`, and several others.

Make sure to include quotation marks if you're using a string as an array index. It will probably work if you don't, but it's bad programming practice and may not work in the future.

Using foreach with associative arrays

It's very common to have a large associative array that you want to evaluate. For example, PHP includes a very useful array called `$_SERVER` that gives you information about your server configuration (things like your hostname, PHP version, and lots of other useful stuff). The following code snippet (from `serverInput.php`) runs through the entire `$_SERVER` array and prints each key/value pair:

```
<?php
print "<dl> \n";

foreach ($_SERVER as $key => $value){
  print <<<HERE
  <dt>$key</dt>
  <dd>$value</dd>

HERE;
} // end foreach
print "</dl> \n";
?>
```

You can see this program running on my work server in Figure 4-5.

Figure 4-5:
This variable stores data in an associative array.

Here's how it works:

1. **Begin the `foreach` loop as normal.**

   The associative form of the `foreach` loop begins just like the regular one:

   ```
   foreach ($_SERVER as $key => $value){
   ```

2. **Identify the associative array.**

   The first parameter is the array name:

   ```
   foreach ($_SERVER as $key => $value){
   ```

3. **Create a variable for the key.**

   Each element of an associative array has a key and a value. I put the key in a variable named `$key`:

   ```
   foreach ($_SERVER as $key => $value){
   ```

4. **Use the `=>` symbol to indicate the associative relationship.**

   This symbol helps PHP recognize you're talking about an associative array lookup:

   ```
   foreach ($_SERVER as $key => $value){
   ```

5. **Assign the value of the element to a variable.**

   The `$value` variable holds the current value of the array item:

   ```
   foreach ($_SERVER as $key => $value){
   ```

6. **Use the variables inside your loop.**

   Each time PHP goes through the loop, it pulls another element from the array, puts that element's key in the `$key` array, and puts the associated value in `$value`. You can then use these variables inside the loop however you wish. I used a definition list because it's a natural way to display key/value pairs. A list of definitions is keys and values.

```
print <<<HERE
  <dt>$key</dt>
  <dd>$value</dd>


HERE;
```

The $ SERVER variable is extremely useful for checking your environment, but you shouldn't make a program that displays this kind of information available on a publicly accessible server. Doing so gives the bad guys information they could use to cause you headaches. Use it for testing and debugging, and then remove it. I have this example disabled on my live site as a security precaution, but you can still look at the source code if you wish.

Introducing Multidimensional Arrays

Arrays in PHP can hold anything, even other arrays. This turns out to be an extremely useful function. A *multidimensional array* is an array that holds arrays. Multidimensional arrays are used when your data is arranged in some sort of tabular form.

We're going on a trip

Some uses for these are to group things or to use as lookup tables. See Book IV, Chapter 4 for one possible use of lookup tables — using multidimensional arrays to hold the distances between cities. You can do exactly the same thing with PHP. Even though the syntax is somewhat different, the concept is exactly the same. Figure 4-6 is an HTML page that lets the user choose what city she is traveling from and to.

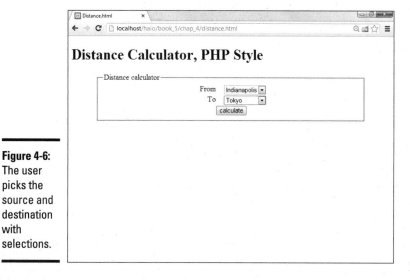

Figure 4-6:
The user picks the source and destination with selections.

The following code shows the basic HTML form:

```html
<!DOCTYPE html>
<html lang="en">
<head>
  <meta charset="UTF-8">
  <title>Distance.html</title>
  <style type="text/css">
  form {
    width: 600px;
    margin: auto;
  }
  label {
    width: 250px;
    float: left;
    clear: left;
    text-align: right;
    margin-right: 1em;
  }
  select {
    float: left;
  }
  button {
    display: block;
    clear: both;
    margin: auto;
  }
  </style>
</head>
<body>
  <h1>Distance Calculator, PHP Style</h1>
  <form action = "distance.php"
        method = "post">
    <fieldset>
      <legend>Distance calculator</legend>
      <label>From</label><p>
      <select name = "from">
        <option value="0">Indianapolis</option>
        <option value="1">New York</option>
        <option value="2">Tokyo</option>
        <option value="3">London</option>
      </select>
      <label>To</label><p>
      <select name = "to">
        <option value="0">Indianapolis</option>
        <option value="1">New York</option>
        <option value="2">Tokyo</option>
        <option value="3">London</option>
      </select>
      <button type = "submit">
        calculate
      </button>
    </fieldset>
  </form>
</body>
</html>
```

There's nothing unfamiliar about this form:

1. **Set the form's action to `distance.php`.**

   That's the program that will actually calculate the distance. Use the post method, as usual.

2. **Create a `select` object to determine where the user is leaving.**

   This form element will be called `from` because it represents the city the user is coming from. Note that the value is an integer that will relate to the various city numbers (`0` for Indianapolis, and so on).

3. **Create a second `select` object for the destination.**

   The second selection is much like the first, but it has the name `to`.

4. **Use CSS for beautification.**

   A little CSS can go a long way to make this page look nicer.

Looking up the distance

When the user submits the form, she is rewarded with the display shown in Figure 4-7.

Distance from Indianapolis to Tokyo is 6476 miles

Figure 4-7:
This clever program calculates the distance.

Of course, you could calculate the distance between cities with `if` statements, switches, and the like, but this kind of problem is really a *lookup table*. That means that the best way to solve it without a computer is to build a table. To use the table, you would use the row to indicate the source and the column to designate the destination, and then see where they cross for a result. It's very easy to get the computer to do exactly the same thing by using a two-dimension array, as shown in the following code:

```
<!DOCTYPE html>
<html lang="en">
<head>
  <meta charset="UTF-8">
  <title>Distance Results</title>
```

```
    </head>
    <body>
      <?php
        //get variables from form
        $cityName = array("Indianapolis", "New York", "Tokyo", "London");
        $from = filter_input(INPUT_POST, "from");
        $to = filter_input(INPUT_POST, "to");

        $distance = array(
          array(0, 648, 6476, 4000),
          array(648, 0, 6760, 3470),
          array(6476, 6760, 0, 5956),
          array(4000, 3470, 5956, 0));

        //calculate and display distance
        $result = $distance[$from][$to];
        print "<h1>Distance from $cityName[$from] to $cityName[$to] is $result
        miles</h1>\n";
      ?>
    </body>
    </html>
```

The two-dimension array simplifies things greatly. Take a look at how the program calculates the result:

1. **Create a standard array to handle city names.**

   The cities all have numbers, so I use an array to help attach the names to the numbers. It's important that this array is in the correct order, so city 0 is Indianapolis throughout.

2. **Retrieve to and from data from the form.**

   These values were sent by the previous form, so get the data and place them in variables.

3. **Build a 2D array to hold the distance data.**

   The distance is stored in a table. A 2D array is a perfect way to hold this data.

4. **Look up the distance in the distance array.**

   A 2D array requires two indices. The first indicates the row, and the second indicates the column.

5. **Print out the result.**

   After you get the data, it's pretty easy to print out.

Breaking a String into an Array

Many times, it can be useful to break a string into an array, especially when reading input from a file.

Here are the two different ways of doing this:

✦ **explode:** explode takes one parameter as a delimiter and splits the string into an array based upon that one parameter.

✦ **preg_ split:** If you require regular expressions, using preg_split is the way to go. split allows you to take complicated chunks of text, look for multiple different delimiters stored in a regular expression, and break it into an array based on the delimiters you specify.

explode works well with comma-separated value (CSV) files and the like, where all the parameters you wish to break the text on are the same. preg_ split works better for when there are many different parameters that you wish to break the text on or when the parameter you're looking for is complex.

Creating arrays with explode

Array creation with explode is very straightforward:

```
explode(" ", $theString);
```

The first value is the parameter on which you're splitting up the string. The second value is the string you would like to split into an array. In this example, the string would be split up on each space. You can put anything you want as the split parameter.

So, if you have the string that you want to store each word as a value in, enter the following code (see Figure 4-8 for the output):

```
<!DOCTYPE html>
<html lang="en">
<head>
  <meta charset="UTF-8">
  <title>explode</title>
</head>
<body>
  <h1>Using explode</h1>
  <?php
    $theString = "Twas brillig and the slithy toves";
    $theArray = explode(" ", $theString);
    print "<pre> \n";
    print_r($theArray);
    print "</pre> \n";
  ?>
</body>
</html>
```

The delimiter can be anything you want. If you're dealing with a CSV file, where each value is separated by a comma, your explode method might look like this:

```
$theArray = explode(",", $theString);
```

You learn more about working with many types of files in Chapter 6 of this minibook.

Figure 4-8:
A string
exploded
into an
array.

Creating arrays with preg_split

preg_split is a bit more complicated. preg_split uses regular expressions to split a string into an array, which can make it a bit slower than explode.

preg_split looks exactly like explode, but instead of one character inside quotations, you can cram all the characters you want to split on into brackets inside the quotations, or you can use a complicated regular expression to determine how the values will split.

If you need a refresher on regular expressions, check Book IV, Chapter 5. Regular expressions work the same in JavaScript and in PHP because both languages derived their regular expression tools from the older language Perl. (The preg part of preg_split stands for "Perl regular expression.")

An instance where you'd want to use preg_split instead of explode could be when processing an e-mail address. A basic e-mail address has dots (.) and an at sign (@). So, to split on either of these characters, you could do the following (see Figure 4-9 for the output):

```
<!DOCTYPE html>
<html lang="en">
<head>
  <meta charset="UTF-8">
  <title>preg_split.html</title>
</head>
<body>
  <h1>Using preg_split</h1>
  <?php
    $theString = "joe@somewhere.net";
    $theArray = preg_split("/[@\.]/", $theString);
```

```
        print "<pre>\n";
        print_r($theArray);
        print "</pre>\n";
    ?>
    </body>
</html>
```

Using preg_split

```
Array
(
    [0] => joe
    [1] => somewhere
    [2] => net
)
```

Figure 4-9:
The e-mail
address
split into an
array.

Recall that regular expressions are encased in the slash character, and the square braces indicate one of a number of options. I want to split on either the at sign or the period. Remember to specify the period with \. because an ordinary period means "any character."

preg_split works well for timestamps, e-mail addresses, and other things where there's more than just one unique delimiter that you wish to split the string on.

Earlier versions of PHP had a function called split. It was much like the preg_split function, but it used a different regular expression syntax. Hardly anybody used it, and it is no longer supported. Use explode for simple patterns and preg_split when you need the power of regular expressions.

Chapter 5: Using Functions and Session Variables

*P*HP programs are used to solve interesting problems, which can get quite complex. In this chapter, you explore ways to manage this complexity. You discover how to build functions to encapsulate your code. You also learn how to use session variables to make your programs keep track of their values, even when the program is called many times.

Creating Your Own Functions

It won't take long before your code starts to get complex. Functions are used to manage this complexity. As an example, take a look at Figure 5-1.

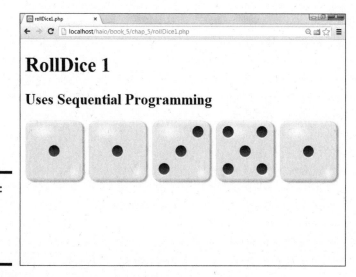

Figure 5-1:
This program rolls five dice.

Rolling dice the old-fashioned way

Before I show you how to improve your code with functions, look at a program that doesn't use functions so you have something to compare with.

The following rollDice.php program creates five random numbers and displays a graphic for each die:

```php
<!DOCTYPE html>
<html lang = "en-US">
  <head>
    <meta charset = "UTF-8">
    <title>rollDice1.php</title>
  </head>
  <body>
    <h1>RollDice 1</h1>
    <h2>Uses Sequential Programming</h2>
    <div>
    <?php
$roll = rand(1,6);
$image = "dado_$roll.png";
print <<< HERE
    <img src = "$image"
        alt = "roll: $roll"
        width = "100px"
        height = "100px" />
HERE;

$roll = rand(1,6);
$image = "dado_$roll.png";
print <<< HERE
    <img src = "$image"
        alt = "roll: $roll"
        width = "100px"
        height = "100px" />
HERE;

$roll = rand(1,6);
$image = "dado_$roll.png";
print <<< HERE
    <img src = "$image"
        alt = "roll: $roll"
        width = "100px"
        height = "100px" />
HERE;

$roll = rand(1,6);
$image = "dado_$roll.png";
print <<< HERE
    <img src = "$image"
        alt = "roll: $roll"
        width = "100px"
        height = "100px" />
HERE;

$roll = rand(1,6);
$image = "dado_$roll.png";
print <<< HERE
    <img src = "$image"
        alt = "roll: $roll"
```

```
            width = "100px"
            height = "100px" />
HERE;

    ?>
  </div>
 </body>
</html>
```

Here are some interesting features of this code:

✦ **The built-in `rand()` function rolls a random number.** Whenever possible, try to find functions that can help you. The `rand()` function produces a random integer. If you use two parameters, the resulting number will be in the given range. To roll a standard six-sided die, use `rand(1,6)`:

```
        $roll = rand(1,6);
```

✦ **I created an image for each possible roll.** To make this program more visually appealing, I created an image for each possible die roll. The images are called `dado_1.png`, `dado_2.png`, and so on. All these images are stored in the same directory as the PHP program.

✦ **The `img` tag is created based on the die roll.** After I have a die roll, it's easy to create an image based on that roll:

```
        $image = "dado_$roll.png";
        print <<< HERE
    <img src = "$image"
        alt = "roll: $roll"
        height = "100px"
        width = "100px" />

    HERE;
```

✦ **The die-rolling code is repeated five times.** If you can roll one die, you can easily roll five. It's as easy as copying and pasting the code. This seems pretty easy, but it leads to problems. What if I want to change the way I roll the dice? If so, I'll have to change the code five times. What if I want to roll 100 dice? The program will quickly become unwieldy. In general, if you find yourself copying and pasting code, you can improve the code by adding a function.

Improving code with functions

Functions are predefined code fragments. After you define a function, you can use it as many times as you wish. As you can see in the following code, the outward appearance of this program is identical to rollDice1.php, but the internal organization is quite different:

```
<!DOCTYPE html>
<html lang = "en-US">
  <head>
    <meta charset = "UTF-8">
    <title>rollDice2.php</title>
```

```
      </head>
      <body>
        <h1>RollDice 2</h1>
        <h2>Uses Functions</h2>
        <?php
          function rollDie(){
            $roll = rand(1,6);
            $image = "dado_$roll.png";
            print <<< HERE
              <img src = "$image"
                    alt = "roll: $roll"
                    height = "100px"
                    width = "100px" />
HERE;
          } // end rollDie

          for ($i = 0; $i < 5; $i++){
            rollDie();
          } // end for loop
        ?>
      </body>
    </html>
```

Here's how things have changed in this version:

1. **Use the `function` keyword to define a function.**

   The `function` keyword indicates that a function definition will follow. The code inside the definition won't be run immediately, but instead, PHP will "remember" the code inside the function definition and play it back on demand:

   ```
   function rollDie(){
   ```

2. **Give the function a name.**

   The function name should indicate what the function does. I call my function `rollDie()` because that's what it does (rolls a die):

   ```
   function rollDie(){
   ```

3. **Specify arguments with parentheses.**

   You can send *arguments* (special variables for your function to work with) by indicating them in the parentheses. This function doesn't need arguments, so I leave the parentheses empty:

   ```
   function rollDie(){
   ```

   For more information on functions, arguments, and the `return` statement, turn to Book IV, Chapter 4. Functions in PHP act almost exactly like their cousins in JavaScript.

4. **Begin the function definition with a left brace ({).**

   The left brace is used to indicate the beginning of the function code.

5. **Indent the code that makes up your function.**

   Use indentation to indicate which code is part of your function. In this case, the function generates the random number and prints an image tag based on that random number:

```
function rollDie(){
    $roll = rand(1,6);
    $image = "dado_$roll.png";
    print <<< HERE
        <img src = "$image"
            alt = "roll: $roll"
            height = "100px"
            width = "100px" />
HERE;
    } // end rollDie
```

6. **Denote the end of the function with a right brace (}).**

7. **Call the function by referring to it.**

   After the function is defined, you can use it in your code as if it were built into PHP. In this example, I call the function inside a loop:

```
for ($i = 0; $i < 5; $i++){
    rollDie();
} // end for loop
```

Because the code is defined in a function, it's a simple matter to run it as many times as I want. Functions also make your code easier to read because the details of rolling the dice are hidden in the function.

Naming functions and variables

It can be hard to come up with a good naming scheme for your variables and functions. Doing so is very important because when you come back to your program, if you haven't named your functions and variables consistently, you'll have a hard time understanding what you wrote. Here are two common naming schemes to make this simple: using underscores (_) between words or camel-casing.

Using underscores is as straightforward as separating_each_word_with_an_ underscore. It's readable, but it's ugly and can cause the variable names to get awfully lengthy.

The method I prefer and use throughout this book is *camel-casing*, where each new word after the first word gets capitalized just-LikeThis. It takes up less space than the underscore method and makes reading the code quicker — and after you get used to it, you won't even notice it anymore.

Tons of naming schemes are out there, and even if you don't use either of these, picking one and being consistent is important. Searching for *naming variables* in Google returns more than one million hits, so plenty of resources are available.

Managing variable scope

Two kinds of scope are in PHP: global and local.

If you define a variable outside a function, it has the potential to be used inside any function. If you define a variable inside a function, you can access it only from inside the function in which it was created. See Book IV, Chapter 4 for more on variable scope.

So, if you have a variable that you want to access and modify from within the function, you either need to pass it through the parentheses or access it with the global modifier.

The following code will print `hello world!` only once:

```php
<?php
$output = "<p>hello world!</p>";

function helloWorld(){
    global $output;

    print $output;
}

function helloWorld2(){
    print $output;
}

helloWorld();
helloWorld2();
?>
```

I left the `global` keyword off in the `helloWorld2()` function, so it didn't print at all because inside the function, the local variable $output is undefined. By putting the `global` keyword on in the `helloWorld()` function, I let it know I was referring to a global variable defined outside the function.

PHP defaults to local inside functions because it doesn't want you to accidentally access or overwrite other variables throughout the program. For more information about global and local scoping, check out `http://us3.php.net/manual/en/language.variables.scope.php`.

Returning data from functions

At the end of the function, you can tell the function to return one (and only one) thing. The `return` statement should be the last statement of your function. The `return` statement isn't required, but it can be handy.

The `getName()` function in the following code example will return `"World"` to be used by the program. The program will print it once and store the text in a variable to be printed multiple times later, as shown in the following code and Figure 5-2:

```html
<!DOCTYPE html>
<html lang="en">
<head>
```

```
  <meta charset="UTF-8">
  <title>helloFunction</title>
</head>
<body>
  <?php
    function getName(){
        return "World";
    }

    print "<h1>Hello, " . getName() . "!</h1>";
    $name = getName();
    print <<<HERE
    <p>$name, welcome to our site. We are so very happy to have you here.</p>
    <p>If you would like to contact us, $name, just use the form on the contact
    page.</p>
HERE;
  ?>
</body>
</html>
```

Figure 5-2:
An example
of a function
with a return
statement.

The example in Figure 5-2 is admittedly contrived. This function could easily be replaced by a variable, but the program that uses the function doesn't know that the function has only one line. Later on, I could make the function much more complicated (maybe pulling the name from a database or session variable). This points out a very important feature of functions that return values: they can feel like variables when you use them.

Managing Persistence with Session Variables

Server-side programming is very handy, but it has one major flaw. Every connection to the server is an entirely different transaction. Sometimes, you'll want to reuse a variable between several calls of the program. As an example, take a look at rollDice3.php in Figure 5-3.

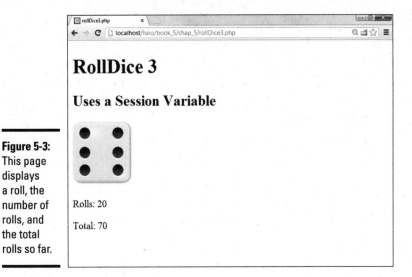

Figure 5-3:
This page
displays
a roll, the
number of
rolls, and
the total
rolls so far.

The interesting feature of rollDice3.php happens when you reload the page. Take a look at Figure 5-4. This is still rollDice3.php, after I refreshed the browser a few times. Take a look at the total. It increases with each roll.

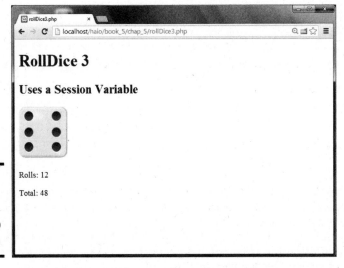

Figure 5-4:
The count
and total
values keep
on growing.

The rollDice3.php program is interesting because it defies normal server-side programming behavior. In a normal PHP program, every time you refresh the browser, the program starts over from scratch. Every variable starts out new.

Understanding session variables

The rollDice3.php program acts differently. It has a mechanism for keeping track of the total rolls and number of visits to the page.

When a visitor accesses your website, she's automatically assigned a unique session id. The session id is either stored in a cookie or in the URL. *Sessions* allow you to keep track of things for that specific user during her time on your site and during future visits if she's not cleared her cache or deleted her cookies.

Any mundane hacker can sniff out your session ids if you allow them to be stored in the URL. To keep this from happening, use the `session.use_only_cookies` directive in your PHP configuration file. This may be inconvenient to users who don't want you to have a cookie stored on their machine, but it's necessary if you're storing anything sensitive in their session.

Sessions are great because they are like a big box that the user carries around with him that you can just throw stuff into. Even if the user comes back to the site multiple times, the variables stored in the session retain their values. If you have hundreds of users accessing your site at the same time, each one will still have access to only their own versions of the variable.

In this example I have one program that is run several times, but you can also use sessions to pass data between programs. All programs coming from the same domain have access to the same session information for each user, so you can use sessions to manage data between programs in a larger system.

Here's the code for rollDice3.php:

```
{<?php
{  session_start();
{?>
{<!DOCTYPE html>
{<html lang = "en-US">

{  <head>
{    <meta charset = "UTF-8">
{    <title>rollDice3.php</title>
{  </head>
{  <body>
{    <h1>RollDice 3</h1>
{    <h2>Uses a Session Variable</h2>
{    <?php
{function init(){
{  global $count;
{  global $total;
{  //increment count if it exists
{  if (isset($_SESSION["count"])){
{    $count = $_SESSION["count"];
```

```
{     $count++;
{     $_SESSION["count"] = $count;
{   } else {
{     //if count doesn't exist, this is our first pass,
{     //so initialize both session variables
{     $_SESSION["count"] = 1;
{     $_SESSION["total"] = 0;
{     $count = 1;
{   } // end if
{} // end init
{function rollDie(){
{   global $total;
{   $roll = rand(1,6);
{   $image = "dado_$roll.png";
{   print <<< HERE
{     <img src = "$image"
{           alt = "roll: $roll"
{           height = "100px"
{           width = "100px" />
{HERE;
{   $total = $_SESSION["total"];
{   $total += $roll;
{   $_SESSION["total"] = $total;
{} // end rollDie
{init();
{rollDie();
{print "     <p>Rolls: $count</p> \n";
{print "     <p>Total: $total</p> \n";
{   ?>
{   </body>
{</html>
```

This program rolls a die, but it uses session variables to keep track of the number of rolls and total value rolled. The session variable is updated every time the same user (using the same browser) visits the site.

Adding session variables to your code

Here's how to incorporate sessions into your programs:

1. **Begin your code with a call to `session_start()`.**

   If you want to use session variables, your code must begin with a `session_start()` call, even before the DOCTYPE definition. I put a tiny `<?php ?>` block at the beginning of the program to enable sessions:

   ```
   <?php
     session_start();
   ?>
   ```

   The most common error with sessions is to not begin with `session_ start()`. Session variables use HTTP headers as part of the communication process, and any other code (even a blank line or innocent HTML code) before the `session_start` will cause the header to be sent without the session information. Every program that includes session variables must begin with a `session_start()` call.

2. **Check for the existence of the session variables.**

   Like form variables, session variables may or may not exist when the program is executed. If this is the first pass through the program, the session variables may not have been created yet. The init() function checks whether the count session variable exists. If so, it will increment the counter; if not, it will initialize the sessions. $_SESSION is a superglobal array (much like $_REQUEST).

   ```
   if (isset($_SESSION["count"])){
   ```

3. **Load session variables from the $_SESSION superglobal.**

   Create a local variable and extract the current value from the $_SESSION associative array:

   ```
   $count = $_SESSION["count"];
   ```

   Note that this line may trigger an error if you haven't already initialized the variable. Some PHP configurations are set up to automatically assign 0 to a nonexistent session variable, and some trigger an error.

4. **Increment the counter.**

   The $count variable is now an ordinary variable, so you can add a value to it in the ordinary way:

   ```
   $count++;
   ```

5. **Store the value back into the $_SESSION superglobal.**

   You can manipulate the local variable, but if you want to use the value the next time the program runs for this user, you need to store the value back into the session after you change it.

   For example, the following code loads the variable $count from the session, adds 1 to it, and stores it back into the session:

   ```
   $count = $_SESSION["count"];
   $count++;
   $_SESSION["count"] = $count;
   ```

6. **Initialize the session variables if they do not exist.**

   Sometimes you need access to a session variable, but that session doesn't already exist. Usually, this will happen on the first pass of a program meant to run multiple times. It will also happen if the user jumps straight into a program without going through the appropriate prior programs (say you have got a system with three PHP programs and the user uses a bookmark to jump straight to program 3 without going to program 1, which sets up the sessions). In these situations, you'll either want to pass an error message or quietly create new session variables. In my example, I simply create a new session if it doesn't already exist. It's an easy matter of assigning values to the $_SESSION superglobal:

```
//if count doesn't exist, this is our first pass,

//so initialize both session variables

$_SESSION["count"] = 1;

$_SESSION["total"] = 0;

$count = 1;
```

If you want to reset your sessions for testing purposes, you can write a quick program to set the variables to 0, or you can clear the history. On most browsers, clearing all history data will also clear cookies and session data, but you may need to check additional options to ensure sessions are cleared in your browser. Note that the session data itself isn't stored in the cookie. The cookie just contains a reference number so the server can look up the session data in a file stored on the server.

Sessions and security

The session mechanism is powerful and easy to use. It isn't quite foolproof, though. Sessions are automatically handled through a browser mechanism called *cookies*. Cookies aren't inherently good or evil, but they've gotten a bad reputation because some programs use them maliciously. You'll occasionally run across a user who's turned off cookies, but this is not a major problem because PHP can automatically use other options when cookies are not available. There's rarely a need to work with cookies directly in PHP because sessions are a higher-level abstraction of the cookie concept.

Like all data passed through the HTTP protocol, session and cookie information is passed entirely in the clear. A person with evil intent can capture your session information and use it to do bad things.

Generally, you should stay away from sensitive information (credit card data, Social Security numbers, and so on) unless you're extremely comfortable with security measures. If you must pass potentially sensitive data in your PHP program, investigate a technology called TLS (Transport Layer Security), which automatically encrypts all data transferred through your site. TLS replaces the older SSL technology and is available as a free plug-in to Apache servers.

Also, session data does not (yet) go through a filter like form input data. The `filter_input` command is scheduled to also allow `INPUT_SESSION` as an option, but it has not yet been implemented, so session data is manipulated through a superglobal with no filtering protection. For this reason, don't read session variable from an untrusted program. Only read session data stored by a program you wrote or understand.

Chapter 6: Working with Files and Directories

An important part of any programming language is file manipulations. Whether you need to create a comma-separated value (CSV) file or generate a dynamic list of files in a directory, or just need a semi-permanent place to log records on the server, file manipulation functions are an indispensable part of your PHP toolbox.

Text File Manipulation

Work with text files is split into two basic categories: writing and reading. Writing and reading come down to six basic functions. See the following bullet list for a brief explanation of the six basic file functions. Each function has an entire subsection in the following "Writing text to files" and "Reading from the file" sections:

+ `fopen()`: Stores a connection to a file you specify in a variable you specify

+ `fwrite()`: Writes text you specify to a file you specify

+ `fclose()`: Closes the connection to a file you specify that you created with `fopen()`

+ `fgets()`: Reads a line from a file you specify

+ `feof()`: Checks whether you have hit the end of a file you specify during a file read

+ `file()`: Puts the entire contents of a file you specify into an array

Writing text to files

This section details the functions needed to access and write to a file, such as how to request access to a file from PHP with the `fopen()` function, write to the file using the `fwrite()` function, and let PHP know you are done with the file with the `fclose()` function.

fopen()

To do any file manipulations, you must tell PHP about the file you would like to manipulate and tell PHP how you would like to manipulate that file.

The `fopen()` function has two required parameters that you must pass to it: the path to the file and the type of file manipulation you would like to perform (the *mode*).

The `fopen()` function returns a connection to the requested file if it's successful. (The connection is called a *pointer* — see the "Official file manipulation terminology" sidebar for more information.) If there is an error, the `fopen()` function returns `False`. Whatever the `fopen()` function returns (the connection or `False`), it should be assigned to a variable (a *stream*).

Here is an example of the `fopen()` function; see the section "Storing data in a CSV file" later in this chapter for an example of the `fopen()` function in action:

```
$fileConnection = fopen($theFile, $theMode);
```

In the preceding example, the file connection returned by the `fopen()` function is assigned to the variable `$fileConnection`. The variable `$theFile` would contain the path to a file; for example, both `C:\\xampp\\htdocs\\inc\\info.txt` and `/inc/log.txt` are valid file paths. The file must be in a place the server can access, meaning that you can put the file anywhere you could put a PHP page for the server to serve.

 Although possible, you probably shouldn't try to connect to a file in the My Documents folder or its equivalent on your operating system. You'll need the actual file path, which can be quite convoluted. It's also not necessary for the files you open to be in the `htdocs` directory. This could be useful if you want to access a file that will not be available except through your program. Use a relative reference if the file will be in the same directory as your program, or use an absolute reference if it will be somewhere else on your system. If you move your program to a remote server, you can only access files that reside on that server.

The variable `$theMode` would contain one of the values from the following list:

✦ `r`: Grants read-only access to the file

✦ `w`: Grants write access to the file

Be careful, though, because if you specify this mode (w) for the `fopen()` function and use the `fwrite()` function, you will completely overwrite anything that may have been in the file. Don't use w if there's anything in the file you want to keep.

✦ a: Grants the right to append text to the file. When you specify this mode for the `fopen()` function and use the `fwrite()` function, the `fwrite()` function appends whatever text you specify to the end of the existing file.

✦ r+ or w+: Grants read and write access to the file. I don't talk about r+ and w+ in this book, except to say that they're a special way of accessing the file, called *random access*. This allows you to simultaneously read and write to the file. If you require this type of access, you probably should be using something more simple and powerful, like relational databases.

fwrite ( )

After you open a file with the `fopen()` function and assign the file connection to a variable (see the "fopen( )" section, earlier in this chapter, for

---

Official file manipulation terminology

If you look at the documentation for `fopen()`, or any of the file manipulation functions, you will see some funny terminology. To keep things simple, I decided to use more recognizable, easily understandable terms. I wanted you to know that I switched things up a little bit to give you a quick primer to help you out if you did happen to look at the official documentation or talk to a more seasoned programmer who might use the official terms.

According to the official online PHP documentation, the `fopen()` function *returns a file pointer, and binds a named resource to a stream.*

What this means is that when you use the `fopen()` function, it opens a file (much like you would do if you opened the file in Notepad) and returns a pointer to that file.

It's as if you had put your mouse arrow at the beginning of the file and clicked there to create the little blinky-line cursor telling Notepad

where you are focusing (where you would like to begin editing the text). The pointer is PHP's focus on the file.

With the `fopen()` function, PHP's focus is *bound to a stream,* which means that it is attached to a variable. When you use the `fopen()` function, you associate the file with a variable of your choosing. This variable is how PHP keeps track of the location of the file and keeps track of where PHP's cursor is in the file. Normally, when you think of a stream, you might think of a one-way flow. But, in this case, the stream can either be read into the program character by character, line by line, or you can move the cursor around to any point in the file that you want. So, rather than being just a one-way flow, the stream is really an open connection to a file.

See `http://us.php.net/manual/en/function.fopen.php` for more detail on the `fopen()` function.

more information), you can use the file in your PHP code. You can either read from the file, or you can write to the file with the `fwrite()` function.

Depending on what mode you specify when you opened the file with the `fopen()` function, the `fwrite()` function either overwrites the entire contents of the file (if you used the `w` mode) or it appends the text you specify to the end of the file (if you used the `a` mode).

The `fwrite()` function has two required parameters you must pass to it: the connection to the file that was established by the `fopen()` function and the text you wish to write to the file. The `fwrite()` function returns the number of bytes written to the file on success and `False` on failure.

Here is an example of the `fwrite()` function (see the section "Storing data in a CSV file" later in this chapter for an example of the `fwrite()` function in action):

```
$writeResults = fwrite($fileConnection, $text);
```

The `fwrite()` function can also be written `fputs()`. `fwrite()` and `fputs()` both do the exact same thing. `fputs()` is just a different way of writing `fwrite()`. `fputs()` is referred to as an *alias* of `fwrite()`.

fclose ()

After you finish working with the file, closing the file connection is important.

To close the connection to a file you've been working with, you must pass the connection to the file you wish to close to the `fclose()` function. The `fclose()` function will return `True` if it is successful in closing the connection to the file and `False` if it is not successful in closing the connection to the file.

Here is an example of the `fclose()` function:

```
fclose($fileConnection);
```

Writing a basic text file

Often, you'll want to do something as simple as record information from a form into a text file. Figure 6-1 illustrates a simple program that responds to a form and passes the input to a text form.

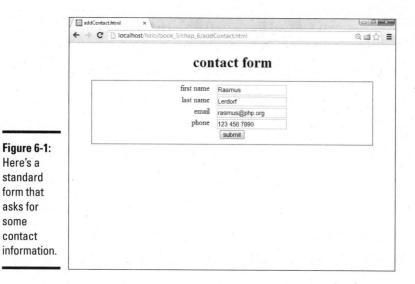

Figure 6-1:
Here's a
standard
form that
asks for
some
contact
information.

I didn't reproduce the code for this form here because it's basic HTML. Of
course, it's available on the book's companion website, and I encourage you
to look it over there. See this book's Introduction for more on the companion
website.

When the user enters contact data into this form, it will be passed to a program that reads the data, prints out a response, and stores the information
in a text file. The output of the program is shown in Figure 6-2.

I'm being attacked by robots!

The basic HTML form shown here is fine, but
you'll find that when you start putting forms on
the web, you'll eventually get attacked by robot
spam programs using your form to post (often
inappropriate) content through your form.

The best solution to this is a technique called
CAPTCHA, which is a mechanism for determining whether a form is submitted by a human or
a computer. When you fill out forms online and
have to type random words or letters from a
weird image, you're using a form of CAPTCHA.

You can implement a very simple form of
CAPTCHA by converting your form to a PHP
page. Create a simple math problem and store
the answer in a session variable. Ask the user
to solve the problem and submit the response
as part of the form. Have your program check
the user's answer against the session.

Although this will not prevent a concerted
attack, it is good enough for basic protection.

Figure 6-2:
This
program has
responded
to the file
input.

The more interesting behavior of the program is not visible to the user. The program opens a file for output and prints the contents of the form to the end of that file. Here are the contents of the data file after a few entries:

```
first: Andy
last: Harris
email: andy@aharrisbooks.net
phone: 111-1111

first: Bill
last: Gates
email: bill@Microsoft.com
phone: 222-2222

first: Steve
last: Jobs
email: steve@apple.com
phone: 333-3333

first: Linus
last: Torvalds
email: linus@linux.org
phone: 444-4444

first: Rasmus
last: Lerdorf
email: rasmus@php.org
phone: 123 456 7890
```

The program to handle this input is not complicated. It essentially grabs data from the form, opens up a data file for output, and appends that data to anything already in the file. Here's the code for addContact.php:

```
<!DOCTYPE html>
<html lang="en">
<head>
```

```html
<meta charset="UTF-8">
<title>addContact.html</title>
<link rel = "stylesheet"
type = "text/css"
href = "contact.css" />
</head>
<body>
<?php
//read data from form
$lName = filter_input(INPUT_POST, "lName");
$fName = filter_input(INPUT_POST, "fName");
$email = filter_input(INPUT_POST, "email");
$phone = filter_input(INPUT_POST, "phone");

//print form results to user
print <<< HERE
<h1>Thanks!</h1>
<p>
Your spam will be arriving shortly.
</p>
<p>
first name: $fName <br />
last name: $lName <br />
email: $email <br />
phone: $phone
</p>
HERE;

//generate output for text file
$output = <<< HERE
first: $fName
last: $lName
email: $email
phone: $phone

HERE;
//open file for output
$fp = fopen("contacts.txt", "a");
//write to the file
fwrite($fp, $output);
fclose($fp);
?>
</body>
</html>
```

The process is straightforward:

1. **Read data from the incoming form.**

    Just use the `filter_input` mechanism to read variables from the form.

2. **Report what you're doing.**

    Let users know that something happened. As a minimum, report the contents of the data and tell them that their data has been saved. This is important because the file manipulation will be invisible to the user.

3. **Create a variable for output.**

    In this simple example, I print nearly the same values to the text file that I reported to the user. The text file does not have HTML formatting because it's intended to be read with a plain text editor. (Of course, you could save HTML text, creating a basic HTML editor.)

4. **Open the file in append mode.**

   You might have hundreds of entries. Using *append mode* ensures that each entry goes at the end of the file, rather than overwriting the previous contents.

5. **Write the data to the file.**

   Using the `fwrite()` or `fputs()` function writes the data to the file.

6. **Close the file.**

   Don't forget to close the file with the `fclose()` function.

The file extension you use implies a lot about how the data is stored. If you store data in a file with an .txt extension, the user will assume it can be read by a plain text editor. The .dat extension implies some kind of formatted data, and .csv implies comma-separated values (explained later in this chapter). You can use any extension you want, but be aware you will confuse the user if you give a text file an extension like .pdf or .doc.

In this program, I joke about sending spam to the user, but of course I don't do it. If you really do want to send e-mails to people in a list, it's not difficult to do. Look up the `mail(to, subject, message)` function in the PHP documentation. Of course just because you *can* do something doesn't mean you *should.* If you send e-mails to folks without their permission, they will consider you a spammer, and often you can get kicked off of your server for this behavior. The ability to send e-mails with PHP has been heavily abused by spammers, so a number of servers have turned off this feature for the cheaper hosting plans.

A note about file permissions

Your programs will be loading and storing files, so you need to know a little about how this works. If you're using a Windows-based server, you will probably have no problems because Windows has a very simplistic file permission system. However, your program will probably be housed on a Unix-like system eventually, so you need to understand a bit about how file permission works on these systems. In the Unix/Linux world, each file has an owner, and that owner can designate who can do what with a file. Typically, if your program creates a file, it can write to it and read from it, but this isn't always the case. If you get a file-access error when testing these programs, it's likely that the operating system is confused about who the file's owner is and what can be done to the file. You should be able to change the ownership of a file and its permissions through the file management system of your server or your FTP client (see Book VIII for more about these tools). Begin by trying to set the permission of your data file to 777 (all permissions for all users). If you cannot do this, you may need to change ownership to yourself. Try right-clicking the filename in your tool and looking for a Properties dialog box for these options.

Reading from the file

If you can write data to a file, it would make sense that you could read from that file as well. The readContact.php program displayed in Figure 6-3 pulls the data saved in the previous program and displays it to the screen.

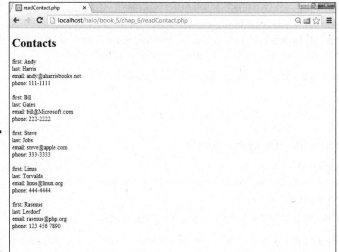

Figure 6-3:
This program reads the text file and displays it onscreen.

It is not difficult to write a program to read a text file. Here's the code:

```
<!DOCTYPE html>
<html lang="en"
<head>
 <meta charset="UTF-8"
 <title>readContact.php</title>
</head>
<body>
<h1>Contacts</h1>
<div>
 <?php
 //open up the contact file
 $fp = fopen("contacts.txt", "r") or die("error");
 //print a line at a time
 while (!feof($fp)){
 $line = fgets($fp);
 print "$line <br />";
 }

 //close the file
 fclose($fp);
 ?>
</div>
</body>
</html>
```

Why not just link to the file?

If this program just prints out the contents of a text file, you might wonder why it's necessary at all. After all, you could just supply a link to the text file. For this trivial example, that might be true, but the process of reading the file gives you many other options. For example, you might want to add improved CSS format-ting. You might also want to filter the contents: for example, only matching the lines that relate to a particular entry. Finally, you may want to do more than print the contents of a file — say, e-mail them or transfer them to another format. When you read the contents into memory, you can do anything to them.

The procedure is similar to writing the file, but it uses a `while` loop.

1. **Open the file in read mode.**

   Open the file just as you do when you write to it, but use the r designa-tor to open the file for read mode. Now you can use the `fgets()` func-tion on the file.

2. **Create a `while` loop for reading the data.**

   Typically, you'll read a file one line at a time. You'll create a `while` loop to control the action.

3. **Check for the end of the file with `feof()`.**

   You want the loop to continue as long as there are more lines in the file. The `feof()` function returns the value `true` if you are at the end of the file and `false` if there are more lines to read. You want to continue as long as `feof()` returns `false`. The exclamation point (`!`) operator is a logical not. The condition `!feof($fp)` is true when there is data left in the file and false when there are no lines left, so this is the appropriate condition to use here.

4. **Read the next line with the `fgets()` function.**

   This function reads the next line from the file and passes that line into a variable (in this case, `$line`).

5. **Print out the line.**

   With the contents of the current line in a variable, you can do whatever you want with it. In this case, I'll simply print it out, but you could format the contents, search for a particular value, or whatever else you want.

Using Delimited Data

This basic mechanism for storing data is great for small amounts of data, but it will quickly become unwieldy if you're working with a lot of information. If you're expecting hundreds or thousands of people to read your forms, you'll need a more organized way to store the data. You can see how to use relational databases for this type of task in Book VI, but for now, another compromise is fine for simpler data tasks. You can store data in a very basic text format that can be easily read by spreadsheets and databases. This has the advantage of imposing some structure on the data and is still very easy to manage.

The basic plan is to format the data in a way that it can be read back into variables. Generally, you store all of the data for one form on a single line, and you separate the values on that line with a *delimiter,* which is simply some character intended to separate data points. Spreadsheets have used this format for many years as a basic way to transport data. In the spreadsheet world, this type of file is called a CSV (for *comma-separated values*) file. However, the delimiter doesn't need to be a comma. It can be nearly any character. I typically use a tab character or the pipe symbol (|) because they are unlikely to appear in the data I'm trying to save and load.

Storing data in a CSV file

Here's how you store data in a CSV file:

1. **You can use the same HTML form.**

   The data is gathered in the same way regardless of the storage mechanism. I did make a new page called addContactCSV.html, but the only difference between this file and the addContact.html page is the `action` property. I have the two pages send the data to different PHP programs, but everything else is the same.

2. **Read the data as normal.**

   In your PHP program, you begin by pulling data from the previous form.

   ```
   $lName = filter_input(INPUT_POST, "lName");
   $fName = filter_input(INPUT_POST, "fName");
   $email = filter_input(INPUT_POST, "email");
   $phone = filter_input(INPUT_POST, "phone");
   ```

3. **Store all the data in a single tab-separated line.**

   Concatenate a large string containing all the data from the form. Place a delimiter (I used the tab symbol \t) between variables and a newline (\n) at the end.

   ```
   //generate output for text file
   $output = $fName . "\t";
   $output .= $lName . "\t";
   $output .= $email . "\t";
   $output .= $phone . "\n";
   ```

4. **Open a file in append mode.**

   This time, I name the file contacts.csv to help myself remember that the contact form is now stored in a CSV format.

5. **Write the data to the file.**

The `fwrite()` function does this job with ease.

6. **Close the file.**

This part (like most of the program) is identical to the earlier version of the code.

Here's the code for addContactCSV.php in its entirety:

```
<!DOCTYPE html>
<html lang="en">
<head>
  <meta charset="UTF-8">
  <title>addContactCSV.php</title>
  <link rel = "stylesheet"
        type = "text/css"
        href = "contact.css" />
</head>
<body>
  <?php
    //read data from form
    $lName = filter_input(INPUT_POST, "lName");
    $fName = filter_input(INPUT_POST, "fName");
    $email = filter_input(INPUT_POST, "email");
    $phone = filter_input(INPUT_POST, "phone");

    //print form results to user
    print <<< HERE
    <h1>Thanks!</h1>
    <p>
    Your spam will be arriving shortly.
    </p>
    <p>
    first name: $fName <br />
    last name: $lName <br />
    email: $email <br />
    phone: $phone
    </p>
HERE;
    //generate output for text file
    $output = $fName . "\t";
    $output .= $lName . "\t";
    $output .= $email . "\t";
    $output .= $phone . "\n";
    //open file for output
    $fp = fopen("contacts.csv", "a");
    //write to the file
    fwrite($fp, $output);
    fclose($fp);
  ?>
</body>
</html>
```

As you can see, this is not a terribly difficult way to store data.

Viewing CSV data directly

If you look at the resulting file in a plain text editor, it looks like Figure 6-4.

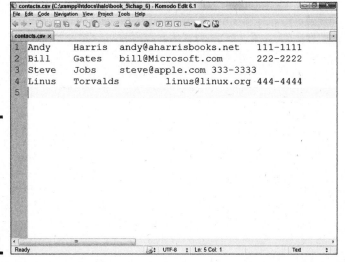

Figure 6-4:
The data is
separated
by tab
characters
and each
entry is on
its own line.

Of course, CSV data isn't meant to be read as plain text. On most operating systems, the .csv file extension is automatically linked to the default spreadsheet program. If you double-click the file, it will likely open in your spreadsheet, which will look something like Figure 6-5.

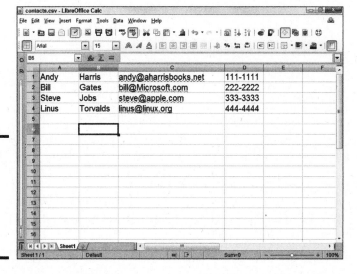

Figure 6-5:
Most
spread-
sheets
can read
CSV data
directly.

This is an easy way to store large amounts of data because you can use the spreadsheet to manipulate the data. Of course, relational databases (described in Book VI) are even better, but this is a very easy approach for relatively simple data sets. I've built many data entry systems by using this general approach.

Reading the CSV data in PHP

Of course, you may also want to read in the CSV data yourself. It's not too difficult to do. Look over the following code for readContactCSV.php:

```
<!DOCTYPE html>
<html lang="en">
<head>
 <meta charset="UTF-8">
 <title>readContactCSV.php</title>
</head>
<body>
 <h1>Contacts</h1>
 <div>
 <?php
 print <<< HERE
 <table border = "1">
 <tr>
 <th>First</th>
 <th>Last</th>
 <th>email</th>
 <th>phone</th>
 </tr>
HERE;
 $data = file("contacts.csv");
 foreach ($data as $line){
 $lineArray = explode("\t", $line);
 list($fName, $lName, $email, $phone) = $lineArray;
 print <<< HERE
 <tr>
 <td>$fName</td>
 <td>$lName</td>
 <td>$email</td>
 <td>$phone</td>
 </tr>
HERE;
 } // end foreach
 //print the bottom of the table
 print "</table> \n";
 ?>
 </div>
</body>
</html>
```

Figure 6-6 shows this program in action.

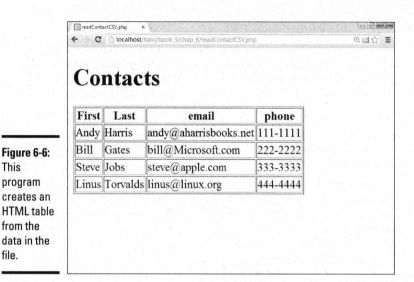

Figure 6-6:
This program creates an HTML table from the data in the file.

In this program, I read the contents of a CSV file and display it in an HTML table. It's not terribly different than reading any other text file, but there are some new twists.

1. **Print the table heading.**

   It's easiest to manually print out the table heading with the field names, because I know what they'll be. A simple heredoc will do the job.

   ```
   print <<< HERE
   <table border = "1">
    <tr>
    <th>First</th>
    <th>Last</th>
    <th>email</th>
    <th>phone</th>
    </tr>
   HERE;
   ```

2. **Load the data into an array.**

   PHP has a marvelous tool called `file`. This function takes a filename as its only input. It then opens that file and places all the contents in an array, placing each line in its own element of the array. There's no need to make a file pointer, or to open or close the file. In this example, I load all the contents of `contacts.csv` into an array called `$data`.

   ```
   $data = file("contacts.csv");
   ```

3. **Use a `foreach` loop to step through the contents.**

   Now I can walk through the contents of the file with a simple `foreach` loop. I place the current line in a variable called (wait for it . . .) `$line`.

   ```
   foreach ($data as $line){
   ```

4. **Explode each line into its own array.**

   You have got to love a function with a violent name, especially when it's really useful. Use the `explode` command to separate the line into its component parts. For this example, I break on the tab (`\t`) character because that's the delimiter I used when storing the file.

   ```
   $lineArray = explode("\t", $line);
   ```

5. **Use the `list()` function to store each element of the array into its own variable.**

   I could just use the array, but I think it's easier to pass the data back to the same variable names I used when creating the program. The `list()` construct does exactly that. Feed it a bunch of variable names and assign an array to it, and now each element of the array will be assigned to the corresponding variable.

   ```
   list($fName, $lName, $email, $phone) = $lineArray;
   ```

6. **Print the variables in an HTML table row.**

   All the variables fit well in an HTML table, so just print out the current row of the table.

   ```
   print <<< HERE
   <tr>
   <td>$fName</td>
   <td>$lName</td>
   <td>$email</td>
   <td>$phone</td>
   </tr>
   HERE;
   ```

7. **Clean up your playthings.**

   There's a little housekeeping to do. Finish the loop and close up the HTML table. There's no need to close the file because that was automatically done by the `file()` function.

   ```
   } // end foreach
   //print the bottom of the table
   print "</table> \n";
   ```

These shortcuts — the `file()` function and `list()` — make it very easy to work with CSV data. That's one reason this type of data is popular for basic data problems.

The `list()` construct works only on numerically indexed arrays and assumes that the array index begins at 0. If you want to use the `list()` function with associative arrays, surround the array variable with the `array_values()` function. Technically, `list()` is not a function but a language construct. (See `http://us3.php.net/list` for more information on the `list()` function.)

Escaping with HTML entities

If you're planning on displaying the user's input to the screen, escape all the special characters before saving the user's input to a file or sending it to the browser. Otherwise, some malicious user could use some simple CSS and HTML to really mess up your page. Remember: Paranoia is your friend. The simplest way to guard against this is to use the `htmlentities()` function:

```
$userInput = htmlentities($userInput);
```

This function converts any HTML characters the user may have entered into the character's HTML entities equivalent. That is, if the user entered `<div>`, it'd be converted to `&lt;div&gt;`. When you display it back to the page, instead of creating a new HTML `div`, the browser will simply output the literal string `<div>` to the user.

If, for some reason, you want to decode these entities, use the `html_entity_decode()` function. This works exactly like its `htmlentities()` counterpart, just in reverse.

The `file()` function is appealing, but it isn't perfect for every situation. It's great as long as the file size is relatively small, but if you try to load in a very large file, you will run into memory limitations. The "line at a time" approach used in readContact.php doesn't have this problem because there's only a small amount of data in memory at any given time.

HTML purists tend to freak out whenever they see an HTML table. It's true that HTML tables were once horribly abused as a layout technique, but that doesn't mean they should *never* be used. It's perfectly suitable to use a table tag to lay out tabular data, which is exactly what I'm doing in this program.

Working with File and Directory Functions

Sometimes, you may need PHP to work with files in a directory. Say you have a reporting tool for a client. Each week, you generate a new report for the client and place it in a directory. You don't want to have to alter the page each time you do this, so instead, make a page that automatically generates a list of all the report files for the client to select from. This is the kind of thing you can do with functions like `opendir()` and `readdir()`.

opendir ( )

Using the `opendir()` function, you can create a variable (technically speaking, this type of variable is called a *handle*) that allows you to work with a particular directory.

The `opendir()` function takes one parameter: the path to the directory you want to work with. The `opendir()` function returns a directory handle (kind of like a connection to the directory) on success and `False` on failure.

Here is an example of the opendir() function (see the "Generating the list of file links" section to see the opendir() function in action). This function stores a directory handle to the C:\xampp\htdocs\XFD\xfd5.7 directory in the $directoryHandle variable:

```
$directoryHandle = opendir("C:\xampp\htdocs\XFD\xfd5.7");
```

readdir ( )

After you open the directory with the opendir() function, you have a cursor pointed at the first file. At this point, you can read the filenames one by one with a while loop. To do this, use the readdir() function.

The readdir() function takes one parameter: the variable containing the directory handle created with the opendir() function. The readdir() function returns the name of a file currently being focused on by the cursor on success and False on failure.

Here is an example of the readdir() function. This function iterates through each file in the directory specified by $dp and assigns the filename of the current file to a new index in $fileArray array:

```
while($currentFile !== false){
 $currentFile = readDir($dp);
 $filesArray[] = $currentFile;
}
```

The actual readdir() function itself is readdir($dp). For more on the readdir() function, see the official PHP online documentation at http://us.php.net/function.readdir.

In some circumstances, the readdir() function might return non-Boolean values which evaluate to False, such as 0 or "". When testing the return value of the readdir() function, use === or !==, instead of == or !=, to accommodate these special cases.

chdir ( )

If you want to create a file in a directory other than the directory that the PHP page creating the file is in, you need to change directories. You change directories in PHP with the chdir() function.

If you want to be absolutely sure that you're in the right directory before writing the file, you can use an if statement with the getcwd() function. This is usually a bit of overkill, but it can be helpful.

The chdir() function takes one parameter: the path to the directory you wish to work with. The chdir() function returns True on success and False on failure.

Here is an example of the `chdir()`. This function changes to the `C:\`
`xampp\htdocs\XFD\xfd5.6` directory:

```
chdir("C:\xampp\htdocs\XFD\xfd5.6");
```

When you change to a directory, you're then free to write to it with the
`fwrite()` function. See the "fwrite( )" section, earlier in this chapter.

Generating the list of file links

Using the `opendir()` and `readdir()` functions, you can generate a list of
links to the files in a directory.

Take a look at the PHP code for the file links list example; see Figure 6-7 for
the HTML generated by this example:

```
<!DOCTYPE html>
<html lang="en">
<head>
 <meta charset="UTF-8">
 <title>fileList.php</title>
</head>
<body>
 <ul>
 <?php
 $dp = opendir(".");
 $currentFile = "";
 while($currentFile !== false){
 $currentFile = readDir($dp);
 $filesArray[] = $currentFile;
 } // end while
 //sort the array in alpha order
 sort($filesArray);
 //write the output
 $output = "";
 foreach($filesArray as $aFile){
 $output .= " <li><a href=\"$aFile\">$aFile</a></li> \n";
 } // end foreach
 print "$output";
 ?>
</ul>
</body>
</html>
```

Here's how the fileList.php program performs its magic:

1. **Open a directory pointer to the current directory.**

   In all major operating systems, the period (`.`) character indicates the
   current directory.

   ```
   $dp = opendir(".");
   ```

2. **Build a loop that repeats until there are no files left.**

   The special `!==` comparison is used to prevent rare problems, such as
   files named `false`. (Yes, believe it or not, that sometimes happens.)

   ```
   while($currentFile !== false){
   ```

Figure 6-7:
A list of links to all files in the directory specified by the opendir() function.

3. **Read the next file from the directory pointer.**

   The readDir() function reads the next file in and stores it to a variable ($currentFile).

   ```
   $currentFile = readDir($dp);
   ```

4. **Append the current file to an array.**

   If you simply assign a file to an array without an index, PHP places the element in the next available space.

   ```
   $filesArray[] = $currentFile;
   ```

5. **Sort the array.**

   The files won't be in any particular order in the array, so use the sort() function.

   ```
   sort($filesArray);
   ```

6. **Print each element of the array.**

   I use an unordered list of links to display each file. Make it a link so that the user can click the file to view it directly.

   ```
   foreach($filesArray as $aFile){
   $output .= " <li><a href=\"$aFile\">$aFile</a></li> \n";
   } // end foreach
   ```

On a Windows server, you have to escape the backslashes in the file path. You do this by adding a backslash before the backslashes in the file path. (For example, you would write C:\\xampp\\htdocs\\XFD\\xfd5.7\\ instead of C:\xampp\htdocs\XFD\xfd5.7\.) On a Unix server, you don't have to do this because file paths use slashes (/) instead of backslashes (\).

If you want just one particular file type, you can use regular expressions to filter the files. If I had wanted only the .txt and .dat files from the directory, I could have run the file's array through this filter to weed out the unwanted file types:

```
$filesArray = preg_grep("/txt$|dat$/", $filesArray);
```

For more on regular expressions, check Book IV, Chapter 5 as well as Chapter 4 of this book.

Chapter 7: Exceptions and Objects

In This Chapter

✔ **Introducing PHP objects**

✔ **Creating a constructor**

✔ **Adding properties and methods to objects**

✔ **Using access modifiers to protect data**

✔ **Building sub-classes with inheritance**

✔ **Trapping for errors with exception handling**

*P*HP has become a critically important part of web programming, and it has undergone a number of important transformations. As PHP becomes more mainstream, it is adopting a number of features from more traditional languages. Two of these important features are object-oriented programming (OOP) and exception handling. Objects are re-usable components that encapsulate data and functions (first mentioned in Book IV, Chapter 4). Exception handling is a mechanism used to detect and gracefully recover from errors. Both object-oriented programming and exception handling are important parts of modern data programming, which is the heart of most practical PHP coding.

Object-Oriented Programming in PHP

After you've written a few programs, you probably begin to notice a few patterns:

✦ **Programming is hard:** Writing code that does what you want is not easy.

✦ **Code should be re-used when possible:** After you get something working, you want to reuse that code as much as possible to avoid the pain of writing completely new code all the time.

✦ **Programs are about data and instructions:** Programs are about both data and the instructions needed to manipulate that data. Data are stored in variables and instructions are stored in functions.

✦ **Abstraction is a good thing:** Functions are great because they hide details and let you solve problems in a bigger way. An even higher level of abstraction (which collects both functions and data) might be even better.

These ideas occurred to computer scientists, too, and the result is a style of programming called *object-oriented programming (OOP)*. OOP was first described in Book IV, Chapter 4 as a feature of JavaScript. PHP also supports object-oriented programming, but does it in a slightly different way.

JavaScript and PHP both support object-oriented programming, but the details are very different. If you're comfortable with OOP in JavaScript, you should still look closely at the way PHP does things. The PHP mechanisms are actually very similar to those in C++, which is one of the most commonly used multi-purpose programming languages, so learning the PHP technique is a great idea. After you get past the differences in details, you'll see that the big ideas of OOP remain the same even when the language implementation changes.

The PHP mechanisms for OOP are important to learn because many of the advanced libraries you're likely to use are object-oriented, and because properly implemented OOP can tame complex programs in a big way.

Building a basic object

Start your experiments in OOP by looking over a simple PHP file:

```php
<?php
//SimpleCritter.php
//meant to be included

class Critter{
  public $name;

  public function __construct($name = "Anonymous"){
    $this->name = $name;
  } // end constructor

  public function sayHi(){
    return "Hi. My name is $this->name.";
  } // end sayHi method

} // end critter def
?>
```

This is an interesting PHP file because it doesn't follow the patterns you've seen before. This code isn't meant to be run directly, but to be reused by other code. Here are the highlights:

1. **No HTML needed here.**

   This file is pure PHP. It doesn't need any HTML at all because it will be called by another PHP program. Code reuse is the goal here, so this is code designed to be reused.

2. **Define a class.**

   Use the `class` keyword to define a class (that is, the recipe for making the object). In this example, I'm defining the `Critter` class. Note that class names are typically capitalized.

3. **Define a property.**

   If you define a variable inside a class, it becomes a *property*. Properties are much like variables, but they live inside a class. The keyword `public` indicates that the variable will be available to any code that wants it. (Not a great idea, as it turns out, but let's keep this first example simple. See the section Protecting your data with access modifiers to see the problems public properties can cause and how to resolve these problems.) Properties are the characteristics of an object.

4. **Define a method.**

   Skip ahead to the function `sayHi()`. For the most part, it looks just like any other function. But when a function is defined inside an object, it becomes a *method*. Methods are things the object can do. Most methods are declared public. Methods, like other functions, can have parameters and return values.

5. **Use `$this` to refer to the current object.**

   Within an object definition, the special keyword `$this` refers to the object currently being defined. The `$this` keyword is normally used to differentiate properties and methods from ordinary variables and functions.

6. **`$this->name` refers to the name property.**

   The special symbol `->` is a *dereference operator*. Really that's fancier than it sounds. It simply indicates that `name` is part of the object. (`$this->name` in PHP works pretty much like `this.name` in JavaScript.)

7. **Build a constructor.**

   In addition to ordinary methods, objects can have a special method called a *constructor*. In PHP, the constructor is called `__constructor` (with two preceding underscores). Constructors are special functions that are automatically called when a class is being instantiated. (That is, you're baking a cookie from the recipe.) Constructors are normally used to initialize all the properties and set up any housekeeping that might be necessary when a new instance of the class is being created. Traditionally, the constructor is listed as the first method in the class even if it isn't always written first.

8. **The constructor takes a parameter.**

   Like any function, a constructor can take one or more arguments. In this case, I want the option to name a critter as soon as it's built, so the constructor has a `$name` parameter.

9. **The parameter has a default argument.**

   If the user doesn't specify a parameter, the constructor will assign "Anonymous" as a default value.

10. **End the class definition.**

    The entire class definition goes inside a pair of squiggly braces, so don't forget to indent your code and comment on end quotes so it's clear what you're ending.

Using your brand-new class

What you did in simpleCritter.php was create the definition of a class. It's like writing a recipe. This file contains the instructions for building a class, but you'll generally use a class in a different project (or many — if your class is useful, you'll use it many times).

Take a look at useCritter.php shown in Figure 7-1. The screenshot doesn't look like much, but there are a lot of interesting things happening behind the scenes. Here's the code:

```
<!DOCTYPE html>
<html lang="en">
<head>
  <meta charset="UTF-8">
  <title>UseCritter</title>
</head>
<body>
  <?php

    require_once("simpleCritter.php");
    $a = new Critter("Jack");

    //referring to a property
    print "Name: $a->name <br />";

    print $a->sayHi();

  ?>
</body>
</html>
```

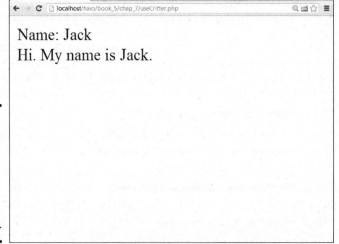

Figure 7-1:
This simple page is the result of some fancy object-oriented shenanigans.

If simpleCritter.php was about defining the class (writing a recipe), useCritter.php is about creating an *instance* (making cookies from the recipe). Here's how it works:

1. **Store useCritter.php and simpleCritter.php in the same directory.**

   You can use complicated directory structures if you want, but when you're getting started, keep things as simple as you can by keeping everything together. This program (useCritter.php) needs simpleCritter.php, so put them in the same place until you've got a good reason to do otherwise.

2. **Require simpleCritter.php file.**

   PHP has a number of tools that allow access to another file. The most commonly used of these functions is require_once(). This function will import an external file and is extremely handy for code reuse.

   ```
   require_once("simpleCritter.php");
   ```

   PHP has four different functions that all seem to do the same thing: include(), include_once(), require(), and require_once(). The differences are subtle, and not terribly important for a beginner, but you should still know what they are. If you use include() or include_once() and the file is not there, the program will keep on going anyway (but will probably crash because something you needed is not available). If you use one of the require functions and the file is not available, the program stops immediately.

   I use require() instead of include() because if I'm calling an external file and it's not there, I want to know right away. The once directive adds another security feature: if you've already required the file once, it won't be loaded into memory again. This seems silly unless you've done some C++ programming and you remember how awkward the mechanism for preventing multiple inclusions of the same file is. For now, stick with require_once(). It almost always serves your needs for file inclusion in PHP.

3. **Create an instance of your new class.**

   Make a variable (I called mine '$a') and use the new keyword to make this variable an instance of the Critter class. Because the Critter constructor takes a single string parameter, I pass a name to the Critter.

   ```
   $a = new Critter("Jack");
   ```

4. **Refer to properties as ordinary variables.**

   Any public properties of a class can be manipulated like ordinary variables, but use the full name ($a->name) to refer to the property. You can think of a property as a sub-variable inside a larger variable (the class). You can read from a property or write to it just like any other variable (although as you see in the next section, this is often discouraged in real life).

   ```
   //referring to a property
   print "Name: $a->name <br />";
   ```

5. **Call a method just like a function call.**

   Methods are very much like functions, except they are attached to a class instance. Call a method just like you would a function, but use the full name ($a->sayHi()).

   ```
   print $a->sayHi();
   ```

The object in this simple example is extremely simplistic, but the power of objects comes when you have a lot of them and they become more complex. Objects allow you to *encapsulate* the data and behavior of entities, which is a very powerful concept.

Protecting your data with access modifiers

The simpleCritter class defined in the previous section does the job, but it can be improved. As computer scientists began working with data, one of the biggest problems they encountered was *trustworthiness*. How can you be sure that the data in your program is what it's supposed to be? The best way to ensure good data is to have some sort of gatekeeping mechanism so that data cannot be changed without going through some sort of filter. Objects have exactly this sort of characteristic. Take a look at the improved Critter. php file:

```php
<?php
//Critter with access modifiers

class Critter{
  //now the property is protected
  protected $name;

  public function __construct($name = "Anonymous"){
    $this->name = $name;
  }

  public function setName($name){
    $this->name = $name;
  }

  public function getName(){
    return $this->name;
  }

  public function sayHi(){
    return "Hi. My name is $this->name.";
  }

} // end critter def
?>
```

This class definition is almost like the last one, but it has one key difference: the name property cannot be changed directly. Here's what the code does:

1. **Defines properties as `protected`.**

   There are three *access modifiers* you can use in PHP, which define the accessibility of a property or method. In the `SimpleCritter` class, you used `public` access throughout. The other modifiers you can use are `private` (which means this element is available only to the current class) and `protected` (for now, you can think of `private` and `protected` as the same). (I describe the difference in the section of this chapter called "How to inherit the wind (and anything else).")

2. **Adds a setter for each property.**

   When you've set a property to `private` or `protected`, you've indicated that element cannot be modified from the outside. However, there's a loophole. You can (and should) write your own methods to allow access to protected properties. A *setter* method is almost always named something like `setPropertyName()` and it takes a single argument. A setter then might check the property for validity, and then will pass it to the instance variable. In this simplistic example, I'll allow any string, but if I had (for example) an angle property that measures in degrees, I might want to check that the input was a numeric value between 0 and 360. A setter allows you to manage data input.

3. **Adds a getter for each property.**

   A *getter* method is almost always named something like `getProperty-Name()` and it doesn't take any arguments. Usually it simply returns the property value. Typically you'll have both a getter and a setter for each property.

Using access modifiers

When you've defined your objects with secure properties, all of the interactions with that object tend to be with methods. Here's an example:

```
<!doctype html>
<html lang="en">
<head>
  <meta charset="UTF-8">
  <title>Use Access Modifiers</title>
</head>
<body>
  <?php
  require_once("Critter.php");

  $a = new Critter("Nobody");
  //this line is no longer legal:
  // print $a->name;

  //Use the methods instead
  $a->setName("Brayden");
```

```
    print "Hi, " . $a->getName() . "! <br />";
    ?>

</body>
</html>
```

Figure 7-2 shows the (underwhelming) output of accessMod.php. A lot of times in programming the most important changes are not obvious to the user.

Figure 7-2: This critter is better-behaved than the last one.

This example is similar to the useCritter.php demonstration, but now I'm using the enhanced critter with protected data. Here are the differences:

1. **This example requires the enhanced Critter file.**

   I stored the protected version of `Critter` in a file called Critter.php so that's the file I require for this example.

2. **You can no longer manipulate the property directly.**

   Attempting to access the property directly (either reading from or writing to the property) will now result in an error.

3. **This example uses the access methods to interact with the property.**

   Use `setName()` to change the name and `getName()` to get the name.

Seriously? You want me to work harder so I can . . . work harder?

I hear you. The first object example (with public properties) was easy to understand and seems to work just fine. Then I suggest making it a little more complicated by protecting the properties, which makes you work a little harder by adding new methods, which makes you work a little harder yet by using those methods. It all seems unnecessary and a bit arbitrary, when the more basic object seems to be working fine.

However, protecting data members as I'm describing here is a really big deal, and it's worth doing (even though that isn't obvious in this very contrived example). Here's why:

✔ **It's hard to repair data errors:** Data errors are notoriously hard to fix after the fact. It's much better to have a mechanism to prevent these errors in the first place. That's what private properties are all about — preventing bad data.

✔ **Some data needs to fall within certain parameters:** Imagine you have some sort of class that needs an angle in degrees. You'll want this to be a numeric value between 0 and 360. With an ordinary variable or public property, there's no way to be certain the value is within the expected range. With

a setter method, you can guarantee that the value will be in the expected range.

✔ **Some "properties" aren't properties at all:** Think about a class that defines a circle. At first you probably think you'd want properties for radius, circumference, and area. However, what if you allowed the user to change all these things? Should we allow a circle with a radius of one and an area of one? (Answer: only if we're extremely close to a black hole and the laws of space and time are breaking down.) Typically, you'd only store the radius, but you supply `getCircumference()` and `getArea()` methods that will calculate these values based on the current radius. To the user, circumference and area are "read-only" properties because they can be read but not changed directly. If you wanted to allow the user to change the area, you could do so, but you'd really reverse-engineer the new radius and change that.

✔ **It's often the law:** Most software shops and computer science teachers are going to require you to protect your data whenever possible, so you might as well learn how to do so now.

You've Got Your Momma's Eyes: Inheritance

Object-oriented programming has another feature which makes it very useful for large projects. Many objects are related to each other, and you can use a family tree relationship to simplify your programming. Consider the following example, shown in Figure 7-3.

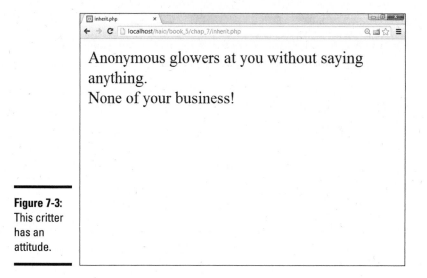

Figure 7-3:
This critter
has an
attitude.

Building a critter based on another critter

There's a new critter in town. This one has the same basic features, but a worse attitude. Take a look at the code to see what's going on:

```
<!doctype html>
<html lang="en">
<head>
  <meta charset="UTF-8">
  <title>inherit.php</title>
</head>
<body>
  <?php
    require_once("Critter.php");

    class BitterCritter extends Critter{

      //all properties and methods inherited from Critter

      //You can add new properties and methods
      public function glower(){
        return "$this->name glowers at you without saying anything.";
      } // end glower

      //if you over-write an existing method, the behavior changes
      public function talk(){
        return "None of your business!";
      } // end talk

    } // end class def

    $a = new BitterCritter();

    print $a->glower() . "<br />";
    print $a->talk() . "<br />";

  ?>
</body>
</html>
```

This example is an illustration of a very common programming situation, where I want a specialization of a previously defined class. I already have a `Critter` class, but I want a new kind of Critter. My new critter (the `BitterCritter`) begins with the same general characteristics of the ordinary critter, but brings a new twist. (I could also develop others — the `GlitterCritter`, `SpitterCritter`, and `HitterCritter` come to mind . . .) The object-oriented idea of *inheritance* is a perfect way to handle this situation.

If you followed the conversation about object-oriented programming in JavaScript, you might wonder why I didn't talk much about inheritance in Book IV. JavaScript supports a different form of object-oriented programming based on an idea called *prototyping* rather than inheritance. People have long and boring conversations about which technique is better, but ultimately it doesn't matter much. Most OOP languages support the form of inheritance used in PHP, so you should really know how it works.

How to inherit the wind (and anything else)

Here's how to implement inheritance:

1. **Begin with an existing class.**

   For this example, I begin with the ordinary `Critter` class, which I import with the `require_once()` function.

2. **Create your new class with the `extends` keyword.**

   As you define the class, if you use the `extends` keyword to indicate which class you are inheriting, your new class will begin with all the properties and methods of the parent class.

3. **You can access public and protected elements of the parent, but not private ones.**

   If a property or method was defined as private in the original class, it's truly nobody else's business. No other code fragments can access that element. Generally though, when you inherit from a class, the new child class should have access to the parent class's elements. That's why I typically create properties as *protected* rather than private.

4. **Add new properties and methods.**

   You can extend your new class with additional properties and methods that the parent did not have. The `BitterCritter` now features a `glower()` method that ordinary critters do not have.

5. **You can also overwrite parent behavior.**

   If you redefine a method that the parent class had, you are changing the behavior of the new class. This allows you to modify existing behaviors (a form of an object-oriented idea called *polymorphism*). In this example, I modify the `bitterCritter`'s talk method to be more bitter.

This demonstration is just the barest glimpse into object-oriented programming. There is much more to this form of software development than I can describe in this introductory chapter, but the basics are all here. Though you might not immediately see the need to build your own objects from scratch, you will definitely encounter object-oriented PHP code as you begin exploring more complex ideas like data programming and content management systems.

Catching Exceptions

Real-life programming is dangerous. Lots of things can go wrong. So the smart way to program data is *defensive programming*. This practice involves anticipating errors and trying to resolve them gracefully. PHP has some advanced error-handling techniques available which are perfect for the task.

Imagine you wrote some code that looked like this:

```
print 5 / 0;
```

I know you wouldn't do that, but sometimes bad code slips through. If your server is set up to pass out error messages, you'll see something like Figure 7-4.

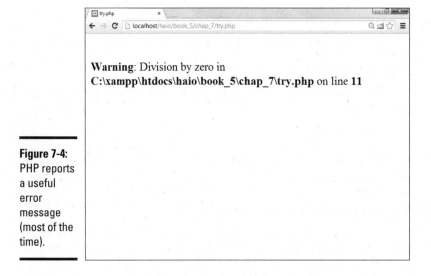

Figure 7-4:
PHP reports a useful error message (most of the time).

Introducing exception handling

There's actually a lot more going on in Figure 7-4 than you might appreciate at first. The default behavior of many PHP installations is to hide errors. (Denial: my favorite coping mechanism.) However, errors occur, especially if you allow user input. This code listing explicitly traps for errors and reports them regardless of server settings:

```
<!doctype html>
<html lang="en">
<head>
  <meta charset="UTF-8">
  <title>try.php</title>
</head>
<body>
  <p>
    <?php
    try {
      5 / 0;
    } catch (Exception $e){
      print $e->getMessage();
    } // end try

    ?>
  </p>
</body>
</html>
```

Here's what's happening:

1. **Use the `try` keyword to indicate potentially dangerous code.**

    The `try` keyword opens up a block of code (like a loop or condition). All the code between `try` and `catch` is considered potentially dangerous.

2. **Place dangerous code in the `try` block.**

    Any code that might cause errors should be placed inside the `try` block. In this (incredibly contrived) example, I put a line of code that would cause any self-respecting math teacher's head to explode. The most dangerous code usually involves things the programmer can't directly control: access to external files, operations on user-defined data, or exposure to external programs and processes.

3. **Use the `catch` clause to anticipate errors.**

    The `catch` clause indicates the end of the dangerous code.

4. **Indicate the exception type.**

    The parameter for the `catch` clause is an object of type `Exception`. PHP has a number of built-in exceptions, and often a library or toolset will include new exceptions (you can also build them yourself if you want). In this generic case, I call the stock `Exception`, which triggers on any kind of exception. (If you want, you can have multiple `catch` statements, each triggering on a different kind of exception.)

5. **Manage the exception.**

    The `catch` clause opens another block of code. Put the code in here that will resolve the problem (or at least die with a little style and grace — informing the user what went wrong before shuffling off this mortal coil).

The most common line here is to call `print($e->getMessage())`. All exception objects have a `getMessage()` method, and this line reports the current error message.

Knowing when to trap for exceptions

If your server is set up for debugging (as XAMPP is by default), it won't usually be necessary to set up exception handling because the default behavior of a debug setup is to report the exceptions anyway. There are a few times you'll still want explicit exception handling:

✦ **You're on a server without debug settings:** You may not have access to the server configuration, so you might not be able to turn on automatic exception reports. Manual exception reports (as done in this unit) still get through.

✦ **You want to do something special:** The automatic exception handler simply reports the problem. If you want to do something else (say, use a default file if a file is not found), you'll need a custom exception handler for that situation.

✦ **You're doing something exotic:** Special libraries (like the PDO library described in Book VI, Chapter 5) often come with their own custom exceptions, and you'll need an exception handler to cover these situations.

Part VI
Managing Data with MySQL

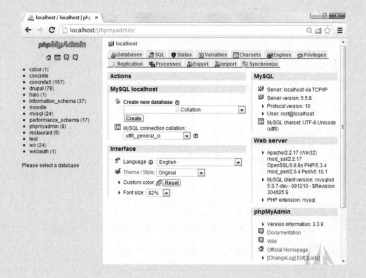

Contents at a Glance

Chapter 1: Getting Started with Data

In This Chapter

✔ Understanding databases, tables, records, and fields

✔ Introducing the relational data model

✔ Introducing a three-tier model

✔ Understanding MySQL data types

✔ Getting started with MySQL and phpMyAdmin

✔ Adding a password to your MySQL root account

✔ Creating new MySQL users

✔ Designing a simple table

✔ Adding data to the table

*M*ost programs and websites are really about data. Data drives the Internet, so you really need to understand how data works and how to manage it well if you want to build high-powered, modern websites.

The trend in web development is to have a bunch of specialized languages that work together. HTML describes page content, CSS manages visual layout, JavaScript adds client-side interactivity, and PHP adds server-side capabilities. You're probably not surprised when I tell you that yet another language, SQL (Structured Query Language), specializes in working with data.

In this minibook, you discover how to manage data. Specifically, you find out how to create databases, add data, create queries to retrieve data, and create complex data models to solve real-world problems. In this chapter, I show you some tools that automate the process of creating a data structure and adding data to it. In later chapters in this minibook, I show how to control the process directly through SQL and PHP code.

Examining the Basic Structure of Data

Data has been an important part of programming since computing began. Many languages have special features for working with data, but through the years, a few key ideas have evolved. A system called *relational data modeling* has become the primary method for data management, and a standard language for this model, called SQL (Structured Query Language), has been developed.

SQL has two major components:

✦ *Data Definition Language* (DDL) is a subset of SQL that helps you create and maintain databases. You use DDL to build your databases and add data to them.

✦ *Data Query Language* (DQL) is used to pull data out of a database after it's been placed there. Generally, your user input is converted to queries to get information from an existing database.

The easiest way to understand data is to simply look at some. The following table contains some basic contact information:

Name	Company	E-mail
Bill Gates	Microsoft	bill@msBob.com
Steve Jobs	Apple	steve@rememberNewton.com
Linus Torvalds	Linux Foundation	linus@gnuWho.org
Andy Harris	John Wiley & Sons	andy@aharrisBooks.net

Note: All these e-mail addresses are completely made up (except mine). Bill Gates hasn't given me his actual e-mail address. He doesn't answer my calls, either . . . (sniff).

It's very common to think of data in the form of tables. In fact, the fancy official database programmer name for this structure is *table*. *A* table (in database terms) is just a two-dimensional representation of data. Of course, some fancy computer-science words describe what's in a table:

✦ **Each row is a *record*.** A record describes a discrete entity. In this table, each record is a person in an e-mail directory.

✦ **A record is made of *fields*.** All the records in this table have three fields: name, company, and e-mail. Fields are a lot like variables in programming languages; they can have a type and a value. Sometimes, fields are also called *columns*.

✦ **A collection of records is a *table*.** All records in a table have the same field definitions but can have different values in the fields.

✦ **A bunch of tables makes a *database*.** Real-world data doesn't usually fit well in one table. Often, you'll make several different tables that work together to describe complex information. The database is an aggregate of a bunch of tables. Normally, you restrict access to a database through a user and password system.

Determining the fields in a record

If you want to create a database, you need to think about what entity you're describing and what fields that entity contains. In the table in the preceding section, I'm describing e-mail contacts. Each contact requires three pieces of information:

✦ **Name:** Gives the name of the contact, in 50 characters or less

✦ **Company:** Describes which company the contact is associated with, in 30 characters or less

✦ **E-mail:** Lists the e-mail address of the contact, in 50 characters or less

Whenever you define a record, begin by thinking about what the table represents and then think of the details associated with that entity. The topic of the table (the kind of thing the table represents) is the record. The fields are the details of that record.

Before you send me e-mails about my horrible data design, know that I'm deliberately simplifying this first example. Sure, it should have separate fields for first and last name, and it should also have a primary key. I talk about these items later in this minibook, as well as in the section "Defining a primary key," later in this chapter. If you know about these items already, you probably don't need to read this section. For the rest of you, you should start with a simple data model, and I promise to add all those goodies soon.

Introducing SQL data types

Each record contains a number of fields, which are much like variables in ordinary languages. Unlike scripting languages, such as JavaScript and PHP (which tend to be freewheeling about data types), databases are particular about the type of data that goes in a record.

Table 1-1 illustrates several key data types in MySQL (the variant of SQL used in this book).

Table 1-1	MySQL Data Types	
Data Type	*Description*	*Notes*
INT (INTEGER)	Positive or negative integer (no decimal point)	Ranges from about –2 billion to 2 billion. Use BIGINT for larger integers.
DOUBLE	Double-precision floating point	Holds decimal numbers in scientific notation. Use for extremely large or extremely small values.

(continued)

Table 1-1 *(continued)*

Data Type	Description	Notes
DATE	Date stored in YYYY-MM-DD format	Can be displayed in various formats.
TIME	Time stored in HH:MM:SS format	Can be displayed in various formats.
CHAR(*length*)	Fixed-length text	Always same length. Shorter text is padded with spaces. Longer text is truncated.
VARCHAR(*length*)	Variable-length text	Still fixed length, but trailing spaces are trimmed. Limit 256 characters.
TEXT	Longer text	Up to 64,000 (roughly) characters. Use LONGTEXT for more space.
BLOB	Binary data	Up to 64K of binary data. Use LONGBLOB for more space.

I list only the most commonly used data types in Table 1-1. These data types handle most situations, but check the documentation of your database package if you need some other type of data.

Specifying the length of a record

Data types are especially important when you're defining a database. Relational databases have an important structural rule: Each record in a table must take up the same amount of memory. This rule seems arbitrary, but it's actually very useful.

Imagine that you're looking up somebody's name in a phone book, but you're required to go one entry at a time. If you're looking for Aaron Adams, things will be pretty good, but what if you're looking for Zebulon Zoom? This sequential search would be really slow because you'd have to go all the way through the phone book to find Zebulon. Even knowing that Zeb was in record number 5,379 wouldn't help much because you don't know exactly when one record ends and another begins.

If your name is really Zebulon Zoom, you have a very cool name — a good sign in the open-source world, where names like Linus and Guido are really popular. I figure the only reason I'm not famous is my name is too boring. I'm thinking about switching to a dolphin name or something. (Hi, my name is "Andy Squeeeeeeek! Click Click Harris.")

Relational databases solve this problem by forcing each record to be the same length. Just for the sake of argument, imagine that every record takes exactly 100 bytes. You would then be able to figure out where each record is on the disk by multiplying the length of each record by the desired record's index. (Record 0 would be at byte 0, record 1 is at 100, record 342 is at 34200, and so on.) This mechanism allows the computer to keep track of where all the records are and jump immediately to a specific record, even if hundreds or thousands of records are in the system.

My description here is actually a major simplification of what's going on, but the foundation is correct. You should really investigate more sophisticated database and data structures classes or books if you want more information. It's pretty cool stuff.

The length of the record is important because the data types of a record's fields determine its size. *Numeric data* (integers and floating-point values) have a fixed size in the computer's memory. Strings (as used in other programming languages) typically have *dynamic length.* That is, the amount of memory used depends on the length of the text. In a database application, you rarely have dynamic length text. Instead, you generally determine the number of characters for each text field.

Defining a primary key

When you turn the contact data into an actual database, you generally add one more important field. Each table should have one field that acts as a *primary key.* A primary key is a special field that's

+ **Unique:** You can't have two records in a table with the same primary key.

+ **Guaranteed:** Every record in the table has a value in the primary key.

Primary key fields are often (though not always) integers because you can easily build a system for generating a new unique value. (Find the largest key in the current database and add one.)

In this book, each table has a primary key. They are usually numeric and are usually the first field in a record definition. I also end each key field with the letters ID to help me remember it's a primary key.

Primary keys are useful because they allow the database system to keep a Table of Contents for quick access to the table. When you build multitable data structures, you can see how you can use keys to link tables together.

Defining the table structure

When you want to build a table, you begin with a definition of the *structure* of the table. What are the field names? What is each field's type? If it's text, how many characters will you specify?

The definition for the e-mail contacts table may look like this:

Field Name	Type	Length (Bytes)
ContactID	INTEGER	11
Name	VARCHAR	50
Company	VARCHAR	30
E-mail	VARCHAR	50

Look over the table definition, and you'll notice some important ideas:

+ **There's now a `contactID` field.** This field serves as the primary key. It's an `INTEGER` field.

+ **`INTEGER`s are automatically assigned a length.** It isn't necessary to specify the size of an `INTEGER` field (as all `INTEGER`s are exactly 11 bytes long in MySQL).

+ **The text fields are all `VARCHAR`s.** This particular table consists of a lot of text. The text fields are all stored as `VARCHAR` types.

+ **Each `VARCHAR` has a specified length.** Figuring out the best length can be something of an art form. If you make the field too short, you aren't able to squeeze in all the data you want. If you make it too long, you waste space.

`VARCHAR` isn't quite variable length. The length is fixed, but extra spaces are added. Imagine that I had a `VARCHAR(10)` field called `userName`. If I enter the name `'Andy'`, the field contains `'Andy'` (that is, `'Andy'` followed by six spaces). If I enter the value `'Rumplestiltskin'`, the field contains the value `'Rumplestil'` (the first 10 characters of `'Rumplestiltskin'`).

The difference between `CHAR` and `VARCHAR` is what happens to shorter words. When you return the value of a `CHAR` field, all the padding spaces are included. A `VARCHAR` automatically lops off any trailing spaces.

In practice, programmers rarely use `CHAR` because `VARCHAR` provides the behavior you almost always want.

Introducing MySQL

Programs that work with SQL are usually called relational database management systems (RDBMS). A number of popular RDBMSs are available:

+ **Oracle** is the big player. Many high-end commercial applications use the advanced features of Oracle. It's powerful, but the price tag makes it primarily useful for large organizations.

+ **MS SQL Server** is Microsoft's entry in the high-end database market. It's usually featured in Microsoft-based systems integrated with .NET programming languages and the Microsoft IIS server. It can also be quite expensive.

✦ **MS Access** is the entry-level database system installed with most versions of Microsoft Office. Although Access is a good tool for playing with data design, it has some well-documented problems handling the large number of requests typical of a web-based data tool.

✦ **MySQL** is an open-source database that has made a big splash in the open-source world. While it's not quite as robust as Oracle or SQL Server, it's getting closer all the time. The latest version has features and capabilities that once belonged only to expensive proprietary systems.

✦ **SQLite** is another open-source database that's really showing some promise. This program is very small and fast, so it works well in places you wouldn't expect to see a full-fledged database (think cellphones and tablets).

The great news is that almost all of these databases work in the same general way. They all read fairly similar dialects of the SQL language. No matter which database you choose, the basic operation is roughly the same.

Why use MySQL?

This book focuses on MySQL because this program is

✦ **Very accessible:** If you've already installed XAMPP (see Book VIII), you already have access to MySQL. Many hosting accounts also have MySQL access built in.

✦ **Easy to use:** You can use MySQL from the command line or from a special program. Most people manipulate SQL through a program called phpMyAdmin (introduced in the section "Setting Up phpMyAdmin," later in this chapter). This program provides a graphical interface to do most of the critical tasks.

✦ **Reasonably typical:** MySQL supports all the basic SQL features and a few enhancements. If you understand MySQL, you'll be able to switch to another RDBMS pretty easily.

✦ **Very powerful:** MySQL is powerful enough to handle typical web server data processing for a small to mid-size company. Some extremely large corporations even use it.

✦ **Integrated with XAMPP and PHP:** PHP has built-in support for MySQL, so you can easily write PHP programs that work with MySQL databases.

✦ **Free and open source:** MySQL is available at no cost, which makes it quite an attractive alternative. MySQL offers other advantages of open-source software. Because the code is freely available, you can learn exactly how it works. The open-source nature of the tool also means there are likely to be add-ons or variations because it's easy for developers to modify open-source tools.

Understanding the three-tier architecture

Modern web programming often uses what's called the *three-tiered architecture,* as shown in Table 1-2.

Table 1-2		**The Three-Tiered Architecture**	
Tier	*Platform (software)*	*Content*	*Language*
Client	Web browser (Chrome)	Web page	HTML/CSS/JS
Server	Web server (Apache)	Business rules and logic	PHP (or other similar language)
Data	Data server (MySQL)	Data content	SQL (through MySQL or another data server)

The user talks to the system through a web browser, which manages HTML code. CSS and JavaScript may also be at the user tier, but everything is handled through the browser. The user then makes a request of the server, which is sometimes passed through a server-side language like PHP. This program then receives a request and processes it, returning HTML back to the client. Many requests involve data, which brings the third (data) tier into play. The web server can package up a request to the data server through SQL. The data server manages the data and prepares a response to the web server, which then makes HTML output back for the user.

Figure 1-1 provides an overview of the three-tier system.

Practicing with MySQL

MySQL is a server, so it must be installed on a computer in order to work. To practice with MySQL, you have a few options:

+ **Run your own copy of MySQL from the command line.** If you have MySQL installed on your own machine, you can go to the command line and execute the program directly. This task isn't difficult, but it is tedious.

+ **Use phpMyAdmin to interact with your own copy of MySQL.** This solution is often the best. phpMyAdmin is a set of PHP programs that allows you to access and manipulate your database through your web browser. If you've set up XAMPP, you've got everything you need. (See Book VIII for more information about XAMPP.) You can also install MySQL and phpMyAdmin

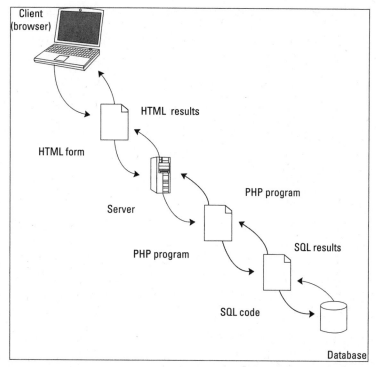

Figure 1-1:
An overview
of the three-
tier data
model.

without XAMPP, but you should really avoid the headaches of manual configuration, if you can. In this chapter, I do all MySQL through phpMyAdmin,
but I show other alternatives in Chapters 2 and 5 of this minibook.

✦ **Run MySQL from your hosting site.** If you're using Freehostia or some
other hosting service, you generally access MySQL through phpMyAdmin.

Setting Up phpMyAdmin

By far the most common way to interact with MySQL is through phpMy-
Admin. If you've installed XAMPP, you already have phpMyAdmin. Here's
how you use it to get to MySQL:

1. **Turn on MySQL with the XAMPP Control Panel, shown in Figure 1-2.**

    You also need Apache running (because XAMPP runs through the
    server). You don't need to run MySQL or Apache as a service, but you
    must have them both running. (Turn on both programs by clicking the
    start button next to the name of the program.)

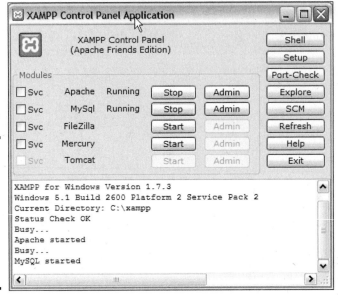

Figure 1-2:
I've turned
on Apache
and MySQL
in the
XAMPP
control
panel using
the buttons.

2. **Go to the XAMPP main directory in your browser.**

   If you used the default installation, you can just point your browser to
   `http://localhost/xampp`. It should look like Figure 1-3.

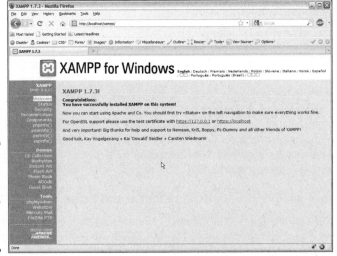

Figure 1-3:
Locating
the XAMPP
subdirectory
through
localhost.

Don't just go through the regular file system to find the XAMPP directory. You must use the `localhost` mechanism so that the PHP code in
phpMyAdmin is activated.

3. **Find phpMyAdmin in the Tools section of the menu.**

   The phpMyAdmin page looks like Figure 1-4.

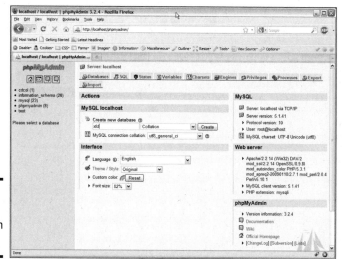

**Book VI
Chapter 1**

Getting Started with Data

Figure 1-4:
The phpMyAdmin main page.

4. **Create a new database.**

   Type the name for your database in the indicated text field. I call my database `haio`. (*HTML All in One* — get it?)

Changing the root password

MySQL is a powerful system, which means it can cause a lot of damage in the wrong hands. Unfortunately, the default installation of MySQL has a security loophole you could drive an aircraft carrier through. The default user is called root and has no password whatsoever. Although you don't have to worry about any pesky passwords, the KGB can also get to your data without passwords.

This section is a bit technical, and it's pretty important if you're running your own data server with XAMPP. But if you're using an online hosting service, you won't have to worry about the data security problems described in this section. You can skip on to the section called "Using phpMyAdmin on a remote server." Still, you'll eventually need this stuff, so don't tear these pages out of the book or anything.

Believe me, the bad guys know that root is the most powerful account on MySQL and that it has no password by default. They're glad to use that information to do you harm (or worse, to do harm in your name). Obviously, giving the root account a password is a very good idea. Fortunately, it's not difficult to do:

1. **Log into phpMyAdmin as normal.**

   The main screen looks like Figure 1-5. Your copy might have a scary warning of gloom at the bottom. You're about to fix that problem.

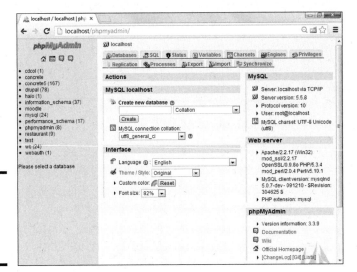

Figure 1-5:
Here's the main phpMyAdmin screen.

2. **Click the Privileges link to modify user privileges.**

   The privileges tab along the top gives you access to change user privileges. The new screen looks something like Figure 1-6.

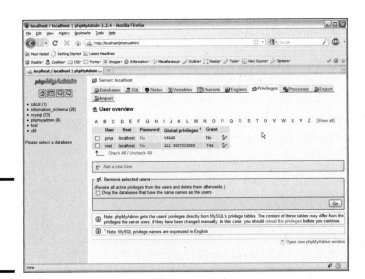

Figure 1-6:
The various users are stored in a table.

3. **Edit the root user.**

   Chances are good that you have only one user, called root (and maybe another called pma which is the phpMyAdmin user). The root account's `Password` field says `No`. You'll be adding a password to the root user. The icon at the right allows you to edit this record. (Hover your mouse over the small icon to see ToolTips if you can't find it.) The edit screen looks like Figure 1-7.

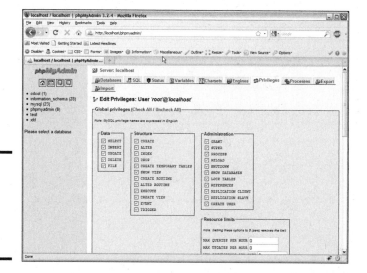

Figure 1-7:
You can use
this tool to
modify the
root user's
permissions.

4. **Examine the awesome power of the root administrator.**

   Even if you don't know what all these things are, root can clearly do lots of things, and you shouldn't let this power go unchecked. (Consult any James Bond movie for more information on what happens with unfettered power.) You're still going to let root do all these things, but you're going to set a password so that only you can be root on this system. Scroll down a bit on the page until you see the segment that looks like Figure 1-8.

5. **Assign a password.**

   Simply enter the password in the Password box, and then reenter it in the next box. Be sure that you type the same password twice. Follow all your typical password rules (six or more characters long, no spaces, case-sensitive).

6. **Hit the Go button.**

   If all went well, the password changes.

7. **Recoil in horror.**

   Try to go back to the phpMyAdmin home (with the little house icon), and something awful happens, as shown in Figure 1-9.

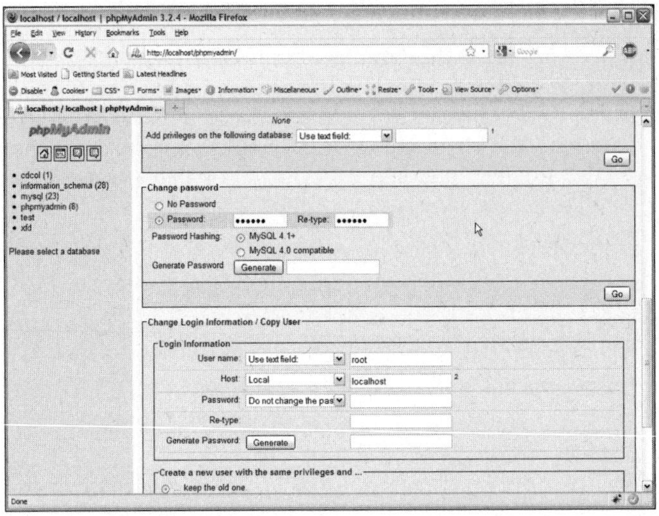

Figure 1-8:
This area
is where
you add the
password.

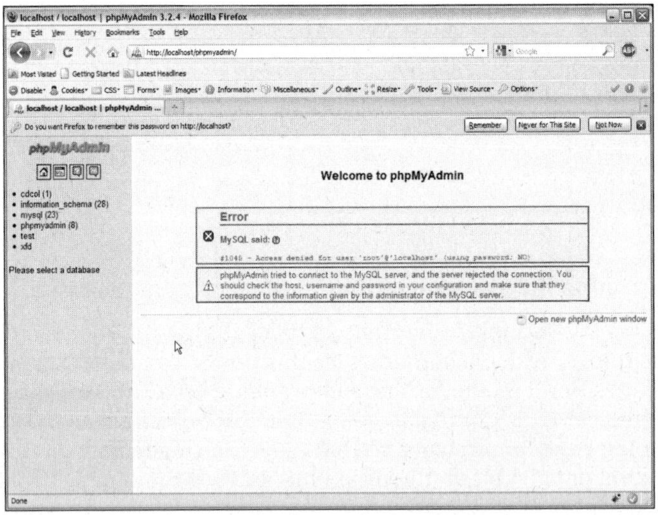

Figure 1-9:
That
message
can't be
good.
Maybe
I should
have left it
vulnerable.

Don't panic about the error in Figure 1-9. Believe it or not, this error is good. Up to now, phpMyAdmin was logging into your database as root without a password (just like the baddies were going to do). Now, phpMyAdmin is trying to do the same thing (log in as root without a password), but it can't because now root has a password.

What you have to do is tell phpMyAdmin that you just locked the door, and give it the key. (Well, the password, but I was enjoying my metaphor.)

1. **Find the phpMyAdmin configuration file.**

   You have to let phpMyAdmin know that you've changed the password. Look for a file in your phpMyAdmin directory called `config.inc.php`. (If you used the default XAMPP installation under Windows, the file is in `C:\Program Files\xampp\phpMyAdmin\config.inc.php`.)

2. **Find the root password setting.**

   Using the text editor's search function, I found it on line 70, but it may be someplace else in your editor. In Notepad++, it looks like Figure 1-10.

Book VI
Chapter 1

Getting Started
with Data

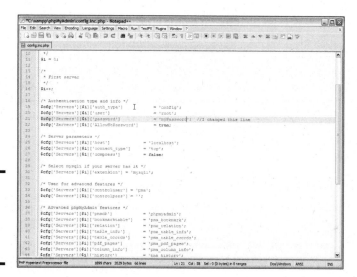

Figure 1-10: Here's the username and configuration information.

3. **Change the root setting to reflect your password.**

   Enter your root password. For example, if your new password is myPassword, change the line so that it looks like

   ```
   $cfg['Servers'][$i]['password']       = 'myPassword';   // MySQL password
   ```

   Of course, myPassword is just an example. It's really a bad password. Put your actual password in its place.

4. **Save the config.inc.php file.**

   Save the configuration file and return to phpMyAdmin. You may need to set the file's permissions to 644 if you're on a Mac or Linux machine.

5. **Try getting into phpMyAdmin again.**

   This time, you don't get the error, and nobody is able to get into your database without your password. You shouldn't have to worry about this issue again, but whenever you connect to this database, you do need to supply the username and password.

Adding a user

Changing the root password is the absolute minimum security measure, but it's not the only one. You can add various virtual users to your system to protect it further.

You're able to log into your own copy of MySQL (and phpMyAdmin) as root because you're the root owner. (If not, then refer to the preceding section.) It's your database, so you should be allowed to do anything with it.

You probably don't want your programs logging in as root because that can allow malicious code to sneak into your system and do mischief. You're better off setting up a different user for each database and allowing that user access only to the tables within that database.

I'm really not kidding about the danger here. A user with root access can get into your database and do anything, including creating more users or changing the root password so that you can no longer get into your own database! You generally shouldn't write any PHP programs that use root. Instead, have a special user for that database. If the bad guys get in as anything but root, they can't blow up everything.

Fortunately, creating new users with phpMyAdmin isn't a difficult procedure:

1. **Log into phpMyAdmin with root access.**

   If you're running XAMPP on your own server, you'll automatically log in as root.

2. **Activate the Privileges tab to view user privileges.**

3. **Add a new user using the Add a New User link on the Privileges page.**

4. **Fill in user information on the new user page (see Figure 1-11).**

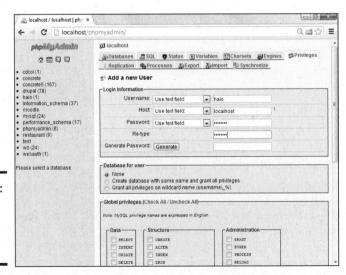

Figure 1-11:
Here's the new haio user being created.

Be sure to add a username and password. Typically, you use `localhost` as the host.

5. **Create a database, if it doesn't already exist.**

   If you haven't already made a database for this project, you can do so automatically with the Create Database Automatically radio button.

6. **Do not assign global privileges.**

   Only the root user should have global privileges. You want this user to have the ability to work only within a specific database.

7. **Create the user by clicking the Go button.**

   You see a new screen like Figure 1-12 (you need to scroll down a bit to see this part of the page).

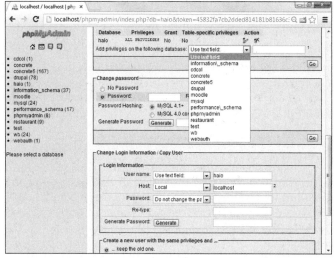

Figure 1-12:
You can specify a specific database for this user.

8. **Specify the user's database.**

   Select the database in the drop-down list. This user (`haio`) will have access only to tables in the `haio` database. Note that you probably don't have many databases on your system when you start out.

9. **Apply most privileges.**

   You generally want your programs to do nearly everything within their own database so that you can apply almost all privileges (for now, anyway). I typically select all privileges except Grant, which lets the user allow access to other users. Figure 1-13 shows the Privileges page.

As you're starting out, your programs have access to one database and are able to do plenty with it. As your data gets more critical, you'll probably want to create more restrictive user accounts so that those programs that should only be reading your data don't have the ability to modify or delete records. This change makes it more difficult for the bad guys to mess up your day.

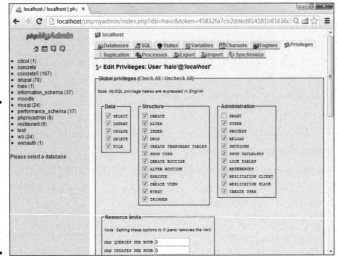

Figure 1-13:
The haio
user can do
everything
but grant
other
privileges
on this
database.

Your database users won't usually be people. This idea is hard, particularly if you haven't used PHP or another server-side language yet. The database users are usually programs you have written that access the database in your name.

Using phpMyAdmin on a remote server

If you're working on some remote system with your service provider, the mechanism for managing and creating your databases may be a bit different. Each host has its own quirks, but they're all pretty similar. As an example, here's how I connect to the system on Freehostia at `http://freehostia.com` (where I post the example pages for this book):

1. **Log onto your service provider using the server login.**

   You usually see some sort of control panel with the various tools you have as an administrator. These tools often look like Figure 1-14.

2. **Locate your database settings.**

   Not all free hosting services provide database access, but most do have free MySQL access. You usually can access some sort of tool for managing your databases. (You'll probably have a limited number of databases available on free servers, but more with commercial accounts.) Figure 1-15 shows the database administration tool in Free Hostia.

3. **Create a database according to the rules enforced by your system.**

   Sometimes, you can create the database within phpMyAdmin (as I did in the last section), but more often, you need to use a special tool like the one shown in Figure 1-15 to create your databases. Free Hostia imposes a couple of limits: The database name begins with the system username, and it can't be more than 16 characters long.

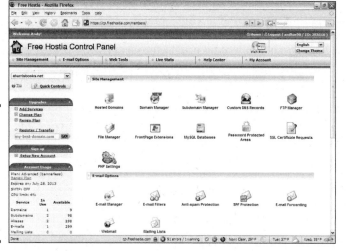

Figure 1-14:
The Free
Hostia site
shows a
number
of useful
adminis-
tration tools.

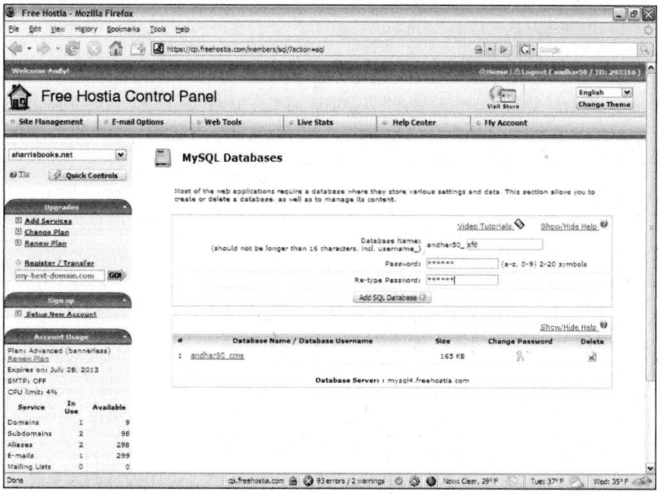

Figure 1-15:
The
database
adminis-
tration tool
lets me
create or edit
databases.

Don't freak out if your screen looks a little different than Figure 1-15.
Different hosting companies have slightly different rules and systems, so
things won't be just like this, but they'll probably be similar. If you get stuck,
be sure to look at the hosting service's Help system. You can also contact
the support system. They're usually glad to help, but they're (understand-
ably) much more helpful if you've paid for the hosting service. Even the free
hosting systems offer some online support, but if you're going to be serious,
paying for online support is a good deal.

4. Create a password for this database.

You probably need a password (and sometimes another username) for
your databases to prevent unauthorized access to your data. Because
the database is a different server than the web server, it has its own

security system. On many hosting services, you must enter a password, and the system automatically creates a MySQL username with the same name as the database. Keep track of this information because you need it later when you write a program to work with this data.

5. **Use phpMyAdmin to add tables to your database.**

    After you've defined the database, you can usually use phpMyAdmin to manipulate the data. With Free Hostia, you can simply click a database name to log into phpMyAdmin as the administrator of that database. Figure 1-16 shows the new database in phpMyAdmin, ready for action.

Figure 1-16:
Now I can access the database in phpMy-Admin.

Typically, a remote server doesn't give you root access, so you don't have to mess around with the whole root password mess described in the "Changing the root password" section of this chapter. Instead, you often either have one password you always use in phpMyAdmin or you have a different user and password for each database.

Implementing a Database with phpMyAdmin

When you've got a database, you can build a table. When you've defined a table, you can add data. When you've got data, you can look at it. Begin by building a table to handle the contact data described in the first section of this chapter, "Examining the Basic Structure of Data":

1. **Be sure you're logged into phpMyAdmin.**

    The phpMyAdmin page should look something like Figure 1-17, with your database name available in the left column.

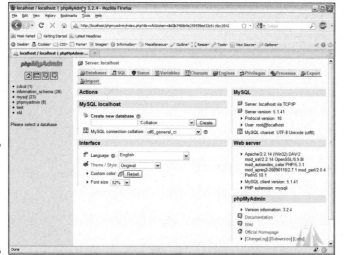

Figure 1-17:
The main
screen of
the phpMy-
Admin
system.

2. **Activate the database by clicking the database name in the left
   column.**

   If the database is empty, an Add Table page, shown in Figure 1-18,
   appears.

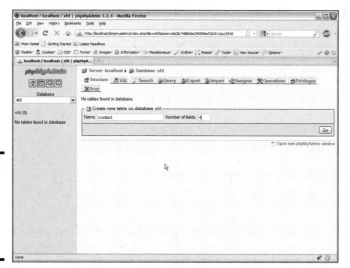

Figure 1-18:
Type a
table name
to begin
adding a
table.

3. **Create a new table using the phpMyAdmin tool.**

   Now that you have a database, add the contacts table to it. The contacts
   database has four fields, so type a **4** into the box and let 'er rip. A form
   like Figure 1-19 appears.

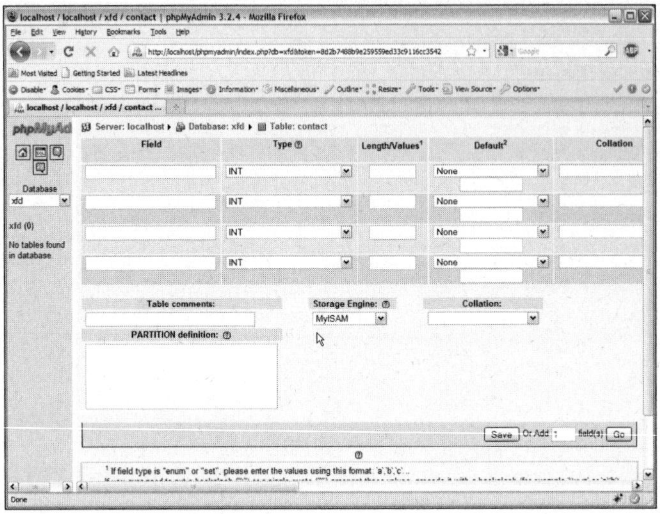

Figure 1-19:
Creating the contacts table.

4. **Enter the field information.**

   Type the field names into the grid to create the table. It should look like Figure 1-20.

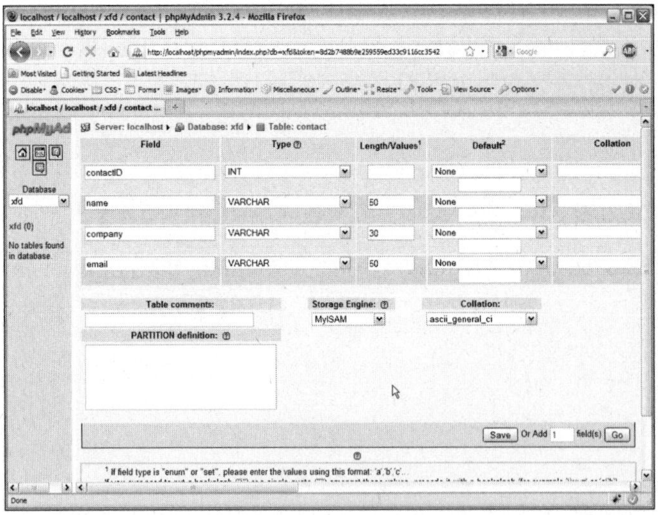

Figure 1-20:
Enter field data on this form.

In Figure 1-20, you can't see it, but you can select the index of contactID as a primary key. Be sure to add this indicator. Also set the collation of the entire table to `ascii_general_ci`.

5. **Click the Save button and watch the results.**

   phpMyAdmin automatically writes some SQL code for you and executes it. Figure 1-21 shows the code and the new table.

Figure 1-21: phpMy-Admin created this mysterious code and built a table.

Now, the left panel indicates that you're in the xfd database, which has a table called Contact.

After you define a table, you can add data. Click Contact in the left column, and you see the screen for managing the contact table, as shown in Figure 1-22.

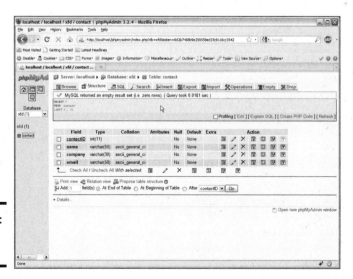

Figure 1-22: I've added the fields.

You can add data with the Insert tab, which gives a form like Figure 1-23, based on your table design.

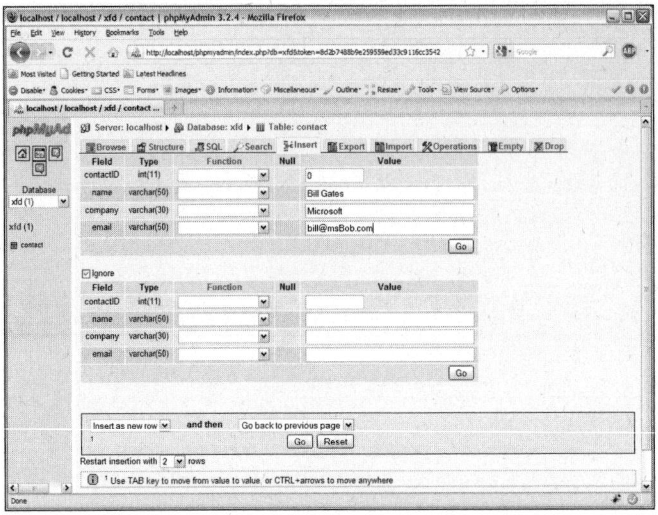

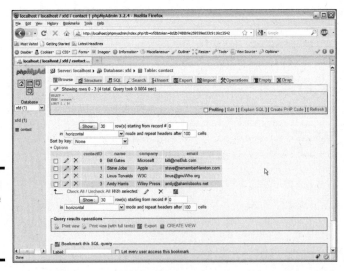

Figure 1-23:
Adding a
record to
the table.

After you add the record, choose Insert Another Row and click the Go button.
Repeat until you've added all the contacts you want in your database.

After you add all the records you want to the database, you can use the
Browse tab to see all the data in the table. Figure 1-24 shows my table after I
added all my contacts to it and browsed.

Figure 1-24:
Viewing the
table data
in phpMy-
Admin.

Chapter 2: Managing Data with MySQL

*A*lthough we tend to think of the Internet as a series of interconnected documents, the web is increasingly about data. The HTML and CSS languages are still used to manage web documents, but SQL (Structured Query Language) — the language of data — is becoming increasingly central. In this chapter, you discover how SQL is used to define a data structure, add data to a database, and modify that data.

Writing SQL Code by Hand

Although you can use phpMyAdmin to build databases, all it really does is write and execute SQL code for you. You should know how to write SQL code yourself for many reasons:

✦ **It's pretty easy.** SQL isn't terribly difficult (at least, to begin with — things do get involved later). Once you know how, I find writing the code in SQL is faster and easier than creating the databases in phpMyAdmin.

✦ **You need to write code in your programs.** You probably run your database from within PHP programs. You need to be able to write SQL commands from within your PHP code, and phpMyAdmin doesn't help much with that job.

✦ **You can't trust computers.** You should understand any code that has your name on it, even if you use a tool like phpMyAdmin to write the code. If your program breaks, you have to fix it eventually, so you really should know how it works.

✦ **SQL scripts are portable.** Moving an entire data structure to a new server is difficult, but if you have a script that creates and populates the database, that script is just an ASCII file. You can easily move a complete database (including the data) to a new machine.

✦ **SQL scripts allow you to quickly rebuild a corrupted database.** As you're testing your system, you'll commonly make mistakes that can harm your data structure. It's very nice to have a script that you can use to quickly reset your data to some standard test state.

Understanding SQL syntax rules

SQL is a language (like XHTML, JavaScript, CSS, and PHP), so it has its own syntax rules. The rules and traditions of SQL are a bit unique because this language has a different purpose than more traditional programming languages:

✦ **Keywords are in uppercase.** Officially, SQL is not case-sensitive, but the tradition is to make all reserved words in uppercase and the names of all your custom elements camel-case (described in Book V, Chapter 6). Some variations of SQL are case-sensitive, so you're safest assuming that they all are.

✦ **One statement can take up more than one line in the editor.** SQL statements aren't usually difficult, but they can get long. Having one statement take up many lines in the editor is common.

✦ **Logical lines end with semicolons.** Like PHP and JavaScript, each statement in SQL ends with a semicolon.

✦ **White space is ignored.** DBMS systems don't pay attention to spaces and carriage returns, so you can (and should) use these tools to help you clarify your code meaning.

✦ **Single quotes are used for text values.** MySQL generally uses single quotes to denote text values, rather than the double quotes used in other languages. If you really want to enclose a single quote in your text, backslash it.

Examining the buildContact.sql script

Take a look at the following code:

```
-- buildContact.sql

DROP TABLE IF EXISTS contact;

CREATE TABLE contact (
  contactID int PRIMARY KEY,
  name VARCHAR(50),
  company VARCHAR(30),
  email VARCHAR(50)
);

INSERT INTO contact VALUES
  (0, 'Bill Gates', 'Microsoft', 'bill@msBob.com');
INSERT INTO contact VALUES
```

```
   (1, 'Steve Jobs', 'Apple', 'steve@rememberNewton.com');
INSERT INTO contact VALUES
   (2, 'Linus Torvalds', 'Linux Foundation', 'linus@gnuWho.org');
INSERT INTO contact VALUES
   (3, 'Andy Harris', 'Wiley Press', 'andy@aharrisBooks.net');

SELECT * FROM contact;
```

This powerful code is written in SQL. I explain each segment in more detail throughout the section, but here's an overview:

1. **Delete the contact table, if it already exists.**

   This script completely rebuilds the contact table, so if it already exists, it is temporarily deleted to avoid duplication.

2. **Create a new table named `contact`.**

   As you can see, the table creation syntax is spare but pretty straightforward. Each field name is followed by its type and length (at least, in the case of VARCHARs).

3. **Add values to the table by using the `INSERT` command.**

   Use a new INSERT statement for each record.

4. **View the table data using the `SELECT` command.**

   This command displays the content of the table.

Dropping a table

It may seem odd to begin creating a table by deleting it, but there's actually a good reason. As you experiment with a data structure, you'll often find yourself building and rebuilding the tables.

The line

```
DROP TABLE IF EXISTS contact
```

means, "Look at the current database and see whether the table `contact` appears in it. If so, delete it." This syntax ensures that you start over fresh as you are rebuilding the table in the succeeding lines. Typical SQL table creation scripts begin by deleting any tables that will be overwritten to avoid confusion.

Creating a table

You create a table with the (aptly named) CREATE TABLE command. The specific table creation statement for the `contact` table looks like the following:

```
CREATE TABLE contact (
 contactID int PRIMARY KEY,
 name VARCHAR(50),
 company VARCHAR(30),
 email VARCHAR(50)
);
```

Creating a table involves several smaller tasks:

1. **Specify the table name.**

   The `CREATE TABLE` statement requires a table name. Specify the table name. Table names (like variables and filenames) should generally not contain spaces or punctuation without good reason.

2. **Begin the field definition with a parenthesis.**

   The left parenthesis indicates the beginning of the field list. You traditionally list one field per line, indented as in regular code, although that format isn't required.

3. **Begin each field with its name.**

   Every field has a name and a type. Begin with the field name, which should also be one word.

4. **Indicate the field type.**

   The field type immediately follows the field name (with no punctuation).

5. **Indicate field length, if necessary.**

   If the field is a `VARCHAR` or `CHAR` field, specify its length within parentheses. You can specify the length of numeric types, but I don't recommend it because MySQL automatically determines the length of numeric fields.

6. **Add special modifiers.**

   Some fields have special modifiers. For now, note that the primary key is indicated on the `contactID` field.

7. **End the field definition with a comma.**

   The comma character indicates the end of a field definition.

8. **End the table definition with a closing parenthesis and a semicolon.**

   Close the parenthesis that started the table definition and end the entire statement with a semicolon.

Adding records to the table

You add data to the table with the `INSERT` command. The way this command works isn't too surprising:

```
INSERT INTO contact VALUES
  (0, 'Bill Gates', 'Microsoft', 'bill@msBob.com');
```

Follow these steps:

1. **Begin with the `INSERT` keyword.**

   Use `INSERT` to clarify that this instruction is a data insertion command.

2. **Specify the table you want to add data to.**

   In my example, I have only one table, so use `INTO contact` to specify that's where the table goes.

3. **(Optional) Specify field names.**

   You can specify a list of field names, but this step is unnecessary if you add data to all fields in their standard order. If you have a list of field names, you're expected to have exactly the same number of values in the `VALUES` list, and they should be in the same order.

4. **Use the `VALUES` keyword to indicate that a list of field values is coming.**

5. **Enclose the values within parentheses.**

   Use parentheses to enclose the list of data values.

6. **Put all values in the right order.**

   Place values in exactly the same order the fields were designated.

7. **Place text values within single quotes.**

   MySQL uses single quotes to specify text values.

8. **End the statement with a semicolon, as you do with all SQL commands.**

9. **Repeat with other data.**

   Add as many `INSERT` commands as you want to populate the data table.

Viewing the sample data

After you've created and populated a table, you'll want to look it over. SQL provides the `SELECT` command for this purpose. `SELECT` is amazingly powerful, but its basic form is simplicity itself:

```
SELECT * FROM contact;
```

This command simply returns all fields of all records from your database.

Running a Script with phpMyAdmin

phpMyAdmin provides terrific features for working with SQL scripts. You can write your script directly in phpMyAdmin, or you can use any text editor.

Once again, your editor can really help you. I recommend a text editor like Notepad++ or Komodo Edit, which both support syntax coloring for SQL. This can really help you find mistakes in your code.

If you've written a script in some other editor, you'll need to save it as a text file and import it into phpMyAdmin.

To run a script in phpMyAdmin, follow these steps:

1. **Connect to phpMyAdmin.**

    Be sure that you're logged in and connected to the system.

2. **Navigate to the correct database.**

    Typically, you use a drop-down list to the left of the main screen to pick the database. (If you haven't created a database, see the instructions in Chapter 1 of this minibook.) Figure 2-1 shows the main phpMyAdmin screen with the haio database enabled.

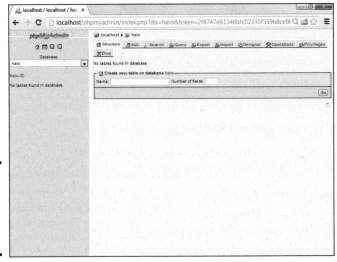

Figure 2-1:
The haio database is created and ready to go.

3. **Activate the SQL pop-up window.**

    You can do so by clicking the small SQL icon in the left-hand navigation menu. The resulting window looks like Figure 2-2.

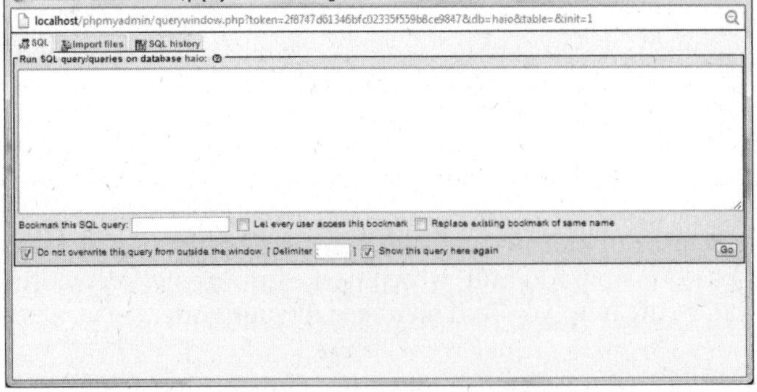

Figure 2-2:
The SQL script window.

4. **(Optional) Type your SQL code directly into this dialog box.**

   This shortcut is good for making quick queries about your data, but generally you create and initialize data with prewritten scripts.

5. **Move to the Import Files tab.**

   In this tab, you can upload the file directly into the MySQL server. Figure 2-3 shows the resulting page. Click the Choose File button to locate your file and the Go button to load it into MySQL.

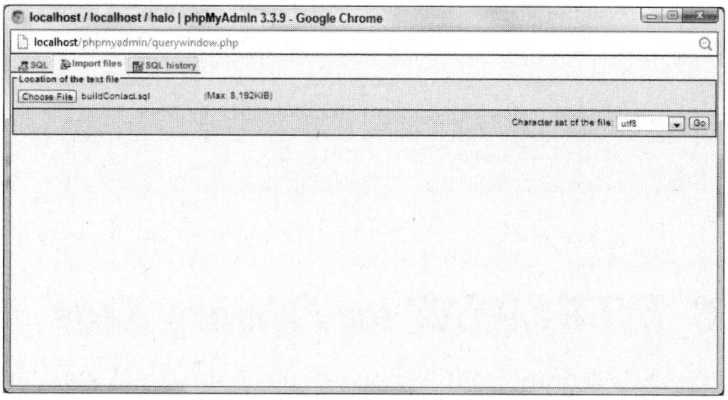

**Book VI
Chapter 2**

Managing Data with MySQL

Figure 2-3:
Importing an externally defined SQL script.

If you've already created the contact database by following the instructions in Chapter 1 of this minibook, you may be nervous that you'll overwrite the data. You will, but for this stage in the process, that's exactly what you want. The point of a script is to help you build a database and rebuild it quickly. After you have meaningful data in the table, you won't be rebuilding it so often, but during the test and creation stage, this skill is critical.

6. **Examine your handiwork.**

   Look back at the phpMyAdmin page, and you see something like Figure 2-4. It shows your script and, if you ended with a SELECT statement, an output of your table. (Later versions of phpMyAdmin display only the last statement in the script, but all are executed unless there is an error in your script.)

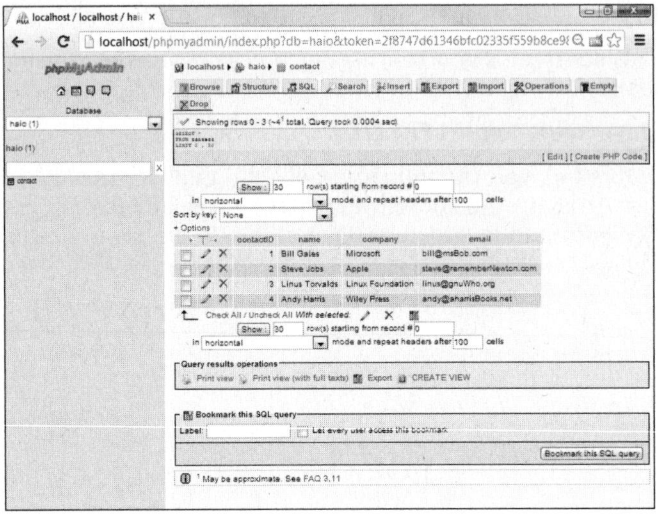

Figure 2-4:
Here's
the script
results,
shown
in php-
MyAdmin.

Using AUTO_INCREMENT for Primary Keys

Primary keys are important because you use them as a standard index for the table. The job of a primary key is to uniquely identify each record in the table. Remember that a primary key has a few important characteristics:

+ **It must exist.** Every record must have a primary key.

+ **It must be unique.** Two records in the same table can't have the same key.

+ **It must not be null.** There must be a value in each key.

When you initially create a table, you have all the values in front of you, but what if you want to add a field later? Somehow, you have to ensure that the primary key in every record is unique.

Over the years, database developers have discovered that integer values are especially handy as primary keys. The great thing about integers is that you can always find a unique one. Just look for the largest index in your table and add one.

Fortunately, MySQL (like most database packages) has a wonderful feature for automatically generating unique integer indices.

Take a look at this variation of the buildContact.sql script:

```
-- buildContactAutoIncrement.sql

DROP TABLE IF EXISTS contact;

CREATE TABLE contact (
```

```
        contactID int PRIMARY KEY AUTO_INCREMENT,
        name VARCHAR(50),
        company VARCHAR(30),
        email VARCHAR(50)
);

INSERT INTO contact VALUES
        (null, 'Bill Gates', 'Microsoft', 'bill@msBob.com');
INSERT INTO contact VALUES
        (null, 'Steve Jobs', 'Apple', 'steve@rememberNewton.com');
INSERT INTO contact VALUES
        (null, 'Linus Torvalds', 'Linux Foundation', 'linus@gnuWho.org');
INSERT INTO contact VALUES
        (null, 'Andy Harris', 'Wiley Press', 'andy@aharrisBooks.net');

SELECT * FROM contact;
```

Here are the changes in this script:

✦ **Add the AUTO_INCREMENT tag to the primary key definition.** This tag indicates that the MySQL system will automatically generate a unique integer for this field. You can apply the AUTO_INCREMENT tag to any field, but you most commonly apply it to primary keys.

✦ **Replace index values with null.** When you define a table with AUTO_INCREMENT, you should no longer specify values in the affected field. Instead, just place the value null. When the SQL interpreter sees the value null on an AUTO_INCREMENT field, it automatically finds the next largest integer.

You may wonder why I'm entering the value null when I said primary keys should never be null. Well, I'm not really making them null. The null value is simply a signal to the interpreter: "Hey, this field is AUTO_INCREMENT, and I want you to find a value for it."

Latin-Swedish?

phpMyAdmin is a wonderful tool, but it does have one strange quirk. When you look over your table design, you may find that the collation is set to latin1_swedish_ci. This syntax refers to the native character set used by the internal data structure. Nothing is terribly harmful about this set (Swedish is a wonderful language), but I don't want to incorrectly imply that my database is written in Swedish.

Fortunately, it's an easy fix. In phpMyAdmin, go to the Operations tab and look for Table Options. You can then set your collation to whatever you want. I typically use latin1_general_ci as it works fine for American English, which is the language used in most of my data sets. (See the MySQL documentation about internationalization if you're working in a language that needs the collation feature.)

I've only run into this problem with some versions of phpMyAdmin. If you create your database directly from the MySQL interpreter or from within PHP programs, the collation issue doesn't seem to be a problem.

Selecting Data from Your Tables

Creating a database is great, but the real point of a database is to extract information from it. SQL provides an incredibly powerful command for retrieving data from the database. The basic form looks as follows:

```
SELECT * FROM contact;
```

The easiest way to practice SQL commands is to use phpMyAdmin. Figure 2-5 shows phpMyAdmin with the SQL tab open.

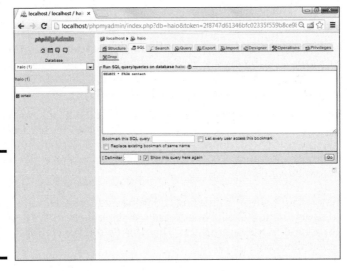

Figure 2-5: You can easily test queries in php-MyAdmin.

Note that you can enter SQL code in multiple places. If you're working with a particular table, you can invoke that table's SQL tab (as I do in Figure 2-5). You can also always enter SQL code into your system with the SQL button on the main phpMyAdmin panel (on the left panel of all phpMy-Admin screens).

If you have a particular table currently active, the SQL dialog box shows you the fields of the current table, which can be handy when you write SQL queries.

Try the `SELECT * FROM contact;` code in the SQL dialog box, and you see the results shown in Figure 2-6.

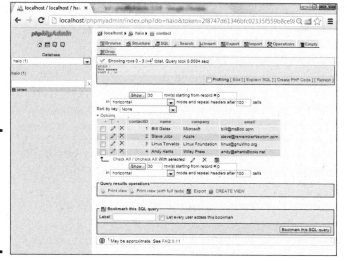

Figure 2-6:
The standard SELECT statement returns the entire table.

Selecting only a few fields

As databases get more complex, you'll often find that you don't want everything. Sometimes, you only want to see a few fields at a time. You can replace the asterisk (*) characters with field names. For example, if you want to see only the names and e-mail addresses, use this variation of the SELECT statement:

```
SELECT name, email FROM contact;
```

Only the columns you specify appear, as you can see in Figure 2-7.

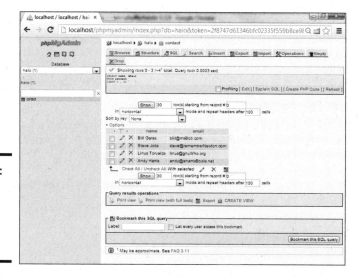

Figure 2-7:
Now, the result is only two columns wide.

Here's another really nice trick you can do with fields. You can give each column a new virtual field name:

```
SELECT
 name as 'Person',
 email as 'Address'
FROM contact;
```

This code also selects only two columns, but this time, it attaches the special labels Person and Address to the columns. You can see this result in Figure 2-8.

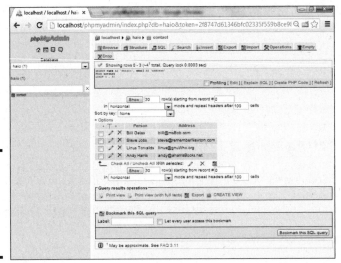

Figure 2-8: You can create virtual titles for your columns.

The capability to add a virtual name for each column doesn't seem like a big deal now, but it becomes handy when your database contains multiple tables. For example, you may have a table named `pet` and another table named `owner` that both have a `name` field. The virtual title feature helps keep you (and your users) from being confused.

Selecting a subset of records

One of the most important jobs in data work is returning a smaller set of the database that meets some kind of criterion. For example, what if you want to dash off a quick e-mail to Bill Gates? Use this query:

```
SELECT *
FROM contact
WHERE
 name = 'Bill Gates';
```

This query has a few key features:

✦ **It selects all fields.** This query selects all the fields (for now).

✦ **A WHERE clause appears.** The WHERE clause allows you to specify a condition.

✦ **It has a condition.** SQL supports conditions, much like ordinary programming languages. MySQL returns only the records that match this condition.

✦ **The condition begins with a field name.** SQL conditions usually compare a field to a value (or to another field).

✦ **Conditions use single equal signs.** You can easily get confused on this detail because SQL uses the single equal sign (=) in conditions, whereas most programming languages use double equals (==) for the same purpose.

✦ **All text values must be within single quotes.** I'm looking for an exact match on the text string 'Steve Jobs'.

✦ **It assumes that searches are case-sensitive.** Different databases have different behavior when it comes to case-sensitivity in SELECT statements, but you're safest assuming that case matters.

Figure 2-9 shows the result of this query.

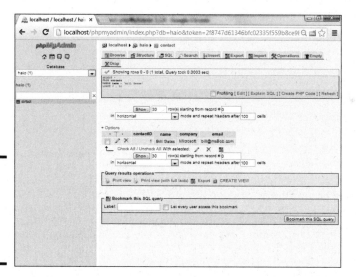

Figure 2-9:
Here's a
query that
returns the
result of a
search.

SQL is pretty picky about the entire text string. The following query doesn't return any results in the contact database:

```
SELECT *
FROM contact
WHERE
  name = 'Bill';
```

The contact table doesn't have any records with a name field containing Bill (unless you added some records when I wasn't looking). Bill Gates is not the same as Bill, so this query returns no results.

Searching with partial information

Of course, sometimes all you have is partial information. Take a look at the following variation to see how it works:

```
SELECT *
FROM contact
WHERE
  company LIKE 'W%';
```

This query looks at the `company` field and returns any records with a `company` field beginning with W. Figure 2-10 shows how it works.

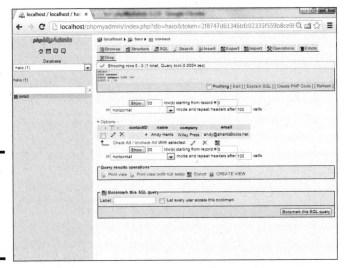

Figure 2-10:
This query returns companies that begin with W.

The LIKE clause is pretty straightforward:

✦ **The keyword `LIKE` indicates a partial match is coming.** It's still the `SELECT` statement, but now it has the `LIKE` keyword to indicate an exact match isn't necessary.

✦ **The search text is still within single quotes, just like the ordinary `SELECT` statement.**

✦ **The percent sign (%) indicates a wildcard value.** A search string of `'W%'` looks for W followed by any number of characters.

✦ **Any text followed by % indicates that you're searching the beginning of the field.** So, if you're looking for people named Steve, you can write `SELECT * FROM contact WHERE name LIKE 'Steve%';`.

Searching for the ending value of a field

Likewise, you can find fields that end with a particular value. Say that you want to send an e-mail to everyone in your contact book with a .com address. This query does the trick:

```
SELECT *
FROM contact
WHERE
    email LIKE '%.com';
```

Figure 2-11 shows the results of this query.

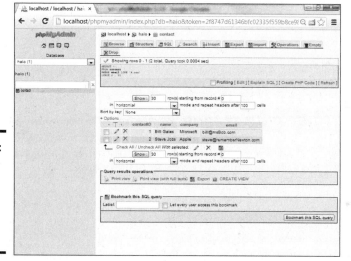

Figure 2-11:
You can
build a
query to
check the
end of a
field.

Searching for any text in a field

One more variant of the LIKE clause allows you to find a phrase anywhere in the field. Say that you remember somebody in your database writes books, and you decide to search for e-mail addresses containing the phrase book:

```
SELECT *
FROM contact
WHERE
    email LIKE '%book%';
```

The search phrase has percent signs at the beginning and the end, so if the phrase "book" occurs anywhere in the specified field, you get a match. And what do you know? Figure 2-12 shows this query matches on the record of a humble, yet lovable author!

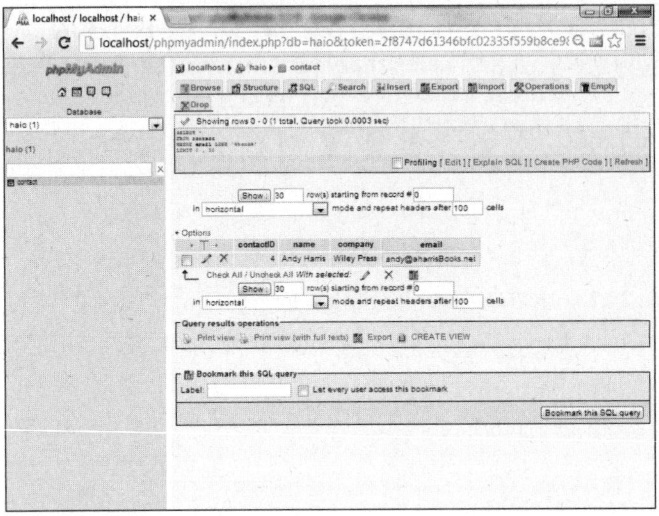

Figure 2-12:
This query searched for the phrase "book" anywhere in the e-mail string.

Searching with regular expressions

If you know how to use regular expressions, you know how great they can be when you need a more involved search. MySQL has a special form of the `SELECT` keyword that supports regular expressions:

```
SELECT *
FROM contact
WHERE
  company REGEXP '^.{9}$';
```

The `REGEXP` keyword lets you search using powerful regular expressions. (Refer to Book IV, Chapter 5 for more information on regular expressions.) This particular expression checks for a `company` field with exactly nine letters. In this table, it returns only one value, shown in Figure 2-13.

Unfortunately, not all database programs support the `REGEXP` feature, but MySQL does, and it's really powerful if you understand the (admittedly arcane) syntax of regular expressions.

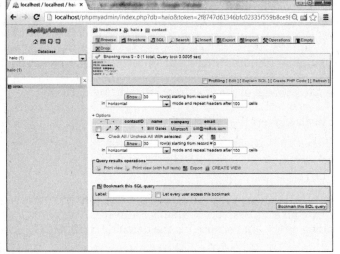

Figure 2-13:
Regular
expressions
are even
more
powerful
than the
standard
LIKE clause.

Sorting your responses

You can specify the order of your query results with the ORDER BY clause. It
works like this:

```
SELECT *
FROM contact
ORDER BY email;
```

The ORDER BY directive allows you to specify a field to sort by. In this
case, I want the records displayed in alphabetical order by e-mail address.
Figure 2-14 shows how it looks.

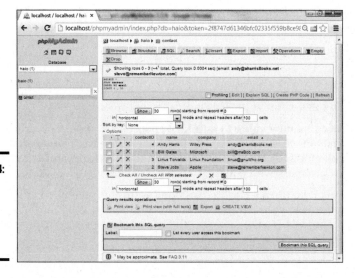

Figure 2-14:
Now, the
result is
sorted
by e-mail
address.

By default, records are sorted in ascending order. Numeric fields are sorted from smallest to largest, and text fields are sorted in standard alphabetic order.

Well, not quite standard alphabetic order . . . . SQL isn't as smart as a librarian, who has special rules about skipping "the" and so on. SQL simply looks at the ASCII values of the characters for sorting purposes.

You can also invert the order:

```
SELECT *
FROM contact
ORDER BY email DESC;
```

Inverting the order causes the records to be produced in reverse alphabetic order by e-mail address. DESC stands for descending order. ASC stands for ascending order, but because it's the default, it isn't usually specified.

Editing Records

Of course, the purpose of a database is to manage data. Sometimes, you want to edit data after it's already in the table. SQL includes handy commands for this task: UPDATE and DELETE. The UPDATE command modifies the value of an existing record, and the DELETE command removes a record altogether.

Updating a record

Say that you decide to modify Bill Gates's address to reinforce a recent marketing triumph. The following SQL code does the trick:

```
UPDATE contact
SET email = 'bill@XBoxOneRocks.com'
WHERE name = 'Bill Gates';
```

The UPDATE command has a few parts:

✦ **The UPDATE command.** This indicates which table you will modify.

✦ **The SET command.** This indicates a new assignment.

✦ **Assign a new value to a field.** This uses a standard programming-style assignment statement to attach a new value to the indicated field. You can modify more than one field at a time. Just separate the field = value pairs with commas.

✦ **Specify a WHERE clause.** You don't want this change to happen to all the records in your database. You want to change only the e-mail address in records where the name is Bill Gates. Use the WHERE clause to specify which records you intend to update.

More than one person in your database may be named Bill Gates. Names aren't guaranteed to be unique, so they aren't really the best search criteria. This situation is actually a very good reason to use primary keys. A better version of this update looks as follows:

```
UPDATE contact
SET email = 'bill@XBoxOneRocks.com'
WHERE contactID = 1;
```

The `contactID` is guaranteed to be unique and present, so it makes an ideal search criterion. Whenever possible, `UPDATE` (and `DROP`) commands should use primary key searches so that you don't accidentally change or delete the wrong record.

Book VI
Chapter 2

Managing Data with MySQL

Deleting a record

Sometimes, you need to delete records. SQL has a command for this eventuality, and it's pretty easy to use:

```
WHERE contactID = 1;
```

The preceding line deletes the entire record with a `contactID` of 1.

Be very careful with the `DELETE` command — it's destructive. Be absolutely sure that you have a `WHERE` clause, or you may delete all the records in your table with one quick command! Likewise, be sure that you understand the `WHERE` clause so that you aren't surprised by what gets deleted. You're better off running an ordinary `SELECT` using the `WHERE` clause before you `DELETE`, just to be sure that you know exactly what you're deleting. Generally, you should `DELETE` based on only a primary key so that you don't produce any collateral damage.

Exporting Your Data and Structure

After you've built a wonderful data structure, you probably will want to export it for a number of reasons:

✦ **You want a backup.** Just in case something goes wrong!

✦ **You want to move to a production server.** It's smart to work on a local (offline) server while you figure things out, but eventually you'll need to move to a live server. Moving the actual database files is tricky, but you can easily move a script.

✦ **You want to perform data analysis.** You may want to put your data in a spreadsheet for further analysis or in a comma-separated text file to be read by programs without SQL access.

✦ **You want to document the table structure.** The structure of a data set is extremely important when you start writing programs using that structure. Having the table structure available in a word-processing or PDF format can be very useful.

MySQL (and thus phpMyAdmin) has some really nice tools for exporting your data in a number of formats.

Figure 2-15 shows an overview of the Export tab, showing some of the features.

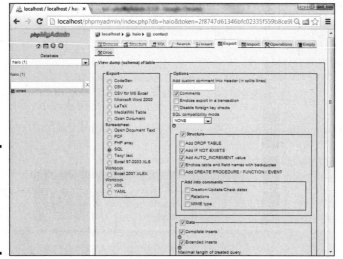

Figure 2-15: These are some of the various output techniques.

The different styles of output are used for different purposes:

✦ **CSV (comma-separated value) format:** A plain ASCII comma-separated format. Each record is stored on its own line, and each field is separated by a comma. CSV is nice because it's universal. Most spreadsheet programs can read CSV data natively, and it's very easy to write a program to read CSV data, even if your server doesn't support MySQL. If you want to back up your data to move to another server, CSV is a good choice. Figure 2-16 shows some of the options for creating a CSV file.

The data file created using the specified options looks like the following:

```
"contactID","name","company","email"
"1","Bill Gates","Microsoft","bill@XBoxOneRocks.com"
"2","Steve Jobs","Apple","steve@rememberNewton.com"
"3","Linus Torvalds","Linux Foundation","linus@gnuWho.org"
"4","Andy Harris","Wiley Press","andy@aharrisBooks.net"
```

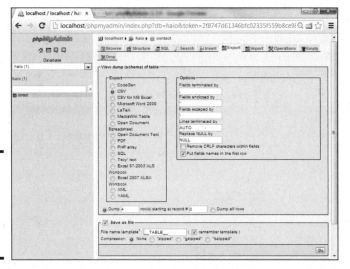

Figure 2-16:
You have several options for creating CSV files.

The CSV format often uses commas and quotes, so if these characters appear in your data, you may encounter problems. Be sure to test your data and use some of the other delimiters if you have problems.

✦ **MS Excel and Open Document Spreadsheet:** These are the two currently supported spreadsheet formats. Exporting your data using one of these formats gives you a spreadsheet file that you can easily manipulate, which is handy when you want to do charts or data analysis based on your data. Figure 2-17 shows an Excel document featuring the contact table.

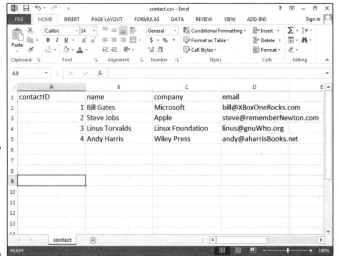

Figure 2-17:
This Excel spreadsheet was automatically created.

✦ **Word-processing formats:** Several formats are available to create documentation for your project. Figure 2-18 shows a document created with this feature. Typically, you use these formats to describe the format of the data and the current contents. LaTeX and PDF are special formats used for printing.

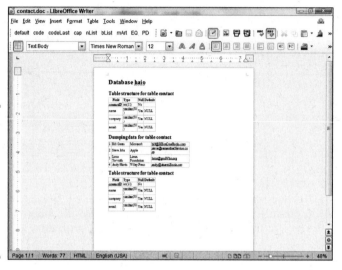

Figure 2-18: Word-processing, PDF, and LaTeX formats are great for documentation.

Exporting SQL code

One of the neatest tricks is to have phpMyAdmin build an entire SQL script for re-creating your database. Figure 2-19 shows the available options.

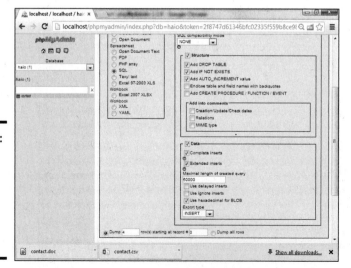

Figure 2-19: You can specify several options for outputting your SQL code.

The resulting code is as follows:

```
-- phpMyAdmin SQL Dump
    -- version 3.3.9
    -- http://www.phpmyadmin.net
    --
    -- Host: localhost
    -- Generation Time: Jul 10, 2013 at 08:30 PM
    -- Server version: 5.5.8
    -- PHP Version: 5.3.5

    SET SQL_MODE="NO_AUTO_VALUE_ON_ZERO";


    /*!40101 SET @OLD_CHARACTER_SET_CLIENT=@@CHARACTER_SET_CLIENT */;
    /*!40101 SET @OLD_CHARACTER_SET_RESULTS=@@CHARACTER_SET_RESULTS */;
    /*!40101 SET @OLD_COLLATION_CONNECTION=@@COLLATION_CONNECTION */;
    /*!40101 SET NAMES utf8 */;


    --
    -- Database: 'haio'
    --

    -- --------------------------------------------------------


    --
    -- Table structure for table 'contact'
    --

    DROP TABLE IF EXISTS contact;
    CREATE TABLE IF NOT EXISTS contact (
      contactID int(11) NOT NULL AUTO_INCREMENT,
      `name` varchar(50) DEFAULT NULL,
      company varchar(30) DEFAULT NULL,
      email varchar(50) DEFAULT NULL,
      PRIMARY KEY (contactID)
    ) ENGINE=InnoDB  DEFAULT CHARSET=latin1 AUTO_INCREMENT=5 ;

    --
    -- Dumping data for table 'contact'
    --

    INSERT INTO contact (contactID, `name`, company, email) VALUES
      (1, 'Bill Gates', 'Microsoft', 'bill@XBoxOneRocks.com'),
      (2, 'Steve Jobs', 'Apple', 'steve@rememberNewton.com'),
      (3, 'Linus Torvalds', 'Linux Foundation', 'linus@gnuWho.org'),
      (4, 'Andy Harris', 'Wiley Press', 'andy@aharrisBooks.net');
```

You can see that phpMyAdmin made a pretty decent script that you can use to re-create this database. You can easily use this script to rebuild the database if it gets corrupted or to copy the data structure to a different implementation of MySQL.

Generally, you use this feature for both purposes. Copy your data structure and data every once in a while (just in case Godzilla attacks your server or something).

Typically, you build your data on one server and want to migrate it to another server. The easiest way to do so is by building the database on one server. You can then export the script for building the SQL file and load it into the second server.

Creating XML data

One more approach to saving data is through XML. phpMyAdmin creates a standard form of XML encapsulating the data. The XML output looks like this:

```
<<?xml version="1.0" encoding="utf-8"?>
<!--
- phpMyAdmin XML Dump
- version 3.3.9
- http://www.phpmyadmin.net
-
- Host: localhost
- Generation Time: Jul 10, 2013 at 08:32 PM
- Server version: 5.5.8
- PHP Version: 5.3.5
-->

<pma_xml_export version="1.0"
    xmlns:pma="http://www.phpmyadmin.net/some_doc_url/">
    <!--
    - Structure schemas
    -->
    <pma:structure_schemas>
        <pma:database name="haio" collation="latin1_swedish_ci" charset="latin1">
            <pma:table name="contact">
                CREATE TABLE `contact` (
                    `contactID` int(11) NOT NULL AUTO_INCREMENT,
                    `name` varchar(50) DEFAULT NULL,
                    `company` varchar(30) DEFAULT NULL,
                    `email` varchar(50) DEFAULT NULL,
                    PRIMARY KEY (`contactID`)
                ) ENGINE=InnoDB AUTO_INCREMENT=5 DEFAULT CHARSET=latin1;
            </pma:table>
        </pma:database>
    </pma:structure_schemas>

    <!--
    - Database: 'haio'
    -->
    <database name="haio">
        <!-- Table contact -->
        <table name="contact">
            <column name="contactID">1</column>
            <column name="name">Bill Gates</column>
            <column name="company">Microsoft</column>
            <column name="email">bill@XBoxOneRocks.com</column>
        </table>
        <table name="contact">
            <column name="contactID">2</column>
            <column name="name">Steve Jobs</column>
            <column name="company">Apple</column>
            <column name="email">steve@rememberNewton.com</column>
        </table>
        <table name="contact">
            <column name="contactID">3</column>
            <column name="name">Linus Torvalds</column>
            <column name="company">Linux Foundation</column>
```

```
                    <column name="email">linus@gnuWho.org</column>
            </table>
            <table name="contact">
                    <column name="contactID">4</column>
                    <column name="name">Andy Harris</column>
                    <column name="company">Wiley Press</column>
                    <column name="email">andy@aharrisBooks.net</column>
            </table>
        </database>
</pma_xml_export>
```

XML is commonly used as a common data language, especially in AJAX applications.

Chapter 3: Normalizing Your Data

In This Chapter

✔ Understanding why single-table databases are inadequate

✔ Recognizing common data anomalies

✔ Creating entity-relationship diagrams

✔ Using MySQL Workbench to create data diagrams

✔ Understanding the first three normal forms

✔ Defining data relationships

*D*atabases can be deceptive. Even though databases are pretty easy to create, beginners usually run into problems as soon as they start working with actual data.

Computer scientists (particularly a gentleman named E. F. Codd in the 1970s) have studied potential data problems and defined techniques for organizing data. This scheme is called *data normalization*. In this chapter, you discover why single-table databases rarely work for real-world data and how to create a well-defined data structure according to basic normalization rules.

On the website, I include a script called buildHero.sql that builds all the tables in this chapter. Feel free to load that script into your MySQL environment to see all these tables for yourself.

Recognizing Problems with Single-Table Data

Packing everything you've got into a single table is tempting. Although you can do it pretty easily (especially with SQL), and it seems like a good solution, things can go wrong pretty quickly.

Table 3-1 shows a seemingly simple database describing some superheroes.

Table 3-1	A Sample Database				
Name	*Powers*	*Villain*	*Plot*	*Mission*	*Age*
The Plumber	Sewer snake of doom, unclogging, ability to withstand smells	Septic Slime Master	Overcome Chicago with slime	Stop the Septic Slime	37
Binary Boy	Hexidecimation beam, obfuscation	Octal	Eliminate the numerals 8 and 9	Make the world safe for binary representation	19
The Janitor	Mighty Mop	Septic Slim Master	Overcome New York with slime	Stop the Septic Slime	41

It seems that not much can go wrong here because the database is only three records and six fields. The data is simple, and there isn't that much of it. Still, a lot of trouble is lurking just under the surface. The following sections outline potential problems.

The identity crisis

What's Table 3-1 about? At first, it seems to be about superheroes, but some of the information is really about things related to the superhero, such as villains and missions. This issue may not seem like a big deal, but it causes all kinds of practical problems later on. A table should be about only one thing. When it tries to be about more than that, it can't do its job as well.

Every time a beginner (and, often, an advanced data developer) creates a table, the table usually contains fields that don't belong there. You have to break things up into multiple tables so that each table is really about only one thing. The process for doing so solves a bunch of other problems, as well.

The listed powers

Take a look at the powers field. Each superhero can have more than one power. Some heroes have tons of powers. The problem is, how do you handle a situation where one field can have a lot of values? You frequently see the following solutions:

+ **One large text field:** That's what I did in this case. I built a massive (255 character) VARCHAR field and hoped it would be enough. The user just has to type all the possible skills.

+ **Multiple fields:** Sometimes, a data designer just makes a bunch of fields, such as `power1`, `power2`, and so on.

Both these solutions have the same general flaw. You never know how much room to designate because you never know exactly how many items will be in the list. Say that you choose the large text field approach. You may have a really clever hero with a lot of powers, so you fill up the entire field with a list of powers. What happens if your hero learns one more power? Should you delete something just to make things fit? Should you abbreviate?

If you choose to have multiple power fields, the problem doesn't go away. You still have to determine how many skills the hero can have. If you designate ten skill fields and one of your heroes learns an eleventh power, you've got a problem.

The obvious solution is to provide far more room than anybody needs. If it's a text field, make it huge; and if it's multiple fields, make hundreds of them. Both solutions are wasteful. Remember, a database can often have hundreds or thousands of records, and each one has to be the same size. If you make your record definition bigger than it needs to be, this waste is multiplied hundreds or thousands of times.

You may argue that this is not the 1970s. Processor power and storage space are really cheap today, so why am I worrying about saving a few bytes here and there? Well, cheap is still not free. Programmers tend to be working with much larger data sets than they did in the early days, so efficiency still matters. And here's another important change. Today, data is much more likely to be transmitted over the Internet. The big deal today isn't really processor or storage efficiency. Today's problem is transmission efficiency, which comes down to the same principle: Don't store unnecessary data.

When databases have listed fields, you tend to see other problems. If the field doesn't have enough room for all the data, people will start abbreviating. If you're looking for a hero with invisibility, you can't simply search for "invisibility" in the `powers` field because it may be "inv," "in," or "invis" (or even "can't see"). If you desperately need an invisible hero, the search can be frustrating, and you may miss a result because you didn't guess all the possible abbreviations. (I guess you can't see the invisible hero.)

If the database uses the listed fields model, you have another problem. Now, your search has to look through all ten (or hundreds of) power fields because you don't know which one holds the "invisible" power. This problem makes your search queries far more complicated and slower than they would have been otherwise.

Another so-called solution you sometimes see is to have a whole bunch of Boolean fields: Invisibility, Super-speed, X-ray vision, and so on. This fix solves part of the problem because Boolean data is small. It's still troublesome, though, because now the data developer has to anticipate every possible power. You may have an `other` field, but it then reintroduces the problem of listed fields.

Listed fields are a nightmare.

Repetition and reliability

Another common problem with data comes with repetition. If you allow data to be repeated in your database, you can have some really challenging side effects. Refer to Table 3-1, earlier in this chapter, and get ready to answer some questions about it. . . .

What is the Slime Master's evil plot?

This question seems simple enough, but Table 3-1 provides an ambiguous response. If you look at the first row (The Plumber), the plot is Overcome Chicago with slime. If you look at The Janitor, you see that the plot is to Overcome New York with slime. Which is it? Presumably, it's the same plot, but in one part of the database, New York is the target, and elsewhere, it's Chicago. From the database, you can't really tell which is correct or if it could be both. I was required to type in the plot in two different records. It's supposed to be the same plot, but I typed it differently. Now, the data has a conflict, and you don't know which record to trust.

Is it possible the plots were supposed to be different? Sure, but you don't want to leave that assumption to chance. The point of data design is to ask exactly these questions and to design your data scheme to reinforce the rules of your organization.

Here's a related question. What if you needed to get urgent information to any hero fighting the Septic Slime Master? You'd probably write a query like

```
SELECT * FROM hero WHERE villain = 'Septic Slime Master'
```

That query is a pretty reasonable request, but it wouldn't work. The villain in The Janitor record is the Septic *Slim* Master. Somebody mistyped something in the database, and now The Janitor doesn't know how to defeat the Slime Master.

If your database allows duplication, this type of mistake will happen all the time.

In general, you don't want to enter anything into a database more than once. If you have a way to enter the Septic Slime Master one time, that should eliminate this type of problem.

Fields with changeable data

Another kind of problem is evident in the Age field. (See, even superheroes have a mandatory retirement age.) Age is a good example of a field that shouldn't really be in a database because it changes all the time. If you have age in your database, how are you going to account for people getting older? Do you update the age on each hero's birthday? (If so, you need to store that birthday, and you need to run a script every day to see whether it's some-body's birthday.) You could just age everybody once a year, but this solution doesn't seem like a good option, either.

Whenever possible, you want to avoid fields that change regularly and instead use a formula to generate the appropriate results when you need them.

Deletion problems

Another kind of problem is lurking right under the surface. Say that you have to fire the Binary Boy. (With him, everything is black and white. You just can't compromise with that guy.) You delete his record, and then you want to assign another hero to fight Octal. When you delete Binary Boy, you also delete all the information about Octal and his nefarious scheme because the only place Octal's information was stored was in Binary Boy's record.

In a related problem, what if you encounter a new villain and you haven't yet assigned a hero to this villain? The current data design doesn't allow you to add villains without heroes. You have to make up a fake hero, and that just doesn't seem right. Villains deserve their own table, and that's exactly what they will get.

Introducing Entity-Relationship Diagrams

You can solve all the problems with the database shown in Table 3-1 by breaking the single table into a series of smaller, more specialized tables.

The typical way of working with data design is to use a concept called an *Entity-Relationship (ER) diagram*. This form of diagram usually includes the following:

✦ **Entities:** Typically, a table is an entity, but you see other kinds of enti-ties, too. An entity is usually drawn as a box with each field listed inside.

✦ **Relationships:** Relationships are drawn as lines between the boxes. As you find out about various forms of relationships, I show you the par-ticular symbols used to describe these relationship types.

Using MySQL Workbench to draw ER diagrams

You can create ER diagrams with anything (I typically use a whiteboard), but some very nice free software can help. One particularly nice program is called MySQL Workbench (`http://dev.mysql.com/downloads/tools/`). This software has a number of really handy features:

+ **Visual representation of database design:** MySQL Workbench allows you to define a table easily and then see how it looks in ER form. You can create several tables and manipulate them visually to see how they relate.

+ **An understanding of ER rules:** MySQL Workbench is not simply a drawing program. It's specialized for drawing ER diagrams, so it creates a standard design for each table and relationship. Other data administrators can understand the ER diagrams you create with this tool.

+ **Integration with MySQL:** After you've created a data design you like, you can have MySQL Workbench create a MySQL script to create the databases you've defined. In fact, you can even have Workbench look at an existing MySQL database and create an ER diagram from it.

Creating a table definition in Workbench

Creating your tables in MySQL Workbench is a fairly easy task:

1. **Create a new model.**

   Choose File ➪ New to create a new model. Figure 3-1 shows the MySQL Workbench model screen.

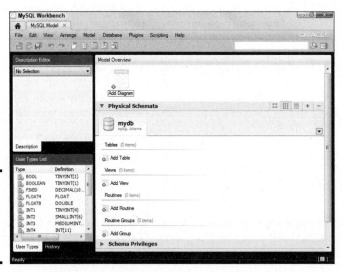

Figure 3-1: MySQL Workbench main screen.

2. **Create a new table.**

   Use the Add Table icon (near the top of the screen) to create a new table. A new dialog box opens at the bottom of the screen, allowing you to change the table name. You see a new table form like the one in Figure 3-2. Change the table name to `hero` but leave the other values blank for now.

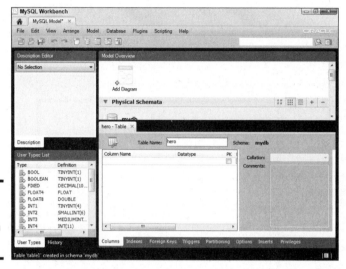

Figure 3-2:
Now your model has a table in it.

3. **Edit the columns.**

    Select the Columns tab at the bottom of the screen to edit the table's fields. You can add field names and types here. Create a table that looks like the `hero` table shown in Figure 3-3. You can use the tab key to add a new field.

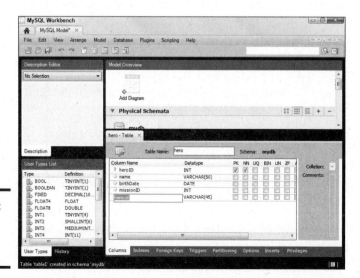

Figure 3-3:
Editing the table definition.

4. Make a diagram of the table.

So far, MySQL Workbench seems a lot like phpMyAdmin. The most useful feature of Workbench is the way it lets you view your tables in diagram form. You can view tables in a couple of ways, but the easiest way is to select Create Diagram from Catalog Objects from the Model menu. When you do so, you'll see a screen, as shown in Figure 3-4.

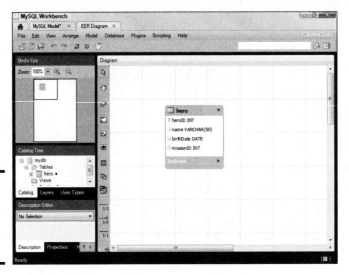

Figure 3-4:
Now you have a diagram of your table.

The diagram doesn't show the *contents* of the table, just the design. In fact, MySQL Workbench doesn't really care that much about what is in the database. The key idea here is how the data is organized. This matters because you will be creating several tables to manage your superheroes.

5. Extract the code.

If you want, you can see the SQL code used to create the table you just designed. Simply right-click the table and choose Copy SQL to Clipboard. The CREATE statement for this table is copied to the Clipboard, and you can paste it to your script. Here's the code created by Workbench:

```
CREATE  TABLE IF NOT EXISTS 'mydb'.'hero' (
  'heroID' INT NOT NULL ,
  'name' VARCHAR(50) NULL ,
  'birthDate' DATE NULL ,
  'missionID' INT NULL ,
  PRIMARY KEY (heroID) )
ENGINE = InnoDB
```

The code generated is similar to the code described in Chapter 2 of this minibook, with a few variations:

This is great and all . . .

But how do I work with an actual database? MySQL Workbench is used to help you design and understand complex databases. So far, you've been working in a local system that isn't attached to a particular database. This is actually a pretty good way to work. Eventually, though, you'll be settled on a design, and you'll want to build a real database from the model. MySQL Workbench has a number of tools to help you with this. First, use the Database – Manage Connections dialog box to create a connection to your database. Then you can use the Forward Engineering option to commit your design to the database, or the Reverse Engineering option to extract a database you've already created and build a diagram from it.

While these options can be handy, they aren't really critical. To be honest, I don't generally use the code engineering features in MySQL

Workbench. In fact, I (like a lot of data developers) do most of my initial data design on a white board and then make cleaner versions of the design with tools like MySQL Workbench. I'm showing you the tool here because it may be helpful to you, and it produces prettier artwork than my white board scribblings.

The hard work is organizing the data. It's pretty easy to convert a diagram to SQL code. Use a tool like MySQL to see how your data fits together. Then if you want, you can either let it build the code for you or simply use it as a starting place to build the code by hand.

As you've seen with other languages, visual tools can help you build code, but they don't absolve you of responsibility. If the code has your name on it, you need to understand how it works. That's most easily done when you write it by hand.

✦ **Default NULL values are indicated:** Most fields are defined with a default value of NULL. (Of course, the primary key can't be NULL, and it's defined that way.)

✦ **Field and table names are quoted:** The auto-generated code uses single quotes around all field and table names. Single quotes are needed when identifiers have spaces in them. Because I rarely use spaces in the name of anything, I tend not to use quotes because they complicate the code.

✦ **The primary key notation is different:** Rather than defining the primary key in the field definition, the primary key is set up as a separate entry in the table definition. This is simply a matter of style.

Introducing Normalization

Trying to cram all your data into a single table usually causes problems. The process for solving these problems is called *data normalization*. Normalization is really a set of rules. When your database follows the first rule, it's said to be in *first normal form*. For this introductory book, you get to the third normal form, which is suitable for most applications.

First normal form

The official definitions of the normal forms sound like the offspring of a lawyer and a mathematician. Here's an official definition of the first normal form:

```
A table is in first normal form if and only if it represents a relation. It does
    not allow nulls or duplicate rows.
```

Yeah, whatever.

Here's what it means in practical terms:

```
Eliminate listed fields.
```

A database is in first normal form if

+ **It has no repeating fields.** Take any data that would be in a repeating field and make it into a new table.

+ **It has a primary key.** Add a primary key to each table. (Some would argue that this requirement isn't necessarily part of first normal form, but it'll be necessary in the next step, anyway.)

In a practical sense, the first normal form means getting rid of listed fields and making a new table to contain powers. You'll need to go back to the model view to create a new table and then create the diagram again. Figure 3-5 shows an ER diagram of the data in first normal form.

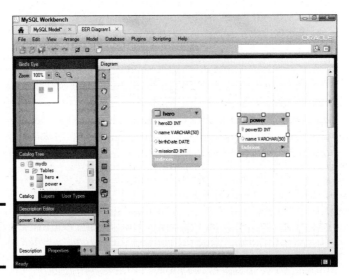

Figure 3-5:
Now I have
two tables.

A couple of things happen here:

1. **Make a new table called** power.

   This table contains nothing but a key and the power name.

2. **Take the** power **field away from the** hero **table.**

   The hero table no longer has a power field.

3. **Add a primary key to both tables.**

   Both tables now have an integer primary key. Looking over my tables, there are no longer any listed fields, so I'm in first normal form.

All this is well and good, but the user really wants this data connected, so how do you join it back together? For that answer, see Chapter 4 of this minibook.

Second normal form

The official terminology for the second normal form is just as baffling as the first normal form:

```
A table is in second normal form (2NF) only if it is in 1NF and all nonkey fields
    are dependant entirely on the entire candidate key, not just part of it.
```

Huh? You've gotta love these computer scientists.

In practical terms, second normal form is pretty easy, too. It really means

```
Eliminate repetition.
```

Look at all those places where you've got duplicated data and create new tables to take care of them.

In the hero data (shown in Table 3-1, earlier in this chapter), you can eliminate a lot of problems by breaking the hero data into three tables. Figure 3-6 illustrates one way to break up the data.

Many of the problems in the badHero design happen because apparently more than one hero can be on a particular mission, and thus the mission data gets repeated. By separating mission data into another table, I've guaranteed that the data for a mission is entered only once.

Note that each table has a primary key, and none of them has listed fields. The same data won't ever be entered twice. The solution is looking pretty good!

Notice that everything related to the mission has been moved to the mission table. I added one field to the hero table, which contains an integer. This field is called a *foreign key reference*. You can find out much more about how foreign key references work in Chapter 4 of this minibook.

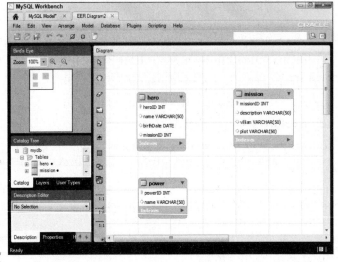

Figure 3-6:
Now I have
three tables:
hero, power,
and mission.

Third normal form

The third normal form adds one more requirement. Here is the official definition:

```
A table is in 3NF if it is in 2NF and has no transitive dependencies on the
    candidate key.
```

Wow! These definitions get better and better. Once again, it's really a lot easier than it sounds:

```
Ensure functional dependency.
```

In other words, check each field of each table and ensure that it really describes what the table is about. For example, is the plot related to the mission or the hero? What about the villain?

The tricky thing about functional dependency is that you often don't really know how the data is supposed to be connected. Only the person who uses the data really knows how it's supposed to work. (Often, they don't know, either, as it turns out.) You have to work with the client to figure out exactly what the *business rules* (the rules that describe how the data really works) are. You can't really tell from the data itself.

The good news is that, for simple structures like the hero data, you're often already in third normal form by the time you get to second normal form. Still, you should check. After a database is in third normal form, you've reduced the possibility of several kinds of anomalies, so your data is far more reliable than it was in the past. Several other forms of normalization exist, but third normal form is enough for most applications.

Identifying Relationships in Your Data

After you normalize the data (see the preceding section), you've created the entities (tables). Now, you need to investigate the relationships among these entities.

Three main types of data relationships exist (and of these, only two are common):

✦ **One-to-one relationship:** Each element of table A is related to exactly one element of table B. This type of relationship isn't common because if a one-to-one relationship exists between two tables, the information can be combined safely into one table.

✦ **One-to-many relationship:** For each element of table A, there could be many possible elements in table B. The relationship between mission and hero is a one-to-many relationship, as each mission can have many heroes, but each hero has only one mission. (My heroes have attention issues and can't multitask very well.) Note that hero and mission are not a one-to-many relationship, but a many-to-one. The order matters.

✦ **Many-to-many relationship:** This type of relationship happens when an element of A may have many values from B, and B may also have many values of A. Usually, listed fields turn out to be many-to-many relationships. In the hero data, the relationship between hero and power is a many-to-many relationship because each hero can have many powers, and each power can belong to multiple heroes.

You can use an ER tool to diagram the various relationship types. Figure 3-7 shows this addition to the `hero` design.

**Book VI
Chapter 3**

**Normalizing Your
Data**

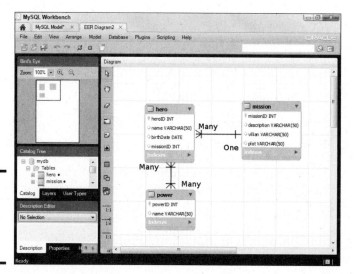

Figure 3-7: Now I've added relationships.

Note that MySQL Workbench doesn't actually allow you to draw many-to-many joins. I drew that into Figure 3-7 to illustrate the point. In the next chapter, I show how to emulate many-to-many relationships with a special trick called a *link table*.

ER diagrams use special symbols to represent different kinds of relationships. The line between tables indicates a *join,* or relationship, but the type of join is indicated by the markings on the ends of the lines. In general, the crow's feet or filled-in circle indicate many, and the double lines indicate one.

ER diagrams get much more complex than the simple ones I show here, but for this introduction, the one and many symbols are enough to get you started.

Chapter 4: Putting Data Together with Joins

In This Chapter

✔ **Using SQL functions**

✔ **Creating calculated fields**

✔ **Working with date values**

✔ **Building views**

✔ **Creating inner joins and link tables**

Single tables aren't sufficient for most data. If you understand the rules of data normalization (see Chapter 3 of this minibook), you know how to break your data into a series of smaller tables. The question remains, though: How do you recombine all these broken-up tables to make something the user can actually use?

In this chapter, you discover several techniques for combining the data in your tables to create useful results.

I wrote a quick PHP script to help me with most of the figures in this chapter. Each SQL query I intend to look at is stored in a separate SQL file, and I can load up the file and look at it with the PHP code. Feel free to look over the code for showQuery on the companion website. If you want to run this code yourself, be sure to change the username and password to reflect your data settings. Use queryDemo.html to see all the queries in action. I also include a script called buildHero.sql that creates a database with all the tables and views I mention in this chapter. Feel free to load that script into your database so that you can play along at home. You learn more about writing your own PHP code for reading SQL data in Chapter 5 of this minibook.

Calculating Virtual Fields

Part of data normalization means that you eliminate fields that can be calculated. In the hero database described in Chapter 3 of this minibook, data normalization meant that you don't store the hero's age, but his or her birthday instead. Of course, if you really want the age, you should be able to find some way to calculate it. SQL includes support for calculating results right in the query.

Begin by looking over the improved `hero` table in Figure 4-1.

Figure 4-1:
The hero
table after
normal-
ization.

The original idea for the database, introduced in Table 3-1 in Chapter 3 of this minibook, was to keep track of each hero's age. This idea was bad because the age changes every year. Instead, I stored the hero's birthday. But what if you really do want the age?

Introducing SQL functions

It turns out SQL supports a number of useful functions that you can use to manipulate date and time data. Table 4-1 shows especially useful MySQL functions. Many more functions are available, but these functions are the most frequently used.

Table 4-1	Useful MySQL Functions
Function	*Description*
CONCAT(A, B)	Concatenates two string results. Can be used to create a single entry from two or more fields. For example, combine firstName and lastName fields.
FORMAT(X, D)	Formats the number X to the number of digits D.
CURRDATE(), CURRTIME()	Returns the current date or time.
NOW()	Returns the current date and time.
MONTH(), DAY(), YEAR(), WEEK(), WEEKDAY()	Extracts the particular value from a date value.

Function	Description
HOUR(), MINUTE(), SECOND()	Extracts the particular value from a time value.
DATEDIFF(A, B)	Frequently used to find the time difference between two events (age).
SUBTIMES(A, B)	Determines the difference between two times.
FROMDAYS(INT)	Converts an integer number of days into a date value.

Typically, you use a programming language, such as PHP, to manage what the user sees, and programming languages tend to have a much richer set of functions than the database. Still, it's often useful to do certain kinds of functionality at the database level.

Knowing when to calculate virtual fields

You calculate data in these situations:

✦ **You need to create a single field from multiple text fields.** You might need to combine first, middle, and last name fields to create a single name value. You can also combine all the elements of an address to create a single output.

✦ **You want to do a mathematical operation on your data.** Imagine that you're writing a database for a vegetable market and you want to calculate the value from the costPerPound field plus the pounds-Purchased field. You can include the mathematical operation in your query.

✦ **You need to convert data.** Perhaps you stored weight information in pounds and you want a query to return data in kilograms.

✦ **You want to do date calculations.** Often, you need to calculate ages from specific days. Date calculations are especially useful on the data side because databases and other languages often have different date formats.

Calculating Date Values

The birthday value is stored in the hero table, but what you really want to know is the hero's age. It's very common to have a date stored in a database. You often need to calculate the time from that date to the current date in years, or perhaps in years and months. Functions can help you do these calculations.

Begin by looking at a simple function that tells you the current date and time, as I do in Figure 4-2.

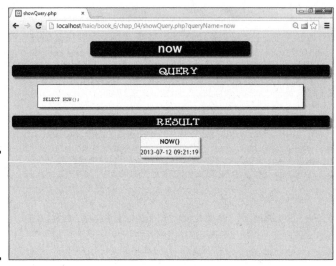

Figure 4-2:
The NOW()
function
returns the
current date
and time.

The current date and time by themselves aren't that important, but you can combine this information with other functions, described in the following sections, to do some very interesting things.

Using DATEDIFF to determine age

The NOW() function is very handy when you combine it with the DATEDIFF() function, as shown in Figure 4-3.

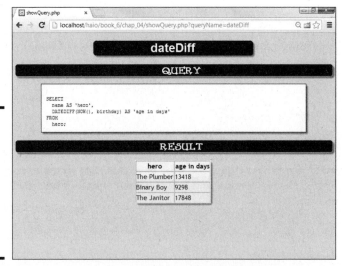

Figure 4-3:
The
DATEDIFF()
function
determines
the
difference
between
dates.

This query calculates the difference between the current date, NOW(), and each hero's birthday. The DATEDIFF() function works by converting both dates into integers. It can then subtract the two integers, giving you the result in number of days.

You normally name the fields you calculate because otherwise, the formula used to calculate the results becomes the virtual field's name. The user doesn't care about the formula, so use the AS feature to give the virtual field a more useful name.

Adding a calculation to get years

Of course, most people don't think about age in terms of days. Age (unless you're talking about fruit flies or something) is typically measured in years. One simple solution is to divide the age in days by 365 (the number of days in a year). Figure 4-4 shows this type of query.

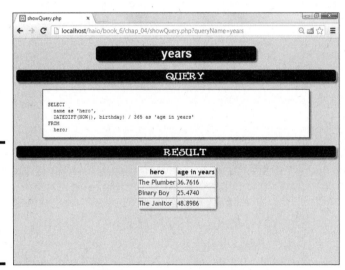

Figure 4-4:
You can divide by 365 to determine the number of years.

This code is almost like the query shown in Figure 4-3, except it uses a mathematical operator. You can use most of the math operators in queries to do quick conversions. Now, the age is specified in years, but the decimal part is a bit odd. Normally, you either go with entire year measurements or work with months, weeks, and days.

Converting the days integer into a date

The YEAR() function extracts only the years from a date, and the MONTH() function pulls out the months, but both these functions require a date value. The DATEDIFF() function creates an integer. Somehow, you need to convert the integer value produced by DATEDIFF() back into a date value.

(For more on this function, see the section "Using DATEDIFF to determine age," earlier in this chapter.)

Figure 4-5 is another version of a query that expresses age in terms of years and months.

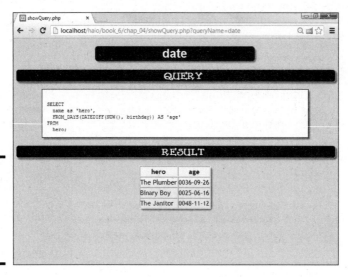

date

Figure 4-5:
The age is now converted back to a date.

This query takes the DATEDIFF() value and converts it back to a date. The actual date is useful, but it has some strange formatting. If you look carefully at the dates, you'll see that they have the age of each hero, but it's coded as if it were a particular date in the ancient world.

Using YEAR() and MONTH() to get readable values

After you've determined the age in days, you can use the YEAR() and MONTH() functions to pull out the hero's age in a more readable way, as illustrated by Figure 4-6.

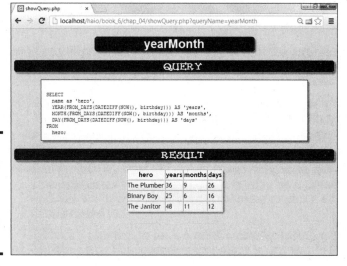

Figure 4-6:
The YEAR(),
MONTH(),
and DAY()
functions
return parts
of a date.

The query is beginning to look complex, but it's producing some really nice
output. Still, it's kind of awkward to have separate fields for year, month,
and day.

Concatenating to make one field

If you have year, month, and day values, it would be nice to combine some of
this information to get a custom field, as you can see in Figure 4-7.

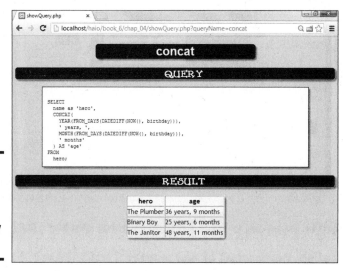

Figure 4-7:
Now, the
age is back
in one field,
as originally
intended.

There's no way I'm writing that every time . . .

I know what you're thinking. All this fancy function stuff is well and good, but there's no stinkin' way you're going to do all those function gymnastics every time you want to extract an age out of the database. Here's the good news: You don't have to. It's okay that the queries are getting a little tricky because you'll write code to do all the work for you. You write it only once, and then your code does all the heavy lifting. Generally, you write PHP code to manage each query inside a function. After you've tested it, you run that function and off you go. . . . You can also use a little gem called the view, described in the "Creating a View" section. Views allow you to store complex queries right in your database.

This query uses the CONCAT() function to combine calculations and literal values to make exactly the output the user is expecting. Even though the birthday is the stored value, the output can be the age.

Creating a View

The query that converts a birthday into a formatted age is admittedly complex. Normally, you'll have this query predefined in your PHP code so that you don't have to think about it anymore. If you have MySQL 5.0 or later, though, you have access to a wonderful tool called the VIEW. A *view* is something like a virtual table.

The best way to understand a view is to see a sample of it in action. Take a look at this SQL code:

```
CREATE VIEW heroAgeView AS
  SELECT
    name as 'hero',
    CONCAT(
      YEAR(FROM_DAYS(DATEDIFF(NOW(), birthday))),
      ' years, ',
      MONTH(FROM_DAYS(DATEDIFF(NOW(), birthday))),
      ' months'
    ) AS 'age'
  FROM
    hero;
```

If you look closely, it's exactly the same query used to generate the age from the birth date, just with a CREATE VIEW statement added. When you run this code, nothing overt happens, but the database stores the query as a view called heroView. Figure 4-8 shows the cool part.

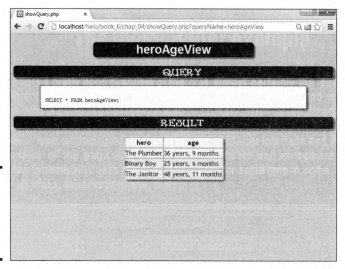

Figure 4-8:
This simple
query hides
a lot of
complexity.

This code doesn't look really fancy, but look at the output. It's just like you had a table with all the information you wanted, but now the data is guaranteed to be in a decent format.

After you create a view, you can use it in subsequent SELECT statements as if it were a table! Here are a couple of important things to know about views:

✦ **They aren't stored in the database.** The view isn't really data; it's just a predefined query. It looks and feels like a table, but it's created in real time from the tables.

✦ **You can't write to a view.** Because views don't contain data (they reflect data from other tables), you can't write directly to them. You don't use the INSERT or UPDATE commands on views, as you do ordinary tables.

✦ **They're a relatively new feature of MySQL.** Useful as they are, views weren't added to MySQL until Version 5.0. If your server uses an earlier version, you'll have to do some workarounds, described in the sidebar "So what if I'm stuck with MySQL 4.0?"

✦ **You can treat views as tables in SELECT statements.** You can build SELECT statements using views as if they were regular tables.

Some database packages make it appear as though you can update a view, but that's really an illusion. Such programs reverse-engineer views to update each table. This approach is far from foolproof, and you should probably avoid it.

So what if I'm stuck with MySQL 4.0?

Views are so great that it's hard to imagine working with data without them. However, your hosting service may not have MySQL 5.0 or later installed, which means you aren't able to use views. All is not lost. You can handle this issue in two ways.

The most common approach is to store all the queries you're likely to need (the ones that would be views) as strings in your PHP code. Execute the query from PHP, and you've essen-

tially executed the view. This method is how most programmers did it before views were available in MySQL.

Another approach is to create a new table called something like `storeQuery` in your database. Put the text of all your views inside this table, and then you can extract the view code from the database and execute it using a second pass at the data server.

Using an Inner Join to Combine Tables

When I normalized the `hero` database in Chapter 3 of this minibook, I broke it up into several tables. Take a quick look at the `hero` table in Figure 4-9.

Figure 4-9:
The hero table has a link to the mission table.

You probably noticed that most of the mission information is now gone from this table, except one important field. The `missionID` field is an integer field that contains the primary key of the `mission` table. A *foreign key* is a field that contains the primary key of another table.

Foreign keys are used to reconnect tables that have been broken apart by normalization.

Look at the `mission` table in Figure 4-10, and the relationship between the `mission` and `hero` tables begins to make sense.

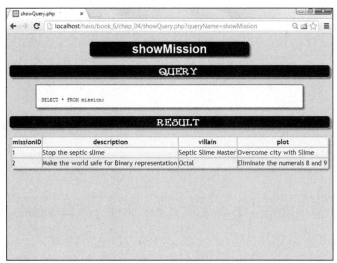

Figure 4-10: The mission table handles mission data but has no link to the hero.

The `mission` table doesn't have a link back to the hero. It can't, because any mission can be connected to any number of heroes, and you can't have a listed field.

Building a Cartesian join and an inner join

Compare the `hero` and `mission` tables, and you see how they fit together. The `missionID` field in the `hero` table identifies which mission the hero is on. None of the actual mission data is in the `hero` field, just a link to which mission the player is on.

Creating a query with both tables, as in Figure 4-11, is tempting. This query appears to join the tables, but it obviously isn't doing the right thing. You have only three heroes and two missions, yet this query returns six rows! What's happened here is called a *Cartesian join*. It's a combination of all the possible values of hero and mission, which is obviously not what you want.

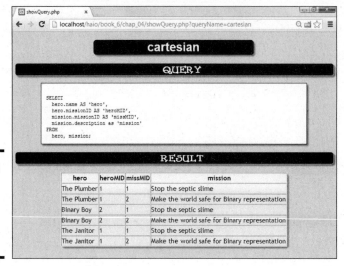

Figure 4-11:
This query joins both tables, but it doesn't seem right.

You don't really want all these values to appear; you want to see only the ones where the `hero` table's `missionID` matches up to the `missionID` field in the `mission` table. In other words, you want a query that says only return rows where the two values of `missionID` are the same. That query may look like Figure 4-12. It's almost identical to the last query, except this time, a `WHERE` clause indicates that the foreign key and primary key should match up.

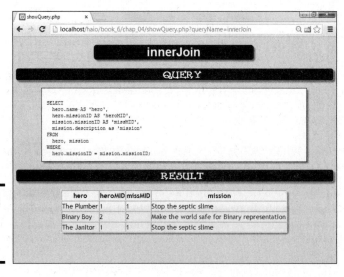

Figure 4-12:
Now, you have an inner join.

This particular setup (using a foreign key reference to join up two tables) is called an *inner join*. Sometimes, you see the syntax like

```
SELECT
  hero.name AS 'hero',
  hero.missionID AS 'heroMID',
  mission.missionID AS 'missMID',
  mission.description AS 'mission'
FROM
  hero INNER JOIN mission
ON
  hero.missionID = mission.missionID;
```

Some of Microsoft's database offerings prefer this syntax, but it really does the same thing: join up two tables.

Enforcing one-to-many relationships

Whenever your ER diagram indicates a many-to-one (or one-to-many) relationship, you generally use an inner join (see the preceding section). Here's how you do it:

1. **Start with the ER diagram.**

   No way are you going to get this right in your head! Make a diagram. Use a tool like MySQL Workbench, some other software, pencil and paper, lipstick on a mirror, whatever. You need a sketch.

2. **Identify one-to-many relationships.**

   You may have to talk with people who use the data to determine which relationships are one-to-many. In the hero data, a hero can have only one mission, but each mission can have many heroes. Thus, the hero is the many side, and the mission is the one side.

3. **Find the primary key of the one table and the many table.**

   Every table should have a primary key. (You'll sometimes see advanced alternatives like multifield keys, but wait until you're a bit more advanced for that stuff.)

4. **Make a foreign key reference to the one table in the many table.**

   Add a field to the table on the many side of the relationship that contains only the key to the table on the one side.

You don't need a foreign key in the table on the one side of the relationship. This concept confuses most beginners. You don't need (or want) a link back to the many table because you don't know how many links you'll need. Multiple links would be a listed field, which is exactly what you're trying to avoid.

If the preceding steps are hard for you to understand, think back to the hero example. Each hero (according to the business rules) can be on only one mission. Thus, it makes sense to put a link to the mission in the hero table because you have only one mission. Each mission can be related to many heroes, so if you try to link missions to heroes, you have listed fields in the `mission` table, violating the first normal form. (For information on the types of normal forms, see Chapter 3 of this minibook.) Figure 4-13 shows how it works in action. The result of this join looks a lot like the original intention of the database, but now it's normalized.

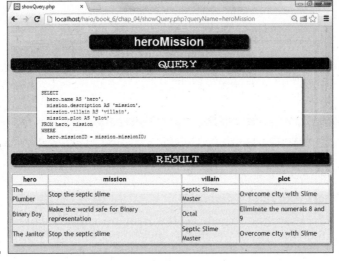

Figure 4-13:
Here's a nice join of the hero and mission tables.

I've had people write to me about this example, saying heroes should be allowed to go on multiple missions, or they're not very good heroes. That's a great point, and it brings up one of the most significant issues in data development. The data programmer's job is to *reflect the business rules in place*. I deliberately made up the business rules in this example to simplify explaining things, so I've got a business rule in place (one mission per hero) that may not be the best from a "saving the world" perspective. However, if that's the business rule you've got, your job is to implement it. There is a time and place for changing the business rules, and a data developer can help with this, but that's a decision that really belongs to the client. For a few companies I've worked with, perhaps the most useful thing I did for them was help them understand their data better and recognize when some of their business rules could be improved. When the client changes the rules, you can implement the new ones, but you shouldn't change the business rules yourself.

Counting the advantages of inner joins

Even though the table in Figure 4-13 contains everything in the original non-normalized data set (except for the repeated field — that's coming up soon), the new version is considerably better for several reasons:

✦ **No data is repeated.** The plot is stored only one time in the database. Even though it may appear several times in this output, each value is stored only once.

✦ **Searching is much more efficient.** Because the data is stored only one time, you no longer have to worry about spelling and typing errors. If the entry is wrong, it is universally wrong, and you can repair it in only one place.

✦ **The data is organized correctly.** Although the user can't see it from this output, the tables are now separated so that each type of data goes where it belongs.

✦ **The output still looks like what the user wants.** Users don't care about the third normal form. (For more on normalization, see Chapter 3 of this minibook.) They just want to get to their data. This table gives them a query that returns the data they're looking for, even though the underlying data structure has changed dramatically.

Building a view to encapsulate the join

The inner join query is so useful, it's a dandy place for a view. I created a view from it:

```
CREATE VIEW heroMissionView AS
  SELECT
    hero.name AS 'hero',
    mission.description AS 'mission',
    mission.villain AS 'villain',
    mission.plot AS 'plot'
  FROM hero, mission
  WHERE
    hero.missionID = mission.missionID;
```

Having a view means that you don't have to re-create the query each time. You can treat the view as a virtual table for new queries:

```
SELECT * FROM heroMissionView;
```

Managing Many-to-Many Joins

Inner joins are a perfect way to implement one-to-many relationships. If you look at ER diagrams, you often see many-to-many relationships, too. Of course, you also need to model them. Here's the secret: You can't really do it. It's true. The relational data model doesn't really have a good way to do many-to-many joins. Instead, you fake it out. It isn't hard, but it's a little bit sneaky.

You use many-to-many joins to handle listed data, such as the relationship between hero and power. Each hero can have any number of powers, and each power can belong to any number of heroes (see the table in Figure 4-14).

Figure 4-14:
The hero table has no reference to powers.

The inner join was easy because you just put a foreign key reference to the one side of the relationship in the many table. (See the section "Using an Inner Join to Combine Tables," earlier in this chapter.) In a many-to-many join, there is no "one" side, so where do you put the reference? Leave it to computer scientists to come up with a sneaky solution.

First, review the `hero` table in Figure 4-14.

Note that this table contains no reference to powers. Now, look at the `power` table in Figure 4-15. You see a lot of powers, but no reference to heroes.

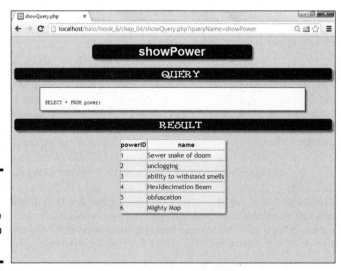

Figure 4-15:
The power table has no reference to heroes.

Here's the tricky part. Take a look at a new table in Figure 4-16.

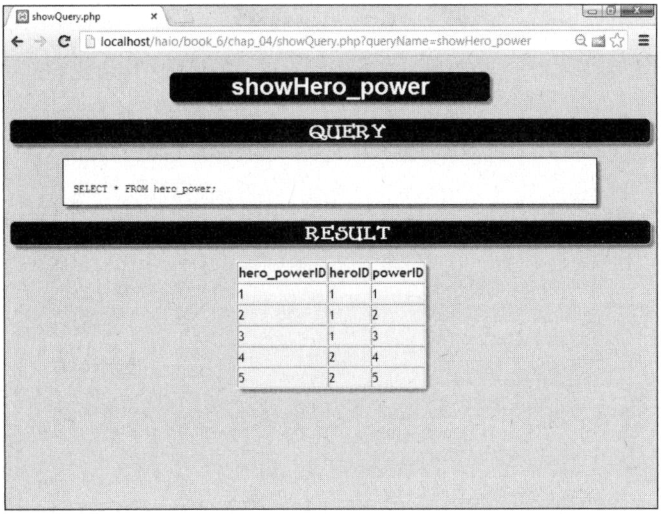

Figure 4-16:
This new
table
contains
only foreign
keys!

The results of this query may surprise you. The new table contains nothing but foreign keys. It doesn't make a lot of sense on its own, yet it represents one of the most important ideas in data.

Understanding link tables

The hero_power table shown in Figure 4-16 is a brand new table, and it's admittedly an odd little duck:

+ **It contains no data of its own.** Very little appears inside the table.

+ **It isn't about an entity.** All the tables shown earlier in this chapter are about entities in your data. This one isn't.

+ **It's about a relationship.** This table is actually about relationships between hero and power. Each entry of this table is a link between hero and power.

+ **It contains two foreign key references.** Each record in this table links an entry in the hero table with one in the power table.

+ **It has a many-to-one join with each of the other two tables.** This table has a many-to-one relationship with the hero table. Each record of hero_power connects to one record of hero. Likewise, each record of hero_power connects to one record of power.

+ **The two many-to-one joins create a many-to-many join.** Here's the magical part: By creating a table with two many-to-one joins, you create a many-to-many join between the original tables!

+ **This type of structure is called a *link table*.** Link tables are used to create many-to-many relationships among entities.

Using link tables to make many-to-many joins

Figure 4-17 displays a full-blown ER diagram of the hero data.

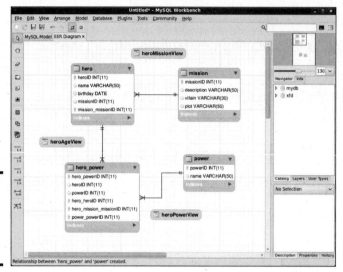

Figure 4-17:
Here's the
ER diagram
of the hero
data.

Link tables aren't really useful on their own because they contain no actual data. Generally, you use a link table inside a query or view:

```
SELECT
  hero.name AS 'hero',
  power.name AS 'power'
FROM
  hero, power, hero_power
WHERE
  hero.heroID = hero_power.heroID
AND
  power.powerID = hero_power.powerID;
```

Here are some thoughts about this type of query:

+ **It combines three tables.** That complexity seems scary at first, but it's really fine. The point of this query is to use the `hero_power` table to identify relationships between hero and power. Note that the `FROM` clause lists all three tables.

+ **The `WHERE` clause has two links.** The first part of the `WHERE` clause links up the `hero_power` table with the `hero` table with an inner join. The second part links up the `power` table with another inner join.

+ **You can use another `AND` clause to further limit the results.** Of course, you can still add other parts to the `AND` clause to make the results solve a particular problem, but I leave that alone for now.

Figure 4-18 shows the result of this query. Now you have results you can use.

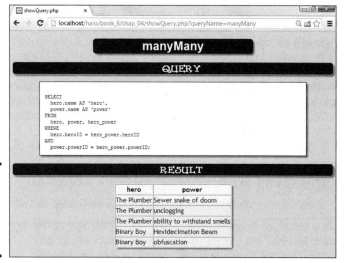

Book VI
Chapter 4

Putting Data
Together with Joins

Figure 4-18:
The Link
Query joins
up heroes
and powers.

Once again, this query is an obvious place for a view:

```
CREATE VIEW heroPowerView AS
  SELECT
    hero.name AS 'hero',
    power.name AS 'power'
  FROM
    hero, power, hero_power
  WHERE
    hero.heroID = hero_power.heroID
  AND
    power.powerID = hero_power.powerID;
```

Typically, you won't do your results exactly like this view. Instead, you display information for, say, Binary Boy, and you want a list of his powers. It isn't necessary to say Binary Boy three times, so you tend to use two queries (both from views, if possible) to simplify the task. For example, look at these two queries:

```
SELECT * FROM heroMissionView WHERE hero = 'binary boy';
SELECT power FROM heroPowerView WHERE hero = 'binary boy';
```

The combination of these queries gives you enough data to describe everything in the original table. Typically, you attach all this data together in your PHP code.

The code is standard PHP data access, except it makes two passes to the database:

```
<!doctype html>
<html lang="en">
<head>
  <meta charset="UTF-8">
  <title>showDetails.php</title>
  <style type = "text/css">
    dt {
       float: left;
       width: 4em;
       clear: left;
    }

    dd {
       float: left;
       width: 20em;
    }
  </style>
</head>

<body>
<?php
//connect

  try {
    $con= new PDO('mysql:host=localhost;dbname=haio', "haio", "haio");
    $con->setAttribute(PDO::ATTR_ERRMODE, PDO::ERRMODE_EXCEPTION);

    //get most information for requested hero
    $hero = "binary boy";

    $query = <<<HERE
SELECT
  *
FROM
  heroMissionView
WHERE
  hero = '$hero'

HERE;

    print "<dl> \n";
    $result = $con->query($query);
    $result->setFetchMode(PDO::FETCH_ASSOC);
    foreach ($result as $row){
      foreach ($row as $field => $value){
        print <<<HERE
  <dt>$field</dt>
  <dd>$value</dd>

HERE;

      } // end field foreach
    } // end row foreach
    print "  <dt>powers</dt> \n";
    print "  <dd> \n";

    //create another query to grab the powers
    $query = <<<HERE
SELECT
  power
```

```
FROM
  heroPowerView
WHERE hero = '$hero'
HERE;

    //put powers in an unordered list
    $result = $con->query($query);
    print "    <ul> \n";
    foreach ($result as $row){
      foreach ($row as $field => $value){
        print "    <li>$value</li> \n";
      } // end foreach
    }  // end while loop
    print "  </ul> \n";
    print "</dd> \n";
    print "</dl> \n";

} catch(PDOException $e) {
    echo 'ERROR: ' . $e->getMessage();
} // end try

?>
</body>
</html>
```

Refer to Chapter 5 of this minibook to read more on PHP and how it's used to access databases.

Chapter 5: Connecting PHP to a MySQL Database

In This Chapter

✓ Building the connection string

✓ Sending queries to a database

✓ Retrieving data results

✓ Formatting data output

✓ Allowing user queries

✓ Cleaning user-submitted data requests

Data has become the prominent feature of the web. As you build more sophisticated sites using HTML and CSS, you will eventually feel the need to incorporate data into your websites. You can do a certain amount of data work with the basic data structures built into PHP, but more sophisticated data problems require more sophisticated tools. Likewise, MySQL is great at data, but is not perfect for getting input from users or preparing HTML output. PHP and MySQL are perfect partners, with very compatible strengths and weaknesses.

This chapter assumes you have a database available and also that you have some basic knowledge of how SQL (Structured Query Language; the language of databases) works. It also assumes you're comfortable with PHP. If you need a refresher on PHP, please check Book V. Book VI covers MySQL in detail.

PHP and MySQL: A Perfect (but Geeky) Romance

PHP programmers frequently use MySQL as their preferred data back end for a number of good reasons:

✦ **MySQL is open source and free.** Like PHP, MySQL is open source, so PHP and MySQL can be used together (with Apache) to build a very powerful low-cost data solution.

✦ **MySQL is very powerful.** MySQL's capability as a data program has improved steadily, and it is now nearly as capable as commercial tools costing thousands of dollars. (And it is better than many that cost hundreds of dollars.)

✦ **PHP has built-in support for MySQL.** PHP includes a number of functions specifically designed to help programmers maintain MySQL databases.

✦ **You probably already have MySQL.** If you installed XAMPP, you probably already have an installation of MySQL ready to go. Check Book VIII, Chapter 1 for installation details.

✦ **MySQL was designed with remote control in mind.** MySQL is meant to be managed from some other program (like the code you write in PHP). It's not designed with a user interface (like Access has), but it's designed from the beginning to be controlled through a programming language like PHP.

Before diving into details, here's an overview of how you get information to and from a MySQL database:

1. Establish a connection.

    Before you can work with a database, you must establish a relationship between your PHP program and the database. This process involves identifying where the database is and passing it a username and password.

2. Formulate a query.

    Most of the time, you'll have some sort of query or request you want to pass to the database. For example, you may want to see all the data in a particular table, or you may want to update a record. In either case, you use SQL to prepare a request to pass to the database.

3. Submit the query.

    After you build the query, you pass it (through the connection) to the database. Assuming that the query is properly formatted, the database processes the request and returns a result.

4. Process the result.

    The database returns a special variable containing the results of your query. You'll generally need to pick through this complex variable to find all the data it contains. For example, it can contain hundreds of records. (For more on records, see the upcoming section "Retrieving data from the database.")

5. Display output to the user.

    Most of the time, you'll process the query results and convert them to some sort of HTML display that the user can view.

As an example, take a look at contact.php in Figure 5-1.

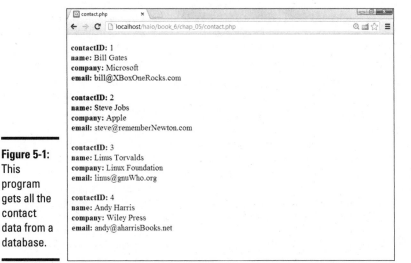

Figure 5-1:
This
program
gets all the
contact
data from a
database.

The contact.php program contains none of the actual contact information. All the data was extracted from a database. Here's an overview of the code:

```
<!DOCTYPE html>
<html lang = "en-US">

  <head>
    <meta charset = "UTF-8">
    <title>contact.php</title>
  </head>
  <body>
    <p>
    <?php
      try {
        $con= new PDO('mysql:host=localhost;dbname=dbName', "user", "pwd");
        $con->setAttribute(PDO::ATTR_ERRMODE, PDO::ERRMODE_EXCEPTION);

        $result = $con->query('SELECT * FROM contact');
        $result->setFetchMode(PDO::FETCH_ASSOC);

        foreach($result as $row){
          foreach ($row as $name=>$value){
            print "<strong>$name:</strong> $value <br />";
          } // end field loop
          print "<br />";
        } // end record loop

      } catch(PDOException $e) {
          echo 'ERROR: ' . $e->getMessage();
      }

    ?>
  </p>
  </body>
</html>
```

If you want to try this program at home, begin by running the build ContactAutoIncrement.sql script (available in Book VI, Chapter 2) in your copy of MySQL. Note that you'll probably have to change the database, username, and password values to make your examples work. This will ensure you have the database created. See Book VI, Chapter 2 if you need more information on creating databases.

Understanding data connections

The key to all database work is the connection. Database connections remind me of the pneumatic tubes at some bank drive-through locations. There's a little container you can stick your request into. You press a button, and the container shoots through a tube to the teller, who processes your request and sends you the results back through the tube.

In data programming, the connection is like that tube: It's the pipeline between your program (your car) and the data (the bank). To establish a data connection, you need to know four things:

✦ **The hostname (where the server is):** Often, the data server will be housed on the same physical machine as the web server and PHP program. In these cases, you can use `localhost` as the server name. Test servers using XAMPP almost always use `localhost` connections. If you're working in a production environment, you may need to ask your service provider for the server address of your database.

✦ **Your database username:** Database programs should always have some type of security enabled. (See Book VI, Chapter 1 for information on setting up database users and passwords.) Your program needs to know the username it should use for accessing the data. (I often create a special username simply for my programs. Book VI, Chapter 1 outlines this process.)

When you first install MySQL through XAMPP, it allows root access with no password. These settings allow anybody to do anything with your data. Obviously, that's not a good solution, security-wise. Be sure to set up at least one username and password combination for your database. If you're using an online hosting service, you probably don't have root access. In this case, you typically have a new user created for each database you build. Book VI explains all.

✦ **A password for the database:** The username isn't secure without a password. Your PHP program also needs a password. This is established when you create the database.

If you're going to make your source code available (as I do on the companion website), be sure to change the username and password so people can't use this information to hack your live data.

✦ **The database name:** A single installation of MySQL can have many databases available. You'll typically have a separate database designed for each project you build. MySQL needs to know which particular database houses the information you're seeking.

Introducing PDO

PHP has used a number of mechanisms for connecting to databases over the years. For a long time, the standard was a series of libraries for the various database types. Many people used the `mysql` library, which was (stay with me here) a library of functions for working with mySQL. If you wanted to use a different database, you'd need a different library with different functions.

The other problem with the `mysql` library was security. The techniques used in that library opened up a number of security holes. There are techniques for closing these holes, but not every programmer used them.

The `mysqli` library (mysql improved) fixed a number of these problems, but was still specific to a single database, and a bit more complex to use than the older library.

PHP5.1 and later now includes a library called PDO (PHP Data Objects) and it's a significant improvement over the `mysql` library. Here are a few key features:

**Book VI
Chapter 5**

Connecting PHP to a
MySQL Database

✦ **It works with multiple backends:** In the old days, changing a database engine meant re-writing all your code. With PDO, you use exactly the same mechanism with all databases, so it's much easier to change data engines.

✦ **It uses object-oriented syntax:** PHP supports object-oriented programming, but it uses a slightly different syntax than JavaScript. Object-oriented programming adds some nice features to data access, so this is generally a good thing.

✦ **It's provides safer access to data:** PDO uses a mechanism called *prepared statements* which prevent the most challenging kinds of data errors. More about this in the section called "Allowing User Interaction" later in this chapter.

Building a connection

With PDO, the connection is an instance of the PDO object. When you make a PDO object, you're making a connection to the database. The data connection command is chock-full of details:

```
$con = new PDO('mysql:host=localhost;dbname=dbname', "username", "password");
```

There's a lot of important stuff happening in this line:

1. **Set up a variable to hold the connection.**

   The entire point of creating a PDO object is to have a connection object, with various methods for modifying the data and making queries. So the first part of the data connection process is to make a connection object. I call mine `$con`.

   ```
   $con = new PDO('mysql:host=localhost;dbname=dbname', "username",
       "password");
   ```

2. **Build a new PDO object.**

   Because PDO is object-oriented, use the `new` keyword to call the PDO object constructor. (See Book V, Chapter 7 for more on objects and constructors in PHP.)

   ```
   $con = new PDO('mysql:host=localhost;dbname=dbname', "username",
       "password");
   ```

3. **Specify the database type.**

   MySQL is the most commonly used database system for PHP programmers, so that's what I specify. However, one of the advantages of PDO is its flexibility. If you change to a different RDBMS, you (theoretically, at least) only need to make one tiny change and the code will still work.

   ```
   $con = new PDO('mysql:host=localhost;dbname=dbname', "username",
       "password");
   ```

4. **Indicate the host.**

   When you're working on a local XAMPP installation, the host will often be `localhost`. If you're on a remote server, you may need to investigate where your databases are hosted. They may be on a completely different machine with its own address.

   ```
   $con = new PDO('mysql:host=localhost;dbname=dbname', "username",
       "password");
   ```

5. **Specify the database name.**

   Within a connection, you might have several databases. Use this part of the connection to determine which database you're using.

   ```
   $con = new PDO('mysql:host=localhost;dbname=dbname', "username",
       "password");
   ```

6. **Indicate the username.**

   Each database will likely have a specific user determined to be that database's administrator. (See Chapter 1 of this mini-book for instructions on setting up users and databases.)

   ```
   $con = new PDO('mysql:host=localhost;dbname=dbname', "username",
       "password");
   ```

7. **Provide the password.**

   Your program is essentially logging in as the user. This is why it's good to build a specific user for each application. This allows you to tightly control access to your database.

   ```
   $con = new PDO('mysql:host=localhost;dbname=dbname', "username",
       "password");
   ```

If you are using the root user with no password, you're setting up your computer to be hacked. Please see my instructions in Chapter 1 of minibook VII to set up a more secure installation.

Retrieving data from the database

After a PDO connection is set up, it's pretty easy to use. Here's the overall plan for retrieving data from the PDO connection:

1. **Put all PDO code in an exception-handler.**

   Data access is inherently dangerous. It's a perfect place for things to go wrong, so use an exception-handler to protect from potential errors. Use the `try` clause to begin your exception-handler. You can learn more about exceptions in Book V, Chapter 7.

   ```
   try {
   ```

2. **Set up your data connection.**

   Create a PDO object, setting up your data connection.

   ```
   $con = new PDO('mysql:host=localhost;dbname=dbname', "userName",
       "password");
   ```

3. **Turn on error-tracking.**

   PDO has some features for tracking errors. These are especially useful because the ordinary PHP error codes don't help with PHP problems. Turn on the PDO error-reporting mechanism with the `setAttribute()` method of the PDO object.

   ```
   $con->setAttribute(PDO::ATTR_ERRMODE, PDO::ERRMODE_EXCEPTION);
   ```

4. **Execute a query.**

   The PDO object's `query()` method allows you to apply a query to the database and returns the result in a special variable.

   ```
   $result = $con->query('SELECT * FROM contact');
   ```

   The `query()` method is one of several techniques for getting data from the database. It's a shortcut meant to be used when you're sending an SQL request that's expected to return a result (like a `SELECT`) statement. Use `execute()` when you want to pass a command that will not return a result (like a `CREATE TABLE` or `UPDATE`) statement.

5. **Set the fetch mode.**

   You can tell PDO to return data in a number of formats. For now, choose `FETCH_ASSOC`. This format returns each record as an associative array. This is the easiest fetch mode to work with. (You can also return each record as a numerically indexed array, both numeric and associative arrays, and as a special object.)

   ```
   $result->setFetchMode(PDO::FETCH_ASSOC);
   ```

6. **Read the data a row at a time.**

   The results of a data query are typically a table, so read the table one row (record) at a time. The `$result` variable is an ordinary array, so you can easily use a `foreach` loop to separate the data into rows.

   ```
   foreach($result as $row){
   ```

7. **Each row is an associative array.**

   Each row can also be thought of as an array. PDO has a number of ways to extract the data, but you set the fetch mode to associative array in Step 5. This means you can use the associative variant of the `foreach` loop to very easily separate each row into its name/value pairs.

   ```
   foreach ($row as $name=>$value){
   ```

8. **Print the field's name and value.**

   Now you can simply print out the name and value of the field. Recall you are building HTML output, so you can go with something simple (as I'm doing in this example) or encode your output in something more sophisticated like a definition list or a table.

   ```
   print "<strong>$name:</strong> $value <br />";
   ```

9. **End all your structures.**

   This is a complicated set of instructions. It's really easy to forget a closing structure. Be sure to indent properly and label all your closing braces.

   ```
   } // end field loop
   print "<br />";
   } // end record loop
   ```

10. **Catch exceptions.**

    Because all this code happens inside a `try` block, you need some sort of `catch` mechanism. Mine simply reports errors.

    ```
    } catch(PDOException $e) {
        echo 'ERROR: ' . $e->getMessage();
    } // end try
    ```

Using HTML tables for output

The basic unit of structure in SQL is called a *table* because it's usually displayed in a tabular format. HTML also has a table structure, which is ideal for outputting SQL data. Figure 5-2 shows contactTable.php, which displays the `contact` information inside an HTML table.

Tables are a very common way to output SQL results. There's one big difference between table output and the basic version shown elsewhere in this chapter. In a table, you have a separate row containing field names. Here's the code:

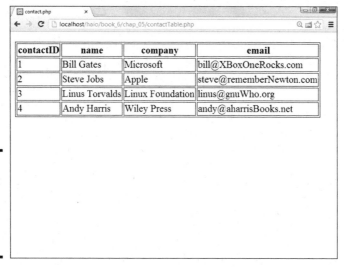

**Book VI
Chapter 5**

**Connecting PHP to a
MySQL Database**

Figure 5-2:
The contact
information
displayed
in an HTML
table.

```
<!DOCTYPE html>
<html lang = "en-US">

  <head>
    <meta charset = "UTF-8">
    <title>contact.php</title>
    <style type = "text/css">
      table, th, td {border: 1px solid black};
    </style>
  </head>
  <body>
    <p>
    <?php
      try {
        $con= new PDO('mysql:host=localhost;dbname=dbName', "user", "pwd");
        $con->setAttribute(PDO::ATTR_ERRMODE, PDO::ERRMODE_EXCEPTION);

        $query = "SELECT * FROM contact";

        //first pass just gets the column names
        print "<table> \n";

        $result = $con->query($query);
        //return only the first row (we only need field names)
        $row = $result->fetch(PDO::FETCH_ASSOC);

        print "  <tr> \n";
        foreach ($row as $field => $value){
          print "    <th>$field</th> \n";
        } // end foreach
        print "  </tr> \n";

        //second query gets the data
        $data = $con->query($query);
        $data->setFetchMode(PDO::FETCH_ASSOC);

        foreach($data as $row){
          print "  <tr> \n";
          foreach ($row as $name=>$value){
            print "    <td>$value</td> \n";
          } // end field loop
```

```
    print "  </tr> \n";
  } // end record loop

  print "</table> \n";

} catch(PDOException $e) {
    echo 'ERROR: ' . $e->getMessage();
} // end try

?>
</p>
</body>
</html>
```

You might be confused that I'm using a table here, seeing as how I argue pretty strongly against use of tables for page layout in the HTML and CSS minibooks. Tables aren't evil: They just aren't designed to be a page layout mechanism. Tables, however, *are* designed to display tabular data, and the result of a data query is pretty much the definition of tabular data. You can (and should) still use CSS for specific layout details of the table. Tables are fine when used to present data, which is what I'm doing here.

This code is still very similar to the basic contact.php program. It extracts data from the database exactly the same way. The main difference is how field names are treated. The field names will go in table headings, and only the values are printed from each row. To make this work, follow these steps:

1. Build a normal MySQL connection.

Begin with the standard connection. Don't worry about formatting until you're reasonably certain that you can read data from the database.

```
$con = new PDO('mysql:host=localhost;dbname=dbName', "user",
"pwd");
$con->setAttribute(PDO::ATTR_ERRMODE, PDO::ERRMODE_EXCEPTION);
```

2. Determine your query.

Create a query that will produce a table, view, or search result. Store it in a variable so you can use it. (You'll use the same query twice in this exercise.)

```
$query = "SELECT * FROM contact";
```

3. Print the `table` tag before extracting any results.

All the query data will be displayed inside the table, so print the `table` tag before you start printing anything that should go inside the table.

```
print "<table> \n";
```

4. Make a first pass to extract field names.

You're actually going to query the database twice. The first time, you simply want the field names, which you'll use to build the table headers, so it only needs one row.

```
$result = $con->query($query);
//return only the first row (we only need field names))
$row = $result->fetch(PDO::FETCH_ASSOC);
```

The `fetch` method pulls the next available record from the `$result` variable. You want the record data in associative array format, so pass the `PDO::FETCH_ASSOC` constant to indicate this.

5. **Print the field names as table headers.**

   Now that you have a single record, walk through that record as an associative array and use the `$field` values to print out field names.

```
print "  <tr> \n";
 foreach ($row as $field => $value){
  print "  <th>$field</th> \n";
} // end foreach
print "  </tr> \n";
```

6. **Make a second query.**

   Now execute the query again with the `$con->query()` method. This time, you're doing an ordinary query with multiple results. Don't forget to set the fetch mode to associative array.

```
//second query gets the data
$data = $con->query($query);
$data->setFetchMode(PDO::FETCH_ASSOC);
```

7. **Use nested loops to print out data elements.**

   Use the ordinary nested-loops trick to print out all of the data elements with each record taking up one row of the HTML table.

```
foreach($data as $row){
  print "  <tr> \n";
  foreach ($row as $name=>$value){
    print "     <td>$value</td> \n";
   } // end field loop
  print "  </tr> \n";
 } // end record loop
```

Allowing User Interaction

If you have a large database, you probably want to allow users to search the database. For example, the form in Figure 5-3 allows the user to search the My Contacts database.

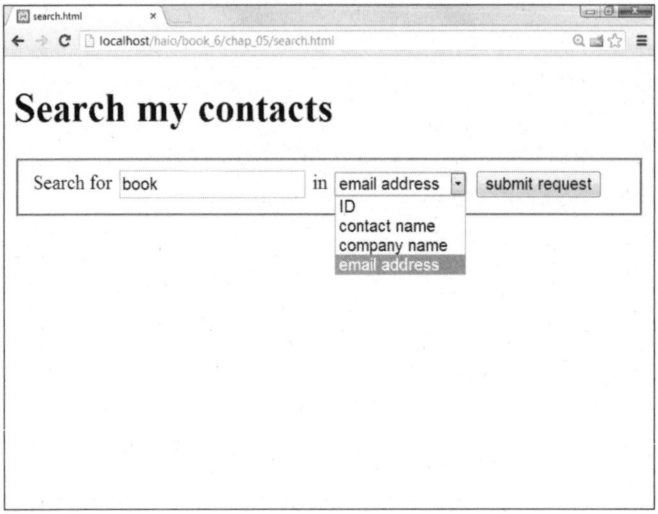

Figure 5-3:
The user
can check
for any
value in any
field.

Here are a couple of interesting things about the form in Figure 5-3:

✦ **The search value can be anything.** The first field is an ordinary text field. The user can type absolutely anything here, so you should expect some surprises.

✦ **The user selects a field with a drop-down menu.** You don't expect the user to know exactly what field names you are using in your database. Whenever possible, supply this type of information in a format that's easier for the user and less prone to error.

✦ **This form is built to fill in a query.** The back-end program (search.php) will be constructing a query from data gathered from this form. The point of the form is to request two pieces of information from the user: a field to search in and a value to look for in that field. search.php uses the data gleaned from this form to construct and submit that query to the database.

✦ **The user doesn't know SQL.** Even if the user does know SQL, don't let him use it. The SQL query should always be built on the server side. Get enough information to build an SQL query, but don't send a query to the PHP. Doing so exposes your database to significant abuse, such as the SQL injection attack described later in this chapter.

✦ **The form uses the `post` mechanism.** From the HTML perspective, it isn't important whether the form uses `get` or `post`, but when you're using forms to construct SQL queries, using `post` is a bit safer because it makes the bad guys work a little bit harder to spoof your site and send bogus requests to your database.

Building an HTML search form

This is what the HTML code for search.html looks like:

```
<!DOCTYPE html>
<html lang = "en-US">

  <head>
    <meta charset = "UTF-8">
    <title>search.html</title>
    <link rel = "stylesheet"
          type = "text/css"
          href = "search.css" />
  </head>
  <body>
    <h1>Search my contacts</h1>
    <form action = "search.php"
          method = "post">
      <fieldset>
        <label>Search for</label>
        <input type = "text"
               name = "srchVal" />
        <label>in</label>
        <select name = "srchField">
          <option value = "contactID">ID</option>
          <option value = "name">contact name</option>
          <option value = "company">company name</option>
          <option value = "email">email address</option>
        </select>
        <button type = "submit">submit request</button>
      </fieldset>
    </form>
  </body>
</html>
```

This is really a pretty basic form. The interesting stuff happens in the search.php program that's triggered when the user submits this form.

Responding to the search request

When the user submits search.html, a page like Figure 5-4 appears, created by search.php.

The search.php program isn't really terribly different from contactTable. php. It takes an SQL query, sends it to a database, and returns the result as an HTML table. The only new idea is how the SQL query is built. Rather than preloading the entire query into a string variable, as I did in all other examples in this chapter, I used input from the form to inform the query.

At one level, this seems pretty easy because an SQL query is just a string, and it's easy to build strings based on input data. However, you should never interpolate user input into an SQL string. If you directly include data from a form into an SQL query, you're opening yourself up to a nefarious type of attack called *SQL injection*. Imagine somebody entering `Andy; DROP TABLE contact` as the search value. This fake name could destroy parts of the database if the programmer is unwary.

Figure 5-4:
The
program
searches
the
database
according
to the
parameters
in search.
html.

Never directly interpolate user input into an SQL statement. Use the sanitizing mechanisms described in the next section instead.

You can use input data to build custom queries, but you must do one of two things first:

✦ **Sanitize the data to ensure it's legit:** There's a couple of ways to do this, including the PDO::quote() method. I show another technique in the next section that ensures the data is in a very specific pre-arranged set of values.

✦ **Use a prepared statement:** Prepared statements are a powerful tool. They not only sanitize your data, they can speed up data requests quite a bit. Prepared statements are described in the next section.

Before going through all the details, here's the general plan.

1. **Ensure the field name is a legitimate value.**

    The user can enter a field name through a drop-down list. Theoretically that should only allow legitimate field names (if I built the form correctly), but an evildoer could build a spoof form with any values in there they wanted. So I'll ensure the field name value matches against a list of fields I know are legit, and quit if they entered something that isn't in my list.

2. **Build a prepared statement.**

    A *prepared statement* is a special database structure. It's like a query, but it has some placeholders in it. For example, you could create the following line:

    ```
    $stmt = $con->prepare("SELECT * FROM contact WHERE $field LIKE ?");
    ```

The database will compile the statement as-is, but will not execute it yet. The question marks indicate values that will be provided later, and you can have as many as you wish.

3. Execute the prepared statement.

When you have a prepared statement, you can execute it by sending it an array of values (one per question mark in the prepared statement). I still need an array even though it has only one value in it.

```
$stmt->execute(array("j%"));
```

4. The values are *not* considered SQL.

One advantage to a prepared statement is the values passed (in this case j%, which looks for a value beginning with J) are never compiled as SQL, so most SQL injection attacks are prevented with this technique.

5. The prepared statement can be reused.

Although it's not needed for this particular application, you can reuse a prepared statement many times, and it's only compiled by the database the first time. This can be very useful because many web applications involve reading data from a form and passing the results into queries.

Theory is good, but an actual example is needed. As usual, I provide the code in its entirety here, and then I point out specific features. Look at the big picture first:

```
<!DOCTYPE html>
<html lang = "en-US">

  <head>
    <meta charset = "UTF-8">
    <title>search.php</title>
  </head>
  <body>
    <h1>My Contacts</h1>
<?php
    try {
      $fieldName = array("contactID", "name", "company", "email");
      //get values from form

      $srchField = filter_input(INPUT_POST, "srchField");
      $srchValue = filter_input(INPUT_POST, "srchVal");

      //don't proceed unless it's a valid field name
      if (in_array($srchField, $fieldName)){
        $field = $srchField;
        //put value inside %% structure
        $value = "%$srchValue%";

        $con= new PDO('mysql:host=localhost;dbname=dbName', "user", "pwd");
        $con->setAttribute(PDO::ATTR_ERRMODE, PDO::ERRMODE_EXCEPTION);

        $stmt = $con->prepare("SELECT * FROM contact WHERE $field LIKE ?");
        $stmt->execute(array($value));
```

```
     $result = $stmt->fetchAll(PDO::FETCH_ASSOC);

     if (empty($result)){
       print "No matches found";
     } else {
       foreach($result as $row){
         foreach ($row as $field => $value){
           print "<strong>$field:</strong> $value <br />";
         } // end field loop
         print "<br />";
       } // end row loop
     } // end 'empty results' if

   } else {
     print "That is not a valid field name";
   } // end if
 } catch(PDOException $e) {
   echo 'ERROR: ' . $e->getMessage();
 } // end try
?>
</body>
</html>
```

There's quite a bit going on in this program, but most of it isn't new.

1. **Enclose the whole thing in a `try` block.**

   As usual, exception-handling is a big part of data access, so be sure to add the standard `try-catch` block.

   ```
   try {
     ...
   } catch(PDOException $e) {
     echo 'ERROR: ' . $e->getMessage();
   } // end try
   ```

2. **Create an array for the valid field names.**

   The easiest way to check if something is within a range of values is to build an array of the legitimate values. I use this array to check to see that the field is legit in Step 4.

   ```
   $fieldName = array("contactID", "name", "company", "email");
   ```

3. **Get input from the user.**

   Grab user input from the form using the normal `filter_input` mechanism. Note that you won't trust the data (yet) in your SQL, but you'll still need to extract the data.

   ```
   $srchField = filter_input(INPUT_POST, "srchField");
   $srchValue = filter_input(INPUT_POST, "srchVal");
   ```

4. **See if the field name is in your list.**

   The `in_array()` function is really useful. If you feed it a value and an array, it will return true if the value appears in the array and false if it does not. (It's kind of like a bouncer for the nightclub of SQL requests.) If the field name is not on the "cool list," code execution jumps to an error message and nothing bad ever gets near the database.

```
        if (in_array($srchField, $fieldName)){
        ..
        } else {
        print "That is not a valid field name";
        } // end if
```

5. Create variables for `$field` and `$value`.

The `$field` value is copied directly from the form (because you've already established that it's legitimate). The `$value` variable will be protected with a different mechanism, so I simply add % to the beginning and end. (Because this value will be used in a LIKE clause, the % symbols indicate that the position of the search string doesn't matter.)

```
        $field = $srchField;
        //put value inside %% structure
        $value = "%$srchValue%";
```

6. Set up a PDO connection.

Set up the PDO connection in the typical way.

```
        $con= new PDO('mysql:host=localhost;dbname=dbName', "user",
    "pwd");
        $con->setAttribute(PDO::ATTR_ERRMODE, PDO::ERRMODE_EXCEPTION);
```

7. Prepare a statement.

The main query will be a prepared statement, so set it up with the question mark placeholder. You can include the `$field` variable directly in the query because it's already been validated.

```
        $stmt = $con->prepare("SELECT * FROM contact WHERE $field LIKE
    ?");
```

8. Execute the statement.

Send an array of values to the `execute()` method to execute the prepared statement. The array should have the same number of entries as question marks in the prepared statement.

```
        $stmt->execute(array($value));
```

9. Fetch the results.

Use the `fetchAll()` method to retrieve all the results from the query. Set the result set to associative arrays with the familiar FETCH_ASSOC constant.

```
        $result = $stmt->fetchAll(PDO::FETCH_ASSOC);
```

10. Test for an empty result set.

If the results of the `fetchAll()` method are empty, there was no match to the query. Send some sort of message to the user so they know what happened.

```
        if (empty($result)){
           print "No matches found";
        } else {
        ...
        } // end if
```

11. **Print out results on success.**

If the result has a value in it, parse it for all the data and print it out as usual.

```
foreach($result as $row){
  foreach ($row as $field => $value){
    print "<strong>$field:</strong> $value <br />";
  } // end field loop
  print "<br />";
} // end row loop
```

You can use the same general techniques to control all SQL statements needed to create and modify a database. In fact, this is exactly how most data programs work on the Internet, maintaining databases and allowing the user to indirectly modify the data.

So why not put the field name in the prepared statement?

If you've been following this example, you can see that you should never directly include content from user input into an SQL query. Prepared statements are the best way to protect your database. So why didn't I just do something like this?

```
$stmt = $con->prepare("SELECT * FROM
      contact WHERE ? LIKE ?");
$stmt->execute(array($field, $value));
```

In fact, I tried to do exactly that, but prepared statements expect the placeholders to be field values, not field names. So I went ahead and interpolated the field name into the SQL, but not until I had ensured it's of a legal value. There are other ways, but the key warning stays in place: Be very careful not to use unsanitized form input in SQL statements.

Part VII

Integrating the Client and Server with AJAX

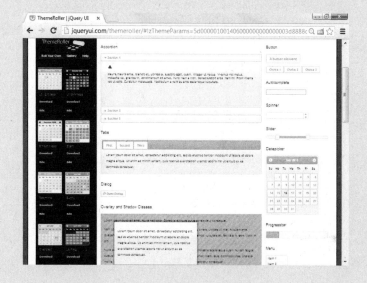

Visit www.dummies.com/extras/html5css3aio for more on fun with jQuery plug-ins.

Contents at a Glance

Chapter 1: AJAX Essentials

In This Chapter

✔ **Understanding AJAX**

✔ **Using JavaScript to manage HTTP requests**

✔ **Creating an XMLHttpRequest object**

✔ **Building a synchronous AJAX request**

✔ **Retrieving data from an AJAX request**

✔ **Managing asynchronous AJAX requests**

*I*f you've been following web trends, you've no doubt heard of AJAX. This technology has generated a lot of interest. In this chapter, I show you what AJAX really is, how to use it, and how to use a particular AJAX library to supercharge your web pages.

The first thing is to figure out exactly what AJAX is and what it isn't. It isn't

✦ **A programming language:** It isn't one more language to learn along with the many others you encounter.

✦ **New:** Most of the technology used in AJAX isn't really all that new; it's the way the technology is being used that's different.

✦ **Remarkably different:** For the most part, AJAX is about the same things you'll see in the rest of this book: building compliant web pages that interact with the user.

So you have to be wondering why people are so excited about AJAX. It's a relatively simple thing, but it has the potential to change the way people think about Internet development. Here's what it really is:

✦ **Direct control of client-server communication:** Rather than the automatic communication between client and server that happens with web forms and server-side programs, AJAX is about managing this relationship more directly.

✦ **Use of the `XMLHttpRequest` object:** This is a special object that's been built into the DOM of all major browsers for some time, but it wasn't used heavily. The real innovation of AJAX was finding creative (and perhaps unintentional) uses for this heretofore virtually unknown utility.

✦ **A closer relationship between client-side and server-side programming:** Up to now, client-side programs (usually JavaScript) did their own thing, and server-side programs (PHP) operated without too much knowledge of each other. AJAX helps these two types of programming work together better.

✦ **A series of libraries that facilitate this communication:** AJAX isn't that hard, but it does have a lot of details. Several great libraries have sprung up to simplify using AJAX technologies. You can find AJAX libraries for both client-side languages, like JavaScript, and server-side languages, like PHP.

Perhaps you're making an online purchase with a shopping-cart mechanism.

In a typical (pre-AJAX) system, an entire web page is downloaded to the user's computer. There may be a limited amount of JavaScript-based interactivity, but anything that requires a data request needs to be sent back to the server. For example, if you're on a shopping site and you want more information about that fur-lined fishbowl you've had your eye on, you might click the More Information button. This causes a request to be sent to the server, which builds an entirely new web page for you containing your new request.

Every time you make a request, the system builds a whole new page on the fly. The client and server have a long-distance relationship.

In the old days when you wanted to manage your website's content, you had to refresh each web page — time-consuming to say the least. But with AJAX, you can update the content on a page without refreshing the page. Instead of the server sending an entire page response just to update a few words on the page, the server *just sends the content you want to update and nothing else.*

If you're using an AJAX-enabled shopping cart, you might still click the fishbowl image. An AJAX request goes to the server and gets information about the fishbowl, which is immediately placed on the current page, without requiring a complete page refresh.

AJAX technology allows you to send a request to the server, which can then change just a small part of the page. With AJAX, you can have a whole bunch of smaller requests happening all the time, rather than a few big ones that rebuild the page in large, distracting flurries of activity.

To the user, this makes the web page look more like traditional applications. This is the big appeal of AJAX: It allows web applications to act more like desktop applications, even if these web applications have complicated features like remote database access.

Google's Gmail was the first major application to use AJAX, and it blew people away because it felt so much like a regular application inside a web browser.

AJAX Spelled Out

Technical people love snappy acronyms. Nothing is more intoxicating than inventing a term. AJAX is one term that has taken on a life of its own. Like many computing acronyms, it may be fun to say, but it doesn't really mean much. AJAX stands for Asynchronous JavaScript And XML. Truthfully, these terms were probably chosen to make a pronounceable acronym rather than for their accuracy or relevance to how AJAX works.

A is for asynchronous

An *asynchronous* transaction (at least in AJAX terms) is one in which more than one thing can happen at once. For example, you can make an AJAX call process a request while the rest of your form is being processed. AJAX requests do not absolutely have to be asynchronous, but they usually are.

When it comes to web design, *asynchronous* means that you can independently send and receive as many different requests as you want. Data may start transmitting at any time without having any effect on other data transmissions. You could have a form that saves each field to the database as soon as it's filled out, or perhaps a series of drop-down lists that generate the next drop-down list based on the value you just selected. (It's okay if this doesn't make sense right now. It's not an important part of understanding AJAX, but vowels are always nice in an acronym.)

In this chapter, I show you how to do both synchronous and asynchronous versions of AJAX.

J is for JavaScript

If you want to make an AJAX call, you simply write some JavaScript code that simulates a form. You can then access a special object hidden in the DOM (the `XMLHttpRequest` object) and use its methods to send that request to the user. Your program acts like a form, even if there was no form there. In that sense, when you're writing AJAX code, you're really using JavaScript. Of course, you can also use any other client-side programming language that can speak with the DOM, including Flash and (to a lesser extent) Java. JavaScript is the dominant technology, so it's in the acronym.

A lot of times, you also use JavaScript to decode the response from the AJAX request.

A is for . . . and?

I think it's a stretch to use *And* in an acronym, but AJX just isn't as cool as AJAX. They didn't ask me.

And X is for . . . data

The *X* is for *XML*, which is one way to send the data back and forth from the server. Because the object you're using is the `XMLHttpRequest` object, it makes sense that it requests XML. It can do that, but it can also get any kind of text data. You can use AJAX to retrieve all kinds of things:

✦ **Plain old text:** Sometimes you just want to grab some text from the server. Maybe you have a text file with a daily quote in it or something.

✦ **Formatted HTML:** You can have text stored on the server as a snippet of HTML/XHTML code and use AJAX to load this page snippet into your browser. This gives you a powerful way to build a page from a series of smaller segments. You can use this to reuse parts of your page (say, headings or menus) without duplicating them on the server.

✦ **XML data:** XML is a great way to pass data around. (That's what it was invented for.) You might send a request to a program that goes to a database, makes a request, and returns the result as XML.

✦ **JSON data:** A newer standard called JSON (JavaScript Object Notation) is emerging as an alternative to XML for formatted data transfer. It has some interesting advantages. You might have already built JSON objects in Book IV, Chapter 4. You can read in a text file already formatted as a JavaScript object.

Making a Basic AJAX Connection

AJAX uses some pretty technical parts of the web in ways that may be unfamiliar to you. Read through the rest of this chapter so that you know what AJAX is doing, but don't get bogged down in the details. *Nobody does it by hand!* (Except people who write AJAX libraries or books about using AJAX.) In Chapter 2 of this minibook, I show a library that does all the work for you. If all these details are making you misty-eyed, just skip ahead to the next chapter and come back here when you're ready to see how all the magic works.

The basicAJax.html program shown in Figure 1-1 illustrates AJAX at work.

Figure 1-1:
Click the
button and
you'll see
some AJAX
magic.

When the user clicks the link, the small pop-up shown in Figure 1-2 appears.

Figure 1-2:
This text
came from
the server.

If you don't get the joke, you need to go rent *Monty Python and the Holy Grail.* It's part of the geek culture. Trust me. In fact, you should really own a copy.

It's very easy to make JavaScript pop up a dialog box, but the interesting thing here is where that text comes from. The data is stored on a text file on the server. Without AJAX, you don't have an easy way to get data from the server without reloading the entire page.

You might claim that HTML frames allow you to pull data from the server, but frames have been deprecated in modern versions of HTML because they cause a lot of other problems. You can use a frame to load data from the server, but you can't do all the other cool things with frame-based data that you can with AJAX. Even if frames were allowed, AJAX is a much better solution most of the time.

You may not be able to run this program without a web server. Like PHP, AJAX requires a server to work properly. If you want to run this program, put it in a subdirectory of your server and run it through `localhost` as you do for PHP programs.

This particular example uses a couple of shortcuts to make it easier to understand:

✦ **The program isn't fully asynchronous.** The program pauses while it retrieves data. As a user, you probably won't even notice this, but as you'll see, this can have a serious drawback. But the synchronous approach is a bit simpler, so I start with this example and then extend it to make the asynchronous version.

✦ **This example isn't completely cross-browser compatible.** The AJAX technique I use in this program works fine for IE 7 and later and all versions of Firefox (and most other standards-compliant browsers). It does not work correctly in IE 6 and earlier. I recommend that you use jQuery or another library (described in Chapter 2 of this minibook) for cross-browser compatibility.

Look over the following code, and you'll find it reasonable enough:

```
<!DOCTYPE HTML>
<html lang="en";>
<head>
  <meta charset="UTF-8">
  <title>basicAJAX.html</title>
  <script type = "text/javascript">
  function getAJAX(){
    var request = new XMLHttpRequest();
    request.open("GET", "beast.txt", false);
    request.send(null);
    if (request.status == 200){
      //we got a response
      alert(request.responseText);
    } else {
      //something went wrong
      alert("Error- " + request.status + ": " + request.statusText);
    } // end if
  } // end function
  </script>
</head>
<body>
<h1>Basic AJAX</h1>
<form action = "">
  <p>
    <button type = "button"
            onclick = "getAJAX()">
      Summon the vicious beast of Caerbannog
    </button>
  </p>
</form>
</body>
</html>
```

Throughout this chapter, I explain exactly how to build an AJAX-enabled web page by hand. It's good to know how this works, but almost nobody does it this way in the real world. Read this chapter to get the basic understanding, but don't worry if the details are a little foggy. The other chapters in this minibook describe a powerful library that greatly simplifies AJAX programming. Feel free to skip ahead if this chapter is too technical. Just come back when you're ready.

Building the HTML form

You don't absolutely need an HTML form for AJAX, but I have a simple one here. Note that the form is not attached to the server in any way.

```
<form action = "">
  <p>
    <button type = "button"
            onclick = "getAJAX()">
      Summon the vicious beast of Caerbannog
    </button>
  </p>
</form>
```

This page is set up like a client-side (JavaScript) interaction. The form has an empty action element. The code uses a button (not a submit element), and the button is attached to a JavaScript function called getAJAX().

All you really need is some kind of structure that can trigger a JavaScript function.

AJAX isn't a complex technology, but it does draw on several other technologies. You may need to look over the JavaScript chapters in Book IV if this material is unfamiliar to you. Although these examples don't require PHP, they do involve server-side responses like PHP does, so AJAX is usually studied by people who are already familiar with both JavaScript and PHP as well as the foundational XHTML and CSS environments. AJAX is most useful when it also incorporates PHP, usually involving a database. So AJAX is one of those tools that's really best at integrating your other tools, and is best studied after you have a basic grasp of these other technologies.

Creating an XMLHttpRequest object

The key to AJAX is a special object called XMLHttpRequest. All the major browsers have it, and knowing how to use it in code is what makes AJAX work. It's pretty easy to create:

```
var request = new XMLHttpRequest();
```

Internet Explorer 5 and 6 had an entirely different way of invoking the XMLHttpRequest object that involved a technology called ActiveX. If you want to support these older browsers, use one of the libraries that I mention in Chapter 2 of this minibook. I've decided not to worry about them in this introductory chapter.

This line makes an instance of the XMLHttpRequest object. You use methods and properties of this object to control a request to the server.

AJAX is really nothing more than HTTP, the protocol that your browser and server quietly use all the time to communicate with each other. You can think of an AJAX request like this: Imagine that you have a basket with a balloon tied to the handle and a long string. As you walk around the city, you can release the basket under a particular window and let it rise. The window (server) puts something in the basket, and you can then wind the string to bring the basket back down and retrieve the contents. The various characteristics of the XMLHttpRequest object are described in Table 1-1.

Book VII
Chapter 1

AJAX
Essentials

Table 1-1   Useful Members of the XMLHttpRequest Object

Member	Description	Basket Analogy
open(protocol, URL, synchronization)	Opens a connection to the indicated file on the server.	Stand under a particular window.
send(parameters)	Initiates the transaction with given parameters (or null).	Release the basket but hang on to the string.

(continued)

Table 1-1 *(continued)*

Member	Description	Basket Analogy
status	Returns the HTTP status code returned by the server (200 is success).	Check for error codes ("window closed," "balloon popped," "string broken," or "everything's great").
statusText	Text form of HTTP status.	Text form of status code.
responseText	Text of the transaction's response.	Get the contents of the basket.
readyState	Describes the current status of the transaction (4 is complete).	Is the basket empty, going up, coming down, or here and ready to get contents?
onReadyStateChange	Event handler. Attach a function to this parameter, and when the readyState changes, the function will be called automatically.	What should I do when the state of the basket changes? For example, should I do something when I've gotten the basket back?

Don't worry about all the details in Table 1-1. I describe these things as you need them in the text. Also, some of these elements only pertain to asynchronous connections, so you won't always need them all.

Opening a connection to the server

The `XMLHttpRequest` object has several useful methods. One of the most important is the `open()` method:

```
request.open("GET", "beast.txt", false);
```

The `open()` method opens a connection to the server. As far as the server is concerned, this connection is identical to the connection made when the user clicks a link or submits a form. The `open()` method takes the following three parameters:

✦ **Request method:** The request method describes how the server should process the request. The values are identical to the form method values described in Book V, Chapter 3. Typical values are `GET` and `POST`.

✦ **A file or program name:** The second parameter is the name of a file or program on the server. This is usually a program or file in the same directory as the current page.

✦ **A synchronization trigger:** AJAX can be done in synchronous or asynchronous mode. (Yeah, I know, then it would just be JAX, but stay with me here.) The synchronous form is easier to understand, so I use it first. The next example (and all the others in this book) uses the asynchronous approach.

For this example, I use the GET mechanism to load a file called beast.txt from the server in synchronized mode.

Sending the request and parameters

After you've opened a request, you need to pass that request to the server. The send() method performs this task. It also provides you with a mechanism for sending data to the server. This only makes sense if the request is going to a PHP program (or some other program on the server). Because I'm just requesting a regular text document, I send the value null to the server. Chapter 6 of this minibook describes how to work with other kinds of data.

```
request.send(null);
```

This is a synchronous connection, so the program pauses here until the server sends the requested file. If the server never responds, the page will hang. (This is exactly why you usually use asynchronous connections.) Because this is just a test program, assume that everything will work okay and motor on.

Returning to the basket analogy, the send() method releases the basket, which floats up to the window. In a synchronous connection, you assume that the basket is filled and comes down automatically. The next step doesn't happen until the basket is back on earth. (But if something went wrong, the next step may *never* happen because the basket will never come back.)

Checking the status

The next line of code doesn't happen until the server passes some sort of response. Any HTTP request is followed by a numeric code. Normally, your browser checks these codes automatically, and you don't see them. Occasionally, you run across an HTTP error code, like 404 (file not found) or 500 (internal server error). If the server was able to respond to the request, it passes a status code of 200.

The XMLHttpRequest object has a property called status that returns the HTTP status code. If the status is 200, everything went fine and you can proceed. If the status is some other value, some type of error occurred.

Fun with HTTP response codes

Just like the post office stamping success/error messages on your envelope, the server sends back status messages with your request. You can see all the possible status codes on the World Wide Web Consortium's website at `www.w3.org/Protocols/rfc2616/rfc2616-sec10.html`, but the important ones to get you started are as follows:

✔ `200 = OK`: This is a success code. Everything went okay, and your response has been returned.

✔ `400 = Bad Request`: This is a client error code. It means that something went wrong on the user side. The request was poorly formed and couldn't be understood.

✔ `404 = Not Found`: This is a client error code. The page the user requested doesn't exist or couldn't be found.

✔ `408 = Request Timeout`: This is a client error code. The server gave up on waiting for the user's computer to finish making its request.

✔ `500 = Internal Server Error`: This is a server error code. It means that the server had an error and couldn't fill the request.

Make sure that the status of the request is successful before you run the code that depends on the request. (Don't get anything out of the basket unless the entire process worked.)

You can check for all the various status codes if you want, but for this simple example, I'm just ensuring that the status is 200:

```
if (request.status == 200){
  //we got a response
  alert(request.responseText);
} else {
  //something went wrong
  alert("Error- " + request.status + ": " + request.statusText);
} // end if
```

The `request.status` property contains the server response. If this value is 200, I want to do something with the results. In this case, I simply display the text in an alert box. If the request is anything but 200, I use the `statusText` property to determine what went wrong and pass that information to the user in an alert.

The `status` property is like looking at the basket after it returns. It might have the requested data in it, or it might have some sort of note. ("Sorry, the window was closed. I couldn't fulfill your request.") There's not much point in processing the data if it didn't return successfully.

Of course, I could do a lot more with the data. If it's already formatted as HTML code, I can use the `innerHTML` DOM tricks described in Book IV to display the code on any part of my page. It might also be some other type of formatted data (XML or JSON) that I can manipulate with JavaScript and do whatever I want with.

All Together Now — Making the Connection Asynchronous

The synchronous AJAX connection described in the previous section is easy to understand, but it has one major drawback: The client's page stops processing while waiting for a response from the server. This doesn't seem like a big problem, but it is. If aliens attack the web server, it won't make the connection, and the rest of the page will never be activated. The user's browser hangs indefinitely. In most cases, the user will have to shut down the browser process by pressing Ctrl+Alt+Delete (or the similar procedure on other OSs). Obviously, it would be best to prevent this kind of error.

That's why most AJAX calls use the asynchronous technique. Here's the big difference: When you send an asynchronous request, the client keeps on processing the rest of the page. When the request is complete, an event handler processes the event. If the server goes down, the browser will not hang (although the page probably won't do what you want).

In other words, the `readyState` property is like looking at the basket's progress. The basket could be sitting there empty because you haven't begun the process. It could be going up to the window, being filled, coming back down, or it could be down and ready to use. You're only concerned with the last state because that means the data is ready.

I didn't include a figure of the asynchronous version because to the user, it looks exactly the same as the synchronous connection. Be sure to put this code on your own server and check it out for yourself.

The asynchronous version looks exactly the same on the front end, but the code is structured a little differently:

```
<!DOCTYPE html>
<html lang="en">
<head>
  <meta charset="UTF-8">
  <title>asynch.html</title>
  <script type = "text/javascript">
  var request; //make request object a global variable
  function getAJAX(){
    request = new XMLHttpRequest();
    request.open("GET", "beast.txt");
    request.onreadystatechange = checkData;
    request.send(null);
  } // end function
  function checkData(){
    if (request.readyState == 4) {
      // if state is finished
      if (request.status == 200) {
        // and if attempt was successful
```

```
          alert(request.responseText);
        } // end if
      } // end if
    } // end checkData
    </script>
</head>
<body>
<h1>Asynchronous AJAX transmission</h1>
<form action = "">
  <p>
    <button type = "button"
            onclick = "getAJAX()">
      Summon the beast of Caerbannogh
    </button>
  </p>
</form>
</body>
</html>
```

Setting up the program

The general setup of this program is just like the earlier AJAX example. The HTML is a simple button that calls the getAJAX() function.

The JavaScript code now has two functions. The getAJAX() function sets up the request, but a separate function (checkData()) responds to the request. In an asynchronous AJAX model, you typically separate the request and the response in different functions.

Note that in the JavaScript code, I made the XMLHttpRequest object (request) a global variable by declaring it outside any functions. I generally avoid making global variables, but it makes sense in this case because I have two different functions that require the request object.

Building the getAJAX() function

The getAJAX() function sets up and executes the communication with the server:

```
function getAJAX(){
  request = new XMLHttpRequest();
  request.open("GET", "beast.txt");
  request.onreadystatechange = checkData;
  request.send(null);
} // end function
```

The code in this function is pretty straightforward:

1. **Create the request object.**

   The request object is created exactly as it was in the first example in the section "Creating an XMLHttpRequest object," earlier in this chapter.

2. **Call request's open() method to open a connection.**

   Note that this time I left the synchronous parameter out, which creates the (default) asynchronous connection.

3. **Assign an event handler to catch responses.**

You can use event handlers much like the ones in the DOM. In this particular case, I'm telling the `request` object to call a function called `checkData` whenever the state of the request changes.

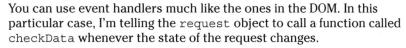

You can't easily send a parameter to a function when you call it using this particular mechanism. That's why I made `request` a global variable.

4. **Send the request.**

As before, the `send()` method begins the process. Because this is now an asynchronous connection, the rest of the page continues to process. As soon as the request's state changes (hopefully because a successful transfer has occurred), the `checkData` function is activated.

Reading the response

Of course, you now need a function to handle the response when it comes back from the server. This works by checking the *ready state* of the response. Any HTTP request has a ready state, which is a simple integer value that describes what state the request is currently in. You find many ready states, but the only one you're concerned with is 4, meaning that the request is finished and ready to process.

Ready, set, ready state!

The `readyState` property of the `request` object indicates the ready state of the request. It has five possible values:

- 0 = Uninitialized: The `request` object has been created, but the `open()` method hasn't been called on.

- 1 = Loading: The `request` object has been created, the `open()` method has been called, but the `send()` method hasn't been called.

- 2 = Loaded: The `request` object has been created, the `open()` method has been called, the `send()` method has been called, but the response isn't yet available from the server.

- 3 = Interactive: The `request` object has been created, the `open()` method has

been called, the `send()` method has been called, the response has started trickling back from the server, but not everything has been received yet.

- 4 = Completed: The `request` object has been created, the `open()` method has been called, the `send()` method has been called, the response has been fully received, and the `request` object is finished with all its request/response tasks.

Each time the `readyState` property of the request changes, the function you map to `readyStateChanged` is called. In a typical AJAX program, this happens four times per transaction. There's no point in reading the data until the transaction is completed, which will happen when `readyState` is equal to 4.

The basic strategy for checking a response is to check the ready state in the aptly named request.readyState property. If the ready state is 4, check the status code to ensure that no error exists. If the ready state is 4 and the status is 200, you're in business, so you can process the form. Here's the code:

```
function checkData(){
  if (request.readyState == 4) {
    // if state is finished
    if (request.status == 200) {
      // and if attempt was successful
      alert(request.responseText);
    } // end if
  } // end if
} // end checkData
```

Once again, you can do anything you want with the text you receive. I'm just alerting it, but the data can be incorporated into the page or processed in any way you want.

Chapter 2: Improving JavaScript and AJAX with jQuery

In This Chapter

✔ **Downloading and including the jQuery library**

✔ **Making an AJAX request with jQuery**

✔ **Using component selectors**

✔ **Adding events to components**

✔ **Creating a simple content management system with jQuery**

*J*avaScript has amazing capabilities. It's useful on its own, and when you add AJAX, it becomes incredibly powerful. However, JavaScript can be tedious. You have a lot to remember, and it can be a real pain to handle multiplatform issues. Some tasks (like AJAX) are a bit complex and require a lot of steps. Regardless of the task, you always have browser-compatibility issues to deal with.

For these reasons, web programmers began to compile commonly used functions into reusable libraries. These libraries became more powerful over time, and some of them have now become fundamental to web development.

As these libraries became more powerful, they not only added AJAX capabilities, but many of them also added features to JavaScript/DOM programming that were once available only in traditional programming languages. Many of these libraries allow a new visual aesthetic as well as enhanced technical capabilities.

A number of very powerful JavaScript/AJAX libraries are available. All make basic JavaScript easier, and each has its own learning curve. No library writes code for you, but a good library can handle some of the drudgery and let you work instead on the creative aspects of your program. JavaScript libraries can let you work at a higher level than plain JavaScript, writing more elaborate pages in less time.

Several important JavaScript/AJAX libraries are available. Here are a few of the most prominent:

✦ **DOJO:** A very powerful library that includes a series of user interface widgets (like those in Visual Basic and Java) as well as AJAX features.

✦ **Prototype:** One of the first AJAX libraries to become popular. It includes great support for AJAX and extensions for user interface objects (through the scriptaculous extension).

✦ **Yahoo User Interface (YUI):** This is used by Yahoo! for all its AJAX applications. Yahoo! has released this impressive library as open source.

✦ **jQuery:** This has emerged as one of the more popular JavaScript and AJAX libraries. It is the library emphasized in this book.

Introducing jQuery

This book focuses on the jQuery library. Although many outstanding AJAX/JavaScript libraries are available, jQuery has quickly become one of the most prominent. Here are some reasons for the popularity of jQuery:

✦ **It's a powerful library.** The jQuery system is incredibly powerful. It can do all kinds of impressive things to make your JavaScript easier to write.

✦ **It's lightweight.** You need to include a reference to your library in every file that needs it. The entire jQuery library fits in 55K, which is smaller than many image files. It won't have a significant impact on download speed.

✦ **It supports a flexible selection mechanism.** jQuery greatly simplifies and expands the `document.getElementById` mechanism that's central to DOM manipulation.

✦ **It has great animation support.** You can use jQuery to make elements appear and fade, move and slide.

✦ **It makes AJAX queries trivial.** You'll be shocked at how easy AJAX is with jQuery.

✦ **It has an enhanced event mechanism.** JavaScript has very limited support for events. jQuery adds a very powerful tool for adding event handlers to nearly any element.

✦ **It provides cross-platform support.** The jQuery library tries to manage browser-compatibility issues for you, so you don't have to stress so much about exactly which browser is being used.

✦ **It supports user interface widgets.** jQuery comes with a powerful user interface library, including tools HTML doesn't have, like drag-and-drop controls, sliders, and date pickers.

✦ **It's highly extensible.** jQuery has a plug-in library that supports all kinds of optional features, including new widgets and tools like audio integration, image galleries, menus, and much more.

✦ **It introduces powerful new programming ideas.** jQuery is a great tool for learning about some really interesting ideas like functional programming and chainable objects. I explain these as you encounter them, mainly in Chapter 4 of this minibook.

✦ **It's free and open source.** It's available under an open-source license, which means it costs nothing to use, and you can look it over and change it if you wish.

✦ **It's reasonably typical.** If you choose to use a different AJAX library, you can still transfer the ideas you learned in jQuery.

Installing jQuery

The jQuery library is easy to install and use. Follow these steps:

1. **Go to** `jquery.com`.

2. **Download the current version.**

   As of this writing, the most current version is 1.10.2. There is a 2.X series, but these versions do not support older browsers, so will not be adopted until the older browsers (particularly IE 6 and less) are no longer used at all.

   You may be able to choose from a number of versions of the file. I recommend the minimized version for actual use. To make this file as small as possible, every unnecessary character (including spaces and carriage returns) was removed. This file is very compact but difficult to read. Download the nonminimized version if you want to actually read the code, but it's generally better to include the minimized version in your programs.

3. **Store the resulting .js file to your working directory.**

   jQuery-1.10.2.min.js is the current file.

To incorporate the library in your pages, simply link to it as an external JavaScript file:

```
<script type = "text/javascript"
        src = "jquery-1.10.2.min.js"></script>
```

Be sure to include the preceding code before you write or include other code that refers to jQuery.

Importing jQuery from Google

Easy as it is to add jQuery support, you have another great way to add jQuery (and other AJAX library) support to your pages without downloading anything. Google has a publicly available version of several important libraries (including jQuery) that you can download from its servers.

This has a couple of interesting advantages:

✦ **You don't have to install any libraries.** All the library files stay on the Google server.

✦ **The library is automatically updated.** You always have access to the latest version of the library without making any changes to your code.

✦ **The library may load faster.** The first time one of your pages reads the library from Google's servers, you have to wait for the full download, but then the library is stored in a *cache* (a form of browser memory) so that subsequent requests are essentially immediate.

Here's how you do it:

```
<script type = "text/javascript"
        src="http://www.google.com/jsapi"></script>
<script type = "text/javacript">
  // Load jQuery
  google.load("jquery", "1");

  //your code here

</script>
```

Essentially, loading jQuery from Google is a two-step process:

1. **Load the Google API from Google.**

   Use the first `<script>` tag to refer to the Google AJAX API server. This gives you access to the `google.load()` function.

2. **Invoke `google.load()` to load jQuery.**

   • The first parameter is the name of the library you want to load.

   • The second parameter is the version number. If you leave this parameter blank, you get the latest version. If you specify a number, Google gives you the latest variation of that version. In my example, I want the latest variation of version 1, but not version 2.

Note that you don't need to install any files locally to use the Google approach.

All these options for managing jQuery can be dizzying. Use whichever technique works best for you. I prefer using the local code rather than the Google solution because I find it easier, and this method works even if I'm offline. For smaller projects (like the demonstrations in this chapter), I don't like the online requirement of Google. In this chapter, I simply refer to a local copy of the jQuery file.

Your First jQuery App

As an introduction to jQuery, build an application that you can already create in JavaScript/DOM. This introduces you to some powerful features of jQuery. Figure 2-1 illustrates the change.html page at work, but the interesting stuff (as usual) is under the hood.

Setting up the page

At first, the jQuery app doesn't look much different than any other HTML/
JavaScript code you've already written, but the JavaScript code is a bit
different:

```
<!DOCTYPE html>
<html lang = "en-US">

<head>
  <title>change.html</title>
  <script type = "text/javascript"
          src = "jquery-1.10.2.min.js"></script>
  <script type = "text/javascript">
    function changeMe(){
      $("#output").html("I changed");
    }
  </script>
</head>
<body onload = "changeMe()">
    <h1>Basic jQuery demo</h1>
    <div id = "output">
      Did this change?
    </div>
</body>
</html>
```

If you're already knowledgeable about jQuery, you may be horrified at my
use of `body onload` in this example. jQuery provides a wonderful alternative to the `onload` mechanism, but I want to introduce only one big, new
idea at a time. The next example illustrates the jQuery alternative to `body
onload` and explains why it is such an improvement.

The basic features of changeme.html are utterly unsurprising:

✦ **The HTML has a div named** `output`. This div initially says, "Did this change?" The code should change the content to something else.

✦ **The HTML calls a function called** `changeMe()` **when the body finishes loading.** This is a mechanism used frequently in DOM programming, although you see a new way to call an initial function in the next section.

✦ **There is a reference to the jQuery library.** Any page that uses jQuery must load it using one of the mechanisms described earlier in this chapter.

✦ **The** `changeMe()` **function looks really crazy.** When you run the program, you can tell what it does. The code gets a reference to the `output` div and changes its `innerHTML` property to reflect a new value ("I've changed."). However, the syntax is really new. All that functionality got packed into one line of (funky-looking) code.

```
$("#output").html("I changed");
```

Meet the jQuery node object

The secret behind jQuery's power is the underlying data model. jQuery has a unique way of looking at the DOM that's more powerful than the standard object model. Understanding the way this works is the key to powerful programming with jQuery.

The jQuery *node* is a special object that adds a lot of functionality to the ordinary DOM element. Any element on the web page (any link, div, heading, or whatever) can be defined as a jQuery node. You can also make a list of jQuery nodes based on tag types, so you can have a jQuery object that stores a list of all the paragraphs on the page or all the objects with a particular class name. The jQuery object has very useful methods like `html( )`, which is used to change the `innerHTML` property of an element.

The jQuery node is based on the basic DOM node, so it can be created from any DOM element. However, it also adds significant new features. This is a good example of the object-oriented philosophy.

Creating a jQuery object

You have many ways to create a jQuery object, but the simplest is through the special `$()` function. You can place an identifier (very similar to CSS identifiers) inside the function to build a jQuery object based on an element. For example,

```
var jQoutput = $("#output");
```

creates a variable called `jQoutput`, which contains a jQuery object-based on the `output` element. It's similar to the following:

```
var DOMoutput = document.getElementById("output");
```

The jQuery approach is a little cleaner, and it doesn't get a reference to a DOM object (as the `getElementById` technique does), but it makes a new jQuery object that is based on the DOM element. Don't worry if this is a little hard to understand. It gets easier as you get used to it.

Enjoying your new jQuery node object

Because `jQoutput` is a jQuery object, it has some powerful methods. For example, you can change the content of the object with the `html()` method. The following two lines are equivalent:

```
jQoutput.html("I've changed"); //jQuery version
DOMoutput.innerHTML = "I've changed"; //ordinary JS / DOM
```

jQuery doesn't require you to create variables for each object, so the code in the `changeMe()` function can look like this:

```
//build a variable and then modify it
var jQoutput = $("#output");
jQoutput.html("I've changed");
```

Or you can shorten it like this:

```
$("#output").html("I've changed");
```

This last version is how the program is actually written. It's very common to refer to an object with the `$()` mechanism and immediately perform a method on that object as I've done here.

Creating an Initialization Function

Many pages require an initialization function. This is a function that's run early to set up the rest of the page. The `body onload` mechanism is frequently used in DOM/JavaScript to make pages load as soon as the document has begun loading. This technique is described in Book IV, Chapter 7. While `body onload` does this job well, a couple of problems exist with the traditional technique:

✦ **It requires making a change to the HTML.** The JavaScript code should be completely separated from HTML. You shouldn't have to change your HTML to make it work with JavaScript.

✦ **The timing still isn't quite right.** The code specified in `body onload` doesn't execute until after the entire page is displayed. It would be better if the code was registered *after* the DOM is loaded but *before* the page displays.

Using $(document).ready()

jQuery has a great alternative to `body onload` that overcomes these short-comings. Take a look at the code for ready.html to see how it works:

```
<!DOCTYPE html>
<html lang = "en-US">

<head>
  <title>ready.html</title>
  <script type = "text/javascript"
          src = "jquery-1.10.2.min.js"></script>
  <script type = "text/javascript">
    $(document).ready(changeMe);
    function changeMe(){
      $("#output").html("I changed");
    }
  </script>
</head>
<body>
  <h1>Using the document.ready mechanism</h1>
    <div id = "output">
      Did this change?
    </div>
</body>
</html>
```

This code is much like change.html, but it uses the jQuery technique for running initialization code:

+ **The body tag no longer has an `onload` attribute.** This is a common feature of jQuery programming. The HTML no longer has direct links to the JavaScript because jQuery lets the JavaScript code attach itself to the web page.

+ **The initialization function is created with the `$(document).ready()` function.** This technique tells the browser to execute a function when the DOM has finished loading (so that it has access to all elements of the form) but before the page is displayed (so that any effects of the form appear instantaneous to the user).

+ **`$(document)` makes a jQuery object from the whole document.** The entire document can be turned into a jQuery object by specifying `document` inside the `$()` function. Note that you don't use quotation marks in this case.

+ **The function specified is automatically run.** In this particular case, I want to run the `changeMe()` function, so I place it in the parameter of the `ready()` method. Note that I'm referring to `changeMe` as a variable, so it has no quotation marks or parentheses. (Look at Book IV, Chapter 7 for more discussion of referring to functions as variables.)

You see several other places (particularly in event handling) where jQuery expects a function as a parameter. Such a function is frequently referred to as a *callback* function because it's called after some sort of event has occurred. You also see callback functions that respond to keyboard events, mouse motion, and the completion of an AJAX request.

Alternatives to document.ready

You sometimes see a couple of shortcuts because it's so common to run initialization code. You can shorten

```
$(document).ready(changeMe);
```

to the following code:

```
$(changeMe);
```

If this code is not defined inside a function and `changeMe` is a function defined on the page, jQuery automatically runs the function directly just like the `document.ready` approach.

You can also create an anonymous function directly:

```
$(document).ready(function(){
  $("#output").html("I changed");
});
```

I think this (anonymous function) method is cumbersome, but you frequently see jQuery code using this technique. Personally, I tend to create a function called `init()` and call it with a line like this:

```
$(init);
```

I think this technique is simple and easy to understand but you may encounter the other variations as you examine code on the web.

Investigating the jQuery Object

The jQuery object is interesting because it is easy to create from a variety of DOM elements, and because it adds wonderful, new features to these elements.

Changing the style of an element

If you can dynamically change the CSS of an element, you can do quite a lot to it. jQuery makes this process quite easy. After you have a jQuery object, you can use the `css()` method to add or change any CSS attributes of the object. Take a look at styleElements.html, shown in Figure 2-2, as an example.

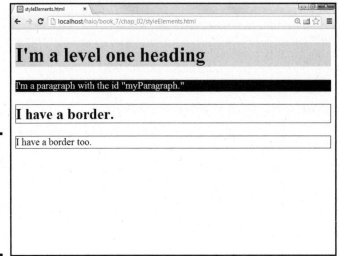

The code displays a terseness common to jQuery code:

```
<!DOCTYPE html>
  <title>styleElements.html</title>
  <meta charset="UTF-8">
  <script type = "text/javascript"
          src = "jquery-1.10.2.min.js"></script>
  <script type = "text/javascript">
    $(init);
    function init(){
      $("h1").css("backgroundColor", "yellow");
      $("#myParagraph").css({"backgroundColor":"black",
                             "color":"white"});
      $(".bordered").css("border", "1px solid black");
    }
  </script>
</head>
<body>
    <h1>I'm a level one heading</h1>
    <p id = "myParagraph">
      I'm a paragraph with the id "myParagraph."
    </p>
    <h2 class = "bordered">
      I have a border.
    </h2>
    <p class = "bordered">
      I have a border too.
    </p>
</body>
</html>
```

You find a few interesting things in this program. First, take a look at the HTML:

✦ **It contains an H1 tag.** I'm aware that's not too exciting, but I use it to show how to target elements by DOM type.

✦ **There's a paragraph with the ID `myParagraph`.** This will be used to illustrate how to target an element by ID.

✦ **There are two elements with the class `bordered`.** You have no easy way in ordinary DOM work to apply code to all elements of a particular class, but jQuery makes it easy.

✦ **Several elements have custom CSS, but no CSS is defined.** The jQuery code changes all the CSS dynamically.

The `init()` function is identified as the function to be run when the document is ready. In this function, I use the powerful CSS method to change each element's CSS dynamically. I come back to the CSS in a moment, but first notice how the various elements are targeted.

Selecting jQuery objects

jQuery gives you several alternatives for creating jQuery objects from the DOM elements. In general, you use the same rules to select objects in jQuery as you do in CSS:

✦ **DOM elements are targeted as is.** You can include any DOM element inside the `$("")` mechanism to target all similar elements. For example, use `$("h1")` to refer to all H1 objects or `$("p")` to refer to all paragraphs.

✦ **Use the # identifier to target a particular ID.** This works exactly the same as in CSS. If you have an element with the ID `myThing`, use the code `$("#myThing")`.

✦ **Use the . identifier to target members of a class.** Again, this is the same mechanism that you use in CSS, so all elements with the class `bordered` attached to them can be modified with the code `$(".bordered")`.

✦ **You can even use complex identifiers.** You can even use complex CSS identifiers like `$("li img");`. This identifier only targets images inside a list item.

These selection methods (all borrowed from familiar CSS notation) add incredible flexibility to your code. You can now easily select elements in your JavaScript code according to the same rules you use to identify elements in CSS.

Modifying the style

After you've identified an object or a set of objects, you can apply jQuery methods. One very powerful and easy method is the `css()` method. The basic form of this method takes two parameters: a style rule and value.

For example, to make the background color of all H1 objects yellow, I use the following code:

```
$("h1").css("backgroundColor", "yellow");
```

If you apply a style rule to a collection of objects (like all H1 objects or all objects with the `bordered` class), the same rule is instantly applied to all the objects.

A more powerful variation of the style rule exists that allows you to apply several CSS styles at once. It takes a single object in JSON notation as its argument:

```
$("#myParagraph").css({"backgroundColor":"black",
                       "color":"white"});
```

This example uses a JSON object defined as a series of rule/value pairs. If you need a refresher on how JSON objects work, look at Book IV, Chapter 4.

Adding Events to Objects

The jQuery library adds another extremely powerful capability to JavaScript. It allows you to easily attach events to any jQuery object. As an example, take a look at hover.html, as shown in Figure 2-3.

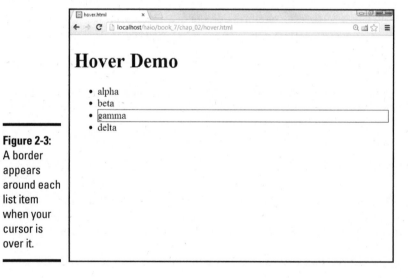

Figure 2-3: A border appears around each list item when your cursor is over it.

When you move your cursor over any list item, a border appears around the item. This isn't a difficult effect to achieve in ordinary CSS but it's even easier in jQuery.

Adding a hover event

Look at the code to see how it works:

```html
<!DOCTYPE html>
<html lang="en">
<head>
  <title>hover.html</title>
  <meta charset="UTF-8">
  <script type = "text/javascript"
          src = "jquery-1.10.2.min.js"></script>
  <script type = "text/javascript">
    $(init);

    function init(){
      $("li").hover(border, noBorder);
    } // end init

    function border(){
      $(this).css("border", "1px solid black");
    }
    function noBorder(){
      $(this).css("border", "0px none black");
    }
  </script>
</head>
<body>
    <h1>Hover Demo</h1>
    <ul>
      <li>alpha</li>
      <li>beta</li>
      <li>gamma</li>
      <li>delta</li>
    </ul>
</body>
</html>
```

The HTML couldn't be simpler. It's simply an unordered list. The JavaScript isn't much more complex. It consists of three one-line functions:

✦ `init()` **is called when the document is ready.** It makes jQuery objects of all list items and attaches the `hover` event to them. The `hover()` function accepts two parameters:

  • The first is a function to be called when the cursor hovers over the object.

  • The second is a function to be called when the cursor leaves the object.

✦ `border()` **draws a border around the current element.** The `$(this)` identifier is used to specify the current object. In this example, I use the `css` function to draw a border around the object.

✦ `noBorder()` **is a function that is very similar to the** `border()` **function, but it removes a border from the current object.**

In this example, I used three different functions. Many jQuery programmers prefer to use anonymous functions (sometimes called *lambda* functions) to enclose the entire functionality in one long line:

```
$("li").hover(
  function(){
    $(this).css("border", "1px solid black");
  },
  function(){
    $(this).css("border", "0px none black");
  }
);
```

Note that this is still technically a single line of code. Instead of referencing two functions that have already been created, I build the functions immediately where they are needed. Each function definition is a parameter to the hover() method.

If you're a computer scientist, you might argue that this is not a perfect example of a lambda function, and you would be correct. The important thing is to notice that some ideas of functional programming (such as lambda functions) are creeping into mainstream AJAX programming, and that's an exciting development. If you just mutter "lambda" and then walk away, people will assume that you're some kind of geeky computer scientist. What could be more fun than that?

Although I'm perfectly comfortable with anonymous functions, I often find the named-function approach easier to read, so I tend to use complete named functions more often. All those braces inside parentheses make me dizzy.

Changing classes on the fly

jQuery supports another wonderful feature. You can define a CSS style and then add or remove that style from an element dynamically. Figure 2-4 shows a page that can dynamically modify the border of any list item.

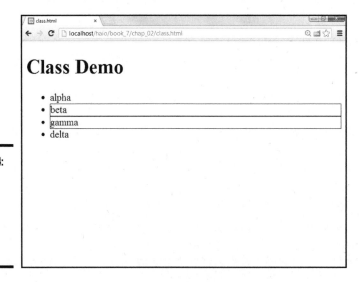

Figure 2-4:
Click list items, and their borders toggle on and off.

The code shows how easy this kind of feature is to add:

```html
<!DOCTYPE html>
<html lang="en">
<head>
  <title>class.html</title>
  <meta charset="UTF-8">
   <style type = "text/css">
     .bordered {
        border: 1px solid black;
     }
   </style>
   <script type = "text/javascript"
           src = "jquery-1.10.2.min.js"></script>
   <script type = "text/javascript">
    $(init);
    function init(){
       $("li").click(toggleBorder);
    } // end init
    function toggleBorder(){
       $(this).toggleClass("bordered");
    }
   </script>
</head>
<body>
    <h1>Class Demo</h1>
    <ul>
      <li>alpha</li>
      <li>beta</li>
      <li>gamma</li>
      <li>delta</li>
    </ul>
</body>
</html>
```

Here's how to make this program:

1. **Begin with a basic HTML page.**

   All the interesting stuff happens in CSS and JavaScript, so the actual contents of the page aren't that critical.

2. **Create a class you want to add and remove.**

   I build a CSS class called `bordered` that simply draws a border around the element. Of course, you can make a much more sophisticated CSS class with all kinds of formatting if you prefer.

3. **Link an `init()` method.**

   As you're beginning to see, most jQuery applications require some sort of initialization. I normally call the first function `init()`.

4. **Call the `toggleBorder()` function whenever the user clicks a list item.**

   The `init()` method simply sets up an event handler. Whenever a list item receives the click event (that is, it is clicked) the `toggleBorder()` function should be activated. The `toggleBorder()` function, well, toggles the border.

jQuery events

jQuery supports a number of other events. Any jQuery node can read any of the following events:

✔ `change`: The content of the element changes.

✔ `click`: The user clicks the element.

✔ `dblClick`: The user double-clicks the element.

✔ `focus`: The user has selected the element.

✔ `keydown`: The user presses a key while the element has the focus.

✔ `hover`: The cursor is over the element; a second function is called when the cursor leaves the element.

✔ `mouseDown`: A mouse button is clicked over the element.

✔ `select`: The user has selected text in a text-style input.

jQuery has several methods for manipulating the class of an element:

- `addClass()` assigns a class to the element.

- `removeClass()` removes a class definition from an element.

- `toggleClass()` switches the class (adds it if it isn't currently attached or removes it otherwise).

Making an AJAX Request with jQuery

The primary purpose of an AJAX library like jQuery is to simplify AJAX requests. It's hard to believe how easy this can be with jQuery. Figure 2-5 shows ajax.html, a page with a basic AJAX query.

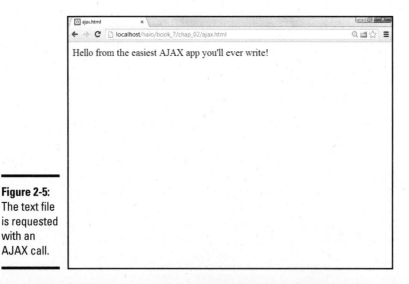

Figure 2-5:
The text file is requested with an AJAX call.

Including a text file with AJAX

This program is very similar in function to the asynch.html program described in Chapter 1 of this minibook, but the code is much cleaner:

```
<!DOCTYPE html>
<html lang="en">
<head>
  <meta charset="UTF-8">
  <title>ajax.html</title>
  <script type = "text/javascript"
          src = "jquery-1.10.2.min.js"></script>
  <script type = "text/javascript">
    $(document).ready(getAJAX);
    function getAJAX(){
      $("#output").load("hello.txt");
    }
  </script>
  </head>
  <body>
    <div id = "output"></div>
  </body>
</html>
```

The HTML is very clean (as you should be expecting from jQuery examples). It simply creates an empty div called `output`.

The JavaScript code isn't much more complex. A standard `$(document).ready` function calls the `getAJAX()` function as soon as the document is ready. The `getAJAX()` function simply creates a jQuery node based on the output div and loads the hello.txt file through a basic AJAX request.

This example does use AJAX, so if it isn't working, you might need to remember some details about how AJAX works. A program using AJAX should be run through a web server, not just from a local file. Also, the file being read should be on the same server as the program making the AJAX request.

The `load()` mechanism described here is suitable for a basic situation where you want to load a plain-text or HTML code snippet into your pages. You read about much more sophisticated AJAX techniques in Chapter 6 of this minibook.

Building a poor man's CMS with AJAX

AJAX and jQuery can be a very useful way to build efficient websites, even without server-side programming. Frequently a website is based on a series of smaller elements that can be swapped and reused. You can use AJAX to build a framework that allows easy reuse and modification of web content.

As an example, take a look at cmsAJAX, shown in Figure 2-6.

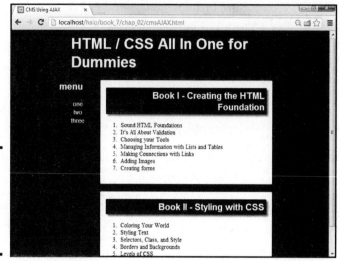

Figure 2-6:
This page
is created
dynamically
with AJAX
and jQuery.

Although nothing is all that shocking about the page from the user's perspective, a look at the code can show some surprises:

```
<!DOCTYPE html>
<html lang = "en">
  <head>
    <meta charset = "UTF-8">
    <title>CMS Using AJAX</title>
    <link rel = "stylesheet"
          type = "text/css"
          href = "cmsStd.css" />
    <script type = "text/javascript"
            src = "jquery-1.10.2.min.js"></script>
    <script type = "text/javascript">
      $(init);
      function init(){
        $("#heading").load("head.html");
        $("#menu").load("menu.html");
        $("#content1").load("story1.html");
        $("#content2").load("story2.html");
        $("#footer").load("footer.html");
      };
    </script>
  </head>
  <body>
    <div id = "all">
      <!-- This div centers a fixed-width layout -->
      <div id = "heading">
      </div><!-- end heading div -->
      <div id = "menu">
      </div> <!-- end menu div -->
      <div class = "content"
           id = "content1">
      </div> <!-- end content div -->
```

```
      <div class = "content"
          id = "content2">
      </div> <!-- end content div -->
      <div id = "footer">
      </div> <!-- end footer div -->
    </div> <!-- end all div -->
  </body>
</html>
```

Look over the code, and you can see these interesting features:

✦ **The page has no content!** All the divs are empty. None of the text shown
  in the screen shot is present in this document, but all is pulled from
  smaller files dynamically.

✦ **The page consists of empty named divs.** Rather than any particular content, the page consists of placeholders with IDs.

✦ **It uses jQuery.** The jQuery library is used to vastly simplify loading data
  through AJAX calls.

✦ **All contents are in separate files.** Look through the directory, and you
  can see very simple HTML files that contain small parts of the page. For
  example, story1.html looks like this:

```
<h2>Book I - Creating the HTML Foundation</h3>

<ol>
  <li>Sound HTML Foundations</li>
  <li>It's All About Validation</li>
  <li>Choosing your Tools</li>
  <li>Managing Information with Lists and Tables</li>
  <li>Making Connections with Links</li>
  <li>Adding Images</li>
  <li>Creating forms</li>
</ol>
```

✦ **The init() method runs on `document.ready`.** When the document is
  ready, the page runs the init() method.

✦ **The init() method uses AJAX calls to dynamically load content.** It's
  nothing more than a series of jQuery load() methods.

This approach may seem like a lot of work, but it has some very interesting
characteristics:

✦ If you're building a large site with several pages, you usually want to
  design the visual appearance once and reuse the same general template
  repeatedly.

✦ Also, you'll probably have some elements (such as the menu and heading) that will be consistent over several pages. You could simply create a
  default document and copy and paste it for each page, but this approach
  gets messy. What happens if you have created 100 pages according to
  a template and then need to add something to the menu or change the
  header? You need to make the change on 100 different pages. (In fact, this
  happened. This is the third edition of this book, and the title has changed
  slightly in each edition. I only needed to change the title one time.)

The advantage of the template-style approach is code reuse. Just like the use of an external style allows you to multiply a style sheet across hundreds of documents, designing a template without content allows you to store code snippets in smaller files and reuse them. All 100 pages point to the same menu file, so if you want to change the menu, you change one file and everything changes with it.

Here's how you use this sort of approach:

1. **Create a single template for your entire site.**

   Build basic HTML and CSS to manage the overall look and feel for your entire site. Don't worry about content yet. Just build placeholders for all the components of your page. Be sure to give each element an ID and write the CSS to get things positioned as you want.

2. **Add jQuery support.**

   Make a link to the jQuery library, and make a default `init()` method. Put in code to handle populating those parts of the page that will always be consistent. (I use the template shown here exactly as it is.)

3. **Duplicate the template.**

   After you have a sense of how the template will work, make a copy for each page of your site.

4. **Customize each page by changing the `init()` function.**

   The only part of the template that changes is the `init()` function. All your pages will be identical, except they have customized `init()` functions that load different content.

5. **Load custom content into the divs with AJAX.**

   Use the `init()` function to load content into each div. Build more content as small files to create new pages.

This is a great way to manage content, but it isn't quite a full-blown content-management system. Even AJAX can't quite allow you to *store* content on the web. More complex content management systems also use databases rather than files to handle content. You'll need some sort of server-side programming (like PHP, covered throughout Book V) and usually a database (like mySQL, covered in Book VI) to handle this sort of work. Content-management systems and complex site design are covered in Book VIII.

Chapter 3: Animating jQuery

In This Chapter

✔ Hiding and showing elements with jQuery

✔ Fading elements in and out

✔ Adding a callback function to a transition

✔ Element animation

✔ Object chaining

✔ Using selection filters

✔ Adding and removing elements

he jQuery library simplifies a lot of JavaScript coding. One of its best features is how it adds features that would be difficult to achieve in ordinary JavaScript and DOM programming. This chapter teaches you to shake and bake your programs by identifying specific objects, moving them around, and making them appear, slide, and fade.

Playing Hide and Seek

To get it all started, take a look at hideShow.html shown in Figure 3-1.

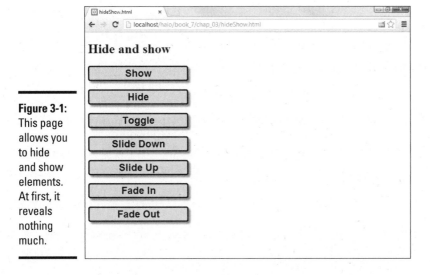

Figure 3-1: This page allows you to hide and show elements. At first, it reveals nothing much.

The hideShow program looks simple at first, but it does some quite interesting things. All of the level-two headings are actually buttons, so when you click them, interesting things happen:

✦ **The show button displays a previously hidden element.** Figure 3-2 demonstrates the revealed content.

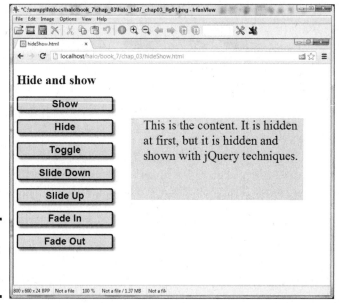

Figure 3-2:
The content
element is
now visible.

✦ **The hide button hides the content.** The behavior of the hide button is pretty obvious. If the content is showing, it disappears instantly.

✦ **The toggle button swaps the visibility of the content.** If the content is currently visible, it is hidden. If it is hidden, it appears.

✦ **The slide down button makes the content transition in.** The slide down transition acts like a window shade being pulled down to make the content visible through a basic animation.

✦ **The slide up button transitions the content out.** This animation looks like a window shade being pulled up to hide the content.

✦ **The speed of the animation can be controlled.** It's possible to adjust how quickly the transition animation plays. This example plays the slide down animation slowly, and the slide up animation more quickly. It's possible to specify exactly how long the transition takes in milliseconds (1/1000ths of a second).

✦ **The fade in button allows the element to dissolve into visibility.** This looks much like a fade effect used in video. As in the sliding animations, the speed of the animation can be controlled.

✦ **The fade out button fades the element to the background color.** This technique gradually modifies the opacity of the element so that it eventually disappears.

You can adjust how quickly the transition animation plays. You can specify exactly how long the transition takes in milliseconds (1/1000 of a second). Also, any transition can have a callback function attached.

Of course, this example relies on animation, which you can't see in a static book. Be sure to look at this and all other example pages on my website: www.aharrisbooks.net. Better yet, install them on your own machine and play around with my code until they make sense to you.

The animations shown in this example are useful when you want to selectively hide and display parts of your page:

✦ **Menus are one obvious use.** You might choose to store your menu structure as a series of nested lists and only display parts of the menu when the parent is activated.

✦ **Small teaser sentences expand to show more information when the user clicks or hovers over them.** This technique is commonly used on blog and news sites to let users preview a large number of topics, kind of like a text-based thumbnail image.

Getting transition support

The jQuery library has built-in support for transitions that make these effects pretty easy to produce. Look over the entire program before digging into the details:

```
<!DOCTYPE html>
<html lang = "en-US">

<head>
  <title>hideShow.html</title>
  <meta charset = "UTF-8">
  <style type = "text/css">
  #content {
    width: 400px;
    height: 200px;
    font-size: 200%;
    padding-left:1em;
    background-color: yellow;
    position: absolute;
    left: 300px;
    top: 100px;
  }
  h2 {
    width: 10em;
    border: 3px outset black;
    background-color: lightgray;
    text-align: center;
    font-family: sans-serif;
    border-radius: 5px;
```

```
    box-shadow: 5px 5px 5px gray;
  }
  </style>
  <script type = "text/javascript"
          src = "jquery-1.10.2.min.js"></script>
  <script type = "text/javascript">
    $(init);
    function init(){
      //styleContent();
      $("#content").hide();
      $("#show").click(showContent);
      $("#hide").click(hideContent);
      $("#toggle").click(toggleContent);
      $("#slideDown").click(slideDown);
      $("#slideUp").click(slideUp);
      $("#fadeIn").click(fadeIn);
      $("#fadeOut").click(fadeOut);
    } // end init
    function showContent(){
      $("#content").show();
    } // end showContent
    function hideContent(){
      $("#content").hide();
    } // end hideContent
    function toggleContent(){
      $("#content").toggle();
    } // end toggleContent
    function slideDown(){
      $("#content").slideDown("medium");
    } // end slideDown
    function slideUp(){
      $("#content").slideUp(500);
    } // end slideUp
    function fadeIn(){
      $("#content").fadeIn("slow", present);
    } // end fadeIn
    function fadeOut(){
      $("#content").fadeOut("fast");
    } // end fadeOut.
    function present(){
      alert("I'm here");
    } // end present
  </script>
</head>
<body>
  <h1>Hide and show</h1>
  <h2 id = "show">Show</h2>
  <h2 id = "hide">Hide</h2>
  <h2 id = "toggle">Toggle</h2>
  <h2 id = "slideDown">Slide Down</h2>
  <h2 id = "slideUp">Slide Up</h2>
  <h2 id = "fadeIn">Fade In</h2>
  <h2 id = "fadeOut">Fade Out</h2>
  <p id = "content">
    This is the content. It is hidden at first, but it is hidden and
    shown with jQuery techniques.
  </p>
</body>
</html>
```

This example may look long and complicated when you view it all at once, but it really isn't hard to understand when you break it into pieces.

Writing the HTML and CSS foundation

The HTML used in this example is minimal, as is common in jQuery development:

✦ A single level-one heading

✦ A series of level-two headings

✦ A paragraph

The level-two headings will be used as buttons in this example. I use a CSS style to make the H2 tags look more like buttons (adding a border and background color). I added an ID attribute to every button so that I can add jQuery events later.

If I wanted the H2 elements to look and act like buttons, why didn't I just make them with button tags in the first place? In this example, I wanted to focus on the jQuery and keep the HTML as simple as possible. jQuery helps make *any* element act like a button easily, so that's what I did. Users don't expect H2 elements to be clickable, so you need to do some styling (as I did) to help them understand that the element can be clicked. For comparison purposes, the other two examples in this chapter use actual HTML buttons.

The other interesting part of the HTML is the `content` div. In this example, the actual content isn't really important, but I did add some CSS to make the content easy to see when it pops up.

The most critical part of the HTML from a programming perspective is the inclusion of the `ID` attribute. This makes it easy for a jQuery script to manipulate the component, making it hide and reappear in various ways. Note that the HTML and CSS do nothing to hide the content. It will be hidden (and revealed) entirely through jQuery code.

**Book VII
Chapter 3**

Animating jQuery

Well-rounded buttons

I used some sneaky CSS tricks to make the H2 elements look like buttons. First, I made them gray (like most buttons are). I also gave them an outset border to make them appear in 3D.

I added the `border-radius` element to get rounded corners, and box shadow to add a little depth.

Initializing the page

The initialization sequence simply sets the stage and assigns a series of event handlers:

```
$(init);

function init(){
  //styleContent();
  $("#content").hide();
  $("#show").click(showContent);
  $("#hide").click(hideContent);
  $("#toggle").click(toggleContent);
  $("#slideDown").click(slideDown);
  $("#slideUp").click(slideUp);
  $("#fadeIn").click(fadeIn);
  $("#fadeOut").click(fadeOut);
} // end init
```

The pattern for working with jQuery should be familiar:

1. **Set up an initialization function.**

   Use the `$(document).ready()` mechanism (described in Chapter 2 of this minibook) or this cleaner shortcut to specify an initialization function.

2. **Hide the `content` div.**

   When the user first encounters the page, the `content` div should be hidden.

3. **Attach event handlers to each H2 button.**

   This program is a series of small functions. The `init()` function attaches each function to the corresponding button. Note how I carefully named the functions and buttons to make all the connections easy to understand.

Hiding and showing the content

All the effects on this page are based on hiding and showing the `content` div. The `hide()` and `show()` methods illustrate how jQuery animation works:

```
function showContent(){
  $("#content").show();
} // end showContent

function hideContent(){
  $("#content").hide();
} // end hideContent
```

Each of these functions works in the same basic manner:

✦ **Identifies the `content` div:** Creates a jQuery node based on the `content` div.

✦ **Hides or shows the node:** The jQuery object has built-in methods for hiding and showing.

The hide and show methods act instantly. If the element is currently visible, the show() method has no effect. Likewise, hide() has no effect on an element that's already hidden.

Toggling visibility

In addition to hide() and show(), the jQuery object supports a toggle() method. This method takes a look at the current status of the element and changes it. If the element is currently hidden, it becomes visible. If it's currently visible, it is hidden. The toggleContent() function illustrates how to use this method:

```
function toggleContent(){
  $("#content").toggle();
} // end toggleContent
```

Sliding an element

jQuery supports effects that allow you to animate the appearance and disappearance of your element. The general approach is very similar to hide() and show(), but you find one additional twist:

```
function slideDown(){
  $("#content").slideDown("medium");
} // end slideDown

function slideUp(){
  $("#content").slideUp(500);
} // end slideUp
```

The slideDown() method makes an element appear like a window shade being pulled down. The slideUp() method makes an element disappear in a similar manner.

These functions take a speed parameter that indicates how quickly the animation occurs. If you omit the speed parameter, the default value is medium. The speed can be these string values:

✦ Fast

✦ Medium

✦ Slow

✦ A numeric value in milliseconds (1/1000 of a second; the value 500 means 500 milliseconds, or half a second)

The show(), hide(), and toggle() methods also accept a speed parameter. In these functions, the object shrinks and grows at the indicated speed.

A slideToggle() function is also available that toggles the visibility of the element, but using the sliding animation technique.

Fading an element in and out

A third type of "now you see it" animation is provided by the `fade` methods. These techniques adjust the opacity of the element. The code should look quite familiar by now:

```
function fadeIn(){
  $("#content").fadeIn("slow", present);
} // end fadeIn

function fadeOut(){
  $("#content").fadeOut("fast");
} // end fadeOut.

function present(){
  alert("I'm here");
} // end present
```

`fadeIn()` and `fadeout()` work just like the `hide()` and `slide()` techniques. The fading techniques adjust the opacity of the element and then remove it, rather than dynamically changing the size of the element as the slide and show techniques do.

 I've added one more element to the `fadeIn()` function. If you supply the `fadeIn()` method (or indeed any of the animation methods described in this section) with a function name as a second parameter, that function is called upon completion of the animation. When you click the fade-in button, the `content` div slowly fades in, and then when it is completely visible, the `present()` function gets called. This function doesn't do a lot in this example but simply pops up an alert, but it could be used to handle some sort of instructions after the element is visible. A function used in this way is a *callback function*.

If the element is already visible, the callback method is triggered immediately.

Changing Position with jQuery

The jQuery library also has interesting features for changing any of an element's characteristics, including its position. The animate.html page featured in Figure 3-3 illustrates a number of interesting animation techniques.

 You know what I'm going to say, right? This program moves things around. You can't see that in a book. Be sure to look at the actual page. Trust me, it's a lot more fun than it looks in this screen shot.

This page illustrates how to move a jQuery element by modifying its CSS. It also illustrates an important jQuery technique called *object chaining* and a very useful animation method that allows you to create smooth motion over time. As usual, look over the entire code first; I break it into sections for more careful review.

Figure 3-3:
Click the
buttons, and
the element
moves.

```
<!DOCTYPE html>

<html lang = "en-US">

<head>
  <title>Animate.html</title>
  <meta charset="UTF-8">
  <style type = "text/css">
  #content {
    width: 300px;
    height: 200px;
    font-size: 200%;
    background-color: yellow;
    position: absolute;
    left: 300px;
    top: 100px;
    padding-left: .5em;
  }
  </style>
  <script type = "text/javascript"
        src = "jquery-1.10.2.min.js"></script>
  <script type = "text/javascript">
    $(init);
    function init(){
      $("#move").click(move2);
      $("#glide").click(glide);
      $("#left").click(left);
      $("#right").click(right);
    } // end init
    function move2(){
      $("#content").css("left", "50px");
      $("#content").css("top", "100px");
    } // end move2
    function move(){
      $("#content").css("left", "50px")
      .css("top", "100px");
    } // end move
    function glide(){
```

```
      //move to initial spot
      $("#content").css("left", "50px")
      .css("top", "100px");
      //slide to new spot
      $("#content").animate({
        "left": "400px",
        "top": "200px"
      }, 2000);
    } // end glide
    function left(){
      $("#content").animate({"left": "-=10px"}, 100);
    } // end left
    function right(){
      $("#content").animate({"left": "+=10px"}, 100);
    } // end left
  </script>
</head>
<body>
<h1>Animation Demo</h1>
<form action = "">
  <fieldset>
    <button type = "button"
            id = "move">
      move
    </button>
    <button type = "button"
            id = "glide">
     glide
    </button>
    <button type = "button"
            id = "left">
      &lt;--
    </button>
    <button type = "button"
            id = "right">
      -->
    </button>
  </fieldset>
</form>
<p id = "content">
  This content will move in response to the controls.
</p>
</body>
</html>
```

Creating the framework

The HTML always forms the foundation. This page is similar to the `hideShow` page, but I decided to use a real form with buttons as the control panel. Buttons are not difficult to use, but they are a little more tedious to code because they must be inside a form element as well as a block-level element, and they require more coding to produce than H2 elements.

Note that I used `&lt;` in one of the button captions. This HTML attribute displays the less-than symbol. Had I used the actual symbol (<), the browser would have thought I was beginning a new HTML tag and would have been confused.

The buttons all have `id` attributes, but I didn't attach functions to them with the `onclick` attribute. After you're using jQuery, it makes sense to commit to a jQuery approach and use the jQuery event techniques.

The only other important HTML element is the `content` div. Once again, this element is simply a placeholder, but I added CSS styling to make it obvious when it moves around. This element must be set to be absolutely positioned because the position will be changed dynamically in the code.

Setting up the events

The initialization is all about setting up the event handlers for the various buttons. An `init()` function is called when the document is ready. That function contains function pointers for the various events, directing traffic to the right functions when a button is pressed:

```
function init(){
  $("#move").click(move);
  $("#glide").click(glide);
  $("#left").click(left);
  $("#right").click(right);
} // end init
```

As usual, naming conventions makes it easy to see what's going on.

Don't go chaining . . . okay, do it all you want

The `move()` function isn't really that radical. All it does is use the `css()` method described in Book VII, Chapter 2 to alter the position of the element. After all, position is just a CSS attribute, right? Well, it's a little more complex than that.

The position of an element is actually stored in *two* attributes, `top` and `left`.

Your first attempt at a `move()` function would probably look like this:

```
function move(){
  $("#content").css("left", "50px");
  $("#content").css("top", "100px");
} // end move
```

Although this approach certainly works, it has a subtle problem. It moves the element in two separate steps. Although most browsers are fast enough to avoid making this an issue, jQuery supports a really neat feature called *node chaining* that allows you to combine many jQuery steps into a single line.

Almost all jQuery methods return a jQuery object as a side effect. So, the line

```
$("#content").text("changed");
```

not only changes the text of the content node but also makes a new node. You can attach that node to a variable like this if you want:

```
var newNode = $("#content").text("changed");
```

However, what most jQuery programmers do is simply attach new function-ality onto the end of the previously defined node, like this:

```
$("#content").text("changed").click(hiThere);
```

This new line takes the node created by $("#content") and changes its text value. It then takes this new node (the one with changed text) and adds a click event to it, calling the hiThere() function when the content ele-ment is clicked. In this way, you build an ever-more complex node by *chain-ing* nodes on top of each other.

These node chains can be hard to read because they can result in a lot of code on one physical line. JavaScript doesn't care about carriage returns, though, because it uses the semicolon to determine the end of a logical line. You can change the complex chained line so that it fits on several lines of the text editor like this:

```
$("#content")
.text("changed")
.click(hiThere);
```

Note that only the last line has a semicolon because it's all one line of *logic* even though it occurs on three lines in the editor.

Building the move( ) function with chaining

Object chaining makes it easy to build the move() function so that it shifts the content's left and top properties simultaneously:

```
function move(){
  $("#content").css("left", "50px")
  .css("top", "100px");
} // end move
```

This function uses the css() method to change the left property to 50px. The resulting object is given a second css() method call to change the top property to 100px. The top and left elements are changed at the same time as far as the user is concerned.

Building time-based animation with animate( )

Using the css() method is a great way to move an element around on the screen, but the motion is instantaneous. jQuery supports a powerful method called animate() that allows you to change any DOM characteristics over a specified span of time. The `glide` button on animate.html smoothly moves the `content` div from (50, 100) to (400, 200) over two seconds:

```
function glide(){
  //move to initial spot
  $("#content").css("left", "50px")
  .css("top", "100px");

  //slide to new spot
  $("#content").animate({
    "left": "400px",
    "top": "200px"
  }, 2000);
} // end glide
```

The function begins by moving the element immediately to its initial spot with chained `css()` methods. It then uses the `animate()` method to control the animation. This method can have up to three parameters:

✦ **A JSON object describing attributes to animate:** The first parameter is an object in JSON notation describing name/value attribute pairs. In this example, I'm telling jQuery to change the `left` attribute from its current value to 400px, and the `top` value to 200px. Any numeric value that you can change through the DOM can be included in this JSON object. Instead of a numerical value, you can use "hide," "show," or "toggle" to specify an action. Review Book IV, Chapter 4 for more details on JSON objects.

✦ **A speed attribute:** The speed parameter is defined in the same way as the speed for fade and slide animations. You find three predefined speeds: slow, medium, and fast. You can also indicate speed in milliseconds; for example, 2000 means two seconds.

✦ **A callback function:** This optional parameter describes a function to be called when the animation is complete. The use of callback functions is described earlier in this chapter in the section "Fading an element in and out."

Couldn't we just use CSS3?

If you recall from Book III, CSS3 has terrific position and animation tools, so why bother with jQuery if it can be done in plain CSS? That's a really good question. jQuery is actually using CSS3 when it can, and defaulting to another technique when it encounters a browser that cannot use jQuery. There's another advantage to the jQuery approach: Because jQuery is really JavaScript code, when you move stuff around with jQuery, you've got all the flexibility of a real programming language, with variables, loops, functions, and all that powerful stuff that a markup language like CSS just doesn't have.

Easing on down

The jQuery `animation()` method supports one more option: *easing.* The term refers to the relative speed of the animation throughout its lifespan. If you watch the animations on the animate.html page carefully, you can see that the motion begins slowly, builds speed, and slows again at the end. This provides a natural-feeling animation. By default, jQuery animations use what's called a `swing` easing style (slow on the ends and fast in the middle, like a child on a swing). If you want to have a more consistent speed, you can specify "linear" as the fourth parameter, and the animation works at a constant speed. You can also install plug-ins for more advanced easing techniques.

Move a little bit: Relative motion

You can also use the animation mechanism to move an object relative to its current position. The arrow buttons and their associated functions perform this task:

```
function left(){
  $("#content").animate({"left": "-=10px"}, 100);
} // end left

function right(){
  $("#content").animate({"left": "+=10px"}, 100);
} // end left
```

These functions also use the `animate()` method, but you see a small difference in the position parameters. The += and -= modifiers indicate that I want to add to or subtract from (respectively) the value rather than indicating an absolute position. Of course, you can add as many parameters to the JSON object as you want, but these are a good start.

Note that because I'm moving a small amount (10 pixels), I want the motion to be relatively quick. Each motion lasts 100 milliseconds, or 1/10 of a second.

Modifying Elements on the Fly

The jQuery library supports a third major way of modifying the page: the ability to add and remove contents dynamically. This is a powerful way to work with a page. The key to this feature is another of jQuery's most capable tools — its flexible selection engine. You can also use numerous attributes to modify nodes. The changeContent.html page, shown in Figure 3-4, demonstrates some of the power of these tools.

**Book VII
Chapter 3**

Animating jQuery

Figure 3-4:
The default
state of
change-
Content is a
little dull.

Of course, the buttons allow the user to make changes to the page dynamically. Clicking the Add Text button adds more text to the content area, as you can see in Figure 3-5.

Figure 3-5:
More text
can be
appended
inside any
content
area.

✦ The clone button is interesting because it allows you to make a copy of an element and place it somewhere else in the document hierarchy. Clicking the clone button a few times can give you a page like that shown in Figure 3-6.

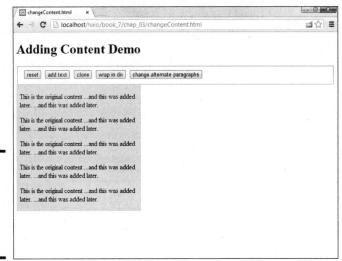

Figure 3-6:
I've made several clones of the original content.

✦ The Wrap in Div button lets you wrap an HTML element around any existing element. The Wrap in Div button puts a div (with a red border) around every cloned element. You can click this button multiple times to add multiple wrappings to any element. Figure 3-7 shows what happens after I wrap a few times.

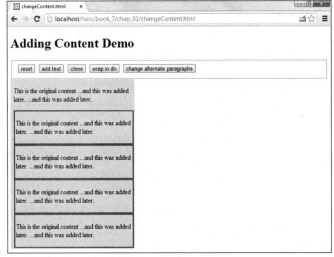

Figure 3-7:
Now you see a red-bordered div around all the cloned elements.

✦ The Change Alternate Paragraphs button increases readability; Sometimes you want to be able to alternate styles of lists and tables. jQuery has an easy way to select every other element in a group and give it a style. The Change Alternate Paragraphs button activates some code that turns all odd-numbered paragraphs into white text with a green background. Look at Figure 3-8 for a demonstration.

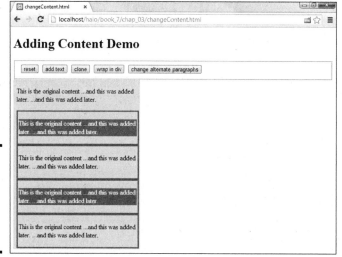

**Book VII
Chapter 3**

Animating jQuery

Figure 3-8:
All odd-numbered paragraphs have a new style.

✦ The Reset button resets all the changes you made with the other buttons.

The code for changeDocument.html seems complex, but it follows the same general patterns you've seen in jQuery programming. As always, look over the entire code first and then read how it breaks down:

```
<!DOCTYPE html>
<html lang = "en-US">

<head>
  <title>changeContent.html</title>
  <meta charset = "UTF-8">
  <style type = "text/css">
  #content {
    width: 300px;
    background-color: yellow;
    left: 300px;
    top: 100px;
    padding-left: .5em;
    border: 0px none black;
  }
  div {
    border: 3px solid red;
    padding: 2px;
  }
  </style>
  <script type = "text/javascript"
          src = "jquery-1.10.2.min.js"></script>
  <script type = "text/javascript">
    $(init);
    function init(){
      $("#reset").click(reset);
```

```
            $("#addText").click(addText);
            $("#wrap").click(wrap);
            $("#clone").click(clone);
            $("#oddGreen").click(oddGreen);
        } // end init
        function reset(){
            //remove all but the original content
            $("p:gt(0)").remove();
            $("div:not(#content)").remove();
            //reset the text of the original content
            $("#content").html("<p>This is the original content</p>");
        } // end reset
        function addText(){
            $("p:first").append(" &#x2026;and this was added later.");
        } // end addContent
        function wrap(){
            $("p:gt(0)").wrap("<div></div>");
        } // end wrap
        function clone(){
            $("p:first").clone()
            .insertAfter("p:last")
            .css("backgroundColor", "lightblue");
        } // end clone
        function oddGreen(){
            //turn alternate (odd numbered) paragraph elements green
            $("p:odd").css("backgroundColor", "green")
            .css("color", "white");
        } // end oddGreen
    </script>
</head>
<body>
    <h1>Adding Content Demo</h1>
    <form action = "">
        <fieldset>
            <button type = "button"
                    id = "reset">
              reset
            </button>
            <button type = "button"
                    id = "addText">
              add text
            </button>
            <button type = "button"
                    id = "clone">
              clone
            </button>
            <button type = "button"
                    id = "wrap">
              wrap in div
            </button>
            <button type = "button"
                    id = "oddGreen">
              change alternate paragraphs
            </button>
        </fieldset>
    </form>
    <div id = "content">
        <p>
          This is the original content
        </p>
    </div>
</body>
</html>
```

Admittedly you see a lot of code here, but when you consider how much functionality this page has, it really isn't too bad. Look at it in smaller pieces, and it all makes sense.

Building the basic page

As usual, begin by inspecting the HTML. The basic code for this page sets up the playground:

1. **Create a form with buttons.**

   This form will become the control panel. Add a button for each function you want to add. Make sure that each button has an ID, but you don't need to specify an `onclick()` function because the `init()` function takes care of that.

2. **Build a prototype `content` div.**

   Build a div called `content`, and add a paragraph to the div.

Be careful with your initial HTML structure. The manipulation and selection tricks you experiment with in this chapter rely on a thorough understanding of the beginning page structure. Be sure that you understand exactly how the page is set up so that you understand how to manipulate it. If your standard HTML page (before any JavaScript/jQuery code is added) doesn't validate, it's unlikely your code will work as expected.

Initializing the code

The initialization section is pretty straightforward. Set up an `init()` function, and use it to assign event handlers to all the buttons:

```
$(init);

function init(){
    $("#reset").click(reset);
    $("#addText").click(addText);
    $("#wrap").click(wrap);
    $("#clone").click(clone);
    $("#oddGreen").click(oddGreen);
} // end init
```

Adding text

It's pretty easy to add text to a component. The `append()` method attaches text to the end of a jQuery node. Table 3-1 shows a number of other methods for adding text to a node.

Table 3-1	Methods That Add Text to a Node
Method	*Description*
append(text)	Adds the text (or HTML) to the end of the selected element(s)
prepend(text)	Adds the content at the beginning of the selected element(s)
insertAfter(text)	Adds the text after the selected element (outside the element)
insertBefore(text)	Adds the text before the selected element (outside the element)

More methods are available, but these are the ones I find most useful. Be sure to check out the official documentation at `http://docs.jquery.com` to see the other options.

```
function addText(){
    $("p:first").append(" &#x2026;and this was added later.");
} // end addContent
```

The `append()` method adds text to the end of the element, but inside the element (rather than after the end of the element). In this example, the text will become part of the paragraph contained inside the `content` div. The more interesting part of this code is the selector. It could read like this:

```
$("p").append(" &#x2026;and this was added later.");
```

That would add the text to the end of the paragraph. The default text has only one paragraph, so that makes lots of sense. If there are more paragraphs (and there will be), the p selector can select them all, adding the text to all the paragraphs simultaneously. By specifying `p:first`, I'm using a special *filter* to determine exactly which paragraph should be affected.

Many of the examples on this page use jQuery filters, so I describe them elsewhere in the following sections. For now, note that `p:first` means the first paragraph. Of course, you also see `p:last` and many more. Read on. . . .

Attack of the clones

You can *clone* (copy) anything you can identify as a jQuery node. This makes a copy of the node without changing the original. The cloned node isn't immediately visible on the screen. You need to place it somewhere, usually with an `append()`, `prepend()`, `insertBefore()`, or `insertAfter()` method.

Take a look at the `clone()` function to see how it works:

```
function clone(){
  $("p:first").clone()
  .insertAfter("p:last")
  .css("backgroundColor", "lightblue");
} // end clone
```

1. **Select the first paragraph.**

   The first paragraph is the one I want to copy. (In the beginning, only one exists, but that will change soon.)

2. **Use the `clone()` method to make a copy.**

   Now you've made a copy, but it still isn't visible. Use chaining to do some interesting things to this copy.

3. **Add the new element to the page after the last paragraph.**

   The `p:last` identifier is the last paragraph, so `insertAfter("p:last")` means put the new paragraph after the last paragraph available in the document.

4. **Change the CSS.**

   Just for grins, chain the `css()` method onto the new element and change the background color to light blue. This just reinforces the fact that you can continue adding commands to a node through chaining.

   Note that the paragraphs are inside `content`. Of course, I could have put them elsewhere with careful use of selectors, but I put them where I want them.

It's hard to keep track of changes to the page because a standard `view source` command shows you the *original* source code, not the code that's been changed by your jQuery magic. jQuery changes the HTML of your page in memory but doesn't change the text file that contains your page. If your page is not doing what you expect, you need to look at the script-generated source code to see what's really going on.

The debugger tools in Chrome or Firebug are the key to debugging all kinds of web coding, especially as things get complex with JavaScript and jQuery. Use the Inspect Element tool to see the actual content of the page. If your jQuery isn't working, be sure to check the console to see if it has sent any error messages. Debugging with the debug tool is described in Book IV, Chapter 3.

Note that the content of the first paragraph is cloned with its current content and style information copied to the new element. If you clone the paragraph and then add content to it and clone it again, the first clone has the default text and the second clone will contain the additional text. If you modify the CSS style of an element and then clone it, the clone also inherits any of the style characteristics of the original node.

It's a wrap

Sometimes you want to embed an object inside another element (or two). For example, the `wrap` button on the `changeContent` page surrounds each cloned paragraph with a `<div></div>` pair. I've defined the `div` tag in my CSS to include a red border. Repeatedly clicking the `wrap` button surrounds all cloned paragraphs with red borders. This would be a very tedious effect to achieve in ordinary DOM and JavaScript, but jQuery makes it pretty easy to do:

```
function wrap(){
  $("p:gt(0)").wrap("<div></div>");
} // end wrap
```

The `wrap()` method is pretty easy to understand. If you feed it any container tag, it wraps that container around the selected node. You can also use multiple elements, so if you wanted to enclose a paragraph in a single item list, you could do something like this:

```
$("p").wrap("<ul><li></li></ul>");
```

The resulting code would surround each paragraph with an unordered list and list item.

Returning to the `wrap()` function, I've decided not to wrap every paragraph with a div, just the ones that have been cloned. (Mainly I'm doing this so that I can show you some other cool selection filters.) The `p:gt(0)` selector means to select all paragraphs with an index greater than 0. In other words, ignore the first paragraph, but apply the following methods to all other paragraphs. You also find these filters:

✦ **Less-than** (`:lt`) isolates elements before a certain index.

✦ **Equals** (`:eq`) isolates an element with a certain index.

Alternating styles

It's a common effect to alternate background colors on long lists or tables of data, but this can be a tedious effect to achieve in ordinary CSS and JavaScript. Not surprisingly, jQuery selectors make this a pretty easy job:

```
function oddGreen(){
  //turn alternate (odd numbered) paragraph elements green
  $("p:odd").css("backgroundColor", "green")
  .css("color", "white");
} // end oddGreen
```

The `:odd` selector only chooses elements with an odd index and returns a jQuery node that can be further manipulated with chaining. Of course, you also see an `:even` selector for handling the even-numbered nodes. The rest of this code is simply CSS styling.

Resetting the page

You need to be able to restore the page to its pristine state. A quick jQuery function can easily do the trick:

```
function reset(){
  //remove all but the original content
  $("p:gt(0)").remove();
  $("div:not(#content)").remove();
  //reset the text of the original content
  $("#content").html("<p>This is the original content</p>");
} // end reset
```

This function reviews many of the jQuery and selection tricks shown in this chapter:

1. **Remove all but the first paragraph.**

   Any paragraph with an index greater than 0 is a clone, so it needs to go away. The `remove()` method removes all jQuery nodes associated with the current selector.

2. **Remove all divs but the original content.**

   I could have used the `:gt` selector again, but instead I use another interesting selector — `:not`. This removes every div that isn't the primary `content` div. This removes all divs added through the `wrap()` function.

3. **Reset the original `content` div to its default text.**

   Set the default text back to its original status so that the page is reset.

All I really need here is the last line of code. Changing the HTML of the `content` div replaces the current contents with whatever is included, so the first two lines aren't entirely necessary in this particular context. Still, it's useful to know how to remove elements when you need to do so.

More fun with selectors and filters

The jQuery selectors and filters are really fun and powerful. Table 3-2 describes a few more filters and indicates how they might be used.

Note that this is a representative list. Be sure to check out the official documentation at `http://docs.jquery.com` for a more complete list of filters.

Table 3-2	Selected jQuery Filters
Filter	*Description*
:header	Any header tag (H1, H2, H3).
:animated	Any element that is currently being animated.
:contains(text)	Any element that contains the indicated text.
:empty	The element is empty.
:parent	This element contains some other element.
:attribute=value	The element has an attribute with the specified value.

Chapter 4: Using the jQuery User Interface Toolkit

The jQuery library is an incredible tool for simplifying JavaScript programming. It's so popular and powerful that developers began adding new features to make it even more useful. Among the most important of these is a framework called jQuery UI (User Interface), sometimes also called the UI toolkit. That's what this chapter's all about.

What the jQuery User Interface Brings to the Table

This tool adds some very welcome features to web development, including new visual elements (widgets), a uniform icon set, and a mechanism for easily generating attractive CSS styles:

✦ **New user interface elements:** As a modern user interface tool, HTML is missing some important tools. Most modern visual languages include built-in support for such devices as scroll bars, dedicated datepickers, and multiple tab tools. Although HTML5 does promise some of these features, support varies greatly by browser. jQuery UI adds versions of these features that work on older and newer browsers in a consistent way.

✦ **Advanced user interaction:** The jQuery widgets allow new and exciting ways for the user to interact with your page. With the UI toolkit, you can easily let users make selections by dragging and dropping elements, and expand and contract parts of the page.

✦ **Flexible theme templates:** jQuery UI includes a template mechanism that controls the visual look and feel of your elements. You can choose from dozens of prebuilt themes or use a tool to build your own particular look. You can reuse this template library to manage the look of your other page elements, too (not just the ones defined by the library).

✦ **A complete icon library:** The jQuery UI has a library of icons for use in your web development. It has arrows, buttons, and plenty of other doo-dads that can be easily changed to fit your template.

✦ **A very clean, modern look:** It's very easy to build forward-looking visual designs with jQuery UI. It supports patterns, shadows, and plenty of special visual effects.

✦ **The power of jQuery:** Because jQuery UI is an extension of jQuery, it adds on to the incredible features of the jQuery language.

✦ **Open-source values:** The jQuery UI (like jQuery itself) is an open-source project with a very active community. This means the library is free to use and can be modified to suit your needs.

The jQuery toolkit is pretty exciting. The best way to get an overview of it is to see an example online. The jQuery website (`http://jqueryui.com`) is a great place to get the latest information about jQuery.

It's a theme park

One of the coolest tools in jQuery UI is a concept called a *theme,* which is simply a visual rule-set. The theme is essentially a complex CSS document designed to be used with the UI library.

Using the themeRoller to get an overview of jQuery

The jQuery website also features a marvelous tool called the *themeRoller.* The themeRoller allows you to select and modify themes, so it's a great place to preview how themes work, as well as see the key features of the UI extension. Figure 4-1 shows this web page, which demonstrates many of the great features of jQuery UI.

Figure 4-1:
The themeRoller lets you review many jQuery UI elements and modify their look.

Before you use themeRoller to change themes, use it to get acquainted with the UI elements. Several useful tools are visible in Figure 4-1:

✦ **Accordion:** The upper-middle segment of the page has three segments (section 1, section 2, and section 3). By clicking a section heading, the user can expand that section and collapse the others.

✦ **Slider:** Sliders (or scroll bars) are an essential user interface element. They allow the user to choose a numeric value with an easy visual tool. jQuery sliders can be adjusted in many ways to allow easy and error-free input.

✦ **Datepicker:** It's very difficult to ensure that users enter dates properly. The datepicker control automatically pops up a calendar into the page and lets the user manipulate the calendar to pick a date. It's a phenomenally useful tool.

✦ **Tabs:** It's common to have a mechanism for hiding and showing parts of your page. The accordion technique is one way to do so, but tabs are another very popular technique. This mechanism allows you to build a very powerful multitab document without much work.

Scrolling down the page, you see even more interesting tools. Figure 4-2 shows some of these widgets in action.

**Book VII
Chapter 4**

**Using the jQuery
User Interface
Toolkit**

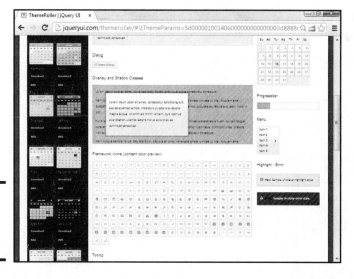

Figure 4-2:
Even more
exciting
widgets.

These widgets demonstrate even more of the power of the jQuery UI library:

✦ **Progress bar:** It's always best to design your code so that little delay exists, but if part of your program is taking some time, a progress bar is a great reminder that something is happening.

✦ **Dialog:** The `open dialog` button pops up what appears to be a dialog box. It acts much like the JavaScript alert, but it's much nicer looking, and it has features that make it much more advanced. In Figure 4-2, the dialog box has a clever title: Dialog Title.

✦ **Formatting tools:** The jQuery UI includes special tools for setting apart certain parts of your page as warnings, as highlighted text, or with added shadows and transparency. If you look carefully at Figure 4-2, you'll see several examples of special formatting, including the red alert box, drop shadows, and the UI-highlight style.

✦ **Icons:** jQuery UI ships with a large collection of icons that you can use on your page. Hover over each of the icons on the themeRoller to see a description of the icon. These can be easily used to allow various user interactions.

This is just a quick preview of the visual elements. Read more about how to implement the various elements in Chapter 5 of this minibook after you understand the basics of how to install and work with jQuery UI in this chapter.

Look at the left column on the themeRoller page. If you click the gallery tab (yep, it's using a jQuery UI tab interface), you can see a list of prebuilt themes. Figure 4-3 shows the themeRoller page with an entirely different theme in place.

Figure 4-3:
Now themeRoller is using the Le Frog theme.

The themeRoller example

themeRoller is a great example for a number of reasons. It offers a pretty good overview of the jQuery UI library, but it's also a great example of where the web is going. It's not really a web page as much as an application that happens to be written in web technologies. Notice that the functionality of the page (the ability to change styles dynamically) uses many jQuery and jQuery UI tricks: tabs, accordions, dialog boxes, and so on. This kind of programming is almost certainly the direction web development is heading, and may indeed be the primary form of application in the future. Certainly it appears that applications using this style of user interface and AJAX for data communication and storage are going to be important for some time to come.

The built-in themes are pretty impressive, but of course, you can make your own. Although you're always free to edit the CSS manually, the whole point of the themeRoller application is to make this process easier.

If you go back to the Roll Your Own tab, you can see an accordion selection that you can use to pick various theme options. You can change fonts, add rounded corners, pick various color schemes, and much more. You can mess around with these options all you want and create your own visual style. You can then save that theme and use it in your own projects.

The themes and widgets are obvious features of the jQuery user interface library, but they aren't the only features. In addition to these more visible tools, jQuery UI adds a number of new behaviors to jQuery nodes. These new behaviors (drag and drop, resize, and more) are used to add functionality to a web page, which is quite difficult to achieve in more traditional programming.

Wanna drag? Making components draggable

The basic idea of this program is completely consistent with the jQuery concepts described in Chapters 2 and 3 of this minibook. The page has very simple HTML code. An initialization function creates a special jQuery node and gives it functionality. That's all there is to it.

Your first building example is a simple application that allows the user to pick up a page element and move it with the mouse. While you do this with JavaScript and DOM in Book IV, Chapter 7, you'll find it's quite easy to get the same effect with jQuery UI. Figure 4-4 shows this page in action.

This example is a good starting place because it's pretty easy. Often, the hardest part of jQuery UI applications is attaching to the library. After that's done (and it's not *that* hard), the rest of the programming is ridiculously easy. Take a look at the code, and you can see what I'm talking about:

```html
<!DOCTYPE html>
<html lang = "en">

<head>
  <title>drag.html</title>
  <meta charset= "UTF-8" />
  <style type = "text/css">
  #dragMe {
    width: 100px;
    height: 100px;
    border: 1px solid blue;
    text-align: center;
  }
  </style>
  <script type = "text/javascript"
          src = "js/jquery-1.9.1.js"></script>
  <script type = "text/javascript"
          src = "js/jquery-ui-1.10.3.custom.min.js"></script>
  <script type = "text/javascript">
    $(init);
    function init(){
      $("#dragMe").draggable();
    }
  </script>
</head>
<body>
  <h1>Drag Demo</h1>
  <div id = "dragMe">
    Drag me
  </div>
</body>
</html>
```

Downloading the library

Writing jQuery UI code isn't difficult, but getting the right parts of the library can be a bit confusing. The jQuery UI library is much larger than the standard jQuery package, so you may not want to include the entire thing if you don't need it.

Figure 4-4:
The user
can simply
drag the box
anywhere
on the page.

Previous versions of jQuery UI allowed you to download the entire package but stored each of the various elements in a separate JavaScript file. It was common to have a half-dozen different `script` tags active just to get the various elements in place. Worse, some dependency issues existed, so you needed to make sure that you had certain packages installed before you used other packages. This made a simple library quite complex to actually use.

Fortunately, the latest versions of the jQuery UI make this process quite a bit simpler:

1. **Pick (or create) your theme.**

    Use the themeRoller site to pick a starting place from the template library. You can then customize your theme exactly to make whatever you want (changing colors, fonts, and other elements).

2. **Download the theme.**

    The themeRoller has a download button. Click this when you're ready to download your theme.

3. **Pick the elements you want.**

    When you're first starting on a project, you'll probably pick all the elements. If you find that the page is loading too slowly, you might build a smaller version that contains only those elements you need. For now, pick everything.

4. **Download the file.**

    After you've chosen the elements you want, you can download them in a zip file.

5. **Install the contents of the zip file to your working directory.**

    The zip file contains a number of files and directories. Copy the `css` and `js` directories into the directory where your web pages will be (often the `public_html` or `htdocs` directory). You do not need to copy the `development-bundle` directory or the index.html page.

6. **If you install multiple themes, copy only the theme information from additional themes.**

    All themes use the same JavaScript. Only the CSS (and related image files) changes. If you want to have multiple themes in your project, simply copy the CSS contents. Each theme will be a different subdirectory of the main CSS directory.

7. **Link to the CSS files.**

    Use the standard link technique to link to the CSS files created by jQuery UI. You can also link to your own CSS files or use internal CSS in addition to the custom CSS. Be sure that you get the path right. Normally, the path looks something like `css/themeName/jquery-ui-1.8.1.custom.css`. (Note I'm not linking to the CSS in this first example. The CSS is explained in the upcoming section called "Resizing on a Theme."

8. **Link to the JavaScript files.**

   The jQuery UI toolkit also installs two JavaScript files: the standard jQuery library and the jQuery UI library. By default, both of these files are installed in the `js` directory. You'll need to link to both files. One will be called something like jquery-1.9.1.js and the other will be called something like jquery-ui-1.10.3.custom.min.js. Sometimes you will see minimized files alongside ordinary versions. The minimized version will have the term `min` embedded. Either version is fine, but the minimized version will load faster.

If something isn't working right, check your file paths again. Almost always, when the jQuery UI stuff isn't working right, it's because you haven't linked to all the right files. Also, note that the CSS files created by jQuery UI also include images. Make sure that your theme has an associated images directory, or your project may not work correctly. If you copied the entire CSS and JS directories from the download, you should be fine.

Writing the program

Here's how you go about putting the program together:

1. **Create a basic HTML document.**

   The standard document doesn't have to be anything special. I created one div with the ID `dragMe`. That's the div I want to make draggable (but of course you can apply dragging functionality to anything you can select with jQuery).

2. **Add the standard jQuery library.**

   The first `script` tag imports the standard jQuery library. The UI library requires jQuery to be loaded first.

3. **Add a link to the jQuery UI library.**

   A second `script` tag imports the jQuery UI library. (See the following section on downloading and installing jQuery for details on how to obtain this library.)

4. **Create an initialization function**.

   Use the standard jQuery techniques to build an initialization function for your page (as usual, I call mine `init()`).

5. **Build a draggable node.**

   Use standard jQuery selection techniques to isolate the element(s) you want to make draggable. Use the `draggable()` method to make the element draggable.

6. **Test your application.**

   Believe it or not, that's all there is to it. As long as everything's set up properly, your element will be draggable! The user can drag it with the mouse and place it anywhere on the screen.

If you're really paying attention, you might notice that the jQuery version that came with the UI is slightly older than the 10.2 version I used in the previous chapter. Really, it's not a big deal because the differences are minor. For UI examples, I go with the version of jQuery bundled with the UI library because I know they're tested to work together.

Resizing on a Theme

The next example demonstrates two important ideas in the jQuery UI package:

✦ **It shows an element that is resizable.** The user can drag on the bottom or right border to change the size of the element. Making an element resizable is very similar to making it draggable.

✦ **It shows the use of a theme.** Take a look at Figure 4-5 to see what's going on.

**Book VII
Chapter 4**

Using the jQuery
User Interface
Toolkit

Figure 4-5:
The size of
this lovely
element can
be changed
by the user.

You can see from Figure 4-5 that the page has a definite visual style. The elements have distinctive fonts and backgrounds, and the headers are in a particular visual style. Although there's nothing earth-shattering about this (after all, it's just CSS), the exciting thing is that these styles are defined by the theme. The theme can easily be changed to another theme (created by hand or via themeRoller), and the visual look of all these elements will reflect the new theme.

Themes provide a further level of abstraction to your websites that make changing the overall visual style much easier.

Figure 4-6 shows the page after the `resize me` element has changed sizes, and you can see that the rest of the page reformats itself to fit the newly resized element.

Figure 4-6:
When the
element
is resized,
the rest of
the page
adjusts.

The following code reveals that most of the interesting stuff is really CSS coding, and the resizing is really just more jQuery UI magic:

```html
<!DOCTYPE html>
<html lang = "en-US">

<head>
  <meta http-equiv="content-type" content="text/xml; charset=utf-8" />
  <link rel = "stylesheet"
        type = "text/css"
        href = "css/ui-lightness/jquery-ui-1.10.3.custom.css" />
  <style type = "text/css">
  h1 {
    text-align: center;
  }
  #resizeMe {
    width: 300px;
    height: 300px;
    text-align: center;
  }
  #sample {
    width: 200px;
    height: 200px;
    margin: 1em;
  }
  </style>
  <script type = "text/javascript"
          src = "js/jquery-1.9.1.js"></script>
  <script type = "text/javascript"
          src = "js/jquery-ui-1.10.3.custom.min.js"></script>
  <script type = "text/javascript">
```

```
    $(init);

    function init(){
      $("#resizeMe").resizable();
      themify();
    } // end init

    function themify(){
      //add theme-based CSS to the elements
      $("div").addClass("ui-widget")
      .addClass("ui-widget-content")
      .addClass("ui-corner-all");
      $(":header").addClass("ui-widget-header")
      .addClass("ui-corner-all");
      $("#resizeMe").append('<span class = "ui-icon ui-icon-star"></span>');
    }
  </script>
  <title>resize.htm</title>
</head>
<body>
  <h1>Resize Demo</h1>
  <div id = "resizeMe">
    <h2>Resize me</h2>
    <p>
      Drag the right or bottom to resize.
    </p>
  </div>
  <div id = "sample">
    <h2>Sample Widget</h2>
    <p>
      This is made to look like a widget
      with the theme css code.
    </p>
  </div>
</body>
</html>
```

Book VII
Chapter 4

**Using the jQuery
User Interface
Toolkit**

Examining the HTML and standard CSS

As usual, the HTML is the foundation of the entire page. It's very clean as usual, and it shows the general structure of the page. The HTML consists of only three primary elements: a heading and two divs. Each div contains its own level-two heading and a paragraph. The divs are given IDs to make them easier to style.

I also included a basic CSS section to handle the general layout of the page. I wanted the widgets to have specified beginning sizes, so I used ordinary CSS to get this effect.

Importing the files

jQuery applications require importation of JavaScript code libraries. In this application (and most jQuery UI applications), I import three files:

✦ **The main jQuery library:** This file is the essential jQuery base library. It is imported as described in Chapter 2 of this minibook, as an ordinary JavaScript file.

✦ **The jQuery UI library:** This file is also a standard JavaScript library. Earlier in this chapter, I describe how to obtain a custom version of this file.

✦ **The theme CSS file:** When you create a theme with themeRoller, you are provided with a CSS file. This file is your theme. Because this is a CSS file rather than JavaScript code, use the `link` tag to attach it to your page.

Not all jQuery UI examples require a theme, but most do. As you see in the following example, themes provide some other really great effects too, so it's worth it to include a theme CSS file whenever you want to use jQuery UI.

Making a resizable element

Surprisingly, the easiest part of the project is making the `resizable` element have the resizable behavior. It's a pretty standard jQuery UI trick:

```
$(init);
function init(){
  $("#resizeMe").resizable();
  themify();
} // end init
```

1. **Begin with an initialization function.**

   Like all good jQuery code, this example begins with standard initialization.

2. **Make an element resizable.**

   Identify the `resizeMe` div as a jQuery node, and use the `resizable()` method to make it resizable. That's all there is to it.

3. **Call a second function to add theming to the elements.**

   Although the `resizable()` method doesn't require use of jQuery themes, the themes do improve the look of the element.

Adding themes to your elements

The jQuery theme tool makes it quite easy to decorate your elements through CSS. The great thing about jQuery themes is that they are *semantic;* that is, you specify the general purpose of the element and then let the theme apply the appropriate specific CSS. You can use the themeRoller application to easily create new themes or modify existing ones. In this way, you can create a sophisticated look and feel for your site and write very little CSS on your own. It's a very powerful mechanism.

Many of the jQuery interface elements (such as the accordion and tab tools described elsewhere in this chapter) automatically use the current CSS theme. Of course, you can also apply them to any of your own elements to get a consistent look.

Themes are simply CSS classes. To apply a CSS theme to an element, you can just add a special class to the object.

For example, you can make a paragraph look like the current definition of the `ui-widget` by adding this code to it:

```
<div class = "ui-widget">
My div now looks like a widget
</div>
```

Of course, adding classes into the HTML violates one of the principles of semantic design (that is, separating the content from the layout), so it's better (and more efficient) to do the work in JavaScript with jQuery:

```
function themify(){
  //add theme-based CSS to the elements
  $("div").addClass("ui-widget")
  .addClass("ui-widget-content")
  .addClass("ui-corner-all");
  $(":header").addClass("ui-widget-header")
  .addClass("ui-corner-all");
  $("#resizeMe")
  .append('<span class = "ui-icon ui-icon-star"></span>');
}
```

The `themify()` function adds all the themes to the elements on my page, applying the pretty jQuery theme to it. I use jQuery tricks to simplify the process:

1. **Identify all divs with jQuery.**

   I want all the divs on my page to be styled like widgets, so I use jQuery to identify all div elements.

2. **Add the `ui-widget` class to all divs.**

   This class is defined in the theme. All jQuery themes have this class defined, but the specifics (colors, font sizes, and so on) vary by theme. In this way, you can swap out a theme to change the appearance, and the code still works. The `ui-widget` class defines an element as a widget.

3. **Add `ui-widget-content` as well.**

   The divs need to have two classes attached, so I use chaining to specify that divs should also be members of the `ui-widget-content` class. This class indicates that the contents of the widget (and not just the class itself) should be styled.

4. **Specify rounded corners.**

   Rounded corners have become a standard of the Web 2.0 visual design. This effect is extremely easy to achieve with jQuery — just add the `ui-corner-all` class to any element you want to have rounded corners.

   Rounded corners use CSS3, which is not yet supported by all browsers. Your page will not show rounded corners in older browsers, but the page will still work fine otherwise.

5. Make all headlines conform to the widget-header style.

The jQuery themes include a nice headline style. You can easily make all heading tags (H1 to H6) follow this theme. Use the `:header` filter to identify all headings, and apply the `ui-widget-header` and `ui-corner-all` classes to these headers.

The jQuery UI package supports a number of interesting classes, which are described in Table 4-1.

Table 4-1	CSS Classes Defined by jQuery UI	
Class	*Used On*	*Description*
ui-widget	Outer container of widget	Makes element look like a widget.
ui-widget-header	Heading element	Applies distinctive heading appearance.
ui-widget-content	Widget	Applies widget content style to element and children.
ui-state-default	Clickable elements	Displays standard (unclicked) state.
ui-state-hover	Clickable elements	Displays hover state.
ui-state-focus	Clickable elements	Displays focus state when element has keyboard focus.
ui-state-active	Clickable elements	Displays active state when mouse is clicked on element.
ui-state-highlight	Any widget or element	Specifies that an element is currently highlighted.
ui-state-error	Any widget or element	Specifies that an element contains an error or warning message.
ui-state-error text	Text element	Allows error highlighting without changing other elements (mainly used in form validation).
ui-state-disabled	Any widget or element	Demonstrates that a widget is currently disabled.
ui-corner-all, ui-corner-tl (etc)	Any widget or element	Adds current corner size to an element. Specify specific corners with tl, tr, bl, br, top, bottom, left, right.
ui-widget-shadow	Any widget	Applies shadow effect to a widget.

A few other classes are defined in UI themes, but these are the most commonly used. Refer to the current jQuery UI documentation for more details.

Adding an icon

Note the small start that appears inside the `resizeMe` element in Figure 4-6. This element is an example of a jQuery UI icon. All jQuery themes support a standard set of icons, which are small (16px square) images. The icon set includes standard icons for arrows as well as images commonly used in menus and toolbars (save and load, new file, and so on). Some jQuery UI elements use icons automatically, but you can also add them directly. To use an icon in your programs, follow these steps:

1. **Include a jQuery UI theme.**

   The icons are part of the theme package. Include the CSS style sheet that corresponds with the theme (as you've already done in this example).

2. **Be sure that the images are accessible.**

   When you download a theme package, it includes a directory of images. The images included in this directory are used to create custom back-grounds as well as icons. The CSS file expects a directory called `images` to be in the same directory as the CSS. This directory should contain several images that begin with `ui-icons`. These images contain all the necessary icons. If the icon image files are not available, the icons will not display. (Of course, you can edit these images in your graphics tool to customize them if you want.)

3. **Create a span where you want the icon to appear.**

   Place an empty span element wherever you want the icon to appear in the HTML. You can place the span directly in the HTML if you want, or you can add it through jQuery. I prefer to add UI elements through jQuery to keep the HTML as pristine as possible.

4. **Attach the `ui-icon` class to the span.**

   This tells jQuery to treat the span as an icon. The contents of the span will be hidden, and the span will be resized to hold a 16-pixel square icon image.

5. **Attach a second class to identify the specific icon.**

   Look at the themeRoller page to see the available icons. When you hover over an icon on this page, you can see the class name associated with the icon.

You can add the code directly in your HTML like this:

```
<p id = "myPara">
  This is my text
  <span class = "ui-icon ui-icon-star"></span>
</p>
```

Or, you can use jQuery to add the appropriate code to your element:

```
$("#myPara").append('<span class = "ui-icon ui-icon-star"></span>');
```

Dragging, Dropping, and Calling Back

jQuery elements look good, but they also have interesting functionality. Most jQuery UI objects have the ability to respond to specialized events. As an example, look over the dragDrop.html page shown in Figure 4-7.

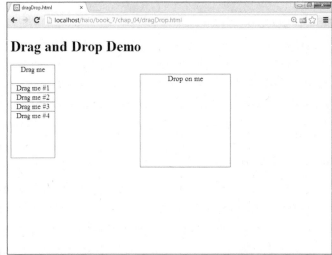

Figure 4-7: The page has a group of draggable elements and a target.

When you drop an element onto the target, the color and content of the target change, as shown in Figure 4-8.

Another interesting aspect of this program is the inclusion of several draggable elements. This program demonstrates how jQuery simplifies working with a number of elements.

Take a look at the entire program before you see the smaller segments:

```
<!DOCTYPE html>
<html lang = "en">

<head>
  <title>dragDrop.html</title>
  <meta charset = "utf-8" />
  <link rel = "stylesheet"
        type = "text/css"
        href = "css/ui-lightness/jquery-ui-1.10.3.custom.css" />
  <style type = "text/css">
  .dragMe {
```

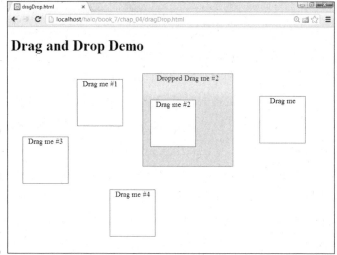

Figure 4-8:
The target
knows when
something
has been
dropped
onto it.

```
    width: 100px;
    height: 100px;
    border: 1px solid blue;
    text-align: center;
    background-color: white;
    position: absolute;
    z-index: 100;
}
#target {
    width: 200px;
    height: 200px;
    border: 1px solid red;
    text-align: center;
    position: absolute;
    left: 300px;
    top: 100px;
    z-index: 0;
}
</style>
<script type = "text/javascript"
        src = "js/jquery-1.9.1.js"></script>
<script type = "text/javascript"
        src = "js/jquery-ui-1.10.3.custom.min.js"></script>
<script type = "text/javascript">
  $(init);

  function init(){
    // make some clones of dragMe
    cloneDragMe();
    //make all drag me elements draggable
    $(".dragMe").draggable();
    //set target as droppable
    $("#target").droppable();
    //bind events to target
    $("#target").bind("drop", changeTarget);
    $("#target").bind("dropout", resetTarget);
  } // end init
```

**Book VII
Chapter 4**

Using the jQuery
User Interface
Toolkit

```
function cloneDragMe(){
for (i = 1; i <= 4; i++){
    zValue = (101 + i) + "";
    yPos = 100 + (i * 20) + "px";
    $("div:first").clone()
      .insertAfter("div:last")
      .css("top", yPos)
      .css("zIndex", zValue)
      .append(" #" + i);
  } // end for loop
} // end cloneDragMe

function changeTarget(event, ui)
$("#target").addClass("ui-state-highlight")
  .html("Dropped ")
  .append(ui.draggable.text());
} // end changeTarget

function resetTarget(event, ui){
    $("#target").removeClass("ui-state-highlight")
      .html("Drop on me");
} // end reset
    </script>
</head>
<body>
  <h1>Drag and Drop Demo</h1>
  <div class = "dragMe">
    Drag me
  </div>
  <div id = "target">
    Drop on me
  </div>
</body>
</html>
```

Building the basic page

As typical with jQuery, the HTML code is simple. It's very striking that you only see a single `dragMe` element. It turns out to be simpler to build a single element in HTML and use jQuery and JavaScript to make as many copies as you need. You also see a single `target` element. I added basic CSS to make the element easy to see (borders) and set them as absolute positioned so that I could control the initial position.

Note that I attached an ID to `target` (because there will be a single target on the page) and made `dragMe` a class (because I want to be able to have several draggable elements on the page).

Initializing the page

The initialization is a bit more elaborate than some of the earlier examples in this chapter, but it still isn't too difficult to follow. The main addition is the ability to respond to some specialty events:

```
$(init);

function init(){
  // make some clones of dragMe
```

```
        cloneDragMe();

        //make all drag me elements draggable
        $(".dragMe").draggable();

        //set target as droppable
        $("#target").droppable();

        //bind events to target
        $("#target").bind("drop", changeTarget);
        $("#target").bind("dropout", resetTarget);

    } // end init
```

The steps here aren't hard to follow:

1. **Make copies of the `dragme` element.**

   This part isn't critical (in fact, I added it after testing with a single element). However, if you want to have multiple copies of the draggable element, use a method to encapsulate the process.

2. **Make all `dragme` elements draggable.**

   Use the jQuery `draggable()` method on all elements with the `dragMe` class.

3. **Establish the target as a droppable element.**

   The `droppable()` method sets up an element so that it can receive events when a draggable element is dropped on it. Note that making something droppable doesn't have any particular effect on its own. The interesting thing comes when you bind events to the element.

**Book VII
Chapter 4**

Using the jQuery
User Interface
Toolkit

4. **Bind a `drop` event to the target.**

   Droppable elements can have events attached to them just like any jQuery object. However, the mechanism for attaching an event to a user interface object is a little bit different than the standard jQuery event mechanism (which involves a custom function for each event). Use the `bind()` method to specify a function to be called when a particular event occurs. When the user drops a node that has been made draggable onto the target element, this triggers the `drop` event, so call the `changeTarget()` function.

5. **Bind a `dropout` event to the target as well.**

   You can bind another event to occur when the user removes all draggable elements from the target. This event is called `dropout`, and I've told the program to call the `resetTarget()` function when this event is triggered.

 You often see programmers using shortcuts for this process. Sometimes, the functions are defined anonymously in the `bind` call, or sometimes the event functions are attached as a JSON object directly in the `droppable()` method assignment. Feel free to use these techniques if you are comfortable with them. I've chosen the technique used here because I think it is the clearest model to understand.

Handling the drop

When the user drags a `dragMe` element and drops it on the target, the target's background color changes and the program reports the text of the element that was dragged. The code is easy:

```
function changeTarget(event, ui){
  $("#target").addClass("ui-state-highlight")
  .html("Dropped ")
  .append(ui.draggable.text());
} // end changeTarget
```

Here's how to put this together:

1. **Create a function to correspond to the `drop` event.**

    The `drop` event is bound to a function called `changeTarget`, so I need to create such a function.

2. **Include two parameters.**

    Bound event functions require two parameters. The first is an object that encapsulates the event (much like the one in regular DOM programming) and a second element called `ui`, which encapsulates information about the user interface. You can use the `ui` object to determine which draggable element was dropped onto the target.

3. **Highlight the target.**

    It's a good idea to signal that the target's state has changed. You can change the CSS directly (with jQuery) or use jQuery theming to apply a predefined highlight class. I chose to use the jQuery theme technique to simply add the `ui-state-highlight` class to the `target` object.

4. **Change the text to indicate the new status.**

    Normally you should do something to indicate what was dropped. (If it's a shopping application, you should add the element to an array so that you can remember what the user wants to purchase, for example.) In this example, I simply change the text of the target to indicate that the element has been dropped.

5. **Use `ui.draggable` to get access to the element that was dropped.**

    The `ui` object contains information about the user interface. `ui.draggable` is a link to the draggable element that triggered the current function. It's a jQuery element, so you can use whatever jQuery methods you want on it. In this case, I extract the text from the draggable element and append it to the end of the target's text.

Beauty school dropout events

Another function is used to handle the `dropout` condition, which occurs when draggable elements are no longer dropped on the target. I bind the `resetTarget()` function to this event:

```
function resetTarget(event, ui){
    $("#target").removeClass("ui-state-highlight")
    .html("Drop on me");
} // end reset
```

All you have to do is this:

1. **Remove the highlight class from the target.**

   One great thing about using the theme classes is how easy they are to remove. Remove the highlight class, and the target reverts to its original appearance.

2. **Reset the HTML text.**

   Now that the target is empty, reset its HTML so that it prompts the user to drop a new element.

Cloning the elements

You can simply run the program as it is (with a single copy of the dragMe class), but more often, drag and drop is used with a number of elements. For example, you might allow users to drag various icons from your catalog to a shopping cart.

The basic jQuery library provides all the functionality necessary to make as many copies of an element as you want. Copying an element is a simple matter of using the jQuery clone() method.

The more elaborate code is used to ensure that the various elements display properly:

```
function cloneDragMe(){
  for (i = 1; i <=4; i++){
    zValue = (101 + i) + "";
    yPos = 100 + (i * 20) + "px";

    $("div:first").clone()
    .insertAfter("div:first")
    .css("top", yPos)
    .css("zIndex", zValue)
    .append(" #" + i);
  } // end for loop
} // end cloneDragMe
```

Here are the steps:

1. **Create a for loop.**

   Anytime you're doing something repetitive, a for loop is a likely tool. In this case, I want to make four clones numbered 1 through 4, so I have a variable named i that can vary from 1 to 4.

2. **Create a zValue for the element.**

   The CSS zIndex property is used to indicate the overlapping of elements. Higher values appear to be closer to the user. I give each element a zOrder of over 100 to ensure that it appears over the target. (If you don't specify the zIndex, dragged elements might go under the target and become invisible.) The zValue variable is mapped to the zIndex.

3. **Determine the y position of the element.**

   I want each successive copy of the dragMe element to be a bit lower than the previous one. Multiplying i by 20 ensures that each element is separated from the previous one by 20 pixels. Add 100 pixels to move the new stack of elements near the original.

4. **Make a clone of the first element.**

   Use the clone() method to make a clone of the first div. (Use the :first filter to specify which div you want to copy.)

5. **Remember to insert the newly cloned element.**

   The cloned element exists only in memory until it is somehow added to the page. I chose to add the element right after the first element.

6. **Set the top of the element with the yPos variable.**

   Use the yPos variable you calculated earlier to set the vertical position of the newly minted element. Use the css() method to apply the yPos variable to the element's left CSS rule.

7. **Set the zIndex.**

   Like the y position, the zValue variable you created is mapped to a CSS value. In this case, zValue is mapped to the zIndex property.

8. **Add the index to the element's text.**

   Use the append() method to add the value of i to the element's HTML. This way you can tell which element is which.

Chapter 5: Improving Usability with jQuery

In This Chapter

✔ **Working with scroll bars**

✔ **Building a sorting mechanism**

✔ **Managing selectable items**

✔ **Using the dialog box tool**

✔ **Creating an accordion page**

✔ **Building a tab-based interface**

The jQuery UI adds some really great capabilities to your web pages. Some of the most interesting tools are *widgets,* which are user interface elements not supplied in standard HTML. Some of these elements supplement HTML by providing easier input options. For example, it can be quite difficult to get the user to enter a date in a predictable manner. The datepicker widget provides an easy-to-use calendar for picking dates. The interface is easy for the programmer to add and makes it hard for the user to enter the date incorrectly. Another important class of tools provided by the jQuery UI helps manage complex pages by hiding content until it is needed.

Multi-Element Designs

Handling page complexity has been a constant issue in web development. As a page gets longer and more complex, navigating the page becomes more difficult. The early versions of HTML had few solutions to this problem. The use of frames was popular for a time because it allows the programmer to place navigation information in one frame and content in another. However, frames added additional usability problems and have fallen from favor. Dynamic HTML and AJAX seem like perfect replacement technologies, but they can be difficult to implement, especially in a reliable cross-browser manner.

The jQuery UI provides two incredible tools for managing larger pages:

✦ The accordion tool allows you to create a large page but display only smaller parts of it at a time.

✦ The tabs tool allows you to easily turn a large page into a page with a tab menu.

These tools are incredibly easy to use, and they add tremendously to your page development options. Both of these tools automate and simplify the DOM and AJAX work it takes to build a large page with dynamic content.

Playing the accordion widget

Some of the most powerful jQuery tools are actually the easiest to use. The accordion widget has become an extremely popular part of the jQuery UI toolset. Take a look at accordion.html in Figure 5-1 to see how it works.

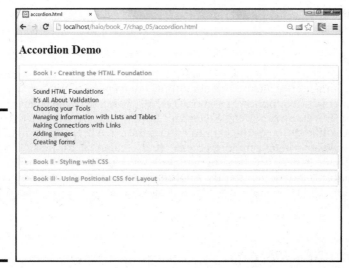

Figure 5-1: This page shows the first minibook outline of a familiar-sounding book.

When you look at Figure 5-1, you see headings for the first three minibooks of this book. The details for the first minibook are available, but the other books' details are hidden. If you click the heading for Book II, Book I is minimized and Book II is now expanded, as you can see Figure 5-2.

This marvelous effect allows the user to focus on a particular part of a larger context while seeing the overall outline. It's called an *accordion* because the various pieces expand and contract to allow the user to focus on a part without losing place of its position in the whole. Collapsible content has become an important usability tool made popular by the system bar in Mac OS and other popular usability tools.

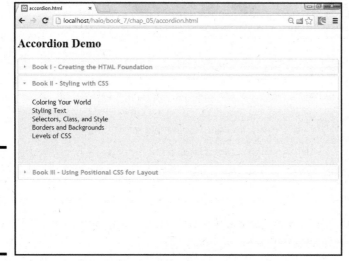

Figure 5-2:
Book I is
minimized,
and Book
II is now
expanded.

The accordion effect is strikingly easy to achieve with jQuery:

```html
<!DOCTYPE html>
<html lang = "en-US">
<head>

  <title>accordion.html</title>
  <meta charset = "UTF-8" />
  <link rel = "stylesheet"
        type = "text/css"
        href = "css/ui-lightness/jquery-ui-1.10.3.custom.css" />
  <script type = "text/javascript"
        src = "js/jquery-1.9.1.js"></script>
  <script type = "text/javascript"
        src = "js/jquery-ui-1.10.3.custom.min.js"></script>
  <script type = "text/javascript">

    $(init);
    function init(){
      $("#accordion").accordion();
    }
    </script>
</head>
<body>
<h1>Accordion Demo</h1>
<div id = "accordion">
  <h2><a href = "#">Book I - Creating the HTML Foundation</a></h2>
  <ol>
    <li>Sound HTML Foundations</li>
    <li>It's All About Validation</li>
    <li>Choosing your Tools</li>
    <li>Managing Information with Lists and Tables</li>
    <li>Making Connections with Links</li>
    <li>Adding Images</li>
    <li>Creating forms</li>
  </ol>
```

```
<h2><a href = "#">Book II - Styling with CSS</a></h2>
<ol>
  <li>Coloring Your World</li>
  <li>Styling Text</li>
  <li>Selectors, Class, and Style</li>
  <li>Borders and Backgrounds</li>
  <li>Levels of CSS</li>
</ol>
<h2><a href = "#">Book III - Using Positional CSS for Layout</a></h2>
<ol>
  <li>Fun with the Fabulous Float</li>
  <li>Building Floating Page Layouts</li>
  <li>Styling Lists and Menus</li>
  <li>Using alternative Positioning</li>
</ol>
</div>
</body>
</html>
```

As you can see by looking over the code, it's mainly just HTML. The effect is really easy to accomplish:

1. **Import all the usual suspects.**

   You need to import the jQuery and jQuery UI JavaScript files, and a theme CSS file. (See Book VII, Chapter 4 if you need a refresher on this process.) You also need to make sure that the CSS has access to the `images` directory with icons and backgrounds because it will use some of these images automatically.

2. **Build your HTML page as normal.**

   Build an HTML page as you would normally do. Pay attention to the sections that you want to collapse. There should normally be a heading tag for each element, all at the same level (Level 2 headings in my case).

3. **Create a div that contains the entire collapsible content.**

   Put all the collapsible content in a single div with an ID. You'll be turning this div into an accordion jQuery element.

4. **Add an anchor around each heading you want to specify as collapsible.**

   Place an empty anchor tag (`<a href = "#"></a>`) around each heading that you want to use as a collapsible heading. The # sign indicates that the anchor will call the same page and is used as a placeholder by the jQuery UI engine. You can add the anchor directly in the HTML or through jQuery code.

5. **Create a jQuery `init()` function.**

   Use the normal techniques to build a jQuery initializer as shown in Chapter 3 of this minibook.

6. **Apply the `accordion()` method to the `div`.**

   Use jQuery to identify the div that contains collapsible content and apply `accordion()` to it:

   ```
   function init(){
     $("#accordion").accordion();
   }
   ```

Building a tabbed interface

Another important technique in web development is the use of a tabbed interface. This allows the user to change the contents of a segment by selecting one of a series of tabs. Figure 5-3 shows an example.

In a tabbed interface, only one element is visible at a time, but the tabs are all visible. The tabbed interface is a little more predictable than the accordion because the tabs (unlike the accordion's headings) stay in the same place. The tabs change colors to indicate which tab is currently highlighted, and they also change state (normally by changing color) to indicate that they are being hovered over. When you click another tab, the main content area of the widget is replaced with the corresponding content. Figure 5-4 shows what happens when the user clicks the Book 3 tab.

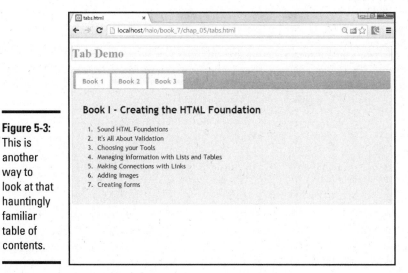

Figure 5-3: This is another way to look at that hauntingly familiar table of contents.

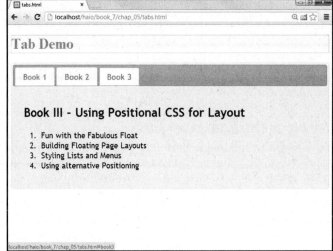

Figure 5-4:
Clicking a
tab changes
the main
content
and the
appearance
of the tabs.

Like the accordion, the tab effect is incredibly easy to achieve. Look over the code:

```
<!DOCTYPE html>
<html lang = "en-US">

<head>
  <meta charset = "UTF-8" />
  <link rel = "stylesheet"
        type = "text/css"
        href = "css/ui-lightness/jquery-ui-1.10.3.custom.css" />
  <script type = "text/javascript"
          src = "js/jquery-1.9.1.js"></script>
  <script type = "text/javascript"
          src = "js/jquery-ui-1.10.3.custom.min.js"></script>
  <script type = "text/javascript">

    $(init);
    function init(){
      $("#tabs").tabs();
    }

  </script>
  <title>tabs.html</title>
</head>
<body>
<h1 class = "ui-state-default">Tab Demo</h1>
<div id = "tabs">
  <ul>
    <li><a href = "#book1">Book 1</a></li>
    <li><a href = "#book2">Book 2</a></li>
    <li><a href = "#book3">Book 3</a></li>
  </ul>
  <div id = "book1">
    <h2>Book I - Creating the HTML Foundation</h2>
    <ol>
      <li>Sound HTML Foundations</li>
      <li>It's All About Validation</li>
      <li>Choosing your Tools</li>
```

```
      <li>Managing Information with Lists and Tables</li>
      <li>Making Connections with Links</li>
      <li>Adding Images</li>
      <li>Creating forms</li>
    </ol>
  </div>
  <div id = "book2">
    <h2>Book II - Styling with CSS</h2>
    <ol>
      <li>Coloring Your World</li>
      <li>Styling Text</li>
      <li>Selectors, Class, and Style</li>
      <li>Borders and Backgrounds</li>
      <li>Levels of CSS</li>
    </ol>
  </div>
  <div id = "book3">
    <h2>Book III - Using Positional CSS for Layout</h2>y<line><![CDATA[    <ol>
      <li>Fun with the Fabulous Float</li>
      <li>Building Floating Page Layouts</li>
      <li>Styling Lists and Menus</li>
      <li>Using alternative Positioning</li>
    </ol>
  </div>
</div>
</body>
</html>
```

The mechanism for building a tab-based interface is very similar to the one for accordions:

1. **Add all the appropriate files.**

   Like most jQuery UI effects, you need jQuery, jQuery UI, and a theme CSS file. You also need access to the images directory for the theme's background graphics.

2. **Build HTML as normal.**

   If you're building a well-organized web page anyway, you're already pretty close.

3. **Build a div that contains all the tabbed data.**

   This is the element that you'll be doing the jQuery magic on.

4. **Place main content areas in named divs.**

   Each piece of content that will be displayed as a page should be placed in a div with a descriptive ID. Each of these divs should be placed in the tab div. (See my code for organization if you're confused.)

5. **Add a list of local links to the content.**

   Build a menu of links. Place this at the top of the tabbed div. Each link should be a local link to one of the divs. For example, my index looks like this:

   ```
   <ul>
     <li><a href = "#book1">Book 1</a></li>
     <li><a href = "#book2">Book 2</a></li>
     <li><a href = "#book3">Book 3</a></li>
   </ul>
   ```

6. **Build an `init()` function as usual.**

   Use the normal jQuery techniques.

7. **Call the `tabs()` method on the main div.**

   Incredibly, one line of jQuery code does all the work.

Using tabs with AJAX

You have an even easier way to work with the jQuery tab interface. Rather than placing all your code in a single file, place the HTML code for each panel in a separate HTML file. You can then use a simplified form of the tab mechanism to automatically import the various code snippets through AJAX calls. Look at the AJAXtabs.html code for an example:

```
<!DOCTYPE html>
<html lang = "en-US">

<head>
  <meta charset = "UTF-8" />
  <link rel = "stylesheet"
        type = "text/css"
        href = "css/ui-lightness/jquery-ui-1.10.3.custom.css" />
  <script type = "text/javascript"
          src = "js/jquery-1.9.1.js"></script>
  <script type = "text/javascript"
          src = "js/jquery-ui-1.10.3.custom.min.js"></script>
  <script type = "text/javascript">

    $(init);
    function init(){
      $("#tabs").tabs();
    }
    //
    </script>
  <title>AJAXtabs.html</title>
</head>
<body>
  <h1>AJAX tabs</h1>
  <div id = "tabs">
      <ul>
        <li><a href = "book1.html">Book 1</a></li>
        <li><a href = "book2.html">Book 2</a></li>
        <li><a href = "book3.html">Book 3</a></li>
      </ul>
  </div>
</body>
</html>
```

Note: I didn't provide a screen shot for the AJAXtabs.html page because it looks exactly like tabs.html, shown in Figure 5-4.

This version of the code doesn't contain any of the actual content! Instead, jQuery builds the tab structure and then uses the links to make AJAX requests to load the content. As a default, it finds the content specified by

the first tab (chap1.html) and loads it into the display area. Here's what
book1.html contains:

```
<h2>Book I - Creating the HTML Foundation</h2>
<ol>
  <li>Sound HTML Foundations</li>
  <li>It's All About Validation</li>
  <li>Choosing your Tools</li>
  <li>Managing Information with Lists and Tables</li>
  <li>Making Connections with Links</li>
  <li>Adding Images</li>
  <li>Creating forms</li>
</ol>
```

As you can see, book1.html is simply a code snippet. It doesn't need all the
complete trappings of a web page (like the doctype or header) because it's
meant to be pulled in as part of a larger page. The AJAX trick is a marvelous
technique because it allows you to build a modular system quite easily. You
can build these code pages separately and include them easily into a larger
page. This is a good foundation for a content-management system.

Improving Usability

Although the UI widgets are good-looking and fun, another important aspect
is how they can improve usability. Web pages are often used to get information from users. Certain kinds of information can be very difficult for the
user to enter correctly. The jQuery UI elements include a number of tools
to help you with this specific problem. The UItools.html page, shown in
Figure 5-5, illustrates some of these techniques.

**Book VII
Chapter 5**

Improving Usability
with jQuery

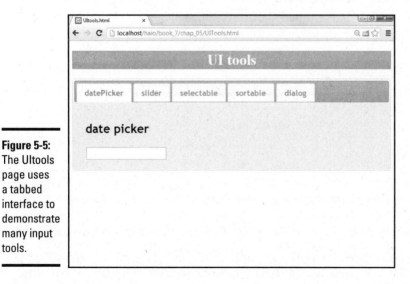

Figure 5-5:
The UItools
page uses
a tabbed
interface to
demonstrate
many input
tools.

A lot is going on in this page, but the tabbed interface really cleans it up and lets the user concentrate on one idea at a time. Using the tabbed interface can really simplify your user's life.

This page is a bit long because it has a number of sections. I demonstrate the code in chunks to make it easier to manage. Be sure to look on the website for the complete code.

Here's the main HTML code so that you can see the general structure of the page:

```
<h1>UI tools</h1>
<div id = "tabs">
  <ul>
    <li><a href = "#datePickerTab">datePicker</a></li>
    <li><a href = "#sliderTab">slider</a></li>
    <li><a href = "#selectableTab">selectable</a></li>
    <li><a href = "#sortableTab">sortable</a></li>
    <li><a href = "#dialogTab">dialog</a></li>
  </ul>
```

You see a main div named `tabs`. This contains a list of links to the various divs that will contain the demonstrations. I describe each of these divs in the section that demonstrates it. The page also imports jQuery, jQuery UI, and the theme CSS. The `init()` method contains most of the jQuery code:

```
$(init);

function init(){
  $("h1").addClass("ui-widget-header");

  $("#tabs").tabs();
  $("#datePicker").datepicker();

  $("#slider").slider()
  .bind("slide", reportSlider);

  $("#selectable").selectable();

  $("#sortable").sortable();

  $("#dialog").dialog();

  //initially close dialog
  $("#dialog").dialog("close");

} // end init
```

The `init` section initializes the various components. The details of the `init()` function are described in each section as they are used.

Most of these special widgets require the standard `jquery` link, `jqueryui`, and a template to be installed. Many of the widgets use features from the template library. Of course, you can start with a default template and tune it up later. You just have to have a template available to see all the effects.

Playing the dating game

Imagine that you're writing a program that requires a birth date. Getting date information from the user can be an especially messy problem because so many variations exist. Users might use numbers for the month, month names, or abbreviations. Some people use month/day/year, and others use day/month/year. They may enter the year as two or four characters. (That silly Y2K thing hasn't really died yet. I still have the bunker in the backyard.) Worse, it's really hard to pick a date without a calendar in front of you.

The datepicker dialog box is one of the coolest elements in the entire jQuery UI library. When you add `datepicker()` functionality to a textbox, that textbox becomes a datepicker. When the user selects the date box, a calendar automatically pops up, as shown in Figure 5-6.

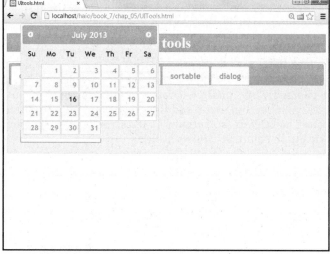

Figure 5-6: The datePicker element turns any text field into a calendar!

Book VII Chapter 5

Improving Usability with jQuery

The user can select a date on the calendar, and it will be placed in the text-box in a standard format. You have no better way to get date input from the user. Building a datepicker can't be much easier:

1. **Begin with a jQuery UI page.**

   You need jQuery, jQuery UI, and a theme to use the datepicker.

2. **Build a form with a text field.**

   Any standard text input element will do. Be sure to give the element an ID so that you can refer to it in JavaScript:

   ```
   <div id = "datePickerTab">
     <h2>date picker</h2>
     <input type = "text"
            id = "datePicker" />
   </div>
   ```

3. **Isolate the text input element with jQuery.**

   Build a standard jQuery node from the input element.

4. **Add the `datepicker()` functionality.**

   Use the `datePicker()` method to convert the text node into a date-picker. This is usually done in some type of `init()` function. The rest is automatic!

   ```
   $("#datePicker").datepicker();
   ```

5. **Retrieve data from the form element in the normal way.**

   When the user has selected the date, it is placed in the text field automatically. As far as your program is concerned, the text field is still an ordinary text field. Retrieve the data in the ordinary way.

The datepicker is a powerful tool with a large number of additional options. Look at the jQuery UI documentation to see how to use it to select date ranges, produce specific date formats, and much more.

Picking numbers with the slider

Numeric input is another significant usability problem. When you want users to enter numeric information, it can be quite difficult to ensure that the data really is a number and that it's in the range you want. Traditional programmers often use *sliders* (sometimes called *scroll bars*) to simplify accepting numeric input. Figure 5-7 shows a slider.

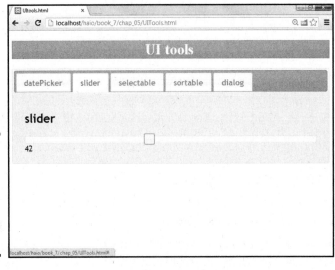

Figure 5-7: The user can choose a number with the mouse using a slider.

The slider is (like many jQuery UI objects) very easy to set up. Here's the relevant chunk of HTML code:

```
<div id = "sliderTab">
  <h2>slider</h2>
  <div id = "slider"></div>
  <div id = "slideOutput">0</div>
</div>
```

The Slider tab is a basic div. It contains two other divs:

✦ The `slider` div is actually empty. It will be replaced by the slider element when the jQuery is activated.

✦ The other div (slideOutput) in this section will be used to output the current value of the slider.

Create the slider element in the `init()` function with some predictable jQuery code:

```
$("#slider").slider();
```

The `slider()` method turns any jQuery element into a slider, replacing the contents with a visual slider.

Note that you can add a JSON object as a parameter to set up the slider with various options. See rgbSlider.html on this book's website for an example of sliders with customization. For more on how to access this book's website, see the Introduction.

You can set up a callback method to be called whenever the slider is moved. In my example, I chained this to the code that created the slider in the first place:

```
$("#slider").slider()
.bind("slide", reportSlider);
```

Use the `bind()` method to bind the `reportSlider()` function (described next) to the `slide` event.

The `reportSlider()` function reads the slider's value and reports it in an output div:

```
function reportSlider(){
  var sliderVal = $("#slider").slider("value");
  $("#slideOutput").html(sliderVal);
} // end reportSlider
```

To read the value of a slider, identify the jQuery node and invoke its `slider()` method again. This time, pass the single word `value`, and you get the value of the slider. You can pass the resulting value to a variable as I did and then do anything you want with that variable.

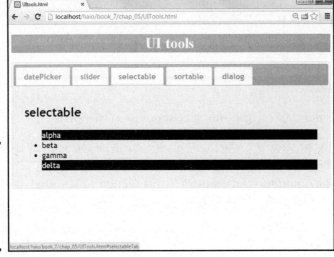

Figure 5-8:
Selectable items are easily chosen with the mouse.

Selectable elements

You may have a situation where you want the user to choose from a list of elements. The `selectable` widget is a great way to create this functionality from an ordinary list. The user can drag or Ctrl+click items to select them. Special CSS classes are automatically applied to indicate that the item is being considered for selecting or selected. Figure 5-8 illustrates the selection in process.

Follow these steps to make a selectable element:

1. **Begin with an unordered list.**

   Build a standard unordered list in your HTML. Give the `ul` an ID so that it can be identified as a jQuery node:

   ```
   <div id = "selectableTab">
     <h2>selectable</h2>
     <ul id = "selectable">
       <li>alpha</li>
       <li>beta</li>
       <li>gamma</li>
       <li>delta</li>
     </ul>
   </div>
   ```

2. **Add CSS classes for selecting and selected states.**

   If you want the selectable items to change appearance when the items are being selected or have been selected, add CSS classes as shown. Some special classes (`ui-selecting` and `ui-selected`) are predefined and will be added to the elements at the appropriate times:

   ```
   <style type = "text/css">
     h1 {
       text-align: center;
   ```

```
    }
    #selectable .ui-selecting {
      background-color: gray;
    }
    #selectable .ui-selected {
      background-color: black;
      color: white;
    }
  </style>
```

3. **In the `init()` function, specify the list as a selectable node.**

    Use the standard jQuery syntax: `selectable()`.

    ```
    $("#selectable").selectable();
    ```

    The `ui-selected` class is attached to all elements when they have been selected. Be sure to add some kind of CSS to this class, or you won't be able to tell that items have been selected.

    If you want to do something with all the items that have been selected, just create a jQuery group of elements with the `ui-selected` class:

    ```
    var selectedItems = $(".ui-selected");
    ```

Building a sortable list

Sometimes you want the user to be able to change the order of a list. This is easily done with the `sortable` widget. Figure 5-9 shows the sortable list in its default configuration. Of course you'll probably want to indicate somehow that the list is sortable, because this feature is not obvious to the user.

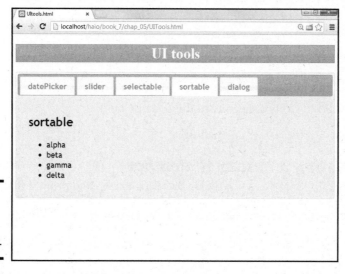

Figure 5-9:
This looks like an ordinary list.

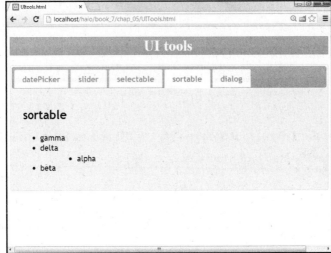

Figure 5-10:
The user
can drag the
elements
into a
different
order.

The user can grab members of the list and change their order, as shown in
Figure 5-10.

Making a sortable list is really easy. Follow these steps:

1. **Build a regular list.**

   Sortable elements are usually lists. The list is a regular list, but with an ID:

   ```
   <div id = "sortableTab">
     <h2>sortable</h2>
     <ul id = "sortable">
       <li>alpha</li>
       <li>beta</li>
       <li>gamma</li>
       <li>delta</li>
     </ul>
   </div>
   ```

2. **Turn it into a sortable node.**

   Add the following code to the init() method:

   ```
   $("#sortable").sortable();
   ```

Creating a custom dialog box

JavaScript supplies a few dialog boxes (the alert and prompt dialog boxes),
but these are quite ugly and relatively inflexible. The jQuery UI includes a
technique for turning any div into a virtual dialog box. The dialog box follows
the theme and is resizable and movable. Figure 5-11 shows a dialog box.

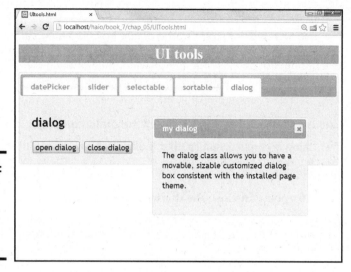

Figure 5-11: This dialog box is actually a jQuery UI node.

Building the dialog box is not difficult, but you need to be able to turn it on and off with code, or it will not act like a proper dialog box (which mimics a window in the operating system):

1. **Create the div you intend to use as a dialog box.**

   Create a div and give it an ID so that you can turn it into a dialog box node. Add the `title` attribute, and the title shows up in the dialog box's title bar.

   ```
   <div id = "dialog"
       title = "my dialog">
     <p>
       The dialog class allows you to have a movable, sizable
       customized dialog box consistent with the installed
       page theme.
     </p>
   </div>
   ```

2. **Turn the div into a dialog box.**

   Use the `dialog()` method to turn the div into a jQuery dialog box node in the `init()` function:

   ```
   $("#dialog").dialog();
   ```

3. **Hide the dialog box by default.**

   Usually you don't want the dialog box visible until some sort of event happens. In this particular example, I don't want the dialog box to appear until the user clicks a button. I put some code to close the dialog box in the `init()` function so that the dialog box will not appear until it is summoned.

Book VII Chapter 5

Improving Usability with jQuery

4. **Close the dialog box.**

   To close a dialog box, refer to the dialog box node and call the `dialog()` method on it again. This time, send the single value "close" as a parameter, and the dialog box will immediately close:

   ```
   //initially close dialog
   $("#dialog").dialog("close");
   ```

5. **Clicking the X automatically closes the dialog box.**

   The dialog box has a small X that looks like the Close Window icon on most windowing systems. The user can close the dialog box by clicking this icon.

6. **You can open and close the dialog box with code.**

   My Open Dialog and Close Dialog buttons call functions that control the behavior of the dialog box. For example, here is the function attached to the Open Dialog button:

   ```
   function openDialog(){
       $(&#x201C;#dialog").dialog(&#x201C;open");
   } // end openDialog
   ```

Chapter 6: Working with AJAX Data

In This Chapter

✔ Understanding the advantages of server-side programming

✔ Getting to know PHP

✔ Writing a form for standard PHP processing

✔ Building virtual forms with AJAX

✔ Submitting interactive AJAX requests

✔ Working with XML data

✔ Responding to JSON data

AJAX and jQuery are incredibly useful, but perhaps the most important use of AJAX is to serve as a conduit between the web page and programs written on the server. In this chapter, you get an overview of how programming works on the web server and how AJAX changes the relationship between client-side and server-side programming. You read about the main forms of data sent from the server, and you see how to interpret this data with jQuery and JavaScript.

Sending Requests AJAX Style

AJAX work in other parts of this book involves importing a preformatted HTML file. That's a great use of AJAX, but the really exciting aspect of AJAX is how it tightens the relationship between the client and server. Figure 6-1 shows a page called AJAXtest.html, which uses a JavaScript function to call a PHP program and incorporates the results into the same page.

Sending the data

The AJAX version of this program is interesting because it has no form. Normally an HTML page that makes a request of a PHP document has a form, and the form requests the PHP page. This page has no form, but a JavaScript function creates a "virtual form" and passes this form data to a PHP page. Normally the result of a PHP program is a completely new page, but in this example the results of the PHP program are integrated directly onto the original HTML page. Begin by looking over the HTML/JavaScript code:

```html
<!DOCTYPE html>
<html lang = "en-US">

<head>
  <title>AJAXTest.html</title>
  <meta charset= "UTF-8" />
  <script type = "text/javascript"
          src = "jquery-1.10.2.min.js"></script>
  <script type = "text/javascript">
    $(init);
    function init(){
      $.get("simpleGreet.php", { "userName": "Andy" }, processResult);
    }
    function processResult(data, textStatus){
      $("#output").html(data);
    }
  </script>
</head>
<body>
<h1>AJAX Test</h1>
<div id = "output">
  This is the default output
</div>
</body>
</html>
```

This program uses a jQuery function to simulate a form. It generates its own virtual form and passes it directly to the PHP program. The PHP program then processes the form data and produces text results, which are available for JavaScript to handle directly. In essence, JavaScript and jQuery are directly managing the server request (rather than allowing the browser to do it automatically) so that the programmer has more control over the process.

Figure 6-1: This page gets data from PHP with no form!

Here's how it works:

1. **Begin with an HTML framework.**

   As always, HTML forms the spine of any web program. The HTML here is quite simple — a heading and a div for output. Note that this example does not include a form.

2. **Include the jQuery library.**

   You can do AJAX without jQuery, but you don't have much reason to do that. The jQuery library makes life much easier and manages cross-browser issues to boot. You can also incorporate the jQuery UI and a theme if you choose, but they aren't absolutely necessary.

3. **Initialize as usual.**

   As soon as this program runs, it's going to get data from the server. (In the next example, I show you how to make this process more interactive.) Set up an `init()` function in the normal way to handle immediate execution after the page has loaded.

4. **Use the `.get()` function to set up an AJAX call.**

   jQuery has a number of interesting AJAX functions. The `.ajax()` function is a very powerful tool for managing all kinds of AJAX requests, but jQuery also includes a number of utility functions that simplify particular kinds of requests. The `get()` function used here sets up a request that looks to the server just like a form submitted with the `get` method. (Yep, there's also a `post()` function that acts like a `post` form.)

5. **Indicate the program to receive the request.**

   Typically your AJAX requests specify a program that should respond to the request. I'm using greetUser.php.

6. **Pass form data as a JSON object.**

   Encapsulate all the data you want to send to the program as a JSON object. (Check out Book IV, Chapter 4 for a refresher on JSON.) Typically this will be a series of name/value pairs. In this example, I'm simply indicating a field named `userName` with the value "Andy".

7. **Specify a callback function.**

   Normally you want to do something with the results of an AJAX call. Use a callback function to indicate which function should execute when the AJAX call is completed. In this example, I call the `processResult()` function as soon as the server has finished returning the form data.

Simplifying PHP for AJAX

One of the nice things about AJAX is how it simplifies your server-side programming. Most PHP programs create an entire page every time. (Check out nameForm.html and greetUser.php on the companion website to compare a more typical HTML/PHP solution. See this book's Introduction for more on the website.) That's a lot of overhead, building an entire HTML page every pass. A lot of material is repeated. However, because you're using AJAX, the PHP result doesn't have to create an entire web page. The PHP can simply create a small snippet of HTML.

Take a look at simpleGreet.php and you can see that it's very stripped down:

```php
<?php
$userName = filter_input(INPUT_GET, "userName");
print "<p>Hi, $userName!</p> ";
?>
```

This is a lot simpler than most PHP programs. All it needs to do is grab the username and print it back out. The JavaScript function takes care of making the code go in the right place. When you're using AJAX, the HTML page stays on the client, and JavaScript makes smaller calls to the server. The PHP is simpler, and the code transmission is generally smaller because there's less repeated structural information. Be sure if the data was sent through the GET method, you extract it with INPUT_GET.

Back in the HTML, I need a function to process the results of the AJAX request after it has returned from the server. The processResult() function has been designated as the callback function, so take another look at that function:

```javascript
function processResult(data, textStatus){
  $("#output").html(data);
}
```

This function is pretty simple with jQuery:

1. **Accept two parameters.**

   AJAX callback functions always accept two parameters. The first is a string that contains whatever output was sent by the server (in this case, the greeting from processResult.php). The second parameter contains the text version of the HTTP status result. The status is useful for testing in case the AJAX request was unsuccessful.

2. **Identify an output area.**

   Just make a jQuery node from the output div.

3. **Pass the data to the output.**

   You sometimes do more elaborate work with AJAX results, but for now, the results are plain HTML that you can just copy straight to the div.

Building a Multipass Application

The most common use of AJAX is to build an application that hides the relationship between the client and the server. For example, look at the multiPass.html page shown in Figure 6-2. This seems to be an ordinary HTML page. It features a drop-down list that contains hero names. However, that list of names comes directly from a database, which can't be read directly in HTML/JavaScript. When the user selects a hero from the list, the page is automatically updated to display details about that hero. Again, this data comes directly from the database. Figure 6-3 shows the page after a hero has been selected.

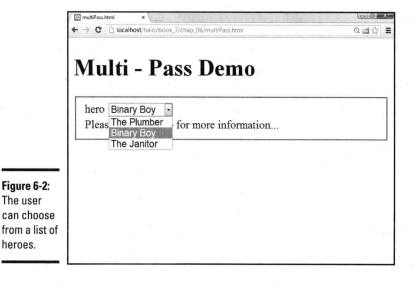

Figure 6-2:
The user can choose from a list of heroes.

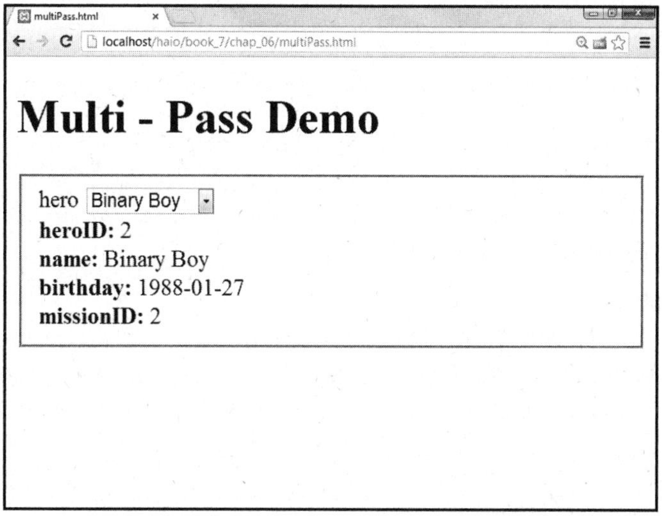

Figure 6-3:
Hero data is automatically updated from the database.

It's certainly possible to get this behavior from PHP alone, but it's interesting to see an HTML/JavaScript page that can access data from a database. Of course, some PHP is happening, but AJAX manages the process. Take a look at the code for multiPass.html to see what's happening:

```
<!DOCTYPE html>
<html lang="en">
<head>
  <title>multiPass.html</title>
  <meta charset="UTF-8">
  <script type = "text/javascript"
          src = "jquery-1.10.2.min.js"></script>
  <script type = "text/javascript">

  $(init);

  function init(){
    //load up list from database
    $("#heroList").load("loadList.php");
  } // end init

  function showHero(){
    //pass a hero id, retrieve all data about that hero
    heroID = $("#heroList").val();
    $("#output").load("showHero.php", {"heroID": heroID});
  } // end showHero
  </script>
</head>
<body>
  <h1>Multi - Pass Demo</h1>
  <form>
    <fieldset>
      <label>hero</label><p>
      <select id = "heroList"
              onchange = "showHero()">
      </select>
      <div id = "output">
        Please select a hero for more information...
      </div>
    </fieldset>
  </form>
</body>
</html>
```

Setting up the HTML framework

As always, the HTML page provides the central skeleton of the page. This site is reasonably simple because it sets up some empty areas that will be filled in with AJAX requests later:

1. **Import jQuery.**

   The jQuery library makes AJAX really simple, so begin by importing the library. Check out Chapter 2 of this minibook if you need a refresher on importing jQuery. You can also include the jQuery UI modules if you want, but it isn't necessary for this simple example.

2. **Build a simple form.**

   The page has a form, but this form is designed more for client-side interaction than server-side. Note that the form does not specify an action parameter. That's because the form won't be directly contacting the PHP program. Let AJAX functions do that.

3. **Don't add a button.**

   Traditional forms almost always have buttons (either standard buttons in client-side coding or submit buttons for server-side). Although you can still include buttons, one of the goals of AJAX is to simplify user interaction. The page will update as soon as the user selects a new hero, so you don't need a button.

4. **Create an empty `<select>` object.**

   Build an HTML `select` element that will contain all the hero names, but don't fill it yet. The hero names should come from the database. Give the `<select>` object an `id` property so that it can be manipulated through the code.

5. **Apply an `onchange` event to the `<select>` object.**

   When the user chooses a new hero, call a JavaScript function to retrieve data about that hero.

6. **Build a div for output.**

   Create a placeholder for the output. Give it an `id` so that you can refer to it later in code.

Loading the select element

The first task is to load the `select` element from the database. This should be done as soon as the page is loaded, so the code will go in a standard `init()` function:

1. **Write an initialization function.**

   Use the standard jQuery technique for this. I just use the `$(init)` paradigm because I think it's easiest.

2. **Build a jQuery node based on the `<select>` object.**

   Use jQuery selection techniques to build a jQuery node.

3. **Invoke the jQuery `load()` method.**

   This method allows you to specify a server-side file to activate. Many AJAX examples in this book use plain HTML files, but in this case, you call a PHP program.

   The `load()` method works just like `get()` (used earlier in this chapter), but it's a bit easier to use `load()` when the purpose of the AJAX call is to populate some element on your web page (as is the case here).

4. **Call `loadList.php`.**

   When you call a PHP program, you won't be loading in the text of the program. Instead, you're asking that program to do whatever it does (in this case, get a list of hero names and `heroIDs`) and place the *results* of the program in the current element's contents. In this situation, the PHP program does a database lookup and returns the `<option>` elements needed to flesh out the `<select>` object.

Writing the loadList.php program

Of course, you need to have a PHP program on the server to do the work. AJAX makes PHP programming a lot simpler than the older techniques because each PHP program typically solves only one small problem, rather than having to build entire pages. The loadList.php program is a great example:

```php
<?php
//connect to database
  try {
    $con= new PDO('mysql:host=host;dbname=dbName', "user", "pwd");
    $con->setAttribute(PDO::ATTR_ERRMODE, PDO::ERRMODE_EXCEPTION);

    $result = $con->query('SELECT * FROM hero');
    $result->setFetchMode(PDO::FETCH_ASSOC);

    foreach($result as $row){
      $id = $row["heroID"];
      $name = $row["name"];

      print <<< HERE
    <option value = "$id">$name</option>

HERE;

    } // end record loop
  } catch(PDOException $e) {
      echo 'ERROR: ' . $e->getMessage();
  } // end try

?>
```

The code for loadList.php is typical of PHP programs using AJAX. It's small and focused and does a simple job cleanly. (I tend to think of PHP programs in AJAX more like external functions than complete programs.) The key to this particular program is understanding the output I'm trying to create. Recall that this example has an empty `select` element on the form. I want the program to add the following (bold) source code to the page:

```
<select id="heroList" onchange="showHero()">
    <option value="1">The Plumber</option>
    <option value="2">Binary Boy</option>
    <option value="3">The Janitor</option>
</select>
```

It should go to the database and find all the records in the `hero` table. It should then assign `heroID` to the `value` attribute of each option, and should display each hero's name. After you know what you want to create, it isn't difficult to pull off:

1. **Make a database connection.**

   In this example, PHP is used mainly for connecting to the database. It's not surprising that the first task is to make a data connection. Build a connection to your database using the techniques outlined in Book VI, Chapter 5.

2. **Create a query to get data from the database.**

   The `<option>` elements I want to build need the `heroID` and `name` fields from the `hero` database. It's easiest to just use a `SELECT * FROM hero;` query to get all the data I need.

3. **Apply the query to the database.**

   Pass the query to the database and store the results in the `$result` variable.

4. **Cycle through each record.**

   Use the PDO associative array-fetching technique described in Book VI, Chapter 5.

5. **Build an `<option>` element based on the current record.**

   Because each record is stored as an associative array, it's easy to build an `<option>` element using fields from the current record.

6. **Print the results.**

   Whatever you print from the PHP program becomes the contents of the jQuery element that called the `load()` method. In this case, the `<option>` elements are placed in the `<select>` object (where all good `<option>` elements live).

Responding to selections

After the page has initialized, the `<select>` object contains a list of the heroes. When the user selects a hero, the `showHero()` function is called by the `select` element's `onchange` event.

The `showHero()` function is another AJAX function. It gathers the details needed to trigger another PHP program. This time, the PHP program needs a parameter. The `showHero()` function simulates a form with a data element in it and then passes that data to the PHP through the AJAX `load()` method:

```
function showHero(){
    //pass a hero id, retrieve all data about that hero
    heroID = $("#heroList").val();
    $("#output").load("showHero.php", {"heroID": heroID});
} // end showHero
```

If the user has selected a hero, you have the hero's `heroID` as the value of the `<select>` object. You can use this data to bundle a request to a PHP program. That program uses the `heroID` to build a query and return data about the requested hero:

1. **Extract the `heroID` from the `select` element.**

   You're building a JSON object which will act as a virtual form, so you need access to all the data you want to send to the server. The only information the PHP program needs is a `heroID`, so use the jQuery `val()` method to extract the value from the `<select>` element.

2. **Use the `load()` method to update the `output` element.**

   Once again, use the exceptionally handy `load()` method to invoke an AJAX request. This time, load the results of `showHero.php`.

3. **Pass form data to the server.**

   The `showHero.php` program thinks it's getting information from a form. In AJAX, the easiest way to simulate a form is to put all the data that would have been in the form in a JSON object. In this case, only one data element needs to be passed: `{ "heroID": heroID}`. This sends a field called `heroID` that contains the contents of the JavaScript variable `heroID`. See Book IV, Chapter 4 if you need a refresher on the JSON format.

The virtual form technique is a common AJAX idiom. It's important because it overcomes a serious usability limitation of ordinary HTML. In old-school programming, the primary way to invoke a server-side program was through an HTML form submission. With AJAX, you can respond to any JavaScript event (like the `onchange` event used in this example) and use JavaScript code to create any kind of fake form you want. You can use variables that come from one or more forms, or you can send data from JavaScript variables. AJAX lets you use JavaScript to control precisely what data gets sent to the server and when that data gets sent. This improves the user experience (as in this example). It's also commonly used to allow form validation in JavaScript before passing the data to the server.

Writing the showHero.php script

The `showHero.php` script is a simple PHP program that has a single task: After being given a `heroID`, pass a query to the database based on that key, and return an HTML snippet based on the query. The code is a standard database access script:

```php
<?php
//get heroID

$heroID = filter_input(INPUT_POST, 'heroID');

    try {
      $con= new PDO('mysql:host=localhost;dbname=dbName', "user", "pwd");
```

```
$con->setAttribute(PDO::ATTR_ERRMODE, PDO::ERRMODE_EXCEPTION);

$stmt = $con->prepare("SELECT * FROM hero WHERE heroID = ?");
$stmt->execute(array($heroID));

$result = $stmt->fetchAll(PDO::FETCH_ASSOC);
foreach($result as $row){
  foreach ($row as $field => $value){
    print <<< HERE
<strong>$field: </strong>$value <br />

HERE;
    } // end field loop
  } // end record loop
} catch(PDOException $e) {
    echo 'ERROR: ' . $e->getMessage();
} // end try
```

As far as the showQuery.php program is concerned, it got a request from an ordinary form. Its job is to produce HTML output based on that input:

1. **Get the `$heroID` value from the form.**

   Use the standard `filter_input` mechanism to extract data from the form. (It doesn't matter to the PHP program that this isn't a normal form. Note that the AJAX call is sending the data through the POST mechanism, so that's how you retrieve it.)

   ```
   $heroID = filter_input(INPUT_POST, 'heroID');
   ```

2. **Build a standard data connection.**

   Create your standard PDO connection, with an exception handler, the PDO connection, and the exception attributes.

   ```
   try {
       $con= new PDO('mysql:host=host;dbname=dbName', "user", "pwd");
       $con->setAttribute(PDO::ATTR_ERRMODE, PDO::ERRMODE_EXCEPTION);
   ```

3. **Build a prepared statement.**

   This query will involve user input (the heroID comes from the user form) so it should use a prepared statement to prevent SQL injection attacks. (See Book VI, Chapter 5 for more about SQL injection and prepared statements.)

   You only want data from the hero identified by $heroID, so build a query that selects a single record.

   ```
   $stmt = $con->prepare("SELECT * FROM hero WHERE heroID = ?");
   $stmt->execute(array($heroID));
   ```

4. **Execute the statement with the `heroID`.**

   Pass the heroID to the prepared statement, place this element in an array, and pass it to the statement.

   ```
   $result = $stmt->fetchAll(PDO::FETCH_ASSOC);
   ```

5. Process the results.

Use the ordinary `foreach` mechanism to print out the results of the query. You can get as fancy as you want with the output, but I'm going for a very standard "print all the contents" approach for now.

```
foreach($result as $row){
    foreach ($row as $field => $value){
        print <<< HERE
<strong>$field: </strong>$value <br />
Xxxxx
HERE;
    } // end field loop
} // end record loop
```

Working with XML Data

Server-side work normally involves storage of data because that's one thing that's easy to do on the server and difficult to do on the client. Data can be stored in many ways:

✦ In plain-text files

✦ In HTML

✦ In JSON

✦ In XML

✦ In a relational database

The database approach is most common because it's incredibly powerful and flexible. Normally programmers use an HTML page to request information from the user, and then use this information in PHP to prepare a request for the database in a special language called SQL (Structured Query Language). The data request is passed to the database management system, which returns some kind of result set to the PHP program. The PHP program then typically builds an HTML page and passes the page back to the browser.

The process can be easier when you use AJAX because the PHP program doesn't have to create an entire web page. All that really needs to be passed back to the JavaScript program is the results of the data query. The examples in this chapter have created HTML snippets as their output, but you often want to make your server-side programs a little more generic so that the data can be used in a number of different ways. Normally, the data is returned using a special data format so that the JavaScript program can easily manage the data.

When a server-side program is designed to simply take some input and produce generic data for output, that program is sometimes called a *web service*. Web services are very popular because they can simplify coding and be re-used. These are good things.

Review of XML

The XML format has become an important tool for encapsulating data for transfer between the client and the server. You might already be familiar with XML because XHTML is simply HTML following the stricter XML standard.

XML is much more than HTML. XML can actually be used to store any kind of data. For example, take a look at the following file (pets.xml):

```
<?xml version="1.0" encoding="utf-8"?>
<pets>
  <pet>
    <animal>cat</animal>
    <name>Lucy</name>
    <breed>American Shorthair</breed>
    <note>She raised me</note>
  </pet>
  <pet>
    <animal>cat</animal>
    <name>Homer</name>
    <breed>unknown</breed>
    <note>Named after a world-famous bassoonist</note>
  </pet>
  <pet>
    <animal>dog</animal>
    <name>Jonas</name>
    <breed>Cairn Terrier</breed>
    <note>The dog that currently owns me</note>
  </pet>
</pets>
```

If you look over pets.xml, you can see that it looks a lot like HTML. HTML tags are very specific (only a few are legal), but XML tags can be anything, as long as they follow a few simple (but familiar) rules:

1. **Begin with a doctype.**

   Formal XML declarations often have very complex doctypes, but basic XML data typically uses a much simpler definition:

   ```
   <?xml version="1.0" encoding="utf-8"?>
   ```

   Anytime you make your own XML format (as I'm doing in this example), you can use this generic doctype.

2. **Create a container for all elements.**

   The entire structure must have one container tag. I'm using `pets` as my container. If you don't have a single container, your programs will often have trouble reading the XML data.

3. **Build your basic data nodes.**

   In my simple example, each pet is contained inside a `pet` node. Each pet has the same data elements (but that is not a requirement).

   Tags are case-sensitive. Be consistent in your tag names. Use camel-case and single words for each element.

4. **Add attributes as needed.**

You can add attributes to your XML elements just like the ones in HTML. As in HTML, attributes are name/value pairs separated by an equal sign (=), and the value must always be encased in quotes.

5. **Nest elements as you do in HTML.**

Be careful to carefully nest elements inside each other like you do with HTML.

You can get an XML file in a number of ways:

- Most databases can export data in XML format.
- More often, a PHP program reads data from a database and creates a long string of XML for output.

For this simple introduction, I just wrote the XML file in a text editor and saved it as a file.

You manipulate XML in the same way with JavaScript, whether it comes directly from a file or is passed from a PHP program.

Manipulating XML with jQuery

XML data is actually familiar because you can use the tools you used to work with HTML. Better, the jQuery functions normally used to extract elements from an HTML page work on XML data with few changes. All the standard jQuery selectors and tools can be used to manage an XML file in the same way that they manage parts of an HTML page.

The readXML.html page featured in Figure 6-4 shows a JavaScript/jQuery program that reads the pets.xml file and does something interesting with the data.

In this case, it extracts all the pet names and puts them in an unordered list. Here's the code:

```
<!DOCTYPE html>
<html lang = "en-US">

<head>
  <meta charset = "UTF-8" />
  <script type = "text/javascript"
          src = "jquery-1.10.2.min.js"></script>
  <script type = "text/javascript">

    $(init);
    function init(){
      $.get("pets.xml", processResult);
    } // end init
```

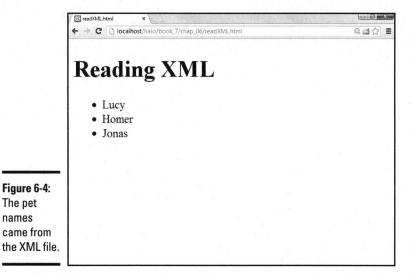

Figure 6-4:
The pet
names
came from
the XML file.

```
function processResult(data, textStatus){
//clear the output
  $("#output").html("");
  //find the pet nodes...
  $(data).find("pet").each(printPetName);
} // end processResult

function printPetName(){
  //isolate the name text of the current node
  thePet = $(this).find("name").text();
  //add list item elements around it
  thePet = "<li>" + thePet + "<\/li>";
  //add item to the list
  $("#output").append(thePet);
} // end printPetName

  </script>
  <title>readXML.html</title>
</head>
<body>
<h1>Reading XML</h1>
<ul id = "output">
 <li>This is the default output</li>
</ul>
</body>
</html>
```

Creating the HTML

Like most jQuery programs, this page begins with a basic HTML framework.
This one is especially simple: a heading and a list. The list has an ID (so that
it can be recognized through jQuery easily) and a single element (that will be
replaced by data from the XML file).

Retrieving the data

The `init()` function sets up an AJAX request:

```
$(init);

function init(){
    $.get("pets.xml", processResult);
} // end init
```

This function uses the `get()` function to request data:

1. **Use the jQuery `get()` mechanism to set up the request.**

   Because I'm just requesting a static file (as opposed to a PHP program), the `get()` function is the easiest AJAX tool to use for setting up the request.

2. **Specify the file or program.**

   Normally you call a PHP program to retrieve data, but for this example, I pull data straight from the pets.xml file because it's simpler and it doesn't really matter how the XML was generated. The `get()` mechanism can be used to retrieve plain text, HTML, or XML data. My program will be expecting XML data, so I should be calling an XML file or a program that produces XML output.

3. **Set up a callback function.**

   When the AJAX is complete, specify a function to call. My example calls the `processResult()` function after the AJAX transmission is complete.

Processing the results

The `processResult()` function accepts two parameters: `data` and `textStatus`:

```
function processResult(data, textStatus){
    //clear the output
    $("#output").html("");
    //find the pet nodes...
    $(data).find("pet").each(printPetName);
} // end processResult
```

The `processResult()` function does a few simple tasks:

1. **Clear the `output` ul.**

   The `output` element is an unordered list. Use its `html()` method to clear the default list item.

2. **Make a jQuery node from the data.**

   The data (passed as a parameter) can be turned into a `jQuery` node. Use `$(data)` for this process.

3. **Find each `pet` node.**

   Use the `find()` method to identify the `pet` nodes within the data.

4. **Specify a command to operate on each element.**

   Use the `each()` method to specify that you want to apply a function separately to each of the `pet` elements. Essentially, this creates a loop that calls the function once per element.

   The `each` mechanism is an example of a concept called an *iterator*, which is a fundamental component of *functional programming*. (Drop *those* little gems to sound like a hero at your next computer science function. You're welcome.)

5. **Run the `printPetName` function once for each element.**

   The `printPetName` is a callback function.

Printing the pet name

The `printPetName` function is called once for each `pet` element in the XML data. Within the function, the `$(this)` element refers to the current element as a jQuery node:

```
function printPetName(){
   //isolate the name text of the current node
   thePet = $(this).find("name").text();

   //add list item elements around it
   thePet = "<li>" + thePet + "</li>";

   //add item to the list
   $("#output").append(thePet);
} // end printPetName
```

Book VII Chapter 6

Working with AJAX Data

1. **Retrieve the pet's name.**

   Use the `find()` method to find the name element of the current pet node.

2. **Pull the text from the node.**

   The name is still a jQuery object. To find the actual text, use the `text()` method.

3. **Turn the text into a list item.**

   I just used string concatenation to convert the plain text of the pet name into a list item.

4. **Append the pet name list item to the list.**

   The `append()` method is perfect for this task.

Of course, you can do more complex things with the data, but it's just a matter of using jQuery to extract the data you want and then turning it into HTML output.

Working with JSON Data

XML has been considered the standard way of working with data in AJAX (in fact, the X in AJAX stands for XML). The truth is, another format is actually becoming more popular. Although XML is easy for humans (and computer programs) to read, it's a little bit verbose. All those ending tags can get a bit tedious and can add unnecessarily to the file size of the data block. Although XML is not difficult to work with on the client, it does take some getting used to. AJAX programmers are beginning to turn to JSON as a data transfer mechanism. JSON is nothing more than the JavaScript object notation described in Book IV, Chapter 4 and used throughout this minibook.

Knowing JSON's pros

JSON has a number of very interesting advantages:

+ **Data is sent in plain text.** Like XML, JSON data can be sent in a plain-text format that's easy to transmit, read, and interpret.

+ **The data is already usable.** Client programs are usually written in JavaScript. Because the data is already in a JavaScript format, it is ready to use immediately, without the manipulation required by XML.

+ **The data is a bit more compact than XML.** JavaScript notation doesn't have ending tags, so it's a bit smaller. It can also be written to save even more space (at the cost of some readability) if needed.

+ **Lots of languages can use it.** Any language can send JSON data as a long string of text. You can then apply the JavaScript `eval()` function on the JSON data to turn it into a variable.

+ **PHP now has native support for JSON.** PHP version 5.2 and later supports the `json_encode()` and `json_decode()` functions, which convert PHP arrays (even very complex ones) into JSON objects and back.

+ **jQuery has a `getJSON()` method.** This method works like the `get()` or `post()` methods, but it's optimized to receive a JSON value.

If a program uses the `eval()` function to turn a result string into a JSON object, there's a potential security hazard: Any code in the string is treated as JavaScript code, so bad guys could sneak some ugly code in there. Be sure that you trust whoever you're getting JSON data from.

The `pet` data described in `pets.xml` looks like this when it's organized as a JSON variable:

```
{
  "Lucy":  { "animal": "Cat",
             "breed": "American Shorthair",
             "note": "She raised me"},
  "Homer": { "animal": "Cat",
             "breed": "unknown",
             "note": "Named after a world-famous bassoonist"},
```

```
"Jonas": { "animal": "Dog",
          "breed": "Cairn Terrier",
          "note": "The dog that currently owns me"}
}
```

Note a couple of things:

+ The data is a bit more compact in JSON format than it is in XML.

+ You don't need an overarching variable type (like `pets` in the XML data) because the entire entity is one variable (most likely called `pets`).

JSON takes advantages of JavaScript's flexibility when it comes to objects:

+ **An object is encased in braces: { }.** The main object is denoted by a pair of braces.

+ **The object consists of key/value pairs.** In my data, I used the animal name as the node key. Note that the key is a string value.

+ **The contents of a node can be another node.** Each animal contains another JSON object, holding the data about that animal. JSON nodes can be nested (like XML nodes), giving the potential for complex data structures.

+ **The entire element is one big variable.** JavaScript can see the entire element as one big JavaScript object that can be stored in a single variable. This makes it quite easy to work with JSON objects on the client.

Reading JSON data with jQuery

As you might expect, jQuery has some features for simplifying the (already easy) process of managing JSON data.

Figure 6-5 shows readJSON.html, a program that reads JSON data and returns the results in a nice format.

Here's the complete code of readJSON.html:

```
<!DOCTYPE html>
<html lang = "en-US">

<head>
  <title>readJSON.html</title>
  <meta charset = "UTF-8" />
  <style type = "text/css">
    dt {
      font-weight: bold;
      float: left;
      width: 5em;
      margin-left: 1em;
      clear: left;
    }
  </style>
  <script type = "text/javascript"
          src = "jquery-1.10.2.min.js"></script>
```

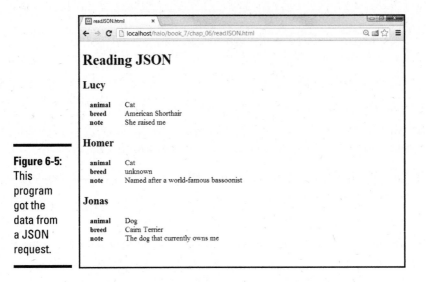

Figure 6-5:
This
program
got the
data from
a JSON
request.

```
<script type = "text/javascript">

  $(init);
  function init(){
    $.getJSON("pets.json", processResult);
  } // end init
  function processResult(data){
    $("#output").text("");
    for(petName in data){
      var pet = data[petName];
      $("#output").append("<h2>" + petName + "<h2>");
      $("#output").append("<dl>");
      for (detail in pet){
        $("#output").append("  <dt>" + detail + "<\/dt>");
        $("#output").append("  <dd>" + pet[detail] + "<\/dd>");
      } // end for
      $("#output").append("<\/dl>");
    } // end for
  } // end processResults
</script>
</head>
<body>
<h1>Reading JSON</h1>
<div id = "output">
 This is the default output
</div>
</body>
</html>
```

Managing the framework

The foundation of this program is the standard XTML and CSS. Here are the
details:

1. **Build a basic HTML page.**

   Much of the work will happen in JavaScript, so an H1 and an output div
   are all you really need.

2. Put default text in the `output` **div.**

Put some kind of text in the `output` div. If the AJAX doesn't work, you'll see this text. If the AJAX does work, the contents of the `output` div will be replaced by a definition list.

3. Add CSS for a definition list.

I print out each pet's information as a definition list, but I don't like the default formatting for `<dl>`. I add my own CSS to tighten up the appearance of the definitions. (I like the `<dt>` and `<dd>` on the same line of output.)

Retrieving the JSON data

The jQuery library has a special AJAX function for retrieving JSON data. The `getJSON()` function makes an AJAX call and expects JSON data in return:

```
$(init);

function init(){
  $.getJSON("pets.json", processResult);
} // end init
```

It isn't difficult to get JSON data with jQuery:

1. Set up the standard `init()` **function.**

In this example, I'm pulling the JSON data in as soon as the page has finished loading.

2. Use the `getJSON()` **function.**

This tool gets JSON data from the server.

3. Pull data from pets.json.

Normally you make a request to a PHP program, which does some kind of database request and returns the results as a JSON object. For this simple example, I'm just grabbing data from a JSON file I wrote with a text editor, so I don't have to write a PHP program. The client-side processing is identical whether the data came from a straight file or a program.

4. Specify a callback function.

Like most AJAX methods, `getJSON()` allows you to specify a callback function that is triggered when the data has finished transferring to the client.

Processing the results

The data returned by a JSON request is already in a valid JavaScript format, so all you need is some `for` loops to extract the data. Here's the process:

```
function processResult(data){
  $("#output").text("");
  for(petName in data){
    var pet = data[petName];
    $("#output").append("<h2>" + petName + "<h2>");
    $("#output").append("<dl>");
    for (detail in pet){
      $("#output").append("  <dt>" + detail + "<\/dt>");
      $("#output").append("  <dd>" + pet[detail] + "<\/dd>");
    } // end for
    $("#output").append("<\/dl>");

  } // end for
} // end processResults
```

1. **Create the callback function.**

   This function expects a `data` parameter (like most AJAX requests). In this case, the `data` object contains a complete JSON object encapsulating all the data from the request.

2. **Clear the output.**

   I replace the output with a series of definition lists. Of course, you can format the output however you wish.

   ```
   $("#output").text("");
   ```

3. **Step through each `petName` in the list.**

   This special form of the `for` loop finds each element in a list. In this case, it gets each pet name found in the data element:

   ```
   for(petName in data){
   ```

4. **Extract the pet as a variable.**

   The special form of `for` loop doesn't retrieve the actual pets but rather the key associated with each pet. Use that pet name to find a pet and make it into a variable using an array lookup:

   ```
   var pet = data[petName];
   ```

5. **Build a heading with the pet's name.**

   Surround the pet name with `<h2>` tags to make a heading and append this to the output:

   ```
   $("#output").append("<h2>" + petName + "<h2>");
   ```

6. **Create a definition list for each pet.**

   Begin the list with a `<dl>` tag. Of course, you can use whichever formatting you prefer, but I like the definition list for this kind of name/value data:

   ```
   $("#output").append("<dl>");
   ```

7. **Get the detail names from the pet.**

   The pet is itself a JSON object, so use another `for` loop to extract each of its detail names (animal, breed, note):

   ```
   for (detail in pet){
   ```

8. **Set the detail name as the definition term.**

   Surround each detail name with a `<dt></dt>` pair. (Don't forget to escape the slash character to avoid an HTML validation warning.)

   ```
   $("#output").append("  <dt>" + detail + "<\/dt>");
   ```

9. **Surround the definition value with `<dd></dd>`.**

   This provides appropriate formatting to the definition value:

   ```
   $("#output").append("  <dd>" + pet[detail] + "<\/dd>");
   ```

10. **Close the definition list.**

    After the inner `for` loop is complete, you're done describing one pet, so close the definition list:

    ```
    $("#output").append("<\/dl>");
    ```

Chapter 7: Going Mobile

In This Chapter

✔ Improving mobile accessibility

✔ Using media queries to build responsive designs

✔ Working with the jQuery mobile library

✔ Building mobile-friendly interfaces

✔ Adding collapsible interface elements

✔ Building multi-page applications with jQuery mobile

✔ Turning mobile pages into iOS apps

Mobile devices are no longer becoming mainstream. They are mainstream. Although people are still using traditional desktop devices to view the web, mobile devices are more prevalent and important than ever. For the most part, you can treat mobile devices like ordinary web browsers, but they do have a few special considerations and tricks. In this chapter you learn how to be sensitive to the needs of mobile users, and how to do some really cool tricks to make a mobile site really stand out.

Thinking in Mobile

A few years back, mobile programming was completely different than ordinary programming. You had to learn entirely different languages and visual toolsets. Although you can still program in native mobile languages, much of what people want to do with mobile devices can be done in HTML5 with CSS and JavaScript. In fact, this was one of the major drivers of HTML5 and CSS3 — making the web more mobile-friendly.

Virtually all mobile devices now ship with an HTML5-compliant browser, so just by learning HTML5, you're well on your way to mobile development. Any of the pages or programs in this book should work fine on a mobile client. (I tested all on an iPad and an Android phone.)

However, there are a few easy things you can do to improve the browsing experience for those who visit your site on a tablet or mobile phone:

✦ **Make text bigger:** Tablets and phones tend to have smaller screens with lower resolution. If your font size is tiny on an ordinary screen, it will but unreadable on a phone. Consider using a larger font size if you expect mobile users.

✦ **Make the user interface larger:** It's also a great idea to make buttons larger because they will need to be pressed by thick fingers rather than a tiny mouse. If you're using check boxes or radio buttons, be sure to use a related label to make the target larger. See the section "Using jQuery Mobile to Build Mobile Interfaces" later in this chapter for some great ways to improve your interface with a special version of jQuery UI specifically designed for mobile devices.

✦ **Consider turning off "helpful" features:** Many phones and tablets come with tools to automatically capitalize input and to autocorrect misspellings. You can turn these elements off by adding these attributes to an input element:

```
<input type = "text" autocorrect = "off" autocapitalize = "off">
```

Think carefully about each input to ensure you've got the best option. For example, a Last Name field would benefit from autocapitalize, but not autocorrect.

✦ **Use specialty input elements:** HTML5 includes some excellent new input types. Many of them were designed with mobile keyboards in mind. For example, the `<input type = "url">` field creates an ordinary-looking textbox, but on many mobile devices, it pops up a custom keyboard containing the special characters normally seen in a web address (/ and : are more prominent, for example). Likewise, the `<input type = "email">` pops up a keyboard that includes the @ sign. Many of the other input elements (date, color, and time) pop up specialty elements designed to work well without a keyboard. Any browser that cannot use these special input types will revert to a standard text input, so this is a very safe tool to use.

✦ **Avoid the `:hover` state:** CSS3 gives nearly every element a `:hover` state, which is activated when the mouse is hovered over an element but has not been clicked. Touch screens don't have a hover state! Most touch screen events feel just like mouse input, but there's no easy way for a touch screen to replicate the `:hover` state. It's fine to use this for special effects, but don't make it a major part of your page design if you intend your project to be used by mobile users.

✦ **Build with responsive CSS:** Much of the time you can build a page once and have it work pretty well on all browsers, but sometimes you really need something different for different browser sizes and capabilities. This is where media queries come in. Essentially, they allow you to apply special rules based on the current screen size (typically the most important variable). Please see the next section, "Building a Responsive Site," to get a feel for how to target specific screen sizes.

✦ **Add a viewport indicator:** The default behavior for many mobile devices is to simply display the standard page on the smaller screen.

Although this can work, it is often difficult to make the screen readable for all screen sizes. If you create a customized layout as described in this chapter, you can set the default behavior of the screen to respond to your improved layout:

```
<meta name="viewport" content="width=device-width, user-
    scalable=false;">
```

Building a Responsive Site

One way to make a site work well on multiple resolutions is to provide different CSS rules based on the detected media type.

CSS3 has a marvelous new feature called the *media query,* which allows you to specify a media type and determine various features of the display. You can use this specification to build a subset of the CSS that should be used when the browser detects a certain type or size of display.

Specifying a media type

The `@media` rule allows you to specify what type of output the included CSS should modify. The most common media types are `screen`, `print`, `speech`, `handheld`, `projection`, and `tv`. There are more, but only `print` and `screen` are universally supported.

For example, the following code will specify the font size when the user prints the document:

```
@media print {
  body {
  font-size: 10pt;
  }
}
```

This CSS can be embedded into a normal CSS document, but it should typically be placed at the end of the document because it holds exceptions to the normal rules. You can place as much CSS code as you wish inside the `@media` element, but you should only put CSS code that's relevant to the specific situation you're interested in. For print output, for example, I might turn off all the colors to save ink, and I might use points (pt) for the character size, as points actually have meaning in printed output.

Adding a qualifier

In addition to specifying the media type, the `@media` rule has another very powerful trick. You can apply a special qualifying condition to the media. For example, look at Figure 7-1.

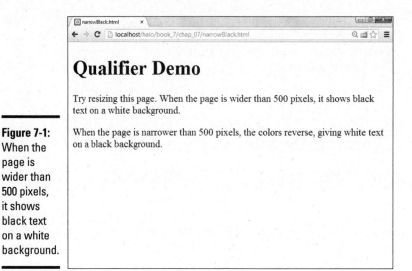

Figure 7-1:
When the
page is
wider than
500 pixels,
it shows
black text
on a white
background.

When the browser is wider than 500 pixels, you can see black text on a white background. But make the screen narrower, and you see something interesting, as shown in Figure 7-2.

Normally you would use this trick to change the layout, but start with this simpler color-changing example. I show how to change the layout in the "Making Your Page Responsive" section later in this chapter. Here's the code for this simpler example:

```
<!doctype html>
<html lang="en">
<head>
  <title>narrowBlack.html</title>
  <meta charset="UTF-8">
<meta name="viewport" content="width=device-width, user-scalable=false;">
  <style type = "text/css">
  body {
    color: black;
    background-color: white;
  }

  @media (max-width: 500px){
    body {
      color: white;
      background-color: black;
    }
  }
  </style>

</head>
<body>
  <h1>Qualifier Demo</h1>
  <p>
    Try resizing this page. When the page is
```

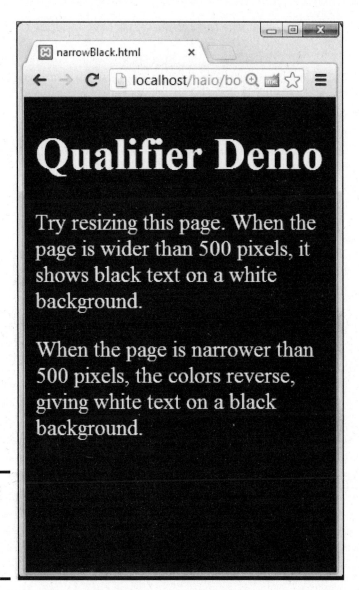

Figure 7-2:
When the
screen is
narrower,
the colors
change!

```
   wider than 500 pixels, it shows black text on a
   white background.
  </p>

  <p>
   When the page is narrower than 500 pixels, the colors
   reverse, giving white text on a black background.
  </p>
 </body>
</html>
```

Here's how to build a page that adapts to the screen width:

1. **Build your site as usual.**

   This is one place where that whole "separate content from layout" thing really pays off. The same HTML will have two different styles.

2. **Apply a CSS style in the normal way.**

   Build your standard style in the normal way — for now, embed the style in the page with the `<style>` tag. Your main style should handle the most common case. (Typically, a full-size desktop.)

3. **Build a `@media` rule.**

   The `@media` CSS rule should go at the end of the normal CSS.

4. **Set a `max-width: 500px` qualifier.**

   This qualifier indicates that the rules inside this segment will only be used if the width of the screen is smaller than 500 pixels.

5. **Place special case rules inside the new style set.**

   Any CSS rules you define inside the `@media` rule will be activated if the qualifier is true. Use these rules to override the existing CSS. Note you don't have to redefine everything. Just supply rules that make sense in your particular context. In this (trivial) example, I'm swapping the color of the foreground and background, but you can do more interesting things here, as you see in the "Making Your Page Responsive" section later in this chapter.

6. **Add a viewport.**

   Mobile browsers will sometimes try to rescale the page so it can all be seen at once. This defeats the purpose of a special style, so use the `viewport` metatag to indicate that the browser should report its true width. It's also often useful to turn off page-scaling because it should no longer be necessary.

In this example, the browser always applies the main (black text on a white background) style. Then it looks at the `@media` rule to see if the qualifier is true. If the width is less than 500 pixels, the `max-width:500px` qualifier is evaluated to true, and all the CSS code inside the `@media` segment is enabled. The browser then stores both sets of CSS and applies the correct CSS based on the status of the rule.

Making Your Page Responsive

The most common use of the media query is to make dramatic changes in the page layout when a smaller screen is encountered. The screen layouts described throughout Book III are already somewhat sensitive to different screen sizes, but true responsive design goes a step farther by recognizing that the entire layout may need to be changed (not just shrunk) in certain circumstances.

As an example, take a look at the page in Figure 7-3.

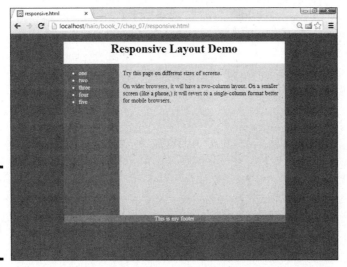

Figure 7-3:
This is a
standard
two-column
page.

When viewed on a normal desktop display, it shows a two-column design, which is a standard design for traditional monitors. However, take a look at the same exact page when viewed on a smaller display (like the ones you would encounter on a mobile phone). Figure 7-4 shows the smaller page.

Multiple-column layouts may look great on the desktop (especially with the proliferation of widescreen monitors), but they can be very frustrating to users with narrow browsers. This page detects when the browser is too narrow to display columns, and automatically switches to a single-column display. It also steps up the overall font size to compensate for the generally weaker resolution of mobile screens, and could do more (resizing buttons, for example, to make them easier to hit with fingers).

If the browser is resized again to a larger size, it will revert to the two-column view.

The responsive technique is not difficult to achieve at all. Begin (as always) by looking over the HTML code.

```
<!doctype html>
<html lang="en">
<head>
  <title>responsive.html</title>
```

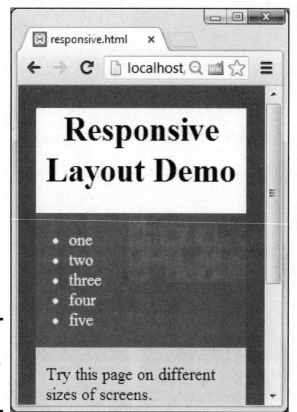

Figure 7-4:
The same page is now in a single column.

```
<meta charset="UTF-8">
<link rel = "stylesheet"
      type = "text/css"
      href = "responsiveWide.css" />
<link rel = "stylesheet"
      type = "text/css"
      href = "responsiveNarrow.css" />
<meta name="viewport" content="width=device-width, initial-scale=1.0">

</head>
<body>
  <div id="all">
    <header>
      <h1>Responsive Layout Demo</h1>
    </header>
    <nav>
      <ul>
        <li>one</li>
        <li>two</li>
        <li>three</li>
        <li>four</li>
        <li>five</li>
      </ul>
    </nav>
```

```
  <div id="content">
    <p>
      Try this page on different sizes of screens.
    </p>

    <p>
      On wider browsers, it will have a two-column layout.
      On a smaller screen (like a phone,) it will revert
      to a single-column format better for mobile browsers.
    </p>

  </div>
  <footer>
    This is my footer
  </footer>
</div>
</body>
</html>
```

Really, the remarkable thing about this HTML is how *unremarkable* it is. There's absolutely nothing in the HTML to indicate it will do something special when the page resizes. I do call two separate CSS files (although I could have used just one, I think it's nice to separate the rules).

As you look over the HTML, it seems pretty standard for an HTML5-based two-column layout. I used native HTML5 elements when I could, and named divs for features that don't have an HTML5 semantic tag.

The one new element is the `meta viewport` attribute in the header. Some mobile browsers automatically zoom into a smaller screen size, and some act like larger browsers and make you zoom in by yourself. If you want the browser to show the smaller size by default, add the `meta viewport` attribute in the document header. This is especially useful for iOS devices.

```
<meta name="viewport" content="width=device-width, initial-scale=1.0">
```

Building the wide layout

If you look over the first CSS file for the responsive example, it will look very much like the kind of two-column design described in Book III. Here's the code for responsiveWide.css:

```
body {
  background-color: red;
}

#all {
  background-color: white;
  width: 600px;
  margin-left: auto;
  margin-right: auto;
}

header {
  text-align: center;
```

```
}
nav {
  background-color: green;
  float: left;
  width: 150px;
  color: white;
  height: 400px;
}

#content {
  background-color: yellow;
  float: left;
  width: 440px;
  height: 400px;
  padding-left: 10px;
}

footer {
  color: white;
  background-color: gray;
  clear: both;
  text-align: center;
}
```

Once again, there's absolutely nothing in this code that would indicate any-thing special is going on. It looks just like the CSS you saw in Book II. That's again a big part of the beauty of responsive design. Build for the base case just like you always do. In this case, I'm building a jello layout with a fixed 600-pixel layout floating in a larger screen. As long as the browser is wider than 600 pixels, the layout will float in the center of the screen. As is typical for this type of layout, I've specified heights for the main containers (`nav` and `#contents`) to make everything look good.

For the sake of visual clarity, I changed the background and foreground colors so the size and position of each element would be obvious, even in a black-and-white screen shot. Obviously these garish color values will need to be changed in production. I don't know, though. I'm kind of liking garish.

Adding the narrow CSS

The second CSS file is where the magic (such as it is) happens. It is also a standard CSS file, except:

+ **The entire file is enclosed in a media query:** This second file is entirely based on the exceptions for a smaller browser.

+ **Trap for a screen less than 600 pixels wide:** Since the standard view expects the screen to be larger than 600 pixels, I will trap for any screen narrower than 600 pixels. (You can try to trap for the size of the typical smart phone, but this is a moving target, as there are too many devices on the market to be certain what the width will be. I simply go for what makes most sense for my design.)

+ **Overwrite any style rules that need to be changed:** If the screen is nar-rower than 600 pixels, I no longer want a jello layout. Instead, I want the page to be in a single column taking up most of the screen width. I also want to slightly increase the overall text size. Only change the CSS necessary to make your page adapt to the narrower screen.

Here's the code for the responsiveNarrow.css file:

```
@media (max-width: 600px) {
  /*special instructions for narrower screens */

  #all {
    display: block;
    width: 90%;
    font-size: 125%;
  }

  nav {
    display: block;
    width: 100%;
    height: auto;
  }

  #content{
    display: block;
    width: 95%;
    height: auto;
    padding-left: 5%;
  }

  footer {
    display: block;
    width: 100%;
  }
}
```

The specific rule changes simply override the style rules defined in responsiveWide.css.

1. **Set the `all` div to take up 90 percent of the screen width.**

   The #all div was set to 600 pixels wide in the main CSS, but here I'm overriding the width to be percentage-based, and to take up 90 percent of whatever the screen width is. I also set the font size to be 125 percent of the standard size, to make the text easier to read on the smaller screen. I don't change anything else about #all because I'm only interested in the screen-width related changes here.

2. **Change the floated elements to `display: block`.**

   The nav and #contents elements were floated in the wide presentation. The easiest way to remove the floating behavior is to assign a new display. Setting the display to block will make the elements act like default divs.

3. **Give each block a relative width.**

   The blocks were assigned pixel-based exact widths in the wide layout. This needs to be overridden with a more flexible scheme. I made every element 100 percent of the parent container, which is 90 percent of the overall screen size.

4. **Set the heights to automatic.**

   In the wide presentation, it made sense to give each column a specific height. That doesn't make sense in the more fluid mobile presentation. Set the height to automatic to override the heights indicated in the wide CSS code.

5. **Season to taste.**

   You'll need to test your code to ensure it's working right. One adjustment is in the padding. In my fixed-width wide version, I specified the padding of the #content div in pixels. In the narrower version, it makes more sense to set this value in percentages.

This is only a very brief introduction to the media query mechanism. There is much more to this specification than I can show in this (already hefty) book. Please check the W3 specification at www.w3.org/TR/css3-mediaqueries/ for more information on the various techniques you can use with media queries.

Using jQuery Mobile to Build Mobile Interfaces

There's another very popular approach to building mobile-friendly websites, and that's to use an add-on library to jQuery called *jQuery Mobile*. Jquery Mobile is a powerful combination of JavaScript and CSS code built on top of the jQuery library.

Building a basic jQuery mobile page

Figure 7-5 shows a basic page using jQuery mobile.

The jQuery library works by taking a normal HTML5 page and modifying it in ways that emulate a native look and feel. The code looks a lot like ordinary HTML:

```
<!doctype html>
<html lang="en">
<head>
  <meta charset="UTF-8">
  <title>Mobile Demo</title>
  <link rel="stylesheet"
       href="http://code.jquery.com/mobile/1.3.1/jquery.mobile-1.3.1.min.css" />
  <script src="http://code.jquery.com/jquery-1.9.1.min.js"></script>
  <script src="http://code.jquery.com/mobile/1.3.1/jquery.mobile-1.3.1.min.js">
  </script>
</head>
<body>
  <div data-role = "page" data-theme = "b">
    <div data-role = "header" data-position = "fixed">
      <h1>JQuery Mobile Demo</h1>
    </div>
    <div data-role = "content">
      <p>
        <a href = "http://jquerymobile.com/"
           data-role = "button">jQuery Mobile web site</a>
```

**Book VII
Chapter 7**

Going Mobile

Figure 7-5:
This looks
almost like
a native
mobile app,
but it's just a
web page.

```
      </p>

    <ul data-role = "listview">
      <li>This is an ordinary list</li>
      <li>Coded to look like</li>
      <li>a mobile list</li>
    </ul>
  </div>
  <div data-role = "footer" data-position = "fixed">
    from <em>HTML All in One for Dummies</em>
  </div>
</div>

</body>
</html>
```

A few details turn this page into a mobile wonder:

1. **Include the jQuery mobile CSS.**

    This is a special CSS file designed to transform HTML elements into
    their mobile counterparts. Although you can download it yourself, most
    developers link straight to the jQuery site (as I do here).

2. **Include the standard jQuery library.**

   Much of the code is based on jQuery, so integrate the `jQuery` library as well. Once again, I pull `jQuery` from the main `jQuery` website.

3. **Incorporate the jQuery mobile library.**

   This is a JavaScript library that extends the `jQuery` library to add new mobile-specific behavior.

4. **Add a `data-role= "page"` attribute to the main div.**

   Create a main div in your page and provide the `data-role` attribute to it. This is a custom attribute added by jQuery mobile. jQuery looks over the data roles of the various elements and applies style and behavior changes to these elements automatically. Assign your main div the data role `page`. This tells the browser to treat the entire div as a page. Look ahead to the "Building a multi-page document" section later in this chapter for more on pages.

5. **Specify a data theme.**

   You can apply a data theme to any element, but you almost always apply a theme to the page. jquery mobile comes with a number of default themes built in, called "a" through "e." Experiment to find the one you like, or you can build your own with the special mobile version of the ThemeRoller found at `http://jquerymobile.com/themeroller/index.php`.

6. **Add more divs inside your page.**

   Add a few more divs inside your page div. Generally you'll have three: header, content, and footer.

7. **Specify the header div with `data-role = "header"`.**

   By placing any of your header information inside a div with a "header" data role, you're telling jQuery to treat this element as a mobile header and apply the appropriate styles. The header typically includes an `<H1>` tag. Look to the section called "Building a multi-page document" for how to add buttons to the header. Typically you'll specify the header to be fixed with the `data-position = "fixed"` attribute. This ensures the header will stay in place if the rest of the content is scrolled, which is typical behavior in a mobile application.

8. **Set up a `content` div.**

   Add a div with `data-role = "content"` to set up the main content area of your page. Any of the main body elements of your site should go in this segment.

9. **Any link can be converted to a button.**

   The standard convention in web apps is to turn links into buttons that have a larger target than mouse-based input. It's easy to convert any link to a button by adding the `data-role = "button"` attribute to the anchor tag.

10. **Convert lists to mobile listviews.**

    Lists also have special conventions in the mobile world. You can use the (sing along with me now . . .) `data-role` attribute to turn any list into a `listView`.

11. **Build a footer.**

    Add one more div with `data-role` set to "`footer`". Normally, the footer (like the header) is fixed with the `data-position` attribute.

Working with collapsible content

The `jQuery` accordion element described earlier in this minibook is ideal for mobile development because it allows you to place an overview of a lot of text on the screen and allows the user to focus on one element at a time. The `jQuery mobile` library makes this a very easy mechanism to build for mobile devices.

Figure 7-6 shows a page hinting at my all-time favorite collapsible content.

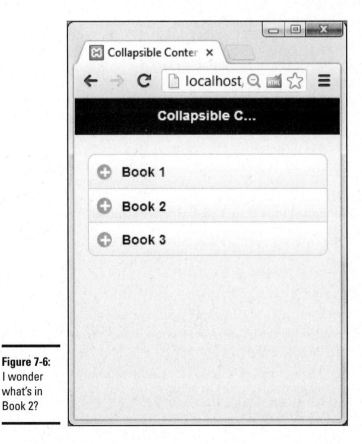

Figure 7-6:
I wonder what's in Book 2?

As the user clicks on a book, the hidden content is revealed, as you can see in Figure 7-7.

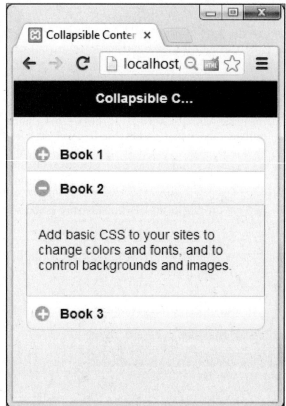

Figure 7-7:
The selected contents expand, and other contents are hidden.

The collapsible content trick is very similar to the standard jQuery mobile example:

```
<!doctype html>
<html lang="en">
<head>
  <meta charset="UTF-8">
  <title>collapsible.html</title>
  <link rel="stylesheet"
       href="http://code.jquery.com/mobile/1.3.1/jquery.mobile-1.3.1.min.css" />
  <script src="http://code.jquery.com/jquery-1.9.1.min.js"></script>
  <script src="http://code.jquery.com/mobile/1.3.1/jquery.mobile-1.3.1.min.js">
  </script>
</head>
<body>
  <div data-role = "page">
    <div data-role = "header" data-position = "fixed">
      <h1>Collapsible Content</h1>
    </div>
```

```
      <div data-role = "content">
        <div data-role = "collapsible-set"
            data-theme = "c" data-content-theme = "b">
          <div data-role = "collapsible">
            <h2>Book 1</h2>
            <p>
              Learn to build a basic site with HTML including new
              HTML5 features.
            </p>
          </div>
          <div data-role = "collapsible">
            <h2>Book 2</h2>
            <p>
              Add basic CSS to your sites to change colors and fonts, and
              to control backgrounds and images.
            </p>
          </div>
          <div data-role = "collapsible">
            <h2>Book 3</h2>
            <p>
              Use positional CSS to build attractive and flexible site layouts
              in a number of different ways.
            </p>
          </div>
        </div>
      </div>
    </div>
  </body>
</html>
```

The code is mostly standard HTML, with a few new attributes in place.

1. **Import the standard jQuery mobile stuff.**

   Import the CSS and JavaScript files from jQuery.com. Of course you can also import your own CSS and JavaScript if you wish, but I keep it simple in this example.

2. **Set up the data roles as normal.**

   All jQuery mobile pages have the same general structure. Build a div for the page, and add a header, content, and footer. Specify each of the segments with the `data-role` attribute.

3. **Set up a div as a collapsible set.**

   If you want the accordion behavior, just build a div inside your content with the `data-role` set to "`collapsible-set`".

4. **Set up the data theme for the collapsed set.**

   Specify a data theme for the collapsed set. It works best if you also explicitly set a `data-content-theme`. (If you don't, sometimes the expanded content will not look like it is part of the main element.)

5. **Place one or more collapsible objects in the set**.

   A collapsible object is simply a div with the `data-role` set to `collapsible`.

6. **Add some sort of header in each collapsible.**

   Any headline tag (`<H1>` through `<H6>`) will be used as the always-visible handle for the collapsible element.

7. **Non-header content will be hidden.**

   Any other content of the collapsible element will be hidden by default and only disclosed when the element is selected.

Building a multi-page document

It's great being able to pare down a web page so it fits on a mobile device, but obviously if the page is smaller, you'll need more of them. Mobile apps often use a page-flipping metaphor to pack more data in a small piece of screen real estate, and the jQuery mobile library has another wonderful tool to make this easy. Take a look at Figure 7-8 to see how to break a single web document into a number of pages.

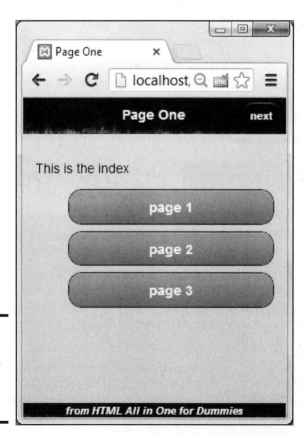

Figure 7-8:
This is the main page. It has a bunch of buttons.

So far, this application looks just like the other jQuery mobile apps you've seen so far. One thing is different, and that's the button in the header. It's very common for mobile apps to have navigation buttons in the header. Press the Next button, and you'll see Figure 7-9.

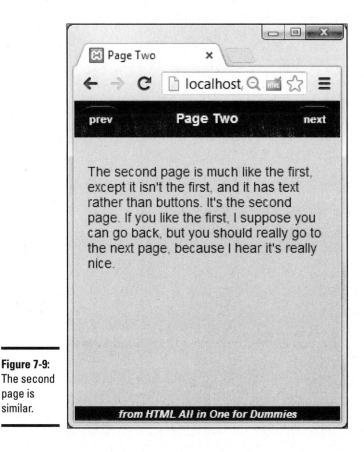

**Book VII
Chapter 7**

Going Mobile

Figure 7-9:
The second page is similar.

After a nifty fade transition, the next page appears. This one has two buttons in the header. Pressing Next again takes the user to the third page, illustrated in Figure 7-10.

The third page is once again very familiar, but this time it has a single button on the left of the header, and another button in the main content area.

The interesting thing about these three pages is they aren't three pages at all! It's all just one page, designed to act like three different pages. There's a couple of advantages to this arrangement.

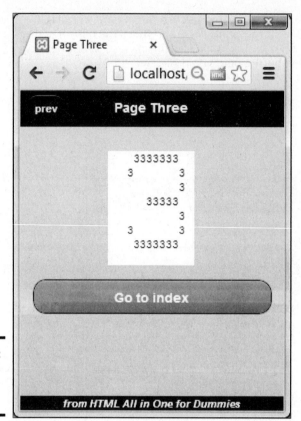

Figure 7-10:
I think this
is the third
page.

✦ **CSS and JavaScript resources only need to be loaded once:** This keeps the system consistent and improves load times slightly.

✦ **There's no lag time:** When the document loads, the whole thing is in memory, even if only one part is visible at a time. This allows you to quickly move between pages without having to wait for server access.

Of course this mechanism doesn't replace ordinary links taking you to new pages. You'd normally implement this type of mechanism when you have a large page you want to treat as several smaller pages so the user doesn't have to scroll.

Here's the code for multiPage.html in its entirety. Of course, I explain each new idea following the listing.

```
<!doctype html>
<html lang="en">
<head>
  <meta charset="UTF-8">
  <title>multiPage.html</title>
```

Book VII
Chapter 7

Going Mobile

```
<link rel="stylesheet"
      href="http://code.jquery.com/mobile/1.3.1/jquery.mobile-1.3.1.min.css" />
<script src="http://code.jquery.com/jquery-1.9.1.min.js"></script>
<script src="http://code.jquery.com/mobile/1.3.1/jquery.mobile-1.3.1.min.js">
</script>
<style type = "text/css">
  #foot {
     font-size: 75%;
     font-style: italic;
     text-align: center;
  }

  pre {
     margin-left: auto;
     margin-right: auto;
     background-color: white;
     width: 8em;
  }
  </style>
</head>

<body>
  <div id = "page1" data-role = "page" data-theme = "b">
    <div id="head" data-role = "header">
      <h1>Page One</h1>
      <a href = "#page2" class = "ui-btn-right">next</a>
    </div>

    <div id="content" data-role = "content">
      <p>
        This is the index
      </p>

    <ul>
      <li><a data-role = "button" href = "#page1">page 1</a></li>
      <li><a data-role = "button" href = "#page2">page 2</a></li>
      <li><a data-role = "button" href = "#page3">page 3</a></li>
    </div>

    <div id="foot" data-role = "footer" data-position = "fixed">
      from HTML All in One for Dummies
    </div>
  </div>


  <div id = "page2" data-role = "page" data-theme = "b">
    <div id="head" data-role = "header">
      <a href = "#page1">prev</a>
      <h1>Page Two</h1>
      <a href = "#page3">next</a>
    </div>

    <div id="content" data-role = "content">
      <p>
        The second page is much like the first, except
        it isn't the first, and it has text rather than
        buttons. It's the second page.
        If you like the first, I suppose you can
        go back, but you should really go to the next
        page, because I hear it's really nice.
      </p>
```

```
      </div>

      <div id="foot" data-role = "footer" data-position = "fixed">
        from HTML All in One for Dummies
      </div>
    </div>

    <div id = "page3" data-role = "page" data-theme = "b">
      <div id="head" data-role = "header">
        <a href = "#page2">prev</a>
        <h1>Page Three</h1>
      </div>

      <div id="content" data-role = "content">
        <pre>
      3333333
    3         3
              3
        33333
              3
    3         3
      3333333
        </pre>

        <p>
          <a href = "#page1" data-role = "button" data-transition = "flip">
            Go to index
          </a>
        </p>

      </div>

      <div id="foot" data-role = "footer" data-position = "fixed">
        from HTML All in One for Dummies
      </div>
    </div>

</body>
</html>
```

While the code for this example is long, it doesn't break a lot of new ground.

1. **Load up the jQuery mobile content.**

   Pull in the necessary CSS and JavaScript files from the jQuery.com site.

2. **Apply your own CSS.**

   Even if you're "borrowing" CSS code from jQuery, you're still allowed to add your own. I added CSS to make the footer and pre elements act the way I want.

3. **Build your pages.**

   You can build as many pages as you want, but they all follow the same general jQuery mobile pattern: Create a page div with header, content, and footer divs. Use the data-role attribute to indicate the role of each div.

4. **Name each of the page-level divs with the `id` attribute.**

   Because the user will be flipping through the pages, each page needs some sort of identifier. Give each page a unique `id` attribute. I went with the rather uninspired `page1`, `page2`, and `page3`. You might think of something more clever than that.

5. **Build buttons inside the headers.**

   The only truly new part of this example (aside from the page-flipping itself) is the buttons in the headers. Skip ahead to the page 2 header, and you'll see something really interesting:

   ```
   <a href = "#page1">prev</a>
   <h1>Page Two</h1>
   <a href = "#page3">next</a>
   ```

   If you define a link inside an element with the `header data-role`, that link will automatically become a button. Furthermore, the first such link defined will automatically be placed to the left of the header, and the second will be placed to the right.

6. **Force a single button to the right.**

   If you want a button to be on the right (as I do on the first page), add a class to the button:

   ```
   <h1>Page One</h1>
   <a href = "#page2" class = "ui-btn-right">next</a>
   ```

7. **Use internal anchors to skip between pages.**

   Take a look at the URLs in all the buttons. They begin with a hash, which indicates an internal link inside the document. Remember, though this feels like three different pages to the user, it's really all one big web page.

8. **Experiment with transitions.**

   Take a careful look at the button on page three:

   ```
   <a href = "#page1" data-role = "button" data-transition = "flip">
       Go to index
   </a>
   ```

   This button has a special `data-transition` attribute. By default, mobile pages swap with a fade. You can set the transition to `slide`, `slideup`, `slidedown`, `pop`, `fade`, or `flip`. You can also reverse the transition by adding another attribute: `data-direction = "reverse"`.

Going from Site to App

Everybody wants to make mobile apps these days. Here's the big secret. Many apps are really written in HTML5, CSS, and JavaScript. You already know everything you need to make apps that work on mobile devices. Better yet, you don't need to learn a new language or get permission from the app store or purchase a license, as you do for native apps.

There's a couple of wonderful tricks you can do for iOS users. You can design your program so the user can add an icon directly to the desktop. The user can then start the program like any other app. You can also make the browser hide the normal browser accoutrements so your program doesn't look like it's running in a browser!

It turns out these effects are quite easy to do.

Adding an icon to your program

Modern versions of iOS (the iPhone/iPad operating system) already have the ability to store any web page on the desktop. Just view the web page in Safari and click the Share button. You'll find an option to save the web page to the desktop. You can instruct your users to do this, and they'll be able to launch your program like a normal app.

However, the default icon for a saved app is quite ugly. If you want a nice-looking icon, you can save a small image as a .png file and put it in the same directory as your program. Then, you can add this line to your page (in the header) and that image will appear on the desktop when the user saves your program:

```
<link rel="apple-touch-icon" href="myImage.png" />
```

As an added bonus, the iPhone or iPad automatically adjust the image to look like an Apple icon, adding the effects appropriate to the installed version of iOS (rounded and glassy in iOS6, flat in iOS7.)

Of course, this icon trick is an Apple-only mechanism. With most versions of Android, any bookmark you've designated with your main browser can be added to the desktop, but there is no custom icon option. The `apple-touch-icon` directive will simply be ignored if you're using some other OS.

Removing the Safari toolbar

Although your program looks good from the main screen, when the user activates the program it's still obvious that the program is part of the web browser. You can easily hide the browser toolbar with another line in the header:

```
<meta name="apple-mobile-web-app-capable" content="yes" />
```

This code will not do anything different unless the program is called from the desktop. However, in that case, it hides the toolbar, making the program look and feel like a full-blown app. As an added bonus, this runs the program in a full-screen mode, giving you a little more room for game play.

Again, this is an Apple-specific solution. There isn't an easy way to achieve the same effect on the Android devices.

Storing your program offline

Now your program is looking a lot like an app, except it only runs when you're connected to the Internet. HTML5 has a wonderful feature that allows you to store an entire web page locally the first time it's run. Then if the user tries to access the program and the system can't get online, the local copy of the game is run instead. In essence, the program is downloaded the first time it is activated and stays on the local device.

This is a relatively easy effect to achieve:

✦ **Make your program stable:** Before you can use the offline storage mechanism, you'll want to make sure your program is close to release-ready. At a minimum, you'll need to ensure you know all of the external files needed by the game.

✦ **Use only local resources:** For this kind of project, you can't rely on the external Internet, so you'll need to have all your files local. This means you can't really use PHP or external files. You'll need to have a local copy of everything on the server.

✦ **Build a cache.manifest file:** Look at the directory containing your game, and create a new text file called cache.manifest.

✦ **Write the first line:** The first line of the cache.manifest file should only contain the text CACHE MANIFEST (all in capital letters).

✦ **Make a list of every file in the directory:** Write the name of every file in the directory, one file per line. Be careful with your capitalization and spelling.

✦ **Add the manifest attribute:** The <html> tag has a new attribute called manifest. Use this to describe to the server where the cache manifest can be found:

```
<html lang = "en"
      manifest = "cache.manifest">
```

✦ **Load the page normally:** You'll need to load the web page once in the normal way. If all is set up correctly, the browser will quietly make a copy of the file.

✦ **Test offline:** The best way to test offline storage is to temporarily turn off wireless access on your machine and then try to access the file. If things worked out, you should be able to see your page as if you were still online.

✦ **Check server settings:** If offline storage is not working, you might need to check with your server administration. The text/manifest MIME type needs to be configured on the server. You might have to ask your server administrator to set this option in the .htaccess file for your account:

```
addtype text/cache-manifest .manifest
```

Note that it can take the cache-manifest mechanism several hours to recognize changes, so when you make changes to your page, these changes aren't automatically updated to the local browser. That's why it's best to save offline archiving for near the end of your project development cycle.

Part VIII

Moving from Pages to Sites

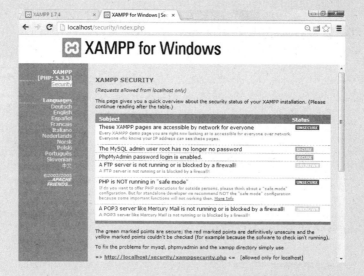

Visit www.dummies.com/extras/html5css3aio for more on what's next for the web.

Contents at a Glance

Chapter 1: Managing Your Servers

*W*eb pages are a complex undertaking. The basic web page itself isn't too overwhelming, but web pages are unique because they have meaning only in the context of the Internet — a vastly new undertaking with unique rules.

Depending where you are on your web development journey, you may need to understand the entire architecture, or you may be satisfied with a smaller part. Still, you should have a basic idea of how the Internet works and how the various technologies described in this book fit in.

Understanding Clients and Servers

A person using the web is a *client*. You can also think of the user's computer or browser as the client. Clients on the Internet have certain characteristics:

+ **Clients are controlled by individual users.** You have no control over what kind of connection or computer the user has. It may not even be a computer but may be instead a cellphone or (I'm not kidding) refrigerator.

+ **Clients have temporary connections.** Clients typically don't have permanent connections to the Internet. Even if a machine is on a permanent network, most machines used as clients have temporarily assigned addresses that can change.

✦ **Clients might have wonderful resources.** Client machines may have multimedia capabilities, a mouse, and real-time interactivity with the user.

✦ **Clients are limited.** Web browsers and other client-side software are often limited so that programs accessed over the Internet can't make major changes to the local file system. For this reason, most client programs operate in a sort of "sandbox" to prevent malicious coding.

✦ **Clients can be turned off without penalty.** It doesn't really cause anybody else a problem if you turn off your computer. Generally, client machines can be turned off or moved without any problems.

Servers are the machines that typically host web pages. They have a much different set of characteristics:

✦ **Servers are controlled by server administrators.** A server administrator is responsible for ensuring that all data on the server is secure.

✦ **Servers have permanent connections.** The purpose of a server is to accept requests from clients. For this reason, a server needs to have an IP number permanently assigned to it.

✦ **Servers usually have names, too.** To make things easier for users, server administrators usually register domain names to make their servers easier to find.

✦ **Servers can access other programs.** Web servers often talk to other programs or computers (especially data servers).

✦ **Servers must be reliable.** If a web server stops working, anybody trying to reach the pages on that server is out of luck. This is why web servers frequently run Unix or Linux because these operating systems tend to be especially stable.

✦ **Servers must have specialized software.** The element that truly makes a computer a server is the presence of web server software. Although several options are available, only two dominate the market: Apache and Microsoft IIS.

Parts of a client-side development system

A development system is made up of several components. If you're programming on the client (using XHTML, CSS, and JavaScript), you need the following tools:

✦ **Web browsers:** You need at least a couple of browsers so that you can see how your programs behave in different ones. Chrome is especially useful for web developers because of its extensive developer toolset.

✦ **Text editor:** Almost all web development happens with plain-text files. A standard text editor should be part of your standard toolkit. I prefer Komodo Edit because it handles all the languages described in this book and works well on all desktop operating systems, and it's free. (I really like Emacs too, but I won't force that monster on anybody.)

For client-side development, you don't necessarily need access to a server. You can test all your programs directly on your own machine with no other preparation. Of course, you'll eventually want a server so that you can show your pages to everyone.

The client-side development tools listed here are described in more detail in Book I, Chapter 3.

Parts of a server-side system

When you start working on the server side (with PHP, MySQL, and AJAX), you need a somewhat more complex setup. In addition to everything you need for client-side development, you also need these items:

✦ **A web server:** This piece of software allows users to request web pages from your machine. You must either sign on to a hosting service and use its server or install your own. (I show you both techniques in this chapter.) By far the most common server in use is Apache. Web server software usually runs all the time in the background because you never know when a request will come in.

✦ **A server-side language:** Various languages can be connected to web servers to allow server-side functionality. PHP is the language I chose in this book because it has an excellent combination of power, speed, price (free), and functionality. PHP needs to be installed on the server machine, and the web server has to be configured to recognize it. See Book VI, Chapter 1 for a review of other server-side languages.

✦ **A data server:** Many of your programs work with data, and they need some sort of application to deal with that data. The most common data server in the open-source world is MySQL. This data package is free, powerful, and flexible. The data server is also running in the background all the time. You have to configure PHP to know that it has access to MySQL.

✦ **A mail server:** If your programs send and receive e-mail, you need some sort of e-mail server. The most popular e-mail server in the Windows world is Mercury Mail, and Sendmail is popular in the world of Unix and Linux. You probably won't bother with this item on a home server, but you should know about it when you're using a remote host.

◆ **An FTP server:** Sometimes, you want the ability to send files to your server remotely. The FTP server allows this capability. Again, you probably don't need this item for your own machine, but you definitely should know about it when you use a remote host.

◆ **phpMyAdmin:** There's a command-line interface to MySQL, but it's limited and awkward. The easiest way to access your MySQL databases is to use the phpMyAdmin program. Because it's a series of PHP programs, it requires a complete installation of PHP, MySQL, and Apache (but, normally, you install all these things together anyway).

Creating Your Own Server with XAMPP

If the requirements for a web hosting solution seem intimidating, that's because they are. It's much more difficult to set up a working server system by hand than it is to start programming with it.

I don't recommend setting up your own system by hand. It's simply not worth the frustration because very good options are available.

XAMPP is an absolutely wonderful open-source tool. It has the following packages built in:

◆ **Apache:** The standard web server and the cornerstone of the package

◆ **PHP:** Configured and ready to start with Apache and MySQL

◆ **MySQL:** Also configured to work with Apache and PHP

◆ **phpMyAdmin:** A data management tool that's ready to run

◆ **Mercury Mail:** A mail server

◆ **FileZilla FTP server:** An FTP server

◆ **PHP libraries:** A number of useful PHP add-ons, including GD (graphics support), Ming (Flash support), and more

◆ **Additional languages:** Perl, another extremely popular scripting and server language, and SQLite, another useful database package

◆ **Control and configuration tools:** A Control Panel that allows you to easily turn various components on and off

This list is a description of the Windows version. The Mac and Linux versions have all the same types of software, but the specific packages vary.

Considering the incredible amount of power in this system, the download is remarkably small. The installer is only 34MB.

XAMPP installation is pretty painless: Simply download the installer and respond to all the default values.

If you use Windows, you may want to change where the package is installed because the program files directory causes problems for some users. I normally install XAMPP in root of the C:\ drive on Windows installations. The default directory is fine for Mac and Linux.

Running XAMPP

After you install XAMPP, you can manage your new tools with the XAMPP Control Panel. Figure 1-1 shows this program in action.

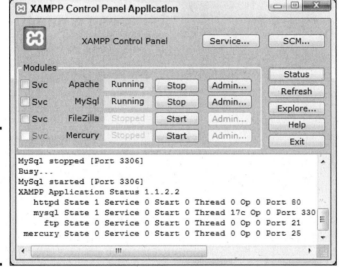

Figure 1-1: XAMPP Control Panel allows you to turn features on and off.

Some components of XAMPP (PHP, for example) run only when they're needed. Some other components (Apache and MySQL) are meant to run constantly in the background. Before you start working with your server, you need to ensure that it's turned on.

You can choose to run Apache and MySQL as a service, which means that the program is always running in the background. This arrangement is convenient, but it slightly reduces the performance of your machine. I generally turn both Apache and MySQL on and off as I need it.

Leaving server programs open on your machine constitutes a security hazard. Be sure to take adequate security precautions. See the section "Setting the security level," later in this chapter, for information on setting up your security features.

Testing your XAMPP configuration

Ensure that Apache and MySQL are running, and then open your web browser. Set the address to `http://localhost`, and you see a screen like the one shown in Figure 1-2.

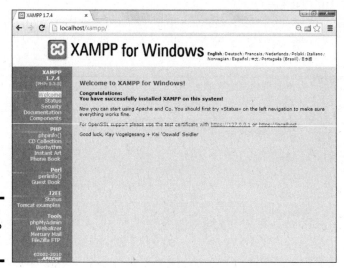

Figure 1-2:
The XAMPP
main page.

This page indicates that XAMPP is installed and working. Feel free to experiment with the various items in the Demos section. Even though you may not know yet what they do, you should know what some of their capabilities are.

Adding your own files

Of course, the point of having a web server is to put your own files in it. Use your file management tool to find the XAMPP directory in your file system. Right under the XAMPP directory is the `htdocs` folder, the primary web directory. Apache serves only files that are in this directory or under it. (That way, you don't have to worry about your love letters being distributed over the Internet.)

All the files you want Apache to serve must be in `htdocs` or in a subdirectory of it.

When you specified `http://localhost` as the address in your browser, you were telling the browser to look on your local machine in the main `htdocs` directory. You didn't specify a particular file to load. If Apache isn't given a filename and it sees the file named index.html or index.php, it displays that file, instead. So, in the default `htdocs` directory, the index.php program is immediately being called. Although this program displays the XAMPP welcome page, you don't usually want that to happen.

Rename index.php to index.php.old or something similar. It's still there if you want it, but now there's no index page, and Apache simply gives you a list of files and folders in the current directory. Figure 1-3 shows my `localhost` directory as I see it through the browser.

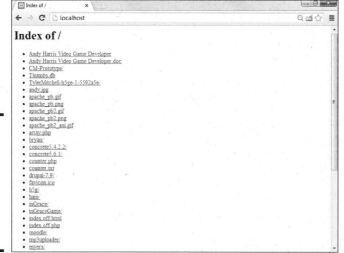

Figure 1-3: After disabling index.php, I can see a list of files and directories.

You typically don't want users to see this ugly index in a production server, but I prefer it in a development environment so that I can see exactly what's on my server. After everything is ready to go, I put together index.html or index.php pages to generate more professional directories.

Generally, you want to have subdirectories to all your main projects. I added a few others for my own use, including `haio`, which contains all the code for this book.

If you want to display the XAMPP welcome screen after you remove the index.php program, simply point your browser to `http://localhost/xampp`.

Setting the security level

When you have a web server and a data server running, you create some major security holes. You should take a few precautions to ensure that you're reasonably safe:

Book VIII Chapter 1

Managing Your Servers

✦ **Treat your server only as a local asset.** Don't run a home installation of Apache as a production server. Use it only for testing purposes. Use a remote host for the actual deployment of your files. It's prepared for all the security headaches.

✦ **Run a firewall.** You should run, at an absolute minimum, the Windows firewall that comes with all recent versions of Windows (or the equivalent for your OS). You might also consider an open-source or commercial firewall. Block incoming access to all ports by default and open them only when needed. There's no real need to allow incoming access to your web server. You only need to run it in `localhost` mode.

The ports XAMPP uses for various tools are listed on the security screen shown in Figure 1-4.

✦ **Run basic security checks.** The XAMPP package has a handy security screen. Figure 1-4 shows the essential security measures. I've already adjusted my security level, so you'll probably have a few more "red lights" than I do. Click the security link at the bottom of the page for some easy-to-use security utilities.

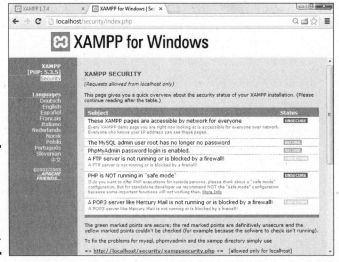

Figure 1-4: The XAMPP Security panel shows a few weaknesses.

✦ **Change the MySQL root password.** If you haven't already done so, use the security link to change the MySQL root password, as shown in Figure 1-5. (I show an alternative way to change the password in Book VI, Chapter 1.)

✦ **Add an XAMPP Directory password.** Type a password into the lower half of the security form to protect your XAMPP directory from unauthorized access. When you try to go to the XAMPP directory, you're prompted for this password.

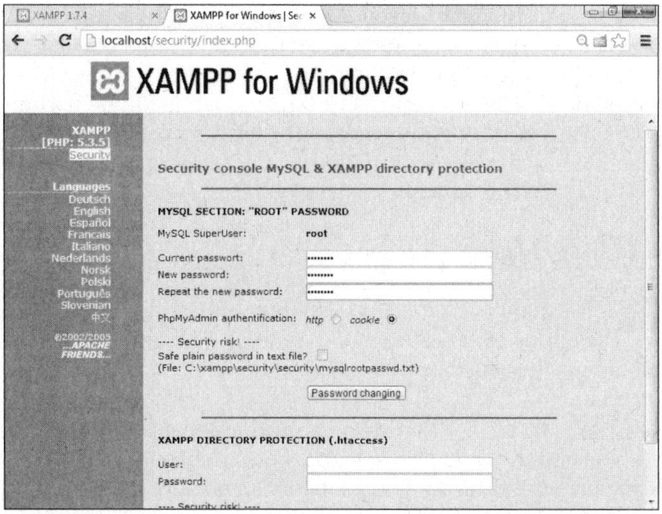

Figure 1-5:
Changing
the MySQL
root
password.

Security is always a compromise. When you add security, you often introduce limits in functionality. For example, if you changed the root password for MySQL, some of the examples (and phpMyAdmin) may not work anymore because they're assuming that the password is blank. You often have to tweak. See Chapter 1 in Book VI for a complete discussion of password issues in MySQL and phpMyAdmin.

Compromising between functionality and security

You may be shocked that my example still has a couple of security holes. It's true, but it's not quite as bad as it looks:

✦ **The firewall is the first line of defense.** If your firewall blocks external access to your servers, the only real danger your system faces is from yourself. Begin with a solid firewall and ensure that you don't allow access to port 80 (Apache) or port 3306 (MySQL) unless you're absolutely sure that you have the appropriate security measures in place.

✦ **I left phpMyAdmin open.** phpMyAdmin needs root access to the MySQL database, so if anybody can get to phpMyAdmin through the web server, they can get to my data and do anything to it. Because my firewall is blocking port 80 access, you can't get to phpMyAdmin from anything other than localhost access, and it's not really a problem.

✦ **I'm not running a mail or FTP server on this machine.** The security system isn't sure whether my FTP or mail system is secure, but because I'm not running them, it isn't really a problem.

If you're having troubles getting Apache to start, take a look at the other programs you have running. Sometimes other programs use the same ports that XAMPP needs, and cause problems. Messaging programs (like Skype) are notorious for this. If you can't start Apache while Skype is running, turn off Skype (or the other offending software) until Apache is turned on. Typically you'll be able to run Skype after Apache is running.

Choosing a Web Host

Creating a local server is useful for development purposes because you can test your programs on a server you control, and you don't need a live connection to the Internet.

However, you should avoid running a production server on your own computer, if you can. A typical home connection doesn't have the guaranteed IP number you need. Besides, you probably signed an agreement with your broadband provider that you won't run a public web server from your account.

This situation isn't really a problem because thousands of web hosting services are available that let you easily host your files. You should consider an external web host for these reasons:

✦ **The host, not you, handles the security headaches.** This reason alone is sufficient. Security isn't difficult, but it's a never-ending problem (because the bad guys keep finding new loopholes).

✦ **The remote server is always up.** Or, at least, it should be. The web server isn't doing anything other than serving web pages. Your web pages are available, even if your computer is turned off or doing something else.

✦ **A dedicated server has a permanent IP address.** Unlike most home connections, a dedicated server has an IP address permanently assigned to it. You can easily connect a domain name to a permanent server so that users can easily connect.

✦ **Ancillary services usually exist.** Many remote hosting services offer other services, like databases, FTP, and e-mail hosting.

✦ **The price can be quite reasonable.** Hosting is a competitive market, which means that some good deals are available. Decent hosting is available for free, and improved services are extremely reasonable.

You can find a number of free hosting services at sites like `http://free-webhosts.com`.

Finding a hosting service

When looking for a hosting service, ask yourself these questions:

✦ **Does the service have limitations on the types of pages you can host?** Some servers are strictly for personal use, and some allow commercial sites. Some have bandwidth restrictions and close your site if you draw too many requests.

✦ **How much space are you given?** Ordinary web pages and databases don't require a huge amount of space, but if you do a lot of work with images, audio, and video files, your space needs increase dramatically.

✦ **Is advertising forced on you?** Many free hosting services make money by forcing advertisements on your pages. This practice can create a problem because you might not always want to associate your page with the company being advertised. (A page for a day care center probably should not have advertisements for dating services, for example.)

✦ **Which scripting languages (if any) are supported?** Look for PHP support.

✦ **Does the host offer prebuilt scripts?** Many hosts offer a series of pre-built and preinstalled scripts. These can often include content management systems, message boards, and other extremely useful tools. If you know that you're going to need Moodle, for example (a course management tool for teachers), you can look for hosting services that have it built in. (If a tool you want isn't there, make sure you have FTP access so you can install it yourself.)

✦ **Does the host provide access to a database?** Is phpMyAdmin support provided? How many databases do you get? What is the size limit?

✦ **What sort of Control Panel does the service provide?** Does it allow easy access to all the features you need?

✦ **What type of file management is used?** For example, determine how you upload files to the system. Most services use browser-based uploading. This system is fine for small projects, but it's quite inconvenient if you have a large number of files you want to transfer. Look for FTP support to handle this.

✦ **Does the host have an inactivity policy?** Many free hosting services automatically shut down your site if you don't do anything with it (usually after 30 to 90 days of inactivity). Be sure you know about this policy.

✦ **Do you have assurances that the server will remain online?** Are backups available? What sort of support is available? Note that these services are much more likely on a paid server.

✦ **How easily can you upgrade if you want?** Does a particular hosting plan meet your needs without being too expensive?

✦ **Does the service offer you a subdomain, and can you register your own?** You may also want to redirect a domain that you didn't get through the service. (See the section "Naming Your Site," later in this chapter, for information on domain names.)

✦ **What kind of support is available?** Most hosting services have some kind of support mechanism with e-mail or ticket systems. Some hosts offer live chat, and some have telephone support. Talking to a real human in real time can be extremely helpful, and this is often worth paying for.

**Book VIII
Chapter 1**

**Managing Your
Servers**

Connecting to a hosting service

The sample pages for this book are hosted on Freehostia.com, an excellent, low-cost hosting service. You can find many great hosting services, but the rest of the examples in this chapter use Freehostia, where the examples for this book are hosted.

Choose whichever hosting service works for you. If you find a free hosting service that you really like, upgrade to a paid service. Hosting is a reasonably cheap commodity, and a quality hosting service is well worth the investment.

Managing a Remote Site

Obviously, having a hosting service isn't much fun if you don't have pages there. Fortunately, there are a lot of ways to work with your new site.

Using web-based file tools

Most of the time, your host has some sort of Control Panel that looks like the one shown in Figure 1-6.

Figure 1-6: This Control Panel allows you to manage your site remotely.

There's usually some sort of file management tool that might look like the one shown in Figure 1-7.

Figure 1-7:
This file
management
tool allows
you to
manipulate
the files on
your system.

In this particular case, all my web files are in the www/aharrisbooks.net directory, so I click to see them. Figure 1-8 shows what you might see in an actual directory.

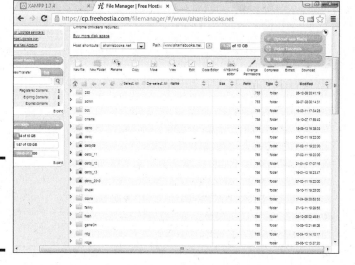

Figure 1-8:
Now, you
can see
some files
here.

**Book VIII
Chapter 1**

**Managing Your
Servers**

This page allows you to rename, upload, and edit existing files and change file permissions.

You can create or edit files with a simple integrated editor: Build a new file with the Create File button. Type a filename into the text area and click the button. You can also click the edit button next to a file, and the file will open in the editor. In either case, the text editor shown in Figure 1-9 appears.

Figure 1-9:
The hosting service has a limited text editor.

You can write an entire website using this type of editor, but the web-based text editing isn't helpful, and it's kind of awkward. More often, you create your files on your own XAMPP system and upload them to the server when they're basically complete. Use server-side editing features for quick fixes only.

Understanding file permissions

Most hosting services use Linux or Unix. These operating systems have a more sophisticated file permission mechanism than the Windows file system does. At some point, you may need to manipulate file permissions.

Essentially, the universe is divided into three populations: Yourself, your group, and everybody else. You can allow each group to have different kinds of permission for each file. Each of the permissions is a Boolean (true or false) value:

✦ **Read permission:** The file can be read. Typically, you want everybody to be able to read your files, or else you wouldn't put them on the web server.

✦ **Write permission:** The file can be written, changed, and deleted. Obviously, only you should have the ability to write to your files.

✦ **Execute permission:** Indicates that the file is an executable program or a directory that can be passed through. Normally, none of your files is considered executable, although all your directories are.

What's with all the permissions?

Permissions are typically treated as binary numbers: 111 means "read, write, execute." This (111 value) is also a 7 permission because 111 binary translates to 7 in base ten (or base eight, but let's skip that detail for now).

A permission is read as three digits, each one a number indicating the permissions, so 644 permission means `rw- r- r-`. This example can be translated as "The owner should be able to read and write this file. Everyone else can read it. Nobody can execute it."

If you don't understand this concept, don't worry about it. The guidelines are very simple: Make sure that each of your files has 644 permission and that each directory has 755 permission. That's all you really need to know.

Using FTP to manage your site

Most of the work is done on a local machine and then sent to the server in a big batch. (That's how I did everything in this book.) The standard web-based file management tools are pretty frustrating when you want to efficiently upload a large number of files.

Fortunately, most hosts have the FTP (File Transfer Protocol) system available. *FTP* is a client/server mechanism for transferring files efficiently. To use it, you may have to configure some sort of FTP server on the host to find out which settings, username, and password you should use. Figure 1-10 shows the Freehostia Control Panel with this information displayed.

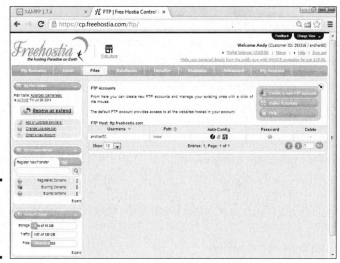

Figure 1-10: Configuring the FTP server.

You also need an FTP client. Fortunately, many free clients are available. I like FileZilla, for a number of reasons:

✦ **It's free and open source.** That's always a bonus.

✦ **It works the same on every OS.** If I'm on Windows, Linux, or Mac, it works the same.

✦ **It's easy to use.** It feels a lot like a file manager.

Figure 1-11 shows FileZilla running in my browser.

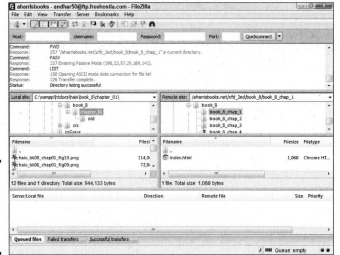

Figure 1-11:
FileZilla is
an excellent
free FTP
client.

Using an FTP client

FileZilla and other FTP programs all do pretty much the same thing. Here's how to use it:

1. **Download and install FileZilla.**

   You can download FileZilla for free at `http://download-filezilla-ftp-free.com/`. (There is also a link at my main page: `www.aharrisbooks.net`.)

2. **Gather the login information.**

   You'll need to get your FTP login information from your service provider. Normally this consists of a special address (like a URL, but it begins with `ftp://`), a username, and a password. These are not necessarily the same credentials used to log in to the server.

3. **Enter host information.**

   Use the site manager (Ctrl+S or File➪Site Manager) to manage your site. Select the New Site button to build a new connection.

There's a place in the dialog box to enter your login information. Put the address (which usually begins with `ftp://`) in the `host` box, with your username and password in the other boxes. You can typically leave the `port` box blank, as this information is normally determined automatically. (If in doubt, try port 21 or 22.) If an ordinary FTP connection doesn't work, check with your server to see if you need to use SFTP (a more secure variant) instead. If so, just select the appropriate encryption method (provided by your server) in the Encryption field. Once you've made the connection, SFTP acts almost exactly like FTP. Figure 1-12 shows the Site Manager dialog box.

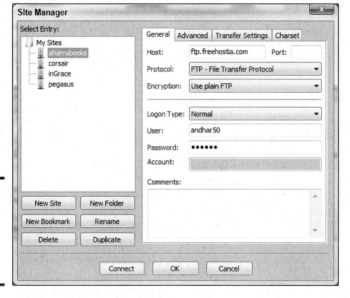

Figure 1-12:
Setting
up an FTP
account
with
FileZilla.

4. **Connect to the FTP server.**

   Click Connect to make the connection. A flurry of obscure messages flies through the top panel. In a few seconds (if all went well), you'll see a directory listing of the remote system in the right-hand panel.

5. **Use the left panel to manage local files.**

   The left-hand panel controls the local file system. Use this to find files on your local computer. It's a normal file management system like My Computer or Finder.

6. **Use the right panel for remote files.**

   The right-hand panel controls the remote server file system. It works exactly like the local system, except it allows you to manipulate files on the remote system. Use this system to move to the appropriate directory on the remote system. You can also create a new directory or rename files with the appropriate buttons on this screen.

7. **Drag files to transfer them.**

   To transfer files between machines simply drag them. Drag from the local machine to the remote machine to upload, or in the other direction to download them. You can move many files at a time in this manner.

8. **Watch for errors.**

   Most of the time, everything works great, but sometimes there is a problem. The bottom panel shows potential error messages. If there is an error, you may need to reload a file.

Most remote servers run some variation of the Unix operating system. You may not be familiar with Unix, but it really works a lot like the systems you already know. However, it has one feature that may be new to you: file permissions. Most of the time, an FTP program automatically gets the file permissions right, but if the browser cannot see a file after you upload it to the server, try right-clicking that file in FileZilla and look at its properties. Most web files should have a permission set called 644 (which means you can read and write the file, everyone else can read it, and nobody can run it on the server). If it is set to something else, try changing it to 644. Web directories should typically have 755 permission, which is almost always the default.

FTP is a completely unsecure protocol. Anything you transfer with FTP is completely visible to any bad guys sniffing the Internet. For this reason, some servers use a different protocol: Secure FTP (SFTP). Filezilla supports this and other protocols your server might use.

Naming Your Site

After you have a site up and running, you need to give it an address that people can remember. The Domain Name System (DNS) is sort of an address book of the entire Internet. DNS is the mechanism by which you assign a name to your site.

Understanding domain names

Before creating a domain name, you should understand the basics of how this system works:

✦ **Every computer on the Internet has an IP (Internet Protocol) address.** When you connect to the Internet, a special number is assigned to your computer. This *IP address* uniquely identifies your computer. Client machines don't need to keep the same address. For example, my notebook has one address at home and another at work. The client addresses are dynamically allocated, and that's fine. But a server needs a permanent address that doesn't change.

✦ **IP addresses are used to find computers.** Any time you request a web page, you're looking for a computer with a particular IP address. For example, the Google IP address is `66.102.9.104`. Type it into your browser address bar, press Enter, and you see the Google main page.

✦ **DNS names simplify addressing.** IP numbers are too confusing for human users. The Domain Name System (DNS) is a series of databases connecting website names with their associated IP numbers. When you type `http://www.google.com`, for example, the DNS system looks up the text `www.google.com` and finds the computer with the associated IP.

✦ **You have to register a DNS name.** Of course, to ensure that a particular name is associated with a page, you need to register that relationship.

Registering a domain name

In this section, I show you how to register a domain using Freehostia.com. Check the documentation on your hosting service. Chances are that the main technique is similar, even if the details are different.

To add a domain name to your site, follow these steps:

1. **Log in to the service.**

   Log in to your hosting service administration panel. You usually see a Control Panel something like the one shown in Figure 1-13.

Figure 1-13: This Control Panel shows all the options, including domain and subdomain tools.

2. **Find the domain manager.**

   In Freehostia, the domain manager is part of the regular administration panel.

3. Pick a subdomain.

In a free hosting service, the main domain (`freehostia.com`, for example) is often chosen for you. Sometimes, you can set a subdomain (like `mystuff.freehostia.com`) for free. The page for managing this process might look like Figure 1-14.

Figure 1-14:
Use this page to create a subdomain for your account.

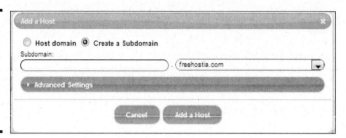

4. Look for a domain search tool.

Often, you have a tool, like the one shown in Figure 1-15, that allows you to search for a domain.

5. Search for the domain name you want.

You can type a domain name to see whether it's available.

Figure 1-15:
I'm searching for aharrisbooks. net — it seems like a good name!

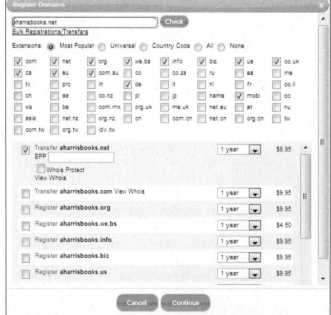

6. **If the domain name is available to register and you want to own it, purchase it immediately.**

   If a domain is available to transfer, it means that somebody else probably owns it.

   Don't search for domains until you're ready to buy them. Unscrupulous people on the web look for domains that have been searched and then buy them immediately, hoping to sell them back to you at a higher price. If you search for a domain name and then go back the next day to buy it, you often find that it's no longer available and must be transferred. I've also seen people offer to sell you a domain that's currently available, then buy it up only after you've agreed to purchase from them and sell it at a huge markup.

7. **Register the domain.**

   The domain-purchase process involves registering yourself as the domain owner. WHOIS information provides your information to people inquiring about the domain name.

8. **Wait a day or two.**

   Your new domain name won't be available immediately. It takes a couple of days for the name to be registered everywhere.

9. **Remember to renew your domain registration.**

   Domain-name registration isn't expensive (typically about $10 per year), but you must renew it or risk losing the name.

Managing Data Remotely

Websites often work with databases. Your hosting service may have features for working with MySQL databases remotely. You should understand how this process works because it's often slightly different from working with the database on your local machine.

Creating your database

Often, a tool like the one shown in Figure 1-16 allows you to pick a defined database or create a new one.

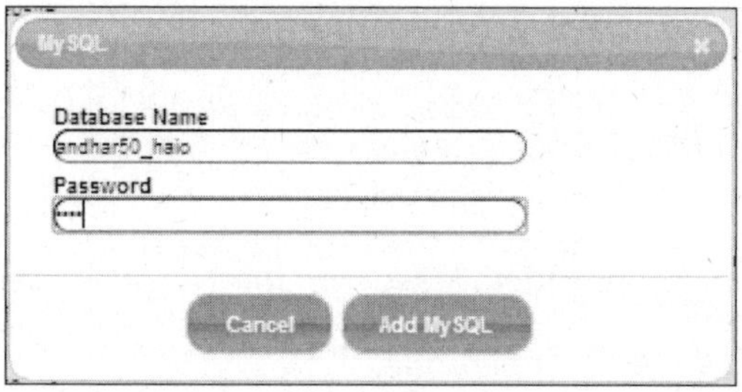

Figure 1-16:
You often have to create a database outside of phpMy-Admin.

This database creation step happens because you don't have `root` access to MySQL. (If everybody had `root` access, chaos would ensue.) Instead, you usually have an assigned username and database name enforced by the server. On Freehostia, all database names begin with the username and an underscore. To create a new database, you need to provide a database name and a password. Usually, a MySQL user is created with the same name as the database name.

After you create the database, you can select it to work with the data in MySQL. Figure 1-17 shows the MySQL screen for my database on Freehostia.

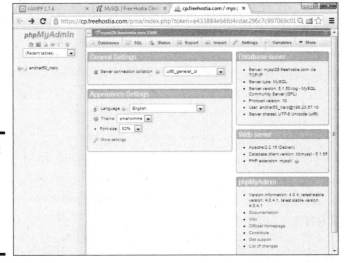

Figure 1-17: phpMy-Admin is just like the one on your home machine!

You can see from Figure 1-17 that phpMyAdmin is somewhat familiar if you read Book VI. Often, public servers remove the Privileges section because you aren't logged in as `root`. Everything else is basically the same. See Book VI for details on how to use phpMyAdmin to work with your databases.

Finding the MySQL server name

Throughout Book VI, I assume that the MySQL server is on the same physical machine as the web server. This situation is common in XAMPP installations, but commercial servers often have separate servers for data. You may have to dig through the documentation or find a Server Statistics section to discover how your PHP programs should refer to your server.

By far the biggest problem when moving your programs to a remote server is figuring out the new connection. Make sure that you know the right combination of server name, username, and password. Test on a simple PHP application before working on a complex one.

Chapter 2: Planning Your Sites

In This Chapter

✔ **Planning multipage websites**

✔ **Working with the client**

✔ **Analyzing the audience**

✔ **Building a site plan**

✔ **Creating HTML and CSS templates**

✔ **Fleshing out the project**

*A*t some point, your web efforts begin to grow. Rather than think about single web documents, you begin to build more complex systems. Most real-life web problems require a lot more than a single page to do the work. How do you make the transition to a site with many different but interconnected pages? How do you think through the process of creating a site that serves a specific purpose?

You might even be thinking about doing commercial web development work. If so, it's definitely time to think about how to put together a plan for a customer.

Creating a Multipage Website

A complete website has these characteristics:

✦ **A consistent theme:** All the pages in a website should be about something — a product, a shop, a hobby. It doesn't matter much what the theme is, but the pages should be unified around it.

✦ **Consistent design:** The site should have a unified color scheme. All pages should have the same (or similar) layout, and the font choices and images should all use a similar style.

✦ **A navigation scheme:** Users must have a clear mechanism to move around from page to page. The organization of the pages and their relationships should be clear.

✦ **A common address:** Normally, all pages in a site are on the same server and have a common DNS name so that they're easy to distinguish.

Obviously, the skills of web design are critical to building a website, but a broader skill set is required when creating something larger than individual pages.

If you're starting to build a more complicated website, you need to have a plan, or else you won't succeed. This plan is even more important if you're building a site for somebody else.

Planning a Larger Site

Here are some questions you need to ask yourself when designing a larger website:

✦ **What's the point of the site?** The site doesn't have to be serious, but it does have to have a theme. If you don't know what your site is about, neither do your users (and they'll leave in a hurry).

✦ **Who am I talking to?** Websites are a form of communication, and you can't communicate well if you don't understand your audience. Who is the primary target audience for this site?

✦ **Which resources do I have available?** Resources involve a lot more than money (but it helps). How much time do you have? Do you have access to a solid technical framework? Can you get help if you need it? Do you have all the copy and raw materials?

✦ **What am I trying to say?** Believe it or not, this question often poses a huge problem. Somebody says, "I need a website." When you ask what she wants on the site, she says, "Oh, lots of things." When you try to pin down the answers, though, people often don't know *what* they want their website to say.

✦ **What are the visual design constraints?** If you're building a page for a small business, it probably has some kind of visual identity (through brochures or signage, for example). The business owner often wants you to stick with the company's current branding, which may involve negotiating with graphic artists or advertisers the business has worked with.

✦ **Where will I put this thing?** Does the client already have a domain name? Will moving the domain name cause a problem? Does content that's already on the web need to be moved? Do you already have hosting space and a DNS name in mind?

Understanding the Client

Often, a larger site is created at the behest of somebody else. Even if you're making a site for your own purposes, you should consider yourself a client. If the project is going to be successful, you need to know a few things about the client, as described in the following sections.

Ensuring that the client's expectations are clear

The short answer to the question of whether a client's expectations are clear is, "Not usually."

A client who truly understands the Internet and knows what it takes to realize her vision for the site probably doesn't need you. Most of the time, a client's own concepts of what should happen on the site are vague, at best. Here are some introductory questions you can ask to get a sense of your client's expectations:

✦ **What are you trying to say with this site?** If the website has a single message that can be boiled down to one phrase or sentence, find out what that message is.

✦ **Who are you trying to reach with this site?** Determine who the client expects to be the typical users of the site. Find out whether she expects others and whether the site has more than one potential type of user. (For example, customers and employees may need different things.)

✦ **What problem is this site trying to solve?** Sometimes, a website is envisioned as a solution to a particular problem (getting the schedule online or keeping an online newsletter updated, for example.)

✦ **What kind of design framework is already in place?** Determine whether the organization already has some sort of branding and design strategy or whether you have freedom in this arena. If the client is already working with a graphic designer or artist, you'll need contact information.

✦ **What is the time constraint?** Find out how quickly the client needs the site completed. Does the client want the entire project at one time, or can it be phased in?

✦ **Do you already have a technical framework in place?** Determine whether the project needs to work with an existing database, web server, website, or domain name and whether you have complete access to those resources.

✦ **Are there security concerns?** First ask whether you will be asked to post data (personal information, credit card numbers, or Social Security numbers, for example) on the Internet that shouldn't be there. Run from any project that requires you to work with this potentially dangerous data, unless you're extremely comfortable with security measures.

✦ **How will you get the copy?** Any professional web developer can tell you that the client usually promises to make the copy available immediately but rarely delivers it without a lot of pleading. If the content is available, it's often incomplete or incorrect. You need to have some plan for getting the material from the client, or else you cannot proceed past a certain point.

✦ **Does the client have a remuneration strategy?** If you will be paid for your work, find out how you will be paid and whether it's hourly or by the project. If you have a business arrangement, treat it as such and write out a contract. Even if the page is written for free for a friend, a written contract is a good idea because you don't want to ruin a friend-ship over something as silly as a website.

Delineating the tasks

Building a website can involve a lot of different tasks. Your contract should indicate which of these tasks is expected. This list describes the potential scope of the project:

✦ **Site layout:** Determine which pages the site has and how they're con-nected to each other.

✦ **HTML coding:** Some projects simply require HTML coding and CSS. Presumably, the copy has already been provided, and you simply need to convert it to HTML format. This work isn't difficult, but it's tedious. Use a text editor with macro capability — after you create an HTML template.

✦ **HTML template design:** Devise an overall page design. The content isn't important here, but the general page design is the issue. This task requires sample data and an editor. It's normally done in conjunction with CSS templating.

✦ **CSS design:** After you have an HTML template or two (so that you know the logical structure of the pages), you can work on the visual design. Start with sketches on paper and maybe images from a paint program. After you have a layout approved, write the CSS to implement it.

✦ **Data design:** If the project will have a database component, take some time to analyze (and, often, rebuild) the data structure to follow the nor-malization rules. Data work is difficult because it doesn't have a visual result, yet it's critical to the overall site. This step is usually put off until the end, and that decision often dooms web projects. If you need data design, start it early.

✦ **Data implementation:** If the project has a data component, write and test the SQL code to build the database, including tables, views, and sample queries. You need time to write PHP code to connect the data-base to the HTML front end.

✦ **Site integration and implementation:** It takes some effort to fit all the pieces back together and make them work. Usually, this process is ongo-ing. The site needs to be set up on a production server and then tested and launched.

✦ **Testing:** Testing your work with live users is critical. You can use formal usability studies, but failing that, you still learn a lot by asking people to use your system and watching them do it (with your mouth shut). This method is the best way to see whether your assumptions are correct and the site is doing what it needs to do.

For this discussion, I'm assuming you're building the entire site manually. In Chapter 3 of this minibook, I explain how to use content management systems to simplify the process of building large websites.

Understanding the Audience

Understanding your audience is one of the trickiest parts of web planning. You need to anticipate the audience in a number of ways, as described in the following sections.

Determining whom you want to reach

Before you make a lot of design decisions, you need to think carefully about the type of person you're trying to reach with the website.

Try to anticipate the mindset that people have when they use a particular site. For example, one of my students simultaneously worked on two sites: one for a graduate program at a university and another for a spa and salon. She had to think quite differently about the users of the two sites, which had implications for how she approached each step of the process.

The graduate program page was part of a website for a university. The university already had its own style and branding guidelines, official colors, and a number of (evolving) standards. The potential users of this site were graduate students seeking online degrees. The focus of this site was all business. People were there to learn about the graduate program and set up their schedules. They wanted information about classes, instructors, and schedules, but they didn't want anything that interfered with the problem at hand. The writing was efficient and official, the color scheme was standard, and the layout was also official.

The spa and salon page had an entirely different feel. The owner loves design and spent long hours picking exactly the right paint color for the walls in the physical space. She's really happy with her brochure, and although she's not sure exactly what she wants, she knows when something isn't right. She wants to give her customers information about the salon, but more importantly, she wants them to get a sense of how invigorating, relaxing, and feminine the experience of visiting her salon can be.

These two sites, although they require the same general technical skills, demand vastly different visual and technical designs because the clients and their users are vastly different.

Of course, someone could simultaneously be a graduate student and a patron of the salon, but the person would still have a different identity in

Book VIII Chapter 2

Planning Your Sites

these different sites. If you're going to a university site, in a student mindset, you want quick, reliable information. If, after you sign up for classes, you're looking for a salon, you likely want to be pampered. Websites are experiences. The design of the site should reflect the experience you're trying to give the user when he visits your site.

Finding out the user's technical expertise

Understanding the user isn't just an exercise in psychology. You also need to estimate the users' technical proficiency because it can have a major impact on your site. Consider these issues for the typical user:

✦ **Whether the user has broadband access:** University students, hard-core gamers, and web developers often have high-speed Internet access, so they don't mind a page with lots of video, multimedia assets, and large file sizes. (In fact, they may *expect* a page like this.) Lots of people still use dialup connections or mobile access with limited bandwidth. If your audience has slower connections, every image creates a delay. Audio and video assets are completely unavailable to this group — and even make your site unattractive to them.

✦ **Whether the user has a recent browser:** You have no way to predict which browser a user has, but think about whether your target audience has a reason to install any of the current browsers. By and large, grandmothers use whichever browsers were on their machines when they purchased them. (I do know some L337 H@XX0R grandmas, however.) If most people in your audience are still using ancient browser — believe it or not, they're still used a lot — using advanced CSS and JavaScript tricks on your page may not be the best choice.

✦ **Whether the user has a recent computer:** As technical people, we tend to assume that everyone else keeps up-to-date on technology. That's not necessarily an accurate assumption.

✦ **Whether the user has certain proficiencies:** If you include a Flash animation, for example, the user might not have the right version of Flash installed. You have to decide whether it's reasonable to expect the user to install a plug-in.

✦ **Whether this will be a largely mobile application:** These days, every website should be considered a potential mobile site, but if a large percentage of your visitors will be using mobile devices to view your page, this will have implications on your design.

This process isn't about stereotyping, but you *must* consider the user while you're building a site. You want to match users' expectations and capabilities, if possible.

Of course, you're making assumptions here, and you may well be wrong. I once did some work for a club for retired professors, and I based my expectations on their being retired. I should have based my assumptions on their being professors. And they let me have it! Be willing to adjust your expectations after you meet real users. (For professional work, you *must* meet and watch real users use your site.)

Building a Site Plan

Often, the initial work on a major site involves creating a plan for the site design. I like to do this step early because it helps me see the true scope of the project. A *site plan* is an overview of a website. Normally, it's drawn as a hierarchy chart.

I was asked to help design a website for an academic department at a major university. The first question I asked was, "What do you want on the website?" I wrote down everything on a whiteboard, with no thought of organization. Figure 2-1 shows a (cleaned-up) version of that sketch.

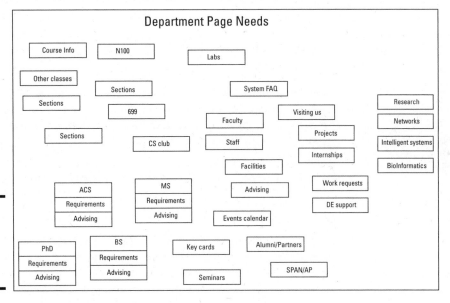

Figure 2-1: We need a lot of stuff on this site. Good grief!

For all the sketches in this chapter, I used Dia, the open-source drawing tool. An excellent tool for this kind of work, I've added a link on the website so that you can play with it.

After all participants suggested everything they thought their site needed, I shooed them out of the room. Using only paper and pencil, I created a more organized sketch based on how *I* thought the information should be organized. My diagram looked like the one shown in Figure 2-2.

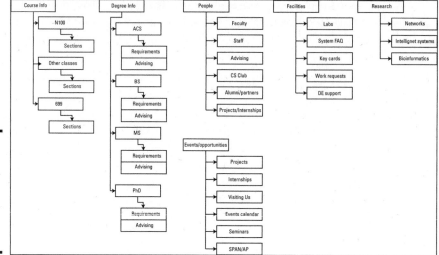

Figure 2-2:
This chart shows an organized representation of the data.

Creating a site overview

Keep these suggestions in mind while creating a site overview diagram:

✦ **Use the Law of Seven.** This law suggests that people generally can't handle more than seven choices at a time. Try not to have more than seven major segments of information at any level. Each of these can be separated into as many as seven chunks, and each of these can have seven chunks.

   Note: Even this book uses the Law of Seven! (Well, sorta — this book has eight minibooks.) The monster you're holding is too intimidating to look at as just one book, but if you break it into smaller segments, it becomes easier to manage. Clever, huh?

✦ **Identify commonalities.** While you look over the data, general groupings emerge. In the university example, I could easily see that we had a lot of course data, degree information, information about faculty, and research. I wanted to consider a few other topics that didn't fit as well, until I realized that they could be grouped as events and opportunities.

✦ **Try to assign each topic to a group.** I'm doing a form of *data normalization* here. This data structure isn't necessarily a formal one, but I'm using the same sort of thinking, so it could be. Clearly, I'm using the principle of functional dependency.

✦ **Arrange a hierarchy.** Group the topics from most general to most specific. For example, the term *course info* is very broad. N100 is a specific course, and it may have many sections (specific date, time, and instructor combinations). Thus, it makes sense to group sections under N100 and to group N100 under courses.

✦ **Provide representative data.** Not every single scrap of information is necessary here. The point is to have enough data so you can see the relationships among data.

✦ **Keep in mind that this diagram does *not* represent the site design.** When I showed this diagram to people, many assumed that I was setting up a menu structure, and they wanted a different kind of organization or menu. That's not the point yet. The purpose of this type of diagram is to see how the data itself fits together. Of course, this diagram tends to inform the page setup and the menu structure, but it doesn't have to.

✦ **Not each box is a page.** It might be, but it doesn't have to be. Later in the process, you can decide how to organize the parts of the site. For example, we decided to put all sections of N100 on one page with the N100 information using AJAX.

Building this sort of site diagram is absolutely critical for larger sites, or else you never really grasp the scope of the project. Have the major stakeholders look it over to see whether it accurately reflects the *information* you're trying to convey.

Building the site diagram

The site diagram is a more specific version of the site overview. At this point, you make a commitment about the particular pages you want in the system and their organizational relationship. Figure 2-3 shows a site diagram for the department site.

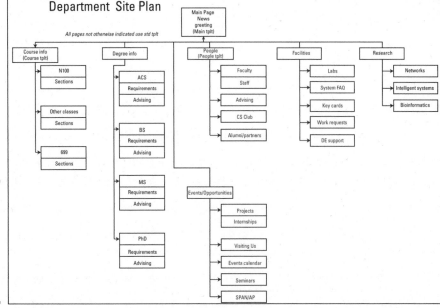

Figure 2-3: Now you have a site diagram for the department site.

The site diagram is a bit different from the overview for these reasons:

✦ **Each box represents a page.** Now you have to make some decisions about how the pages are organized. Determine at which level of the overview you have separate pages. For example, are all the course sections on one page, or all the sections of N100? Does each section of each course have a different page? These decisions will help you determine which technologies to use in constructing the page.

✦ **The site diagram still doesn't need every page.** If you have 30 classes, you don't need to account for each one if you know where they go and they all have the same general purpose and design.

✦ **The navigation structure should be clear.** The hierarchy should give you a clear navigation structure. (Of course, you can, and often should, add a secondary navigation structure. See the sidebar "Semantic navigation.")

✦ **Name each box.** Each page should have a name. These box names translate to page titles and help you form a unified title system. This arrangement is useful for your navigation scheme.

✦ **Identify overall layout for each box.** Generally, a site uses only a few layouts. You have a standard layout for most pages. Often, the front page has a different layout (for news and navigation information). You may have specialty layouts, as well. For example, the faculty pages all have a specific layout with a prominent image. Don't plan the layout here — just identify it.

✦ **Sort out the order.** If the order of the pages matters, the site diagram is the place to work it out. For example, I organized the degrees from undergraduate to PhD programs.

The goal for this part of the site-planning process is to have a clear understanding of what each page requires. This information should make it easy for you to complete the data and visual design steps. The site diagram is an absolutely critical document. After you have it approved, print it and tape it to your monitor. It's your map for the rest of the project.

Semantic navigation

One idea that has been popular in web design circles is the notion of *semantic navigation,* where you set up your menu structure so that it reflects the jobs people are trying to do, rather than reflect the hierarchy of your sites. For example, a university department site might have a menu for common student activities, alumni, and faculty.

This idea can be quite helpful if done properly, but don't try to set up your entire site this way because it involves too much duplication of data. (Students and faculty both need course information, but you don't want to post that in two different places.) Instead, set up your site in a normalized way, and then put another menu system on your site that allows users to choose the section of the site they want based on problems they're trying to solve. Then, you create the best of both worlds.

Creating Page Templates

If you've developed a site diagram, you should have a good feel for the over-all requirements of the web development project. You should know how many layouts you need and the general requirements for each one. Your next task is to think about the visual design. Here are some guidelines:

✦ **Get help if you need it.** Visual design is a skill that requires insight and experience. If you "design like a programmer" (I sure do!), don't be afraid to get help from a person who has design sensibility. You still need to translate the design into code, however.

✦ **Identify unifying design goals.** All pages on the site have certain char-acteristics in common. Find out the overall color scheme, whether you will have a logo, and whether all pages will have the same header and retain the same fonts throughout.

✦ **Identify a primary layout.** Generally, a website requires one major layout that's repeated throughout the site. Often, the main page does not use this primary layout, but most internal pages do. Determine, for example, which broad design elements can be shared by most of the pages, whether every page has a headline, whether you need columns, and how important images are.

✦ **Identify specialty designs.** The main page is often a bit different from the other pages because it serves as an overview to the site. Likewise, if you will be repeating certain kinds of pages (the course pages and faculty pages in my university example), you have to know how these designs differ from the primary layout. Keep design elements as consis-tent as you can because unity makes your job easier and ties the site pages together.

Sketching the page design

Do not write even a single line of code before sketching out some design ideas. Figure 2-4 shows a page sketch for my sample site.

Your page sketch gives you enough information to create HTML and CSS code. It needs to start showing some detail, such as the following details:

✦ **Draw out each element on the page.** Any major page element (head-lines, menus, columns) must be delineated.

✦ **Include the class or ID identifier for each element.** If you have a seg-ment that will be used as a menu, name it "menu," for example. If you have a content area, identify that name now. Write all names directly on the diagram so that you're clear about what belongs where.

✦ **Include all relevant style information.** Describe every font, the width of every element (including measurement units), the foreground and back-ground colors (with hex codes), the background images (including sizes), and anything else you might need in order to code CSS styles for the page.

✦ **Build a page sketch following these guidelines for each page template in your site.** If you have three page designs, for example, you need three separate diagrams.

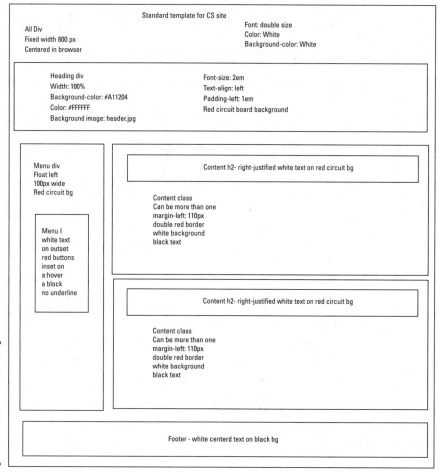

Figure 2-4:
Here's a sample sketch for the standard template on this site.

These diagrams are finished only if they give you everything you need to build the HTML and CSS templates. The idea is to do all your design work on paper and then implement and tweak your project with code. If you plan well, the coding is easy.

TIP

The design sketch isn't a page mock-up. It's not meant to look exactly like the page. Instead, it's a sketch that explains with text all the various details you need to code in HTML and CSS. Often, designers produce beautiful mock-ups that aren't helpful in development because you need to know sizes and colors, for example. If you want to produce a mock-up, by all means do so, but also make a design sketch that includes things like actual font names and hex color codes so that you can re-create the mock-up with live code.

Building the HTML template framework

With a page layout in place, you can finally start writing some code. Begin with your standard page layout diagram and create an HTML template to implement the diagram in working code. The HTML template is quite simple because most of the design should happen in the CSS. Keep these guidelines in mind:

✦ **Remember that the template is simply a framework.** The HTML is mainly blank. It's meant to be duplicated and filled in with live data.

✦ **It has a reference to the style sheet.** External CSS is critical for large web projects because many pages refer to the same style sheet. Make a reference to the style sheet, even though it may not actually exist yet.

✦ **Include all necessary elements.** The elements themselves can be blank, but if your page needs a list for a menu, add an empty list. If you need a content div, put it in place.

✦ **Create a prototype from the template.** You'll need sample data in order to test the CSS. Build a prototype page that contains typical data. The amount of data should be typical of the actual site so that you can anticipate formatting problems.

It's very possible that you'll never manually put content in your template. There are several options for automating this process, which can be found in Chapter 4 of this minibook.

The HTML template should be easy to construct because everything you need is in the page template diagram. Figure 2-5 shows an HTML prototype.

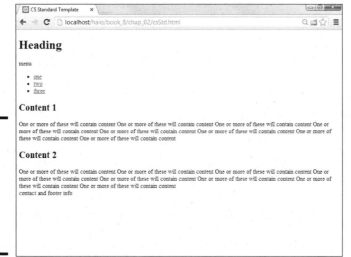

Figure 2-5: An HTML prototype for my site (with no CSS attached yet).

Here's the HTML code for my prototype:

```html
<!DOCTYPE html>
<html lang = "en-US">

  <head>
    <meta charset = "UTF-8">
    <title>CS Standard Template</title>
    <link rel = "stylesheet"
          type = "text/css"
          href = "csStd.css" />
  </head>
  <body>
    <div id = "all">
      <!-- This div centers a fixed-width layout -->
      <div id = "heading">
        <h1>Heading</h1>
      </div><!-- end heading div -->
      <div id = "menu">
        menu
        <ul>
          <li><a href = "#">one</a></li>
          <li><a href = "#">two</a></li>
          <li><a href = "#">three</a></li>
        </ul>
      </div> <!-- end menu div -->
      <div class = "content">
        <h2>Content 1</h2>
        One or more of these will contain content
        One or more of these will contain content
        One or more of these will contain content
        One or more of these will contain content
        One or more of these will contain content
        One or more of these will contain content
        One or more of these will contain content
        One or more of these will contain content
      </div> <!-- end content div -->
      <div class = "content">
        <h2>Content 2</h2>
        One or more of these will contain content
        One or more of these will contain content
        One or more of these will contain content
        One or more of these will contain content
        One or more of these will contain content
        One or more of these will contain content
        One or more of these will contain content
        One or more of these will contain content
      </div> <!-- end content div -->
      <div id = "footer">
        contact and footer info
      </div> <!-- end footer div -->
    </div> <!-- end all div -->
  </body>
</html>
```

People commonly start writing pages at this point, but that's a dangerous idea. Don't use any real data until you're certain of the general HTML structure. You can always change the style later, but if you create 100 pages and then decide that each of them needs another <div> tag, you have to go back and add 100 divs.

Creating page styles

With an HTML framework in place, you can start working on the CSS. The best way to incorporate CSS is by following these steps:

1. **Begin with the page template diagram.**

   It should have all the information you need.

2. **Test your CSS in a browser.**

   Begin with a simple CSS implementation that ensures you have the right names for all the page elements. (I like to give each element a different background color, for example.) Then modify each element according to your design document, testing as you go.

3. **Implement the CSS from your diagram.**

   You should be *implementing* the design you already created, not *designing* the page. (That already happened in the diagramming process.)

4. **Save the design.**

   For multi-page projects, external CSS in a separate file is definitely the way to go. As you work, save the CSS in the normal way so the browser will be able to read it. (See Book II for information on implementing external style sheets.)

5. **Test and tweak.**

   Things are never quite what they seem with CSS because browsers don't conform to standards equally. You need to test and tweak on other browsers. If users with older technologies are a concern, you may have to use a secondary style sheet for older versions of IE. You may also want to make a mobile version.

6. **Repeat for other templates.**

   Repeat this process for each of the other templates you identified in your site diagram.

The result of this process should be a number of CSS files that you can readily reuse across your site.

Here's the CSS code for my primary page:

```
body {
  background-color: #000000;
}

h1 {
  text-align: center;
  font-family: sans-serif;
  color: white;
  text-shadow: 0 0 10px black;
}
```

```css
#all {
  background-color: white;
  border: 1px solid black;
  width: 800px;
  margin-top:2em;
  margin-left: auto;
  margin-right: auto;
  min-height: 600px;
}

#heading {
  background-color: #A11204;
  background-image: url("cbBackground.png");
  color: #FFFFFF;
  height: 100px;
  font-size: 2em;
  padding-left: 1em;
  border-bottom: 3px solid black;
  margin-top: -1.5em;
}

#menu {
  background-image: url("cbBackground.png");
  background-color: #A11204;
  color: #FFFFFF;
  float: left;
  width: 100px;
  min-height: 500px;
}

#menu li {
  list-style-type: none;
  margin-left: -2em;
  margin-right: .5em;
  text-align: center;
}

#menu a {
  color: #FFFFFF;
  display: block;
  border: #A11204 3px outset;
  text-decoration: none;
}
#menu a:hover {
  border: #A11204 3px inset;
}

.content {
  border: 3px double #A11204;
  margin: 1em;
  margin-left: 110px;
  padding-left: 1em;
  padding-bottom: 1em;
  padding-right: 1em;
  border-radius: 5px;
  box-shadow: 5px 5px 5px gray;
}

.content h2 {
  background-color: #A11204;
  background-image: url("cbBackground.png");
  color: #FFFFFF;
  text-align: right;
}
```

```
#footer {
  color: #FFFFFF;
  background-color: #000000;
  border: 1px solid #A11204;
  float: left;
  clear: both;
  width: 100%;
  text-align: center;
}
```

Figure 2-6 shows the standard template with the CSS attached.

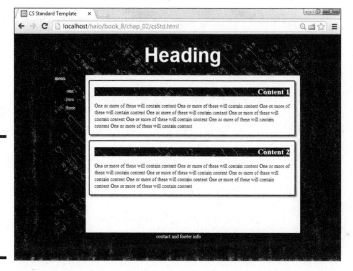

Figure 2-6:
The HTML
template
looks
good with
the CSS
attached.

Building a data framework

The examples throughout this chapter assumed that a large web project can be done in straight HTML and CSS. That's always a good starting point, but if your program needs data or interactivity, you probably have a data back end.

Most data-enabled sites fail because they weren't planned properly.

The reason is almost always that the data normalization wasn't incorporated into the plan early enough, and the other parts of the project inevitably depend on a well-planned data back end.

If you suspect your project will involve a database, you should follow these steps early in the process (during the early site-planning phase):

1. **Identify the true data problem to be solved.**

   Data gets complicated in a hurry. Determine why exactly you need the data on the site. Keep the data as simple as you can, or else you'll become overwhelmed.

2. **Identify data requirements in your site diagram.**

   Find out where on the site diagram you're getting data. Determine which data you're retrieving and record this information on the site diagram.

3. **Create a third normal form ER diagram.**

   Don't bother building a database until you're sure that you can create an ER diagram in third normal form. Check Book VI, Chapter 3 for details on this process. If you're spotty on data design, get help.

4. **Implement the data structure.**

   Create an SQL script that creates all the necessary data structures (including tables and views) and includes sample data. Implementing the design is easy after you've made it. (That seems to be a theme, doesn't it?)

5. **Create PHP middleware.**

   After the database is in place, you usually need PHP code to take requests, pass them to the database, and return the results. Most of the PHP code for the main site consists of simple queries from the database. If you can use AJAX or SSI, it simplifies the process because your PHP code doesn't have to create entire pages — it simply creates snippets of code.

   See Chapter 3 of this minibook for help on implementing these technologies.

6. **Consider update capabilities.**

   Usually, when you have a database, you need another part of the site to allow the client to update information. It's often an administrative site with password access. An administrative site is much more complex than the main site because it requires the ability to add, edit, and update records.

Fleshing Out the Project

If you completed all the steps in the preceding section, it becomes relatively easy to create the page: It's simply a matter of forming the copy into the templates you created, tying it all together, and launching the site.

Making the site live

Typically, you do the primary development on a server that isn't in public view. Follow these steps to take the site to production:

1. **Test your design.**

   Do some usability testing with real users. Watch people solve typical problems on the site and see what problems they encounter.

2. **Proofread everything.**

   Almost nothing demolishes credibility as quickly as sloppy writing. Get a quality proofreader or copy editor to look over everything on the site to check for typos and spelling errors. If your page contains a specific type of content (technical information or company policy, for example), have an expert familiar with the subject check the site for factual or content errors.

3. **Prepare the online hosting environment.**

   Be sure that you have the server space to handle your requirements. Make a copy of your database and test it. Check the domain name to be sure that you have no legal encumbrances.

4. **Move your site online.**

   Move the files from your development server to the main server.

5. **Test everything again.**

   Try a *beta* test, where your page is available to only a few people. Get input and feedback from these testers and incorporate the best suggestions.

6. **Ensure you have a maintenance agreement.**

   Websites are complicated, and they will have a long lifespan. Make sure you have an agreement in place that clearly indicates your ongoing relationship with the project. You should generally have the client sign off that the project is complete and build in some kind of contract for on-going support.

7. **Take a vacation. You earned it!**

Contemplating efficiency

When you start working with the site, you'll probably encounter repeated code. For example, each page may have exactly the same title bar. You obviously don't want to write exactly the same code for 100 different pages because it might change, and you don't want to make the change in 100 different places. You have three options in this case:

✦ **Use AJAX to import the repeated code.** Follow the AJAX instructions in Chapter 3 of this minibook to import your header (or other repeated code).

✦ **Use Server-Side Includes (SSI) to import code on the server.** If your server allows it, you can use the SSI technology to import pages on the server without using a language like PHP. SSI is explained in Chapter 3 of this minibook.

✦ **Build the pages with PHP.** Put all segments in separate files and use a PHP script to tie them together. When you do this, you're creating a content management system, which is the topic of Chapters 3 and 5 of this minibook.

Chapter 3: Introducing Content Management Systems

In This Chapter

✔ **Understanding the need for content management systems**

✔ **Previewing typical content management systems**

✔ **Installing a content management system**

✔ **Adding content to a content management system**

✔ **Setting up the navigation structure**

✔ **Adding new types of content**

✔ **Changing the appearance with themes**

✔ **Building a custom theme**

*I*f you've ever built a large website, you'll probably agree that the process can be improved. Experienced web developers have discovered the following maxims about larger projects:

✦ **Duplication should be eliminated whenever possible.** If you find yourself repeatedly copying the same HTML code, you have a potential problem. When (not if) that code needs to be changed, you have a lot of copying and pasting to do.

✦ **Content should be separated from layout.** You've already heard this statement, but it's taken to a new level when you're building a large site. Separating *all* content from the layout would be helpful so that you could create the layout only one time and change it in one location.

✦ **Content is really data.** At some point, the content of the website is really just data. It's important data, to be sure, but the data can — and should — be separated from the layout code.

✦ **Content belongs to the user.** Developing a website for somebody can become a long-term commitment. If the client becomes dependent on the site, he frequently pesters you for changes. It would be helpful if the client could change his own content and ask you only for changes in structure or behavior.

✦ **A website isn't a collection of pages — it's a framework.** If you can help the client own the data, you're more concerned with the framework for manipulating and displaying that data. It's a good deal for you and the client.

A content management system (CMS) is designed to address exactly these issues, as this chapter will show you.

Overview of Content Management Systems

CMSs are used in many of the sites you use every day. As you examine these CMSs, you start to recognize them all over the web. If you have your own server space, a little patience, and a little bit of knowledge, you can create your own professional-looking site using a CMS.

This list describes the general characteristics of a CMS:

✦ **It's written in a server-side language.** The language is usually PHP, but CMSs are sometimes written in other languages. Stick with PHP for now because it's described in this book, it's easy to use, and it's the most frequently used CMS language.

✦ **All content is treated as data.** Almost all the content of the CMS is stored in text files or (more commonly) a MySQL database. A CMS usually has few HTML files.

✦ **The layout consists of data, too.** The CSS and HTML templates, and everything else the CMS needs, are also stored as data, in either text files or the database.

✦ **All pages are created dynamically.** When a user logs in to a CMS, she is normally talking to a PHP program. This program analyzes the current situation and generates an HTML document on the fly.

✦ **There are different levels of access.** Most CMSs allow anonymous access (like regular web pages) but also allow users to log in for increased access, and usually a special form of administrative access to modify the site.

✦ **The content can be modified from within the system.** Users with the appropriate access can modify the content of the CMS without knowing anything about PHP or databases. Often, you don't even need to know HTML or CSS.

✦ **The layout can be modified from within the system, too.** Many CMSs allow you to change the layout and design from within the system, although the process is usually more involved.

✦ **CMSs can be expanded.** Most CMSs are easily modified with hundreds of visual themes, add-in modules, and new capabilities available for free. In most cases, if you need something that isn't there, you can make it yourself.

✦ **Many of the best CMSs are open-source.** CMSs are a shocking value. When you consider how much they can contribute to your online presence, it's amazing that most CMS programs are absolutely free.

Previewing Common CMSs

To get a true feel for the power of CMSs, you should test-drive a few. The wonderful resource www.opensourcecms.com allows you to log in to hundreds of different CMSs as a user and as an administrator to see how they work. I show you a few typical CMSs so that you can get a feel for how they work.

Moodle

Often, you have a special purpose in mind. For example, I wanted to teach an online course without purchasing an expensive and complicated course management system. I installed the special-purpose CMS Moodle. Figure 3-1 shows the Moodle screen for one of my courses.

Figure 3-1: Moodle is useful for managing online courses.

Moodle has a lot of features that lend it to the educational setting:

✦ **Student and instructor management:** The system already understands the roles of student and instructor and makes appropriate parts of the system available.

✦ **Online assignment creation and submission:** One of the biggest problems with online courseware is getting assignments to and from students. Moodle has a complete system for handling this problem.

✦ **Online grade book:** When a teacher grades an assignment (online through Moodle), the student's grades are automatically updated.

✦ **Online testing support:** Moodle has built-in modules for creating, managing, and scoring online quizzes and exams.

✦ **Communication tools:** Moodle includes a *wiki* (a collaborative documentation tool), online chat, and forum tools you can set up for improved communication with your students.

**Book VIII
Chapter 3**

Introducing Content
Management
Systems

✦ **Specialized educational content:** Moodle was put together by hundreds of passionate (and geeky) teachers, so it has all kinds of support for various teaching methodologies.

Community-created software can be very good (as Moodle is) because it's built by people who know exactly what they want, and anybody with an idea (and the skills to carry them out) can add or modify the features. The result is an organic system that can often be better than the commercial offerings.

I find Moodle easier to use and more reliable than the commercial course management system that my university uses. I keep a Moodle backup for my classes because when the "official" system goes down, I can always make something available for my students.

WordPress

WordPress is another specialty CMS, meant primarily for blogging (short for *web logging,* or keeping an online public diary). WordPress has become the dominant blogging tool on the Internet. Figure 3-2 shows a typical WordPress page.

Figure 3-2:
Woot! I'm
blogging!

WordPress takes one simple idea (blogging) and pushes it to the limit. Unregistered users see the blog output, but if you log in, you gain access to a complete set of tools for managing your online musings.

Figure 3-3 illustrates the administrator view of WordPress.

Additionally, you can change the layout and colors, add new templates, and do much more, as you can in a more traditional CMS.

Of course, hundreds of other specialized CMSs are out there. Before you try to build your own CMS from the ground up, take a look at the other available offerings and see whether you can start by using the work of somebody else.

Figure 3-3:
You can
easily get
started with
WordPress —
just start
writing.

Drupal

Drupal is one of the most popular multipurpose CMSs out there. Intended for larger sites, it's more involved than the specialty CMSs — although it can do almost anything.

Figure 3-4 shows a basic site running Drupal.

Figure 3-4:
Drupal is
intended
to support
online
communities.

Drupal was designed primarily for managing community websites. It is commonly used in the following types of sites:

✦ **Gaming sites:** Many game communities are based around a CMS like Drupal because it allows opportunities for users to share information, opinions, news, and files.

✦ **Software sites:** A CMS like Drupal is an ideal place to post information about your software, including downloads, documentation, and user support.

✦ **Forums:** Although you can find many dedicated forum packages, Drupal supports several good forum tools.

✦ **Blogging:** You can also use Drupal as a news site and a location to post your blog. You can add community features when you want or need them.

Drupal is powerful and extremely popular. However, this power has led to increased complexity. Learning everything you can do with Drupal will take some time and effort.

Building a CMS site with WebsiteBaker

For the rest of this chapter, I take you through the installation and customization of a complete website using the WebsiteBaker CMS. This is one of my favorite CMSs for a number of reasons:

✦ **It's easy to understand:** Systems like Drupal have gotten so complicated that you often require entire books on how to use them. WebsiteBaker (as you'll see) is not complicated at all, even for somewhat advanced features.

✦ **It's easy to modify:** WebsiteBaker uses a reasonably simple template system that's primarily HTML and CSS (with a few PHP functions thrown in). This makes it very easy to adapt pages that were not designed in WebsiteBaker to a CMS format.

✦ **It's easy to teach to clients:** When you're building a commercial site, it's critical that your customer learns how to manage the site. The easier you can make managing the site for the customer, the easier your job is down the road.

✦ **It's reasonably complete:** The basic install of WebsiteBaker is not large, but you can customize your installation with hundreds of modules and templates to get exactly the look and behavior you want.

✦ **It's free and open source:** Like almost all the software I recommend, WebsiteBaker is entirely free and open source, even for commercial use.

I focus on WebsiteBaker in the upcoming section, but it's just a sample CMS. Look over this section, but if you want to use a different CMS other than WebsiteBaker, by all means do so. You'll see the overall steps are pretty much the same regardless of the particular package you use. (I used almost exactly the same steps to install Drupal and WordPress on my demo server.)

Installing your CMS

A CMS package typically contains many different kinds of files. Most are primarily PHP programs with HTML/HTML pages and CSS. Most CMSs also include databases written in MySQL. To install a CMS, you need to download these components and install them on your server.

1. **Download the latest version of WebsiteBaker at `www.website baker2.org/en/home`.**

   Download the .zip file. (The CMS is all web code, so it doesn't matter which operating system you use.)

2. **Create a subdirectory on your web root.**

   If you use a local server, create a new subdirectory under `htdocs` (or wherever you save your web files). If you're on a remote server, use FTP or the file management tool to create the subdirectory you want the files to go in.

3. **Copy all WebsiteBaker files to the new directory.**

   The .zip file you download from WebsiteBaker contains a `wb` directory. Copy all files and folders in this directory to your new directory.

4. **Navigate to the new directory in your browser.**

   Be sure you have Apache and MySQL turned on. If you're on a local machine, be sure to use the `localhost` mechanism to find the directory.

   If all is well, you see the WebsiteBaker Installation Wizard, as shown in Figure 3-5.

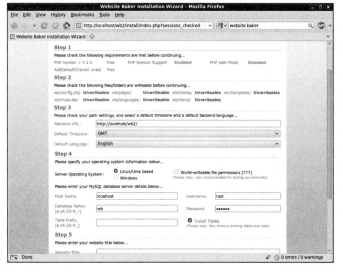

Figure 3-5:
The Website-Baker Installation Wizard helps you get started.

Most CMSs work in a similar way: You install a set of base files to the server, and then the system helps you get the other systems configured. Here's how to install WebsiteBaker:

1. **Check system configuration.**

   The Step 1 section of the installation wizard ensures all the needed components are available on your server.

2. **Ensure folders are writable.**

   The CMS will need to write files to the server. If you're in a Unix-based system, you may have to check the file permissions to ensure all files and folders specified in this section can be written to. Each specified file or folder can be set to 777 permission.

   See Chapter 1 of this minibook for more on changing Unix permissions. (Even if you use a Windows or Mac at home, your web server might use Linux or Unix.)

3. **Set default settings.**

   Specify the path to the CMS, the default time zone, and the default language.

4. **Specify your operating system.**

   Windows has its own way of doing things, so let WebsiteBaker know whether you're using Windows or a Unix-based system. (Mac OSX and Linux are both Unix-based.)

5. **Include database information.**

   Supply the information needed so WebsiteBaker can get to your database. Supply a database name as well as the username and password you want to use to access the database. Check the Install Tables option to have WebsiteBaker automatically build the database you need.

6. **Enter the website name.**

   This name appears on all the site's pages (but you can change it later).

7. **Create an administrator account.**

   The admin account will have the ability to change the site. Create a user named admin with a password you can remember.

8. **Install the CMS.**

   Press the Install WebsiteBaker button to install the CMS. Figure 3-6 shows the installation wizard after I filled in the contents.

   If all goes well, you're greeted by the administration page shown in Figure 3-7.

The final step of installing your CMS is to remove the install directory. This directory contains the scripts and tools you used to install the CMS. If you leave it in place, bad guys can reinstall your CMS from the web and destroy your settings. Use your file management or FTP tool to delete the install directory from your WebsiteBaker directory as soon as you're satisfied the installation went well. When you do this, the warning about the installation directory will disappear.

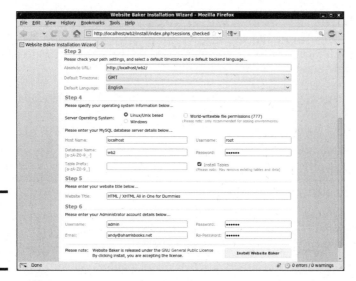

Figure 3-6:
The CMS
is ready to
install.

Instead of installing the CMS manually, many hosting services have automated installation scripts for popular CMSs that you can use. Freehostia has built-in support for WebsiteBaker, but I find the automated systems tend to have older versions of the software. You should still know how to set up the CMS by hand.

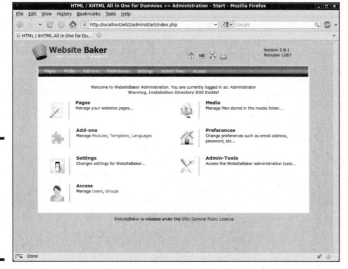

Figure 3-7:
Congrat-
ulations!
You now
own a
bouncing
baby CMS!

Getting an overview of WebsiteBaker

The administration page (refer to Figure 3-7) is the control panel you and other administrators use to build the site. The administration page's tools are the foundation of the entire site:

✦ **Pages:** Where you add the primary content for the site. Each page is built here. WebsiteBaker features a few standard page types, and you can install hundreds more through the module feature.

✦ **Add-ons:** The core installation of WebsiteBaker is reasonably basic, but you can customize it in many ways. The most important techniques are to add new types of pages (modules) and new visual themes (templates). I describe both techniques later in this chapter.

✦ **Settings:** Allows you to change global settings for the site. You can modify the site name, description, theme, and other settings from this panel.

✦ **Access:** Allows you to add new users and groups and grant various users access to different parts of the system. For example, if you're setting up a site for a church, you might want the children's pastor to have access to only the site's children's ministry parts.

✦ **Media:** You can add images and video to your site. This section allows you to manage and upload the various media to your server.

✦ **Preferences:** Allows you to change a few more settings, including the e-mail address and password of the admin account.

✦ **Admin-Tools:** Contains advanced options for improving the administration experience.

Adding your content

The point of a content management system is to manage some content, so it's time to add pages to the system.

1. **From the administration page, choose Pages.**

   A screen similar to Figure 3-8 appears.

2. **Type** main **as the first page name.**

   Each page you create needs to have a name.

3. **Keep the page type WYSIWYG.**

   You can make many different kinds of pages, but most of your pages will be the standard WYSIWYG format.

4. **Leave all other settings at their default.**

   The other settings available here don't mean much until you have multiple pages.

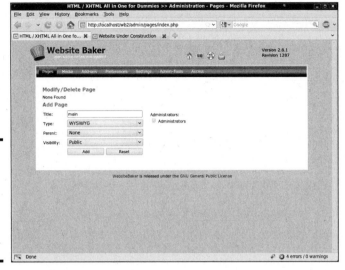

Figure 3-8:
This page
allows you
to add,
modify,
and delete
pages.

5. **Click the Add button to add the page.**

   A screen similar to Figure 3-9 appears.

Figure 3-9:
Now you're
at a nice
page editor.

**Book VIII
Chapter 3**

Introducing Content
Management
Systems

Using the WYSIWYG editor

The purpose of the CMS is to make editing a website without any technical skills easy. You can give admin access to an HTML novice, and he can use the system to build web pages with no knowledge of HTML or CSS. The editor has a number of useful tools that make creating and editing much like working with a word processor.

✦ **Predefined fonts and styles:** The user can choose fonts and styles from drop-down menus, unaware that these options are taking advantage of predefined CSS styles.

✦ **The ability to add lists, links, and images:** The editor includes the ability to add lists, links, and images (and other types of content) without any knowledge of HTML. If you add an image, the editor includes a wizard that helps you upload the image to the server. If you add a link, a wizard helps you specify the URL of the link.

✦ **Multiple paste options:** Many users create content in Microsoft Word. A Paste from Word button attempts to delete all the excess junk Word adds to a file and paste the content cleanly, which is a major lifesaver.

✦ **A plain source editor:** My favorite button on the WYSIWYG editor is the one that turns off the WYSIWYG features. The Source button displays the page as plain HTML/HTML text. The automated features are nice, but I can usually build a page a lot faster and more accurately by hand. This feature is especially useful when the visual tools aren't doing what you want.

When you finish building your page, click the Save button to save the contents of the page.

Along the top of the editor is a series of icons: a house, a blue screen, a life ring, and a lock. Click the blue screen (which is the View icon) to open your new page and see it the way the user will see it. Figure 3-10 shows the results of my simple page.

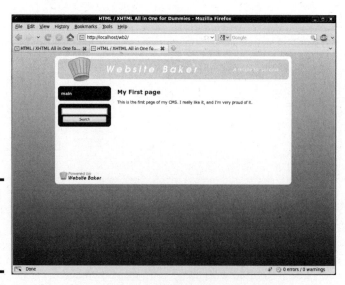

Figure 3-10:
This is how the page looks to the user.

The WYSIWYG page is the most commonly used page type (especially by nontechnical users) but it's not the only option. The standard edition of WebsiteBaker also comes with a number of other default page types:

✦ **Code:** Interprets the page as PHP code. This is any easy way to enter any PHP code you wish, including database lookups. The code is interpreted as PHP, so if you want it to be HTML, you can just use a giant heredoc. Figure 3-11 shows a PHP snippet being written, and Figure 3-12 shows the results.

Figure 3-11:
The code page allows you to write any PHP code you wish.

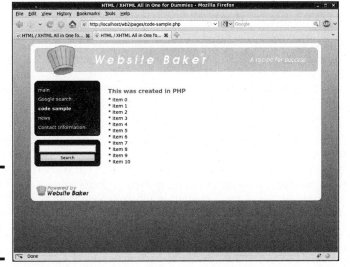

Figure 3-12:
How the code page looks to the user.

✦ **Form:** Allows you to build a basic HTML form without knowing any HTML. The administrator can add all the normal form elements. Figure 3-13 shows the form editor in action. When the user enters form data, the content is automatically e-mailed to the administrator and stored in a database that can be retrieved via the CMS. This feature is one of the most important factors of a CMS because it's something that plain HTML websites simply can't do.

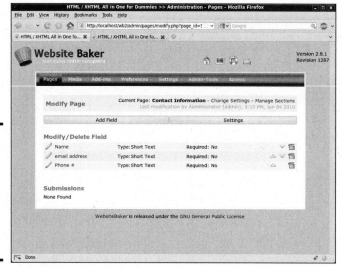

Figure 3-13:
The form editor simplifies creating forms and collecting form data.

✦ **Menu Link:** This placeholder (it isn't really a page type) allows you to create a menu item that helps organize other pages. Use the parent attribute of a page to make it a child of a menu or an ordinary page. The menu structure adapts automatically.

✦ **News V3.5:** A blog feature that allows the user to write blog articles. I often use it for other things, such as sermon archives for church sites, specials of the week for commercial sites, and so on. A blog feature is good any time you're working with repetitive, dated material. You can add multiple blogs to the same site easily. Figure 3-14 shows the news page in action.

✦ **Wrapper:** This incredibly versatile page type allows you to do all kinds of interesting things. Essentially, it allows you to embed any page into the CMS. Figure 3-15 shows the wrapper used to embed a Google search into my site. The wrapper is handy when you want to access an external ordering or newsgroup system but keep within the visual structure of the CMS.

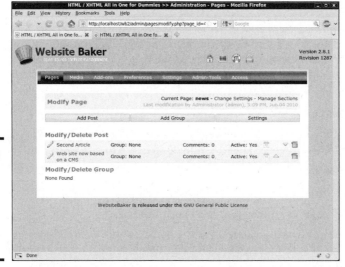

Figure 3-14:
The news page type allows you to build a blog-like document.

Figure 3-15:
Use the wrapper page type to embed other pages into your system.

You are not limited to these page types. See the section "Adding new functionality" later in this chapter for information on how to add additional page types to your system.

Changing the template

One of the primary goals of a CMS is to separate the visual layout from the contents. So far, you've seen how to modify the contents, but you'll also want to change the appearance of the page. The visual settings of a site are all based on a *template* concept. You can easily overlay a new template onto the existing site without changing the contents at all.

1. **Log in as the administrator.**

   Obviously, the administrator has the ability to change the template (although you can allow individual users to change their own templates).

2. **Go to the system menu.**

   Templates are set in the system menu.

3. **Change template under Default Settings.**

   Don't worry about the Backend Theme and Search Settings templates. It's best to leave these alone until you're a bit more experienced because they don't have a major impact on the user experience.

4. **Choose a template from the drop-down list.**

   All the templates installed in the system are available in a drop-down list. For this example, I chose the All CSS template (the default). See the section "Adding additional templates" for how to download and install templates that aren't already installed in the system.

5. **Preview the site with your new template in place.**

   Figure 3-16 shows the contents of the site with the All CSS template in place. The template essentially encapsulates core HTML code and the CSS used to display each file.

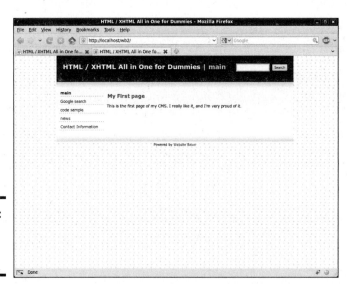

Figure 3-16: The same site has a new look!

Adding additional templates

The standard installation of WebsiteBaker includes only a few templates. Typically, you'll want to work with additional templates. Fortunately, there are hundreds of great templates available, and you can easily build your own. Here's how to add additional templates.

1. **Locate the template you want online.**

   A number of web places offer great, free templates for WebsiteBaker. My favorite is the Templates repository available at `www.websitebaker2.org/template/pages/templates.php`. The templates in this archive are approved by the WebsiteBaker community and meet minimum quality standards. (Note that many of these templates have been adopted from other CMS systems so you can often get the same general look and feel regardless of the CMS you choose.)

2. **Download a template or two that you like.**

   When browsing templates, remember that you will be able to modify them. If you don't like the particular colors or images, you can change them later. Save the downloaded .zip file somewhere on your local machine.

3. **Log in to WebsiteBaker as admin.**

   Only the administrator can add new templates to the system.

4. **Navigate to the Templates page of the Add-ons section**.

   This is where you install and uninstall downloaded templates.

5. **Click the Browse button to locate the .zip file on your local system.**

   Load the entire .zip file containing the template onto the server.

6. **Click the Install button to begin the process.**

   You receive a notification when the installation is complete.

7. **Navigate to the Settings section.**

   Installing a template does not apply the template automatically.

8. **In Settings, apply the new template.**

   Specify the template to display from the drop-down list of templates.

9. **Preview your new look.**

   Use the Preview button (or reload the currently showing version of the CMS) to see the new look. Figure 3-17 shows my site with the Multiflex-3 template installed.

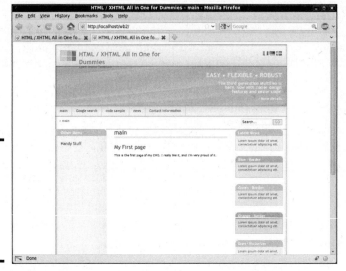

Figure 3-17:
You can
install any
template
onto your
existing
system.

The Multiflex-3 template is one of the most commonly used templates on the Internet. The original design (`www.oswd.org/design/preview/id/3626`) was built with plain HTML/CSS implementation in mind but has been ported to nearly every CMS including WebsiteBaker. The design is a solid and very flexible starting place. I've used it as the foundation of dozens of sites. After you get to know it, you'll recognize it all over the place.

Adding new functionality

In addition to custom templates, you can add modules to your system. A module is a new page type that adds additional functionality. Dozens of add-ons are available at the WebsiteBaker AMASP (All Modules and Snippets Project) at `www.websitebakers.com`.

The add-on modules include many new types of functionality, including online shopping modules, image galleries, event calendars, and many more. In addition to full-fledged modules, the AMASP also includes PHP snippets you can copy into your code for advanced functionality and *droplets,* which are small, self-contained PHP modules to add features to your site. It's probably best you start with full modules because they require the least effort to get working. As you become more proficient with WebsiteBaker, you'll want to investigate how to add more features.

Many of my clients like to have image galleries. I use them for a number of things, including a simple form of an online catalog and for viewing sample work for craft or artist sites. Here's how to add a basic but full-featured image gallery:

1. **Find a module you wish to test.**

   Go to the AMASP site and browse the various modules until you find one you like; there's about a dozen. For this example, I'm looking at the (unimaginatively named) Image Gallery module. This one works very well, looks pretty good, and is very easy for my clients to use, so I almost always install it on commercial sites.

2. **Download the module.**

   Modules are installed much like templates. Download the module, which is usually PHP and HTML code in a .zip file, and then save the .zip file somewhere on your local file system.

3. **Log in as admin.**

   As usual, anything that involves changing the site requires administrator access.

4. **Navigate to the Add-ons section.**

   You add modules in the same section you add templates; that is, the Modules page of the Add-ons section.

5. **Browse to find the .zip file you downloaded.**

   Click the Browse button to look on your local system for the .zip file containing the module. Click the Install button when you locate the file. WebsiteBaker uploads the module to the server and places the files in the correct location.

6. **A new page type will appear.**

   When you go to the Pages section, you see a new type of page. In this case, you can now add image galleries.

Building Custom Themes

WebsiteBaker is an outstanding way to build a complex and fully featured website easily and quickly. With over a hundred templates, you're bound to find something you like. However, you almost never find something *exactly* the way you want it. This is especially important if you're developing for somebody else. Usually, you find a template that is close, but you still need to modify the colors and images. For that reason, it's important to understand the general structure of a WebsiteBaker template and how to make your own.

Starting with a prebuilt template

Although it's possible to build a WebsiteBaker template from scratch, it's generally not a good idea. It's much smarter to begin with a template that's close and add those features you need to make it your own. That way the general structure is already proven, and you only need to customize it to your specifications.

1. **Find a starting template you like.**

   Often I have clients look over the Templates repository (`www.website baker2.org/template/pages/templates.php`) and tell me their favorite three templates. I also like to have them explain what they like or dislike about each template. I tell them we can change colors or banner graphics in a template, so to focus more on the general look and feel.

   If you don't have another place to start, I like the templates built into the WebsiteBaker core (especially All CSS and Round). Blank Template is especially designed for customizing. I often build commercial sites based on Multiflex-3 because it's well known throughout the web community and has some great features.

2. **Install the template on your local system.**

   It's much easier to work with a template on your local system than on a remote server.

3. **Locate the local copy of the template.**

   Normally, templates are stored in the `wb/templates` directory of your server. Each template will have its own folder.

4. **Copy the folder of the template you want to modify.**

   It's generally smarter to work with a copy rather than the original. Paste the copied folder in the templates directory.

5. **Rename the new folder to reflect your new template name.**

   Your new template needs a different name than the original template.

At this point, you have a copy of the original template, but this copy will not be reflected in the CMS yet. You need to make a few changes before the new template is available. Before you do that, take a look at the file structure of a typical WebsiteBaker template. Figure 3-18 shows my copy of the Multiflex-3 template.

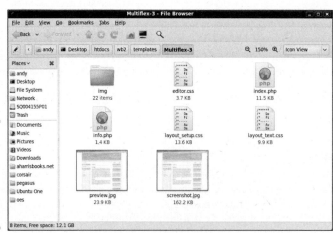

Figure 3-18: Typical file structure for Website-Baker templates.

One of the reasons I like WebsiteBaker so much is how relatively simple the template structure is compared to other CMSs. The directory contains a relatively small number of files:

✦ **index.php:** This PHP file is the basic file that's used as the foundation of every page in the system. It's essentially an HTML page with a few special PHP functions built in. You can edit any of the HTML you wish, and the resulting changes will be reflected in every page of the site.

✦ **info.php:** This simple PHP file contains a number of variables used to control the overall behavior of the template. You'll make a few changes in this file to give your template an official name.

✦ **layout_setup.css:** This CSS file describes the CSS used for the overall page design. You can change the contents of this CSS file to change font colors or other big-picture CSS.

✦ **layout_text.css:** This CSS file is used to define the styles of the various text elements in the site. If you're looking for a class that isn't defined in layout_setup.css, you may find it here. *Note:* The names of the CSS files may change in other templates, but there will be at least one CSS file.

✦ **editor.css:** This file is used to modify the internal WYSIWYG editor. It describes how various elements are displayed in the editor.

✦ **images directory:** Often a template will include a number of images. These are stored in a subdirectory for convenience. You may need to change some of these images to create the look you're going for.

Some templates are more complex, some less so. Really, you can have as many or as few files as you want. You'll always need to have index.php and info.php. You'll almost always have at least one CSS page. You can have anything else you wish in the template, but nothing else is absolutely necessary.

Changing the info.php file

The info.php file contains a few PHP variables. You can modify these variables to identify this template as your own. You must change the template name to a unique value, and you can also change such variables as the developer name and version number. I typically claim any substantial changes I make to a template, but I always give credit to the original developer. It's great to stand on the shoulders of giants, and you should give them their due in the documentation. Here's the info.php file after I made a few changes:

```php
<?php

/*

Website Baker Project <http://www.websitebaker.org/>
Copyright (C) 2004-2006, Ryan Djurovich

Website Baker is free software; you can redistribute it and/or modify
it under the terms of the GNU General Public License as published by
```

Book VIII Chapter 3

Introducing Content Management Systems

```
the Free Software Foundation; either version 2 of the License, or
(at your option) any later version.

Website Baker is distributed in the hope that it will be useful,
but WITHOUT ANY WARRANTY; without even the implied warranty of
MERCHANTABILITY or FITNESS FOR A PARTICULAR PURPOSE.  See the
GNU General Public License for more details.

You should have received a copy of the GNU General Public License
along with Website Baker; if not, write to the Free Software
Foundation, Inc., 59 Temple Place, Suite 330, Boston, MA  02111-1307  USA

*/


$template_directory = 'aio';
$template_name = 'aio';
$template_version = '1.1';
$template_platform = '2.x';
$template_author = 'Andy Harris, from Erik Coenjaerts (WB port)';
$template_license = '<a href="http://www.1234.info/webtemplates/">Open Source</
    a>';
$template_description = 'Original design from <a href="http://www.1234.info/
    webtemplates/">1234.info</a>. Ported to Website Baker by <a href="http://
    www.coenjaerts.com">Erik Coenjaerts</a>.';
$menu[1]='Main Menu';
$menu[2]='Top Menu';
$menu[3]='Extra Menu';
$block[2]='Sidebar';
$block[3]='News';

?>
```

Note that the template has the potential for three different types of menus and three blocks of information. ($block[1] is the main content block and is available by default.)

Modifying index.php

For the most part, you can leave index.php alone. However, there are a few modifications you might make. If you look over the file, it's basically plain HTML/HTML with a few PHP functions thrown in. Generally, you can change the HTML code without any worries, but be more careful about the PHP code. The PHP code tends to call special functions defined in the WebsiteBaker code base. Here are the functions and variables you're likely to run across:

✦ **TEMPLATE_DIR:** This constant contains the template directory. Use it to make links to the template directory.

✦ **WEBSITE_TITLE:** Use this constant to display the website name anywhere in your template.

✦ **PAGE_TITLE:** The title of the current page as defined in the menu.

✦ **WEBSITE_HEADER:** This constant displays the header defined in the admin panel.

✦ **show_menu(*menuID*):** This is a powerhouse of a function. It analyzes your site structure and uses it to build a navigation structure. It takes a parameter, which is the level of menu. (Typically the left menu is level 1 and the top menu is level 2, but this can be changed.) ***Note:*** Some templates use the more advanced show_menu_2() function, which has additional parameters, like the ability to define template code for how the menu displays.

✦ **page_content(*blockID*):** This function is used to display content for the current page. The parameter describes which block of content should display. Use 1 for the main page content, 2 for block 2, and so on.

✦ **page_footer():** Display the page footer identified in the admin panel.

WebsiteBaker features many more constants and functions, but these are the basic ones used in nearly all templates. See the online documentation at www.websitebaker2.org/ for complete documentation. Other CMS systems use the same idea (HTML templates with PHP functions embedded), but of course the function names are a bit different in a different CMS.

You may want to make other modifications of the default template. For example, the Multiflex-3 template includes multilanguage support and a large number of different "Post-it note" features. I generally remove the multilanguage content (because I only speak one language) and change all the "Post-it notes" to use the same CSS style (or remove them all).

Modifying the CSS files

Of course, the most powerful way to change the appearance of your pages is to modify the CSS files. Here's how:

1. **Make a backup first.**

   You're very likely to break things when you go mucking around in unfamiliar code, so make a backup first so when you (inevitably) destroy something, you'll be able to get back to a sensible starting place.

2. **Identify the class you want to modify.**

   This can be surprisingly difficult in a system you didn't create. Use the Inspect feature of the Chrome or Firebug developer tools to quickly identify which styles act on a particular element and what its class hierarchy is.

3. **Find the class definition in the CSS sheets.**

   Note that a system may have more than one CSS file, so find the one containing the class information you're interested in.

4. **Make incremental changes.**

   Make small changes and test frequently.

5. **Test on a local server.**

You can make changes directly on the files in your local server. Just reload the page after every change to make sure the changes are being reflected. Of course, you need to have the template installed in your system.

Packaging your template

A template is nothing more than a set of PHP and CSS files (and perhaps some images and other files). It's pretty easy to port a template for installation. Just follow these steps:

1. **Create a stable version of the template.**

It doesn't have to be perfect before you package it, but at a minimum you need to change the info.php page to reflect the new template's name.

2. **Package the entire directory into a .zip file.**

Use a utility like IZArc for Windows or the xip utility that comes installed with Linux or Mac. Save the .zip file with the same name as your template. *Note:* Don't include the template directory itself in the template; just include any contents of that directory (including subdirectories, if you have them).

3. **Install the template into your copy of WebsiteBaker.**

Install your template the way you do any other template.

Chapter 4: Editing Graphics

In This Chapter

✔ **Introducing Gimp**

✔ **Managing the main tools**

✔ **Selecting image elements**

✔ **Working with layers**

✔ **Understanding filters**

✔ **Creating a tiling background**

✔ **Building banner images**

HTML and CSS are powerful tools, but sometimes you still need to use a graphics editor to get the look you want. In this chapter, you learn to use Gimp, a free and powerful graphic editor.

Using a Graphics Editor

You'll find using a graphics editor handy for a number of tasks:

+ **Modifying an image:** The obvious use of a graphical tool is to modify or create an image that will be used on your web page. This could involve changing the image size, correcting the color balance, changing the file type, or cropping the image.

+ **Preparing a background image:** As I discuss in Book II, Chapter 4, background images can be distracting if you aren't careful. Making a lower contrast image (either lighter or darker than normal) might make sense so the text is easier to read. You might also want to prepare a tiled background.

+ **Building banners:** Many websites include a special banner image that's prominent on every page. The banner image usually has a very specific size requirement.

+ **Modifying existing graphics:** You might be modifying a template from the jQuery UI project (see Book VII, Chapter 4) or from a CMS (see Chapter 3 in this minibook). In both cases, you often have images that are close to, but not exactly, what you need.

+ **Changing colors:** Frequently, you have the right pattern, but not the right colors. Modifying colors with a modern graphical tool is surprisingly easy.

Choosing an Editor

Fortunately, great programs that make all these tasks quite easy to perform are available. Raster-based graphics editors are designed to solve exactly this type of problem and many more. A number of important graphics tools are used in web development:

✦ **Adobe Photoshop:** The industry standard for web graphics, and indeed for all digital imagery, Photoshop is powerful and capable but quite expensive. A slightly cheaper and less powerful version called Adobe Photoshop Elements is available.

✦ **Adobe Fireworks:** Designed specifically for web developers, Fireworks features the ability to slice an image to make a graphical web page from an image — and it's relatively inexpensive.

✦ **Windows Paint:** This simple image editor is available in all versions of Microsoft Windows. Although easy to use and already available to Windows users, Paint is relatively limited. It only supports a few image formats and doesn't have full support for transparent images or layers.

✦ **Paint.net:** A group of computer science students decided to create an improvement to Microsoft Paint that evolved into a very robust image-editing program. It is free (although, technically, not open source) and has all the features you might need for editing web images. However, the primary version is available only for Windows.

✦ **Gimp:** A popular alternative to Photoshop, Gimp has all the features you might need for web image editing. It is completely free, open source, and available for all major operating systems. For these reasons, I use Gimp throughout this chapter (and indeed throughout the book — nearly every graphic was created using Gimp).

People are passionate about their graphics programs. If you love Photoshop, you might find the Gimp interface strange and unfamiliar. I think learning how Gimp works is worth the time, but if you prefer, you can download GimpShop, a version of Gimp modified to use the same menus and keyboard shortcuts as Photoshop.

Note that in this list I'm only considering full-blown graphics editors. I describe image manipulation programs, such as IrfanView (which is simpler and has fewer features), in Book II, Chapter 4.

I'm also confining the conversation to *raster-based* image editors, which use a different mechanism for managing images than *vector-based* image editors. The vector-based approach is slowly gaining popularity on the web, especially with the support for SVG in HTML5. However, most web graphics are in a raster format, even those that were originally created in a vector format. If you are interested in playing with vector graphics, I recommend looking into the excellent free program Inkscape. It has native support for SVG, which is the most universal vector standard for web browsers.

Introducing Gimp

If you haven't already installed Gimp, get a recent copy from this book's web-site or `www.gimp.org`. Install the program and take a look at it. The Gimp interface's multiple windows are shown in Figure 4-1.

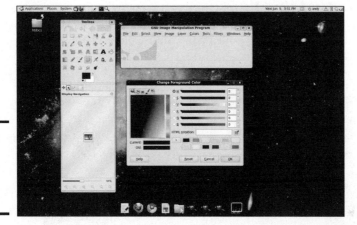

Figure 4-1:
Gimp uses a multiple window model.

Gimp sure seems cluttered . . .

Gimp doesn't reside in a single window like most programs. Instead, it uses a number of windows. Some find this jarring, but after you get used to it, this can be a useful feature. You can make any window as large or as small as you wish and combine windows to get less screen clutter. I configure Gimp in a way that combines the most common windows into the Toolbox, so I have one window showing the Toolbox and most of the dialog boxes and a separate window showing each picture I'm working on.

If you click the Configure Tab button (a small arrow at the top right of the tabs section), you can add new tabs to the main Toolbox window. I normally add my favorite tools (Navigation, Layers, Tool Options, and Brushes) to the Toolbox so the features are readily available and appear here instead of in separate windows.

Recent versions of Gimp have a single-window mode you can use if you prefer. Just select Single Window Mode from the Windows menu.

Book VIII
Chapter 4

Editing Graphics

I have the Change Foreground Color dialog open in Figure 4-1, and I simply double-clicked the foreground color in the main toolbox to open this dialog. Gimp tends to open a lot of dialogs, which might bother some people. Also, I want to illustrate how powerful the color chooser is. Like most features in Gimp, it has a lot of options.

The Toolbox is Gimp's main control panel. It manages all the tools you use to create images. Gimp also creates an image window, which contains the menu elements, but no image (by default). You can load an image into the image window or create a new image.

Creating an image

You choose the File ➪ New menu command to create a new image. After you specify the size of your image, a new, blank image appears, as shown in Figure 4-2.

Figure 4-2:
It's easy to create a new, blank image.

Of course, you can also load an existing image into Gimp. Gimp accepts all major image formats (and dozens more with optional plug-ins). Use the File ➪ Open menu command to open an image, or simply drag an image file onto the Gimp Toolbox.

Painting tools

Gimp includes a number of useful tools to create or modify an image. Figure 4-3 shows a few of these tools.

✦ **Pencil:** The Pencil tool is the standard drawing tool. It draws hard edges in the exact shape of the pen. You can choose from many pen shapes in the Tool Options panel (described in the next section).

✦ **Paintbrush:** The Paintbrush tool is similar to the Pencil tool, but it uses a technique called *anti-aliasing* to make smoother edges. Like the Pencil tool, the Brush tool can use many different pen shapes.

✦ **Eraser:** The Eraser tool is used to remove color from a drawing. If the current layer has transparency enabled, the Eraser tool makes things transparent. If transparency is not turned on, the Eraser tool "draws" in the background color.

✦ **Airbrush:** The Airbrush tool allows you to paint with a virtual airbrush. You can modify the flow and size of the paint. This tool is especially effective with a pressure-sensitive drawing tablet.

✦ **Ink:** The Ink tool simulates a calligraphy brush. The speed of drawing indicates the width of the stroke. It seems quite realistic because everything I draw with it looks just as bad as what I create when I try real calligraphy.

Working with existing images

It's very common in web development to work with images that already exist. For example, I've built a couple of sites for office supply companies. It's nice to sprinkle the site with colorful images of staplers, Post-it notes, and the like. The question is, how do you get these graphics? If you're a skilled photographer or artist, you can create them yourself, but this takes more time and talent than I typically have. You could reuse images you find on the web, but this is not respectful of these elements' owners.

The best solution is to use an image-supply site like `www.freedigitalphotos.net` or `www.istockphoto.com`. Be sure to search for royalty-free artwork, and check the license to ensure you can use and modify the work. I'm a big fan of stock art. Typically, I can find a dozen images to spruce up a site for less than $20, and I have the satisfaction of knowing I'm completely legal. Often, stock art is designed for both print and digital use. Generally, you can purchase the smallest size for digital work, which is economical and perfectly fine for use on the web. (*Note:* Monitors have much less resolution than printed paper, so you can get away with a smaller image.)

To reuse an image in a legitimate way, consider the following:

✔ **Acknowledge the source:** Generally, this acknowledgment isn't necessary for images you purchase, but it is polite if you receive an image for free. You can place the acknowledgment in the source code.

✔ **Get permission if needed:** It's always best to get permission from the original developer. Sometimes this isn't possible or necessary, but you should always try. Of course if you've purchased a stock photo, you're also purchasing permission to use it.

✔ **Make the image your own:** Do something to modify the image. If it's a stock photo, this isn't necessary, but you might want to change the colors, move things around, and make the image fit the theme of your project a little better. Modifying an image does not make it legal if you did not have permission.

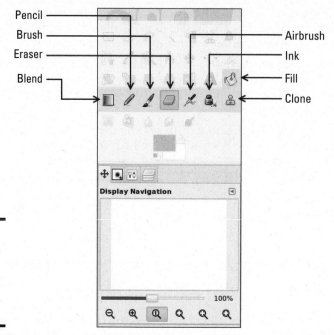

Pencil

Brush ——— Airbrush

Eraser ——— Ink

Blend ——— Fill

——— Clone

Figure 4-3:
These tools
are used
to draw or
modify an
image.

✦ **Clone:** The powerful Clone tool allows you to grab content from one part of an image and copy it to another part of the image. This tool is often used in photo retouching to remove scars and blemishes.

✦ **Fill:** The Fill tool is used to fill an area with a color or pattern. It has multiple options that allow you to pick the pattern, the color, and the method of filling. (You can fill the current selection or all areas with the same color, for example.)

✦ **Blend:** This Blend tool allows you to fill an area with color patterns, similar to the Fill tool. There are numerous options that allow you to determine what pattern is used and how it is distributed. (Many programs call this the Gradient tool.)

A complex program like Gimp deserves (and has) entire books written about it. There's no way I can describe everything in this brief introductory chapter. Still, this should give you an indication of what you can do. Check the many excellent user tutorials at www.gimp.org/tutorials and the manual at www.gimp.org/docs.

Selection tools

Often, you'll be working on specific parts of an image. It's critical to have tools to help you grab a particular part of an image and work with it in isolation. Gimp (like any high-quality graphics tool) has a number of useful selection tools. Figure 4-4 shows where they are in the Toolbox.

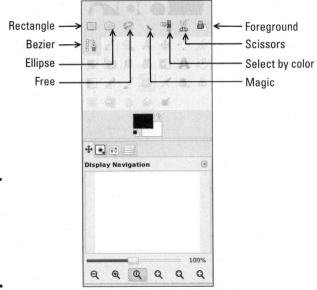

Rectangle ———→
Bezier ———→
Ellipse ————
Free ————

———← Foreground
———— Scissors
———— Select by color
———— Magic

Display Navigation

100%

Figure 4-4:
These tools
are used for
selecting
parts of an
image.

✦ **Rectangle Select:** The Rectangle Select tool is used to (wait for it . . .) select rectangles. Rectangle selections are easy, and they're pretty common, so this is a good, basic selection tool.

✦ **Ellipse Select:** The Ellipse Select tool is like the Rectangle Select tool, but (you're catching on here) it selects ellipses. You can set the aspect ratio to 1:1 to select perfect circles.

✦ **Free Select:** Also called the Lasso tool, the Free Select tool allows you to draw a selection by hand. It takes an incredibly steady hand to use well, so it's usually only used for rough selections that are fine-tuned using other techniques.

✦ **Magic Select:** Also called the Fuzzy Select, the Magic Wand tool allows you to grab contiguous sections of similar colors. It's handy when you have a large section of a single color that you want to select. (You might want to select a white background and replace it with a pattern, for example.) Hold down the Shift key and make further selections if you want to select more than one color.

✦ **Select by Color:** Similar to the Fuzzy Select tool, the Select by Color tool grabs all the pixels of a chosen color, whether they're touching the selected pixel or not, and removes them. (It's ideal for use with a green screen, for example.)

✦ **Scissors Select:** The Scissors Select tool uses image-processing techniques to automatically select part of an image. Click along the edge of an element you want to select, and (if you're lucky) the selection will follow the edge. This works fine for high-contrast elements, but conditions have to be perfect.

Book VIII
Chapter 4

Editing Graphics

✦ **Foreground Select:** The Foreground Select tool is a multipass tool that simplifies pulling part of an image from the rest. On the first pass, use the Lasso tool to choose the general part of the image you want to select. The image will show a selection mask with selected parts in white and nonselected parts blue. Click the colors you want to keep and then press Enter to commit the selection.

✦ **Bezier Select:** The Bezier Select tool is my favorite. Click an image to create a general outline of the selection. (You're actually making a *Bezier path,* which uses math formulas to draw a curved shape.) Modify the path until it's exactly how you want it and then you can convert it to a selection.

Modification tools

A number of tools are used to modify parts of an image. Figure 4-5 illustrates the main modification tools:

✦ **Move:** This tool allows you to move a selection, a layer, or some other element.

✦ **Rotate, Scale, Shear, Perspective, and Flip:** These tools all apply transformations to a selection. Use them to rotate or resize a part of your image, or to change the perspective of a section so it appears to be on an angled surface, for example.

✦ **Heal:** This tool takes a sample area and applies it to other parts of an image (much like the Clone tool). It is often used in photo retouching to give skin a clean, unblemished look. It's great for fixing the rectangular artifacts that often appear in JPG images.

✦ **Blur/Sharpen:** This tool is used to blur (reduce contrast) or sharpen (increase contrast) a small part of the image selectively with the current pen. This tool is often used for quick touch-ups to remove scratches or other blemishes.

✦ **Smudge:** This allows you to push a color into adjacent pixels to clean up an image. I frequently use this tool when trying to build a tiled background to help line pixels up in a seamless way.

✦ **Dodge/Burn:** This tool is named after a photography darkroom tool. It's used to darken or lighten parts of an image and to remove unwanted shadows.

Managing tool options

Most tools have options available. For example, when you choose the Pencil or Brush tool, you can select which brush tip to use. When you use the Fill tool, you can determine whether the tool fills with the current color or the current selection. You can also determine whether the tool fills with a color or a pattern.

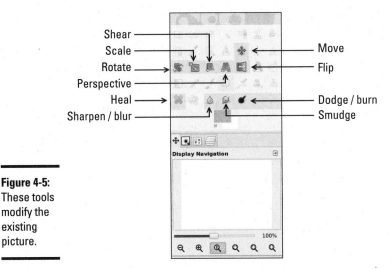

Shear
Scale
Rotate
Perspective
Heal
Sharpen / blur

Move
Flip
Dodge / burn
Smudge

Display Navigation

100%

Figure 4-5:
These tools
modify the
existing
picture.

You can see the Tool Options dialog box for any tool by double-clicking the tool in the Toolbox. Generally, I dock the Tool Options dialog box to the main Toolbox tabs because it's so frequently used.

Utilities

Gimp also comes with a number of handy utilities. The tools highlighted in Figure 4-6 have a variety of uses:

+ **Color Selector:** The two overlapping rectangles show the current foreground and background color. Click one of the rectangles to pick a new color to work with. You can choose colors in a number of ways, using RGB and HSV schemes, as well as prefilled color palettes and a very cool watercolor tool.

+ **Color Picker:** Allows you to determine the RGB value of any pixel on the image and pick that color as the current drawing color. It's very handy when you want to match colors precisely.

+ **Zoom:** Allows you to quickly zoom in and out of your image. Drag around an area, and the selected area will fill the entire window. Hold down the Ctrl key while dragging to zoom out. Hold the center mouse button (often also the scroll wheel) to pan your zoomed-in view in any direction. It's very helpful to zoom in close when you're doing detail work.

+ **Measure:** Drag the mouse on an image, and you can find the distance and angle between any two points. The Move tool is useful for precise placement.

+ **Move:** Allows you to move a selection or layer.

✦ **Align:** The Align tool simplifies lining up various elements with each other.

✦ **Crop:** Used to crop unwanted border areas from an image.

✦ **Text:** Adds editable text to the image. The Text tool works with layers, so check the upcoming "Understanding Layers" section for more detail.

✦ **Perspective Clone:** This tool combines the Perspective tool and the Clone tool. Although it's cool, the applications are a bit rare, so I don't use it often in web development.

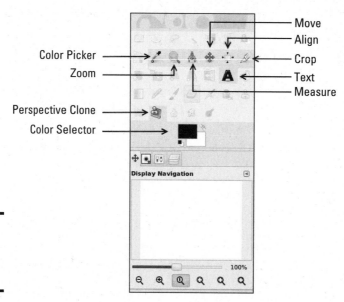

Figure 4-6: These tools often come in handy.

Understanding Layers

Gimp has an astonishing variety of tools, but most of the interesting things you can do with a raster graphics tool involve a concept called *layers.* Layers are really pretty simple: Imagine the old animated movies (before digital animation was possible). Painters would create a large background, but the characters were drawn on transparent sheets (called *cels* in animation). A single frame of an animation might contain a single opaque background with a large number of mainly transparent layers on top. Each layer could be manipulated individually, providing a great deal of flexibility.

Any high-end graphics editor will support some form of layer mechanism. (In fact, support for layers is a primary differentiator between basic and advanced graphics tools.) Figure 4-7 shows the Layers panel in Gimp.

Figure 4-7:
The Layers panel allows you to manipulate layers.

The primary area of the Layers panel is the window, showing a stack of layers. The background is on the bottom of the stack, and any other layers are on top. Anything on an upper layer obscures a lower layer. Imagine a camera at the top of the stack pointing down at the stack of layers. If a higher layer has transparency (as it usually does) the lower layer will show through any transparent pixels.

The Opacity slider in the Layers panel allows you to adjust the overall transparency of the layer. This can be useful for quickly lightening or darkening a layer, and for other effects, such as shadows.

Only one layer is active at a time. The current layer is highlighted in the window at the bottom of the Layers panel. Most operations will occur on the active layer only. Click a layer in the layers window to make that layer active.

Be sure you know which layer is active. Many times I try to draw on a layer and nothing happens. I then typically scribble harder, thinking that will help. Almost always when this happens, I've selected the wrong layer and made a big mess somewhere. It's possible (and common) to have a layer active which is not visible. Fortunately, the Undo command (Ctrl+Z) is quite powerful. If in doubt, keep the Layers panel visible so you can tell which layer is active.

Each layer has two icons next to it that you can activate. The eye icon toggles the layer's visibility. The link icon allows you to link two or more layers together. Each layer also has a name. You can double-click the layer name to change it. This is especially useful when you have a complex image with many layers.

The bottom of the Layers panel has the following buttons to help you manage various layers:

+ **New Layer:** This button creates a new layer. The default type is transparent, but you can also choose to have the layer appear in the foreground or background color.

+ **Up and down buttons:** Allow you to move a layer up or down in the stack. The position of a layer in the stack is important because higher layers have precedence.

+ **Duplicate Layer:** Makes a copy of the currently active layer. If you're modifying a layer, working on a duplicate is a great idea because if you mess up, you still have a backup.

+ **Anchor:** When you copy and paste a part of an image, the pasted segment is placed into a temporary layer. Use the anchor button to nail down the selection to the current layer.

+ **Delete:** Allows you to delete the currently active layer. Be careful you delete the correct layer.

Introducing Filters

Digital editors include a number of other very useful tools. Generally, these tools apply mathematical filters to an image to change the image in some way. The standard installation of Gimp comes with dozens of filters, but here are a few most common to web developers:

+ **Blur filters:** Blur filters reduce the contrast between adjacent pixels to make the image less defined, and can often be used to hide imperfections or scratches. The most common blur is Gaussian blur, but there are many others, including Motion blur, which simulates the blur seen in a slow camera taking a picture of something moving quickly.

+ **Unsharp mask:** A class of filters called *sharpen* filters are the opposite of blur filters. They increase contrast between adjacent pixels. I don't know why the sharpen filter is called the "Unsharp mask," but it is.

  Note: There is no "enhance" filter like the ones so common on crime dramas. Sadly, you can't just "zoom and enhance" endlessly to see the killer's eye color on the reflection of a spoon.

+ **Colorize:** This marvelous tool allows you to keep the contrast of a layer and change the color, which can be perfect for changing the color of hair, eyes, or clothing.

+ **Brightness/Contrast:** Lets you adjust the brightness (overall value) and contrast of a particular layer.

+ **Color balance:** Allows you to adjust the relative amounts of red, green, and blue in a layer, which can be used to improve pictures with poor lighting.

Solving Common Web Graphics Problems

Gimp, and tools like it, can be used in many ways. The rest of this chapter is a cookbook of sorts, showing how to build a number of graphics commonly used in web development.

Changing a color

Frequently, you'll have an image that's good, but not the right color. For example, you may want to change the color of a person's clothing, or make part of a logo fit the color scheme of the rest of your site. Gimp makes performing this effect quite easy:

1. **Load your starting image into Gimp and make any other adaptations you wish to the original image.**

2. **Use the Fuzzy Select tool to select the part you want to modify.**

   You might need to use the Shift key to add several variants of the color to the selection.

3. **Use the Copy command (Ctrl+C) to copy the section of the image you just selected.**

4. **Use the Paste command (Ctrl+V) to paste the selected area into a new layer.**

   The pasted area goes into a new "pseudo-layer" by default. In the Layers panel you'll see layer called Floating Selection – Pasted Layer. Click the New Layer button and you'll create a new layer containing only the section you need.

5. **Colorize the new layer by applying the Colorize filter (Colors ⇨ Colorize).**

   Play with the color sliders until you get the color you want. Because you made the changes on a new layer, you can always remove or hide the layer to return to the original. (Or have several different color layers so you can play with various options.)

Figure 4-8 shows an example of this technique using an image of a glass of orange juice by Graur Razvan Ionut I found at FreeDigitalPhotos.net. The original image contained only the picture of orange juice, but I duplicated the juice glass and changed the color of the second glass to look like coffee. Of course you'll need to see this effect online at the companion website because the color change will not be apparent in this black-and-white book. See the book's Introduction for more on the companion site.

Building a banner graphic

Nearly every commercial website has a *banner graphic* — a special graphic, usually with a set size (900×100 is common), that appears on every page. Normally, if you're modifying a CSS template, you have a default banner graphic. You'll want to copy this graphic in order to start with the right size and shape.

You can build a banner many ways, but here's a simple technique you can modify (Figure 4-9 shows the banner's progression):

1. **Load or create the basic shape.**

   If you have a starting graphic to use, load it into Gimp. If not, create a new image of the size you need. Mine is 100 pixels tall by 900 pixels wide.

2. **Create a plasma background.**

   Use the Plasma filter (Filters ➪ Render ➪ Clouds ➪ Plasma) to create a semi-random pattern. Use the New Seed and Turbulence buttons to change the overall feel. Don't worry about the colors; you remove them in the next step.

3. **After the plasma background is in place, use the Colorize filter to apply a color to the background.**

   Pick a color consistent with your theme. For this example, go for a lighter color because you're using shadows, which require a light background. Use the Lightness slider to make a relatively light color. (I'm going for a cloudy sky look, so I set Hue to 215, Saturation to 100, and Lightness to 75.)

4. **Create a text layer using the Text tool.**

   Text in a graphic should be large and bold. The Text tool automatically creates a new layer. After you type your text, specify the font and size.

5. **Duplicate the text layer.**

   In the Layers panel, make a copy of the text layer. Select the lower of the two text layers (which will become a shadow).

6. **Blur the shadow.**

   With the shadow layer selected, apply the Gaussian blur (Filters ➪ Blur ➪ Gaussian Blur).

7. **Move the shadow.**

   Use the Move tool to move the relative positions of the text and the shadow. Typically, users expect a shadow to be slightly lower and right of the text (simulating light coming from the top left). The farther the shadow is from the text, the higher the text appears to be floating.

8. **Make the shadow semitransparent.**

   With the shadow layer still selected, adjust the Opacity slider to about 50 percent. This will make the shadows less pronounced and allow part of the background to appear through the shadow layer.

9. **Season to taste; make additions based on your needs.**

   For example, one client wanted a picture of his sign to appear on the banner. I took a photo of the sign, brought it in as a layer, cleaned it up, and rotated and scaled the image until it fit in place.

10. **Save in a reusable format.**

    The native format for images in Gimp is XCF. (I have no clue what XCF stands for, but every time I try to make up an acronym, it comes out dirty. There must be something wrong with me.) XCF stores everything — layers, settings, and all. If you need to modify the banner later (and you will), you'll have a good version to work from.

    Choose File ➪ Save As to save the file. If you specify the .xcf extension, Gimp automatically saves in the full format.

11. **Export to a web-friendly format.**

    Generally, I save banner graphics as PNG or GIF files. (Gimp supports both formats.) I prefer PNG unless the bottom layer has transparency (because some browsers still don't support the advanced transparency features of the PNG format). Do not save images containing text in JPG format. The JPG compression scheme is notorious for adding artifacts to text.

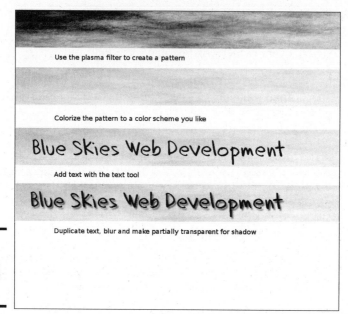

Figure 4-9:
The steps
for building
a banner.

TIP

Normally, when you save to another format, a dialog box of options appears. If in doubt, go with the default values.

Figure 4-10 shows the final banner image. I included the XCF and PNG files on the website. Feel free to open my files in Gimp and experiment.

Figure 4-10:
This is a
simple but
reasonably
cool banner.

Building a tiled background

Often, you want a background image to cover the entire page. This can be harder than it seems because you don't know how large the page will be in the user's browser. Worse, large images can take a huge amount of space and slow down the user's experience. The common solution is to use a tiled image that's designed to repeat in the background. Gimp has some very useful tools for building tiled images.

Recall that the `background-repeat` CSS property allows you to specify how a background repeats. The default setting repeats the background infinitely in both the X and Y axes. You can also set the background to repeat horizontally (`repeat-x`), vertically (`repeat-y`), or not at all (`no-repeat`).

The goal of a tiled background is to make a relatively small graphic fill the entire page and look like a larger image. The secret is to create the image so it's difficult to see where the image repeats. Here's one way to make a tiled background in Gimp (Figure 4-11 shows the background's progression). Of course, you can adapt this technique for your own purposes.

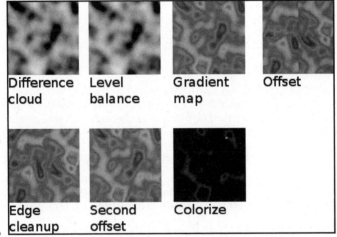

Figure 4-11:
Building
a tiled
background
image.

1. **Create a new image.**

   The size of your image is important. Smaller images are much more effi-cient to download, but the pattern is much more obvious. Start with 256 by 256 pixels.

2. **Build a random pattern.**

   You can use the Plasma filter technique described in the previous sec-tion or try a similar technique by choosing Filters ➪ Render ➪ Clouds ➪ Difference Clouds. The Difference Clouds filter creates a grayscale image but with a number of interesting options. The Tileable option creates a pattern that's ready to tile. Play with these options until you get some-thing interesting.

3. **Adjust the contrast.**

   For the best effect, you want a relatively even distribution of values from light to dark. The easiest way to do this is through the automatic nor-malization tool (Colors ➪ Auto ➪ Normalize).

4. **Pick a gradient.**

   You'll add colors to your pattern using a technique called *gradient map-ping*. Use the Gradient dialog box (Windows ➪ Dockable Dialogs ➪ Gradients) to pick a gradient. Darker colors on your image map to colors on the left of the gradient, and lighter colors map to the left. You can adjust colors, so don't worry if the colors aren't exactly what you want. (If you want, you can make your own gradient with the gradient editor by clicking the Gradient dialog box's New Gradient button.)

5. **Use the Gradient Map tool (Colors ➪ Map ➪ Gradient Map) to map the colors of the gradient to your cloud pattern.**

6. **Offset the image to check for tiling**.

   The easiest way to see whether the image tiles well is to offset the image. This puts the edges in the center so you can see how the image will look when multiple copies are next to each other. Open the Offset dialog by choosing Layer ➪ Transform ➪ Offset. The Offset dialog has a handy x/2, y/2 button. Click the button to see how your image looks.

7. **Clean the image if necessary.**

   If you chose the Tileable option when you built the cloud image, the new image will look fine. If not, you may have some visible seams. Use the Smudge and Clone tools to clean up these seams if necessary. Apply the Offset tool a second time to check whether your seams look good.

8. **Apply filters to get the effect you want.**

   You may want to colorize your image or blur it a bit to cover any artifacts of your cleanup. Remember that background images should be extremely dark or extremely light with very low contrast if you want readable text.

9. **Test the image by saving the image in XCF format and a web-friendly format (like PNG), build a simple page using the image as a background, and load the page into your browser to ensure it tiles the way you expect.**

   Figure 4-12 shows a sample page containing my tiled image as the background.

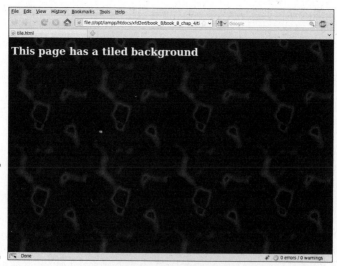

Figure 4-12: This page features my new tiled background.

Chapter 5: Taking Control of Content

In This Chapter

✔ Approximating CMS with Server Side Includes (SSI)

✔ Reviewing client-side includes using AJAX

✔ Using PHP includes to build a basic CMS-style system

✔ Building a data-based CMS

✔ Creating a form for modifying content

Commercial sites today combine many skills and tools: HTML, CSS, JavaScript, AJAX, databases, and PHP. This book covers many of these techniques. In this chapter you combine all these techniques to build your own content management systems. Some are very simple to build, and some are quite sophisticated.

Building a "Poor Man's CMS" with Your Own Code

The benefits of using a CMS are very real, but you may not want to make the commitment to a full-blown CMS. For one thing, you have to learn each CMS's particular way of doing things, and most CMSs force you into a particular mindset. For example, you think differently about pages in Drupal than you do in WebsiteBaker (both described in Chapter 3 of this minibook). You can still get some of the benefits of a CMS with some simpler development tricks, as described in the following sections.

The examples in this chapter build on information from throughout the entire book. All of the CMSs (and pseudo-CMSs) built in this chapter use the design developed in Chapter 2 of this minibook.

Using Server Side Includes (SSIs)

Web developers have long used the simple SSI (Server Side Include) trick as a quick and easy way to manage content. It involves breaking the code into smaller code segments and a framework that can be copied. For example, Figure 5-1 shows a variation of the website developed in Chapter 2 of this minibook.

Figure 5-1:
This web page appears to be a standard page.

Even if you view the source code in the browser, you don't find anything unusual about the page.

However, if you look at the code in a text editor, you find some interesting discoveries:

```
<!DOCTYPE html>
<html lang = "en-US">

  <head>
    <meta charset = "UTF-8">
    <title>csSSI.shtml</title>
    <link rel = "stylesheet"
          type = "text/css"
          href = "csStd.css" />
  </head>
  <body>
    <div id = "all">
      <!-- This div centers a fixed-width layout -->
      <div id = "heading">
        <!--#include virtual = "head.html" -->
      </div><!-- end heading div -->

      <div id = "menu">
        <!--#include virtual = "menu.html" -->
      </div> <!-- end menu div -->

      <div class = "content">
        <!--#include virtual = "story1.html" -->
      </div> <!-- end content div -->

      <div class = "content">
        <!--#include virtual = "story2.html" -->
      </div> <!-- end content div -->
```

```
        <div id = "footer">
          <!--#include virtual = "footer.html" -->
        </div> <!-- end footer div -->
      </div> <!-- end all div -->
    </body>
</html>
```

Some interesting things are happening in this code snippet:

+ **The page has no content!** All the actual content (the menus and the book information) are gone. This page, which contains only structural information, is the heart of any kind of CSS — the structure is divorced from the content.

+ **A funky new tag is in place of the content.** In each place that you expect to see text, you see an `<!-#include ->` directive, instead. This special instruction tells the server to go find the specified file and put it here.

+ **The filename is unusual.** The server doesn't normally look for include tags (because most pages don't have them). Typically, you have to save the file with the special extension .shtml to request that the server look for include directives and perform them. (It's possible to use special server configurations to allow SSI with normal .html extensions.)

+ **Servers don't always allow SSI technologies.** Not every server is configured for Server Side Includes. You may have to check with your server administrator to make this work.

The nice thing about Server Side Includes is the way that it separates the content from the structure. For example, look at the code for the first content block:

```
        <!--#include virtual = "story1.html" -->
```

This code notifies the server to look for the file story1.html in the current directory and place the contents of the file there. The file is a vastly simplified HTML fragment:

```
<h2>Book I - Creating the HTML Foundation</h2>
<ol>
  <li>Sound HTML Foundations</li>
  <li>It's All About Validation</li>
  <li>Choosing your Tools</li>
  <li>Managing Information with Lists and Tables</li>
  <li>Making Connections with Links</li>
  <li>Adding Images</li>
  <li>Creating Forms</li>
</ol>
```

This approach makes it very easy to modify the page. If I want a new story, I simply make a new file, story1.html, and put it in the directory. Writing a program to do this automatically is easy.

Like PHP code, SSI code doesn't work if you simply open the file in the browser or drag the file to the window. SSI requires active participation from the server; to run an SSI page on your machine, therefore, you need to use localhost, as you do for PHP code.

If you view the source code of csSSI.shtml you won't see the include lines; they'll be replaced with the included HTML snippets. I've placed a special source view of this program on the website so you can see the source code as I do for PHP programs.

Using AJAX and jQuery for client-side inclusion

If you don't have access to Server Side Includes, you can use AJAX to get the same effect.

Figure 5-2 shows what appears to be the same page, but all is not what it appears to be.

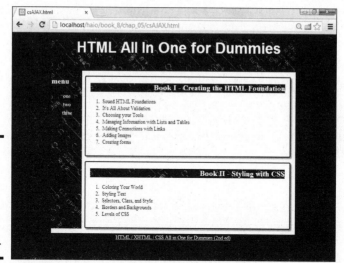

Figure 5-2: This time, I grabbed content from the client side using AJAX.

Figures 5-1 and 5-2 look identical, but they're not. I used totally different means to achieve exactly the same output, from the user's point of view.

The code reveals what's going on:

```
<!DOCTYPE html>
<html lang = "en-US">

  <head>
    <meta charset = "UTF-8">
    <title>csAJAX.html</title>
    <link rel = "stylesheet"
          type = "text/css"
```

```
       href = "csStd.css" />
 <script type = "text/javascript"
         src = "jquery-1.10.2.min.js"></script>
 <script type = "text/javascript">
   $(document).ready(function() {
     $("#heading").load("head.html");
     $("#menu").load("menu.html");
     $("#content1").load("story1.html");
     $("#content2").load("story2.html");
     $("#footer").load("footer.html");
   });
 </script>
</head>
<body>
  <div id = "all">
    <!-- This div centers a fixed-width layout -->
    <div id = "heading">
    </div><!-- end heading div -->
    <div id = "menu">
    </div> <!-- end menu div -->
    <div class = "content"
         id = "content1">
    </div> <!-- end content div -->
    <div class = "content"
         id = "content2">
    </div> <!-- end content div -->
    <div id = "footer">
    </div> <!-- end footer div -->
  </div> <!-- end all div -->
</body>
</html>
```

Once again, the page content is empty. All the contents are available in the
same text files as they were for the Server Side Includes example. This time,
though, I used a jQuery AJAX call to load each text file into the appropriate
element.

Here's the plan:

1. **Import the jQuery library.**

   The jQuery library is by far the easiest way to work with AJAX, so
   import jQuery any time you want to work with AJAX. See Book VII,
   Chapter 2 for more on importing the jQuery library.

2. **Add an initialization function.**

   There are many ways to call initial functions in jQuery (discussed in
   Book VII, Chapter 2). It doesn't matter which mechanism you use as long
   as it occurs after the page has loaded but before any other JavaScript. I
   use the standard $(document).ready mechanism in this example.

3. **Load each div with the load() method.**

   The jQuery library has a load() method that allows you to make an
   AJAX call and place the document in the indicated element. Use this
   mechanism on each element in your page.

The same document structure can be used with very different content by changing the JavaScript. If you can't create a full-blown CMS (because the server doesn't allow SSI, for example) but you can do AJAX, this is an easy way to separate content from layout. See Book VII, Chapter 2 for more information on using jQuery and AJAX for page includes.

Building a page with PHP includes

Of course, if you have access to PHP, it's quite easy to build pages dynamically.

The csInclude.php program shows how this is done:

```
<!DOCTYPE html>
<html lang = "en-US">

  <head>
    <meta charset = "UTF-8">
    <title>CS PHP Includes</title>
    <link rel = "stylesheet"
          type = "text/css"
          href = "csStd.css" />
  </head>
  <body>
    <div id = "all">
      <!-- This div centers a fixed-width layout -->
      <div id = "heading">
        <?php include("head.html"); ?>
      </div><!-- end heading div -->
      <div id = "menu">
        <?php include("menu.html"); ?>
      </div> <!-- end menu div -->
      <div class = "content">
        <?php include("story1.html"); ?>
      </div> <!-- end content div -->
      <div class = "content">
        <?php include("story2.html"); ?>
      </div> <!-- end content div -->
      <div id = "footer">
        <?php include("footer.html"); ?>
      </div> <!-- end footer div -->
    </div> <!-- end all div -->
  </body>
</html>
```

As you can see, using PHP is almost the same as using the SSI and AJAX approaches from the last two sections of this chapter:

1. **Start by building a template.**

   The general template for all three styles of page inclusion is the same. There's no need to change the general design or the CSS.

2. **Create a small PHP segment for each inclusion.**

   In this particular situation, it's easiest to write HTML code for the main site and write a small PHP section for each segment that needs to be included.

3. **Include the HTML file.**

   Each PHP snippet does nothing more than include the appropriate HTML.

Creating Your Own Data-Based CMS

If you've come this far in the chapter, you ought to go all the way and see how a relational database can add flexibility to a page-serving system. If you really want to turn the corner and make a real CMS, you need a system that stores all the data in a data structure and compiles the pages from that structure dynamically. That sounds like a project. Actually, creating your own CMS neatly ties together most of the skills used throughout this book: HTML, CSS, PHP, and SQL. It's not nearly as intimidating as it sounds, though.

Using a database to manage content

The first step is to move from storing data in files to storing in a relational database. Each page in a content management system is often the same structure, and only the data is different. What happens if you move away from text files altogether and store all the content in a database?

The data structure might be defined like this in SQL:

```sql
DROP TABLE IF EXISTS cmsPage;
CREATE TABLE cmsPage (
  cmsPageID INTEGER PRIMARY KEY AUTO_INCREMENT,
  title VARCHAR(30)
);

DROP TABLE IF EXISTS cmsBlock;
CREATE TABLE cmsBlock (
  cmsBlockID INTEGER PRIMARY KEY AUTO_INCREMENT,
  blockTypeID INTEGER,
  title VARCHAR(50),
  content TEXT,
  pageID INTEGER

);

DROP TABLE IF EXISTS blockType;
CREATE TABLE blockType (
  blockTypeID INTEGER PRIMARY KEY AUTO_INCREMENT,
  name VARCHAR(30)
);

DROP VIEW IF EXISTS pageView;
CREATE VIEW pageView AS
  SELECT
    blockType.name as 'block',
    cmsBlock.title as 'title',
    cmsBlock.content as 'content',
    cmsBlock.pageID as 'pageID',
    cmsPage.title as 'page'
  FROM
```

```
      cmsBlock, blockType, cmsPage
    WHERE
      cmsBlock.blockTypeID = blockType.blockTypeID;

INSERT INTO cmsPage VALUES (
  null,
  'main page'
);

INSERT into blockType VALUES (null, 'head');
INSERT into blockType VALUES (null, 'menu');
INSERT into blockType VALUES (null, 'content1');
INSERT into blockType VALUES (null, 'content2');
INSERT into blockType VALUES (null, 'footer');

INSERT INTO cmsBlock VALUES (
  null,
  1,
  'it\'s a binary thing',
  null,
  1
);

INSERT INTO cmsBlock VALUES (
  null,
  2,
  'menu',
  '
        <ul>
        <li><a href = "dbCMS.php?pageID=1">one</a></li>
        <li><a href = "dbCMS.php?pageID=2">two</a></li>
        <li><a href = "dbCMS.php?pageID=1">three</a></li>
        </ul>
  ',
  1
);

INSERT INTO cmsBlock VALUES (
  null,
  3,
  'Book I - Creating the HTML Foundation',
  '
<ol>
  <li>Sound HTML Foundations</li>
  <li>It\'s All About Validation</li>
  <li>Choosing your Tools</li>
  <li>Managing Information with Lists and Tables</li>
  <li>Making Connections with Links</li>
  <li>Adding Images</li>
  <li>Creating forms</li>
</ol>
  ',
  1
);

INSERT INTO cmsBlock VALUES (
  null,
  4,
  'Book II - Styling with CSS',
  '
<ol>
  <li>Coloring Your World</li>
  <li>Styling Text</li>
```

```
   <li>Selectors, Class, and Style</li>
   <li>Borders and Backgrounds</li>
   <li>Levels of CSS</li>
</ol>
   ',
   1
);

INSERT INTO cmsBlock VALUES (
  null,
  5,
  null,
  'see <a href = "http://www.aharrisbooks.net">aharrisbooks.net</a> for more
    information',
  1
);
```

This structure has three tables and a view:

+ **The `cmsPage` table:** Represents the data about a page, which currently isn't much. A fuller version might put menu information in the page data so that the page would "know" where it lives in a menu structure.

+ **The `cmsBlock` table:** Represents a block of information. Each block is the element that would be in a miniature HTML page in the other systems described in this chapter. This table is the key table in this structure because most of the content in the CMS is stored in this table.

+ **The `blockType` table:** Lists the block types. This simple table describes the various block types.

+ **The `pageView` view:** Ties together all the other information. After all the data is loaded, the `pageView` view ties it all together, as shown in Figure 5-3.

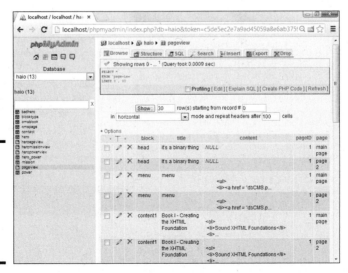

Figure 5-3:
This view describes all the data needed to build a page.

Most of the data is being read as HTML, but it's still text data. I included the entire SQL file, including the INSERT statements, on the companion website as buildCMS.sql.

Writing a PHP page to read from the table

The advantage of using a data-based approach is scalability. In using all the other models in this chapter, I had to keep copying the template page. If you decide to make a change in the template, you have to change hundreds of pages. If you use data, you can write one PHP program that can produce any page in the system. All this page needs is a page-number parameter. Using that information, it can query the system, extract all the information needed for the current page, and then display the page. Here's the (simplified) PHP code for such a system:

```
<!DOCTYPE html>
<html lang = "en-US">

  <head>
    <meta charset = "UTF-8">
    <title>CS Basic CMS</title>
    <link rel = "stylesheet"
          type = "text/css"
          href = "csStd.css" />
  </head>
<?php
//get pageID from request if possible
$pageID = filter_input(INPUT_POST, "pageID");

if ($pageID == ""){
  $pageID = 1;
} // end if

try {
  //connect to database
  $con= new PDO('mysql:host=host;dbname=dbName', "user", "pwd");
  $con->setAttribute(PDO::ATTR_ERRMODE, PDO::ERRMODE_EXCEPTION);

  //read current page information from the db
  $stmt = $con->prepare("SELECT * FROM pageView WHERE PageID = ?");
  $stmt->execute(array($pageID));
  $result = $stmt->fetchAll(PDO::FETCH_ASSOC);

  //make page variables based on the current record
  foreach ($result as $row){
    if ($row["block"] == "head"){
      $head = $row["title"];
    } else if ($row["block"] == "menu"){
      $menu = $row["content"];
    } else if ($row["block"] == "content1"){
      $c1Title = $row["title"];
      $c1Text = $row["content"];
    } else if ($row["block"] == "content2"){
      $c2Title = $row["title"];
      $c2Text = $row["content"];
    } else if ($row["block"] == "footer"){
      $footer = $row["content"];
    } // end if
```

```
    } // end foreach
} catch(PDOException $e) {
    echo 'ERROR: ' . $e->getMessage();
} // end try
?>

    <body>
      <div id = "all">
        <!-- This div centers a fixed-width layout -->
        <div id = "heading">
          <h1>
            <?php print $head; ?>
          </h1>
        </div><!-- end heading div -->
        <div id = "menu">
          <?php print $menu; ?>
        </div> <!-- end menu div -->
        <div class = "content">
          <h2>
            <?php print $c1Title; ?>
          </h2>
          <div>
            <?php print $c1Text; ?>
          </div>
        </div> <!-- end content div -->
        <div class = "content">
          <h2>
            <?php print $c2Title; ?>
          </h2>
          <div>
            <?php print $c2Text; ?>
          </div>
        </div> <!-- end content div -->
        <div id = "footer">
          <?php print $footer; ?>
        </div> <!-- end footer div -->
      </div> <!-- end all div -->
    </body>
</html>
```

Here's the cool thing about dbCMS. This page is all you need! You won't have to copy it ever. The same PHP script is used to generate every page in the system. If you want to change the style or layout, you do it in this one script, and it works automatically in all the pages. This is exactly how CMS systems work their magic!

Looking at all the code at one time may seem intimidating, but it's quite easy when you break it down, as explained in these steps:

1. **Pull the `pageID` number from the request.**

   If possible, extract the `pageID` number from the GET request. If the user has sent a particular page request, it has a value. If there's no value, get page number 1:

   ```
   //get pageID from request if possible
   //note this is a GET request, for flexibility
   $pageID = filter_input(INPUT_GET, "pageID");
   ```

```
if ($pageID == "") {
  $pageID = 1;
} // end if
```

Note that I'm using a sneaky trick to indicate the page. The menu links will all call the same program, but with a different `pageID`:

```
<ul>
  <li><a href = "dbCMS.php?pageID=1">one</a></li>
  <li><a href = "dbCMS.php?pageID=2">two</a></li>
  <li><a href = "dbCMS.php?pageID=1">three</a></li>
    </ul>
```

2. **Query `pageView` to get all the data for this page.**

   The `pageView` view was designed to give you everything you need to build a page with one query.

3. **Make a data connection.**

   Build a standard PDO connection to the database. (Check Book VI, Chapter 5 if you need more on building a PDO connection.) Don't forget to set up an exception handler and the appropriate error constants.

```
try {
 //connect to database
 $con= new PDO('mysql:host=localhost;dbname=haio', "haio", "haio");
 $con->setAttribute(PDO::ATTR_ERRMODE, PDO::ERRMODE_EXCEPTION);

 // OTHER CODE WILL GO HERE

} catch(PDOException $e) {
    echo 'ERROR: ' . $e->getMessage();
} // end try
```

4. **Form and execute the query.**

   Use the prepared statement mechanism to build a statement that will return all records for the current page. Execute the statement and fetch all the results in a variable called `$results`.

```
//read current page information from the db
$stmt = $con->prepare("SELECT * FROM pageView WHERE PageID = ?");
$stmt->execute(array($pageID));
$result = $stmt->fetchAll(PDO::FETCH_ASSOC);<Warning>
```

   Don't simply interpolate the `$pageID` variable into the SQL query. Doing so would open yourself up to SQL injection attacks. Use the prepare/execute mechanism to prevent this type of attack.

5. **Use the entry to populate page variables.**

   Each entry contains two fields: `block` and `content`. The `block` field determines the type of content, and the `content` field shows what content is there. Use this data to populate the variables used to build the page:

```
//make page variables based on the current record
foreach ($result as $row) {
  if ($row["block"] == "head") {
```

```
          $head = $row["title"];
        } else if ($row["block"] == "menu"){
          $menu = $row["content"];
        } else if ($row["block"] == "content1"){
          $c1Title = $row["title"];
          $c1Text = $row["content"];
        } else if ($row["block"] == "content2"){
          $c2Title = $row["title"];
          $c2Text = $row["content"];
        } else if ($row["block"] == "footer"){
          $footer = $row["content"];
        } // end if

      } // end foreach
```

6. **Write out the page.**

   Go back to HTML and generate the page, skipping into PHP to print the necessary variables.

```html
<body>
  <div id = "all">
    <!-- This div centers a fixed-width layout -->
    <div id = "heading">
      <h1>
        <?php print $head; ?>
      </h1>
    </div><!-- end heading div -->
    <div id = "menu">
      <?php print $menu; ?>
    </div> <!-- end menu div -->
    <div class = "content">
      <h2>
        <?php print $c1Title; ?>
      </h2>
      <div>
        <?php print $c1Text; ?>
      </div>
    </div> <!-- end content div -->
    <div class = "content">
      <h2>
        <?php print $c2Title; ?>
      </h2>
      <div>
        <?php print $c2Text; ?>
      </div>
    </div> <!-- end content div -->
    <div id = "footer">
      <?php print $footer; ?>
    </div> <!-- end footer div -->
  </div> <!-- end all div -->
</body>
```

Allowing user-generated content

The hallmark of a CMS is the ability of users with limited technical knowledge to add content to the system. My very simple CMS illustrates a limited way to add data to the CMS. Figure 5-4 shows the buildBlock.html page. This page allows authorized users to add new blocks to the system and produces the output shown in Figure 5-5.

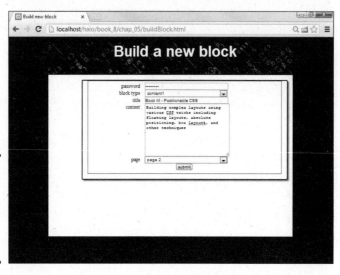

Figure 5-4:
A user can add content, which updates the database.

Figure 5-5:
The result of a successful page update.

After a few entries, a user can build a complete second page, which might look similar to Figure 5-6.

Figure 5-6:
This page
is simply
another
set of page
blocks
added by
the user.

The system is simple but effective. The user builds blocks, and these blocks
are constructed into pages. First, look over the buildBlock.html page.

```html
<!doctype html>
<html lang="en">
<head>
  <meta charset="UTF-8">
  <title>Build new block</title>

  <link rel = "stylesheet"
        type = "text/css"
        href = "csStd.css" />

  <style type = "text/css">
  label {
    float: left;
    width: 10em;
    clear: left;
    text-align: right;
    padding-right: 1em;
  }

  input, select, textarea {
    float: left;
    width: 20em;
  }

  button {
    display: block;
    clear: both;
    margin: auto;
  }

  </style>
</head>
<body>
```

**Book VIII
Chapter 5**

Taking Control of
Content

```
<div id = "all">
  <div id = "heading">
    <h1>Build a new block</h1>
  </div>

  <div class = "content">
    <form action = "buildBlock.php"
          method = "post">
      <fieldset>

        <label>
          password
        </label>
        <input type = "password"
               name = "password" />

        <label>block type</label>
        <select name = "blockType">
          <option value = "1">head</option>
          <option value = "2">menu</option>
          <option value = "3">content1</option>
          <option value = "4">content2</option>
          <option value = "5">footer</option>
        </select>

        <label>title</label>
        <input type = "text"
               name = "title" />

        <label>content</label>
        <textarea name = "content"
                  rows = "10"
                  cols = "40"></textarea>

        <label>page</label>
        <select name = "pageID">
          <option value = "1">main page</option>
          <option value = "2">page 2</option>
        </select>

        <button type = "submit">
          submit
        </button>
      </fieldset>
    </form>
  </div>
  </div>
</body>
</html>
```

This code is a reasonably standard HTML form. Here are the highlights:

✦ **Add CSS for consistency:** It's important that the user understands she is still in a part of the system, so I include the same CSS used to display the output. I also add local CSS to improve the form display.

✦ **Build a form that calls buildBlock.php:** The purpose of this form is to generate the information needed to build an SQL INSERT statement. The buildBlock.php program provides this vital service.

◆ **Ask for a password:** You don't want just anybody modifying your forms. Include a password to make sure only those who are authorized add data.

◆ **Get other data needed to build a block:** Think about the INSERT query you'll be building. You'll need to get all the data necessary to add a new record to the cmsBlock table.

Honestly, this page is a bit sloppy. I hard-coded the block types and page IDs. In a real system, this data would be pulled from the database (ideally through AJAX). However, I decided to go with this expedient to save space.

Adding a new block

When the page owner submits the buildBlock.html form, control is passed to buildBlock.php. This program reads the data from the form, checks the password, creates an INSERT statement, and passes the query to the database.

Here's the code and then the details:

```php
<!doctype html>
<html lang="en">
<head>
  <title>buildBlock.php</title>
  <meta charset="UTF-8">
</head>
<body>
  <?php
  //retrieve data from form
  $password = filter_input(INPUT_POST, "password");
  $blockType = filter_input(INPUT_POST, "blockType");
  $title = filter_input(INPUT_POST, "title");
  $content = filter_input(INPUT_POST, "content");
  $pageID = filter_input(INPUT_POST, "pageID");

  //check password
  if ($password == "allInOne"){
    manageResults();
  } else {
    print "<h2>Unauthorized access...</h2>";
  } // end if

  function manageResults(){
    global $blockType, $title, $content, $pageID;

    //return output
    print <<<HERE
    <h2>Page input:</h2>
    <p>
      blockType: $blockType <br />
      title: $title <br />
      content: $content <br />
      pageID: $pageID
    </p>
HERE;

    try {
```

```
//connect to database
$con= new PDO('mysql:host=host;dbname=dbName', "user", "pwd");
$con->setAttribute(PDO::ATTR_ERRMODE, PDO::ERRMODE_EXCEPTION);

//create an INSERT statement based on input
$stmt = $con->prepare('INSERT INTO cmsBlock VALUES(null, ?, ?, ?, ?)');
$result = $stmt->execute(array($blockType, $title, $content, $pageID));

//provide feedback
if ($result){
  print "System updated";
} else {
  print "There was an error";
} // end if


} catch(PDOException $e) {
    echo 'ERROR: ' . $e->getMessage();
} // end try
} // end function


?>
<p>
<a href = "dbCMS.php">return to the CMS</a>
</p>
</body>
</html>
```

Here's how you use the PHP code with the HTML form to update the database:

1. **Retrieve data from the form.**

   Use the `filter_input` or `$_REQUEST` mechanism to extract all data from the previous form.

2. **Filter all input that's used in the query.**

   All form variables except the password are used in an SQL query, so pass each variable through the `mysql_filter_input()` function to prevent SQL injection attacks. (See Book VI, Chapter 5 for information about SQL injection attacks and how to prevent them.)

3. **Check the password.**

   You obviously don't want just anybody to change your system. Check the password and continue only if the user is authorized.

4. **Print the form contents.**

   Ensure the form contents are what you expect before passing data to a database.

5. **Connect to the database.**

   Build a standard database connection so you can pass the query to the database.

6. **Build and execute the query.**

Send the query to the database with the prepare/execute mechanism. Note that an INSERT command doesn't return a data result, so there's no need to do a fetch command. However, the $result variable will still contain a true or false value, so compare this value to ensure the insertion worked correctly.

Improving the dbCMS design

Although the simple PHP/MySQL combination described in the last section is a suitable starting point, you probably want to do a bit more to make a complete CMS because a better CMS might have the following features:

✦ **Automatic menu generation:** The menu system in dbCMS is too static as it is. Your database should keep track of where each page is located in the system, and your menu code should be dynamically generated based on this information.

✦ **Better flexibility:** To keep the code simple, I made only one page type, and the page always has exactly two content blocks. You'll want a much more flexible design.

✦ **Error-checking:** This program isn't nearly robust enough for real use (yet). It crashes if the data isn't complete. Before you can use this system in a real application, you need a way to improve its "crash-worthiness."

✦ **Improved data input:** The very basic input form described in this chapter is fine, but it could certainly be improved. Loading the block type and page data directly from the database would be better. It would also be nice if the user could create new block types. Still, this basic CMS shows how you can start building your own content systems.

Book VIII
Chapter 5

Taking Control of Content

Index

Special Characters and Numerics

H

M

N

O

T

X

About the Author

Andy Harris began his teaching life as a special education teacher. As he was teaching young adults with severe disabilities, he taught himself enough computer programming to support his teaching habit with freelance programming. Those were the exciting days when computers started to have hard drives, and some computers began communicating with each other over an arcane mechanism some were calling the Internet.

All this time Andy was teaching computer science part time. He joined the faculty of the Indiana University-Purdue University Indianapolis Computer Science department in 1995. He serves as a Senior Lecturer, teaching the introductory course to freshmen as well as numerous courses on web development, general programming, and game programming. As manager of the Streaming Media Laboratory, he developed a number of online video-based courses, and worked on a number of international distance education projects including helping to start a computer science program in Tetevo, Macedonia FYR, and collaboration with Sun-Yat-Sen University in Guangzhou, China.

Andy is active in home schooling, and is the technology columnist for a national homeschool magazine.

Andy is the author of several other computing books including *HTML5 Game Development For Dummies, JavaScript/AJAX for Dummies,* and *Game Programming: The L Line.* He invites your comments and questions at andy@aharrisbooks.net. You can visit his main site and find a blog, forum, and links to other books at www.aharrisbooks.net.

Dedication

I dedicate this book to Jesus Christ, my personal savior, and to Heather, the joy in my life. I also dedicate this project to Elizabeth, Matthew, Jacob, and Benjamin. I love each of you.

Author's Acknowledgments

Thank you first to Heather. Even though I type all the words, this book is a real partnership, like the rest of our life. Thanks for being my best friend and companion. Thanks also for doing all the work it takes for us to sustain a family when I'm in writing mode.

Thank you to Connie Santisteban. I've really enjoyed working with you on this project.

Thank you to the copy and development editor, Linda Morris. I appreciate your efforts to make my geeky mush turn into something readable. Thanks for improving my writing.

A special thanks to Claudia Snell for technical editing. I appreciate your vigilance. You have helped to make this book as technically accurate as possible.

Thank you to the many people at Wiley who contribute to a project like this. The author only gets to meet a few people, but so many more are involved in the process. Thank you very much for all you've done to help make this project a reality.

A big thank you to the open-source community which has created so many incredible tools and made them available to all. I'd especially like to thank the creators of Firefox, Firebug, Aptana, HTML Validator, Komodo Edit, Notepad++, PHP, Apache, jQuery, and the various jQuery plug-ins. This is an amazing and generous community effort.

Thanks to those I've gotten to learn and teach with, from the graduate students, to the math homework girls: Graciela and Vanesa.

I'd finally like to thank the IUPUI computer science family for years of support on various projects. Thank you especially to all my students, current and past. I've learned far more from you than the small amount I've taught. Thank you for letting me be a part of your education.

Publisher's Acknowledgments

Acquisitions Editor: Constance Santisteban

Project Editor: Linda Morris

Copy Editor: Linda Morris

Technical Editor: Claudia Snell

Editorial Assistant: Annie Sullivan

Sr. Editorial Assistant: Cherie Case

Project Coordinator: Sheree Montgomery

Cover Image: © iStockphoto.com/Marina Strizhak

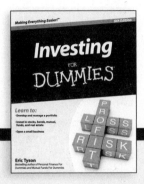
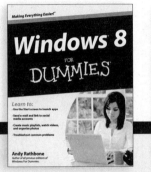

Math & Science

Algebra I For Dummies,
2nd Edition
978-0-470-55964-2

Anatomy and Physiology
For Dummies,
2nd Edition
978-0-470-92326-9

Astronomy For Dummies,
3rd Edition
978-1-118-37697-3

Biology For Dummies,
2nd Edition
978-0-470-59875-7

Chemistry For Dummies,
2nd Edition
978-1-1180-0730-3

Pre-Algebra Essentials
For Dummies
978-0-470-61838-7

Microsoft Office

Excel 2013 For Dummies
978-1-118-51012-4

Office 2013 All-in-One
For Dummies
978-1-118-51636-2

PowerPoint 2013
For Dummies
978-1-118-50253-2

Word 2013 For Dummies
978-1-118-49123-2

Music

Blues Harmonica
For Dummies
978-1-118-25269-7

Guitar For Dummies,
3rd Edition
978-1-118-11554-1

iPod & iTunes
For Dummies,
10th Edition
978-1-118-50864-0

Programming

Android Application
Development For
Dummies, 2nd Edition
978-1-118-38710-8

iOS 6 Application
Development For Dummies
978-1-118-50880-0

Java For Dummies,
5th Edition
978-0-470-37173-2

Religion & Inspiration

The Bible For Dummies
978-0-7645-5296-0

Buddhism For Dummies,
2nd Edition
978-1-118-02379-2

Catholicism For Dummies,
2nd Edition
978-1-118-07778-8

Self-Help & Relationships

Bipolar Disorder
For Dummies,
2nd Edition
978-1-118-33882-7

Meditation For Dummies,
3rd Edition
978-1-118-29144-3

Seniors

Computers For Seniors
For Dummies,
3rd Edition
978-1-118-11553-4

iPad For Seniors
For Dummies,
5th Edition
978-1-118-49708-1

Social Security
For Dummies
978-1-118-20573-0

Smartphones & Tablets

Android Phones
For Dummies
978-1-118-16952-0

Kindle Fire HD
For Dummies
978-1-118-42223-6

NOOK HD For Dummies,
Portable Edition
978-1-118-39498-4

Surface For Dummies
978-1-118-49634-3

Test Prep

ACT For Dummies,
5th Edition
978-1-118-01259-8

ASVAB For Dummies,
3rd Edition
978-0-470-63760-9

GRE For Dummies,
7th Edition
978-0-470-88921-3

Officer Candidate Tests,
For Dummies
978-0-470-59876-4

Physician's Assistant Exam
For Dummies
978-1-118-11556-5

Series 7 Exam
For Dummies
978-0-470-09932-2

Windows 8

Windows 8 For Dummies
978-1-118-13461-0

Windows 8 For Dummies,
Book + DVD Bundle
978-1-118-27167-4

Windows 8 All-in-One
For Dummies
978-1-118-11920-4

Available in print and e-book formats.

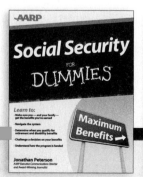
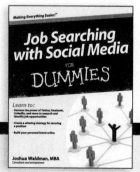

Available wherever books are sold. For more information or to order direct: U.S. customers visit www.Dummies.com or call 1-877-762-2974.
U.K. customers visit www.Wileyeurope.com or call (0) 1243 843291. Canadian customers visit www.Wiley.ca or call 1-800-567-4797.
Connect with us online at www.facebook.com/fordummies or @fordummies

Take Dummies with you everywhere you go!

Whether you're excited about e-books, want more from the web, must have your mobile apps, or swept up in social media, Dummies makes everything easier .

Visit Us

Like Us

Follow Us

Watch Us

Join Us

Pin Us

Circle Us

Shop Us

Dummies products make life easier!

- DIY
- Consumer Electronics
- Crafts
- Software
- Cookware
- Hobbies
- Videos
- Music
- Games
- and More!

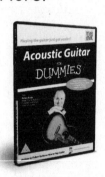

For more information, go to **Dummies.com**® and search the store by category.

FOR
DUMMIES®

A Wiley Brand